GUIDELINES FOR INVESTIGATING OFFICER-INVOLVED SHOOTINGS, ARREST-RELATED DEATHS, AND DEATHS IN CUSTODY

As unrest over officer-involved shootings and deaths in custody takes center stage in conversations about policing and the criminal justice system, *Guidelines for Investigating Officer-Involved Shootings, Arrest-Related Deaths, and Deaths in Custody* addresses critical investigation components from an expert witness perspective, providing the insights necessary to ensure a complete investigation. Investigating a custodial death or an officer involved in a shooting presents unique and complex issues: estate, community, judicial, agency, involved officer, and public policy interests are all at stake. These types of deaths present various emerging medical, psychological, legal and liability, technical, and investigatory issues that must be addressed through a comprehensive investigation. This book is ideal for students in criminal investigation, death investigation, crime scene investigation, and special topic courses in custodial deaths and officer-involved shootings, as well as for death investigators, law enforcement officers, police administrators, and attorneys.

Darrell L. Ross, Ph.D., is a Professor and Department Head of Sociology, Anthropology, and Criminal Justice, and the Director of the Center for Applied Social Sciences (CASS) at Valdosta State University. Ross worked for the Michigan Department of Corrections as an officer, cell block supervisor of mentally impaired prisoners, probation officer, and instructor in the training academy. He also taught in the Police Academy at Ferris State University as a certified instructor teaching subject control techniques, mechanics of arrest, and responding to the mentally ill person. He directed the forensic science program at East Carolina University and served as the Director of the School of Law Enforcement and Justice Administration at Western Illinois University.

Ross has published over 95 articles, books, book chapters, and monographs on the use of force, stress and human factors during use-of-force incidents, liability issues, officer-involved shootings, excited delirium syndrome, prone restraint and asphyxiation, sudden arrest-related deaths, and custodial suicides. Ross has provided technical assistance and consultation to local, county, state, federal, and private criminal justice agencies nationally and internationally, as well as to various branches of the military. He regularly provides training to line level officers and administrators and makes presentations at national and international conferences on officer-involved shootings, use-of-force issues, sudden arrest-related deaths, and custodial deaths. Since 1987, Ross has provided expert witness services regarding these and other topics.

Gary M. Vilke, M.D., is a Professor in the Department of Emergency Medicine at the University of California, San Diego (UCSD) and is the former Medical Director for the County of San Diego Emergency Medical Services. Vilke served as the Director for Custody Services at UCSD for over 15 years and is the Director for Clinical Research for the Emergency Department. His research focus has been in the areas of prehospital care and in-custody deaths, and he has published over 215 original articles and 65 book chapters, including more than 50 articles on topics including positional asphyxia, weight force on the back, OC spray, neck holds, restraint chairs, excited delirium syndrome, and the TASER. He has lectured internationally on these topics. Additionally, he has over 35 grant-funded projects, including funding by several national organizations to perform research on in-custody deaths, including the Police Executive Research Forum (PERF), the Institute for the Prevention of In-Custody Deaths (IPICD), and the National Institute of Justice.

GUIDELINES FOR INVESTIGATING OFFICER-INVOLVED SHOOTINGS, ARREST-RELATED DEATHS, AND DEATHS IN CUSTODY

Darrell L. Ross and Gary M. Vilke

Routledge
Taylor & Francis Group
NEW YORK AND LONDON

First published 2018
by Routledge
711 Third Avenue, New York, NY 10017

and by Routledge
2 Park Square, Milton Park, Abingdon, Oxon, OX14 4RN

Routledge is an imprint of the Taylor & Francis Group, an informa business

Library of Congress Cataloging-in-Publication Data
Names: Ross, Darrell L. (Darrell Lee), 1951- editor. | Vilke, Gary M., 1966- editor.
Title: Guidelines for investigating officer-involved shootings, arrest-related deaths, and deaths in custody / [edited by] Darrell L. Ross, Gary M. Vilke.
Description: New York, NY : Routledge, 2017. | Includes index.
Identifiers: LCCN 2017003250| ISBN 9781138674967 (hardback) | ISBN 9780323296236 (pbk.)
Subjects: LCSH: Police shootings--United States. | Police misconduct--United States. | Criminal investigation--United States. | Arrest (Police method)
Classification: LCC HV8141 .G845 2017 | DDC 363.2/32--dc23
LC record available at https://lccn.loc.gov/2017003250

ISBN: 978-1-138-67496-7 (hbk)
ISBN: 978-0-323-29623-6 (pbk)
ISBN: 978-1-315-56095-3 (ebk)

Typeset in Bembo
by Saxon Graphics Ltd, Derby

CONTENTS

CONTRIBUTORS

Alexis Artwohl, Ph.D., is an internationally recognized behavioral science consultant to law enforcement as a trainer, researcher, and author. She has done extensive training in the United States, Canada, Mexico, the United Kingdom, and Jordan. Artwohl is co-author of the book *Deadly Force Encounters* and other publications. During her 16 years as a private practice clinical and police psychologist, she provided consultation to multiple agencies throughout the Pacific Northwest as well as traumatic incident debriefings and psychotherapy to numerous public safety personnel and their family members.

Michael Brave, J.D., M.S., Member/Manager of LAAW International, LLC, is an attorney, consultant, trainer, and sworn police officer. His experience includes involvement in a wide range of comprehensive law enforcement risk/liability and litigation management services. He has been retained as an expert in over 220 cases, and has been involved in reviewing over 500 law enforcement temporal death cases. He has presented on force options and other subjects over 1,000 times in the United States, as well as Mexico, Canada, Panama, Austria, and the United Kingdom. He serves as National/International Litigation Counsel for TASER International, Inc., and Director of the TASER Science and Medical Research Group. He is a TASER Master Instructor, TASER's designated Person Most Knowledgeable, and Legal Advisor Member of the TASER Scientific and Medical Advisory Board and TASER Training Board. He formerly served as Chief, Intelligence and Investigative Operations Unit, Office of Enforcement Operations, United States Department of Justice.

Theodore Chan, M.D., is Professor and Chair of the Department of Emergency Medicine at the University of California, San Diego. A graduate of the University of California at Berkeley and the University of California, San Francisco, School of Medicine, Chan worked previously in Washington, DC, in the Office of the Assistant Surgeon General, and the state capitol at the California State Senate. He is board-certified in Emergency Medicine and has collaborated with numerous community health and law enforcement agencies. He has conducted seminal research on the physiologic effects of physical restraint and less lethal weapons in humans, and his research has been supported by grants from the National Institutes of Health, Department of Justice, and Robert Wood Johnson Foundation. Chan is editor of the Cardiology section of the *Journal of Emergency Medicine*; and has authored and edited three textbooks: *Atlas of Emergency Procedures*, *ECG in Emergency Medicine and Acute Care*, and *Sudden Deaths in Custody*.

Christopher J. Coyne, M.D., M.P.H., is an attending physician and clinical researcher in the Department of Emergency Medicine at the University of California San Diego (USCD). Coyne has several years of experience treating patients in custody, both at the LAC/USC Medical Center Emergency Department in Los Angeles, California, as well as multiple San Diego County Jail facilities. He has written several peer-reviewed manuscripts on a variety of emergency medicine topics, including a review of the medical and legal literature on restraint chairs, deaths related to conducted energy weapons, and the recommended medical therapy for agitated patients. Coyne is an active member of the American College of Emergency Physicians and the Society of Academic Emergency Medicine. He currently serves as the Associate Fellowship Director for the Clinical Research Scholar Fellowship in the Department of Emergency Medicine at UCSD. In January of 2017, Coyne became director of the Department of Emergency Medicine Behavioral Emergencies Research (DEMBER) lab.

Michael A. Darracq, M.D., M.P.H., is a practicing emergency physician, medical toxicologist, and faculty at the University of California, San Francisco (UCSF)-Fresno Medical Education Program. His experience and expertise includes medical education, emergency medicine, clinical and forensic toxicology, and legal consultation. He has presented on topics related to medical toxicology, emergency medicine, medical education, and hazardous materials medical management throughout the United States, Mexico, and Kuwait. Michael is a veteran of the United States Navy Medical Corps and Operation Enduring Freedom, having served as a subject matter expert and consultant to the Afghan National Army for the development of emergency medicine capability and services in Afghanistan.

Mark S. Dunston is the Chief of Police for the Ocean Springs, Mississippi, Police Department. Beginning his career in 1984, Dunston has served in numerous positions and assignments throughout his career. These positions include undercover narcotics, uniformed patrol, uniformed patrol supervisory ranks, investigations, academy instructor and director, and law enforcement executive. Dunston has trained over 50,000 law enforcement and military personnel throughout the United States, its territories, and foreign governments, including Hong Kong, China, Canada, and Brazil in areas of use of force, firearms, officer survival, and problem solving, as well as the leadership and management issues that direct those topics. Dunston has designed and implemented many other training programs for law enforcement agencies, including firearms, pursuit driving, field supervision, and executive leadership.

Dunston has published numerous articles in law enforcement periodicals and journals on the topics of use of force and officer survival, the management of the use of force, and liability issues concerning the use of force and vehicle pursuits. He is a graduate of the 191st FBI National Academy and the 20th Police Executive Research Forum's Senior Management Institute for Police conducted with Harvard University's Kennedy School of Government. As an expert witness and litigation consultant, Dunston has been retained in over 100 cases in both federal and state courts throughout the United States.

R. Edward Geiselman, Ph.D., is the co-developer of the Cognitive Interview technique. He has been a Professor of Psychology at the University of California, Los Angeles (UCLA), for 34 years. He earned his Bachelor's degree from Purdue University in 1972, where he studied engineering and psychology. Subsequently, he earned both Masters and Doctoral degrees from Ohio University in experimental psychology. Since joining the faculty at UCLA, he has published over 100 research papers in social science and police science journals. He is the author of several books, including *The Psychology of Murder*; *Intersections of Psychology, Psychiatry, and Law* (Volumes 1, 2, & 3); *Eyewitness Expert Testimony*; and *Memory Enhancing Techniques for Investigative Interviewing: The Cognitive Interview*. Geiselman has conducted training and offered other consulting services for numerous investigative agencies including the FBI, Homeland Security, U.S. Secret Service, U.S. State Department, Los Angeles Police Department, Los Angeles Sheriff's Department, Singapore Police Force, Health and Human Services, National Transportation Safety Board, Los Angeles Metropolitan Transit Authority, U.S. Marine Corps, Walter-Reed Army Hospital, Black Hat, and Hong Kong's Independent Commission Against Corruption. He also conducts investigative interviews for local police departments in ongoing cold-case investigations. Geiselman was awarded the Mary-Ellen McCormick award by the Los Angeles Sheriff's Department in 2013 for his career contributions to the investigation of child abuse cases.

Michael Holman, M.D., is an Emergency Physician at Sharp Chula Vista Hospital in San Diego. He graduated from University of California, San Diego (UCSD), Emergency Medicine Residency in 2016 and spent time studying patterns of injury in neck trauma. He was Chief Resident of UCSD Emergency Residency from 2015 to 2016. He has worked as a San Diego County Jail physician and for Kaiser Permanente. He has testified as an expert witness for the District Attorney's Office in strangulation cases. He has lectured to other emergency and trauma physicians on the topic. He has researched the safety of law enforcement neck holds and presented his research at academic emergency medicine conferences. He also has interest in carotid artery injury in strangulation injuries.

Mark Kroll, Ph.D., is a Biomedical scientist specializing in Bioelectricity. His primary scientific focus is the effect of electrical shocks on the human body and electrical devices to diagnose and treat heart disease and cancer. He is an adjunct Full Professor of Biomedical Engineering at the University of Minnesota and Cal Poly University (San Luis Obispo). Kroll holds over 360 issued U.S. patents, currently holding the most patents on electrical medical devices. Over 1,000,000 people have had devices with these patented features in their chest. In 2010 he received the international Biomedical Career Achievement Award/Fellow of both the American College of Cardiology and the Heart Rhythm Society. His experience includes taking a TASER Conducted Electrical Weapon probe deployment directly to the midline of the chest as well as drive-stuns. Kroll is a member of TASER Scientific and Medical Advisory Board and Corporate Board. He is a frequent consultant with larger U.S. federal and municipal law enforcement legal counsel. Kroll has also testified in Australian and Canadian legal proceedings.

Todd Lough, Ph.D., earned his doctorate in Political Science (1998) from Loyola University in Chicago. After finishing his schooling, Lough worked for nine years as a Chicago Police Officer. During his tenure with the Chicago Police Department (CPD), he worked in a number of different capacities, including patrol officer, gang and tactical officer, neighborhood relations officer, and gang violence analyst. As a gang violence analyst Lough worked in the CPD's Deployment Operations Center, where he conducted a weekly analysis of street gang-related shootings in an effort to deploy department resources to combat gang violence and reduce the city's homicide rate. Since 2007, Lough has served as an Associate Professor in the School of Law Enforcement and Justice Administration at Western Illinois University. His research interests include a variety of municipal policing issues such as communication in law enforcement, police training, and the effect of education on police performance.

Binh T. Ly, M.D., is physician with board certification in Emergency Medicine as well as subspecialty certification in Medical Toxicology. His primary academic appointment is as a Professor of Emergency Medicine at the University of California, San Diego, where he has been the residency training program director since 2008. He previously served from 2005–2014 as the training program director for the Medical Toxicology fellowship training program. In addition to his academic appointments, Ly provides consultation services in the specialty of Medical Toxicology at numerous hospitals in the San Diego community as well as the California Poison Control System. He is currently a legal consultant in toxicology with expertise in alcohol intoxication and drugs of abuse for both criminal and civil ligation.

Randall L. Murphy, MSM, is the former Director of Advanced Immersion Technologies for Meggitt Training Systems, and designed/directed the groundbreaking research on combat stress and its impact on police officers in a virtual environment under an institutional review board with the University of South Florida in 2008. The research has been peer-reviewed both nationally and internationally, with papers presented in Australia, Singapore, England, Canada, Taiwan, and the United States. Murphy replicated the stress research on soldiers for NATO Forces and U.S. Forces as part of Bold Quest 2011. During Bold Quest 2012, he assisted the U.S. Army Expeditionary Warrior Experiment Maneuver Battle Lab, Fort Benning, with scientific human observation research of the Advanced Situational Awareness Training program. He designed and directed the Human Factors research on soldiers during a live fire training exercise. The United States Army used the successful results to modify their doctrine of firearms training. Murphy served as the past president of the Kansas Criminal Justice Professors Association and was a college professor for 18 years teaching criminal justice, ethics, management, and constitutional law. He has instructed courses at John Jay College, Washburn University, and Kansas University. He obtained a B.A. in Administration of Justice with a minor in Public Administration from Avila University and a Master's of Science Management from Friends University. His law enforcement experience includes service as a police officer, detective, administrator of the police academy, and the Major over the Crime Scene Unit with the Kansas City, Kansas, Police Department for 30 years retiring in 2002. Murphy received the Good Neighbor Award from the Kansas Attorney General for assistance in writing the victims' rights constitutional amendment and three Officer of the Year awards. He is a lifetime member of the Police Officer's Hall of Fame as a Surviving Spouse and holds the Purple Heart from the Military Order of Purple Heart.

Darrell L. Ross, Ph.D., is a Professor and Department Head of Sociology, Anthropology, and Criminal Justice, and the Director of the Center for Applied Social Sciences (CASS) at Valdosta State University. Ross worked for the Michigan Department of Corrections as an officer, cell block supervisor of mentally impaired prisoners, probation officer, and instructor in the training academy. He also taught in the Police Academy at Ferris State University as a certified instructor teaching subject control techniques, mechanics of arrest, and responding to the mentally ill person. He directed the forensic science program at East Carolina University and served as the Director of the School of Law Enforcement and Justice Administration at Western Illinois University.

Ross has published over 95 articles, books, book chapters, and monographs on the use of force, stress and human factors during use-of-force incidents, liability issues, officer-involved shootings, excited delirium syndrome, prone restraint and asphyxiation, sudden arrest-related deaths, and custodial suicides. Ross has provided technical assistance and consultation to local, county, state, federal, and private criminal justice agencies nationally and internationally, as well as to various branches of the military. He regularly provides training to line-level officers and administrators and makes presentations at national and international conferences on officer-involved shootings, use-of-force issues, sudden arrest-related deaths, and custodial deaths. Since 1987, Ross has provided expert witness services regarding these and other topics.

Christian Sloane, M.D., grew up in the San Francisco Bay Area and attended University of California, Berkeley, for his undergraduate degree in Molecular Biology. He attended medical school at University of California, San Diego (UCSD), graduating in 1997. His transitional internship was at Scripps Mercy Hospital, followed by residency in Emergency Medicine at UCSD, where he was Chief Resident. Sloane is a member of Disaster Medical Assistance Team CA-4 and deployed with the team to the Louis Armstrong New Orleans International Airport in support of the medical evacuation after Hurricane Katrina, and also went to Haiti immediately after the 2010 earthquake with International Relief Teams. Currently he is the Medical Director for Mercy Air Services in San Diego and the director of Quality and Performance Improvement for the emergency department. He enjoys practicing Wilderness Medicine, and ran the medical student elective for the Wilderness Medical Society. Current research interests include less lethal weapons, with particular focus on the TASER and other law enforcement tools, and positional restraint. He was a cast member on an episode of *Fight Science* that examined the use of some of the devices. He has also done work with respect to injury prevention in police officers that wear body armor.

Stephen Thornton, M.D., is residency-trained, board-certified emergency medicine physician and fellowship-trained, board-certified medical toxicologist. He is an associate professor at the University of Kansas Hospital and the medical director for the University of Kansas Hospital Poison Control Center. He is an attending medical toxicologist at the University of Kansas Hospital and the Children's Mercy Hospital in Kansas City, Missouri. He has an interest in drugs of abuse, particularly in novel psychoactive substances, and has multiple peer-reviewed publications on the topic.

Gary M. Vilke, M.D., is a Professor in the Department of Emergency Medicine at the University of California, San Diego (UCSD) since 1996 and is the former Medical Director for the County of San Diego Emergency Medical Services. Vilke served as the Director for Custody Services at UCSD for over 15 years and is the Director for Clinical Research for the Emergency Department. His research focus has been in the areas of prehospital care and in-custody deaths, and he has published over 215 original articles and 65 book chapters, including more than 50 articles on topics including positional asphyxia, weight force on the back, OC spray, neck holds, restraint chairs, Excited Delirium Syndrome, and the TASER. He has lectured internationally on these topics. Additionally, he has over 35 grant-funded projects, including funding by several national organizations to perform research in in-custody deaths, including the Police Executive Research Forum (PERF), the Institute for the Prevention of In-Custody Deaths (IPICD), and the National Institute of Justice.

James F. Wilson, Esq., is a retired police defense litigator who still works as a part-time deputy city attorney for the City of Stockton, California, where he is a legal advisor to the Police Department and a litigator who oversees the defense of "police misconduct" cases brought against the city and its peace officers. In addition, Wilson is a faculty member at the California Specialized Training Institute at San Luis Obispo, California, where he lectures on officer preparation for handling the civil liability aspects of police uses of force in the Officer Safety and Field Tactics Course. He has approximately 35 years of experience as a litigator, including stints as both a prosecutor and a defense attorney in criminal litigation, and as both plaintiff's and defense counsel in civil litigation. He served as a police officer in Southern California for seven years before becoming an attorney, and has conducted training for California peace officers on a variety of subjects for approximately 30 years. Wilson has consulted with and represented many law enforcement agencies in California over the years. He also is certified by the Force Science Institute in Force Science Analysis, and is a member of the International Law Enforcement Educators and Trainers Association (ILEETA).

PREFACE

Given the annual number of contacts between the police and citizens, the numbers of detainees confined in jails and prisons across the country, and the health condition of these individuals, a custodial death is not unexpected. Although rare in occurrence, an officer-involved shooting, an arrest-related death, or a death in custody are considered high-profile incidents requiring a detailed investigation. This book exposes the reader to the numerous investigatory issues which emerge from these incidents, a focused insight into the nature of these deaths, and provides specific guidelines for performing the investigation.

Any one of the three categories of death comprises multiple and complex components of forensic science which can pose potential problems during the investigation. There is extreme pressure and scrutiny focused on the agency in which the death occurred and the agency tasked for conducting the investigation by the public, the media, the estate of the decedent, and the criminal justice system to ensure the investigation follows applicable protocols. Compounding the investigation is the fact that these incidents rarely occur and the assigned investigator, the agency administrator, the medical examiner, and involved officer may experience such a death only once in their career. Performing an investigation in any one of these types of death for the first time requires current knowledge and skills in numerous disciplines and techniques. Without the requisite knowledge the result can be an increase in the potential for errors to occur, which can significantly impact the ultimate outcome of the investigation. Regardless, getting it right is of utmost importance to the assigned investigator.

The primary objective of this book is to improve the investigations of arrest-related deaths, officer-involved shooting deaths, and in-custody deaths, by examining the relevant research in each topic, and accepted practices and procedures which will enhance the effectiveness of performing such an investigation. The chapters of the book go beyond other types of investigation books, as a major goal of the book provides the current status of the science, guidelines, and relevant checklists for the investigator tasked with performing the investigation. Investigatory bodies like the National Transportation and Safety Board (NTSB), National Center for Missing and Exploited Children (NCMEC) First Responder Investigators, National Association of Medical Investigators (NAMI), and the National Forensic Science Technology Center (NFSTC), have all developed investigation checklists to assist in performing the most thorough investigation possible. Checklists can provide a framework of actions, considerations, and activities that may assist the investigator in performing competent, productive, and thorough investigations. The outcome will simultaneously assist in mitigating errors that can impact the investigation.

The intent of the book is to address the emerging components of each death category under one cover. The book is designed around seven broad themes: (1) it meets the needs of investigators and administrators in acquiring a comprehensive perspective regarding the nature of these unique death investigations; (2) the book addresses the important role of the investigator and the agency administrator and their respective duties when performing the investigation; (3) the book provides the current status of the research on the science of each topic area which will enhance an investigator's knowledge base on the subject matter; (4) the book provides investigation guidelines for the investigator to consider when conducting the investigation; (5) the book addresses the human factors of the involved officers which should be considered by the investigator; (6) the book describes the interview methods investigators should consider when performing officer interviews; and (7) the book provides checklists for the investigator to use in the field and when writing the investigation report in order to mitigate the chance of error. The content of the book is both technical and applied and is based on the recent research and protocols impacting each death category.

An important theme integrated within the entire book as in all endeavors of the criminal justice system is the investigator's responsibility to adhere to professional ethics and accountability, and to perform their duties within the parameters of the Constitution. Not only must the investigator follow appropriate professional ethics and investigatory guidelines but the performance of the investigation must comport with the law and legal decisions. As a result, applicable United States Supreme Court and appellate court decisions and case studies are presented to guide the investigator in carrying out the legal aspects of the investigation.

Like many projects the book is not the work of just one, but assistance was provided by numerous professionals in their respective fields. First, this book is the culmination of the efforts of the co-author and numerous contributing authors. A special note of gratitude goes to Gary Vilke, M.D. whose medical knowledge and expertise are unparalleled. Dr. Vilke not only significantly assisted in the completion of the book but he oversaw the chapters which addressed varying medical issues involved in the death investigations.

Second, the book presents lessons learned from all of the contributing authors who have performed these types of investigations as practitioners, have been involved in varying aspects of these investigations, and have conducted research and published previous works on the subject. In addition, numerous contributing authors have trained investigators, medicolegal personnel, administrators, and officers on the topics, provided technical assistance to criminal justice agencies on the topics of the book, provided numerous conference presentations on the subject, and have provided expert courtroom testimony on the subject matter. Collectively, the contributing authors have provided expert witness services in over 2,000 cases on all of the varying topics addressed in the book. Further, the book provides lessons learned by all of the authors and each chapter presents case examples, which illustrate the varying types of arrest-related and custodial deaths addressed. These authors are all working professionals in their respective disciplines who volunteered their expertise and time to contribute to the success of the book. I am extremely grateful for their contributions, which will maximize the success of the investigation.

Finally, I thank Deborah Robinson, Ph.D., professor in Criminal Justice at Valdosta State University for her time devoted to reviewing each chapter. Her assistance in ensuring that all of the chapters were structured properly is sincerely appreciated.

Darrell L. Ross, Ph.D.

1

ARREST-RELATED DEATHS, EMERGING QUESTIONS, AND COMPETING EXPECTATIONS IN INVESTIGATIONS

Darrell L. Ross, Michael Brave, and Mark Kroll

Introduction

Ask most any medicolegal investigator, investigating an arrest-related death, officer-involved shooting, or suicide death in custody, and he or she will comment that these classifications of deaths present some of the most complex and challenging death investigations they are required to perform. Prior researchers have reported that deaths classified into these categories are among the most highly charged and emotional cases investigated by coroners or medical examiners (Lifschultz & Donoghue, 1991). Luke and Reay (1992) noted that investigating deaths in police custody is considered a "perilous and a slippery slope, in the never-never land of death." Reay (1998) further reported that a death in police custody, due to unsubstantiated facts and rumors surrounding the death, has the potential for controversy, and major disturbances have erupted because of alleged police misconduct. Moreover, Southall et al. (2008) reported that a death during arrest or while in police custody is one of the most contentious and controversial cases facing the medical examiner.

An arrest-related death is defined as a person who dies during the process of arrest, who may be under restraint and custody, and dies on scene, during transport, or at the hospital (Burch, 2011). The sudden death may also occur during arrest or confinement, which involved a violent and combative detainee who vigorously fought with the police during control and restraint, and was under the influence of a chemical substance and/or was experiencing symptomologies of a mental illness. A sudden custodial death may also occur in a mental health facility during the course of controlling and restraining a combative mental health patient. An officer-involved shooting most generally occurs during a police arrest/intervention of a person, or during the police investigation of a suspicious person or circumstance which poses an imminent threat to the officers or others, requiring the use of lethal force. Some officer-involved shootings may also involve, although rarely, a corrections officer or parole officer discharging his or her firearm while performing sworn duties. A custodial death by suicide generally occurs during the confinement of a detainee or prisoner in a jail or correctional facility. Detainees have also died in custody due to an excessive use/abuse of chemical substances. While any one of these death classifications is a statistically rare event, they can present significant problems for those tasked with conducting varying aspects of the investigation. Graham (2014) noted that the medicolegal investigator assigned to investigate and certify the custodial death bears a heavy responsibility to the decedent's family, the public, law enforcement, and other institutions while performing the investigation.

Concerns about arrest-related custodial deaths and officer-involved shootings stem not only from their limited frequency of occurrence, but from the potential consequences and aftermath of the incident. In a police use of lethal force shooting incident, and in a custodial suicide death, the cause of death is generally clearly identifiable. In an arrest-related death, where the individual suddenly died after a violent restraint confrontation, the cause of death may not be so apparent. The responding and restraining officers may use the same control techniques and less-lethal force equipment they have used on previous occasions, without significant injury sustained by the arrestee, let alone a death. But in an arrest-related death, the person suddenly and unexpectedly dies within a short time after restraint on scene, during transport to the hospital, or at the hospital.

Compounding the incidence of many sudden death cases, a negative autopsy may result, indicating no definitive cause of death was determined. As a result, pathologists are left to theorize about the potential contributing factors or causes of death, including the person's underlying medical (cardiac or pulmonary disease), the acute state of the person (drug-induced state or psychosis), and the use of force and restraint equipment and devices used by law enforcement officers (Chan, 2006).

Regardless of the cause of death, the involved officers, their supervisors, the agency administrator, and ultimately the city and/or county of the involved officers, will be blamed. Veteran officers, administrators, investigators, and medical examiners know too well of the potentially devastating aftermath of these death incidents, as they involve: loss of life; bereavement of the affected family; emerging questions regarding the involved officers' actions and involvement in the incident; strained police and community relations and trust; protests and rioting, which result in social and economic crises in the affected cities; riots and disturbances in confinement facilities; internal affairs investigations; prosecutorial investigations and potential criminal charges filed against the officers, which could result in a criminal trial; initiation of civil litigation filed against the officers and the agency; possible termination of the involved officers; and possible civil rights investigations by the Department of Justice (DOJ).

Frequently, following an arrest-related death, death in custody, or officer-involved shooting, protests and riots have erupted, causing destruction to property and businesses, for example: the police shooting in Ferguson, MO in 2014 of Michael Brown; the custodial restraint death of Eric Garner in 2014 in New York City, NY; the custodial death of Freddie Gray in 2015 in Baltimore, MD; the shooting of two motorists in Cleveland, OH in 2012, followed by the acquittal of the officer criminally charged in the shooting; a shooting in Cleveland, OH of a youth with a starter pistol, where the involved officer was acquitted; and the prosecution of an officer who shot a youth with a knife in Chicago, IL in 2015, which was captured on video. All of these incidents represent examples of community members protesting and rioting. In the Freddie Gray custodial death incident, six Baltimore police officers were prosecuted, which resulted in three officers being acquitted, one trial resulted in a mistrial, and the charges were dropped against the other two officers (Stolberg & Bidgood, 2016). In addition to community unrest, criminal prosecution of the involved officers and filing of §1983 civil federal lawsuits against the involved officers and the law enforcement or correctional agency also occur.

Since the passage of the Violent Crime Control and Law Enforcement Act of 1994 by Congress, the common trend following an arrest-related death is for the Department of Justice to conduct a civil rights investigation into the incident, in accordance with Title 42 U.S. Code §14141. The past trend had been for the DOJ to conduct a civil rights investigation after the grand jury convened or after the conclusion of a criminal trial. However, the DOJ commenced its investigation into the Baltimore, MD police department prior to the criminal trial of the six accused involved officers. To date, the DOJ has conducted investigations into each of the aforementioned departments, except in the incidents in New York, and found a systematic pattern and practice of violating the constitutional rights of citizens, resulting in the departments entering into legal agreements to remedy those identified practices. As of 2016, there are 39 law enforcement agencies under some level of federal oversight in accordance with §14141 since 2009 (Department of Justice, 2016). Even though the officers' conduct was exonerated in Ferguson, Baltimore, and Cleveland, the DOJ conducted investigations into the police departments and all resulted in consent decrees (Department of Justice, 2016).

Prior to 1998, little research had been conducted on the nature of arrest-related deaths, officer-involved shootings, and custodial suicide deaths. Since 1998, a plethora of research has been performed on varying components of arrest-related deaths, enhancing not only our understanding regarding the nature of these deaths, but also enhancing the investigatory protocols for those who perform these investigations. For example, Laub (2011a), based on the collective research of medical and police experts, provided recommended and applicable protocols appropriate for conducting an investigation of a death after the use of the TASER. The Psychological Services Section of the International Association Chiefs of Police (2013) has published its recommended protocols for investigation of officer-involved shootings. Moreover, Hall et al. (2012; 2015) and Ross and Hazlett (2016) reported similar but independent findings of prospective analysis of the outcomes of violent prone restraint incidents in policing and detention centers. The field research findings confirmed what past reputable laboratory experiments have found since 1998, that controlling and restraining a combative person in the prone position is not associated with positional asphyxia, causing the death of the person. Neither study reported a death from placing the person in the prone position, even when a significant number of the individuals were under the influence of a chemical substance or exhibited symptomologies of a mental illness, and various force measures were used like the TASER, aerosols, empty-hand control techniques, and various restraint equipment.

Conducting an investigation into any of these death categories can pose problems and significant challenges for the investigator (Ross, 2015). The National Academy of Sciences (2009) recommended that efforts be targeted toward improving medicolegal death investigations. While efforts have been instituted to improve the skills of death investigators since this recommendation, no text has been published since the NAS recommendation, which specifically addresses the investigation issues surrounding arrest-related deaths, officer-involved shootings, and custodial suicide deaths in confinement. This book is specifically designed to address the many associated issues involved in performing an investigation on these topic areas. In this chapter the questions which emerge from these investigations are addressed and the expectations of those involved or impacted by the investigation are presented.

Medicolegal Death Investigations

The tasks of collecting and analyzing information about the circumstances and causes of death have been referred to as medicolegal death investigation. This term combines the dual relationship which exists between medical science and the law (Hanzlick, 2007). The primary purpose of the medicolegal investigation is to establish the cause and the manner of death (Wagner, 2008). The medicolegal investigation of death in custody requires precise and detailed examination (Hiss & Kahana, 1996). Because the death occurred during a police contact, arrest, or during custodial confinement, questions of whether the police abused their authority will also be examined.

All states, by law, require a medicolegal investigation of deaths which involve injury or that are sudden and unexplained (Hanzlick, 2007). Deaths due to homicide, suicide, and accidents, and unexplained causes are common examples. For example, the Georgia Death Investigation Act, §45-16-20 (Official Code of Georgia Annotated, 2010) requires that a medical examiner's inquiry be made into deaths that meet the following criteria: death as a result of violence; a suicide; sudden death of a person in apparent good health; when a prisoner dies in a state hospital, or a state, county, or city penal facility; death by any suspicious or unusual manner, with particular attention to those persons 16 years of age and under; and a death of a patient under hospice care, and after having been admitted to a hospital in an unconscious state and without regaining consciousness within 24 hours of admission. Arrest-related deaths, officer-involved shootings, and custodial suicide deaths in confinement facilities fall within the purview of a medicolegal death investigation. The protocols for performing the medicolegal death investigations in these death classifications are addressed in this book.

A system for investigating these classifications of death is in place in all states, and comprises many individuals representing local, county, and state agencies. The medicolegal death investigation process includes numerous activities, which start at the crime scene and follow through to the court process. The process generally comprises the following components: securing the scene; collecting and analyzing scene evidence; taking measurements at the scene; estimating times associated with the incident; examining the body; performing numerous laboratory tests and diagnosis; interviewing witnesses; examining the history of the decedent; and court testimony (Di Maio, 2006).

In most states, the medical examiner/coroner possesses the statutory responsibility to determine the cause and manner of death. In death incidents involving the activity of law enforcement officers, the involved agency will generally investigate the scene and collect the associated evidence, but the medical examiner will maintain control of the body. Individuals responsible for investigating the arrest-related death from the involved agency may include the following: internal affair investigators, homicide investigators, crime scene technicians, and various command personnel. Individuals representing the prosecutor's office will generally be involved and may be on scene, as well as the agency's legal counsel and risk manager. It is important that all responding agencies represented and tasked with conducting the investigation recognize the varying jurisdictional and statutory responsibilities which apply to individual agency representatives, and that these individuals work together toward accomplishing the common goal, which is to discover the facts of the death (Laub, 2011b; Wagner, 2008). Once the investigation is finalized, the medical examiner may select among the following manners of death, including: natural causes, homicide, suicide, accident, and undetermined. This can only be accomplished by conducting a competent and thorough death-scene investigation that provides the basis for a comprehensive medicolegal autopsy, and together, the scene investigation and autopsy provide the basis for an accurate determination of cause and manner of death (Laub, 2011b).

Emergent Questions Involving Arrest-Related Death Investigations

An arrest-related death, officer-involved shooting, or custodial suicide death are considered high-profile cases requiring a detailed and complete investigation to be completed. Because the incident involved law enforcement and/or correctional officers, and since they will be under extreme scrutiny and possibly facing criminal charges, a thorough investigation by police and the medical examiner's office is critical. Performing less than a professional and detailed investigation, and rushing to conclusions, jeopardizes the ultimate goal of any investigation, that of seeking the truth. Many probing questions emerge from these deaths, and following proper investigation protocols can assist in assuring that as many as possible of these questions are addressed as thoroughly as possible.

In an arrest-related death where the officers responded with varying degrees of force, including lethal force, some of the many probing questions will include:

- What type of decedent behaviors prompted the officer's use of force?
- What was the physiological and mental health history of the decedent?
- What was the chemical substance abuse history of the decedent?
- What measures did the officer use in assessing the behaviors of the decedent?
- Did the officer over-react in determining the degree of force selected?
- Did the officer's response follow a predetermined plan when encountering violent and combative individuals?
- What force control technique or force equipment did the officer decide to use and were they justified?
- How did the officer restrain the decedent and in what position was the restrained decedent placed?
- Did the officer misuse or misapply the force technique or equipment used?
- Did the officer's use of force contribute to the death of the decedent?
- Why did the officer resort to the use of lethal force and were other options available at the time?
- Did the decedent possess a weapon at the time that the officer used the force measure?
- Was the decedent an imminent threat to the officer at the time the level of force was used?
- When did the officer radio for medical assistance?
- Did the officer fail to monitor the restrained person?
- What type of medical intervention did the officer provide?
- How was the decedent transported?
- Was the decedent transported to the jail rather than to a hospital?
- Was a competent investigation completed?

These are among some of the multitude of questions that will emerge during and after the investigation regarding the arrest-related death and/or officer involved shooting. In cases of a custodial suicide death or other death in custody, some of the many questions that may emerge include:

- Did the booking officer fail to properly process the detainee at the time of booking?
- Did the booking officer fail to attend to any obvious signs of intoxication, signs of a serious injury, or signs of a serious medical or mental illness?
- What was the mental health history of the decedent?
- What was the substance abuse history of the decedent?
- When was the decedent assessed by a medical health provider?
- Was the decedent provided prescribed medications during confinement?
- Did the officer fail to properly house the detainee based on appropriate classification protocols?

- What preventative measures did the officers take to minimize the risk of self-harm to the decedent?
- Did the officer deny access to appropriate medical or mental health care to the decedent?
- Did the officers perform security checks in accordance with the security classification of the decedent?
- Were the officers deliberately indifferent to the medical and mental health needs of the decedent?
- Was a competent investigation completed?

Answering these questions, and many others, can create challenges for the investigator, and like other investigations, some questions may ultimately remain unanswered. When this occurs, concerns about the adequacy of the investigation emerge, giving the impression that the investigator or the medical examiner completed a less than thorough investigation. Concerns and additional questions are further raised when an officer is acquitted of alleged wrongdoing in a court, or after an internal affairs investigation by the department. Additional questions may emerge about the integrity of the investigation and the ethical behavior of the investigators.

A thorough investigation is not only owed to, but also expected by the estate of the decedent and the involved officers, as well as the citizens in the community, the department administrators, the media, the investigator, the medical examiner's office, and the criminal justice system (Peckitt, 2016). Due to the media's coverage of sensational cases and the portrayal of conducting an investigation as shown on popular TV shows like *CSI* and *NCIS*, the expectation by society is that any death investigation can be solved in a short period of time, using the most sophisticated forensic science equipment and techniques. When an arrest-related death investigation, officer-involved shooting, or custodial suicide death investigation fails to bring conclusive or even contrary findings, not matching the expectations of one of the aforementioned entities, further suspiciousness of a cover-up further erodes the trust amongst any members of the group.

Competing Expectations of Arrest-Related Death Investigations

The classifications of death investigations present situations where the investigator must get it right the first time, even though there is no absolutely perfect investigation. Margins of error and error rates are part of the forensic science testing process, although all tests strive for high reliability (James & Nordby, 2012). Part of the problem, however, is that these classifications of death occur so infrequently and involve numerous complex variables that the investigator may miss an important component due to his or her unfamiliarity with the associated factors during the investigation. With less than one officer-involved shooting or a sudden arrest-related death occurring out of a million citizen contacts, the investigator may only conduct one investigation of this type in his or her career. Yet, the same level of high-caliber investigation is expected, regardless of the frequency of performing the investigation (Hargrove & Bowman, 2009). The lack of frequency of conducting such an investigation can subsequently increase the risk of error. Some of the more common errors made in arrest-related death and officer-involved shooting investigations may include:

- failing to protect and manage the incident scene allowing for scene contamination;
- responding to a scene with a preconceived notion, which aids in confirmation bias;
- failing to take enough incident scene photographs;

- failing to interview all witnesses;
- failing to ensure identification, collection, analysis, documentation, and maintenance of all evidence;
- failing to investigate or consider other cause-of-death possibilities. Hargrove and Bowman (2009) reported that 33 percent of all autopsies performed are flawed with major errors;
- failing to explain and support the precise alleged mechanism of cause of death, which has confused temporality with causation;
- failing to test for, or inability to test for newer designer drugs;
- failing to exclude research involving junk science and anecdotes, which influence the cause of death classifications; and
- allowing the media and the public to influence a rush to judgment and incorrect decision (Geberth, 2007; Karch & Brave 2015).

Recognizing this problem does not diminish the fact that investigators must meet the implied expectations and their responsibility of performing a thorough investigation. Part of the primary objective of this book is to minimize the error rate impacting the outcomes of these investigations. An arrest-related death, an officer-involved shooting, or a custodial suicide death in jail or prison, activates a series of concerns and expectations for the criminal justice system, various groups, agencies, and the community. The expectations and concerns of these entities are discussed below without any ascribed priority.

Expectations of the Medical Examiner

For an arrest-related death or death in custody, it is expected that a competent death investigation will be conducted, as the conclusions made as to the cause of death will impact the officer's career and the department's image in the community, as well as impacting the involved family members and the judicial system. The expectation of the medical examiner is to ensure that he or she uses his or her forensic expertise in a manner that provides integrity and accuracy, and is free from bias when determining the cause and manner of death. Di Maio (2003) reports that medical expertise is critical in death investigations, and begins with preserving the crime scene, examining the body, collecting evidence at the crime scene, performing a thorough autopsy, conducting laboratory tests, and determining the cause and manner of death.

While the officers, the family, the department, and others expect the medical examiner to reach a definitive cause of death in an arrest-related death, it is not always possible, as about 25 to 30 percent of these deaths result in a negative autopsy. It is not uncommon for the medical examiner to report on the death certificate in a violent use of force restraint death, that the cause of death is undetermined (Chan, 2006; Tester & Ackerman, 2012). This is understandable, as a restraint death involving a person who is under the influence of an illicit chemical, in the throes of a severe psychosis, or both, comprises a multitude and a confluence of factors which may contribute to the death. Therefore, it is critical that the medical examiner be fully knowledgeable about these factors in an effort to provide a thorough, competent, and bias-free examination of all evidence.

Despite the training, education, and experience of the medical examiner, given the rarity of arrest-related deaths, many medical examiners have never performed an autopsy of a person exhibiting symptomologies of excited delirium or a death after the use of the TASER or other force equipment.

Hence, it is easy for confirmation bias to creep into the investigation. Confirmation bias refers to the tendency to search for, interpret, or recall information in a way that confirms one's preconceived belief or hypothesis (Karch & Brave, 2015).

Medical examiners frequently base their conclusions on the "balance of probabilities," "differential diagnosis," or "exclusion," but commonly fail to include: all possible causes/contributors; a clear statement of limitations, including tests not done and factors not considered; statement of degree of medical/scientific certainty being used; and clear statement of general and specific incident causation. Further, medical examiners investigating arrest-related deaths frequently add modifiers to death certificates, such as: "while prone," "during police restraint," or "following the application of a TASER." Additionally, medical examiners seldom include the exact mechanism of cause or contribution to death, an explanation of general and specific causation of mechanism, evidence that supports this speculation, or methodologically reliable supporting literature citations. As a result, many errors may emerge during the investigation, and may include the following:

- failing to test for all types of illicit and/or prescription drugs;
- failing to perform detailed tests of all internal organs, including the brain;
- relying on junk science, which has been shown to be unreliable and discredited research;
- relying on case reports or hearsay, which are not accepted by the court as reliable evidence;
- failing to explain and support the precise alleged mechanism of cause of death, confusing temporality with causation;
- failing to investigate or consider other cause of death possibilities, such as exertional stress and genetic abnormalities;
- failing to utilize experts when appropriate (e.g., cardiac pathologist, forensic toxicologist, bioelectrical scientist);
- failing to consider toxidrome (signs and symptoms of poisoning) of substances in relation to mortality;
- failing to keep abreast of the current science and police use of force measures pertaining to arrest-related deaths, and;
- decisions made to a degree of certainty of "possibility" and not to an appropriate degree of professional certainty (*Hasler v. U.S.*, 1983; Ho, Peterson, & Masoudi, 2008; Karch & Brave, 2015; Krexi et al., 2015).

A classic example depicting errors performed by a medical examiner is illustrated in *TASER International, Inc. v. Chief Medical Examiner of Summit County* (2009). The civil action involved the deaths of three men while in custody of several law enforcement agencies in Summit County in 2005 and 2006. All three incidents involved the application of a TASER and the medical examiner determined that the use of the TASER contributed to each death and the manner of death in each was ruled as a homicide. TASER International brought suit and requested that the court order the medical examiner to remove any reference to any TASER causing or contributing to the cause of death with respect to each decedent. The court entered a judgment in favor to TASER International and ordered the medical examiner to amend the death certificate in each case. In two of the cases, the court ordered the medical examiner to change the cause of death from homicide to accident, and in the third from homicide to undetermined.

The medical examiner proposed the theory of causation of death in the incidents from using the TASER as: impaired respiration and asphyxia caused by contraction of the muscles in the diaphragm; acidosis brought about by the TASER, and the possibility that the decedents were scared to death by the use of TASER. During the trial, the errors were admitted by the medical examiner and some included: agreed that no research specifically supports that the use of the TASER will cause death; agreed that the TASER will not specifically contribute to asphyxia; agreed that the autopsy of one of the decedents was the first one she ever conducted where the TASER was applied; that she did not know how a TASER operates nor did she do any research to familiarize herself with the use of the TASER; and that one of the decedent's behaviors was consistent with excited delirium. Expert witnesses from various disciplines used by TASER International found scientific fault with the investigation, and rejected the theories of causation of death advanced by the medical examiner. The court agreed and found, based on the evidence, the testimony of the expert witnesses, and the testimony of the medical examiner, that a minimal investigation was conducted into the cause and manner of death, and that various errors were made in the three incidents. The court noted that the medical examiner could not opine to a reasonable degree of scientific certainty the mechanism through which TASER deployments contributed to the deaths.

While it may not be possible to expect an investigation to be perfect and free from any error, ill-informed medical examiners should not be able to go unchallenged when rendering their opinions, which may be based on bias and outside the current scientific literature. Police officers are expected to make split-second decisions under stressful conditions when deciding to use a level of force, and are expected to get it right. Conversely, medical personnel, who have the luxury of time and the full record and resources at their disposal, should be held to a higher standard to ensure that a full, complete and competent investigation is conducted, which will assist in mitigating the risk of error.

Expectations of the Department

When an arrest-related death, an officer-involved shooting, or a custodial death occurs, numerous expectations of the department are triggered. The department is expected and is obligated to commence a complete investigation and guarantee that agency personnel fulfill their investigative responsibility. Trust and accountability to the community, the decedent's family, to the involved officers, and to the criminal justice system are paramount in initiating and completing the investigation.

Expectations of department activity related to these death investigations should be addressed pre- and post-incident. The involved agency is expected to be proactive and develop policies and procedures which guide the officers' actions in the field, and should be in place and investigators should be trained in them prior to a death incident occurring. Too often, in many arrest or custodial death incidents, appropriate policies and protocols are missing and/or outdated, which can negatively impact the investigation. Current policies appropriate to the incident should be reviewed.

Prior to the death incident occurring, department administrators should build and maintain relationships that are evidenced on several levels. First, administrators should build a close relationship with agency command personnel and investigators in developing the policies and protocols which guide them in conducting arrest-related investigations. Administrators should further provide investigators with ongoing advanced training commensurate to their tasks and responsibilities as they relate to these death categories. It is expected that the agency administrator develop and structure a team approach in responding to an arrest-related death, which prepares and directs all personnel involved in how to perform their specific responsibilities when required to do so.

Second, administrators should build a close relationship with city and county management personnel. In doing so, these entities will be informed of the department's philosophy in preparing and responding to death investigations, and will assist in keeping these entities abreast of the ongoing resources needed. Third, department administrators should build and maintain relationships with outside law enforcement agencies who may also conduct death investigations which occur with their department personnel. In many states, an outside agency may be called in or required to conduct the death investigation. For example, in Michigan, the Michigan State Police perform many investigations of arrest-related deaths and officer-involved shootings on behalf of the involved department. In Georgia, the Georgia Bureau of Investigation generally performs the death investigations. Also in Michigan, the Mission Team, comprised of many investigators from participating sheriff departments, are called in to conduct an independent investigation into custodial jail deaths and some arrest-related deaths. Further, in 2014, the state legislature of Wisconsin signed statutory law requiring all custody death investigations involving a law enforcement officer be performed by an independent agency (Wisconsin State Legislature, 2014). Wisconsin is the first state to pass such legislation to date.

Fourth, agency administrators should maintain a close relationship with the medical examiner/coroner's office. The medical examiner is authorized to examine the death scene location and the body to determine the cause and manner of death. Since agency investigators will be working closely with the medical examiner, a solid relationship should be fostered prior to the incident occurring. Jurisdictional and statutory responsibilities should be determined prior to the death incident occurring and administrators should seek to have the medical examiner provide basic and advanced training to agency investigators where feasible.

Fifth, department administrators should build relationships with key leaders and groups in the community, which can foster a relationship of trust prior to an arrest-related death occurring. Arrest-related deaths, officer-involved shootings, and custodial deaths in jail are more likely to draw more scrutiny and criticism than other citizen and police incidents (Katz, 2015). As a result of the death incident, trust can be eroded and when the community perceives that the investigation was performed with bias or that the investigation resulted in a cover-up, distrust of the police is enhanced. Such community dissatisfaction can periodically result in protests and riots. As previously mentioned, the arrest-related deaths of Michael Brown in 2014, in Ferguson, MO and Eric Garner in 2014 in New York City, both African American men, illustrate the perception of distrust between the community and the police. When the grand jury decided not to bring criminal charges against the involved officers, some community citizens decided to riot, which lasted several days and resulted in millions of dollars of property destruction. The perception by many of the rioters was that the death investigation was tainted, due to collusion between the police department and the prosecutor.

Sixth, it is expected that agency administrators maintain close relations with the media. The media represent a most powerful method with which to communicate with the community. Accountability and trust can be further entrenched with the community by the agency administrator or designated person, like a public information officer (PIO), by communicating to the community how the investigation is progressing, providing appropriate information about the investigation on a regular basis, and by telling the department's story rather than allowing the media to "convey their story." Getting ahead of the media early, as appropriate, is suggested in order to inform the community about the incident and the progress of the investigation, in order to dispel distortions of the public perception.

Where law enforcement agencies have procrastinated in providing timely information to the community through the media about the incident and the investigation, the delay has been more likely to fuel the perception of the community that the police are involved in a cover-up, are being less than truthful, or are engaged in a corrupt investigation process, and has assisted in magnifying the distrust of the police. The agency spokesperson should regularly speak to the community through the media explaining the progress of the investigation, which can assist in dissuading some in the community from engaging in violence, while at the same time, protecting the integrity of the investigation and concomitantly protecting the rights of the involved officers. Engagement with the community through the assistance of the media can go a long way in demonstrating trust and accountability during a highly emotional and volatile incident.

Seventh, after an arrest-related death, the department is expected to conduct a "complete investigation." A complete investigation is one that includes all relevant information required to achieve the purpose of the inquiry (Community Oriented Policing Services, 2008). It is expected that a complete investigation is free from bias and prejudice, is performed in a timely manner, and is regularly monitored to ensure quality control and integrity. Agency administrators can ensure a complete investigation is performed, thus keeping investigators accountable by periodically requiring them to report on the progress of the investigation. Simultaneously, the administrator must balance the standards of quality control by permitting investigators the latitude to perform their investigation duties without micromanaging them. Further, a complete investigation is one that assists the agency head in making the appropriate decision based on a final report, which clearly presents all of the evidence and information discovered through the investigation. Agency administrators should also maintain a close relationship with the prosecuting attorney who will be examining the case to determine if criminal charges should be filed against the involved officer(s).

Once the department is notified that an arrest-related or custodial death has occurred, the department is expected to notify the appropriate command personnel, investigators, and crime scene technicians so they may respond to the incident location. A notification tree, which identifies the following individuals, should be developed prior to an arrest-related death incident occurring: dispatch; senior precinct supervisor; emergency medical services; the police chief or sheriff (department head); immediate supervisor of the involved officer(s); agency investigators and external investigators; the medical examiner; the prosecutor; crime scene technicians; attorney for the officer(s); agency risk manager and legal counsel; the public information officer; the police union as appropriate; and the peer support team.

Involved Officer Expectations

It is expected that the agency protect the interests of the involved officer as the investigation proceeds. The involved officer is entitled to a complete and thorough investigation at the same level as the decedent's family, and it is expected that investigators maintain the investigation integrity and follow all of the investigation protocols. At the appropriate time after the incident, the involved officer should be allowed to make a "public safety statement" and be encouraged to exercise his or her right to counsel, but should not be encouraged to waive Fifth Amendment rights. The agency must balance the need to obtain the truth through conducting a lawful investigation, while also ensuring that the officer's rights are protected.

After the incident, the officer should be asked if he or she requires medical attention and provided with medical assistance as warranted; allowed to render his or her firearm and be provided with another; be transported to a non-stressful location; allowed to contact his or her family members; and allowed to go home and rest from 24 to 72 hours prior to participating in an interview with investigators. Prior to conducting an internal department interview, the involved officer must be provided with warnings in accordance with the United States Supreme Court's decision in *Garrity v. New Jersey* (1967). If the officer is being criminally charged, he or she must be provided with his or her Miranda warnings and afforded the same rights of a person charged with a criminal offense prior to the interview.

Expectations of the Investigator

The overarching expectation of an arrest-related death investigation is the search for the truth and adhering to professional procedures (Hanzlick, 2007; Lee, 2002; Lyons, 2015; Wangmo et al., 2014). The outgrowth of these two important principles results in indicators of ethical conduct, which comprise honesty, fairness, accountability, public scrutiny, and self-awareness, as well as professional accountability and responsibility. Regardless of the category of death leading to the investigation, the investigator will be examining an incident which involves investigating the actions of fellow agency officers or another department's officers. When the investigator and the officer of the investigation are part of the same agency, a problem may emerge in which the investigator may interpret the evidence and officer statements in a preconceived manner, providing evidence that a less than thorough investigation was performed (Kahan, 2011). Performing such an investigation requires the investigator to maintain objectivity and impartiality, while objectively examining all pieces of evidence, and strictly following accepted investigation protocols and guidelines. Failing to follow investigation protocols can place the entire investigation at risk.

When an arrest-related death occurs, the decedent's family, members of the community and the criminal justice system expect that the investigation will be conducted in accordance with acceptable protocols and within the boundaries of ethics and the law. Maintaining a focus and a commitment to remaining unbiased in assessing the evidence, no matter where the evidence leads, is expected of all investigators. Adhering to the profession's ethical standards will assist in keeping the investigation free of bias, and will ensure that a non-prejudicial investigation is performed. One reason why ethics is so important in the field of forensic investigations is because the results yielded by physical evidence discovered have a great impact on the lives of others (Barnett, 2001). A classic example of this was observed in the O.J. Simpson case. Due to various mistakes made during the investigation, the evidence collected did not hold up in court, and O.J. Simpson was cleared of all charges. Following the tenets of ethics in performing an investigation serves to hold investigators accountable, and will assist in strengthening the trust of those being investigated and trust within the community. An ethical investigation is not only expected, but also serves the interest of the decedent's family, the interest of the involved officers, the interests of the community, and the interests of the criminal justice system.

The basic components of a death investigation involving an arrest-related death are similar to those in other death-related investigations, which include: scene investigation, collecting and preserving evidence, examining the decedent's history, interviewing witnesses and officers, and examination of the body with various lab tests performed (Graham, 2014). In many law enforcement agencies, an arrest-related death investigation may be assigned to internal affairs investigators or a homicide investigator. Investigators assigned to either unit may have experience in investigating officer misconduct, a citizen complaint, or a criminal homicide, but may have little or no experience in investigating an arrest-related death occurring from a use of force encounter, or an officer involved shooting, or a custodial suicide. Regardless, the expectation of the investigator is to perform a thorough and complete investigation in order for a competent adjudicator to make a final determination without resorting to surmise, prejudice, or assumption of facts at issue (Community Oriented Policing Services, 2008).

Beyond being competent in the basic components of death investigations, the investigator, however, is also expected to be knowledgeable of the agency's policy on using force and all of the use of force measures allowed. Arrest-related deaths and officer-involved shooting incidents include the involved officers using a myriad of force options depending on the totality of the circumstances. Hence, when investigating a violent arrest-related death, the investigator should be knowledgeable of the following important components: state and federal laws guiding the appropriate use of force; all of the authorized empty-hand control techniques; all intermediate weapons; all restraint equipment; all authorized firearms; and the training of the officers in the appropriate use of these items. Further, investigators should be knowledgeable of the research on human factors science and the various perceptual distortions which occur in a stressful use of force encounter, which impact decision making and the officer's performance before and during the incident.

Moreover, when an arrest-related death occurs after a period of violent restraint and control by officers, the investigator is expected to be knowledgeable of the factors surrounding the death, such as Excited Delirium Syndrome (ExDS), mental illness and anti-psychotic medications, illicit substances, and the theory of positional/restraint asphyxiation. It is expected that the investigator will consult with the agency's use of force and firearms instructors in cases of arrest-related deaths and officer-involved shootings. Investigators are also expected to be knowledgeable about confinement-related issues when assigned to investigate a custodial death in confinement.

The death investigator is expected to maintain quality control and integrity of the investigation. The following underscore these principles: maintaining chain of custody of the evidence collected; compiling and retaining notes; interviewing witnesses and officers in a timely manner; keeping supervisors abreast of the progress of the investigation; maintaining a current file and securing it; keeping a current log of items addressed in the investigation; protecting the rights of the involved officers; and detailed documentation of performing the investigation. Part of the maintenance of quality control in any investigation includes the investigator keeping abreast of the investigation protocols and techniques, relevant research, policy, and laws by attending training on a regular basis and following the training and the protocols when performing the investigation.

Of equal importance for the investigation is producing a high-quality report. Investigators are expected to write a comprehensive report, which at the least answers the questions that emerge from the incident (Community Oriented Policing Services, 2008). Compiling and structuring a thorough report is often difficult for many investigators. Training, experience, and professional judgment can assist in gauging the scope of the report. The investigator's report should provide appropriate information so that the decision maker may arrive at the best decision possible. A comprehensive report should present, at a minimum, the following: relevant facts which are underscored with the evidence; all questions which emerged from the investigation surrounding the death; all evidence collected and assessed; all tests that were performed and all photographs taken; all interviews and statements of witnesses and involved officers; a clear and precise explanation of all measurements and distances taken, and estimates of time involved in the incident; and a detailed and impartial summary, while also avoiding conclusionary statements where possible and unless authorized, avoiding interjecting personal opinions (Community Oriented Policing Services, 2008). It is customary to provide an explanation of inconsistencies amongst statements and inconsistencies between statements and the evidence.

Finally, the investigator is expected to prepare to testify in court. Depending on the outcome of the investigation, the investigator may have to testify in criminal and/or in civil court. The investigator is expected to be knowledgeable of the rules in both courts. Regardless of the type of court proceedings, the investigator must be prepared to fully describe: the outcome of the investigation and the report submitted; the investigation standards and protocols relied upon; his or her knowledge of the Federal Rules of Evidence and state laws; how all evidence was collected; all tests and analysis performed; and his or her training attended and certifications completed (Wells, 2012). The investigator should also be knowledgeable of how to provide testimony in civil court when a deposition is required and when the case proceeds to trial. Complete documentation of all evidence and retention of notes and other documents is recommended as the plaintiff's attorney in a civil case will submit a request to produce all documents pertinent to the case. Prior to testifying in a deposition or court trial in civil court, it is highly recommended that the investigator meet with the defense counsel.

Expectations of the Decedent's Family

One of the most important issues involved in the investigation of an arrest-related death, officer-involved shooting or in custody suicide is the expectation of the decedent's family members that the investigation will be professionally performed. Like other elements comprised in the investigation, the family not only expects that the investigation be completed in accordance with appropriate protocols, but also in accordance with integrity and ethical values. The trauma associated with a sudden unexpected tragedy will place the family of the decedent under immense personal pressures. It is essential therefore that family members be treated with respect and their individual needs taken into account. Those charged with the investigation should provide information to family members and respond to their questions and inquiries in a timely manner. These principles should be reflected at all levels within police department. Due regard should be given to any police action that may impinge on the decedent's family throughout the investigation.

As time progresses in the investigation, family members will have many questions which will require answers. One individual from the department should be assigned to convey information and respond to the questions of the family members. Assigning one spokesperson to communicate with the family will assist in maintaining a steady flow of accurate information throughout the investigation, and will ensure that the family is provided with updated information on a regular basis.

Expectations of the Criminal Justice System

While the American criminal justice system has experienced many changes since its inception, the philosophical foundation has remained unchanged—to protect the innocent and to ensure that the truth emerges for any matter before the court, thereby ensuring that justice is done (James & Nordby, 2012). Even though investigators work for a particular law enforcement or correctional agency, they must always keep in mind that they work for the common good of society in search of the truth. As part of the criminal justice system, the medicolegal investigator works as one member of a larger team toward the same end goal of discovering the truth. The investigator's responsibility to perform a competent and complete investigation serves to keep the overall mission of the criminal justice system intact.

Police, corrections, and court personnel comprise the criminal justice system and each component possesses the inherent power to maintain public order and public safety. The overall purpose of the criminal justice system is to protect the innocent and punish law violators, as the criminal justice system's foundation is grounded in the law. In a democratic society, the principles and ideals of the society are achievable through a system of laws that protect the rights of all individuals, while meeting the needs of a greater society. The duty of each component of the criminal justice system is to perform its responsibility within the confines of the law, which serve the will of the people. The criminal justice system works more efficiently when citizens believe that laws are fair, are enforced equitably, and when each component performs its responsibility within the confines of the Constitution.

The criminal justice system in the United States is premised on the adversarial system, which places oppositional sides against one another. Through knowledge of and appropriate application of the law, the goal is for one side to prevail and in this sense, the system is outcome based. In the legal system, the truth is determined by the verdict of the jury or the judge.

The medicolegal death investigation is part of the criminal justice system and combines medical science and the law. Of equal importance to forensic investigators and to lawyers is an assessment of the truth of the available evidence being presented. The central focus for the law and in the courts is on the evidence and its reliability. However, the law and science are often on contrasting sides of the issue as both observe the evidence from differing perspectives. On the law side, attorneys view the evidence, arguing to accept or reject the evidence based on their position and the facts they are asserting. Attorneys examine the evidence from a black or white perspective, true or false, right or wrong, and admissible or inadmissible. Attorneys often rely upon their skills and abilities of persuasion and again are outcome based.

Conversely, on the forensic science investigation side, the evidence is presented based on the collection and analysis of the data and tests performed, which is presented all within a degree of medical or scientific certainty. The science involved in the medicolegal process generates reasoned conclusions. This means that the conclusions found in the examination of the evidence by investigators are tentative, probable, and statistically likely, based on the scientific methods used. The investigator presents all of the evidence and sees it comprising several components, with various degrees of significance. For example, in an arrest-related death, the medicolegal investigator may find, after performing an autopsy and toxicology tests, that the decedent's death was more likely caused by an enlarged heart and the combination of drugs contained in his system leading to a cardiac arrest, rather than the restraint position he was placed in by the police. An opposing counsel would likely challenge the reliability of the finding and challenge the investigation methods used, the completeness of the autopsy, and how the toxicology tests were administered.

In our system of criminal justice, the medicolegal death investigation process involves the law and science. Both of these entities serve the philosophical foundations of our democratic society system of justice. The law is outcome based and science is justification based. These two entities are in contrast to one another, but serve to underscore the adversarial process and achieving the goal of a democratic system, which is to determine the truth and seek justice for the involved parties. The medicolegal death investigation meets the expectations of the criminal justice system and serves the interest of the decedent's family, the interests of the involved agency, the interests of the involved officers, and the interests of the community when investigators adhere to the scientific process and the law when performing their investigation duties.

Summary

Conducting an investigation into an arrest-related death, custodial death, or an officer-involved shooting will be one of the most challenging investigations the investigator will be tasked to complete. These types of deaths contain numerous issues to examine and, because the frequency of these types of deaths is low, mitigating the potential errors in conducting the investigation is a critical concern for the investigator. This chapter has introduced the nature of these classifications of deaths, and has identified many of the emerging questions surrounding them. These deaths have the capacity to prompt riots and further widen the gap of mistrust between the public and the law enforcement community. Recognizing this and recognizing competing expectations of the investigation from varying perspectives provides a reminder for considering how to approach and conduct the most professional and ethical investigation possible. Further, following the appropriate investigatory protocols in these death investigations will demonstrate that the integrity of investigation was maintained, assisting to mitigate errors.

References

Barnett, P. D. (2001). *Ethics in forensic science: Professional standards for the practice of criminalistics*. Boca Raton: CRC Press.

Burch, A. M. (2011). *Arrest-related deaths: 2003–2009, statistical tables*. Washington, DC: Bureau of Justice Statistics.

Chan, T. C. (2006). Medical overview of sudden in custody deaths. In D. L. Ross & T. C. Chan (eds), *Sudden deaths in custody* (pp. 9–14). Totowa, NJ: Humana Press.

Community Oriented Policing Services. (2008). *Standards and guidelines for internal affairs: Recommendations from a community of practice*. Washington, DC: United States Department of Justice.

Di Maio, V. (2003). *Medicolegal death investigation system: Workshop summary*. Washington, DC: National Institute of Justice.

Di Maio, V. (2006). Deaths in custody investigations. In D. L. Ross & T. C. Chan (eds.), *Sudden deaths in custody* (pp. 167–172). Totowa, NJ: Humana Press.

Department of Justice, Civil Rights Division. (2016). Special litigation section case summaries, law enforcement agencies. Retrieved from www.justice.gov/crt/special-litigation-section-case-summaries.

Garrity v. New Jersey, 385 U.S. 493 (1967).

Geberth, V. J. (2007). 10 most common errors in death investigations: Part 1 and 2. *Law and Order*, *55*(11), 1–10.

Graham, M. A. (2014). Investigation of deaths temporally associated with law enforcement apprehension. *Academic Forensic Pathology*, *4*, 366–389.

Hall, A. C., McHale, M. D., Kam, A. S., Stewart, L. C., McCarthy, C. S., & Fick, G. H. (2012). Incidence and outcome of prone positioning following police use of force in a prospective, consecutive cohort of subjects. *Journal of Forensic and Legal Medicine*, *19*(2), 83–89.

Hall, A. C., Votova, K., Heyd, C., Walker, M., McDonald, S., Eramian, D., & Vilke, G. M. (2015). Restraint in police use of force events: Examining sudden in custody deaths for prone and not-prone positions. *Journal of Forensic and Legal Medicine*, *5*(April), 29–35.

Hanzlick, R. (2007). *Death investigation: Systems and procedures*. Boca Raton, FL: CRC Press.

Hargrove, T. & Bowman, L. (2009). Cause of death investigations often dead wrong. *Scripps Howard News Service*. Retrieved from www.asotincounty.net/threads/669-Cause-of-death-investigations-often-dead-wrong.

Hasler v. U.S., 718 F.2d 202, 205 (6th Cir. 1983).

Hiss, J. & Kahana, T. (1996). Medicolegal investigation of death in custody: A postmortem procedure for detection of blunt force injuries. *American Journal of Forensic Medicine and Pathology, 17*(4), 312–314.

Ho, M. P., Peterson, P. N., & Masoudi, F. A. (2008). Evaluating the evidence: Is there a rigid hierarchy? *Circulation, 118*, 1675–1684.

International Association of Chiefs of Police. (2013). *Officer involved shooting guidelines*. Philadelphia, PA: IACP Police Psychological Services Section, 1–12.

James, S. H. & Nordby, J. J. (2012). *Forensic science: An introduction to scientific and investigative techniques* (3rd ed.). Boca Raton, FL: CRC Press, Taylor & Francis.

Kahan, D. M. (2011). Neutral principles, motivated cognition, and some procedures for constitutional law. *Harvard Law Review, 125*(1), 1–10.

Karch, S. & Brave, M. (2015). *Confirmation bias and investigation of arrest-related deaths*. Presentation at the International Symposium on Forensic Science Error Management: Detection, Measurement and Mitigation; National Institute of Standards and Technology (NIST) conference, Washington, DC.

Katz, W. (2015). Enhancing accountability and trust with independent investigation of police lethal force. *Harvard Law Review Forum, 128*(F. 235), 1–20.

Krexi, L., Georgiou, R., Krexi, D., & Sheppard, M. N. (2015). Sudden cardiac death with stress and restraint: The association with sudden adult death syndrome, cardiomyopathy and coronary artery disease. *Medicine, Science and the Law, 56*(2), 85–90.

Laub J. H. (2011a). *Study of deaths following electro muscular disruption*. Washington, DC: National Institute of Justice.

Laub, J. H. (2011b). *Death investigation: A guide for the scene investigator, a technical update*. Washington, DC: National Institute of Justice.

Lee, H. C. (2002). *Cracking cases: The science of solving crimes*. Amherst, NY: Prometheus Books.

Lifschultz, B. D. & Donoghue, E. R. (1991). Deaths in custody. *Legal Medicine*, 45–71.

Luke, J. & Reay, D. T. (1992). The perils of investigating and certifying deaths in police custody. *American Journal of Forensic Medicine and Pathology, 13*(2), 98–100.

Lyons, D. P. (2015). *Fundamentals of jail and prison administrative/internal investigations: For correctional administrators and managers*. Bloomington, IN: AuthorHouse Publisher.

National Academy of Sciences (2009). *Strengthening forensic science in the United States: A path forward*. Washington, DC: Department of Justice.

Official Code of Georgia Annotated. (2010). *Georgia Death Investigation Act* (§45-16-20).

Peckitt, B. (2016). Investigating death in custody. *Medico-Legal Journal, 84*(2), 60–73.

Reay, D. T. (1998). Deaths in custody. *Clinics in Laboratory Medicine, 18*(1), 1–21.

Ross, D. L. (2015). *Investigation arrest-related deaths*. Presentation at the International Symposium on Forensic Science Error Management: Detection, Measurement and Mitigation; National Institute of Standards and Technology (NIST) conference, Washington, DC.

Ross, D. L. & Hazlett, M. (2016). A prospective analysis of the outcomes of violent prone restraint incidents in policing. *Forensic Research and Criminology International, 2*(1), 1–10.

Southall, P., Grant, J., Fowler, D., & Scott, S. (2008). Police custody deaths in Maryland, USA: An examination of 45 cases. *Journal of Forensic and Legal Medicine, 15*(4), 227–230.

Stolberg, D. G. & Bidgood, J. (2016). All charges dropped against Baltimore officers in the Freddie Gray case. *New York Times*, July 27, 2016, www.nytimes.com.

Taser v. International, Inc. and City of Akron v. Chief Medical Examiner of Summit County, Ohio, Court of Appeals of Ohio, CA No. 24233 (9th Dist., 2009).

Tester, D. J. & Ackerman, M. J. (2012). The molecular autopsy: Should the evaluation continue after the funeral? *Pediatric Cardiology, 33*(3), 461–470.

Violent Crime Control and Law Enforcement Act of 1994. United States Congress, 108 Statute, 1796 (Pub. L. 103–322).

Wagner, S. A. (2008). *Death scene investigation.* Boca Raton, FL: CRC Press, Taylor & Francis.

Wangmo, T., Ruiz, G., Sinclair, J., Mangin, P., & Elger, B. S. (2014). The investigation of deaths in custody: A qualitative analysis of problems and prospects. *Journal of Forensic and Legal Medicine, 25*(July), 30–37.

Wells, D. (2012). *In brief: Law 101: Legal guide for the forensic expert.* Washington, DC: National Institute of Justice.

Wisconsin State Legislature (2014). Statute 165.855, Investigation of deaths involving a law enforcement officer.

2

VITAL STATISTICS AND ARREST-RELATED DEATHS

Darrell L. Ross and Michael Brave

Introduction

Since 1933, the Centers for Disease Control and Prevention (CDC) annually reports on national health vital statistics (National Center for Health Statistics, 2015). As part of the CDC, the National Center for Health Statistics (NCHS) provides a systematic statistical system for collecting and disseminating the nation's official vital statistics. The vital statistical system is defined as including the legal registration, statistical recording, and reporting of the occurrence of, and the collection, compilation, analysis, and distribution of statistics pertaining to the "vital events," which include live births, deaths, fetal deaths, marriages, divorces, adoptions, annulments, and legal separations. Published official statistics are accessible dating back to 1890, and include data pertaining to: marriages, births, divorces, mortality, diseases, fetal deaths, and special reports on other societal health statistics. The reports provide a broad perspective of the nation's health, the influences on health, and health outcomes.

Vital statistics place in perspective the trends and patterns of health-related issues in order to identify and classify diseases and manners of death, focus research and assessment, and identify treatment and prevention efforts. Collecting, analyzing, and disseminating vital statistical information serve several useful functions, including: providing a source of data for the measurement of the incidence and prevalence of disease; providing for comparisons of disease rates in different populations or within the same population over time; identifying groups of people at high risk of a particular disease; assessing strategies for preventing disease; and providing for the effective use for scientific analysis (National Center for Health Statistics, 2015). The Vital Statistic data also provide an important benchmark for comparison purposes longitudinally. The practice of epidemiology would be most problematic and inconceivable without access to vital and health statistics. For example, it has been reported by the CDC that the leading cause of death for Americans is heart disease, a reported vital statistic that has remained stable for many years, and males are more likely to die from it than females (National Center for Health Statistics, 2015). The Vital Statistic data are reported to be 99 percent accurate (Quinn, 2014).

Arrest-related deaths and custodial deaths have created a public concern about the force measures and practices used by the police and correctional personnel. The concern focuses on whether the force measure or technique applied caused or contributed to the death. Continuing the concern is the fact that an autopsy may show that the medical condition or levels of chemical substance consumed by the decedent caused the death, further elevating public concern and creating speculation about the true cause of death. An arrest-related death and a custodial suicide represent high-profile events where criminal prosecution and civil litigation are common, whereby officers and administrators must always justify the actions of the involved officers.

Unlike the Vital Statistical System, there has not been a similar system in place that has an extensive history in recording, collecting, analyzing, and distributing statistical information regarding arrest-related deaths, officer-involved shootings, and custodial deaths in general. Prior to 2000 and the passage of the Deaths in Custody Reporting Act, only limited data were collected on these deaths by the Department of Justice (Banks et al., 2015). This lack of historical and reliable statistical information has added to the public's impression that an arrest-related death may be a common occurrence in citizen and police contacts. As such, misconceptions and misunderstandings abound, allowing the public to infer that the police use brutal and excessive force techniques during arrests, leading to custodial deaths, or that the police frequently target and use lethal force against younger minority populations, or that a prisoner frequently dies in confinement due to abuse or neglect.

The concern about the prevalence and the nature of arrest-related deaths and custodial deaths stems from the fact that statistical data about these deaths had not been recorded, collected, or made accessible to the public on a historical basis, with databases such as the National Vital Statistical System, until recently. With limitations, there are several sources that have published statistical data over varying time periods, which provide limited insights into the nature of arrest-related deaths, officer-involved shootings, and custodial deaths. However, due to underreporting or no reporting by many criminal justice agencies, reporting inconsistencies and inaccuracies over many years, and with jurisdictional definitional problems, reliable data collected on these deaths are inconsistent. This chapter provides an overview of what is known about the reported frequency and nature of arrest-related deaths, officer-involved shootings, and custodial deaths in jails and prisons. Statistical information reported by various governmental data sources and a discussion about their implications are presented.

Contacts Between the Police and Citizens

An important starting point is to review the data reported about the nature of citizen and police contacts. Questions arise about the frequency of use of force during a contact between the police and citizens. Prompted by the Rodney King incident in 1992, and due to a lack of reliable data on the extent of the police use of excessive force, the U.S. Congress enacted the Violent Crime Control and Law Enforcement Act (VCCLEA) in 1994. The act, through §14142, requires the Attorney General to collect data on excessive force by the police and to publish an annual report from the data (Violence Crime Control and Law Enforcement Act, 1994). As such, the Department of Justice has been researching contacts between the police and citizens since 1996. In 1996, the survey began through a pilot-test with citizens 12 years of age and older. Beginning in 1999, the questionnaire changed, citizens 16 years and older were included, and not all questions were posed each reporting year. About half of the survey addresses police contacts that result in the police threatening or using varying force measures.

The Bureau of Justice Statistics (BJS) researchers have analyzed and reported the contact survey data on five occasions (Durose, Schmitt, & Langan, 2005; Durose, Smith, & Langan, 2007; Eith & Durose, 2011; Greenfeld, Langan, & Smith, 1997; Langan et al., 2001). Table 2.1 displays comparisons of

TABLE 2.1 Force used in police contacts with citizens: 1996, 1999, 2002, 2005, and 2008 (in percentages)

Component	*1996**	*1999*	*2002*	*2005*	*2008*
Citizen felt contact legitimate	88	80	84	80	81
Threatened/used force by officer	500,000 (1%)	422,000 (1%)	664,500 (1.5%)	707,520 (1.6%)	574,000 (1.4%)
Traffic-related	–	45	50	48	59
Reported crime to police	–	35	26	20	21
Suspicious behavior	–	20	18	24	20
Investigate crime	–	6	18	21	19
White citizen	64	59	56	53	54
Black citizen	15	23	26	28	28
Hispanic citizen	16	16	15	13	13
Other citizen	5	3	3	6	5
% Male/female	87/13	87/13	78/22	72/28	75/25
Average age of citizen	21	23	27	27	28
Curse, insult/verbal threat to officer and argue		59	23	22	22
Disobeyed the officer		30	34	14	15
Attempt to elude officer		5	4	5	4
Resist handcuffing/arrest		7	6	5	6
Active resistance		23	24	–	26
Under influence of chemical substance	–	21			
Push/grabbed by officer		40	42	55	60
Struck by officer		45	8	9	17
Gun pointed by officer		15	19	15	26
Gun fired by officer		0	0	0	0
Aerosol used by officer		5	5	3	6
Conducted Energy Device applied		–	–	5	8
Handcuffed	80	52	30	41	54
Arrested		42	38	30	40
Citizen believed force excessive		76	75	83	74
Injury sustained to citizen		15	14	15	19
Citizen filed complaint/lawsuit		19	19	13	14
Total contacts	45 mil	44 mil	45.3 mil	43.5 mil	40 mil

Note: *Pilot test.

survey results for the years of 1996, 1999, 2002, 2005, and 2008 in which force was threatened or used by the police during citizen contact.

Over the 12-year period, common trends have emerged and averages of the results are reported. As shown in Table 2.1, on average, police have contact with 44 million citizens annually, and the use of force is threatened or used, on average, in 573,604 of the encounters. This equates to about 1.3 percent of the contacts. Contacts where the police used or threatened force decreased by 14 percent from 2002 to 2008. Males are three times more likely than females to have force used or threatened against them. A white male, aged 16 to 29 is twice as likely as a black male and three times as likely as any other race to have force used or threatened. A significant number of contacts emerged from incidents involving the following: traffic related (52%); reporting a crime to the police (20%); responding to suspicious person/behaviors (21%); and investigating a crime (16%). During the contact, police commonly encountered the following types of citizen resistance: verbal insults, cursing, and threats; noncompliance to officer commands; attempts to elude the officer; active physical resistance; and resistance during handcuffing.

Responding officers used empty-hand control techniques in over 50 percent of the use of force contacts. Officers used intermediate weapons in about 8 percent, pointed their firearm at a citizen in about 20 percent, and there were no reports of a firearm being fired during any of the contacts. The use of a TASER by the police began being reported in 2005 and 2008 and, on average, the device was used in about seven percent of the contacts. The use of any aerosol reported by citizens was the least reported form of force applied by an officer. The citizen was arrested in about 42 percent and handcuffed in about 36 percent of the contacts. Citizens sustained an injury in about 16 percent of the contacts where force was used or threatened. While citizens believed that the contact was legitimate, about 78 percent believed the force used by the police was excessive, even though only about 16 percent on average filed a complaint or lawsuit. Although not shown in Table 2.1, citizens reported that in about 25 percent of the contacts, their behavior provoked a force response from the police.

Arrest-Related Deaths

On October 13, 2000, Congress passed the Death in Custody Reporting Act (DCRA), Public Law 106-297. The law mandates that all in-custody deaths be counted and that BJS researchers collect data annually on these incidents. This represents a second data set that collects data relevant to arrest-related deaths. Reports on persons who die in custody or under the restraint of state or local law enforcement personnel have been tabulated since 2003 and reported through 2009 (Burch, 2011). Data are collected regarding deaths occurring during arrest and during confinement, providing national-level information on deaths of suspects and offenders from their initial contact with law enforcement officers through completion of their confinement (Planty et al., 2015).

In 2006, the DCRA reporting requirements expired but BJS personnel continued to collect data and report on custodial deaths. In December 2014, Congress reauthorized the reporting with the Death in Custody Reporting Act of 2013. All arrest-related deaths (ARD) are included in the count regardless of whether physical custody had been established or whether a formal arrest process had been initiated prior to the time of the death. The BJS defines "in the process of arrest" to include all circumstances in which a person is in the custody or under the restraint of police officers. The definition also includes deaths that involve law enforcement assistance in restraining or transportation of individuals in need of medical or mental health care. Collected data also include those deaths of persons attempting to elude law enforcement during the course of apprehension. Excluded from the report are deaths that occur in a long-term holding facility and deaths that did not involve either a state or local law enforcement agency.

Criminal suspects represent the majority of individuals included in the ARD program, although persons not considered an arrested subject but who are detained are also included. For example, a person stopped, frisked, and search or detained during a vehicle stop can be included. According to the ARD, the most common types of reported noncriminal deaths include a call for assistance or during a transport, such as responding to requests for medical or mental health assistance. Frequently, these types of calls involve a person who is suicidal or displays erratic and bizarre behaviors necessitating police intervention. Law enforcement personnel may have to use a degree of force to control and restrain the person to assist in providing care, assist with an involuntary commitment to a medical or mental health facility, or assist emergency medical personnel to restrain the person in order to render care so that transport to a medical facility may be facilitated.

The types of deaths included in the ARD program emerge from the following: barricaded and standoff situations; deaths related to police use of force, including physical control measures, restraints, and intermediate weapons; officer-involved shootings; vehicle accidents caused by either the subject, intervening officer, or other third party; other types of fatal accidents while attempting to evade capture by the police; and suicides committed during standoffs and barricaded situations (Planty et al., 2015). Further, deaths that occur during a police field intervention or during confinement in a detention facility, including suicides, deaths attributed to alcohol and drug intoxication, sudden medical conditions, choking on ingested objects, or other forms of asphyxiation are included (Planty et al., 2015).

Like other death reporting programs, there are limitations, and caution should be used in assessing the data due to variations in reporting. Participation in the reporting program is voluntary and incidents resulting in deaths are under-reported. Slightly less than 4,000 agencies with 100 or more sworn officers have provided data for the report. Law enforcement agencies account for 73 percent (municipal, state police, and special jurisdiction police) and sheriff's departments account for about 20 percent of the incidents. ARD data are more representative of the nature of the death than the volume in which they occur (Burch, 2011). Any ARD which did not involve either a state or local law enforcement agency is excluded from the report.

An evaluation of ARD in relation to the number of arrests that occurred in the United States between the years 2003 and 2009 is reported in Table 2.2. As shown in Table 2.2, during the reporting period, about 98 million arrests were made, and of these arrests, 4,813 resulted in an ARD (Burch, 2011; Snyder, 2012). The evaluation revealed six types or manners of death. Of all ARD occurring, about 61 percent of the deaths were classified as a homicide by law enforcement officers. Deaths from suicide and intoxication each accounted for about 11 percent. About 6 percent of the deaths were classified as undetermined or were under-reported. Accidental deaths accounted for about 6 percent and natural causes and unknown deaths accounted for about 6 percent. Males account for more of the arrests and are more likely to die during arrest than a female.

Table 2.3 shows arrest-related death decedent characteristics (Burch, 2011).

TABLE 2.2 Arrest-related deaths in the US, 2003–2009 (in percentages)

Characteristic	*2003–2009*	*2003*	*2004*	*2005*	*2006*	*2007*	*2008*	*2009*
Homicide by LEO	61	60	56	55	62	61	64	68
Homicide by other	0.6	0.5	0.6	0.6	0.3	0.9	0.5	0.5
Suicide	11	10	13	12	9	11	12	13
Intoxication	11	13	12	13	11	12	9	7
Accidental injury	6	9	6	7	5	5	5	4
Natural causes	5	4	7	5	5	5	5	4
Unknown	6	4	6	8	8	5	5	3
Male/female	96/4	95/5	96/4	97/3	95/5	95/5	95/5	95/5
Estim # of arrests	97,954,000	13.6 mil	14 mil	14 mil	14.3 mil	14.2 mil	13.7 mil	13.1 mil
Total	4,813	627	673	689	721	745	629	729

TABLE 2.3 Arrest-related deaths by decedent characteristic, manners of death, and circumstance, 2003–2009 (in percentages)

	Manner of death					
Variable	*Homicide*	*Suicide*	*Intoxication*	*Accident*	*Natural causes*	*Unknown*
Male	62	11	11	6	5	6
Female	49	11	16	6	12	6
Unknown	1	0	0	0	0	1
White	42	60	34	35	45	30
Black	32	15	41	41	35	36
Hispanic	20	20	21	20	12	17
Other	4	2	3	2	2	2
Unknown	3	2	1	3	7	14
≤17	3	1	1	5	0	2
18–24	23	15	10	20	4	10
25–34	30	26	34	24	17	28
35–45	22	30	36	29	27	32
55+	6	8	2	4	21	4
Unknown	2	1	1	2	0	6
Violent offense	75	54	27	27	25	31
Property offense	3	9	11	13	20	11
Drug offense	3	4	20	16	12	9
Public-order offense	8	22	24	32	34	18
No criminal charge	7	5	5	2	7	7
Unreported	4	6	13	10	6	25
Total ARD = 4,813	2,958 (61%)	541 (11%)	525 (11%)	272 (6%)	244 (5%)	273 (6%)

On average, white males account for 42 percent of the ARD, 32 percent were black, and Hispanics accounted for about 20 percent. Other or unknown ethnic groups accounted for the remaining 6 percent. About 55 percent of the persons were between 25 and 44 years of age. The incident circumstances of the arrest were classified into five types. Each manner of ARD was higher for violent crime arrests, accounting for 60 percent, including: homicide, sexual assault, robbery, assault, and other violent crimes. Offenders engaged in property offenses and drug offenses accounted for 6.4 percent. Deaths resulting from public order offenses accounted for 14.5 percent and 3.4 percent accounted for no criminal charges, including medical and mental health transport. In about 9 percent of the ARD, an offense was not reported. The manner of death for white males was higher than other races in the classifications of homicide, suicide, and natural causes. Unknown deaths and deaths from intoxication and accidents were reported more often for black decedents.

Officer-Involved Shootings

State laws require that a medical examiner or coroner investigate all homicides and other sudden unexpected deaths (Quinn, 2014). Information collected from a death certificate, including manner of death, is reported and the information is forwarded for analysis. There are three sources of data that report justifiable homicides by the police, also known as "legal intervention deaths." First, the Uniform Crime Report (UCR) has been published annually by the Federal Bureau of Investigation (FBI) since 1930, and provides data on the total number of crimes known to law enforcement in the United States. The UCR provides aggregate annual counts of homicides occurring in the United States. In the 1960s, the FBI began collecting more detailed information regarding homicides and reporting it in the Supplemental Homicides Report (SHR). The SHR reports the circumstances about specific types of homicides, characteristics of the event, and the victim-offender relationships as reported to them by the police. The SHR reports on all murders (including justifiable homicides) and negligent manslaughter.

Second, justified law enforcement homicides committed in self-defense are reported in the SHR (Brown & Langan, 2001). The FBI first published justifiable homicide data in 1968 as more law enforcement departments began submitting information through the SHR. The first homicide records were received in 1966 and 1967, but because only a few police agencies submitted reports, the FBI did not disseminate statistical information. The SHR data base contained information on the age, race, and gender of persons killed by police, but it did not include information on the officers involved in these incidents. After 1975, the FBI expanded information on the SHR and included more demographic information about the officer who was involved in the shooting.

The SHR captures deaths by location of the offense and includes all homicides occurring in state and local law enforcement jurisdictions. There are limitations with the data reported in the SHR and caution must be used when reviewing the data. First, reporting information to the FBI is voluntary and many law enforcement agencies either do not consistently submit SHR forms or just do not submit any forms at all. Second, some SHR forms reporting a homicide are incomplete and are missing data. Third, SHR data forms have changed over the years, increasing or deleting some features of the event. Fourth, the SHR does not include homicide information pertaining to federal law enforcement agencies, federal prisons, military bases, or Indian reservations. Fifth, the SHR data are reflective of a homicide investigation conducted by the police and do not reflect the outcome of decisions made by a prosecutor or the courts. Sixth, the number of incidents involving a non-justifiable homicide by police in the United States is unknown. There is nothing that distinguishes murders by an officer from murders committed by another. Seventh, there are no official statistics recorded of where a police officer was justified in killing a suspect but instead decided to use non-lethal force. Due to these limitations, reliable information regarding the number of justifiable homicides committed by the police does not exist, general estimates therefore are made on the available data, and caution should be used when examining the data (Geller & Geller, 1992; Klinger, 2012; Loftin et al., 2003).

Annually, SHR data are published in the FBI's UCR and the report is always one year behind the year of publication. Available SHR data on justifiable homicides by police have been published since 1976. The Department of Justice has published reports on two occasions regarding the number of justifiable homicides committed by law enforcement officers (Brown & Langan, 2001; Cooper & Smith, 2011; Smith & Cooper, 2013). Justifiable homicides committed by the police are considered justified when it is done to prevent imminent death or serious bodily injury to the officer or another person (Brown & Langan, 2001). Based on reported data collected by the FBI through the UCR and SHR, trends of justifiable homicides committed by the police from 1968 to 2014 are shown in Figure 2.1 (Brown & Langan, 2001; Cooper & Smith, 2011; Federal Bureau of Investigation, 2015; Fox and Zawitz, 2006; Smith & Cooper, 2013).

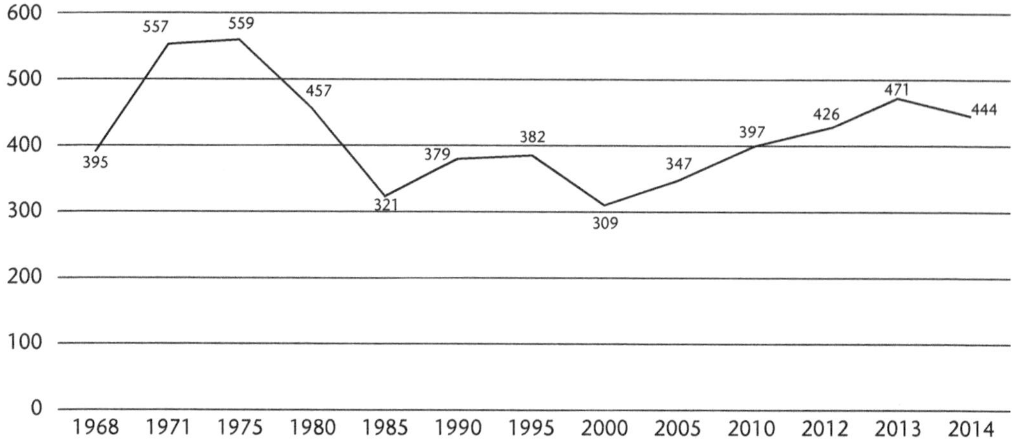

FIGURE 2.1 Justifiable homicide by police, 1968–2014.

According to the FBI, from 1968 to 2014, the police justifiably killed a total of 18,382 persons, averaging 390 per year (Federal Bureau of Investigation, 2015). As shown in Figure 2.1, the highest number of persons killed by the police was in 1975 at 559. The least number killed was 300 in 1987, not shown. From 1970 to 1975, police shootings averaged 430, making it the highest reported period; from 1976 to 1998, 373 persons on average were killed; and from 2006 to 2014, an average of 412 persons were killed by the police. From 1980 to 1985, police killings of citizens declined by 30 percent, the largest percentage decline during the 47-year reporting period. From 2000 to 2014, the percentage of police shootings increased by 30 percent, from 309 to 444, averaging about 390 shooting incidents.

The SHR reports that from 1978 to 2008, white males with an average age of 27 were more likely than others to be killed by the police (Cooper & Smith, 2011). Indeed, 98 percent of the persons killed by the police were male. In 1978, of persons killed by police 49 percent were African-American males while 48 percent were white males. In 1988, 57 percent of men killed by police were white, while 39 percent were African-American, and in 1998, 61 percent of those killed by police were white males compared to 34 percent African-American males (Brown & Langan, 2001). Over this 30-year period, 61 percent of the justifiable homicides were of white males and African-American males accounted for 38 percent. Other races accounted for three percent of the police killings. The percentages for white males killed by the police have increased by 21 percent and the police killing of African-American males has declined by 22 percent. The probability of the police killing an African-American male is about one in three of police shootings. In 64 percent of the shooting incidents, the person attacked the police; in about 24 percent the person fled or resisted the police officer; and 16 percent the circumstances were undetermined (Brown & Langan, 2001; Cooper & Smith, 2011; Federal Bureau of Investigation, 2015; Fox & Zawitz, 2006).

The third data source which collects data and reports on "deaths by legal intervention" (homicides) is the National Vital Statistics System (NVSS) and is reported by the National Center of Health Statistics (NCHS). This is a mortality category which is intended to capture homicidal deaths caused by law enforcement personnel. The data reported in the NVSS are less reliable than the UCR and the SHR. For example, Sherman and Langworthy (1979) reported that in comparing police-involved shootings in a sample of states and counties, which was generated by law enforcement agencies for the years 1970 to 1976, the numbers were grossly underreported, and estimated the underreporting by about 51 percent nationwide. Further, Loftin et al. (2003) performed a comparative analysis of justifiable homicides committed by the police by examining data from the NVSS and the SHR. The researchers found that both data sources underreported homicides committed by the police, although findings from the SHR data showed a higher reporting of justifiable homicides than the NVSS, by 29 percent.

The researchers also reported that data generated by the NVSS were underreported as certifiers of the death certificate failed to indicate that police caused the death, and if there is mention of police involvement, the case may be misclassified as a homicide. The biggest problem with the SHR data showed that not all law enforcement agencies submit homicide reports for counting and/or submit incomplete data, revealing a bias count downward. In addition, the SHR may not always include data in which the death occurred during a confrontation with federal law enforcement agencies. The authors concluded that because data on justifiable homicides committed by the police are systematically underreported, caution should be used when reviewing the data (Loftin et al., 2003).

A fourth source of collected data pertaining to officer-involved shootings is reported by the CDC (2013). From 2003 through 2012, 4,285 deaths were attributed to legal interventions by the police as reported by doctors and medical examiners. The average number of fatal police shootings averaged about 429 annually during the reporting period.

Police Officers Killed and Assaulted in the Line of Duty

During the 47-year reporting period of 1968–2014, an average of 71 police officers were feloniously killed in the line of duty (see Figure 2.2) (Federal Bureau of Investigation, 2014, 2015). As shown in Figure 2.2, the highest number of officers feloniously killed occurred in 1974 with 132 deaths. The highest average for officers killed occurred from 1971 to 1976, at 126, while the lowest period of officer killings occurred from 2005 to 2010, averaging 50 deaths. From 2000 to 2014, an average of 54 officers were feloniously killed. Since 1968, numbers of officers feloniously killed have declined by about 46 percent. The Federal Bureau of Investigation (2015) reported that from 1987 to 2014 officers were killed in the line of duty during the following circumstances: while making an arrest (29%); responding to a disturbance call (26%); conducting a traffic stop (18%); from an ambush (14%); investigating a suspicious person/circumstance (11%); while transporting an arrestee (1%); and from contacting a mentally ill person (1%). Weapons used by offenders who killed the law enforcement officers included: firearm (84%), motor vehicle (7%), cutting instruments (3%), other involved about 6%.

Further, from 1990 to 2014, an average of 59,000 officers annually were assaulted in the line of duty (Federal Bureau of Investigation, 2015). The largest percentage of victim officers (31 percent) were assaulted while responding to disturbance calls. Assailants used personal weapons (hands, fists, feet, etc.) in 80 percent of the incidents, firearms in 4.0 percent of the incidents, and knives or other cutting instruments in 2.0 percent of the incidents. Other types of dangerous weapons (i.e., clubs, bricks, and bats) were used in about 14 percent of the assaults.

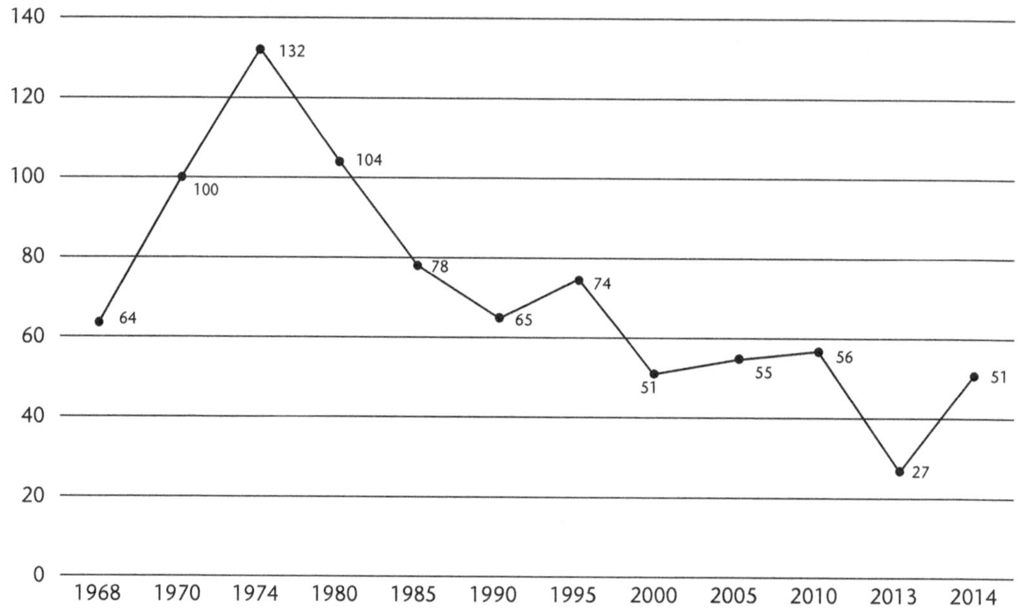

FIGURE 2.2 Law enforcement officers killed in the line of duty, 1968–2014.

Census of State and Local Law Enforcement Agencies

It is important to also review the police and citizen contacts, arrest-related deaths, and officer-involved shootings in perspective by reviewing the number of law enforcement agencies, the number of sworn officers, trends in the United States population, and the number of reported crimes. As shown in Table 2.4, data collected by BJS researchers show that from 1976 to 2013, the number of law enforcement agencies has increased by about 28 percent and the number of sworn officers has increased by about 31 percent (Reaves, 2011, 2015). The population in the United States has increased by 31 percent (US Census Bureau, 2015), while the reported crimes have decreased by about 11 percent overall (Reaves, 2015). The average population in the United States from 1976 to 2013 is about 280 million residents.

TABLE 2.4 Census of state and local law enforcement agencies

	Year								
Variable	*1976*	*1987*	*1990*	*1993*	*1997*	*2000*	*2003*	*2007*	*2013*
LE agencies	13,000	15,000	17,360	17,501	17,784	17,876	17,881	17,985	17,991
Sworn officers	330,150	355,290	363,001	373,554	420,152	440,920	451,737	463,147	487,317
US pop. in millions	218.04	240.13	256.51	269.39	272.65	282.16	290.11	301.23	317.01
Crimes reported, in millions	11.4	13.2	14.4	13.5	12.6	11.8	11.4	11.1	10.2

Skeptical of the reported FBI and SHR data, media outlets have collected their own data on officer-involved shooting incidents. Data reported by various news outlets must be observed with caution as they are likely to be fraught with errors, relying on unofficial information, and may make conclusions prior to all of the facts being reported. Generally, media outlets do not perform longitudinal analysis of police shootings but will generally "cherry pick" selected years to advance a particular point after a high-profile incident occurs. For example, after the police shooting in Ferguson, Missouri the *Washington Post* (2015) assessed the police shootings in 2015 and reported that the police shot and killed 991 individuals. Using the census data average from 1976 to 2013 and the number of annual police shootings during that time as reported by the FBI and SHR, there is about a 0.00014 percent likelihood a citizen would be shot and killed by the police. Using the *Washington Post* estimate of 991 deaths as the result of police intervention, there would be a 0.00035 percent likelihood of being shot and killed by the police. Both estimate calculations show that the chance of being shot and killed by the police is less than a fraction of one percent chance occurrence and is a rare occurrence.

Custodial Deaths in Jails

Since 1978, the primary source for assessing mortality patterns in jails has been the Bureau of Justice Statistics. This dataset provides the third general source for examining data available, which assesses reported deaths in jail custody pertinent to this text. From 1978 to 1998, the manners of death in jails were reported as part of the census assessment of the nation's jails and the profile of jail inmates by the BJS (1978–1998). As part of the Death in Custody Reporting Program (DCRP) and starting in 2000, the BJS annually reports on the causes of prisoner deaths in jails and prisons (Noonan, Rohloff, & Ginder, 2015). The BJS uses the DCRP data to track the trends in the number and manners of death occurring in local jails and state prisons. Respondents of the facilities submit completed survey instruments to the BJS on an annual basis and report any death for the referenced calendar year. Besides reporting the manner of the prisoner's death, data are submitted regarding the circumstance of the death, time and location of the death, and autopsy report information. A response rate of about 92 percent is reported by the BJS and since 2007 participation in the DCRP became voluntary. The data collection instrument has changed several times, incorporating new and additional items for collection.

Results are compiled from county sheriffs' departments which operate a jail or detention facility and that confine detainees before or after adjudication for more than 72 hours, excluding temporary lock-ups (Noonan et al., 2015). Table 2.5 combines the two data sources to show trends in the deaths of local jail prisoners from 1978 to 2012 (Bureau of Justice Statistics, 1981, 1996, 2002; Noonan et al., 2015).

As shown in Table 2.5, during the 34-year reporting period, an average of 2,800 jails of the 3,100 facilities annually reported a detainee death in the facility. During the reporting period, an average of 10 million detainees were admitted into the nation's jails (Minton et al., 2015). The detainee population increased by about 79 percent and the average daily population (ADP) was about 685,000 detainees confined. The total number of reported deaths was 17,544, which averaged about 800 deaths annually. Detainee deaths increased 36 percent over the period, which followed the increase in the detainee population. From 2000 to 2013, an average of 978 detainees died in custody, but the ADP detainee population increased by 21 percent, averaging about 721,143. The increase in the average number of detainee deaths increased by 18 percent while the ADP increased by 21 percent. From 2000 to 2013, about 50 percent of the responding jails reported no deaths.

TABLE 2.5 Deaths in jails, 1978–2013

				Cause				
Year	*All*	*Illness*	*Suicide*	*Drug/alcohol*	*Accident*	*Homicide*	*Other*	*ADP*
1978	611	223	297	–	–	–	91	158,000
1986	277	145	107	–	–	11	14	266,000
1988	472	219	147	–	–	3	37	336,000
1990	494	208	148	–	0	–	53	408,075
1992	445	170	124	–	0	–	44	442,000
1994	647	290	234	–	–	19	41	490,000
1996	306	124	76	–	5	3	19	550,000
1999	919	385	324	–	–	28	104	601,000
2000	904	516	289	37	25	17	17	599,000
2001	942	485	313	58	36	19	24	640,000
2002	970	508	314	54	34	18	35	668,000
2003	1,002	512	296	89	28	15	52	688,000
2004	1,021	529	299	76	33	25	50	716,000
2005	1,045	501	286	83	24	22	110	742,000
2006	1,094	604	278	87	33	36	52	772,000
2007	1,100	608	284	79	18	20	71	782,000
2008	958	444	228	43	15	16	8	780,000
2009	960	491	304	64	26	23	24	749,000
2010	918	477	305	54	23	20	13	734,000
2011	889	425	311	73	27	21	22	723,000
2012	958	529	300	57	18	22	24	746,000
2013	967	482	327	70	31	28	18	757,120
Total	17,544	8,875	5,591	924	376	376	1,402	

The majority of jail deaths occur in jail and the detainee is found dead in a cell. Counting a death in jail is problematic. Not all jail deaths occur in the jail nor do all prisoner deaths actually take place in the jail. For example, if the detainee dies during transport to the hospital or at the hospital, jail personnel may not count the death as a "death in jail/custody." For example, the BJS reported that about 10 percent of the jails were unable to report whether any prisoners died at the jail in 1993. Further, as shown in Table 2.5, seven classifications of manners of death are reported. Of these manners of death, drugs/alcohol, homicides, and accidents were not reported for each year, making accounting of these deaths problematic on a yearly basis.

About 51 percent of the deaths were caused by an illness, followed by about 32 percent from a suicide. In comparison of the manners of death, suicides have remained stable at about 32 percent, while deaths from illnesses have increased by about 24 percent. Deaths from an illness include the following: heart disease, cancer, liver disease, respiratory disease, AIDS-related disease, and unspecified illness. Deaths from AIDS accounted for about 5 percent of the total deaths, but have been declining (by about 60 percent) since 2003. Deaths from drugs/alcohol accounted for 5 percent, and accidents and homicides accounted for 2 percent of the deaths, respectively. Deaths classified as other or unknown accounted for about 8 percent of the deaths. About 75 percent of the deaths are unconvicted prisoners and 38 percent die within seven days or fewer of admission.

Decedent detainee characteristics show that males comprised 88 percent of the jail population. Race of decedent detainees shows that 55 percent were white, 30 percent were African-American, 12 percent were Hispanic, and 3 percent were identified as other. Males are about eight times more likely to die in jail than females. White male detainees with an average age of 40 are more likely to die in jail from all manners of death. White (80%) and Hispanic (25%) detainees are more likely to commit suicide and whites are more likely to die of accidents and drugs/alcohol. African-American detainees are more likely to die of heart disease and AIDS.

Prisoner Deaths in Prison

Using data collected from the DCRP, the BJS has reported on the mortality rates of prisoners confined in state and federal prisons since 2001 (Carson, 2013; Noonan et al., 2015). The same seven manners of death are reported for the state prisons as they were for jail facilities, as shown in Table 2.6.

As the prison population increased, so too have the deaths in custody. Prisoner deaths increased 14 percent during the evaluation period. Similar to their jail counterparts, state prisons observed more deaths from illness than from any other manners of death, and other manners of death in prison follow a similar pattern as the jail deaths. About 90 percent of the prisoner deaths are from an illness and natural causes. Death due to cancer comprised the highest percentage of prisoner death followed by heart disease. Prisoner suicides accounted for about 6 percent of the deaths and homicides accounted for one percent of the deaths. Prisoner deaths from AIDS declined by about 70 percent, the most of any reported manners of death. Deaths by drugs/alcohol remained stable throughout the period.

TABLE 2.6 Mortality of state prisoners, 2001–2013

					Cause				
Year	*All*	*Illness*	*Suicide*	*AIDS*	*Drug/ alcohol*	*Accident*	*Homicide*	*Other*	*Pop.*
2001	2,869	2,594	168	275	35	22	39	37	1,187,800
2002	2,934	2,374	168	241	37	29	48	37	1,199,900
2003	3,152	2,621	199	209	23	26	49	25	1,225,700
2004	3,123	2,636	199	147	22	34	49	36	1,239,700
2005	3,168	2,661	213	156	37	28	56	17	1,252,400
2006	3,233	2,698	219	132	56	32	55	41	1,297,200
2007	3,389	2,860	215	120	41	28	57	68	1,321,000
2008	3,450	2,933	197	99	58	26	40	97	1,327,000
2009	3,414	2,927	202	98	50	32	54	51	1,326,500
2010	3,232	2,794	216	73	40	32	70	7	1,320,600
2011	3,353	2,925	185	57	58	38	70	20	1,290,200
2012	3,351	2,879	205	74	32	50	85	26	1,267,000
2013	3,479	3,082	192	52	56	34	90	18	1,261,000
Total	42,439	35,984	2,578	1,732	492	411	762	480	

The average annual prisoner population in state prison was 1,172,175 and averaged 4,523 deaths annually. African-American prisoners made up about 44 percent and white prisoners made up about 40 percent of the prisoner population. Male prisoners accounted for 97 percent of the deaths, and 55 percent of those who died were 55 years or older.

During the period, the average annual mortality rate for male prisoners was 1.7 times higher than for female prisoners. With the exception of AIDS-related deaths, white prisoners had the highest average annual mortality rate for all illness-related causes of death. AIDS-related deaths were the highest among African-American prisoners, and were at least two times higher than for prisoners of Hispanic origin.

Discussion

The consistent theme of the reported data on arrest-related deaths, officer-involved shootings, and custodial deaths in confinement show that these incidents are under-reported and therefore contain limitations, thus making definitive conclusions problematic. An arrest-related death or a death in custody is an expected occurrence, although such deaths are rare, given the frequency of police and citizen contacts, the number of arrests performed annually, and the number of prisoners confined in a jail or prison (Graham, 2014). However, based on data source limitations, only general estimations can be made regarding their occurrence.

The police-citizen contact data reported since 1996 consistently show that such contacts result in use of force or threatened use of force in only 1.3 percent of the contacts. This also means that 98.7 percent of the police-citizen contacts do not result in the police use of force (Hyland, Langton, & Davis, 2015). Since citizens completed a survey regarding the nature of these contacts, no citizen died during the contact. Overwhelmingly, the police used empty-hand control techniques (70%) during these force contacts, and any type of intermediate weapon was used in about 10 percent. The use of restraints was applied in about 85 percent of the contacts and in about 16 percent, an injury was reported during contact. The officers pointed their firearms but did not discharge their firearm in about 20 percent of the contacts. These reported findings are similar to what Ross (2011) found when he reviewed 60 published predominant use of force studies conducted from 1966 to 2011. In their collective totality, the studies showed that the police use of force is rare; that the force officers used is in response to the resistive behaviors of the person and the totality of the dynamic and changing circumstances; that the contextual variables underscore the officers' perception in using a degree of force; and that when officers use a level of force, they routinely use less force than what the incident allowed.

The reported ARD data show that such a death is a rare occurrence. From 2003 to 2009, police reported making about 98,000,000 arrests and 4,813 of these arrests resulted in a death (see Table 2.2). The annual reported ARD averaged about 688 deaths, resulting in a 0.005 percent likelihood of such a death occurring. A homicide committed by the police accounted for about 61 percent of the ARD (n = 420). There are, however, limitations to this estimate. Banks et al. (2015) reported that the ARD and SHR programs reported during 2003 to 2009 only captured about 49 percent of law enforcement homicides and the SHR program only captured about 46 percent. It is estimated that about 50 percent of the law enforcement homicides in the United States are not captured by either of the two reported programs. On average, about 43 states report ARD and some annual reports are incomplete.

Also, the SHR and the FBI have reported that from 1968 to 2014, officer-involved justified shootings averaged about 390 persons killed annually (see Figure 2.1). Even though the number is slightly less than what is reported in the ARD program, the time period covered is more than double the amount of time of the ARD data. From 2000 to 2014, reported justifiable homicides by the police have increased by about 30 percent, while the number of arrests made averages about 14 million annually. Dividing the number of total arrests made from 2003 to 2009 (98,000,000) by the number of total reported justifiable police homicides during the same time period (2,651) equals a 0.0003 percent likelihood that a person will be killed by the police. Banks et al. (2015) estimate, however, that about 50 percent of the police justifiable homicides are not captured in the official reporting programs. By doubling the number of police justifiable homicides to 5,302 (over seven years) and dividing it by 98,000,000 reported arrests, the likelihood of a person being shot and killed by the police is estimated to be 0.0005 percent, which remains statistically negligible. This would align with the number of police shootings reported by *The Washington Post*. But even tripling the number to 7,953 killings, the likelihood still remains at less than one percent likelihood, at 0.0008 percent.

Using *The Washington Post* numbers of 991 individuals killed by the police in 2015, as previously presented, showed that a citizen has a 0.0003 percent likelihood being shot and killed by the police. Additionally, it has been postulated that citizen and police contacts have been under-estimated by the DOJ and it is difficult to actually know how many contacts occur annually. Johnson (2016), using the Census Bureau information, calculated that there may be as many as about 193,000,000 calls for service but also including other proactive stops and other informal citizen contacts made by the police which could double the number to about 385,000,000 police and citizen annual contacts. Combining the number of arrests made by the police reported in the Uniform Crime Reports of 11,285,833 with the average number of annual reported assaults on officers of about 48,000, and the 991 deaths of citizen shootings by police, the likelihood of a citizen being shot by the police is calculated at about 0.0003%.

While it is acknowledged that these data sources have their limitations and caution must be used when reviewing them, even tripling the number of justifiable police homicides shows that the likelihood of being killed by the police is still less than one percent. The recalculated data support what former research on the police use of force has shown, that the police use of force during a citizen contact is rare, an officer-involved shooting is statistically rare, and a death during an arrest is also rare.

Moreover, given the millions of jail detainees admitted annually, their medical and mental health condition and unhealthy lifestyles, it is not surprising that a death in confinement may occur. For example, Maruschak, Berzofsky, and Unangst (2015) reported that 45 percent of the jail population enters jail with varying chronic medical conditions, including: cancer, heart disease, high blood pressure, diabetes, kidney problems, AIDS, and respiratory disease. About 62 percent of admitted detainees are overweight, obese, or morbidly obese, and it is estimated that about 54 percent enter jail with a chemical substance abuse dependency (alcohol, illicit drugs, and prescription drugs). In addition, about 25 percent have been diagnosed with a mental illness, and of those, about 76 percent abuse chemical substances (James & Glaze, 2006).

Still, the likelihood of such a death occurring in jail is statistically rare. The reported custodial deaths in jails showed that from 1978 to 2013, 17,544 detainees died in jail custody, which averaged about 800 deaths annually. The average daily population (ADP) during this time was 685,000 detainees, and the estimated likelihood of a custodial death in jail is 0.0012 percent, although the detainee population increased by 79 percent. From 2000 to 2013, however, detainee deaths averaged 978 and the ADP was 721,143, an increase of average deaths of 18 percent. The statistical likelihood of a jail death is 0.0014 percent, still a negligible percentage and less than one percent. Even allowing for under-reporting and by doubling the average number of jail deaths to 1,956, the estimated likelihood of a death occurring in a jail remains negligible at 0.0027 percent. Of the six reported manners of death, about 80 percent of these deaths included natural illness, suicides, and AIDS. Deaths due to alcohol/drug intoxication accounted for about 5 percent. Among the reported manners of a jail death, about 38 percent of deaths occur within seven days of admission. A detainee death by homicide accounted for less than one percent of the total deaths in jail. The argument that a custodial death during jail confinement is highly likely is not supported by the reported data and remains at less than one percent annually of the ADP.

The occurrence of a death of state prisoners followed similar trends as their jail detainee counterparts. Deaths from natural causes and natural illnesses accounted for 61 percent of the deaths, followed by suicides and AIDS-related deaths, equaling a total of about 68 percent of the prisoner deaths. Based on the reported prisoner deaths, it is estimated that likelihood of a death in prison is 0.005 percent.

Comparing the age, race, and gender of ARD, an officer-involved shooting, and custodial deaths show varying patterns. Being male and white is associated with a greater likelihood of dying during arrest or confinement than being female. The average age of a jail detainee decedent is about 40 years old, compared to about 55 years old in prison. The average age of an ARD prior to confinement is about 34 years old, and the average age of the decedent in an officer-involved shooting is 27 years of age.

Of the data sources reporting a death in custody or during confinement, officer-involved shootings have been more scrutinized. Beyond criticizing the lack of and the limitations of the reported data, scrutiny has also focused on the perception that the police shoot young black males more frequently than other races. Police officers have been accused of discriminately and disproportionately using deadly force against young black males. While the numbers of reported justifiable homicides by the police are annually reported by the FBI, they have been reported inconsistently. However, the reported data and research show that the race of the officer and race of the offender are statistically negligible in use of force encounters, including deadly force.

Fryer (2016), a Harvard economist, researched racial differences in the police use of force and found that race was statistically insignificant in officer-involved shootings. He examined four data sets including: New York City's Police Department's Stop-Question-and-Frisk Program (2003– 2013); The Police-Public Contact Survey (1996–2011); fifteen police departments' data on officer-involved shootings; and Huston Police Department's Arrest Data (2000–2015). Fryer reported that the data sets in their collective totality showed that the police use of high levels of force was rare. Coefficient statistics showed that when the police used empty-hand control techniques, the use of the TASER, pepper spray, or the baton, African-American and Hispanic suspects were slightly more likely to be the recipient of force than whites (5% more likely). Further, Fryer reported that African-Americans were 23.8 percent less likely and Hispanics were 8.5 percent less likely to be shot by the police and the coefficient was statistically insignificant. The Fryer study aligns with prior studies on officer-involved shootings showing that the use of deadly force is not correlated with the race of the suspect.

Examining the nature of officer-involved shooting must extend beyond just the reported numbers and must be placed in a "contextual perspective" which involves examining several factors. First, as noted in Table 2.4, the population of the United States has dramatically increased over the last 47 years. While the number of sworn police officers has also generally increased, that increase does not match the US population growth. Indeed, in some regions of the country, police agencies have laid officers off or have not replaced retiring or terminated officers since 2008.

Second, while violent crime has declined since 1993, some major larger metropolitan cities have not totally experienced the national decline. For example, cities with populations over 200,000, which have not experienced the same levels of decline in homicide, rapes, and aggravated assaults, include: Detroit, Memphis, Baltimore, St. Louis, Cleveland, Newark, NJ, and Kansas City, MO, to name a few (Federal Bureau of Investigation, 2013). In many cities, "hot spot" crime areas account for higher volumes of violent crime, and trends generally revolve around issues of the drug culture, underscored by gang violence, disturbance calls, and/or family violence calls, and calls involving firearms and other weapons. In these hot spot crime areas, calls for police services are more frequent than in other sectors of the city (or the county), and these calls are more likely to involve a police response to a violent crime.

Third, the reported rate of African-Americans killed by the police in justifiable homicides has declined from 49 percent in 1978 to 34 percent in 1998 (Brown & Langan, 2001). Further, according to the Centers for Disease Control and Prevention (2014), the rate of police killings of African-Americans has fallen by 70 percent from 1969 to 2011. While the CDC reported that the younger African-Americans were the victims in one in four killings by police from 1968 to 1974, one in seven from 1975 to 1984, and one in ten from 2000 to 2011, the data reported by Brown and Langan (SHR), the CDC, the FBI, and the BJS, all consistently show that younger black males, ages 17 to 30, are at a higher risk of a contact with the police and arrest (see Table 2.1). The pertinent question, however, is, does the risk reflect discrimination by the police in these incidents or can the variations be explained in the disparity that is associated with other contact variables?

The answer to this question is assessed on several levels. First, women are at a lower risk of being killed by the police as they have a lower involvement in violent crimes and violent crimes which involve a firearm. Second, young men are at a greater risk of police contact, which impacts the likelihood of a police shooting because they are more likely to engage in violent crimes. The police citizen contact data (Table 2.1) showed that young males (16 to 29) were more likely than females to have force used or threatened against them, while white males were twice as likely as black males and three times more likely than any other race to have force used or threatened against them. Young white males accounted for about 42 percent of all of the reported ARD and black individuals accounted for about 33 percent. In this data set, white males accounted for about 42 percent of the justifiable police homicides and black individuals accounted for about 32 percent.

Further, Snyder (2012) reported nine significant arrest-related crime trends from 1980 to 2009, which would increase the likelihood of a police contact and which may lead to a justified police shooting. During the time period, the black arrest rate for murder averaged seven times the white rate and the victimization rate was about six times higher than the rate for whites, although the rate is declining. The black forcible rape arrest rate declined 70 percent, while the white arrest rate fell by 31 percent. On average, the black arrest rate for robbery was ten times the white rate but was declining. On average, 61 percent of all arrests for aggravated assaults were white arrests, 37 percent were black arrests, and the remaining included other races. On average, the black arrest rate for burglary was three times the white arrest rate. The black arrest rate for motor vehicle theft averaged four times the white arrest rate. The black arrest rate for weapon law violations increased and resulted in a ratio of five black arrests to one white arrest. In about 20 percent of the weapon law violations, the arrestee was under 18 years old. Also during the time period, the increase in the arrest rate for drug sale, manufacturing, and possession was greater for adults than juveniles. Overall, the racial disparity in arrests for drug sale or manufacture was greater than for drug possession or use, and the black arrest rate was about four times greater than for whites, a trend that has remained constant since 1980.

While total arrests for whites generally account for about 69 percent of the arrests, blacks comprise about 28 percent, and Native Americans or Asians account for about 3 percent. The African-American population comprises about 13 percent of the United States population and the arrest-related data in eight of nine categories showed a disproportionate arrest rate over white arrests. African-American males are more likely to be arrested on weapons-related charges and are at a greater risk of being a victim of homicide than other races, while whites are more likely to be a victim in a sex-related homicide.

Youth in the United States comprise about 18 percent of the population, but account for about 40 percent of the violent crime, and the use of firearms by these youth accounts for over 70 percent of the Part I Index Crimes. The homicide victimization rates for white and black young males were significantly higher between the ages of 15 to 25. The homicide rate for white youth peaked at age 20, while it peaked at age 25 for black males. Homicide victimization rates for young black males was about nine times higher than for young white males, although both rates have been declining from 2001 to 2011 (Cooper & Smith, 2011). The likelihood of youth-on-youth killings in hot spots may triple over other areas. A black youth is significantly more likely to be killed by another black youth than by a police officer. Also, the CDC (National Center for Health Statistics 2015) reported that African-American males are about 10 to 14 times more likely to die from a traffic accident, a drowning, an accidental poisoning, and/or a criminal homicide than from being shot by the police.

The arrest trends indicate a disparity for arrests of African-Americans in many crime categories, but the issue of racial discrimination is not supported by the trends and is countered by the contextual and situational variables of the call and the arrest. Consistent with a majority of the calls for service with a high frequency occurring in hot spots of a given city, younger males are more likely to commit a higher volume of crime, which places them at a higher rate of risk of engaging in criminal behavior. The criminological theory is replete with supportive research that younger males are more likely to engage in risk taking behaviors, including committing violent crimes. Of these calls for service, a disproportionate number of younger males are more likely to be involved with the call, particularly if the call is associated with drugs, crimes of violence, firearms, and other weapons.

These factors exponentially multiply the risk that the police may use lethal force in response to the associated criminal behaviors. Research on the use of lethal force shows that using lethal force parallels not only the hot spot violent crime trends, but also aligns with the contextual variables associated with these hot spot violent crime trends. The potential for the police using lethal force increases in these situations, underscoring the disparity of the police using lethal force. Calls for service and crime trends analysis places the disparity issue in context, while concomitantly rebuffing the perception that the use of lethal force is used discriminately (MacDonald, 2003). For at least the last 40 years, the research on the use of force and the contacts between the police and citizens consistently show that the use of force, including lethal force, is not racially motivated, but rather is associated with the location of the arrest, the situational nature and dynamics of the arrest, and the behaviors and resistance exhibited by the person. Rather, as mentioned previously, the officer's use of force is determined by the contextual variables impacting the circumstances, such as: a high crime/violent crime location/hot spot area of the community, the level of perceived citizen resistance and behaviors, age of the citizen, weapons violations, involvement of drugs, and the demeanor of the citizen, and the dynamics of the contact (Fryer, 2016; MacDonald, 2016; Walker, Spohn, & DeLone, 2012).

Summary

Using multiple sources, the available reported data demonstrate that during contacts between the police and citizens, the use of force is rare and that an ARD or an officer-involved shooting is even more rare. In addition, the data indicate that death in custody is also rare. In comparison, underappreciated statistics of other types of deaths or sudden deaths place an ARD in its proper perspective. For example, the FBI has reported that on average there are about 18,000 criminal homicides which have occurred from 1990 to 2014. The CDC (National Center for Health Statistics 2015) reported on average, there is about one death per 56 hospital emergency room admissions (all causes, weekends) and 63 hospital emergency room admissions (all causes, weekdays); there were 33,000 deaths from traffic accidents; about 39,000 deaths caused by accidental poisoning; about 30,000 deaths from falls; and about 250,000 deaths due to medical errors, which are the third leading cause of death in the United States.

Additional factors which may increase sudden death rates over the broader population include: severe mental illness (two to three times); antipsychotic drugs (three times); epilepsy (24 times); cocaethylene from a combination of alcohol and cocaine (18–25 times); and African-American adolescents and athletes (five times) (De Hert et al., 2009; Maron et al., 1998; Straus et al., 2004). Duckworth (2013) reported about one in four, or 62 million, people experience mental illness annually, about 2.4 million adults are diagnosed with schizophrenia, about 6.1 million are diagnosed with bi-polar, about 14.8 million are diagnosed with major depression, and about 46 percent of the homeless are considered mentally ill. The mentally ill population has an increased risk of exhibiting various medical conditions and is likely to die 25 years early.

Further, Rudd et al. (2015) reported that from 2000 to 2014, the rate of deaths from drug overdoses increased 137 percent. They reported that more persons in the United States died from a drug overdose in 2014 than in any other year on record. From 2000 to 2014, about half a million persons in the United States died from a drug overdose, which equates to approximately 1.5 times more drug overdose deaths than automobile fatalities. Deaths from opioids (pain relievers) and heroin account for 61 percent of the deaths in 2014, and these deaths have tripled since 2010. The top four categories of death from chemical abuse include: alcohol (29,000), prescription drugs (16,235), heroin (8,200), and cocaine (5,100).

The rate of death for Hispanic and African-Americans, aged 25 to 44, increased by 8 percent, regardless of gender. Also, the Centers for Disease Control and Prevention (National Center for Health Statistics 2015) reports that annually, about 2.6 million deaths in the United States are attributed to heart disease (956,494), cancer (585,000), respiratory disease (149,000), accidents (130,000), suicide (40,000), and homicide (16,000).

In other scenarios, on average, about one sudden cardiac death occurs per 7,692 military recruits a year, per 1,300 NCAA Division 1 male basketball players over an average four-year career, and per 72,000 high school athletes over a three-year high school career (Bell & Redeimeier, 2001; Eckart et al., 2004; Harmon, et al., 2012; Maron, Gohman, & Aeppli, 1998).

These statistics provide additional insight into the frequency of sudden deaths outside law enforcement activities. There is no comparison between the frequency of these deaths and an ARD, as sudden deaths outside law enforcement occur at a significantly higher rate. An individual has over 250 times the likelihood of dying from a medical error by a physician than from being shot and killed by the police. However, there is no public outcry when a person dies from a faulty medical procedure.

As shown by the available collected data on ARD, both law enforcement officers and detention officers have less than one percent chance of being involved in a contact during their career where the citizen or detainee dies during the contact or in custody. Yet, an ARD or a custodial death generates wide scrutiny, initiates a critical investigation, and possible criminal prosecution and civil lawsuits emerge after an occurrence.

Law enforcement officers endure the brunt of the negative criticisms and consequences of these events and they deserve a competent, objective, fair, and complete analysis of the ARD before any conclusions are reached and negative actions are taken. The ARD can be complicated and complex, and frequently involves numerous variables to examine. The investigator should be knowledgeable of the role of these variables and their significance when performing the investigation.

References

Banks, D., Couznes, L., Blanton, C., & Cribb. D. (2015). *Arrest-related deaths program assessment: Technical report.* Washington, DC: United States Department of Justice, Bureau of Justice Statistics.

Bell, C. M. & Redeimeier, D. A. (2001). Mortality among patients admitted to hospitals on weekends as compared with weekdays. *New England Journal of Medicine, 345*(9), 663–668.

Brown, J. M. & Langan, P. A. (2001). *Policing and homicide, 1976–1998: Justifiable homicide by police, police officers murdered by felons.* Washington, DC: United States Department of Justice, Bureau of Justice Statistics.

Burch, A. M. (2011). *Arrest-related deaths, 2003–2009: Statistical tables.* Washington, DC: United States Department of Justice, Bureau of Justice Statistics.

Bureau of Justice Statistics. (1978, 1984, 1989, 1995). *Jails and jail inmates.* Washington, DC: U.S. Department of Justice.

Bureau of Justice Statistics. (1981, 1986, 1987, 1988, 1990, 1991, 1992, 1993, 2002). *Profile of jail inmates.* Washington, DC: U.S. Department of Justice.

Carson, A. (2013). *Prisoners in 2012.* Washington, DC: Bureau of Justice Statistics, US Department of Justice.

Center for Disease Control's searchable mortality data (2016), accessed at: http://wonder.cdc.gov/ucd-icd10.html.

Cooper, A. & Smith, E. L. (2011). *Homicide trends in the United States, 1980–2008.* Washington, DC: United States Department of Justice, Bureau of Justice Statistics.

Death in Custody Reporting Act of 2000, Public Law No: 106-297 (2000).

Death in Custody Reporting Act of 2013, Public Law No: 113-242 (2014).

De Hert, M., Dekker, J. M., Wood, D., Kahl, K. G., Holt, R. I. G., & Moller, H.-J. (2009). Cardiovascular disease and diabetes in people with severe mental illness: Position statement from the European Psychiatric Association (EPA), supported by the European Association for the Study of Diabetes (EASD) and the European Society of Cardiology (ESC). *European Psychiatry, 24*(6), 412–424.

Duckworth, K. (2013). *Mental illness: Facts and numbers.* Arlington, VA: National Alliance on Mental Illness.

Durose, M. R., Schmitt, E. L., & Langan, P. A. (2005). *Contacts between police and the public: Findings from the 2002 national survey.* Washington, DC: United States Department of Justice, Bureau of Justice Statistics.

Durose, M. R., Smith, E. L., & Langan, P. A. (2007). *Contacts between police and the public, 2005.* Washington, DC: United States Department of Justice, Bureau of Justice Statistics.

Eckart, R. E., Scoville, S. L., Campbell, C. L., Shry, E. A., Stajduhar, K. C., Potter, R. N., Pearse, L.A., & Virmani, R. (2004). Sudden death in young adults: A 25-year review of autopsies in military recruits. *Annals of Internal Medicine, 141*(11), 829–834.

Eith, C. & Durose, M. R. (2011). *Contacts between police and the public, 2008.* Washington, DC: United States Department of Justice, Bureau of Justice Statistics.

Federal Bureau of Investigation. (2013). *Crime in the United States: Expanded homicide data* (tables 13 and 14). Washington, DC: United States Department of Justice.

Federal Bureau of Investigation. (2014). *Crime in the United States (1968–2014)*. Washington, DC: United States Department of Justice.

Federal Bureau of Investigation. (2015). *Law enforcement officers killed and assaulted, statistical tables, 1987–2014*. Washington, DC: United States Department of Justice.

Fox, J. A., & Zawitz, M. W. (2006). *Homicide trends in the United States: 2002 Update*. Washington, DC: United States Department of Justice, Bureau of Justice Statistics.

Fryer Jr., R. G. (2016, July). An empirical analysis of racial differences in police use of force. *National Bureau of Economic Research*, Working Paper 22399, www.nber.org/papers/w22399, Cambridge, MA: 1–61.

Geller, W. A. & Geller, M. S. (1992). *Deadly force: What we know, a practitioner's desk reference on police-involved shootings*. Washington, DC: Police Executive Research Forum.

Graham, M. A. (2014). Investigation of deaths temporally associated with law enforcement apprehension. *Academic Forensic Pathology*, *4*(3): 366–389.

Greenfeld, L. A., Langan, P. A., & Smith, S. K. (1997). *Police use of force: Collection of national data*. Washington, DC: United States Department of Justice, Bureau of Justice Statistics.

Harmon, K. G., Asif, I. M., Maleszewski, J. J., Owens, D. S., Prutkin, J. M., Salerno, J. C., & Drezner, J. A. (2012). Incidence, etiology, and comparative frequency of sudden cardiac death in NCAA athletes: A decade in review. *Circulation*, *132*(1), 10–19.

Hyland, S., Langton, L., & Davis, E. (2015). *Police use of nonfatal force, 2002–2011*. Washington, DC: United States Department of Justice, Bureau of Justice Statistics.

James, D. J. & Glaze, L. E. (2006). *Mental health problems of prison and jail inmates*. Washington, DC: United States Department of Justice, Bureau of Justice Statistics.

Johnson, R. R. (2016, July). *Dispelling the myths of surrounding police use of lethal force*. Dolan Consulting Group, 1–20, accessed at www.DolanConsultingGroup.com.

Klinger, D. A. (2012). On the problems and promise of research on lethal police violence: A research note. *Homicide Studies*, *16*(1), 78–96.

Langan, P. A., Greenfeld, L. A., Smith, S. K., Durose, M. R., & Levin, D. J. (2001). *Contacts between police and the public: Findings from the 1999 national survey*. Washington, DC: United States Department of Justice, Bureau of Justice Statistics.

Loftin, C., Wiersema, B., McDowall, D., & Dobrin, A. (2003). Underreporting of justifiable homicides committed by police officers in the United States, 1976–1998. *American Journal of Public Health*, *93*(7), 1117–1121.

MacDonald, H. (2003). *Are cops racist? How the war against the police harms black Americans*. Chicago, IL: Ivan R. Dee Publisher.

MacDonald, H. (2016). *The war on cops: How the new attack on law and order makes everyone less safe*. New York, NY: Encounter Books.

Maron, B. J., Gohman, T. E., & Aeppli, D. (1998). Prevalence of sudden cardiac death during competitive sports activities in Minnesota high school athletes. *Journal of the American College of Cardiology*, *32*(7), 1881–1884.

Maruschak, L. M., Berzofsky, M., & Unangst, J. (2015). *Medical problems of state and federal prisoners and jail inmates, 2011 to 2012*. Washington, DC: United States Department of Justice, Bureau of Justice Statistics.

Minton, T. D., Ginder, S., Brumbaugh, S. M., Smiley-McDonald, H., & Rohloff, H. (2015). *Census of jails: Population changes, 1999–2013*. Washington, DC: United States Department of Justice, Bureau of Justice Statistics.

National Center for Health Statistics. (2015). *Compressed mortality file, 1968–2014*. Atlanta, GA: Centers for Disease Control and Prevention.

Noonan, M., Rohloff, H., & Ginder, S. (2015). *Mortality in local jails and state prisons: 2000–2013: Statistical tables*. Washington, DC: United States Department of Justice, Bureau of Justice Statistics.

Planty, M., Burch, A. M., Banks, D., Couzens, L., Blanton, C., & Cribb, D. (2015). *Arrest-related deaths program: Data quality profile.* Washington, DC: United States Department of Justice, Bureau of Justice Statistics.

Quinn, B. (2014). *The nation's two measures of homicide.* Washington, DC: United States Department of Justice, Bureau of Justice Statistics.

Reaves, B. A. (2011). *Census of state and local law enforcement agencies, 2008.* Washington, DC: United States Department of Justice, Bureau of Justice Statistics.

Reaves, B. A. (2015). *Local police departments, 2013: Personnel, policies, and practices.* Washington, DC: United States Department of Justice, Bureau of Justice Statistics.

Ross, D. L. (2011). What we know about police use of force: Dispelling the myths. *Law Enforcement Executive Forum Monograph*, 1–26.

Rudd, R. A., Aleshire, N., Zibbell, J. E., & Gladden, R. M. (2015). Increases in drug and opioid overdose deaths in the United States, 2000–2014. *Morbidity and Mortality Weekly Report, 64*(50), 1378–1382.

Sherman, L. W. & Langworthy, R. H. (1979). Measuring homicide by police officers. *Journal of Criminal Law and Criminology, 70*(4), 546–560.

Smith, E. L. & Cooper, A. (2013). *Homicide in the U.S. known to law enforcement, 2011.* Washington, DC: United States Department of Justice, Bureau of Justice Statistics.

Snyder, H. N. (2012). *Arrest in the United States, 1980–2009.* Washington, DC: United States Department of Justice, Bureau of Justice Statistics.

Straus, S. M. J. M., Bleumink, G. S., Dieleman, J. P., van der Lei, J., 't Jong, G. W., Kingma, J.H., & Stricker, B. H. C. (2004). Antipsychotics and the risk of sudden cardiac death. *Archives of Internal Medicine, 164*(12), 1293–1297.

US Census Bureau. (2015). United States population. Available at www.census.gov. Accessed 1.5.16. *Violent Crime Control and Law Enforcement Act,* Title 42 U.S.C., §14141 and §14142 (1994).

Walker, S., Spohn, S., & DeLone, M. (2012). *The color of justice: Race, ethnicity, and crime in America* (5th ed.). Belmont, CA: Wadsworth Cengage Learning.

Washington Post. (2015). *Police shootings*, accessed at www.WashingtonPost.com/policeshootings.

3

LEGAL AND LIABILITY ISSUES SURROUNDING THE USE OF FORCE

Darrell L. Ross

Introduction

The police use of threatened or actual use of force is rare during a citizen contact (Eith & Durose, 2011). Moreover, an arrest-related death (ARD) during the contact is also rare (Mumola, 2007). Despite the rare occurrence, an ARD will most likely trigger a number of legal questions. It is common for the decedent's estate to file a civil legal action, attempting to hold the responding involved officers and their agency administrators liable for the wrongful death. Counsel for the plaintiff and the defendant officers frequently retain medical experts to render opinions regarding the cause of death, and police experts will also be retained to opine on the use of force measures used by the officers.

As this text emphasizes, an ARD initiates an extensive investigation of the involved officers' actions. Nothing draws the public's attention and scrutiny of law enforcement more than an ARD (Katz, 2015). The investigation outcomes of some past high-profile cases where grand juries have declined to file charges against the involved officers have sparked mistrust between some community members and the police, resulting in the loss of the public's trust in the investigations and reviews of ARD (Warren, 2015). Therefore, the investigator tasked with the duty of the investigation must adhere to proper investigation procedures, maintain integrity of the investigation, and work within the ethics of the profession in order to meet the expectations of the decedent's family, the involved officers, the involved agency, and the community. Where the public believes an investigation was completed in accordance with fundamental due process, the public will support the legitimacy of the agency. Conversely, legitimacy and support of the agency can erode when the public believes the investigation was performed unfairly and unimpartially (Sullivan, 2014).

For many years, the police use of force has continued to be a major societal issue, as some members in varying communities perceive that the police abuse their official authority to use force and that an agency's investigation is less than professional, "protects their own," thereby ratifying the actions of their officers. In response to the Rodney King incident in Los Angeles, the subsequent Christopher Commission Report (1991) of the Los Angeles Police Department found that supervisors exercised "lax supervision" and performed inadequate investigations into use of force incidents. As a result,

Congress enacted the Violent Crime Control and Law Enforcement Act of 1994 (VCCLEA). Section §14141 of the act authorizes the Civil Rights Division of the Department of Justice to initiate civil actions against law enforcement agencies to remedy allegations of policies and actions that show a "pattern and practice" of violating the constitutional rights of citizens. Among others, a majority of these civil actions involve allegations of the use of excessive force measures during citizen contacts. Since 1997, there have been 22 police agencies that have entered into consent decrees and memoranda of agreement (MOA) to address systemic policing issues, and there are currently 20 agencies under investigation by the DOJ (Wesler, 2013; United States Department of Justice, 2015). A review of these consent decrees and MOAs shows that the DOJ found a majority of the agencies systematically abused their authority of using force measures and about 50 percent conducted insufficient investigations into their officers' actions.

Since an ARD represents a major use of force incident requiring an investigation, the investigator should be knowledgeable about the varying facets of police use of force. Frequently, in a civil liability case alleging excessive force, an investigator's testimony in a deposition shows the lack of knowledge pertaining to varying facets of the use of force, yet the investigator was assigned the task of conducting the investigation. Hence, the investigator must be knowledgeable of the agency's policy on using force and all of the authorized use of force measures; all of the authorized empty-hand control techniques; all intermediate weapons; all restraint equipment; all authorized firearms; the training of the officers in the appropriate use of force measures; and state and federal laws guiding the appropriate use of force. Moreover, since an ARD may implicate potential criminal conduct of the involved officers, will involve administrative disciplinary issues for potential violation of departmental policies and tactics, and ultimately may result in a civil lawsuit, the investigator must be aware of the legal issues impacting the investigation.

It is important for the investigator to be mindful that a criminal and an administrative investigation may be running concurrently, and agency administrators may desire to request that an outside agency conduct the criminal investigation and the prosecutor's office conduct the interview (Schmidt, 2004). Using an outside agency to conduct the criminal investigation assists in ensuring that the integrity of the investigation is not questioned and reduces the potential of bias of the investigator when investigating a fellow officer. It is also important for investigators to acknowledge the distinction between criminal and noncriminal activities, as ARDs emerge from officers engaged in performing their sworn duties and not from intentional criminal acts of violence (Hatch & Dickson, 2007).

This chapter addresses the pertinent legal issues involved in an ARD investigation. Failure to be aware of these legal distinctions could severely damage the investigation, while understanding the law and procedures will assist in ensuring the evidence obtained will not be suppressed in future proceedings. The first section describes the investigation considerations associated with a criminal investigation, the second section addresses administrative investigation issues, and the last section describes the relevant use of force civil liability issues that may emerge.

Criminal Investigation

Prior to an officer being interviewed in an investigatory setting, the officer should be advised as to the nature of the interview. If the interview is criminal in nature and the officer is under arrest and in custody, the officer must be provided with warnings in accordance with the United States Court decision in *Miranda v. Arizona* (1966). If the officer is not considered a criminal suspect, the Miranda warnings are not required as the interview is a non-custodial interview. Frequently, investigators needlessly provide the officer with the Miranda warnings when it is not required.

Miranda allows a criminal suspect in custody the right to an attorney and the suspect is not required to answer any questions. If the officer is not in custody, he or she is not afforded the right to an attorney and the investigator should not provide the Miranda warnings. In the absence of the Miranda warnings, the officer should be provided with a modified version of warnings consistent with the Court's decision in *Beckworth v. United States* (1976). In its eight to one decision, the Court held that a criminal suspect, who was being interviewed at his home but was not under arrest, is not entitled to the Miranda warnings. In a case involving the *Bureau of Engraving* (1999), the Federal Impasses Panel applied the warnings from the *Beckworth* decision to afford federal employees due process and to reduce exposure to future possible litigation (Schmidt, 2004). According to Schmidt (2004, 2–3), the *Beckworth* warnings provided to federal employees state:

> You have the right to remain silent if the answer would tend to incriminate you. Anything you may say may be used in an Administrative proceeding or any criminal proceeding involving you. If you refuse to answer the questions on the grounds that they may incriminate you, you cannot be discharged solely for remaining silent. However, your silence can be considered in an administrative proceeding for its evidentiary value that is warranted by the facts surrounding your case.

While *Beckworth* is not binding on local and state law enforcement agencies, Schmidt (2004) recommends that a modified version be used as a matter of policy in non-custodial criminal investigation interviews of officers. First, the investigator should provide the officer with timely notice of the interview, the nature of the allegations, and that the officer may have an attorney present during the interview. Second, any reference about the officer choosing to assert his Fifth Amendment right should be omitted, as an officer can never be required to forfeit his or her protection against self-incrimination. Department administrators should consider providing officers with an Advice of Rights notice when an officer is participating in a criminal investigation, which includes:

1. this interview is part of a criminal investigation and you have the right to remain silent if your answer might incriminate you;
2. anything you say can be used against you as evidence in a disciplinary or civil proceeding or any future criminal prosecution involving you;
3. if you refuse to answer a question because the answer may incriminate you, you cannot be disciplined solely for remaining silent;
4. you do not have the right to remain silent about another person's commission of a crime, unless that information also implicates your involvement in a criminal offense; and
5. you have the right to consult an attorney of your choosing, and to have that attorney present to advise you during the interview.

In a criminal investigation, there is no moral or professional obligation for the officer to participate. An officer has the right to remain silent in a criminal investigation and has the right for an attorney to be present during the questioning. It should be expected that, once the Advice of Rights is provided to an officer, he or she will likely request that the attorney be present. Further, the investigator should always review the collective bargaining unit's agreement, the state's statutory requirements as warranted, and the agency's protocols for conducting investigations.

Administrative Investigation

Interviewing an officer as a suspect in a criminal investigation is quite different from interviewing the officer for possible disciplinary reasons due to policy violations. Even so, anytime an internal affairs (IA) officer interviews an officer, a coercive climate may exist, and because the officer is anxious and desires to be truthful and to get his or her "story" out, he or she may not totally realize the process involved in an administrative disciplinary interview. Equally, the investigator needs to be aware of the protocols for conducting an administrative interview when policy violations are being questioned, as the involved officer(s) career is at stake. Unlike a criminal investigation, an officer may not refuse a lawful order from a superior's question regarding the performance of his sworn duties. Doing so will almost certainly lead to disciplinary action and most likely will lead to termination (Aitchison, 2013).

There are two United States Supreme Court decisions addressing the administrative interview process. In *Garrity v. New Jersey* (1967), police officers were accused of fixing tickets. During the interview, the officers were ordered to respond to questions and threatened that if they did not, their employment would be terminated. The officers answered the incriminating questions and their responses were used against them in a subsequent criminal prosecution. The Court ruled that the officers' Fifth Amendment protection from self-incrimination was violated, and that the administrative process forced the officers to choose between forfeiting their employment and their protection against self-incrimination. The Court held that "policemen, like teachers and lawyers, are not relegated to a watered-down version of constitutional rights," and ruled that "compelled statements made by law enforcement officers under threat of possible forfeiture of employment cannot be used against the officers in criminal prosecutions" (*Garrity v. New Jersey*, 1967, 5).

In *Gardner v. Broderick* (1968), the Court took occasion to further address the issue of compelled statements ordered by an agency investigator and employment termination. An officer was being questioned for alleged bribery and corruption and refused to sign a waiver of immunity that would have been used in a subsequent criminal prosecution. The Court reversed the officer's discharge and held that the officer was discharged solely for his refusal to waive a constitutional right. With language that has since become a guidepost for disciplinary investigations of law enforcement officers, the Court ruled that while a law enforcement agency can conduct an administrative investigation of an officer, it cannot, in the course of that investigation, compel the officer to waive the immunity guaranteed by the *Garrity* decision. The issue of immunity is protected in the Fifth Amendment and it states that no person shall be compelled in a criminal case to be a witness against himself. The "compulsion" is the threat of disciplinary action if the employee fails to cooperate in an administrative process. An officer can be compelled to answer questions in an administrative interview and in a civil case, unless the response will be used in a criminal prosecution.

The *Garrity* decision involves the following components and applies: whenever the employing agency requires an employee to respond to job-related questions; when the statement is being compelled and not voluntary; when threat of job loss for not answering the questions can only be based after advising the employee that the results will not be used in a criminal prosecution; when it is recommended to provide the employee with an advisory statement prior to questioning; when Miranda warnings are not required; and when the investigator may be required to comply with bargaining units and statutory requirements. Moreover, responses to the compelled job-related questions cannot be used later in a criminal prosecution.

Garrity interviews do not allow the officer to lie or to provide false statements. If the employee is provided *Garrity* warnings and a compelled statement is obtained, the employee could be subject to criminal charges if the employee made false statements during the interview. If, after being given *Garrity* warnings, the employee chooses not to answer questions narrowly tailored to the officer's job duties, the agency can impose strong disciplinary action for this act of insubordination up to and including termination (Daigle, 2012). For example, in *McKinley v. City of Mansfield* (2005), the police department was investigating unlawful scanner use by numerous officers. Officer McKinley was subjected to a compulsory interview during which he made exculpatory statements. Because his statements were inconsistent with a fellow officer's and a victim's, he was subjected to a second compulsory interview, which he alleged was a lying and falsification interview. At that interview, McKinley was accused of lying; he was confronted with the specific statements alleged to be lies; and he was told the basis for the conclusion that each statement was false. He admitted his earlier statements were false, and he corrected them with truthful statements, all of which were taped. He was prosecuted and convicted of falsification and obstructing official business. One of the IA investigators not only revealed McKinley's two compelled statements to the prosecutor, he also testified in detail about the content of McKinley's two statements. The conviction was overturned and McKinley filed a §1983 lawsuit, alleging that his Fifth Amendment rights were violated. The Court of Appeals overturned summary judgment in favor of the defendants, concluding that there was a genuine issue of material fact whether the second interview was a scannergate follow-up interview or a new investigation centered on McKinley's apparent lies in the first interview. If a jury concludes that the matter under investigation in the second interview was falsification as defined by *McKinley*, the combination of the compulsion and the courtroom usage of the officer's compelled statements (from interview two) establish a Fifth Amendment violation.

Prior to performing the administrative interview, it is recommended that the investigator read Advisory Statements to the officer as a matter of practice so that it is clearly stated, at the beginning, as to the nature of the interview and the responsibility of the officer. A majority of law enforcement departments have instituted Advisory Statements to be read to the officer under *Garrity* and generally include the following:

> You are hereby ordered to fully cooperate with the investigating official(s). Your failure to cooperate will create an objective and subjective fear of termination. You have the following rights and responsibilities during this investigation: (1) You have the right to be informed of the allegations involved; (2) You will be asked questions specifically directed and narrowly related to the performance of your official duties; (3) Statements made during any interviews may be used as evidence of misconduct or as the basis for seeking disciplinary action against you; (4) Any statements made by you during these interviews cannot be used against you in any subsequent criminal proceeding, nor can the fruits of any of your statements be used against you in any subsequent criminal proceeding; (5) If you so request, a person of your choice may be present to serve as a witness during the interviews; and (6) If you refuse to answer questions relating to the performance of your official duties, you will be subject to dismissal.

The investigator should have the officer sign, date, and place the time on the form indicating when the statement was read

The second United States Supreme Court decision impacting administrative investigations is *NLRB v. J. Weingarten* (1975). The decision applies only to agencies that are under collective bargaining. Under *Weingarten*, an employee is granted union assistance and representation (steward) at an investigatory interview where disciplinary or other adverse action may reasonably result. *Weingarten* rights only arise when an employee is the focus of an administrative disciplinary investigation and is asked questions of an investigatory nature. The Court did not rule that the employee must be informed in advance by the employer that he or she is entitled to union representation. Employees who are on probation and who are in administrative positions are not entitled to *Weingarten* protections. Generally, the union steward informs employees of this provision in written union documents and/or at union meetings (Aitchison, 2013).

Union representation in an investigatory interview may be useful to serve as a witness to the interview, assist the employee in avoiding making fatal admissions, may object to intimidating tactics by the investigator, and discourage an employee from informing on others. The employee must request that he or she desires to have union representation. In accordance with *Weingarten* rights, the supervisor: must advise the steward of the nature of the interview and the alleged violations, must allow the steward to meet with the employee prior to the interview, and must allow the steward to speak during the interview but may not end it; while the steward can ask for clarification or object to confusing questions and can advise the employee not to answer badgering, misleading, or abusive questions. If an employee feels that the *Weingarten* protections were violated, the employee should file a grievance. When in doubt, management should grant the employee their *Weingarten* rights.

Use of Force and Civil Liability

When examining an officer's decision to use a degree of force in a particular incident, the primary focus becomes whether the force applied was justified. Because there are innumerable variables which emerge from any force incident, numerous questions will arise concerning the legitimacy of the force measures used. Some of the more common questions include: what was the need to use the force selected; did the officer follow the agency's policy; did the officer follow the training provided; did the officer create the need to use the level of force; did the officer fail to wait for back-up; did the officer misuse a physical control technique, misuse a non-deadly force device, and use deadly force without justification; did the officer continue to use force after the need stopped; was the force used disproportionate to the need; what was the nature of the circumstances, the confrontational environment, and the type of threat and resistance of the subject encountered; what was the reactionary time needed; what was the perception of the officer at the moment force was used; and what was the totality of circumstances of the confrontation, to mention a few. These are complex questions and not always easy to answer.

Since 1985, the United States Supreme Court has established standards of review, which guide officers in deciding a level of force to use. The Court's decisions in the following cases provide the foundation for assessing the officer's use of force. Investigators should become knowledgeable of these standards and their application when conducting a use of force analysis. Further, understanding how the courts apply these standards in accordance with the relevant Constitutional amendments will be useful to the investigator when assisting counsel to defend a civil action for excessive force filed against agency officers and administrators. An agency policy violation does not equate to a constitutional rights violation.

Table 3.1 shows the applicable case decisions and the standards applied by the Court to the use of force claims (Brave, 2011; modified).

TABLE 3.1 Use of force status matrix

Free person	*Pre-trial detainee*	*Convicted person*
Fourth Amendment	Fourteenth Amendment	Eighth Amendment
Objective Reasonableness	Objective Reasonableness	Cruel and Unusual Punishment
TN v. Garner (1985)	Kingsley v. Hendrickson (2015)	Whitley v. Albers (1986)
Graham v. Connor (1989)		Hudson v. McMillian (1992)
Saucier v. Katz (2001)		Hope v. Pelzer (2002)
Brosseau v. Haugen (2004)		Wilkins v. Gaddy (2010)
Scott v. Harris (2007)		
Plumhoff v. Rickard (2014)		
Tolan v. Cotton (2014)		
City and County of San Francisco v. Sheehan (2015)		
*Mullenix v. Luna, 557 U.S. __ (2015)		

Note: *Not strictly a use of force decision.

In *Tennessee v. Garner* (1985), the Court ruled that the use of deadly force constituted a seizure in accordance with the Fourth Amendment. In response to a prowler call, two officers from the Memphis police department responded. To prevent the youth from fleeing, one officer shot and killed an unarmed youth who was scaling a fence. The officers acted pursuant to the state fleeing statute, which authorized the use of deadly force to prevent subjects from fleeing—known as the "fleeing felon" law. The Court opined that the rule was unconstitutional, served no important governmental function, and held that it is not permissible to use deadly force to prevent the escape of a felony suspect in all circumstances.

The Court further held that if an officer had probable cause to believe that the suspect poses a threat of serious physical harm, either to the officer or to others, in other words is dangerous, it is not unconstitutionally unreasonable to prevent the escape by using deadly force. The primary issue, therefore, in excessive force claims becomes the issue of seizure under the Fourth Amendment. Writing for the majority, Justice White explained that in excessive force claims, the matter of a seizure arises under the Fourth Amendment and a court must balance the need for the seizure against the nature and quality of the seizure to determine whether the seizure was reasonable. The Court outlined several rules to guide officers in deciding to use deadly force including: deadly force may be warranted to prevent an escape or to protect a citizen when an officer has probable cause to believe the person is escaping; if a suspect threatens an officer with a weapon or there is probable cause to believe that he has committed a crime involving the infliction or threatened infliction of serious physical harm; and when feasible, the officer should give a warning prior to using deadly force.

In *Graham v. Connor* (1989), the Court held that the Fourth Amendment governs all use of force against free citizens. This holding was updated in subsequent decisions that will be discussed later in the chapter. In *Graham*, the Court acknowledged the right to make an arrest or investigatory stop necessarily carries with it the right to use some degree of physical coercion or threat to effect it. The Court held use of force claims fall within the purview of a seizure under the Fourth Amendment (*Brower v. County of Inyo*, 1989) and are assessed against the standard of "objective reasonableness," first decided in *Malley v. Briggs* (1986).

Importantly, *Graham* underscores that under the Fourth Amendment, officers are authorized to use objective reasonable force and such degree of force will be assessed on a case-by-case basis, within the totality of the circumstances, and based on the following criteria: (1) the severity of the crime at issue; (2) whether the suspect was actively resisting arrest; (3) whether the suspect was attempting to evade the arrest by flight; (4) whether the suspect posed an immediate threat to the officer or others; and (5) whether circumstances were tense, uncertain, and rapidly evolving. The Court ruled that objective reasonableness is not capable of precise definition or mechanical application and stated that judging the officer's use of force must allow for the fact that police officers are often forced to make split-second decisions. The Court noted that the type of degree of force to use in a given situation must be based upon the perception of the officer and not through hindsight. The Court endorses a "reasonableness at the moment" standard that requires fact finders to take into account the unpredictable and rapid dynamics of the arrest environment. The case decision is in deference to police officers.

The Court emphasized that a claim of excessive force must be evaluated by assessing the "objective reasonableness" of the officer's actions in light of the facts and circumstances confronting him or her, without regard to his or her underlying intent or motivation. From a broad perspective, the *Graham* decision is important for use of force investigators as the officer's response in a given confrontation must be fully assessed by examining the nature of the circumstances of the confrontation, the confrontational environment in which the officer was operating (totality of circumstances), the suspect's behaviors and actions (threat posed, furtive movements, access to weapons, and officer's/others' safety), and the officer's perception and reaction time needed to decide a course of action (split-second decision making, human factors, fear, belief of bodily injury, imminent or immediate threat).

In *Saucier v. Katz* (2001), the Court used an excessive force claim to further establish that officers may be granted qualified immunity when the facts show that the officer's conduct violated a constitutional right and that the right was clearly established at the time. Katz attended a speech of Vice President Al Gore at a military base, approached the podium, and two military police officers grabbed him and escorted him from the area. Katz filed a lawsuit claiming the officers used excessive force, although he did not sustain any injuries. Using the two-pronged question approach, the Court awarded the officers with qualified immunity, finding that they did not use excessive force and only used force to protect Vice President Gore.

The Court has rendered decisions in six additional cases in accordance with the Fourth Amendment, affirming their decision in *Graham*. In *Brosseau v. Haugen* (2004), Officer Brosseau attempted to physically restrain Haugen, who ran to his jeep and attempted to flee. Brosseau instructed Haugen to stop and to exit the jeep, pointed her firearm at him, and tapped the gun on the window, shattering it. Haugen began driving the jeep forward and Brosseau fired one round, which struck Haugen in the back. Officer Brosseau stated that she fired her firearm because she feared Haugen might run over other officers or citizens in the immediate area. The Court overturned the lower court's decisions of denial of qualified immunity, holding that Brosseau had probable cause to believe deadly force was justified based on Haugen's dangerous actions, which posed a threat to others. The Court opined that qualified immunity should have been awarded as the facts of the case followed similar fact patterns in other cases where qualified immunity was granted.

In *Scott v. Harris* (2007), the Court ruled that a suspect driving recklessly at excessive speeds attempting to elude police officers posed a risk of danger to the police and citizens. After attempting to stop Harris covering nine miles, reaching speeds over 90 mph, while Harris narrowly missed striking oncoming motorists, Officer Scott bumped the back bumper of Harris' vehicle after acquiring authorization, causing him to run off the roadway and crash. Harris survived the crash but was rendered a quadriplegic and sued, claiming Scott used excessive deadly force. The Court overturned the lower court's denial of qualified immunity. As part of their review, the Court watched the video of the pursuit and noted that Harris led the officers on a Hollywood car chase, and placed the officers and the citizens at great risk of serious injury. The Court held that Harris' vehicular flight represented a deadly hazard for the public and that the officers had a duty to protect them from suspects who may kill or seriously injure others. The Court emphasized that in judging whether the officer's force was reasonable, the risk of bodily harm to the officer posed by the actions of the suspect must be considered in light of threat to the public that the officer was trying to eliminate. The Court concluded that Harris' actions posed a "dangerousness risk of flight" and that Scott's action of bumping Harris' car was a reasonable use of force under the Fourth Amendment and awarded him qualified immunity.

In *Plumhoff v. Rickard* (2014), the Court affirmed its decisions in *Graham*, *Garner*, and *Scott*, holding that analyzing a claim of excessive force must be performed from the perception of a reasonable officer on the scene and not from 20/20 hindsight, as police officers are often forced to make split-second decisions in circumstances which are tense, uncertain, and rapidly evolving. Rickard was stopped in his vehicle and sped off after twice being instructed to exit his car for a sobriety test, after which he led officers on a high-speed pursuit, lasting about five minutes, reaching speeds of about 100 mph. Officer Plumhoff joined the pursuit and Rickard struck his patrol car twice. Rickard drove his vehicle into a parking lot and drove head first into Plumhoff's vehicle, and Rickard stopped momentarily. As officers approached Rickard's car, he spun the tires, moved forward and struck another patrol car, and Plumhoff fired three rounds at Rickard with his firearm. Rickard fled down the street away from the officers, nearly struck Officer Gardner, who fired ten rounds from his firearm, while Officer Galtelli fired two rounds into Rickard's vehicle. Rickard lost control of his car, crashed into a building, died from multiple gunshot wounds, and the passenger in the car, Allen, died from a combination of one gunshot and the effects from the crash.

Rickard's estate filed a civil action and the lower courts concluded that the undisputed facts did not support the assertion that their actions were in compliance with the Fourth Amendment. The lower courts held that Rickard's actions and fleeing from the officers did not pose a risk of danger to others or to them, and the officers appealed. Relying on its decision in *Scott*, the Court overturned the lower courts' decisions and ruled that Rickard's own actions of eluding the police initiated the chase with the police in which he exceeded 100 mph, lasting over five minutes, passing more than two dozen motorists, in which several had to move out of the way. The Court opined that Rickard posed a grave public risk by driving outrageously and recklessly, striking police officer vehicles, and that he temporarily stopped the chase but quickly spun his tires and drove off in an attempt to escape. The Court ruled that given Rickard's dangerous actions, the officers' use of deadly force, even firing 15 rounds, was objectively reasonable, concluding that the officers did not fire more rounds than was necessary to end the public safety risk, and that it made sense that if they were justified in shooting, the officers needed to shoot until the threat of risk had ended.

In *Tolan v. Cotton* (2014), the Court reviewed a police officer's use of deadly force in response to the actions of the suspect and also examined the legal principle of qualified immunity. Officer Edwards observed a vehicle abruptly make a turn into a residential area and ran the license plate but entered one digit incorrectly from the actual plate number. The incorrect number came back indicating that it was stolen and matched the vehicle stopped by Edwards. Officer Edwards stopped the two occupants of the vehicle and ordered to them to the ground. Tolan, the driver, explained that the car was his and complied with the officer. The stop was in front of Tolan's house and his mother and father came out and informed Edwards that Tolan was their son and the car was not stolen but actually belonged to the family. Officer Cotton responded to Edwards' call for assistance. Tolan's mother again reiterated that the car was not stolen, Cotton ordered her to stand against the garage door and she resisted, stating that it was her house. Officer Cotton grabbed her arm, escorted her to the garage, whereby she jerked her arm away, which left bruises on her arm (Tolan's mother claimed she was slammed into the garage door and Cotton reported that the mother flipped her arm up and told him to get his hands off of her). Tolan either stood up or rose to his knees, from about 15 to 20 feet away, and yelled at Cotton to "get his F•••ing hands off of his mother." Cotton then drew his firearm and fired three shots at Tolan, with Tolan surviving the shooting.

Tolan filed a civil action claiming that Cotton used excessive deadly force and the Fifth Circuit Court of Appeals affirmed the lower court's award of summary judgment. The appellate court ruled that Tolan's mother had resisted and that his words amounted to a verbal threat, whereby Cotton could have reasonably feared for his life, and accordingly, Cotton did not violate clearly established law when he shot Tolan. The Court examined Tolan's appeal and held it is undisputed that a police officer may use deadly force in self-defense, agreeing with the lower courts. However, the Court remanded the case back to the lower court, stressing that in accordance with qualified immunity, the court examining the motion must give the weight of the facts of the case as presented by the plaintiff, even if the officer's version is in disagreement with those facts.

In *City and County of San Francisco v. Sheehan* (2015), the Court examined the use of deadly force when confronted by a mentally ill person. Officers responded to a mental health facility to effect a temporary detention application of Sheehan, who had stopped taking her medications, refused to speak with her psychiatrist, and refused to eat. The officers were advised of the situation by the facility social worker, went to Sheehan's room, knocked and announced themselves, did not obtain a response, and they used a key to enter the room. Inside the room, Sheehan grabbed a kitchen knife, approached the officers, yelled at them to leave and that she would kill them. The officers then exited the room. The officers called for backup, but while waiting for their arrival, the officers became concerned that Sheehan would gather more weapons, was a danger to herself and others as she had already threatened to kill the social worker prior to their arrival and to kill them, and determined that the situation required immediate attention. The officers opened the door and the first officer sprayed Sheehan in the face with pepper spray, but she did not drop the knife. Sheehan was only a few feet away and one officer fired two shots, the second officer fired multiple shots, and Sheehan fell to the floor. Sheehan survived.

Sheehan filed a civil lawsuit asserting several claims: (1) that the officers violated the Americans for Disability Act (ADA) for failing to accommodate her disability; (2) the officers used excessive force; and (3) that the officers failed to follow their training to minimize their force when encountering a mentally ill person. The Court decided not to address the ADA claim. The Court further held that the officers' decision to re-enter the room a second time did not violate the Fourth Amendment, reasoning that Sheehan's action presented a continuous exigent circumstance, that the officers knew she possessed weapons, had threatened to kill them and others, and delaying their actions would make the situation more dangerous. The Court ruled that the officers used pepper spray first but Sheehan advanced toward them, was within several feet from the officers, and that the use of deadly force was justified. Relying on prior decisions, the Court noted that an officer may make a warrantless entry in order to protect someone from an imminent injury or to provide emergency assistance to someone who is injured, and noted that nothing in the Fourth Amendment precludes the officers from using deadly force to protect themselves (i.e., *Michigan v. Fisher*, 2009; *Scott v. Harris*, 2007).

In granting qualified immunity to the officers, the Court reasoned that Sheehan could not:

> establish a Fourth Amendment violation based merely on bad tactics that result in a deadly confrontation that could have been avoided; that courts must not judge officers with "the 20/20 vision of hindsight," even if an officer acts contrary to the training, however, (and here, given the generality of that training, it is not at all clear that they did so), that does not itself negate qualified immunity where it would otherwise be warranted.
>
> (City and County of San Francisco v. Sheehan, 2015, *1190*)

Considering the specific circumstances confronting the officers, the Court ruled that they had sufficient reason to believe that their conduct was justified.

In *Mullenix v. Luna* (2015), the Court granted Trooper Mullenix qualified immunity, holding that the law was not clearly established when he used deadly force against Lejia, who was fleeing and subsequently died. The Court ruled that it reviewed the case to affirm the principles of determining the granting of qualified immunity, although it used a deadly force incident to do so. The Court did not rule on the justifiable use of force, yet the majority opined that they have never found the use of deadly force in connection with a dangerous car chase to violate the Fourth Amendment, let alone to be a basis of denying qualified immunity.

Officer Baker of the Tulia, TX police department attempted to serve a warrant on Lejia for his arrest and he fled away in his vehicle. Officer Baker followed Lejia onto the interstate and was joined by Trooper Rodriquez of the Texas Department of Public Safety (DPS). The pursuit lasted about 18 minutes, reaching speeds of over 100 mph over 25 miles. During the pursuit, Lejia called the Tulia police dispatch and threatened to shoot at the officers if they did not stop chasing him, and the dispatcher informed all involved officers. Dispatch also advised officers that Lejia may be intoxicated.

An officer from Canyon Police Department set up spike strips in order to stop Lejia. DPS Trooper Mullenix arrived at the location with the Canyon PD officer, but decided to shoot at Lejia's vehicle as it approached to disable it. Trooper Mullenix was trained in the use of spike strips but was not trained in shooting at a car to disable it. Trooper Mullenix radioed Trooper Rodriquez of the idea, he acknowledged the transmission and slowed down. Trooper Mullenix then requested the DPS dispatch to inform the sergeant of the plan and before he obtained authorization, Trooper Mullenix exited his patrol car armed with his rifle, took up a position, and could hear the sergeant state over the radio to wait and see if the spikes would work. Trooper Mullenix observed Lejia approach his area with Trooper Rodriquez pursuing him. Trooper Mullenix fired six rounds at Lejia's vehicle. Lejia's vehicle contacted the spike strips, hit the median, and rolled over two and half times. It was determined that Lejia died from four of the gun shots and none of the shots struck the engine, radiator, or hood. Lejia's estate filed a §1983 lawsuit alleging excessive force under the Fourth Amendment. The Fifth Circuit Court of Appeals affirmed the denial of qualified immunity by the lower court, holding that there were issues of fact as to whether Trooper Mullenix acted recklessly or unreasonably and whether Lejia posed an immediate risk of harm.

Relying on past decisions in *Brosseau*, *Scott*, and *Plumhoff*, the Court's majority held that the officers confronted an intoxicated person, who traveled on the roadway at excessive speeds, would not stop, was speeding away, allegedly threatened to shoot the officers twice, and posed an immediate threat. The Court ruled that whatever can be said of the wisdom of Trooper Mullenix's choice, past precedents do not place the conclusion that he acted unreasonably in these circumstances. Because the constitutional rule applied by the Fifth Circuit was not beyond debate, the Court granted Trooper Mullenix's qualified immunity.

Pre-Trial Detainees

Until its decision in *Kingsley v. Hendrickson* (2015), the Court had not issued a decision on what standard should apply when a pre-trial detainee asserted a claim of excessive force against a detention officer. By their classification, pre-trial detainees are confined, are not free citizens, are awaiting arraignment, or are proceeding through trial, therefore are not convicted and sentenced prisoners. Many lower federal courts struggled with which standard to apply and the period between arrest and conviction had been considered as the "Twilight Zone" (Ross, 2016). A majority of the courts applied the shocks-the-conscience test in accordance with the Fourteenth Amendment (i.e., *Johnson v. Glick*, 1973), while other courts applied the *Graham* standard until the detainee was arraigned and then applied the shocks-the-conscience standard, while yet other courts applied the Eighth Amendment standard, which requires a showing of malice, sadism, and intent to cause harm. The uncertainty of what standard to apply created confusion amongst the lower courts and the Court reviewed the case to provide a uniform standard across the circuits.

Kingsley was confined in jail and refused to comply with the jail rules after repeated instructions to remove paper covering a light fixture. Officers instructed Kingsley to exit the cell, he refused, and four officers and a supervisor handcuffed him, forcibly removed him from the cell and relocated him to a receiving cell. Kingsley claimed the officers placed him prone on a bed, placed a knee in his back, and then slammed his head into the concrete to remove the handcuffs. The officers denied the allegations but they and Kingsley agreed that one officer applied one application of the TASER in the drive stun mode for five seconds, left the cell, and came back about 15 minutes later and removed the handcuffs. Kingsley filed a §1983 excessive force claim under the Fourteenth Amendment, and a jury found in favor of the officers, as did the appellate court, holding that Kingsley failed to show that the officers actually intended to use excessive force and recklessly violated his rights.

The Court reviewed the case to determine what standard should apply when a detainee files an allegation of excessive force. Citing its decision in *Graham*, the Court held that a pre-trial detainee must show only that the force purposely or knowingly used against him was "objectively unreasonable" in accordance with the Fourteenth Amendment. In a five to four decision, the Court ruled that the standard cannot be applied mechanically, that the totality of circumstances of the incident must be considered, and the evaluation must be based on the perception of a reasonable officer on scene, including what the officer knew at the time and not with 20/20 hindsight. The Court concluded that the analysis of an officer's use of force must account for the legitimate interests that stem from the government's need to manage the facility, in which jail officials are needed to preserve internal order and discipline to maintain institutional security. In combination with the *Graham* criteria, additional objective circumstances, which may potentially be relevant to assessing reasonableness of the use of force, include: (1) the relationship between the need for the use of force and the amount of force used; (2) the extent of the detainee's injury; (3) any effort made by the officer to temper or to limit the amount of force; (4) the severity of the security problem at issue; (5) the threat reasonably perceived by the officer; and (6) whether the detainee was actively resisting.

Convicted and Confined Prisoners

A claim of excessive force stemming from an incident inside a prison with a convicted prisoner is assessed in accordance with the Eighth Amendment purview of the cruel and unusual punishment clause. In *Whitley v. Albers* (1986), the Court examined the use of deadly force by prison officers who shot a prisoner in the knee when he refused commands to release an officer hostage. Albers brought a §1983 action, claiming excessive force and that his rights were violated under the Eighth and Fourteenth Amendments. The lower courts found in favor of Albers and the Court overturned their decisions, holding that the infliction of pain in the course of a prison security measure is only an Eighth Amendment violation if it is inflicted unnecessarily and wantonly. The Court ruled that whether the force used inflicted unnecessary and wanton pain and suffering ultimately turns on whether the force was applied in a good faith effort to maintain or restore discipline, or whether the use of force was applied maliciously and sadistically for the purpose of causing harm. The Court held that liability would only attach in a deadly force situation if a prisoner could show that such force was applied maliciously and sadistically to create harm.

The Court's decision in *Whitley* only addressed incidents involving deadly force. In *Hudson v. McMillian* (1992), the Court held that an officer's use of excessive force can constitute cruel and unusual punishment under the Eighth Amendment when such force is used maliciously and sadistically for the purposes of causing harm. While handcuffed and during an escort by two officers to another cell, Hudson was repeatedly punched in the head and face, sustaining minor bruising and swelling to his face, and cracking his dentures. The Court held that the officer's action violated Hudson's constitutional rights, despite the fact that he sustained only minor injuries. The Court opined that injuries sustained by a prisoner are irrelevant but the applicable standard in prison force incidents is whether the officer maliciously and sadistically used force to cause harm and when such force is applied, contemporary standards of decency are violated, regardless of whether significant injury is evident.

Using the malicious and sadistic use of force to cause harm clause, the Court established the standard with which to assess all claims of excessive force under the Eighth Amendment. The extent of the injury sustained by the prisoner is irrelevant. The intent of the officer is examined along with the legitimate objective and rationale for application of force and the standard is applied on a case-by-case basis within the circumstances encountered. The Court reaffirmed their decision in *Hudson* with its decision in *Hope v. Pelzer* (2002), which involved the cruel and unusual use of the hitching post as punishment, and in *Wilkins v. Gaddy* (2010), reemphasizing that when prison officials maliciously and sadistically use force to cause harm, contemporary standards of decency are always violated.

From 1985 to 2015, the United States Supreme Court has opined 13 times on legal issues pertaining to the use of force, with a significant majority of the opinions in deference to law enforcement. Of these cases, nine opinions have addressed deadly force issues, including one in the correctional environment, and three opinions addressed issues of the officers firing their firearm at a moving vehicle. Of these opinions, nine have addressed issues in accordance with the Fourth Amendment, while the remainder have addressed use of force issues of incarcerated and convicted prisoners in accordance with the Eighth Amendment.

A review of the United States Supreme Court decisions shows that an assessment of a claim of excessive force occurring in a street arrest confrontation and jail confinement situation will be reviewed in accordance with the Fourth Amendment and the "objective reasonableness" standard. The Court's decision in *Graham* is the controlling case, and guidance for assessing the use of reasonable force was created through the five established criteria. These criteria underscore the importance that the subject dictates the degree of force and justification of using force is in response to the actions or inactions, and resistance of the subject. The Fourth Amendment reasonableness assessment requires a fact finder to focus on only one question: was the force used by the officer objectively reasonable based on the subject actions? The Court stressed in *Graham* that reasonableness cannot be mechanically applied, must be assessed within the perspective of the officer at the moment he or she used it, and within the totality of the circumstances. An officer's motivation in using a level of force is irrelevant.

The Court's decision in *Hudson* is the controlling case to assess claims of excessive force arising out of the prison context. In accordance with the Eighth Amendment and within the context of the cruel and unusual punishment clause, the Court has established the standard of using force in good faith or maliciously and sadistically for the purpose of causing harm. By establishing the standard under the Eighth Amendment, the Court has made a distinction for assessing claims of excessive force between pre-trial detainees and convicted and incarcerated prisoners. The Court has held that pre-trial detainees cannot be punished (*Bell v. Wolfish*, 1979), and that significant or severe injury is not required for a legitimate excessive force claim to be made. The Court reaffirmed this standard in their decision in *Wilkins*.

Application by the Lower Courts in Arrest-Related Deaths

Although the Court has established standards with which to review claims of excessive force, it is the lower federal courts that actually apply the standards. There are divergent applications of the objective reasonableness standard across the circuits, which can pose problems on how a particular circuit court may apply the standard. Use of force investigators are encouraged to review case decisions in their jurisdiction to keep abreast of how the court applies the *Graham* decision to varying use of force situations. Some lower courts have developed a "hybrid approach" in their excessive force analysis by adding other factors beyond the *Graham* factors.

For example, the Sixth Circuit Court added the "quantum of force" used by the officer to its force assessment. Generally this means that: within the totality of circumstances, did the types of force measures and the amount used match the resistance of the subject; was the force used disproportionate to the need; and was it reasonably foreseeable to the officer that the effects from the application of the chosen force option under the totality of the circumstances would result in the sustained injuries (*Bryan v. McPherson*, 2009; *Hagans v. Franklin Sheriff's Office*, 2012; *Martin v. City of Broadview Heights*, 2013). The Eleventh Circuit Court adds the factors of: risk of flight by the suspect and the danger posed; what was the need for the application of force; was the force used proportionate to the need for its use; and what was the extent of the injury inflicted (*Buckley v. Haddock*, 2008). The Eleventh Circuit also uses the "quantum of force" employed by the officer to evaluate a claim of excessive force (*Salvato v. Miley*, 2015). The Ninth Circuit Court adds: were there other alternative methods of capturing or subduing the suspect; what did the officer know about the subject's health and/or mental condition; and did the subject have the capacity to comply with the officer's commands (*Bryan v. McPherson*, 2009).

The following sections provide a brief assessment of how the lower courts apply the *Graham* criteria in deadly force cases and sudden arrest-related restraint deaths.

Deadly Force

Ross (2013) studied 1,100 published §1983 decisions by the lower federal courts from 1989 to 2012 to examine the trends in how the courts assess the human factors in deadly force confrontations. Of these published cases, the courts ruled in favor of the defendant officer in about 82 percent of the litigation. A brief summary of the highlights of some of the deadly force decisions that investigators should further review are discussed below.

An emerging trend associated with a number of officer involved shootings is the suspect using a vehicle as a deadly force instrument against the officer and such published decisions accounted for about 30 percent. Suspects who flee from an officer will take desperate measures and risk their lives and others' to avoid capture by speeding, driving into oncoming traffic, speeding through stop signs, red lights and intersections, ramming oncoming motorists, ramming the officer, and driving at the officer. The United States Supreme Court ruled in *Sykes v. United States* (2011) that a vehicle can be used as a lethal instrument against an officer, which is underscored with their holdings in *Brosseau*, *Scott*, and *Plumhoff*. In *Smith v. Freland* (1992), an officer acted reasonably when he shot and killed a motorist who had fled from him at speeds in excess of 90 mph, when the officer reasonably believed he and citizens were in imminent danger. The motorist attempted to run over the officer and went through a roadblock. When the officer had him cornered in a cul-de-sac, he turned around on a lawn and drove right at the officer, at which point the officer fired his firearm. The officer's use of lethal force was measured against the facts at the time the force was used, as opposed to what may have been done or what was possible by way of hindsight. The court concluded that a car can be used as a deadly weapon, that the officer, fearing for his life, fired in self-defense, and to prevent the motorist's escape, as it presented a threat to others.

In the following case decisions, the lower courts determined that the officer possessed probable cause to believe that the vehicle posed an immediate threat of serious physical harm or death to the officer or others. In *Pace v. Capobianco* (2002), the driver of a vehicle recklessly advanced toward the officer. The court concluded that the officer used reasonable force within seconds when he confronted a "gravely dangerous" situation and fired in self-defense. In *Robinson v. Arrugueta* (2005), the court noted that the officer had 2.72 seconds to react before getting crushed between two cars and fired his weapon based on that perception in self-defense. In *Wilkinson v. Torres* (2010), the court found that the officer confronting a van accelerating at him on a slippery yard, formed the perception within three seconds that he was in immediate threat of serious physical harm, and had probable cause to believe, in this tense, uncertain, and rapidly evolving situation, that the threat to his safety justified the use of deadly force.

Similarly, in *Terrell v. Smith* (2012), the court granted summary judgment to an officer who shot and killed the driver of a vehicle endangering his safety. Officer Smith ordered the driver to stop several times as he drove toward him, near enough to crush him, with the car door actually striking Officer Smith. The court noted that the officer quickly formed the perception that he was in immediate danger and had to make a split-second decision in response to a rapidly unfolding and uncontrolled situation. Further cases which affirm an officer's use of deadly force when faced with a vehicle include: *Beets v. County of Los Angeles* (2012); *Cann v. Baltimore Co. MD* (2011); *Edmunson v. Keesler* (1996); *Hill v. Nigro* (2008); *Long v. Slaton* (2007); *Marion v. City of Corydon* (2009); *Smith v. Cupp* (2005); *Williams v. City of Grosse Pointe Park* (2007).

When confronting an individual, police officers are taught to perform a visual assessment of the individual, to watch the person's hands, to be alert to sudden furtive movements, and to maintain a reactionary distance between themselves and the person as feasible. A common gesture alerting an officer to use a level of force is when a person suddenly reaches toward a pocket or the waistband area. The officers' justification of using deadly force is supported by developing the perception of a threat to themselves or others based on the suspect's movements alone. The axiom is that action always beats reaction and an officer's response will always be slower than the action that prompted the response. The courts agree that an officer may use deadly force in self-defense and in defense of another and that frequently the decision to use force has to be made within a split-second. The officer has discretion to determine the amount of force required under the circumstances based on the perception developed at the moment force was required. Police officers are required to react to apparent dangers and apparent weapons, because normal conditions and lag time do not often allow an officer to ascertain with certainty, whether a weapon is present and the conditions in which an officer operates heighten the likelihood to make mistakes.

In *Deluna v. City of Rockford* (2006), an officer responded to a domestic disturbance call and, as he exited his vehicle, he observed the suspect outside of the house, shirtless, approaching him, and stating that he had "something for the officer." The officer commanded him to raise his hands and he refused. The officer drew his firearm, began to walk backward as the suspect continued to approach him. As the officer walked backward he stumbled on a black plastic pipe and struggled to maintain his balance. The officer observed the suspect reach behind his back and lunge toward him as he stumbled. Fearing that he was reaching for a weapon, the officer shot the suspect one time from a distance of about 5 to 15 feet. The appellate affirmed the lower court's summary judgment decision holding that the use of deadly force was justified. The court ruled that regardless of whether the officer saw a gun or believed he was reaching for a weapon, the action of the decedent lunging toward him after the bizarre conduct, established the real danger of imminent serious bodily injury should the decedent actually reach the officer. The court noted that the officer need not wait until there is a serious physical struggle for control of his weapon before the situation presents an imminent danger of serious physical injury. Further cases affirming the officer's decision to use lethal force when a suspect displayed furtive movements include: *Blossom v. Yarbrough* (2005); *Johnson v. City of Memphis* (2010); *Manis v. Lawson* (2009); *Ontiveros v. City of Rosenberg* (2009).

Under a split-second decision-making circumstance, a police officer will inevitably make an occasional mistake, and may use deadly force believing that a suspect possessed a weapon when in fact they did not. Court decisions have examined whether the officer used reasonable force when confronted with a cell phone or some other object which could be mistaken for a firearm. In *Hudspeth v. City of Shreveport* (2008), officers were engaged in a pursuit with Hudspeth, which lasted about five minutes at night. Hudspeth pulled into a convenience store parking lot and exited his vehicle, holding a silver cell phone. Officers followed him and he extended his arm with the cell phone and pointed it like a handgun. An officer began to struggle with him, whereby Hudspeth pulled away, aiming the cell phone at a second officer who shot Hudspeth twice. Hudspeth continued to walk toward the convenience store, turned quickly toward the officers, with both hands outstretched, as if to point a handgun. The officers instinctively crouched, and fired their weapons, hitting Hudspeth in the back and killing him. The court ruled in favor of the officers and noted that the officers were forced to make a split-second judgment in a circumstance which was tense, uncertain, and rapidly evolving. The court noted that the officers had an articulable basis to believe that based on Hudspeth's behaviors, suddenly turning toward the officers and extending his arms with a cell phone, as if to point a weapon, the officers could have reasonably perceived him as posing a threat of serious bodily harm, and their actions were reasonable.

Similar cases where the courts have ruled in favor of the officer under these circumstances include: *Berbue v. Conley* (2007); *Carnaby v. City of Houston* (2011); *Estate of Escobedo v. City of Fort Wayne* (2008); *Loch v. City of Litchfield* (2012); *Simmonds v. Genesee County* (2012); *Summerland v. County of Livingston* (2007). These cases and others represent human factors of perceptional distortions in vision, reaction time, and cognitive processing when the officer is forced to make a split-second decision under rapidly unfolding circumstances, and when the operational environment is less than optimal.

Pointing a firearm at an officer generally justifies the use of deadly force and displaying a potential deadly weapon unusually justifies the use of deadly force (McGuiness, 2009). An officer is not required to wait for the threat to actually materialize before stopping the threat, as long as the officer has formed the perception that there is imminent danger of death or serious bodily injury. In *DeMerrell v. City of Cheboygan* (2006), officers responded to a domestic violence call, began to approach the house, and DeMerrell came out with a pellet gun. DeMerrell was waving the gun above his head, began to walk toward the officers, came within about 18 feet of the officers, and lowered the gun. One officer fired one round from a shotgun, killing DeMerrell. The appellate court affirmed the lower court's summary judgment, holding that it did not matter what distance existed between the subject and the officer when he shot, as DeMerrell pointed the gun at the officers. The court opined that there was overwhelming evidence that the officers confronted a dangerous, volatile situation involving an intoxicated, armed, aggressive suspect who was advancing on the police and defying commands to stand down. The court held that officers are entitled to qualified immunity when they fire on a person who is pointing a gun at them.

In *Buchanan v. City of Gulfport Police Department* (2013), three officers confronted a mentally ill man who was swinging a bat at cars driving through the takeout window at a fast food restaurant. The officers instructed him to drop the bat, he refused, and two officers activated their TASERs. Buchanan dropped the bat, pulled the lead wires out of his chest, picked the bat up, charged the officers with the bat raised, and two officers shot four rounds from their firearms. Buchanan survived. The court opined that the officers confronted a mentally agitated and dangerous subject at night, in a busy public area, attempted to use less lethal means to control him but were rebuffed when he pulled the TASER probes from his chest, picked up the bat, and charged the officers, and that the officers were forced to make a split-second decision when the subject charged the officers with the bat raised. The court awarded summary judgment to the officers, noting that the subject, although mentally disturbed, posed a risk of danger to the public and the officers, and that the officers had less than two seconds to form the perception that the subject posed an immediate threat of harm to the officers. Similar decisions by various courts affirming an officer's decision to use deadly force when faced with a deadly weapon or being shot at, include: *Blanford v. Sacramento County* (2005); *Brooks v. Gaenzle* (2010); *Buchanan v. State of Maine* (2006); *Butler v. City of Tulsa* (2007); *Connors v. Graves* (2008); *Estate of Escobedo v. Martin* (2012); *Flynn v. Mills* (2005); *Gaddis v. Redford Township* (2004); *Garczynski v. Bradshaw* (2009); *Sudac v. Hoang* (2005).

Sudden Arrest-Related Restraint Deaths

A sudden death in custody after a violent confrontation where police or detention officers used non-deadly force measures and devices, and the individual was placed prone and restrained, is filed in accordance with the Fourth Amendment. Claims often assert that the officer used excessive force during the restraint process, and include: the misuse of physical control techniques, the misuse of restraints and the restraint chair, the misuse of less-lethal force equipment (i.e., aerosols, conducted energy weapons, impact weapons, canines, projectiles), the officers failed to provide medical and/or psychological care, the officers failed to properly follow agency policies and practices, and the officer's agency failed to properly train, supervise, and guide the officers through comprehensive policies and procedures. A sudden custodial death after a violent restraint incident occurring in a prison is evaluated under the Eighth Amendment's standard of malicious and sadistic conduct for the purposes of causing harm.

Ross (2010) examined 215 published §1983 lawsuits from 1985 to 2010 and an additional 35 published decisions from 2011 to 2015 on sudden restraint custodial deaths. The nature of these claims involved: violent subjects whose condition appeared to be mentally ill, intoxicated on an illicit chemical substance, or both, the subject's prone position set up a situation for compressional or restraint asphyxia, or the subject showed signs of excited delirium. The courts awarded summary judgment to the officers in about 60 percent of the cases. A brief overview of the highlights of some of the court decisions are discussed below, and investigators are encouraged to review the full case.

In *May v. Township of Bloomfield* (2013), officers confronted a 6' 1", 235-pound, bi-polar man (Gillard), who was hallucinating due to not taking his prescribed lithium for about five days. While driving his van, Gillard caused several accidents of other motorists and led officers on an eight-mile pursuit, reaching speeds over 70 mph through residential and business areas. Gillard stopped his vehicle after crashing into a motorist at an intersection, and sustained a broken leg. He exited the van, punched the first responding officer in the face, pinned her by her throat against the van, continued to punch her, and a second officer deployed his conducted electrical weapon (CEW). The CEW did not penetrate his back as Gillard wore several layers of clothing. Five other officers responded, and one struck him with the baton eight times in the thigh of the broken leg, with no effect. Gillard fought with the officers over the course of about seven minutes, striking and kicking at them and attempting to disarm one officer. Four other officers applied their CEWs, totaling 31 trigger pulls over the period. The officers were finally able to ground Gillard prone and he fought against control and being handcuffed. An officer activated two applications of the CEW in the drive stun mode on his calf and the officers were finally able to restrain Gillard with four sets of handcuffs behind his back. After several minutes, Gillard became unresponsive and officers began rescue breathing. Paramedics arrived, provided medical intervention, and transported Gillard to the hospital where he was pronounced dead.

After the autopsy, the medical examiner concluded that Gillard died from positional/compressional asphyxia with acute psychosis contributing. Gillard had an enlarged heart with atherosclerosis and narrowing of the arteries, was diagnosed as bi-polar and had a long history as a poly-substance abuser. The estate filed a civil action claiming that the officers violated the Fourth Amendment by using excessive force, and violated the Fourteenth Amendment by failing to provide adequate medical treatment. Several medical experts opined that Gillard did not die from positional asphyxia but rather he was in a state of excited delirium and died from complications associated with his cardiovascular condition during restraint. The court awarded summary judgment, holding that: Gillard posed a severe and potentially lethal threat to the public and the officers, that using the CEWs was reasonable given the violent and resisting behaviors of Gillard and it did not cause or contribute to his death, that it was reasonable to use the CEW while Gillard was prone as he continued to resist control and being restrained, that the use of the baton strikes was reasonable, and that it was reasonable to prone Gillard as one officer only applied an incidental amount of weight on his back during the handcuffing process. The court ruled that the officers were properly trained and were not deliberately indifferent to Gillard's medical needs.

Compare, however, *Martin v. City of Broadview Heights Police Department* (2013) where the Sixth Circuit Appellate Court denied officers qualified immunity. An officer responded to a call of a naked man attempting to enter an apartment at about 2:00 am. The officer responded and encountered Martin, wearing only jeans, who briefly spoke gibberish to the officer as he was attempting to handcuff him, and he fled. The officer caught Martin, fell on him, Martin began to stand up resisting control, and a second officer responded. The officer placed his knee on Martin's side to keep him on the ground, wherein Martin bit the officer's knuckles, and the officer delivered five closed fist punches to Martin's face, back, and ribs. The officer pinned Martin's legs with his legs and gripped Martin's chin with his right arm, in which the estate claimed that he wrapped his arm around Martin's neck. A third officer responded and the three officers controlled and handcuffed Martin. The officers heard a gurgling sound from Martin, turned him on his side, observed that he was unresponsive, attempted to resuscitate him, called for the paramedics, and Martin was pronounced dead.

The County Coroner determined that Martin died from an acute psychotic episode with excited delirium due to intoxication by lysergic acid diethylamide (LSD) and cardiopulmonary arrest and not from the physical control measures used by the officers. The pathologist who conducted the autopsy found numerous injuries suggesting asphyxiation and three months later ordered an investigator in the coroner's office to conduct an investigation. The pathologist concluded that the officers' collective actions resulted in a "compressive event," causing Martin's asphyxiation. The estate hired an independent pathologist to review the case and he too concluded that Martin died of asphyxiation and not from excited delirium.

The estate filed a civil lawsuit claiming that the officers used excessive force, failed to train officers about positional asphyxiation, that the officers failed to follow department policies, that the department administrators failed to train officers on how to respond to emotionally disturbed persons, and they failed to properly investigate the use of force. The appellate court affirmed the lower court's denial of summary judgment, holding that the officers' use of force measures on a person who was agitated and acting erratically, was disproportionate to Martin's behaviors and the threat that he posed, holding him in the prone position with their weight on his back and striking him in the face and body, placing legs around Martin's legs, placing an arm on his chin and restraining him, and failing to adhere to the department's policy on positional asphyxia, all reinforced that the force applied was unreasonable. The court opined that the "quantum of force" the officers used was constitutionally excessive, violating the Fourth Amendment. The court did not address claims against the administration for failure to train and a failure to investigate.

These two case examples exhibit polar opposite decisions made by the courts when examining similar fact patterns of sudden arrest-related deaths in police custody. The decisions show similar subject behaviors, officer responses, but underscore how varying courts may assess the officers' use of force in response to the subjects' behaviors, and differ in their conclusions. Rather than assess the officer's response from the perception of the officers engaged with the suspect at the moment they were struggling with the violent subject, and in accordance with the *Graham* standard and review criteria, some courts ignore the criteria and rely on junk science when the notion of positional asphyxia was debunked in 1998 (i.e., *Price v. County of San Diego*, 1998).

For example, the following case decisions represent similar fact patterns of a sudden restraint death in police custody as illustrated in the *May* case, and the courts awarded qualified immunity to the officers and their departments: *Burdine v. Sandusky County, OH* (2013); *Deshotels v. Marshall* (2011); *Hagans v. Franklin County Sheriff's Office* (2012); *Hill v. Carroll County, Mississippi* (2009); *Hoyer v. City of Southfield and Oakland County* (2003); *Jones v. City of Cincinnati* (2012); *Khan v. Normand* (2012); *Lewis v. City of West Palm Beach, FL* (2009); *Mann v. TASER, Inc.* (2009); *Turner v. City of Toledo* (2012); and *Williams v. Chambers* (2009). Compare, however, the court's denial of qualified immunity to the officers in the following cases: *Aldaba v. Pickens and Board of Marshall County Commissioners* (2015); *Champion v. Outlook Nashville, Inc.* (2004); *Cruz v. City of Laramie, Wyoming* (2001); *Estate of Booker v. Gomez* (2014); *Richman v. Sheahan* (2008); *Sallenger v. Oakes* (2007); and *Swans v. City of Lansing* (1998).

Litigating a sudden arrest-related death in custody comprises numerous complex medical, use of force, and legal issues. Courts which deviate from or tack on additional factors to the *Graham* criteria and simultaneously rely on junk science and spurious theories regarding using a CEW and controlling and restraining a violent person prone, create a conflicting playing field where law and science intersect when evaluating the use of force resulting in a sudden arrest-related death incident. It becomes important for investigators assigned to these cases to be knowledgeable about the numerous issues which emerge and to perform a detailed and thorough investigation to avert claims of an inadequate investigation.

The Fourth Circuit Appellant Court's decision in *Estate of Armstrong v. Village of Pinehurst and TASER International, Inc.* (2016) provides a classic example of the court ignoring the science regarding an arrest-related death. Armstrong had been off his medications for five days, and during the commitment to a hospital to treat his bi-polar disorder and paranoid schizophrenia, he became frightened and left. The admitting physician issued an involuntary commitment order compelling him to return. On the order, the physician noted that Armstrong was a danger to himself, but did not indicate that he was a danger to others, although he did consider him to be a danger to others. Three Pinehurst officers responded and observed Armstrong near the hospital eating grass.

Once the commitment papers were authorized, the three officers approached Armstrong and he sat down and held onto a stop sign post. The officers and two hospital security officers used verbal instructions and physical force measures to remove him, but he refused to comply. Armstrong's sister appeared on scene and pled with him to comply. An officer drew his TASER and warned Armstrong that he would use it (Drive Stun), but the warning had no effect. The officer activated the TASER over two minutes with five five-second applications, but the applications actually increased Armstrong's resistance. The officer ceased the applications and the five officers physically removed him from the post. The officers placed him in the prone position, one officer stood on his back, while another officer placed a knee on his back to control and restrain him as handcuffs were placed and hobbled to his ankles. The officers stood up, left Armstrong prone, observed that he was unresponsive, and they initiated CPR immediately. Emergency medical personnel responded, initiated intervention, and transported him to the hospital, where he was pronounced dead. From the time the officers engaged Armstrong and until EMS responded, about six and one-half minutes had elapsed.

The federal district court granted summary judgment to the claim of excessive force and the appellate court reversed, holding that the officers' use of force was excessive. Applying the *Graham* criteria, the court ruled that Armstrong did not commit a crime, did not threaten the officers, and he was not actively resisting. The court opined that mental illness is not necessarily a safety risk and that minimal physical resistance does not equate to a risk of immediate danger. The court ruled that the force used by the officers is considered "serious injurious force" (TASER in any mode, pepper spray, strikes, grounding, tackling, wrestling, canine), that it was "disproportionate" to the minimal type of resistance confronted, and that Armstrong's mental capacity was a mitigating factor that was not considered by the officers. The court held that the officers should have slowed down their response, that Armstrong was not an immediate threat, the officers needed to consider other force options, and the officers should have simply pulled him from the post without using other force measures, particularly the TASER.

The court did not consider the science about the use of the TASER and placing arrestees in the prone position. Armstrong was 5'11" and weighed about 262 pounds, with a significantly enlarged heart (cardiomegaly). The cause of death was listed as complications of Excited Delirium Syndrome and not from the use of the TASER. Yet, in the court's published opinion, these factors and their implications were not addressed. The court confused the application of Drive Stun mode with the Probe mode and did not fully appreciate the differences with pain compliance and muscle control in the Probe mode. This ruling is mandatory in the Fourth Circuit Court of Appeals and requires responding officers to consider other force options prior to using the TASER, to slow down their response, not to use serious injurious force techniques, and if the TASER is to be applied on the mentally impaired, it should only be considered when the person is exhibiting aggressive resistance. The application of the case is that using any force measure which inflicts any type of pain, and not just the use of the TASER, will be considered disproportionate force and excessive.

Claims of Failing to Investigate

Claims of failing to perform an adequate investigation have been filed by plaintiffs in arrest-related deaths beyond the claim of excessive force. These types of claims are filed against an agency administrator's policies in accordance with *Monell v. New York Department of Social Services* (1978) and attach to allegations for failing to discipline errant officers, which may ratify the misconduct of the officers, and that such failure was the moving force which created a constitutional violation (*Salvato v. Miley*, 2015).

In *Salvato*, Deputy Miley and Deputy Brown responded to a call of a man yelling and cussing at cars. On location, the deputies got involved in a physical struggle with Salvato and as he was backing away, Deputy Miley shot him once without warning. The Eleventh Circuit Court of Appeals held that Deputy Miley used excessive force. A second claim was lodged against the sheriff for not performing an internal investigation of the shooting ratifying the excessive force used by Deputy Miley. The sheriff testified that he did not order an investigation as the Florida Department of Law Enforcement (FDLE) conducted the investigation and the grand jury did not indict Deputy Miley. The investigation by FDLE focused on criminality and not on possible department policy violations. The sheriff concluded that the FDLE and the grand jury's report was sufficient to address the department's policies, did not take any disciplinary actions against Deputy Miley, but did reassign her to work in the jail. At the trial, the jury found the sheriff liable for failing to conduct an investigation into the shooting which ratified Deputy Miley's use of excessive force. The sheriff appealed, arguing that one instance of failing to investigate an excessive force incident is insufficient to ratify a constitutional violation.

Referencing the United States Supreme Court's decision in *City of St. Louis v. Praprotnik* (1988), the appellate court held that: a local government may be held liable for a constitutional tort when policymakers have had the opportunity to review a subordinate's decisions before they become final and that the plaintiff must show that a policy, custom, or practice of the agency caused the violation. Since the plaintiff could not show evidence that the sheriff failed to conduct an investigation in former cases of excessive force, that a single failure to investigate a use of force incident was not actionable, and that the sheriff did not approve the shooting before it occurred, the court reversed the lower court's decision holding that the sheriff was entitled to summary judgment.

In *James v. Harris County* (2009), Deputy Wilkinson stopped Harrison for speeding, placed him in his patrol car, returned to Harrison's vehicle, searched the inside, discovered a gun on the floor, and left it there. Wilkinson returned to the patrol car, informed Harrison that he was under arrest, attempted to handcuff him, and a struggle ensued. Harrison began grabbing for Wilkinson's firearm and Wilkinson, fearing for his life, shot Harrison in the back, then in the face three times, and waited for backup. The estate of Harrison filed a civil lawsuit claiming the officers used excessive force, that the sheriff failed to conduct an adequate investigation, and that such lax official policy or failure in investigating the incident was the moving force behind the use of excessive deadly force. A police expert opined that he reviewed 36 investigations of officer-involved shootings by the County and found that a substantial number fell below investigatory standards and attempted to connect those cases to the Wilkinson shooting incident. The expert opined that the sheriff turning the investigation over to the County District Attorney's office was an abdication of his responsibility.

The Fifth Circuit Court of Appeals affirmed the lower court's awarding of summary judgment to the County, holding there was sufficient evidence to establish that Wilkinson used excessive force but there was insufficient evidence to hold the County liable for Wilkinson's actions and the claim of a policy for failure to investigate the use of force. The court held that a governmental policy must be the "moving force" behind or actually caused a constitutional injury and a plaintiff must show direct causation between the policy and the violation. The court ruled that Wilkinson was not personally aware of any failure to investigate a deputy's excessive force conduct in the department or a failure to discipline them. The court granted summary judgment to the sheriff as the plaintiff must prove a direct causation between the policy and the conduct of the officer and it must be the moving force of the misconduct to prevail. The sheriff's policy on conducting investigations was not the moving force behind Wilkinson's use of deadly force.

As observed in these case decisions, claims of failing to investigate are examined by the courts in accordance with *Monell* and fall within the governmental entity's policy and practice and responsibility for disciplining officer misconduct. Plaintiffs claiming a failure to investigate the ARD must show that the governmental entity maintained an official policy in which no investigation was conducted into an officer's use of force, that the policy and the practice of the agency deliberately ignored the results of an investigation which ratified the misconduct, that the policy and practice was the "moving force" behind an officer's misuse of force, and that the administrator had constructive knowledge of the practice (see also, *Backe v. City of Galveston, TX*, 2014; *Harrison v. City of Dickson, TN*, 2013; *Lee v. City of Richmond*, 2013).

The plaintiff must show a direct causation between the policy and the conduct of the officer and it must be the moving force of the misconduct. This is often difficult for a plaintiff to prove as the administrator must approve the misconduct or be aware of the misconduct prior to it occurring in order to show ratification by the administrator. Generally, more than a single act of a failing to investigate an alleged claim of excessive force is needed before liability will attach. Further, many law enforcement agencies request that an external independent agency conduct the investigation which follows professional practices, does not invoke a constitutional violation, and agency administrators do not abdicate their responsibility by doing so.

The court's decision in *Backe v. City of Galveston, TX* (2014), however, provides an "exceptional" example to the general trend of claims of failing to investigate. Claims of excessive force, a custom of underreporting and under-investigating acts of force, and failure to train officers were filed after multiple officers encountered 13 individuals attending a wedding, who fought with the police in an effort to prevent them from arresting a 19-year-old who was intoxicated and underage. When an undercover officer attempted to arrest the youth in a bar next to the reception room, family members and others attending the wedding physically intervened and the officer called for backup. Other city officers arrived and began using pepper spray, their batons, chokeholds, and body strikes, while also throwing people on the floor, kicking and pulling individuals away by their hair, using their TASERs, handcuffing and throwing them on a car, and generally manhandling the individuals. Over the 13 minutes, 34 city and other local and federal officers responded, and 13 individuals reported the police used force against them. The new chief conducted an internal affairs investigation of the incident and a lieutenant who participated in using force during the incident led the investigation. Of the 34 officers responding, 20 officers used 49 acts of force during the incident, 36 acts of force were not reported, and 43 acts were not reported by officers on scene. Of the reports submitted, only a few officers indicated using any force, giving the appearance that little to no force was used, which was contrary to the complaints.

The district court found that the officers used excessive force during the incident, that a custom and a culture in the department of using excessive force was well known by the chief, that the city council had constructive knowledge of the officers' abuse of force and, along with the new chief, did nothing to correct it. The court found the chief and the city liable for officers under-reporting and under-investigating this incident as ample evidence was shown that a half-hearted investigation was conducted and only a few officers actually reported using force during the incident. The court found evidence to support the department's custom of under-reporting and under-investigating acts of officer use of force, and it was the moving force behind the plaintiff's constitutional violation. Even though this case was an example of a single incident, it was such a unique circumstance which exemplified a custom and practice of ignoring excessive force misconduct, the court denied qualified immunity. The court granted summary judgment on the failure to train claim.

Summary and Use of Force Principles

This chapter has addressed the common legal and liability issues which emerge from an ARD. Investigators are encouraged to review the cited cases, become familiar with their agency policies, and applicable collective bargaining agreements prior to conducting an interview with an officer, which may involve criminal conduct or involve internal administrative issues. Advising the officer of the nature of the interview prior to conducting the interview is recommended. Investigators are also encouraged to seek further legal training from their agency legal counsel to obtain additional knowledge on conducting investigations with agency officers.

Second, the chapter has discussed 14 United States Supreme Court decisions pertaining to the use of force, including the criteria established to review claims of excessive force. In its decision in *Graham*, the Court established the standard of "objective reasonableness" and five criteria used in analyzing claims of excessive force in accordance with the Fourth Amendment. In its decision in *Kingsley*, the Court reaffirmed its decision in *Graham*, and also applied the objective reasonableness standard to assess claims of excessive force filed by pre-trial detainees. Further, in accordance with the Eighth Amendment and its decision in *Hudson*, the Court reviewed claims of excessive force filed by convicted prisoners by assessing whether the force was used in a good faith effort or maliciously and sadistically for the purpose of causing harm. Investigators are encouraged to review the full decisions of these cases.

Lower court decisions have shown divergent interpretation and application of the objective reasonableness standard. Generally, the courts have held: that an officer's decision to use force must include an analysis of the perception of the officer at the moment force was required; that an officer may have to make a split-second decision to use force and the decision is not measured against a clock; that an officer does not have to possess omniscience; that an officer need not wait for back-up; that an officer need not move sequentially in a force matrix; that an officer need not see a weapon prior to using force; and that an officer is not required to use minimal force but objective reasonable force. The application of force by an officer is assessed on a case-by-case basis and the facts unique to the incident.

The following general use of force principles emerge from these court decisions. Investigators are encouraged to consider them when reviewing a use of force incident:

- the criteria established by the Court depending on the status of the person (Fourth, Eighth, or Fourteenth Amendment);
- the officer's perception and belief of imminent or immediate threat of the subject;
- the resistance and behaviors of the person;
- objective for using force: self-defense, defense of another, to prevent a crime, to effect an arrest, medical intervention, to prevent/quell a riot or disturbance, to overcome unlawful resistance, or to maintain security and enforce discipline in a correctional facility;
- nature of the circumstance, dynamics of the confrontation, and the associated variables;
- safety of the officer(s) and others jeopardized by the subject;
- incident operating environmental variables;
- the response time of the officer;
- the subject's resistance dictates the officer response;
- officer's response to subject resistance/behaviors, and justification for each application of empty-hand control force measures, non-deadly force equipment and aerosol, restraints, restraint chair, canine, projectiles, and use of deadly force;
- the number of subjects involved in the confrontation;
- the subject's possession of and access to weapons or potential weapons;
- threat posed by the subject to the officers and others;
- dangerousness of flight posed by the subject;
- an officer's ability to use verbal commands and warnings prior to and during the application of force;
- the "quantum of force," proportionate force used, and foreseeable consequences of force measures applied;
- escalation and de-escalation of the use of force and whether force was used after the need diminished;
- incident tense, rapidly evolving situation and the reaction time of the officer;
- exigent circumstances;
- injury and exhaustion of the officer; and
- the totality of circumstances and the nature and quality of the intrusion by the officer.

Finally, the justification of an officer's decision to use force turns on the facts and circumstances known to the officer at the time the force was used. What was discovered or determined after the incident cannot be used to justify the use of force and would normally not be admissible evidence. An officer's motivation is irrelevant, and evil intent does not make an otherwise reasonable use of force bad and, conversely, the absence of evil intent does not make an objectively unreasonable use of force appropriate.

References

Aitchison, W. (2013). Applying *Garrity* and *Weingarten*. Presentation at the Labor Relations Information Systems Training Seminar, Las Vegas, NV.

Aldaba v. Pickens and Board of County Commissioners, U.S. App. LEXIS 1822 (10th Cir. 2015).

Backe v. City of Galveston, TX, No. 10-CV-388 (2014).

Beckworth v. United States, 325 U.S. 341 (1976).

Beets v. County of Los Angeles, 669 F. 3d 1038 (9th Cir. 2012).

Bell v. Wolfish, 441 U.S. 520 (1979).

Berbue v. Conley, 506 F. 3d 79 (1st Cir. 2007).

Blanford v. Sacramento County, 406 F. 3d 1110 (9th Cir. 2005).

Blossom v. Yarbrough, 429 F. 3d 963 (10th Cir. 2005).

Brave, M. (2011). Use of force status matrix. In D. L. Ross, *Liability issues in criminal justice* (pp. 258–259). Waltham, MA: Anderson Publishing.

Brooks v. Gaenzle, U.S. App. Lexis 16488 (10th Cir. 2010).

Brosseau v. Haugen, 543 U.S. 194 (2004).

Brower v. County of Inyo, 489 U.S. 593 (1989).

Bryan v. McPherson, 630 F. 3d 805 (9th Cir. 2009).

Buchanan v. City of Gulfport Police Department, No. 108-CV-1299 (5th Cir. 2013).

Buchanan v. State of Maine, U.S. App. Lexis 28352 (1st Cir. 2006).

Buckley v. Haddock, No. 06-00053CV-5-RS—MD (11th Cir. 2008).

Burdine v. Sandusky County, OH, No. 12-3672 (6th Cir. 2013).

Bureau of Engraving v. Graphic Communications International Union, 164 F.3d 427 (8th Cir. 1999).

Butler v. City of Tulsa, U.S. App. Lexis 27332 (10th Cir. 2007).

Cann v. Baltimore Co. MD, No. 10-2213 (E.D. MD, 2011).

Carnaby v. City of Houston, 636, F.3d (5th Cir. 2011).

Champion v. Outlook Nashville, Inc., 380 F. 3d 893, 901 (6th Cir. 2004).

Christopher Commission Report (1991). *Report of the Independent Commission on the Los Angeles Police Department.*

City and County of San Francisco v. Sheehan, 575 U.S. ___ (2015).

City of St. Louis v. Praprotnik, 485 U.S. 112 (1988).

Connors v. Graves, U.S. App. Lexis 16480 (5th Cir. 2008).

Cruz v. City of Laramie, Wyoming, 239 F. 3d 1183 (10th Cir. 2001).

Daigle, E. (2012). *Garrity* warnings: To give or not to give, that is the question. *The Police Chief*, *79*, 12–13.

Deluna v. City of Rockford, Ill., 447 F. 3d 1008 (7th Cir. 2006).

DeMerrell v. City of Cheboygan, No. 05-2325 (6th Cir. 2006).

Deshotels v. Marshall, No. 11-301-10 (5th Cir. 2011).

Edmunson v. Keesler, Nos. 95-3125, 95-3132, WL 683888 (4th Cir. 1996).

Eith, C. & Durose, M. R. (2011). *Contacts between police and the public, 2008.*

Washington, DC: U.S. Department of Justice.

Estate of Armstrong v. Village of Pinehurst and TASER International, Inc. F. 3d WL 105386 (C. A. 4th Cir. 2016).

Estate of Booker v. Gomez and City and County of Denver Health Hospital, 12-1496 (10th Cir. 2014).
Estate of Escobedo v. City of Fort Wayne, No. 05: CV-424-TS (N.D. Ind. 2008).
Estate of Escobedo v. Martin, U.S. App. Lexis 25443 (7th Cir. 2012).
Flynn v. Mills, 361 F. Supp. 2d 866 (S. D. Ind. 2005).
Gaddis v. Redford Township, 363 F. 3d 763 (6th Cir. 2004).
Garczynski v. Bradshaw, U.S. App. Lexis 15179 (11th Cir. 2009).
Gardner v. Broderick, 329 U.S. 273 (1968).
Garrity v. New Jersey, 385 U.S. 493, 500 (1967).
Graham v. Connor, 490 U.S. 386 (1989).
Hagans v. Franklin County Sheriff's Office, WL 3608510 (6th Cir. 2012).
Harrison v. City of Dickson, No. 3:11-CV-01044 (M.D. Ten. 2013).
Hatch, D. E. & Dickson, R. (2007). *Officer-involved shootings, and use of force: Practical investigative techniques* (2nd ed.). Boca Raton, FL: CRC Press.
Hill v. Carroll County, Mississippi, U.S. App. Lexis 23730 (6th Cir. 2009).
Hill v. Nigro, U.S. App. Lexis 4407 (3rd Cir. 2008).
Hope v. Pelzer, 536 U.S. 730 (2002).
Hoyer v. City of Southfield and Oakland County, U.S. Dist. Lexis 5835 (E.D. Mich. 2003).
Hudson v. McMillian, 503 U.S. 1 (1992).
Hudspeth v. City of Shreveport, No. 07-30260 (5th Cir. 2008).
James v. Harris County, No. 07-207525 (5th Cir. 2009).
Johnson v. City of Memphis, 617 F. 3d 864 (6th Cir. 2010).
Johnson v. Glick, 481 F. 2d 1028 (2nd Cir. 1973).
Jones v. City of Cincinnati, No. 11-4174 (6th Cir. 2012).
Katz, W. (2015). Enhancing accountability and trust with independent investigations of police lethal force. *Harvard Law Review Forum, 128*, 1–20.
Khan v. Normand, No. 11-30112, WL 1949216 (5th Cir. 2012).
Kingsley v. Hendrickson, 576 U.S. ___ (2015).
Lee v. City of Richmond, VA, No. 3:12-cv-471 (E.D. VA, 2013).
Lewis v. City of West Palm Beach, FL, No. 08-12348 (11th Cir. 2009).
Loch v. City of Litchfield, U.S. App. Lexis 18099 (8th Cir. 2012).
Long v. Slaton, 508 F. 3d 576, 580 (11th Cir. 2007).
Malley v. Briggs, 475 U.S. 335 (1986).
Manis v. Lawson, 585 F. 3d 839 (5th Cir. 2009).
Mann v. TASER, Inc., 402 Fed. Appx. 514 (11th Cir. 2009).
Marion v. City of Corydon, 559 F. 3d 693 (7th Cir. 2009).
Martin v. City of Broadview Heights, 712 F. 3d 951 (6th Cir. 2013).
May v. Township of Bloomfield, et al., No. 11-14453 (E.D. Mich. 2013).
McGuiness, J. M. (2009). A primer on North Carolina and federal use of force law: Trends in Fourth Amendment doctrine, qualified immunity, and state law issues. *Campbell Law Review, 31*(3), 431–501.
McKinley v. City of Mansfield, 404 F.3d 418 (6th Cir. 2005).
Michigan v. Fisher, 558 U.S. ___ (2009).
Miranda v. Arizona, 384 U.S. 486 (1966).
Monell v. NY Department of Social Services, 436 U.S. 658 (1978).
Mullenix v. Luna, 557 U.S. ___ (2015).
Mumola, C. (2007). *Arrest-related deaths in the United States, 2003–2005*. Washington, DC: Bureau of Justice Statistics Special Report.
NLRB v. J. Weingarten, 420 U.S. 251 (1975).
Ontiveros v. City of Rosenberg, 564 F. 3d 379 (5th Cir. 2009).

Pace v. Capobianco, 283 F. 1275 (2002).
Plumhoff v. Rickard, 571 U.S. ___ (2014).
Price v. County of San Diego, 990 F. Supp. 1230 (S.D. Cal. 1998).
Richman v. Sheahan, 512 F. 3d 586 (7th Cir. 2008).
Robinson v. Arrugueta, 415 F. 3d 1252 (11th Cir. 2005).
Ross, D. L. (2010). The use of force, science, liability, and restraint asphyxia. *Law Enforcement Executive Forum, 10*(1), 35–56.
Ross, D. L. (2013). Assessing lethal force liability decisions and human factors research. *Journal of Law Enforcement Executive Forum, 13*, 85–107.
Ross, D. L. (2016). Examining *Kingsley v. Hendrickson*: Ending the "twilight zone." *Criminal Law Bulletin, 52*, 818–837.
Sallenger v. Oakes, 473 3d. 731 (7th Cir. 2007).
Salvato v. Miley, No. 14-12840 (11th Cir. 2015).
Saucier v. Katz, 533 U.S. 194 (2001).
Schmidt, W. (2004). Interviews and interrogations of public employees: *Beckworth, Garrity, Miranda, and Weingarten* rights. *Law Enforcement Executive Forum, 4*(7), 1–19.
Scott v. Harris, 550 U.S. 127 (2007).
Simmonds v. Genesee County, U.S. App. Lexis 12347 (6th Cir. 2012).
Smith v. Cupp, 430 F. 3d 766 (6th Cir. 2005).
Smith v. Freland, 954 F. 2d 343, 347 (6th Cir.1992).
Sudac v. Hoang, 378 F. Supp. 2d 1298 (D. Kan., 2005).
Sullivan, J. (2014). Clearing the cops: Do district attorneys rubber-stamp police use of deadly force? *Common Wealth Magazine, Winter*, 29–36.
Summerland v. County of Livingston, No. 06-1975 (6th Cir. 2007).
Swans v. City of Lansing, 63 F. Supp. 2d 625 (W.D. Mich. 1998).
Sykes v. United States, 550 U.S 192 (2011).
Tennessee v. Garner, 471 U.S. 1 (1985).
Terrell v. Smith, No. 10-14908 (11th Cir. 2012).
Tolan v. Cotton, 572 U.S. __ (2014).
Turner v. City of Toledo, 3:07-CV-274 (W.D. OH, 2012).
United States Department of Justice, Civil Rights Special Litigation Division. (2015). *Consent decrees*. Retrieved from www.justice.gov/crt/special-litigation-section.
Warren, V. (2015). *Public comment before the President's Task Force on 21st Century Policing*. Washington, DC.
Wesler, C. (2013). *Civil rights investigations of local police agencies: Lessons learned*. Washington, DC: Police Executive Research Forum.
Whitley v. Albers, 475 U.S. 312 (1986).
Wilkins v. Gaddy, 559 U.S. ___ (2010).
Wilkinson v. Torres, 610 F. 3d 546 (9th Cir. 2010).
Williams v. Chambers, No. 4:07-CV-01409-ERW (E.D. MO 2009).
Williams v. City of Grosse Pointe Park, U.S. App. Lexis 18599 (6th Cir. 2007).

4

STRESS, PERCEPTUAL DISTORTIONS, AND HUMAN PERFORMANCE

Darrell L. Ross and Randall L. Murphy

Introduction

In *Graham v. Connor* (1989), the United States Supreme Court established that all claims of excessive force are to be examined in accordance with the Fourth Amendment's "objective reasonableness" standard, and such degree of force will be assessed on a case-by case basis, within the totality of the circumstances, and based on the following criteria: the severity of the crime at issue; whether the suspect was actively resisting arrest; and whether the suspect was attempting to evade arrest by flight. The Court ruled that objective reasonable force is not capable of precise definition or mechanical application, and stated that judging an officer's use of force must allow for the fact that police officers are often forced to make split-second decisions in circumstances that are tense, uncertain, and rapidly evolving. In addition, the type and degree of force to use in a given situation and from the perspective of a reasonable officer on the scene should be the focus, rather than 20/20 hindsight. The Court has also re-affirmed this standard of review in eight subsequent decisions.

A key component included within the legal standard of review by the Court is the "officer's perception." The problem in many major use of force confrontations, including officer-involved shootings, is the limitation of the reaction time necessary for the officer to fully cognitively process incoming stimuli, which can create perceptual distortions (Artwhol & Christensen, 1997; Klinger & Brunson, 2009; Lewinski, 2008; Ross & Siddle, 2003; Ross, Murphy, & Hazlett, 2012). Scientific research has shown that making a decision under stress and time pressures can affect a person's sensory perception and ultimately his or her performance (Horowitz, 1976; Hsieh, 2002; Kavanagh, 2006; Miller & Low, 2001). A significant number of officers involved in a deadly force shooting incident have described numerous alterations in perception, thinking, and performance which occurred during the incident (Artwhol, 2002; Honig & Roland, 1998; Miller, 2006; Ross & Siddle, 2003). Experiencing these physiological and psychological changes occurs as a natural adaptive reaction of the sympathetic nervous system, which activates resources throughout the body when extreme cognitive and emotional demands require it, like a deadly force circumstance (Miller, 2006; Selye, 1959).

As discussed in the chapter on legal issues, an officer-involved shooting civil liability case may be won or lost on the officer's perception or misperception justifying the use of deadly force. For example, in *McKinney v. Duplain* (2008), Officer Duplain shot and killed a suspect who attempted to gain entrance through the back door of a residence. The incident occurred in a small back yard at 1:30am with limited lighting, which cast large shadows. Duplain responded to the backyard and confronted a subject from about 16 feet away. Within two seconds, the subject charged the officer with his hands in his pockets, wearing a heavy Carhart coat. Duplain had less than two seconds to determine whether the suspect had a weapon or not. Based on the circumstances, Duplain formed the perception that he was in immediate danger, feared for his life and survival, and discharged his firearm four times as the suspect closed to within four feet.

Two of the rounds struck the suspect, killing him instantly. It was determined that the suspect was unarmed. After the shooting, Duplain stated that he could not recall how many rounds he fired, stated that time seemed to slow down immensely, that he did not recall seeing the suspect's face, that he did not know how close the suspect was when he fired, that he moved to his right as he fired, and just pointed the firearm at the suspect and fired. After four years of discovery, the jury at the civil trial determined that Duplain formed the perception that he fired to protect himself and awarded a no cause for action. Defense experts were able to testify to the human factors and the stress components experienced by Duplain just before and during the time he fired his firearm.

This chapter presents a review of the research literature, which addresses the impact of stress on the human body and how stress may impact an officer's perception and performance when faced with a survival stress situation. Just as the investigator must be knowledgeable of the many facets of conducting the incident investigation, the investigator must be as knowledgeable about the science of human performance under stress. Understanding how stress impacts human performance will assist the investigator in obtaining the most accurate assessment of the incident, will assist later when the investigator conducts an interview with the involved officer, and will assist in obtaining the most complete and accurate analysis which can be cross-checked against other evidence collected.

The Science of the Stress Response

In interviews with officers after a shooting incident, reviewing their internal affairs investigation videos or transcripts, and reviewing their deposition testimony, Ross (2016) found that officers commonly reflect that: "I had little time to think; I thought he would kill me or my partner; I thought he had a gun in his hand; I had no concept of time; I never saw my sights, I just pointed the gun and fired; I could feel my heart racing; I have no idea how many rounds I fired; everything just slowed down; I never heard my partner's gun fire; I don't recall hearing others giving commands; I feared for my own life; I feared for my partner's life; and I had little time to think." Officers also commented that the behavioral cues of the subject assisted in the formation of perception, including: reaching in the waist band or reaching toward the center of a vehicle; unexpectedly charging the officer; charging the officer with an object; quickly turning toward the officer with an object; raising a firearm or other weapon, and the subject stating he/she would assault the officer, to mention a few.

These statements and others are among the many comments officers discuss which relate to their perception and experience during the shooting incident. They are indicative of their recall of having survived a deadly force incident and are consistent with the numerous perceptional distortions experienced by officers surviving an officer-involved shooting. In the following section, an overview is given of the various bodily responses which occur during a perceived stressful and deadly encounter.

The Brain

To gain a better appreciation of how a stressful and traumatic situation impacts the body, like experiencing the need to defend oneself in a threatening circumstance, a brief overview of how the brain processes information is helpful. Hippocrates commented over 2,400 years ago that the brain has the most power for man ... the eyes, the ears, the tongue, the feet and the hands do whatever the brain determines, it is the brain that is the messenger to the understanding, and the brain that interprets the understanding (Schwartz & Begley, 2002). Little did Hippocrates know at the time how modern research would prove him correct.

The human brain is a dynamic ecosystem and is constantly receiving information from the senses about its current state, concerning environmental and internal stimuli, various organs, and the chemical and nutritive state of the blood (Carter, 1998; Kandel, 2006; Ratey, 2001; Schwartz & Begley, 2002). The brain seeks to maintain homeostasis amidst a changing environment and it is constantly interpreting all incoming stimuli (Howard, 2000). The brain comprises 100 billion nerve cells or neurons, which provide mechanisms for processing, interpreting, and directing bodily responses. The primary functions of the brain are cognition, memory, movement, language, and emotion, and it is bombarded with information through our senses, which has to be processed. The brain's dictum is "survival" first.

MacLean (1967) has commented that the brain is the most adaptive mechanism in the universe and has divided it into three general parts, known as the Triune Brain. The base of the brain known as the Reptilian Brain houses the command centers for living, including: controlling sleep, walking, respiration, temperature regulation, basic automatic movements, and coordinating sensory input. The Paleomammalian Brain or the neocortex, the mid-brain (including the limbic system), promotes survival and refines and coordinates movements. In this area, memory and emotions are formed, which further enhance internal regulations of the body. The third area is known as the Neomammalian Brain, or cortex, and is responsible for fine-tuning the body's lower functions and for abstract thinking, planning abilities, and assists in responding to new challenges. Further, the cerebellum (little brain) plays a major role in thinking, speaking, memory, movement, and emotions.

The focus of the discussion in this chapter will center on the limbic system and will address how the brain processes danger and shifts the body into survival. The environment which a person traverses constantly changes, and an important responsibility of the brain is to process the incoming stimuli, which is accomplished through the senses and internal messages from organs. The five senses all receive and send messages to the brain and a significant amount of sensory information is gleaned through vision and hearing.

The limbic system is responsible for the functions of arousal, emotions, and memories. It deals with high and low functions and is found in the brain stem within the cerebrum. The major components include the thalamus, hypothalamus, amygdala, hippocampus, and basal ganglia. The thalamus lies deep inside the brain and is responsible for several functions. With the exception of smell, the thalamus serves to pick up sensory and motor stimuli and relays it to other portions of the brain, while regulating sleep and consciousness. The thalamus is associated with the visual system, receiving input from the retina and then transmitting information through the optic nerve and onto the occipital lobe. It is involved in sensory perception and movement.

The hypothalamus is the link between the endocrine system and the nervous system and it maintains the body's homeostasis. It acts like the body's thermostat. It is referred to as the "brain of the brain" and it is one of the busiest regions of the brain. It produces, releases, and regulates hormones throughout the body and assists in regulating the heart, body temperature, sleep, fluid and electrolyte balance, appetite and body weight, and pituitary gland function. The hypothalamus is responsible for regulating the body's hunger, thirst, response to pain, levels of pleasure, sexual satisfaction, anger and aggressive behavior. It also regulates the functioning of the autonomic nervous system, which regulates pulse, blood pressure, breathing, and arousal in response to emotional circumstances.

The hypothalamus receives input from several sources. From the vagus nerve, it obtains information about blood pressure and the distension of the stomach. From the reticular formation in the brainstem, it receives information about skin temperature. From the optic nerve, it gets information about light and darkness. From neurons lining the ventricles, it obtains information about the contents of the cerebrospinal fluid, including toxins that lead to vomiting. And from the other parts of the limbic system and the olfactory (smell) nerves, it gets information that helps regulate eating and sexuality. The hypothalamus also has some receptors of its own, that provide information about ion balance and temperature of the blood.

The hypothalamus is responsible for the "fight or flight" response and sends instructions to the rest of the body in two ways. The first is to the autonomic nervous system. This allows the hypothalamus to have ultimate control of things like blood pressure, heartrate, breathing, digestion, sweating, and all the sympathetic and parasympathetic functions. The second way the hypothalamus controls things is through the pituitary gland. It is neurally and chemically connected to the pituitary, which in turn pumps hormones into the bloodstream. The hypothalamus directs the pituitary gland to distribute chemicals throughout the body when survival thinking is necessary.

The amygdala receives information from the thalamus and the cerebral cortex and attaches meaning to sensory information for survival and serves as the brain's alarm system. It is involved in the processing of fear, anger, and pleasure. The amygdala is involved in autonomic responses associated with fear and hormonal secretions, and determines what memories to store. The amygdala can heighten sensory sound perceptions and if the sound is startling, it will activate the automatic fight or flight response. The functions of the amygdala include arousal, autonomic response system to fear, hormonal secretions, and memory. Associated with the limbic system structures is the basal ganglia, which is responsible for focusing attention, repetitive behaviors, and rewarding experiences.

Shaped like a horseshoe, the hippocampus is involved with storing, forming, and organizing memory. It is located within the temporal lobe adjacent to the amygdala. The hippocampus serves as a memory indexer and sends out memories to the cerebral portion of the brain for long-term storage and retrieval when needed. It communicates with the reticular activating system. It converts things in the mind (at the moment), short-term to things to recall for the long term.

Perception

Perception is critical to existing, which translates to survival. Ratey (2001) reported that scientists are still far away from completely understanding how perception works. Perception is the mental process by which the brain interprets and gives meaning to information received from the sensory organs. It depends on both the psychological and physiological characteristics of the perceiver, in addition to the nature of the stimulus. Perception is the condition of being aware and the product of careful mental activity (Gibson, 1950, 1960; James, 1890). Perception is the process of applying stored knowledge to the sensory input and forming an interpretation (Green, 2011). Past experiences (and past learning) impact human perception and help to match what was previously experienced to a present situation. The brain's neural network responds in a specific pattern to past experiences and in response to a stimulus (Ratey, 2001).

The senses of vision, touch, taste, smell, and hearing all assist in developing a person's perception. Smells can have powerful effects, as they may frighten, comfort, or intrigue a person. Through the hypothalamus, the smell of cinnamon rolls baking in the mall at the Cinnabon Bakery shop can, at the same time, trigger the perception in the brain of comfort and joy and that of desiring to eating several. The receptors in the nose receive the odor and meaning is attached to it based on the past experience of the person. Smell can also trigger memories because the olfactory nerves are wired directly to the hippocampus and the amygdala and can send the person back to a past experience.

Sound is processed through the brain and through the eardrum as it responds to air-pressure changes as incoming sound waves are received. The inner ear picks up the pressure of the sound and the thalamus sends the information to the auditory cortex of the temporal lobe for further processing. Sounds are processed in the brain by sorting tones and by spatial characteristics. The cells in the auditory cortex are highly sensitive and the cortex then compares the pattern of firing to stored patterns, which make sense to the person. Emotional meaning is attached to the sound, underscoring the many levels of sophisticated processing necessary to develop the perception. Like other senses, sounds can trigger memories of past experiences. For example, a particular song can trigger a memory of the first date or other significant meaningful experience of the person.

Vision is impacted by light rays as they hit the eye. The electrochemical energy is sent to the brain via the optic nerve, transmitted through the thalamus, and the eye and head are adjusted to maximize the input of information. The retina assists in filtering the proper amount of light that enters and the rods and the cones also assist in the intensity of the light's wavelength. The retina contains about 120 million rods and about 6 million cones (Breedlove, 1995, 2013). The cones are responsible for color vision and for most of the human visual perception in normal and bright light. The rods have less visual acuity but provide the better portion of vision at night or when it is dark. The neural signals created by the rods and cones depart from the back of the eye via the optic nerve and on to other centers of the brain. The eyes take snapshots from the external environmental stimuli and separate them into millions of bits of information and segregate them according to color and light and direction of the light (Ratey, 2001). Once the job of the thalamus is completed, the processed visual information is sent back to the occipital cortex in the brain. V1, the secretarial function of the brain, specializes the sensory information and makes distinctions of the color, shape, size, and orientation. Among the senses, visual information takes longer to process. As the visual system processes the stimuli, motion is perceived before color and color is processed before shape. The color of yellow is processed faster than other colors.

The brain is shaped by the perceptions it experiences and requires varying degrees of expectation of anticipating what is about to be confronted and then preparing for it. Anticipation is the mental process of being aware of environmental stimuli, which produces a situational awareness and activates the amygdala and hippocampus regions of the brain. Expectation may be part of anticipation in the environment and it precedes perception. Anticipation serves as a proactive mental process and provides preparatory consciousness and alertness, or excitement or warning to external stimuli and cues, prior to an event or incident occurring. It is an initial part of the survival stress response assisting in increasing assessment of the immediate and the future. For example, an officer may be patrolling and suddenly receives a radio call to proceed to shots fired at a school by an active shooter. During the response to the location and with limited information received, the anticipatory phase of cognition is automatically activated, placing the officer on alert to anticipate or expect future danger.

Stress Response

Stress has been described as both an environmental variable and an emotional response to a specific situation (Gould et al., 1987; Selye, 1978). Selye (1936) first termed external pressures on the body as "stressors" and biological response as "stress." He defined stress as the non-specific response of the body to any demand made upon it. He believed that eustress (positive) and distress (negative) produced the same initial response in the body (Selye, 1936).

McGrath (1970) designed a four-stage model to explain the process of how stress interacts with a person's response. The process involves a sequence of events that begins with an environmental demand on the person, his/her perception and placing value to the event, the mental response (decision-making) and physical response. Martens (1977) defined stress as a substantial imbalance between (environmental) demand and response capability, under conditions where the demand has important consequences. Combining McGrath's model and Martens' definition of stress, stress may be viewed as positive or negative, but the emphasis is placed on the situational environment, the individual's perception of the situation, and the ability to respond physically or mentally.

Cannon (1929) explained that the body's response to stressful stimuli is through a process known as "fight or flight." This automatic response is an adaptive response mechanism alerting an individual's body to danger and begins to prepare the body to mentally and physically respond. The process is virtually uncontrollable and it dominates all voluntary and involuntary systems until the threat perception has been eliminated or avoided. He was the first to recognize that the brain was the center for interpreting (perceiving) a dangerous stimulus and responding to it (reaction and movement) (Cannon, 1929).

The autonomic nervous system is responsible for processing an individual's response to a perceived stressful situation. The autonomic nervous system is comprised of two components, the Sympathetic Nervous System (SNS) and the Parasympathetic Nervous System (PNS) (Sapolsky, 2004). The brain and the body are hardwired to respond to a perceived stressful situation and a pathway to receive, process, transfer, and respond to the stressors automatically occurs through the SNS. The SNS controls the body's response during perceived threat. An environmental demand will be first processed through the brain and it evaluates the degree of threat through an integrated network of regions in the brain involving the thalamus, amygdala, hypothalamus, hippocampus, and frontal lobes of the cortex. During arousal (stressful event), information from the perceptual senses is first processed through the reticular activating system (RAS), which relays emotional stimuli to the cortex. The information is routed to the thalamus and emotion is attached to the perception of the level of threat through the amygdala, the body's alarm system (Carter, 1998; Ratey, 2001; Sapolsky, 2004). In a non-spontaneous threat situation, the threat is processed cognitively and physically, normally without difficulty. In a spontaneous, startled, fearful situation however, the amygdala, which is hardwired for survival, primes the body with adrenaline for an automatic response. The triggering of the amygdala is directly responsible for what many consider (post-incident) as irrational responses, such as panic, flight, freezing in place, aggressive actions that utilize untrained skills, repeating an action time and again (a motor skill feedback loop), or an inappropriate physical response.

Generally, the response to stress and activation of an SNS discharge results in a release of norepinephrine and epinephrine, an increase in cortisol and glucose levels, an increase in heart rate and heart rate variability, blood pressure, breathing rate, perspiration, muscle tension, respiration, palms sweating, muscle tension, and improved blood flow to the brain, heart, and large muscles (Asken, Vonk, & Sterland, 2009; Salas & Driskell, 1996; Violanti et al., 2007). Under high levels of stress, the eyes dilate, the lenses flatten, and the eyes begin to move in a saccadic manner (Vickers, 2007). When experiencing a high stress event, it is common for the heart rate to increase to over 135 BPM. Cortisol promotes an increase in the hormones released throughout the body's bloodstream as a natural response to an increase in arousal and plays a key role in the maintenance of adequate blood pressure during a stressful circumstance (Groer et al., 2010; Hellhammer, Wust, & Kudielka, 2009). Fine motor skills, which require eye/hand coordination, begin to deteriorate as resources are shifted to larger muscles necessary to carry out gross motor skills. A reduction in full scope of vision also occurs, and the other four senses are also affected. The cognitive system is also affected and the fight or flight response is activated.

After the stressful situation abates, the other half of the autonomic nervous system responds. The PNS takes over and the body is returned to homeostasis as the heart rate and blood pressure return to pre-event levels, muscles relax, respirations abate, digestive system returns to normal, pupil size decreases, and urinary tract returns to normal levels. The time needed to return to equilibrium is idiosyncratic.

Stress Response in a Deadly Force Situation

A perceived threat of death in a deadly force encounter will automatically activate the SNS. In a real-life deadly force scenario, the officer will be faced with a multitude of rapidly incoming stimuli, threatening the officer's life or others, circumstances that are ambiguous, dynamic, and evolving, occurring in varying confrontational environments, under poor lighting conditions, and often forcing the officer to make a split-second decision. Cognitive processing impacts perception during a perceived stressful situation (Artwohl, 2002; Damasio, 1994; Honig & Lewinski, 2008; Kandel, 2006; LeDoux, 1996). A person's response to the perception formed from the senses is directly related to their performance (Ratey, 2001).

When a person perceives a high level of stress, the brain transfers from thinking to reacting and the SNS is activated (McGaugh, 1990). The stress response of fight, flight, or freeze is involuntarily activated as part of the survival response hardwired into the brain (Sapolsky, 2004). Epstein (1994) and Artwohl (2002) concluded that individuals have two distinct modes of processing and interpreting stimuli and information. First, under the rational thinking model, which applies to low to moderate levels of stress, a person generally is able to calmly engage in conscious, deliberate, and analytical cognitive processing, which underscores rational thinking. Second, when an individual experiences and perceives a high stress situation requiring quick decision-making, the cognitive processing of information in the brain automatically transfers to experiential thinking. The interpretation and perception of the information processed by the person automatically speeds up the cognitive process based on the urgency, life threatening, or survivability of the stimuli or situation, requiring an immediate response. This rapid cognitive process is characterized by intuitive and holistic rather than logical or analytical thought, focused on immediate action rather than reflection, seized by emotion and rapid thinking rather than slow and deliberate thinking, and fragmented memory of the event may result.

Fear can evoke the SNS response. Fear is the automatic emotional reaction to perceived danger or threat and beyond the person's control (Solomon, 2001). Ratey (2001) reported that the amygdala is responsible for assessing fearful and threatening stimuli, which brings the total circumstance into perspective. The emotion of fear is associated with the fight or flight response. Many fears are learned. For example, being bitten by a dog as a youth may condition a person to be fearful of dogs later in life. Fear of heights may also be learned and may cause someone to freeze when confronted with the danger.

Fear can also cause someone to freeze, but in law enforcement, this is not always a viable option. Fear, however, can assist the officer as it can help him or her to maintain alertness, it can focus the attention to action and to respond to a perceived threat of danger, it can mobilize tremendous strength, information can still be processed, and it serves as a basic instinct to survive. The startle response to an unexpected stimulus provides an example of the adaptive response to fear. A sudden loud noise can create an automatic startle response and is often associated with a threat of danger. As the noise is picked up, the head rotates to the direction of the sound and the optic system scans to determine the source and the automatic response occurs. Instantaneously, the SNS has been activated, the amygdala screams, "DANGER," and the person responds instinctively to protect him/herself.

In policing, hesitation can get an officer killed or significantly injured and cueing into contextual cues of a deadly force incident is critical (Pinizzotto et al., 2012). Part of the cognitive process is the ability to recognize patterns or cues of threatening behaviors in order to compare them against past experiences and training. Contextual cues are those patterns of subject behaviors and movements which may provide circumstance indicators of an impending assault (Ross, 2016). For example, an officer may make a traffic stop and observe the driver suddenly rotate his upper body and arms and reach for the console. The furtive movement may be the driver reaching for a weapon or for a driver license.

Under stress, perception is influenced by several factors, including intensity, physical dimensions of the stimulus, and past experiences of the person. Experiences shape a person's perception and match a perception of an event to schemas or heuristics, also referred to as recognized patterns (LeDoux, 1996; Ratey, 2001). Humans see the world in patterns and cues and they are helpful in assisting in making judgments under limited time, but they may also result in an error of judgment. In police work, patterns or contextual cues are taught to officers about observing a suspect's behaviors, motions, statements, and facial gestures. Police officers are taught to assess human behaviors, patterns of movements, assault cues, and statements in order to gauge the threat level of a person to enhance their own safety. Threatening assault cues during an encounter may include a subject's stance, arms folded across the chest, assuming a power stance, a blank stare, looking back and forth, making direct eye contact, failing to make eye contact, facial gestures, body movements, quick furtive movements, not showing the hands, hands at the waist, making quick reaching motions with the hands, charging/lunging forward, reaching into pockets or waistbands, and statements and verbal threats, to mention a few. All of this is occurring in milliseconds without the luxury of time to deliberate the actions of the person and it is common for the encounter to be fluid and dynamic in nature.

In police work, confrontation contextual cues are the only cues an officer can rely on. If the officer focuses on a quick motion of reaching into the waist as a subject approaches him or her through the visual system, the brain scans to match the contextual cue or patterns in order to properly interpret the motion. Several outcomes exist. First, if the officer delays the physical response, the subject could pull a firearm and shoot the officer. Second, the officer may freeze, further delaying a physical response, thus placing him or her in physical jeopardy. Third, the officer may discharge his or her firearm and kill the subject who was just reaching for their wallet. The net result is that contextual cues and patterns of human behaviors can assist the officer in anticipating and developing the perception that an assault is imminent, thus preparing the officer to respond appropriately. However, there is the potential for the officer misperceiving the action, which could result in a mistake of fact shooting. Thus, the focus of the officer's attention to the contextual cues and behavioral patterns of the subject, under time pressures, and interpreting the bodily patterns, will impact the officer's perception and decision making in physically responding.

Perceptual distortions or selective attention can significantly impede the brain from processing threat information correctly, impeding an officer's appropriate survival response. Salas and Driskell (1996) found that cognitive effects of stress may include narrowing of attention, tunnel vision, increased errors, longer reaction time to peripheral stimuli, and memory defects. Perceptual distortions, which involve cognitive processing, can include tunnel vision, visual clarity, auditory problems, color distortion, decision making, and time factors surrounding the incident.

It is not uncommon for a police officer in a deadly force encounter to experience limited reaction time (Blair et al., 2011; Broome, 2013; Hillman, 1995; Hontz, 2000; Ross, 2016). It is well known that action beats reaction and in most officer-involved shootings, the officer operates behind the reactionary curve. Reaction time comprises three phases (Ratey, 2001): analyzing and evaluating the external threat information, formulating a response selection, and initiating a motor response. Each stage must be completed in sequence and each stage is dependent on the former. These stages align with the effects of SNS and vision. As perception of the threat commences, vision narrows and the brain's ability to evaluate the threat level also diminishes. If impairment occurs in the first two stages, response selection and motor response may also be impaired.

Activation of the SNS can significantly alter reaction time, which is defined as the process of perceiving a threat and initiating a survival response. Smith (1990) and Lewinski (2002) report that it can take from about 0.5 to 1.5 seconds to form a perception, acquire target acquisition, and respond by firing when the officer's firearm is holstered. A majority of officer-involved shootings occur within three seconds and within ten feet of the subject, and the subject can fire at least two rounds at the officer before the officer can fire. A subject can close the distance of nine feet within about 0.5 seconds (Dysterheft et al., 2013). This means that an officer can be slashed by a subject brandishing a knife in half a second.

In these situations where the officer has limited reaction time, stress can impact the officer's decision making. Stress does not per se cause an officer to make a poor decision, but it directly impacts the way information is processed (Klein, 1998). Stressors such as limited reaction time, time pressures, noise, ambiguity, and poor vision can result in the following: they limit the time to gather as much information as is needed; they limit the ability to sample as many cues, forcing the officer to attend to the cues as he or she perceives them; and they force the officer to attend to the most threatening stimuli when multiple threats are present. They can also cause an officer to misperceive an object.

Varying degrees of stress can significantly affect perception (Dror, 2007; Kavanagh, 2006). Perception is influenced by several factors, including intensity, physical dimensions of the stimuli, the person's past experiences, the emotional state of the person, attention factors, stress levels, and the person's readiness to respond to the stimulus. Vision is influenced from perceived patterns (contextual cues) and the ability to perceive completed figures and ability to distinguish important figures from background. Stress can also impact the visual system (Ratey, 2001) and it is not uncommon for a police officer to miss or misperceive something during a fast-paced stressful situation (Ross, Murphy,

& Hazlett, 2012; Simons & Levin, 1998). In a stressful situation, vision can be affected and the brain directs the focus of attention to that stimulus requiring immediate attention, while excluding peripheral stimuli. Under stress, the vision generally overrides the other senses by 80 to 90 percent (Breedlove, 2013). This tunneling effect is known as selective attention, occurring involuntarily, and in response to an SNS discharge (Chabris & Simons, 2009).

Selective attention (or misperception) explains how a person may miss observing something that is in his or her direct line of vision, or not hearing something because the brain has focused the vision directly on the immediate stressor that requires attention. Peripheral vision then may be narrowed by as much as 70 percent (Breedlove, 1995, 2013; Easterbrook, 1959). This response is also referred to as inattentional blindness or visual noise, which is an unconscious rejection of competing visual input. It can occur across all of the senses but primarily affects vision (Honig & Lewinski, 2008; Williams, Allen, & Stein, 1999). Accordingly, this phenomenon occurs from an overload of visual sensory input or from focusing primarily on the task at hand. If a weapon is involved or an object is perceived to be a weapon, a "weapon focus" phenomenon may be created, which aligns with the tunnel vision effect. This can explain why a person may misperceive a situation and actually be blind to seeing the obvious. Perceptual narrowing suggests that as the level of demand increases, there will be a corresponding decrease in the visual area as the number of visual cues is reduced (Godnig, 2001).

Inattentional blindness may result in a type I or a type II error, impacting perception, recall, and performance. A type I error, or a false negative, involves rejecting something that is apparent or obvious. For example, a person may miss obvious cues while driving a car and strike an object. Conversely, a type II error is a false positive, such as, a person incorrectly perceives a cell phone as a firearm. Type I or II errors are at risk of occurring and may increase as stress levels increase, affecting perception and further impacting a response (Lewinski, 2008).

Environmental factors such as visibility, operating conditions, and low lighting may also intensify selective attention as vasoconstriction of the retina occurs. Many deadly force incidents occur during low level light and at night. As the perception of fear of surviving the encounter increases, the SNS is activated, placing the officer on alert and the vision system loses some of its ability to maintain clear focus on a target at close distance. An optical shift occurs in the lens as it changes its shape, losing some of its optical power. During low light conditions, the cones are unable to send precise signals for the brain to process. Depth perception can be a problem for the officer and the ability to discern detail is reduced. The pupil of the eye increases, creating less depth of field in the visual system of the officer. This can cause threat cues to be missed. SNS activation also inhibits the ability to maintain near vision and the ability to focus, which leads to the loss of depth perception, the loss of night vision, and the loss of monocular vision (Godnig, 2001; Siddle & Breedlove, 1995).

Other low lighting factors play a role in vision and can include: contrast of an image, which reduces the ability to discriminate a dark visual image from a lighter visual image; shadows, which can emerge from low lighting limiting eye focus; being able to closely focus on moving targets, causing problems with fixation ability; inhibiting the ability to maintain near vision and to focus; the loss of night vision; problems with reflected light; and the loss of monocular vision (Godnig, 2001; Siddle & Breedlove, 1995). All of these factors are significant in that they are likely to cause inaccuracy of shooting skills, limitations with physical skills, altered reaction time, and the inability to be aware of environmental surroundings, which may pose additional threats to the officer.

The effects of stress on performance include the accuracy of task performance as well as the speed at which tasks are performed. The stress of noise may affect cognitive processes as well as motor skills

(Thackery & Touchstone, 1983). Hearing diminishes, causing auditory exclusion. If hearing is the dominant source of information, when a loud sound occurs, visual exclusion may occur. Other senses may also be tuned out, which further diminishes the officer's ability to feel cuts, scratches, strikes, or bullet wounds, and can also impair performance and recall.

The impact of stress has been shown to affect motor performance (Ratey, 2001). Yerkes and Dodson (1908) proposed that arousal (stress) and performance were associated. Creating a model known as the inverted-U hypothesis, they explained that as arousal increased, performance also increased to a certain point, but that continued increase in arousal would lead to a detriment in performance (noting a curvilinear relationship). Gould et al. (1987) found anxiety to have a curvilinear relationship with pistol-shooting performance, supporting the inverted-U hypothesis.

Stress and Memory

It is an understatement to state that human memory is complex. For example, prior experiences and the psychological state of the person, as well as the stress of the incident, can all alter memory. The effects of stress can impact a person's perception and can reduce the ability to receive and recall details of the event (Bremner, 1999; British Psychological Society Research Board, 2008; Gray & Lombardo, 2001; Janis & Mann, 1977; Miller, 2015; Salas & Driskell, 1996; Sharps, 2010). De Quervain, Roozendall, and McGaugh (1998), Violanti et al. (2007), and Groer et al. (2010) report that cortisol hormones released under stress may inhibit memory retrieval. The World Health Organization (WHO) (1998) reveals that the effects of acute stress reaction, including temporary memory loss, may subside after hours or may last several days. Grossman and Siddle (2004) report that acute stress can create amnesia after a critical incident. The greater the trauma, the greater the impact of the post-incident amnesia will likely be.

Memory is the product of information processing and is associated with attention (Ebbinghaus, 1885). When processing a life-threatening encounter, such as facing a deadly force encounter, an emotional arousal stimulus is produced. Either through vision and/or through hearing, the stimulus is sent to the brain and after the amygdala has attached emotional meaning like fear and/or survival, the stimulus is passed onto the hippocampus. The hippocampus organizes the information and processes it in association with prior memories of similar sensory details. The more emotional significance attached to the event, the more intently the memory is recorded by the hippocampus (LeDoux, 1996; Ratey, 2001). However, if the perceived fear arousal is perceived to be high (like an unexpected startle response) the hippocampus may be hindered from recording a complete and thorough memory of the experience (Kim & Diamond, 2002; Plihal & Born, 1999).

When a high survival stress situation occurs, the hypothalamus releases high levels of cortisol to adequately respond to the circumstance. Cortisol is bound to receptors in the hippocampus but when the emotional attachment is too high, neurons are flooded with cortisol, causing the metabolism of the cells to overheat and die (Ratey, 2001). High levels of cortisol may contribute to false memories (Payne & Nadel, 2004; Payne et al., 2002). This may result in the hippocampus storing fragmentation and portions of the event and with the passage of time, with sleep, and as the cortisol abates, the more likely the person is to recall more details of the incident (Maquet, 2000; Xie et al., 2013).

Moreover, high levels of arousal can affect attention, and when combined with the flood of cortisol, memory impairment may occur. As discussed earlier, as the visual system narrows to attend to the perceived threat, vision is focused on the threat and the brain filters out information deemed unimportant for survival (Shomstein & Yantis, 2004). Inattentional blindness can commonly occur across the senses, but when affecting vision, the brain will subconsciously suppress all other information, failing to encode a concrete memory of the situation. The brain selectively excludes peripheral information in order to give full attention to the immediacy of the threat. The officer's perception and memory of the event are significantly influenced more by what the focus of the attention was prior to and during the encounter. Gray (2004) found that the more the focus is on something during high stress, the less likely the person is able to recall peripheral information which occurred during the event.

The split-second nature of the high arousal survival stress encounter may further impair the officer's memory of the event as the brain automatically adjusts itself from rational thinking to experiential thinking. Experiential thinking is dominant over rational thinking in response to the emotion of fear during a high stress situation and includes the following components: being seized by emotion, oriented toward immediate action, framed within intuition, and fragmented memory can result (Epstein, 1994). Research in cognitive psychology has shown that memory of some aspects of the incident can be recalled with clarity like "flashbulb memory," meaning that snapshots can be specifically recalled, depending on the officer and confrontation variables. In other situations, recall of the stressful event may be spotty (Loftus, 1996; Loftus, Greene & Doyle, 1989). Hence, what can be expected of an officer regarding his or her memory after surviving a deadly force encounter is that memory is as likely to be inaccurate as accurate (Honig & Lewinski, 2008). After an officer-involved shooting, memory is commonly fragmented, errors in recall may occur, and after the passing of time, as homeostasis of the body returns to pre-event levels and there is time for cortisol and hormone levels to return to normal levels, recall of the details of the event can increase. This explains why investigation interviews with involved officers should be delayed for 24 to 48 hours (International Association of Chiefs of Police, 2013).

Research on Perceptual Distortions in Policing

An important dimension of an officer-involved shooting is how the stress of the incident may impact the perception of the officer. Police officers, like other humans, may experience several perceptual distortions, which may impact their cognitive processing of the circumstance, facts, and the operating environment, which may ultimately impact their response (Klinger & Brunson, 2009). Experiencing a life-threatening incident during an officer-involved shooting where the SNS response is activated, perceptual distortions including a slowness or an increase in time, loss or partial loss of auditory ability, and narrowing of the field of vision are all frequently experienced by officers, along with memory impairment. Recognizing perceptual distortions, which commonly occur in an officer-involved shooting or a major use of force incident, must be considered when analyzing whether the force was justified (Artwhol, 2002; Lewinski, 2008; Ross, Murphy, & Hazlett, 2012; Ross, 2016). Distortions of perceptions occurring during an officer-involved shooting have been limitedly researched. The main findings of ten published studies, which have specifically researched the common types of perceptual distortions associated with an officer-involved shooting, are presented in Table 4.1.

The methodology used in the studies included surveying the involved officers, while the Ross (2016) and Klinger and Brunson (2009) studies used officer interviews, and the Campbell (1992) study combined surveys with officer interviews. Ross, Murphy, and Hazlett (2012) measured the physiological and psychological stress reactions of 150 officers prior to, during, and after completing a deadly force scenario, using a force simulator. Respondents also completed two surveys regarding

TABLE 4.1 Studies on perceptional distortions in lethal force confrontations (in percentages)

Variables	*Study*									
	Neilson (1981)	Solomon & Horn (1986)	Campbell (1992)	Artwhol & Christensen (1997)	Honig & Roland (1998)	Ross & Siddle (2003)	Honig & Sultan (2004)	Klinger & Brunson (2009)	Ross, Murphy, & Hazlett (2012)	Ross (2016)
Tunnel vision	43	56	44	79	51	56	42	31	81	56
Loud sounds	NR	59	NR	16	82	29	21	6	22	NR
Quieter sounds	27	39	NR	84	51	34	51	45	NR	31
Auditory exclusion	NR	63	42	88	NR	41	NR	79	24	45
Time slow	64	61	34	62	41	64	41	45	61	70
Time increase	NR	22	21	17	20	16	19	17	15	23
Heightened visual clarity	NR	NR	NR	71	41	25	41	39	55	21
Visual	NR	56	NR	NR	NR	NR	NR	41	22	27
Depth perception	NR	NR	NR	NR	NR	61	NR	NR	40	80
Threat focus	NR	NR	NR	NR	NR	78	NR	NR	86	86
Misperception	NR	NR	NR	NR	NR	NR	NR	NR	30	26
Fear/need to survive	NR	NR	NR	NR	40	48	45	NR	36	50
Memory	NR	NR	NR	52	25	30	31	29	32	39
# of officers studied (N)	63	86	167	72	340	165	982	113	150	150

Note: NR = Not Reported.

their perceptions of being exposed to the scenario, with the first survey within 30 minutes of completion and the second survey after 48 hours of completing the scenario. An overview of the study is discussed in the next section. The studies, in their collective totality, comprised 2,288 officers. The sample size ranged from 63 officers in the Neilson (1981) study to 982 officers in the Honig and Sultan (2004) study, and the average study sample size was 214 officers.

Based on the various study methods used and the focus of the study, 15 different perceptual distortions were reported with varying frequencies. Each of these studies was independently researched and revealed similar findings. Irrespective of the study methods, all ten reported officers involved in a deadly force encounter experienced various types of perceptual distortions. These perceptual distortions account for what the officers recalled experiencing during the encounter. A wide range of frequencies of perceptual distortions occurred, ranging from 22 to 88 percent, underscoring that a majority of the officers may experience multiple distortions in a deadly force encounter. Other possible distortions in lighting, distance, color, and face recognition were not part of the research.

First, the most common perceptual distortion experienced by officers involved varying aspects of vision. Every study reported that the officer experienced "tunnel vision" and the frequency of experience averaged 54 percent of the incidents. Tunnel vision, referred to as selective attention, is the loss of peripheral vision and the field of vision is narrowed. In many incidents, the officer may lose about 75 percent of the peripheral vision, allowing the ability to keenly cue into the threat, but be oblivious to actions going on around him or her. This would be consistent with Breedlove's (2013) findings that when the SNS is activated in response to a survival stress encounter, an officer will lose about 70 percent of his or her vision. Breedlove (2013) reports that when the SNS is activated, vasoconstriction to the blood vessels on the periphery of the retina occurs, which results in narrowing of the peripheral field known as tunnel vision.

Related to the findings on tunnel vision, 30 percent of the studies found, on average, that in about 81 percent of the incidents, officers focused on the threat or the weapon/object presented and officers had problems with depth perception in about 60 percent of the incidents. Distortions in vision, which included color distinction, object recognition, and the inability to see the full movements of the subject, were reported in 60 percent of the studies, occurring in about 30 percent of the encounters. In 80 percent of the studies, officers reported a sense of heightened detail. Associated with vision distortions is officer misperception and two studies reported this distortion. Ross, Murphy, and Hazlett (2012) reported that 30 percent of the officers experienced misperception and Ross (2016) reported that about 33 percent of the officers misperceived seeing an object in the subject's hand, a subject's description, number of subjects on scene, number of officers on scene, the quality of information provided by others, and the number of weapons a subject may possess. Equally, depth perception, which is associated with vision, was only measured in three studies. The average of these three studies showed that about 60 percent of the respondents reported having distortions in depth perception.

These studies confirm that under stress and an SNS activation, distortions in vision will be significantly affected and vision is one of the primary perceptional senses impacted. This will cause associated distortions to occur, including tunnel vision, weapon focus, selective attention, and depth perception, all impacting the perception and misperceptions of the officer during the stressful encounter. Distortions in vision are also associated with inattentional blindness, but it can occur across all of the senses. The implication of this phenomenon is that under stress, an officer whose peripheral vision has narrowed can be looking directly at something and literally be blind to it (Simons, 2003). Further, because of the attention of focus, the officer would be unlikely to accurately identify others or objects in close proximity to him or her, and also this has the implications for a deadly crossfire situation to occur (Honig & Lewinski, 2008). Moreover, distortions in vision will also be impacted by the quickness of the furtive movements of the subject threatening the officer as well as the environmental conditions under which the confrontation occurs, including bright versus low lighting, distance from the subject, angle of the subject, and visibility.

Second, an effect on the perception of time was reported in every study. A majority of the responding officers reported that during the encounter, time moved slowly and was found, on average, in about 54 percent of the incidents. Reporting officers were more than twice as likely to experience time moving slowly as opposed to believing that time increased, which averaged about 20 percent of the incidents.

Distortions of sound were the third most commonly reported perception. In eight of the studies, officers reported, on average, believing sounds were quieter in about 52 percent, and in about 30 percent, the officers reported that sounds were louder. In seven of the studies, the officers reported, on average, that their auditory perceptions were blunted or excluded in 55 percent of the incidents. Officers commonly reported not being able to hear clearly or their hearing was muted when they fired their own firearm and/or when other officers on scene may have fired their firearms. Officers reported that the sound of the gunshots resembled a cap gun and often stated that the gunfire did not sound like what they experienced on the range. Other officers reported not recalling hearing their own firearm being fired.

The distortion of sound or auditory exclusion is also associated with selective attention when the officer experiences high levels of physiological arousal. Due to the focus of attention to the perceived threat facing the officer, the officer will automatically attend to the immediate salient information perceived as the threat at the time and will filter out peripheral noise determined to be irrelevant. Officers commonly reported not hearing verbal commands being voiced by other officers, even though they were within close proximity of each other, or other environmental noises at the time the officer confronted the threat. During the high stress encounter, the officer's vision and focus of attention will narrow to the threat and the brain will subconsciously reject other senses, determining them unnecessary for survival of the situation at the moment. Experiencing selective attention limits the brain to attending to only one source of information at a time (Simons & Levin, 1998; Shomstein & Yantis, 2004).

Fourth, seven studies revealed that officers had memory distortions and fragmented recall. Officers reported distortion in memory, on average, in about 35 percent of the encounters. Altered memory of the event was reported in various forms, which included: the number of rounds fired by the officer or other officers, commands given by other officers, statements made by the subject, gaps in the sequence of how the event transpired, description of the subject, location of additional officers at the time of the shooting, where the subject was exactly standing or moving when the officer shot, the color of the weapon the subject may be holding, the distance between the officer and the subject at the time the rounds were shot, and where the hands of the subject were when the rounds were fired.

Memory is a product of information processing and is connected to attention. Experiencing a perceived higher arousal situation, like a deadly force encounter, which occurs within split seconds, the officer is less likely to be able to process all of the incoming stimuli impacting memory. Selective attention focuses the vision on the immediate threat, allowing the officer to form a specific and vivid memory of the incident, although not accurately. During the moment the officer perceives an immediate bodily survival threat, the brain acts to protect itself, selects the sense(s) to address the threat, and actively rejects other stimuli, resulting in memory distortion and fragmentation (Epstein,

1994). Sapolsky (2004) and Ratey (2001) observe that as stress increases in a traumatic situation, memory declines. Time pressure and the stress attached to the incident limit the ability to process the information adequately and reduce cue sampling. As vision narrows to attend to the threat and survival, competing stimuli will not be processed. The important component is that the focus of attention through the senses under high arousal determines what is perceived directing the officer's response. If something is not perceived, it cannot be remembered. Although there may be idiosyncratic variances which impact memory, prior research and the ten research studies presented above show substantial support that officers commonly experience distortions of recall of the stressful encounter.

Fifth, 50 percent of the studies reported that it was common for officers to experience the emotion of fear and felt the need to survive. In these studies, the officers reported, on average, in about 54 percent of the encounters the officers experienced these feelings. All of the officers in the Ross (2016) study reported that just prior to shooting the subject, they experienced fear for their safety, the safety of other officers or others in the area, and also experienced the need to survive the confrontation. In the shooting incident, the subject's behaviors, verbal threats, quick furtive bodily movements, lunging and charging actions, observing an object in the subject's hand presented in a rapid motion, or observing a weapon in the subject's hand, caused the officer to be in fear for his or her life and to believe the subject was a threat to the officer, their partner, or others in the community. As the officers' attention is drawn to the movements and actions of the subject, meaning will be attached, which can impact the emotion of fear. The emotion of fear is attached with the fight or flight response. Hence, as these studies report, it would be common for an officer to experience the emotion of fear and respond to protect him or herself.

The findings of these studies align with the general human anatomy research of how the stress response impacts officer perception when confronting a deadly force situation. It is not uncommon for officers to experience varying perceptual distortions, but as the level of stress perceived increases, so do the corresponding intensity of the perceptional distortions, underscoring the notion that "perception is reality." Decision-making, performance, and errors may be observed in some situations and varying levels of memory impairment are expected.

Testing Perceptual Distortions

The ten studies previously discussed on perceptual distortions experienced during an officer-involved shooting provide useful information about the officer's response during a survival stress encounter. To further examine the perceptual distortions experienced by police officers, a randomized experiment was conducted to assess whether the SNS could be triggered in a virtual use of force simulator environment and assess whether the physiological responses to deadly force scenarios could be measured (Ross, Murphy, & Hazlett, 2012). The following research questions guided the study:

1. Does a lethal force virtual simulator create a measurable stress response in participants?
2. Will the virtual simulator scenarios produce a high percentage of reported perceived stress as induced stressors intensify?
3. To what degree did participants misperceive events during the scenario? and
4. Were respondents more likely to misperceive a significant amount of manifest content as the stress within the scenario increased?

Using a new simulator designed by the Meggitt Corporation (Suwanee, GA), 150 veteran police officers participated in one of two different lethal force scenarios. A randomized experimental design was developed and human subject research authorization was secured. Respondent officers volunteered and were paid for their participation and randomly assigned to one of three scenarios. Over 93 percent of the departments employed from 151 to 500 officers. Of these officers, 80 percent were male, 20 percent were female, 75 percent were Caucasian, 10 percent were African-American, and 8 percent were Hispanic. Upon arrival at the experiment site, respondents were provided with an overview of their participation, and reviewed and signed informed consent forms. They were administered a questionnaire regarding their personal lifestyle history.

Baseline physiological information was obtained from each respondent, including: resting heart rates, blood pressure, thoracic capacity, and measurement of waist circumstance. Saliva biomarkers were taken from each participant to assess their stress responses to the events encountered during the scenario. Saliva provides an effective mechanism to measure the degree of the stress response and provides a non-intrusive method for collecting the samples. Saliva biomarker samples using the drool method into polypropylene tubes were taken pre-scenario and at 10 and 30 minutes post-scenario. Saliva biomarker samples were refrigerated immediately. Saliva biomarker samples were transported on ice back to their lab and later analyzed.

Participants were outfitted with a wireless harness device (Biograph Infinity) that tracked respiratory rate, electrocardiographs, skin temperature, heart rate, and heart rate variability to track physiological data. Respondents were fitted with Mobile Eye tracking glasses to monitor eye movement. Each participant was provided with a police uniform shirt, a portable two-way radio, and a Blue Fire® Glock simulator weapon with the officer's department gun belt system. Officers were dispatched real time to the call using two-way radios and their agency's own 10-code system. Information on the participant's perceptions and memory of the scenario was collected within 30 minutes of completion and they also completed and submitted the same questionnaire within 48 hours of the experiment. Return rate of the second questionnaire achieved 100 percent. From time of arrival to departure amounted to about 1.5 hours per respondent.

Scenarios

Two scenarios were developed to measure the impact of stress on officer perception. The scenarios were filmed using live actors and shown to the officers in a testing lab housing a new stress induction system. The lab was about 20 feet by 18 feet with all but one wall being black. The scenario was projected on a white wall in the lab, which was about 16 feet tall and 10 feet wide. Figure 4.1 shows a respondent officer in the lab going through the scenario (upper left corner), the scenario shown in the lab of what the officer observes (upper right corner), the recorded physiological responses of the officer as he progresses through the scenario (bottom left corner), and the same video shown on the computer outside the lab.

FIGURE 4.1 Simulator scenario.

To perform the experiment the respondents were randomly assigned to one of three groups as follows:

Group 1: Motorcycle (n = 52/150 participants)

The duration of the scenario was about two minutes and involved a traffic stop of a person on a motorcycle. Upon being stopped by the officer, the driver dismounts from the bike, faces toward and confronts the officer verbally, while standing next to the bike. Within a few seconds the driver reaches over the bike with his right hand, grabs a firearm, and brings it around quickly, firing at the officer. No inducement of stressors was added to this scenario.

Group 2: Workplace Violence/Limited Stressors (n = 25/150 participants)

Officers are dispatched via a real time dispatcher to a building and informed by a security officer that a gunman is inside. The officer makes contact with employees in offices and in the hallways. The officer observes a person standing facing him from about 20 feet. The subject observes the officer and flees further into the building. The officer approaches the location where the subject fled and observes a male on the floor bleeding. The officer continues to pursue the subject and makes contact with an employee who directs him down another hallway. The officer observes the subject push a female to the floor who begins screaming, and the subject continues to flee. The subject opens a back door of the building, runs into the street, attempts to hijack a vehicle, continues to run into a wooded area, and turns and fires a handgun at the officer from chest level. Two back-up officers arrive, one toward the back of the subject (about 15 feet) and the other officer arrives at a right oblique angle to the subject's position. These position alignments place the subject in the middle of the pursuing officer and one back-up officer, as he fires at the respondent officer. The scenario duration is about five minutes. Limited inducement of stressors throughout the scenario was employed.

Group 3: Workplace Violence w/Stressors (n = 73/150 participants)

The same scenario as explained for Group 2 was used with the infusion of high intensity stressors. High intensity stressors included: several blasts of air from two vortex cannons directed at the officer, shoot back cannon of pellets directed at the officer at appropriate time to simulate hostile fire, a phone book thrown at the officer by an employee, changes from moderate lighting in the building to extreme sunlight leaving the building, a truck passes close by with a loud horn honking with a blast of air from the vortex cannons, and distracting sounds of a beating heart rhythm with sound increasing throughout the scenario.

Findings

Analysis of the saliva biomarkers revealed that the workplace scenario with stressors produced the largest responses in biomarkers, with significant rises in cortisol, alpha-amylase, and Interleukin (IL-6). Cortisol, alpha-amylase, and IL-6 are major enzymes contained in saliva and during acute stress will show elevated in secretion. While each scenario showed some levels of elevation in the stress response, Group 3 produced the most statistically significant correlation between amylase and IL-6 at 10 minutes ($r = .47$, $p < .001$) and at 30 minutes ($r = .34$, $p < .001$) (see Figures 4.2 and 4.3). These data show the connection between a sympathetic nervous system response and elevated levels of alpha amylase and IL-6 secretions. Perceptions of respondents self-reported perceived scenario stressors (i.e. a stressful scenario, safety, fear, need to apprehend, and felt threatened) were correlated with alpha amylase at 10 and 30 minutes ($r = .25$, $p < .001$). These data affirmatively answered the first research question, that a virtual simulator did produce significant measurable stress associations, most noticeably in Group 3.

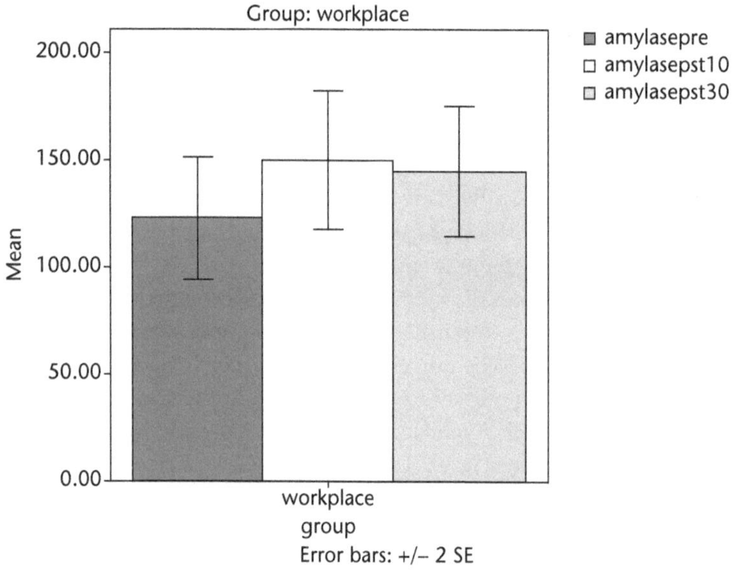

FIGURE 4.2 Workplace w/stressors: Alpha Amylase.

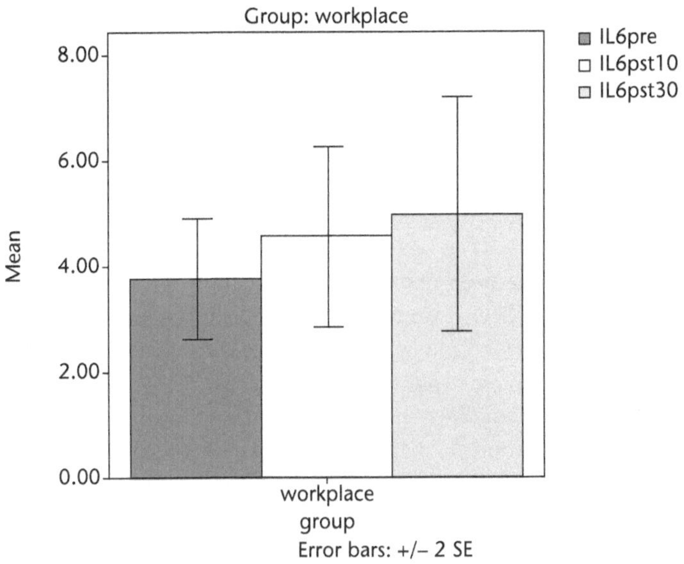

FIGURE 4.3 Workplace w/stressors: IL-6.

Self-Reported Perceived Stressors

After each scenario, respondents answered a series of questions regarding their perception of the scenario. Table 4.2 reveals the differences in self-reported perceptions by scenario as reported by the participants. Percentages of each variable are reported, reflecting whether the respondent experienced the identified stressor.

TABLE 4.2 Self-reported perceptions of selected experienced stressors-post scenario (in percentages)

Variable	*#1 Motorcycle*	*#2 Workplace violence-limited stress*	*#3 Workplace violence stress*
Safety-self	40	72	82
Safety-others	24	68	80
Apprehend	21	84	84
Threatened	34	58	71
Fear	22	35	40
Demanding	24	59	66
Stressful scenario	40	66	86
Able to cope	95	94	96
Thinking	12	14	14
Moving	9	10	10
Increase heart rate	13	58	68
Breathing difficulty	10	20	23
Vision distortion	12	18	18
Auditory distortion	10	16	18

Table 4.2 shows percentage responses to 14 self-reported respondent-perceived stressors completed within 30 minutes of exiting the scenarios. Regardless of scenario, the respondents reported and biomarker results showed that all respondents incurred associated levels of stress. Overall, the motorcycle (Group 1) respondents reported the least amount of perceived threat during the two-minute scenario. A significant percentage of all of the respondents reported concern for personal safety ($r = .45$, $p = <.001$) and that the scenario was stressful ($r = .34$). Respondents in Group 2 and Group 3 reported the need to apprehend the subject, believed the subject presented a threat to themselves and others, and experienced perception of fear ($r = .41$, $p < .001$).

Table 4.3 reveals selected items that should have been observed during each of the scenarios, but were missed by the officer and/or in which the officer had no recollection of the occurrence of the item during the scenario. Each of the items in Table 4.3 can be categorized in seven broad perception distortions: (1) circumstance of the scenario; (2) environment of the scenario; (3) information pertaining to the subject; (4) vision difficulties; (5) auditory difficulties; (6) time distortions; and (7) reaction time. For example, in the motorcycle Group, 1, many respondents missed observing what the subject was wearing, the nature of the traffic stop, the subject reaching across the bike for the firearm, the number of rounds fired by the subject at the officer, and the comments/threats made to the officer by the subject. Officers reported experiencing auditory difficulties with the subject when

TABLE 4.3 Misperceptions of selected stressors encountered by scenario

#1 Motorcycle (N=52) variable / % incorrect	*#2 Workplace violence-limited stress (N=25) variable / % incorrect*	*#3 Workplace violence stress (N=73) variable / % incorrect*
Subject clothes / 61	Subject description / 36	Subject description / 47
Traffic stop / 30	Number of doors checked (4) / 65	Number of doors checked (4) / 67
Verbal threats / 65	Perception of lighting / 76	Perception of lighting / 83
Perception of subject initially / 39	Others encountered (3 males & 3 females) / 53	Others encountered (3 males & 3 females) / 61
Subject reached across bike / 65	Number of fired shots in building by subject / 76	Perception of blood on floor / 82
Rounds fired by subject / 72	Subject assaulted (2 men & 1 woman) / 50	Elderly man said "gun" / 52
Duration of the scenario / 36	Subject had 2 weapons / 79	Subject had 2 weapons / 83
Threatened to cut throat / 59	Subject fired 2 shots (outside) / 60	Subject assaulted (2 men & 1 woman) / 68
	Subject fired from chest level / 65	Subject fired 2 shots (outside) / 71
	Zero rounds fired by responding officers / 67	Subject fired from chest level / 72
	Recall number of rounds fired / 75	Zero rounds fired by responding officers / 68
	Duration of scenario / 64	Recall number of rounds fired / 89
		Duration of scenario / 68
		Sounds in building / 54
Mean (8/29 items) 27% Incorrect perception	Mean (12/40 items) 30% Incorrect perception	Mean (14/44 items) 32% Incorrect perception

he spoke to the officers and when he threatened them. Group 1 respondents misperceived about 29 percent of 28 items contained within the scenario.

In Group 2 and Group 3, the percentage of items misperceived by reporting respondents increased as stressors intensified. Common items misperceived included the actual number of persons encountered during the scenario, failing to observe blood on the floor from a male that had been assaulted by the subject, difficulty recalling statements made by occupants in the building, difficulty in recalling the position the subject pointed the weapon, experiencing auditory difficulties, perception that the subject fired his gun in the building when he actually fired outside, and failing to note that they had fired at the subject with a back-up officer standing directly behind the subject. Group 2 and 3 respondents reported experiencing difficulties with perceived lighting during the scenario, and experienced time distortions regarding the duration of the scenario; they could not recall how many individuals they confronted inside the building, and were unaware that they fired at their back-up officer as the subject positioned himself between the back-up officer and the respondent officer.

Respondents in Group 3 reported that they experienced an increase in heart rates during the scenario (68%). A small percentage of respondents in all three groups reported experiencing difficulties in vision, hearing, or breathing during the scenario. Further, after 48 hours of completing the scenarios, all of the respondents submitted their questionnaires. The overall analysis revealed that recall of the misperceived events improved by about 21 percent in all three groups ($r = .29$; $p < .05$).

Implications

This research has shown that a use of force virtual simulator can induce stress during a lethal force scenario. The results showed an affirmative answer to each research question posed. An important finding in this study was the elevation in the salivary cortisol concentrations (alpha-amylase and IL-6) over a 30-minute period, illustrating that the brain did perceive the scenario as significantly stressful and activated a measurable SNS discharge in the respondents. A significant finding of the study overwhelmingly showed that perceptions of respondents in Group 2 and Group 3 were affected throughout the scenario, as they reported developing a strong concern for their own and others' safety, that the scenario was actually threatening, they felt the need to actually apprehend the suspect, believed that the scenario was demanding, and a moderate number of respondents reported experiencing a perception of fear.

Respondents misperceived a collective total of about 29 percent of the activities within the scenarios. It was shown that perhaps due to the Hawthorne effect, respondents self-reported experiencing varying physiological effects of stress, such as an increase in heart rate, visual and auditory distortions. When these self-reported perceptions are compared with the unobtrusive measurements, the degree of misperceptions increased over self-reported perceptions. The findings of this research reveal that there are varying levels of stress experienced across all three groups, but as scenario stressors intensified, Group 2 and Group 3 respondent perceptions deteriorated. A significant three-way association was evidenced between the respondents' self-reported perceptions during the scenarios, with the biomarker results, and amongst the misperception results. These findings reveal that performance and recall is related to perception and show that as the intensity and the frequency of stressors increased, perception deteriorated.

The misperception or perceptual distortion findings also show that in high stress situations, officers are commonly responding behind the reactionary curve. When an officer is faced with a time pressure decision in response to a subject's motions and actions, it will take a moment to form a perception, process it, and respond. These factors have a direct bearing on the officer's reaction time. The faster the dynamics of a situation unfold, the more likely the officer may form a misperception of the events. In some cases, the officer may not see the action at all. For example, Group 1 respondents reported that the motion the suspect made to reach across the motorcycle was so fast that many of them missed observing the firearm being shot at them. Respondents in Group 2 and Group 3 reported missing seeing that the suspect possessed a second weapon, and reported that the suspect fired in the building when he actually had not.

The operating environment of the officer, combined with confrontational circumstances, can also impact the formation of perceptions and misperceptions. In the workplace violence scenario, the respondents experienced changes in lighting on four occasions and in sounds. The officer entered the building from the outside, pursued the subject through the low lighting of the building, encountered red flashing and clanging security lights, and then abruptly exited the darkened building into glaring sunlight, and as the respondent continues outside, a passing truck blasts its horn. A significant number of the respondents reported that they experienced misperceptions about the incident activities when the lighting of the scenario was considered.

Additional important misperceptions can also be experienced under high levels of stress, which can impact descriptions of individuals or a suspect, misperceive information provided by others, create an inability to recall certain components of the encounter, and misperceive elements of distance and depth perception. For example, a number of respondents in Group 2 and in Group 3 misreported the actual description of the suspect, experienced problems in recalling the number of shots the suspect fired or that they fired, experienced difficulty in recalling the number or gender of the occupants in the building, and experienced difficulty in recalling the number of offices and doors checked. In their collective totality, the respondents experienced distortions or misperceptions including: time, sensory distortions (including visual, auditory), ambiguity of processing information, time distortions and time pressures needed to cognitively process the information, environmental conditions variables, and recall of important elements of the scenario. These misperceptions were associated with respondents' self-reported perceptions of the encounter and with the salivary biomarker findings.

The findings of this research confirm prior studies as perceptual distortions were experienced by a significant number of respondents, demonstrating that the SNS was activated, impacting their recall. The perceptual distortions and misperceptions experienced impaired the respondents' ability to correctly recall certain events during the scenario. The scenarios were continuously flowing, dynamic, injected with frequent stressors, and forced the respondents to make judgments quickly. A significant number of respondents in Group 2 and Group 3 reported they experienced the actual belief to apprehend the subject, developed the need to protect themselves and others, and believed that the suspect presented a threat of harm personally and to others. A moderate number of respondents in these groups experienced a sense of fear during the scenario. Respondents were so focused on the threat the subject posed, misperceptions of some of the events developed, underscoring the principle of selective attention and Type I errors.

These reported perceptions and misperceptions were common across the three groups, were not just endemic of a specific respondent, but based on the situational factors contained within the scenarios. Respondents' recall of reported misperceptions did improve by 21 percent after 48 hours.

Summary

This chapter has provided an overview of the basic physiological and some of the psychological factors which are involved in responding to stressful stimuli and how the brain processes threatening stimuli, preparing a person to respond accordingly. The chapter further addressed how these factors impact an officer-involved shooting. There are many physiological and psychological factors which come into play which are associated in processing stress, and ten published studies demonstrate the frequency and the intensity of these factors commonly experienced by police officers in an officer-involved shooting. These studies rebuff the speculation that experiencing perceptual distortions in an officer-involved shooting is a myth generated in an attempt to otherwise explain why an officer decided to fire his or her firearm during a survival stress encounter. Documenting these stressors in a use of force simulator with veteran officers further underscored the studies' findings as significant. Investigators are encouraged to become familiar with the scientific research presented in this chapter to gain a better understanding of the limits of human performance, which will provide better guidance in conducting the investigation and preparing to interview the involved officer. It is unrealistic to expect that every officer will perform flawlessly under stress and will have total recall in all stressful circumstances, including making a split-second decision involving life or death (Honig & Lewinski, 2008). The investigation checklist in appendix A should be considered by the investigator prior to and after the interview of the involved officers.

Appendix A: Human Factors Checklist

Type of Circumstance

☐ Traffic ☐ Disturbance call ☐ Investigate suspicious person
☐ Welfare check ☐ Making an arrest ☐ Handling/transporting a prisoner
☐ Tactical situation ☐ Cell check ☐ Cell extraction ☐ Booking/intake
☐ Behaviors of subject ☐ Contextual cues ☐ Subject threats
☐ Number of officers ☐ Circumstances quickly changed ☐ Other

Operating Environment

☐ Day ☐ Night ☐ Low light ☐ Shadows ☐ Terrain conditions ☐ Indoors
☐ Outdoors ☐ Low visibility ☐ Contrast of light/objects ☐ Cover/lack of cover
☐ Environmental hazards/conditions ☐ Other

Perceptual Distortions

☐ Spatial distortions ☐ Visual ☐ Auditory ☐ Tactile ☐ Olfactory
☐ Selective attention ☐ Inattentional blindness ☐ Focus on threat
☐ Color distortion ☐ Situational awareness ☐ Memory ☐ Reactionary time
☐ Time pressures ☐ Incident stress ☐ Task overload ☐ Cognitive overload
☐ Ability to communicate ☐ Decision making ☐ Other

Personal

☐ Fatigue ☐ Job stress ☐ Personal stress ☐ Medications ☐ Illness
☐ Time on shift ☐ Days worked in a row ☐ State of mind
☐ Cognitive process ☐ Training history ☐ Overall health ☐ Workload
☐ Other

References

Artwhol, A. (2002). Perceptual and memory distortions during officer involved shootings. *FBI Law Enforcement Bulletin*, 18–24.

Artwhol, A. & Christensen, L. W. (1997). *Deadly force encounters: What officers need to know to mentally and physically prepare for a gun fight*. Boulder, CO: Paladin Press.

Asken, M., Vonk, K., & Sterland, T. (2009). Heart rate variability and police performance. *PoliceOne*. Retrieved from www.policeone.com/healthfitness/articles/1793270-Heart-rate-variability.

Blair, J. P., Pollock, J., Montague, D., Nichols, T., Curnutt, J., & Burns, D. (2011). Reasonableness and reaction time. *Police Quarterly*, *14*(4), 323–343.

Breedlove, H. W. (1995). *The effects of survival stress on the visual system*. Presentation at the PPCT Use of Force Conference, St. Louis, MO.

Breedlove, H. W. (2013). *Tactical Vision*. Presentation at the Tactical Strength and Conditional Conference, Virginia Beach, VA.

Bremner, J. D. (1999). Does stress damage the brain? *Biological Psychiatry*, *45*(7), 797–805.

British Psychological Society Research Board (2008). *Guidelines on memory and the law*. London: The British Psychological Society.

Broome, R. E. (2013). A phenomenological psychological study of the police officer's lived experience of the use of deadly force. *Journal of Humanistic Psychology*, *54*(2), 158–181.

Campbell, J. H. (1992). *A comparative analysis of the effects of post-shooting trauma on the special agents of the Federal Bureau of Investigation*. (Unpublished doctoral dissertation.) Michigan State University, East Lansing, MI.

Cannon, W. B. (1929). *Bodily changes in pain, hunger, fear, and rage*. New York, NY: Appleton.

Carter, R. (1998). *Mapping the mind*. Berkeley: University of California Press.

Chabris, C. & Simons, D. (2009). *The invisible gorilla: How our intuitions deceive us*. New York, NY: Random House.

Damasio, A. R. (1994). *Descartes' error: Emotion, reason, and the human brain*. New York, NY: HarperCollins.

de Quervain, D. J., Roozendall, B., & McGaugh, J. (1998). Stress and glucocorticoids impair retrieval of long-term spatial memory. *Nature*, *394*(6695), 787–790.

Dror, I. E. (2007). Perception of risk and the decision to use force. *Policing*, *1*(3), 265–272.

Dysterheft, J. L., Lewinski, W. J., Seefeldt, D. A., & Pettitt, R. W. (2013). The influence of start position, initial step type, and usage of a focal point on sprinting performance. *International Journal of Exercise Science*, *6*(4), 320–327.

Easterbrook, J. (1959). The effects of emotion on cue utilization and the organization of behavior. *Psychological Review*, *66*, 187–201.

Ebbinghaus, J. A. (1885). *Memory: A contribution to experimental psychology*. New York, NY: Columbia University Press.

Epstein, S. (1994). The integration of the cognitive and psychodynamic unconscious. *American Psychologist*, *49*(8), 709–724.

Gibson, J. J. (1950). *Perception of the visual world*. Boston, MA: Houghton Mifflin.

Gibson, J. J. (1960). *The senses as perceptual senses*. Boston, MA: Houghton Mifflin.

Godnig, E. (2001). Body alarm reaction and sports vision. *Journal of Behavioral Optometry, 12*(1), 3–6.

Gould, D., Petlichkoff, L., Simons, J., & Vevera, M. (1987). Relationship between competitive state anxiety inventory-2 subscale scores and pistol shooting performance. *Journal of Sport Psychology, 9*, 33–42.

Graham v. Connor, 490 U.S. 386 (1989).

Gray, M. J. & Lombardo, T. W. (2001). Complexity of trauma narratives as an index of fragmented memory in PTSD. *Applied Cognitive Psychology, 15*(7), S171-S186.

Gray, R. (2004). Attending to the execution of a complex sensorimotor skill: Expertise differences, choking and slumps. *Journal of Experimental Psychology: Applied, 10*(1), 42–54.

Green, M. (2011). Inattentional blindness and conspicuity. *Human Factors, 53*, 1–6.

Groer, M., Murphy, R. L., Bunnel, W., Solomon, K., Van Eepoel, J., Rankin, B., White, K., & Bykowski, C. (2010). Salivary measures of stress and immunity in police officers engaged in simulated critical incident scenarios. *Journal of Occupational and Environmental Medicine, 52*(6), 595–602.

Grossman, D. & Siddle, B. K. (2004). Critical incident amnesia: The physiological basis and the implications of memory loss during extreme survival stress situations. *The Firearms Instructor, 31*.

Hellhammer, D., Wust, D., & Kudielka, B. (2009). Salivary cortisol as a biomarker in stress research. *Psychoneuroendocrinology, 34*(2), 163–171.

Hillman, M. (1995). Physical lag time and their impact on the use of deadly force. *The Tactical Edge*, 28–31.

Honig, A. & Lewinski, W. J. (2008). A survey of the research on human factors related to lethal force encounters: Implications for law enforcement training, tactics, and testimony. *Law Enforcement Executive Forum, 8*(4), 129–152.

Honig, A. L. & Roland, J. E. (1998). Shots fired: Officer involved. *The Police Chief, 65*, 116–119.

Honig, A. L. & Sultan, S. E. (2004). Reactions and resilience under fire: What an officer can expect. *The Police Chief, 71*(12), 54–60.

Hontz, T. (2000). Justifying the deadly force response. *Police Quarterly, 2*(4), 462–476.

Horowitz, M. J. (1976). *Stress response syndromes*. New York, NY: Jason Aronson Publishers.

Howard, P. J. (2000). *The owner's manual for the brain*. Austin, TX: Bard Press.

Hsieh, S. (2002). Task shifting in dual-task settings. *Perceptual and Motor Skills, 94*(2), 407– 414.

International Association of Chiefs of Police. (2013). *Officer involved shooting guidelines*. Philadelphia, PA: IACP Police Psychological Services Section, 1–12.

James, W. (1890). *The principles of psychology, Vol I*. New York, NY: Henry Holt and Co.

Janis, I. L. & Mann, L. (1977). *Decision making: A psychological analysis of conflict, choice, and commitment*. New York, NY: The Free Press.

Kandel, E. R. (2006). *In search of memory: The emergence of a new science of mind*. New York, NY: W. W. Norton and Company.

Kavanagh, E. L. (2006). A cognitive model of firearms policing. *Journal of Police and Criminal Psychology, 21*(2), 25–36.

Kim, J. J. & Diamond, D. M. (2002). The stressed hippocampus, synaptic plasticity and lost memories. *Neuroscience, 3*, 452–462.

Klein, G. (1998). *Sources of power: How people make decisions*. Cambridge, MA: The MIT Press.

Klinger, D. A. & Brunson, R. K. (2009). Police officers' perceptual distortions during lethal force situations: Informing the reasonableness standard. *Criminology & Public Policy, 8*(1), 117–140.

LeDoux, J. (1996). *The emotional brain*. New York, NY: Touchstone.

Lewinski, B. (2002). Biomechanics of lethal force encounters. *The Police Marksman, 27*(6), 19–23.

Lewinski, B. (2008). The attention study: A study on the presence of selective attention in firearms officers. *Law Enforcement Executive Forum, 8*(6): 107–138.

Loftus, E. F. (1996). *Eyewitness testimony*. Cambridge, MA: Harvard University Press.

Loftus, E. F., Greene, E. L., & Doyle, J. M. (1989). The psychology of eyewitness testimony. In D. C. Raskin (ed.), *Psychological methods in criminal investigations and evidence*. New York, NY: Springer Press.

MacLean, P. (1967). *The triune brain in evolution: Role in paleocerebal functions.* New York, NY: Plenum Press.

Maquet, P. (2000). Sleep on it. *Neuroscience, 3*(12), 1235–1236.

Martens, R. (1977). *Sport competition anxiety test.* Champaign, IL: Human Kinetics.

McGaugh, J. L. (1990). Significance and remembrance: The role of neuromodulatory systems. *Psychological Science, 1*(1), 15–25.

McGrath, J. E. (1970). Major methodological issues. In J. E. McGrath (ed.), *Social and psychological factors in stress.* New York, NY: Rhinehart and Winston.

McKinney v. Duplain, Lexis 87821(C.D. Ind. 2008).

Miller, J. O. & Low, K. (2001). Motor processes in simple, go/no go, and choice reaction time tasks: A psychophysiological analysis. *Journal of Experimental Psychology: Human Perception and Performance, 27*(2), 266–289.

Miller, L. (2006). Officer involved shooting: Reaction patterns, response protocols, and psychological intervention strategies. *International Journal of Emergency Mental Health*, 8(4), 239–254.

Miller, L. (2015). Why cops kill: The psychology of police deadly force encounters. *Aggression and Violent Behavior, 22*, 97–111.

Neilson, E. (1981). *The law enforcement officer's use of deadly force and post-shooting reactions.* Salt Lake City, UT: Salt Lake City Police Department.

Payne, J. D. & Nadel, L. (2004). Sleep, dreams, memory consolidation: The role of the stress hormone cortisol. *Learning and Memory, 11*, 671–678.

Payne, J. D., Nadel, L., Allen, J. J. B., Thomas, K. G. F., & Jacobs, W. J. (2002). The effects of experimentally induced stress on false recognition. *Memory, 10*(1), 1–6.

Pinizzotto, A. J., Davis, E. F., Bohrer, S. B., & Infanti, B. J. (2012). Law enforcement restraint in the use of deadly force within the context of "the deadly mix." *International Journal of Police Science & Management, 14*(4), 285–298.

Plihal, W. & Born, J. (1999). Effects of early and late nocturnal sleep on priming and spatial memory. *Psychophysiology, 36*(5), 571–582.

Ratey, J. J. (2001). *A user's guide to the brain: Perception, attention, and the four theatres of the brain.* New York, NY: Pantheon Books.

Ross, D. L. (2016). Assessing officer involved shootings: Contextual cues and responses. Presentation at the Academy of Criminal Justice Sciences conferences, Denver, CO.

Ross, D. L., Murphy, R. L. & Hazlett, M. H. (2012). Analyzing perceptions and misperceptions of police officers in lethal force virtual simulator scenarios. *Law Enforcement Executive Forum, 12*(3), 53–73.

Ross, D. L. & Siddle, B. K. (2003). An analysis of the effects of survival stress in police use of force encounters. *Law Enforcement Executive Forum, 3*(2), 9–26.

Salas, H. & Driskell, J. (1996). *Stress and human performance.* Mahwah, NJ: L. Erlbaum Associates.

Sapolsky, R. M. (2004). *Why zebras don't get ulcers* (3rd ed.). New York, NY: St. Martin's.

Schwartz, J. M. & Begley, S. (2002). *The mind and the brain.* New York, NY: HarperCollins.

Selye, H. (1936). A syndrome produced by nocuous agents. *Nature, 138*, 32–36.

Selye, H. (1959). *The stress of life.* New York, NY: McGraw-Hill.

Selye, H. (1978). *The stress of life* (2nd ed.). New York, NY: McGraw-Hill.

Sharps, M.J. (2010). *Processing under pressure.* Flushing, NY: Looseleaf Law Publications, Inc.

Shomstein, S. & Yantis, S. (2004). Control of attention shifts between vision and audition in human cortex. *The Journal of Neuroscience, 24*(47), 10702–10706.

Siddle, B. K. & Breedlove, H. (1995, May/June). How stress affects vision and shooting stance. *The Police Marksman*, 16–20.

Simons, D. J. (2003). *Surprising studies of visual awareness* (DVD). Champaign, IL: Visco Productions.

Simons, D. J. & Levin, D. T. (1998). Failure to detect changes to people during a real-world interaction. *Psychonomic Bulletin and Review, 5*, 644–649.

Smith, G. (1990). Evaluation of law enforcement officer combat handgun skills. *Smith and Wesson Academy Newsletter, 15*, 5–9.

Solomon, R. M. (2001). *Coping with vulnerability: The dynamics of fear in critical incidents and training, implications.* Tacoma, WA: Washington State Patrol.

Solomon, R. M. & Horn, J. M. (1986). Post-shooting traumatic reactions: A pilot study. In J. T. Reese & H. A. Goldstein (eds), *Psychological services for law enforcement*. Washington, DC: U.S. Government Printing Office.

Thackery, R. L. & Touchstone, R. M. (1983). *Rate of initial memory recall and monitoring performance following a simulated emergency involving startle.* Washington, DC: Federal Aviation Administration, Office of Aviation Medicine.

Vickers, J. N. (2007). *Perception, cognition and decision training: The quiet eye in action.* Champaign, IL: Human Kinetics.

Violanti, J. M., Andrew, M., Burchfiel, C. M., Hartley, T. A., Charles, L. E., & Miller, D. B. (2007). Posttraumatic stress symptoms and cortisol patterns among police officers. *Policing: An International Journal of Police Strategies and Management, 30*(2), 169–188.

Williams, J., Allen, R., & Stein, A. (1999). *Air traffic specialist: Visual scanning.* Washington, DC: U.S. Department of Transportation.

World Health Organization (WHO). (1998). *WHO international classification of diseases* (10th ed.). Atlanta, GA: World Health Organization.

Xie, L., Kang, H., Oiwu, X., Chen, M. J., Yonghong, L., Meenakshiunearam, T., & Nedergarrd, M. (2013). Sleep drives metabolic clearance from the adult brain. *Science*, 342, 373–377.

Yerkes, R. M. & Dodson, J. D. (1908). The relation of strength of stimulus to rapidity of habit-formation. *Journal of Comparative Neurology and Psychology, 18*(5), 459–482.

5

MEMORY AND DECISION MAKING UNDER STRESS

Alexis Artwohl

Introduction

Human cognitive processes such as attention and perception, memory, and decision making are incredibly complex. Although behavioral scientists have discovered much over the past century, we are still in the early stages of understanding what many scientists consider one of the most complex structures in the known universe: the human brain.

How the mind works is highly relevant to the criminal justice system. The criminal justice system is concerned primarily with human behavior and issues such as memory, eyewitness recall, and how people make decisions are often brought to bear. Unfortunately, sometimes myths, assumptions, and personal opinions are used to make judgments of human behavior, including memory, rather than facts which have been validated by research.

Unreliability of Memory for Detail

Research shows that memory is often quite unreliable (Artwohl, 2002, 2003; British Psychological Society Research Board, 2008; Chabris & Simons, 2010; Deffenbacher et al., 2004; Fisher & Geiselman, 1992; Morgan et al., 2004; Sapolsky, 2004; Schacter, 2001; Sharps, 2010; Sharps et al., 2003; Terry, 1997; U.S. Department of Justice, 1999; Wells & Olson, 2003; Wells & Quilivan, 2009).

One misconception is that memories are like recordings of an event that can simply be replayed later; however, this is not true. Memory is in fact a creative, reconstructive process, quite prone toward gaps, errors, false memories, emotional influences, and bias. This is why each time a person recalls a memory the details may change from one telling to another. Another misconception is that faulty memory of dramatic events is due to "stress." While stress can indeed influence the formation and retrieval of memory, it is a fallacy that this is the only reason. In fact, memory for details of ordinary, everyday life is also highly prone to error (Schacter, 2001).

Two research-based books written for lay people on this topic are *The Seven Sins of Memory* by Dr. Daniel Schacter (2001), a psychologist who runs a memory lab at Harvard University, and *The Invisible*

Gorilla by Dr. Christopher Chabris and Dr. Daniel Simons (2010), who are research psychologists at Union College and the University of Illinois, respectively. Chabris and Simons (2010) point out that people often overestimate the accuracy of memory. They call this the "illusion of memory." We are unaware of how faulty our memory is because most of the time, quite frankly, no one really cares exactly what we remember and no one is motivated to find out what really happened.

As Schacter (2001, 1) points out, "Memory plays such a pervasive role in our daily lives that we often take it for granted until an incident of forgetting or distortion demands our attention." This is exactly what happens to officers involved in shootings and other events (Artwohl, 2002; Artwohl, 2003; Honig & Sultan, 2004; Hope et al., 2016; Klinger, 2001; Lewinski, 2008; Lewinski et al., 2016; Ross, Murphy, & Hazlett, 2012; Ross & Siddle, 2003), and to other witnesses in the criminal justice system. The criminal justice system now takes a very keen interest in every detail of witnesses' memories and this sometimes does not bode well for everyone involved. Chabris and Simons (2010, 76) report:

> In many cases, memory distortions and embellishments are minor matters, but in some contexts they have tremendous consequences, precisely because of the illusion of memory. When people are subject to the illusion of memory, they impugn the intentions and motivations of those who are innocently misremembering.

Schacter (2001, 10) remarks that once people are educated about how error-prone memory is,

> you might easily conclude that evolution burdened mankind with an extremely inefficient memory system—so prone to error that it often jeopardizes our well-being. ... I take issue with this conclusion, and argue instead that the seven sins of memory are by-products of otherwise adaptive properties of memory.

It appears that evolution has programmed our brain for survival, not for the convenience of the criminal justice system. Our brain wants us to remember the gist of events, especially dangerous events, and the important take-away lesson for our future survival. It doesn't really care about the details. However, when our brain starts to interface with the criminal justice system, all of sudden everybody wants highly historically accurate, detailed memory from the witnesses and now "the devil's in the details."

Wells and Quilivan (2009) reviewed the many factors that can influence the accuracy of eyewitness memory and how this research intersects with the current legal standards as defined by *Manson v. Brathwaite* (1977). They concluded that:

> Manson was a reasonable proposition in 1977, but we know much more today. ... Both biological science (via DNA) and social science (via eyewitness identification experiments) have shed new light on the eyewitness identification errors and have revealed these errors to be much more prevalent than the 1977 court could have surmised. ... In a joint effort between social science and the law, we should be able to create a system that provides stronger incentives to eliminate unnecessarily suggestive procedures without excluding reliable identifications.
>
> *(Wells & Quilivan, 2009, 21)*

Terry (1997, 21) agrees and states,

> An eyewitness's testimony can be inaccurate. Human memory is not like physical recorders. Instead, memory is active, not passive; dynamic, not static; reconstructive, not reproductive. Eyewitnesses, with limiting preconceptions and limited perceptual systems, process only a small part of a scene. Their impressions are recorded in memory where they risk being contaminated by previously and subsequently acquired information.

He recommends that, "The cause of justice can be advanced by introducing expert eyewitness testimony on the state of scientific knowledge of eyewitness behavior so that the triers of fact can critically evaluate the specific eyewitness evidence before them" (Terry, 1997, 23).

Narrative vs. Historical Truth

The criminal justice system is obviously invested in finding out if witnesses are telling the "truth." As many philosophers have pointed out, determining what is "true" can be a complicated undertaking.

One way of looking at the truth is to remember that everyone has a "Narrative Truth," which is defined as their sincere beliefs about what they think happened. Another kind of truth is "Historical Truth," which is what really happened. We know from the research on how memory for details is highly prone to error that the Narrative Truth of eyewitnesses and the Historical Truth are unlikely to perfectly match. These differences between the two kinds of truth will range from small to large for any given eyewitness or event. *If witnesses provide statements during which they are honestly relating their Narrative Truth as they know it, and it is not consistent with Historical Truth as determined by objective evidence, that does not mean they are lying.*

What is more important, Narrative Truth or Historical Truth? This is a fascinating question and the answer depends on the perspective of the person answering it. Investigators are tasked with determining Historical Truth, i.e., what happened as best they can determine. This important task is fraught with obstacles, including conflicting honest eyewitness statements, witnesses who lie to mislead the investigators, lack of physical evidence, seemingly objective evidence such as videotapes that in themselves can actually distort reality and lead to erroneous conclusions, the human limitations of the investigators themselves, and the human limitations of all the other humans representing the criminal justice system. The criminal justice system has to deal with the reality that there will be parts of the Historical Truth of some events that will simply remain unknowable.

Although finding out what really happened is certainly important, Narrative Truth is also important, especially to those who are being investigated. There are multiple human performance factors that will influence the perceptions and judgment of officer decision making that can lead to honest mistake-of-fact officer-involved shooting (OIS) situations, such as an uncooperative and potentially dangerous suspect in low light conditions who turns on officers, pulls out a dark object and points it at them, and gets shot because the contextual cues lead officers to sincerely believe that the suspect's cell phone was a gun. Should the officers be held accountable for shooting an "unarmed" suspect, or are their reactions justified based on the "totality of the circumstances"?

Attorney Mike Stone, who has represented many police officers, addresses this issue in an article discussing the legal issues involved in whether or not multiple officers involved in an OIS have the right to jointly consult with their attorneys and representatives before speaking to investigators (Stone & Berger, 2008). He states that:

> Based on hundreds of such events over 30 years, we do not permit involved officers and deputies to "commingle" their statements, even if their agencies permit them the opportunity to do so. … It is far better to keep individual recollections pure, and it is necessary that the officers be held accountable *only for what they saw or perceived.*
>
> *(Stone & Berger, 2008, 5)*

The answer to the question of which is more important, Narrative Truth or Historical Truth, is that they are both important in the complicated journey to find justice in any given situation. Given that they are both important, it is complicated to come to a firm conclusion about whether or not officers should be allowed to, or should even want to, confer, view videotapes, and be exposed to other physical evidence before they participate in providing a statement. Although all these can help officers and other witnesses have a better knowledge about the Historical Truth of an event, they also have the potential to contaminate the witnesses' Narrative Truths. This may or may not be in the best interest of the officers and/or the investigation. This is a decision that all the stakeholders in an OIS, including the officers, will have to make based on the unique circumstances of each event.

Videotapes and other physical evidence can provide valuable information for investigators. However, a critical point to remember about videotapes is that although they can be very compelling, and many people in and out of the criminal justice system believe that they somehow represent absolute reality, *nothing could be further from the truth.* Force Science News (2015) provides a discussion on the limitations and problems with videotapes.

> Certainly, a camera can provide more information about what happened on the street. But it can't necessarily provide all the information needed to make a fair and impartial final judgment. There still may be influential human factors involved, apart from what the camera sees.
>
> *(Force Science News, 2015)*

Cameras also have inherent problems themselves, such as camera speed, recording in 2D instead of 3D, etc.

The Steps of Memory

The criminal justice system is commonly concerned with events and what participants and eyewitnesses remember about these events—who, what, where, when, how. A greatly simplified model about how memories are formed and retrieved is that memory involves a series of three steps: (1) *encoding*, (2) *retention*, and (3) *retrieval* (Fisher & Geiselman, 1992). During *encoding*, people must be paying attention to the information in the first place and then hold it in short-term memory (also known as working memory) long enough to use it to respond to the demands of the situation. During the second step, *retention*, the information has to be transferred into long-term memory storage where it may be available for future use. During the third step, *retrieval*, the information has to be remembered, i.e., retrieved from memory storage, if it is to be used or transmitted to other individuals. Although this sounds simple, it is a very complex process and much of it is still not well understood. We will review some of the basics in this process, as they are currently known.

Encoding

Paying Attention

People often think they are paying attention to most, or even all, of what is happening right in front of them, but this is rarely true. Research has shown that people are only capable of paying attention to very limited amounts of information at any one point in time (Chabris & Simons, 2010; Lewinski, 2008; Mack & Rock, 1998; Shomstein & Yantis, 2004; Simons & Chabris, 1999). This is known as selective attention. The brain cannot pay 100 percent attention to all information all the time, so it will pick only certain stimuli and ignore the rest. Which stimuli it will pick totally depends on the judgments the brain is constantly making about what is most relevant for the person's well-being and survival from one millisecond to another. This is happening all the time, not just during shootings or other high stress events.

Chabris and Simons (2010) vividly illustrated this with their famous series of "invisible gorilla" experiments, in which they showed people a video and gave them a visual task to perform, such as counting cars or counting passes of a basketball between players. For those who followed the instructions, many totally failed to see a person in a gorilla suit sauntering right through the middle of the scene. They point out that

> the gorilla study illustrates, perhaps more dramatically than any other, the powerful and pervasive influence of the illusion of attention. We experience far less of our visual world than we think we do. … we assume that visually distinctive or unusual objects will draw our attention but in reality they often go completely unnoticed.
>
> *(Chabris & Simons, 2010, 7)*

There are also visual limitations, such as the fact that the eye actually has only a narrow field of vision that it can clearly focus on at one time (Vickers, 2007). Much of what you see at any one time is in your blurry peripheral vision and it is easy to not see or to misinterpret that visual data, especially for things that are novel or unexpected.

The individuals who did not see the obvious gorilla sauntering through the videos were experiencing a form of selective attention called "inattentional blindness." There are many ways the brain can allocate attentional resources: attention can be internal vs. external, narrow vs. broad, voluntary vs. captured, focused on one sensory modality over another, etc. Besides inattentional blindness, people also experience inattentional deafness (i.e., "auditory exclusion"), inattentional numbness, fail to notice that things are changing right before their eyes, and a host of other attention phenomena that greatly influence what they perceive and remember later (Fougnie, 2008; Lewinski, 2008; Mack & Rock, 1998).

Interpretations of Stimuli

Stimuli that are meaningful to an individual are the most likely to be noticed (Chabris & Simons, 2010; Vickers & Lewinski, 2012). What is meaningful? That will obviously vary depending on the individual and the situation. Each person's brain is constantly filtering all incoming information and using each unique lifetime of experience to decide what it means and to which it is the most important to pay attention. In looking at the difference between amateurs and experts on any given task, research shows that experts excel in part because they are much better able to immediately grasp and pay attention to meaningful stimuli and filter out those that are not relevant to the task at hand (Vickers, 2007; Vickers & Lewinski, 2012). This finely tuned ability to focus on the most relevant stimuli comes from effortful practice and experience over time, and it may or may not be done in a conscious manner (Vickers & Lewinski, 2012). People are also more likely to notice things that they expect to see but miss things that are unexpected (Chabris & Simons, 2010).

Perceptual Bias

Through a lifetime of experience, the brain becomes wired to interpret input in certain ways. In their discussion of visual illusions, Purves, Wojtack, and Howe (2008) point out that,

> The hypothesis is that all visual percepts are generated empirically to facilitate successful behavior, and were never intended to correspond to the physical properties of the world or our measurements of these properties. From this perspective, illusions do not reflect any inadequacy or imperfection of visual function, but are rather signatures of its core strategy.

There are many types of optical illusions that can powerfully fool the brain into seeing things in certain ways that are not actually true. Even when people are shown that their perceptions are false, the optical illusion is so overwhelming that they still cannot force themselves to see it accurately.

These optical illusions occur frequently in real life as well, and the resulting perceptual bias can cause people to see or hear things that will prove inaccurate when compared to objective evidence that might be available.

Context

The context in which the information is received can powerfully influence the interpretation of the information, the action people take, and their memory of the event. The Supreme Court refers to context as "the totality of the circumstances" (Ross, 2013; Sharps & Hess, 2008). It can lead to lightning quick correct decisions or tragic misunderstandings. For example, let's assume a man is home alone in the evening and he hears someone coming up the front steps onto the porch. He looks out the peephole and sees a masked individual holding a gun and a bag. He immediately opens the door. Foolish? What if it is Halloween Night? Chances are high that it is simply another trick or treater and there will be no harm done. However, what if it is *not* Halloween and the now frightened homeowner immediately calls the police. The police shortly arrive and see the masked individual on the porch. The police order him to put down the gun but instead he runs down the stairs, pointing the gun in their direction and they shoot him. When it all gets sorted out, it turns out the masked individual was a drunken friend of the homeowner. The gun is a fake and the drunken friend was trying to play a practical joke. In this example, the context was partly determined by whether or not it was occurring on Halloween.

In addition to the situational and external context of an event, each individual has a lifetime of experiences that will cause him or her to frame the event based on his or her own internal context. Let's assume the homeowner in the above example has repeatedly been the butt of his drunken friend's practical jokes in the recent past and he now believes the masked stranger may well be his friend playing yet another practical joke on him. Instead of immediately calling the police, he might talk to the masked individual through the closed door to try and determine his identity. If it is determined that it is indeed his friend, the police may not be called at all. If the homeowner can't determine the masked individual's identity, the police are called and, as in the above example, they shoot the masked individual, the officers' behavior can also be judged based on the internal context as interpreted by each observer. For instance, if the masked individual was in fact a stranger getting ready to break in, the homeowner will be inclined to see this behavior as threatening and believe the police were totally justified in shooting him. If the masked individual turns out be his drunken friend, the homeowner's grief and guilt may result in him perceiving this same behavior as erratic, but not dangerous, and lead him to believe that the "trigger-happy" police were overly quick to shoot him. The event is exactly the same, but changing the external and internal contexts of the situation can result in dramatically different interpretations and outcomes.

Sharps and Hess (2008) highlighted the importance of context in a series of experiments designed to test people's ability to rapidly process information in a scene likely to be encountered by police officers. They showed a series of photographs depicting a potentially violent crime to college students, who then had to make a quick "shoot—no shoot" decision by pressing a button. They manipulated several variables, including whether or not the "perpetrator" was brandishing a gun vs. a power screwdriver, a simple vs. a more complex scene, and the presence or absence of a potential victim. They found that in the condition where a lone perpetrator was armed with a gun in a simple environment with *no* potential victim present, 64 percent of the students decided to shoot the perpetrator. Adding a potential victim and bystanders to the scene raised the shoot decisions to 88 percent. Again, using the same scene, this time with the perpetrator holding a power screwdriver instead of a gun, resulted in 84.8 percent of the students deciding to shoot the unarmed perpetrator. Although the students were untrained, they were operating in a well-lighted, relatively low stress environment. Sharps and Hess (2008) pointed out that police officers are often forced to make the same decisions in highly stressful, dynamic situations, frequently under conditions of darkness or semidarkness, with stimuli which may be occluded or partially occluded by objects in the environment, including the suspect's clothing and posture. It's not surprising that uncooperative suspects brandishing objects that are not guns are occasionally shot by police who are influenced by complex contextual cues to perceive the object as a weapon. The same thing can happen to citizens caught up in sudden, stressful situations.

Short-term Memory

Once people have noticed and interpreted stimuli, they briefly keep them in short-term memory, also called working memory (LeDoux, 1996; Schacter, 2001). This is called short-term because the information is necessary to complete a task at hand but is not necessarily something that needs to be retained for future reference. People can retain only a small amount of information in working memory so the brain will choose only a few bits and ignore the rest. An example is trying to remember a novel phone number just long enough to dial it. In order to not instantly forget the phone number, people will often repeat it over and over on their way to the phone to keep the digits in their short-term memory. However, within a short period of time after dialing, they will have forgotten the phone number because it did not get transferred into long-term memory storage. This forgetting can happen very rapidly, in a matter of seconds, and is complicated by the fact that people often engage in behavior that is outside of their own conscious awareness. Not all information in short-term memory gets transferred into long-term memory. Thus, individuals may experience or even do things during an event of which they later have no conscious memory. There are many factors that will influence whether or not information is stored into long-term memory where it is retained for future use. Here is an actual case in point:

> I was in a high speed pursuit with a bunch of other officers, chasing a known felon with a long history of violent behavior. When he started firing the gun out the window, I had the disturbing thought that I may not live through this. In spite of the fear, my training kicked in, I performed well, and we killed the suspect before he killed us.
>
> When I finally got home, my wife made a comment about listening to the pursuit over the phone. I had no idea what she was talking about. It turns out that during the pursuit, I had called her on the cellular phone in my patrol car to tell her I loved her in case I didn't make it. My wife said she told me to hang up and concentrate on my driving.
>
> I had no memory at all of making that call.
>
> *(Artwohl & Christensen, 1997, 43)*

Retention

Declarative vs. Procedural

Memory is very complex. As LeDoux (1996, 180) points out, "there are multiple memory systems in the brain each devoted to different memory functions." There are many ways to categorize the types of long-term memories that people retain. One distinction is between declarative and procedural memory. Declarative memory refers to conscious, specific memories about people, places, events, etc. An example would be remembering what you ate for breakfast. Procedural memory refers to our ability to remember how to do things without consciously thinking about them, such as riding a bicycle.

If a person is driving a car and something darts out in front of the car, he or she will pretty reliably slam on the brakes without conscious thought. Thanks to repeated practice, the procedural memory of slamming on the brake to avoid hitting something comes to the rescue. The declarative memories would consist of exactly what it was that darted out in front of car, where it came from, how fast was it going, how fast was the car going, how long the event took, how far did the car travel, etc. Not surprisingly, many people in this situation would be fuzzy on many of these details, thus having an imperfect declarative memory of the event in spite having no hesitation in hitting the brakes based on procedural memory.

LeDoux (1996) recounts a fascinating example of this distinction. Nearly 100 years ago, Swiss psychologist Claparede had a patient who had anterograde amnesia, which is the inability to form new memories. Patients with this devastating disability cannot transfer any information from short-term to long-term memory and thus very quickly forget everything they are exposed to. You could meet these patients hundreds of times and each time they would think they were meeting you for the first time. Dr. Claparede's patient had this experience—she had met him numerous times, yet each time she saw him, it was like a brand new introduction. One day Dr. Claparede concealed a pin in his palm so when the patient met the "new" doctor, she got a painful prick. When Dr. Claparede showed up the next day for his usual new introduction, the patient refused to shake his hand even though she could not tell him why. She had no declarative memory of the event, the doctor, or why she subconsciously (i.e., procedurally) refused to touch his hand. The literature of neuroscience is full of people with all types of unusual and seemingly illogical memory performances such as this one, illustrating the multi-layered complexity of memory formation and retrieval.

The criminal justice system is often mostly concerned with declarative memories. However, it is important to always remember that there are many subconscious influences that can bias declarative memory, even if the eyewitness and the investigator have no direct conscious knowledge of them.

The Effects of Stress on Memory

Memory for details of everyday life is often unreliable. What about when people are under stress?

There is no question that events which have a strong emotional component, positive or negative, will form memories that are more vivid and long lasting than everyday humdrum experiences (Porter & Peace, 2007). There is evidence that this is particularly true for memories connected with fear and other negative emotions. People will forget most of what happens in their daily life, yet will always remember their wedding day or the car wreck they were in, even if they get some of the details wrong. There are a variety of reasons for this. Events that are distinctive and unusual, that stand out from the background of everyday life, are more likely to be "memorable." McGaugh (2003) and LeDoux (1996) both point out that highly emotional events, especially fearful events, are subject to the influence of stress hormones that have been shown to make memories more vivid and persistent. Memorable events are also likely to be thought of more often than everyday humdrum events, and thus benefit from rehearsal of the memory, thereby strengthening them. However, the criminal justice system is often concerned with the *details* of emotionally laden, high stress events, and how well eyewitnesses can remember and *accurately* report those details. As we can see from the discussion above, normal everyday memory is fraught with errors from myriad sources. Cooperative eyewitnesses are frequently trying to provide information about upsetting events, often of short duration, that are usually experienced under high levels of emotional and physiological arousal caused by stress. So what is the effect of stress on memory for details? Research shows the answer is not simple, and it depends on how much perceived stress the eyewitness is experiencing.

Sapolsky (2004, 28) sums up the research on stress and memory accuracy, stating that, "Recent research shows just how short-term stressors of mild to moderate severity enhance cognition and memory, whereas major or prolonged stressors disrupt them." He points out that mild to moderate stressors can be experienced as stimulating, helping people become more alert and focused. However, "memory formation and retrieval go awry when stressors become too big or too prolonged" (Sapolsky, 2004, 32).

Deffenbacher et al. (2004) agree with his summary. Their literature review and research points out that mild levels of stress result in the *arousal* level of attention, that "the arousal mode of neuronal control functions to support alert wakefulness and responsiveness to environmental change and novel stimulation. … Presumably nonthreatening eyewitness events would elicit the arousal mode" (Deffenbacher et al., 2004, 688). They point out this is likely to result in enhanced memory.

However, at higher levels of stress, Deffenbacher et al. (2004) state that people switch into a defensive response set that they refer to as the *activation* mode of attention, which is more likely to be characterized by processing under tight attention controls and a bias against stimulus change, resulting in impaired memory in individuals who are experiencing higher levels of perceived threat and resulting anxiety. They did a series of experiments which supported the finding that higher levels of stress resulted in more memory impairment. They also point out that:

> we would be remiss if we did not issue a further caveat concerning the modest obtained effect size. ... All stress manipulations in the literature that we have examined quite likely do not reach the stress-inducing levels of extra-laboratory violent crime scenes. Thus an effect size of −.31 is perhaps serious underestimate of the debilitating effects of stress engendered by violent crime.
>
> *(Deffenbacher et al., 2004, 703)*

Deffenbacher et al. (2004) also point out the difficulty of replicating lab conditions that are stressful enough to simulate real life stressors that would approach the magnitude often experienced by eyewitnesses in the criminal justice system. However, Morgan et al. (2004) capitalized on a naturally occurring source of real life stress, namely, military training. The US military has developed reality training designed to help combat personnel who are trapped in enemy territory evade capture and, if captured, to endure being a prisoner of war (POW). Morgan et al. (2004) developed a training exercise in which 509 military personnel volunteered to be research subjects. The subjects were "captured" and taken to a simulated POW camp and interrogated by the "enemy." To test the effect of stress on eyewitness recall accuracy, the subjects were interrogated twice during captivity. One was a high stress interrogation, which included real physical confrontations, and the other was a low stress interrogation without physical confrontation. Each interrogation lasted 40 minutes and was completed four hours apart, with the order randomized among subjects. After the training exercise was complete, the subjects were allowed access to food and rest for 24 hours. They were then asked to identify their interrogators. The researchers found that for more than half of the subjects, their ability to correctly identify their interrogator was significantly better in the low compared to the high stress interrogation. A minority had better memory in the high stress condition, and the rest had the same level of accuracy for both the low and high stress interrogation. They concluded their research confirms the significantly deleterious effects of high stress levels on memory, as subjects who had spent 40 minutes with interrogators failed to correctly identify them. Furthermore, the researchers point out that the subjects, special-operations military personnel subjected to rigorous selection and training, are arguably more stress resistant and level headed than the average citizen caught up in a sudden stressful event. So if these military personnel can experience memory impairment from high levels of stress, it is probably even more true for the average person and the average cop (Morgan et al., 2004).

It should be noted that a minority of the military personnel in this study actually had better memory in the high stress interrogations. This speaks to the fact that stress is, to some degree, in the hearts, minds, and even the genes of the individuals. A situation that may overwhelm one individual and degrade memory may be pleasantly exciting to another and thus enhance memory. The degree of stress experienced by each of the individuals in a stressful event will be a complex combination of the event itself and the individual characteristics of those who are experiencing it.

Memory and Post-Traumatic Stress Disorder

Sometimes the inevitable memory gaps, errors, and other phenomena associated with participants and witnesses involved in a shooting are explained as being caused by trauma. There is no question that shootings are stressful and potentially traumatizing and this can have an influence, but research shows that only a minority of recovery and rescue workers in critical incidents, even one as severe as the World Trade Center event, will develop post-traumatic stress disorder (PTSD) (Neria, DeGrande, & Adams, 2011). Neria et al. (2011, 442) point out that:

> Humans possess an impressive capacity to adapt to extremely adverse situations. Most studies of 9/11-related PTSD documented that significant proportions of the samples studied were either not affected or only minimally affected by the attacks. Resilient individuals have been found to manifest mild stress reactions in the immediate aftermath of disasters, but it has been shown that these reactions are not likely to significantly interfere with continued functioning and are typically of short duration.

So, the influence of selective attention, perception, short-term memory limitations, etc., is more important in explaining the memory gaps and errors of individuals in critical incidents. However, for the minority who will develop PTSD, the literature on how it might impact memory can be relevant.

There is ongoing debate over the nature of memories in PTSD as to whether they are special, or simply a natural variation on all the factors mentioned above that can influence memory in any high stress situation. Most agree that memories of traumatic events tend to be unusually persistent and vivid, which is to be expected from a highly emotional event that represents danger. Porter and Peace (2007) did a prospective study of memory for traumatic events at intervals of 3 months, 3.45 years, and 5.0 years. They found that ratings of vividness, overall quality, and sensory components of the memories were virtually unchanged for traumatic memories but declined for positive memories. In reference to the historical accuracy of the memories, they pointed out "in the absence of video recordings of the original events, we could not establish the ground truth and were limited to examining the memory consistency, not necessarily the reliability" (Porter & Peace, 2007, 440). So, the memories may be vivid and persistent, but not necessarily a totally accurate representation of what actually happened. Also, the details of the traumatic memories may change over time.

Ehlers, Hackmann, and Michael (2004), in their review of the literature on PTSD and memory, distinguish two kinds of memory in individuals with PTSD. One is *intrusive re-experiencing*, which usually consists of "sensory impressions and emotional responses from the trauma that appear to lack a time perspective and a context" (Ehlers et al., 2004, 403). This type of memory is typically involuntary and not wanted by the eyewitness. The other type is *intentional recall*, which they found "may be characterized by confusion about temporal order, and difficulty in accessing important details, both of which contribute to problematic appraisals" (Ehlers et al., 2004, 403).

Decision Making Under Stress

Scientists studying cognition have known for years that people process information and make decisions using two different decision-making methods. These are often known as *rational* vs. *intuitive*, but are given different names by different researchers (Artwohl & Christensen, 1997; Epstein, 1994;

Kahneman, 2011; Klein, 1998; Sharps, 2010). *Rational* decision making is often characterized as slow, logical, deliberate, sequential, conscious, analytical, effortful, thoughtful, fact-based, open to rapid change based on new information, reflective, oriented toward delayed action, and based on rules. This powerful analytical tool enables humans to build skyscrapers, send people to the moon, make them less likely jump to conclusions, and helps detectives solve complex investigative cases. However, it has a potentially fatal flaw, which is it takes so long that it may get someone killed or injured if he or she faces an emergency situation that requires an immediate response. Therefore, humans have another method of decision making, often known as *intuitive*, that can happen much faster than rational thought. When faced with a sudden, potentially threatening event, the brain switches to this intuitive mode of processing, which is characterized as very fast, emotionally-based, effortless, automatic, decreased conscious thought, associative rather than sequential, less open to change, more likely to respond based on previous experience, less reflective and introspective, action oriented, and more influenced by immediate contextual cues. Although rational decision making may be more powerful in non-emergency situations, many people revert to the intuitive method anyway because it is easier. The intuitive system is often referred to by people as "gut instinct," "sixth sense," and other terms, which highlight the fact that the decision making is experienced at a subconscious level.

The research of LeDoux (1996) has highlighted that these two types of decision making are biologically different, and this difference allows people faced with sudden danger to get a "sixth sense" that something is immediately wrong before the conscious mind is aware of it. Therefore, the intuitive system can make a lightning fast judgment and take immediate action that can be lifesaving before the conscious, rational mind can figure out what is even going on.

Dr. Daniel Kahneman of Princeton University is one of the leading researchers in this area. His book, *Thinking, Fast and Slow* (2011), distills the research into a book written for lay people. He calls intuitive thinking "System 1" and points out that it "operates automatically and quickly, with little or no effort and no sense of voluntary control" (Kahneman, 2011, 20). Rational thinking is "System 2" and "allocates attention to the effortful mental activities that demand it, including complex computations. The operations of System 2 are often associated with the subjective experience of agency, choice, and concentration" (Kahneman, 2011, 21). Kahneman (2011) points out that because intuitive decision making requires less effort than rational thinking, people are inclined to rely on the intuitive decision-making process, resulting in fairly lax monitoring of the rational system over the intuitive system. This can lead to errors in logic but, in those who have high levels of training and practice, intuitive decision making can also be "powerful and accurate" in spite of being done without conscious thought. He points out that Systems 1 and 2 are rarely operating totally independently, so it's a matter of which one is predominant at any moment in time (Kahneman, 2011).

Epstein (1994) calls the intuitive system *experiential* and points out that people are usually compelled to use this system when presented with emotionally arousing events. "The transformation that occurs in people's thinking when they are emotionally aroused provides a dramatic illustration of a very different way of thinking from the way people think when they are unemotional" (Epstein, 1994, 710). He agrees with Kahneman that people are likely to rely more often on the intuitive system because it requires less effort, and the rational system fails to control it because intuitive influences are outside of conscious awareness. However, when faced with an emotionally arousing event, intuitive decision making will automatically become the default option. He also agrees with Kahneman that intuitive decision making can often be more powerful and accurate if people have sufficient subconscious experiences to draw upon. Thus people "often have intuitive knowledge that they can effectively apply without being aware of the principles that are involved" (Epstein, 1994, 719).

For his book *Sources of Power*, Klein (1998) studied individuals who make effective decisions in high stress situations. The purpose was to determine how they make decisions, with the goal of being able to teach others to do the same. He stated the initial study was poorly designed because he assumed that effective decision makers would be using some version of rational thought. He studied firefighters and became frustrated because not only were the effective incident commanders not following a rational model, one even startled the researcher by stating "I don't make decisions." The commander pointed out that if he took the time to try and make a decision, the structure would burn down while he was figuring out what to do. Further analysis led Klein to conclude that in situations that are characterized by time pressure, dynamic conditions, ambiguous information, unclear goals, and poorly defined procedures, people rely on a form of *intuitive* decision making, which he calls "recognition primed decision making." Klein (1998, 31) points out that

> intuition depends on the use of experience to recognize key patterns that indicate the dynamics of a situation. Because patterns can be subtle, people often cannot describe what they noticed, or how they judged a situation as typical or atypical … This is one basis for what we call intuition: recognizing things without knowing how we do the recognizing.

He also found that emergency responders did *not* mull over what might be the "optimal" solution because research has shown that "optimizing is hard, and takes a long time" (Klein, 1998, 20).

If the incident commanders delayed action until they could figure out the "optimal" solution, disaster would ensue. Instead, they seized upon the first option that came to mind that would work, a decision strategy that Klein termed "satisficing," based on earlier work by Herbert Simon. This means incident commanders were using rapid, intuitive decision making to find a *satisfactory* solution, not logically analyzing the situation until they could find the *optimal* solution. Klein (1998) reported that later studies of military commanders found that they used the same intuitive "recognition primed" decision-making strategies as the firefighter incident commanders.

Research Specific to Officer-Involved Shootings (OIS)

Klein (1998) documented intuitive decision making in firefighters, while Pinizotto, Davis, and Miller (2004) documented this same phenomenon in police officers who are faced with sudden danger. They point out that officers in these situations are sometimes "unable to articulate, their accurate reactions that may represent building blocks to reasonable suspicion or probable cause indicators" and/or unable to "explain their reasons for reacting in such appropriate ways that actually saved their lives or prevented an offender from assaulting them" (Pinizotto et al., 2004, 2).

Lewinski (2008) put 46 constables with the London Metropolitan Police through shooting scenarios, then tested their recall of the event by comparing it to videotapes of their reactions. He found that selective attention with an external and narrow focus resulted in inattentional blindness and deafness in all the officers except for one who was physically removed from the action. He pointed out that this intense focus on the perceived threat facilitated their performance but impaired their ability to recall details of the event. He also found that officers relied on intuitive decision making, which allowed them to perform quickly and effortlessly, yet impaired their ability to think critically and perform logical analysis, including elements of the scenario and their own behavior (Lewinski, 2008).

Artwohl (2002), in her survey of 157 officers involved in justified officer involved shootings, found that 75 percent reported they gave little or no conscious thought to what they did during the shooting, but simply responded on "autopilot," obviously relying on intuitive decision making. As Klein (1998) points out, conscious rational decision making simply takes too much time, so in sudden emergencies like most officer-involved shootings, the participants simply won't have the luxury of time and must rely on intuitive decision making. As a case in point,

> As soon as I saw the suspect's gun, I found myself behind cover returning fire. I don't remember actually moving to the cover position or drawing my gun. It just happened like I had rehearsed in my mind and during training. The whole event happened way too suddenly and quickly for me to even begin to think about what I was doing. ... It's really true; you'll only do what you have trained to do because there's no time to think up anything else.
>
> *(Artwohl & Christensen, 1997, 43)*

Police officers are trained observers and in tasks for which the veteran officers have ample training and experience, they may in fact be able to quickly focus on the most relevant and important cues and ignore the rest. This can make their responses more effective. However, they are human beings and subject to biological limitations on what their brains can pay attention to. Many researchers (Artwohl, 2002, 2003; Honig & Sultan, 2004; Klinger, 2001; Lewinski, 2008; Lewinski et al., 2016; Ross, 2013; Ross et al., 2012; Ross & Siddle, 2003) have documented cognitive phenomena in officers involved in shootings, such as attentional narrowing, resulting in auditory exclusion and inattentional blindness, memory gaps for part of the event, memory gaps for some of their own behavior, time distortion, intrusive thoughts, and false memories. As a case in point:

> A suspect with a gun got the drop on my partner and was getting ready to shoot him. As I shot the suspect, I could see blood spurting out of my partner as the suspect shot him. After the suspect had been neutralized, I ran over to help my partner, praying that he would survive his gunshot wound. As it turns out, he had also shot the suspect but the suspect never got off a round.
>
> *(Artwohl & Christensen, 1997, 44)*

Artwohl (2003) has also documented cases of officers at the scene of a critical incident who discharged their weapons, yet have no memory of having done so. For example,

> A male gangster was holding a couple in their 90s as hostages. A patrol sergeant shot the suspect along with two other officers. He remembers seeing a muzzle flash and thought it was the suspect firing at him. He was shocked to find out the suspect had not actually shot at him. It was really his own muzzle flash that he saw. He had to look at his own magazine to see if he had really fired or not.
>
> *(Artwohl, 2003, 42)*

These studies have yielded the consistent finding that the involved officers often experience a multitude of attention and memory influences that impair their ability to have complete and accurate memories of the event. Across multiple studies, the most common of these is inattentional deafness, including total auditory exclusion of very loud sounds like gunshots, people screaming, etc. The research on the perils of divided attention explains why this would be the most common effect. For example, an officer-involved shooting is almost always a primarily visual event, with the officers intensely focusing on visual threat cues. The life or death demand of this visual task leaves little left over in those moments for paying attention to auditory cues, so the brain not only ignores them, but even suppresses them from conscious awareness. The active suppression of sound recognition was demonstrated in research by Shomstein and Yantis (2004), which showed that when research subjects were given a visual task to perform, not only did their visual cortex become more active, but their auditory cortex actually became less active. Thus, the brain was actually suppressing the person's ability to recognize sounds to allocate more resources to vision. And this was in a simple lab experiment. One can assume that the effect would be even more pronounced when one's life depended on paying attention to visual threat recognition cues.

Rapid intuitive decision making can be powerful and accurate with proper training and/or experience. However, it can also lead to poor snap judgments with unfortunate results, especially since people often rely on it because it is easier than the effort required for logical decision making. Sharps and Hess (2008) illustrated this in an experiment where they studied the question of how untrained people believed a police officer should respond to a given situation involving gun violence. The subjects were college students who were presented with photographs in which a police officer was confronting an armed perpetrator. The photographs depicted a variety of scenes. These scenes depicted a threat, which a panel of police use of force experts had all unanimously agreed absolutely required the police officer to shoot the perpetrator. The results of the experiment found that only 11.36 percent of the subjects believed the police officer should shoot the suspect. Sharps and Hess (2008, 63) pointed out that,

> The results of this experiment indicate that 9 out of 10 people, within the experimental framework employed, were of the opinion that an officer should not fire in this situation, although all of the senior police officers consulted stated that the situation absolutely required a shooting response. This result may have important implications for situations in which 12-person juries must evaluate a given police shooting.

What is of particular interest is that Sharps and Hess (2008) found that the reasons given for the subjects' opinions were illogical and unrealistic. This included concocting elaborate rules under which an officer might fire, expecting the officer to be able to read the perpetrator's mind or be clairvoyant, etc. Sharps and Hess (2008, 63) commented that, "It is suggested that many of these unrealistic responses may have derived from confusion of media depictions of police work." This is an example of people observing a life and death situation for which they are very likely to have no experience and training to evaluate. Yet, they were willing to make snap intuitive judgments based on exposure to faulty information and even to justify that judgment using illogical reasoning. Since intuitive judgments are often not open to introspection and not easily changed, people may not only make poor judgments, but may be unaware of how illogical these judgments really are and stubbornly stick to illogical conclusions. This may not bode well for those who are judged.

This well researched distinction between intuitive and rational decision making is important for the criminal justice system. The events that come to the attention of the criminal justice system are often events that are sudden, high stress, time pressured events that will cause people to react based on intuitive responses rather than rational thought. This means that it will become more difficult for the participants and observers to explain what happened or why they reacted as they did. For instance, officers involved in shootings or citizens trying to defend themselves are expected to justify their use of force and investigators usually want a logical, sequential, analysis that will clearly explain their thought process during the event. The literature shows that this will be a difficult task for both the participant and the investigator (Fisher & Geiselman, 1992; Klein, 1998).

Emergency services personnel may also be criticized for failing to respond based on the "optimal" solution as thought up by those who apply rational hindsight judgment in the days, weeks, or months after the event. Research shows that the time it takes to reach an "optimal" decision is a luxury that can be fatal during a time pressured emergency, so participants will instead rely on intuitive thinking and "satisficing" to seize upon the first effective solution that intuitively comes to mind. However, they will then be judged by those who have the luxury of time to engage in rational thinking and "optimizing" in their critique of the event and officer's behavior. This does not mean that emergency services personnel should not be held accountable for their actions, but that the criminal justice system needs to be aware and respectful of human limitations.

Investigators need to be educated about how the mind works during emergencies, and trained in the cognitive interview techniques developed by Fisher and Geiselman (1992) that will facilitate retrieval of memories and intuitive thought processes. The research by Sharps and Hess (2008, 63) points out that intuitive snap judgments of officer-involved shootings by a poorly informed public can create problems and they proffer that "there is substantial need for better education in the realities of crime and police work for the public from which, of course, all jurors are selected." In response to these issues, Lane County, Oregon produced an excellent video to help achieve this goal, titled *Hollywood vs. Reality: Officer Involved Shootings* (Force Science News, 2011).

Investigators and Others Are Not Themselves Immune

Much of the memory research appropriately focuses on the participants and eyewitnesses in events with which the criminal justice system is likely to come in contact. However, other human beings like detectives, judges, and juries are also subject to the same influences on attention, perception, bias, memory, and decision making that can impact the participants and eyewitnesses.

This includes detectives who investigate the cases. Dr. Kim Rossmo, as presented in his book *Criminal Investigative Failures* (2009), did extensive research on the many cognitive and emotional factors that contribute to investigative failures. He points out that law enforcement personnel are not immune to these universal human performance factors that lead to organizational failures in all occupations. He identified three groups of key factors that influence human beings working within the criminal justice system: cognitive biases, organizational traps, and probability errors. Under cognitive biases, he identified several. Perception and memory limitations may cause investigators to forget relevant details. Over-reliance on intuition can lead to incorrect snap judgments instead of careful, effortful, logical analysis. Heuristics, i.e., mental shortcuts that allow people to function efficiently in daily life, may result in errors. Multiple types of biases can interfere with people's abilities to perceive facts in a rational and objective manner. As we have seen, these types of mental processes can often have a procedural, emotional component that makes them subtle and hard to detect at a conscious level. Dr. Rossmo provides multiple case examples where these and other factors led to investigative failures and he makes recommendations to minimize these problems and help investigators and prosecutors stay on track with their cases.

Retrieval

There are many human performance factors and situational variables that will influence what parts of an event will be put into long-term memory storage, and how those memories will be interpreted and altered based on the sum total of each person's life experiences. This happens during the *encoding* and *storage* steps of forming memories. Some of these will enhance memory, while others will cause missing, distorted, or even false memories. For the most part, the criminal justice system does not have much control over these variables. However, the criminal justice system can control variables that influence *retrieval* during the investigation. Many factors can influence the ability of cooperative witnesses to recall information, such as sleep deprivation, timing of the interviews, how rested the witness feels, anxiety levels, and the behavior of the interviewer (Fisher & Geiselman, 1992; Geiselman, 2010). Fisher & Geiselman (1992) developed an interview technique they recommend for cooperative witnesses, which they named the Cognitive Interview. A description of the cognitive interview, and review of their research which they used to derive and validate it, can be found in their book titled *Memory-Enhancing Techniques for Investigative Interviewing* (1992).

Summary and Key Findings

Officers are professionals and trained observers. They are also human beings who must cope with the same biological limitations of the human brain as everyone else. Research on memory and decision making under stress teach us some key points:

- Eyewitnesses are never reporting what *actually happened.* They can only report what they perceived, interpreted, stored in their memory, and what they can retrieve at any given moment. The details of their report may or may not be an accurate representation of reality.
- Honest witnesses can provide reports based on their Narrative Truth that are not historically accurate and may vary significantly from what the physical evidence indicates actually happened. This lack of accuracy does not in itself mean that the eyewitness is being untruthful.
- Videotapes and other physical evidence can be valuable investigative tools, but videotapes can distort reality and physical evidence can be misinterpreted. Caution must be used to ensure that these tools are carefully and appropriately used based on scientific research.
- Eyewitnesses will *not* be able to pay attention to, and therefore *not* remember, every single feature of an event. They will typically remember the gist with a limited number of details.
- Eyewitnesses may briefly hold features of the event in their short-term memory that may influence their behavior, but will not be transferred to long-term memory storage and therefore will not be available for future retrieval.
- Memory formation and decision making are strongly influenced by many features of the event, such as lighting, contextual cues, and stimuli that may capture the eyewitnesses' attention such as the presence of weapons.

- The interpretation and subsequent memory formation of an event is strongly influenced by cognitive features of the individual eyewitnesses, including their biases, expectations, biological limitations, and the sum total of their previous life experiences.
- The conditions under which people attempt to retrieve memories can strongly influence the amount, the content, and the accuracy of their memories. The criminal justice system can manipulate these conditions to enhance the ability of eyewitnesses to remember and accurately report what they observed.
- It is normal for people to have memory errors for events, including memory gaps for part of the event, memory gaps for their own behavior, confusion, and false memories.
- Mild levels of stress can enhance memory, but severe or prolonged stress can impair memory formation and retrieval.
- Sleep deprivation can impair memory formation and the ability of witnesses to retrieve memories.
- It is normal for memories to change over time based on internal cognitive processes and external influences.
- It is normal for memories to change from one recounting to another based on the conditions under which retrieval is attempted.
- It is normal for multiple eyewitnesses to have different memories and interpretations of the same event.
- Eyewitnesses can have vivid and compelling memories during high stress events that are totally false.
- The confidence an eyewitness has in a memory is not a reliable predictor of how accurately it represents what actually happened.
- Research has confirmed that eyewitness memory is unreliable and should be used with caution in absence of other confirmatory physical evidence.
- Decision making during sudden, time pressured, high stress events is made under the influence of subconscious intuitive thinking which can make it difficult for the decision maker to consciously articulate the rationale for their behavior.
- Even in the absence of high stress, people often revert to intuitive thinking because it is easier. This can result in faulty and illogical eyewitness interpretations of an event, especially in individuals who have limited and/or faulty training and experience with the observed event.
- The same cognitive processes that cause memory and reasoning errors in eyewitnesses can also influence professionals in the criminal justice system. Errors can be minimized by recognition of these processes and training and procedures designed to minimize them.

References

Artwohl, A. (2002). Perceptual and memory distortions in officer involved shootings. *FBI Law Enforcement Bulletin, 18*, 18–24.

Artwohl, A. (2003). No recall of weapons discharge. *Law Enforcement Executive Forum, 3*(2), 41–49.

Artwohl, A. & Christensen, L. C. (1997). *Deadly force encounters.* Boulder, CO: Paladin Press.

British Psychological Society Research Board. (2008). *Guidelines on memory and the law.* London: The British Psychological Society.

Chabris, C. & Simons, D. (2010). *The invisible gorilla: And other ways our intuitions deceive us.* New York, NY: Crown Publishers.

Deffenbacher, K. A., Bornstein, B. H., Penrod, S. D., & McGorty, E. K. (2004). A meta-analytic review of the effects of high stress on eyewitness memory. *Law and Human Behavior, 28*(6), 687–706.

Ehlers, A., Hackmann, A., & Michael, T. (2004) Intrusive re-experiencing in post-traumatic stress disorder: Phenomenology, theory, and therapy. *Memory, 12*(4), 403–415.

Epstein, S. (1994). Integration of the cognitive and psychodynamic unconscious. *American Psychologist, 49*(8), 709–721.

Fisher, R. P. & Geiselman, R. E. (1992). *Memory-enhancing techniques for investigative interviewing.* Springfield, IL: Charles C. Thomas.

Force Science News. (2011). Hollywood vs. reality: Officer involved shootings (#194). Retrieved from www.forcescience.org/fsnews/194.html.

Force Science News. (2015). 10 limitations of body cams you need to know for your protection (#265). Retrieved from www.forcescience.org/fsnews/265.html.

Fougnie, D. (2008). The relationship between attention and working memory. In N. B. Johanesen (ed.) *New research on short-term memory.* Hauppauge, NY: Nova Science Publishers.

Geiselman, R. E. (2010). Rest and eyewitness recall. *American Journal of Forensic Psychiatry, 28*(1), 65–69.

Honig, A. L. & Sultan, S. E. (2004). Reactions and resilience under fire: What an officer can expect. *The Police Chief, 71*(12), 54–60.

Hope, L., Blocksidge, D., Gabbert, F., Sauer, J. D., Lewinski, W., Mirashi, A. & Atuk, E. (2016). Memory and the operational witness: Police officer recall of firearms encounters as a function of active response role. *Law and Human Behavior, 40*(1–2), 25–35.

Kahneman, D. (2011). *Thinking, fast and slow.* New York, NY: Farrar, Straus, and Giroux.

Klein, G. (1998). *Sources of power: How people make decisions.* Cambridge, MA: MIT Press.

Klinger, D. (2001). *Police responses to officer-involved shootings.* Washington, DC: U.S. Government Printing Office: NCJ 19228.

LeDoux, J. (1996). *The emotional brain.* New York, NY: Touchstone/Simon Schuster.

Lewinski, W. (2008). The attention study: A study on the presence of selective attention in firearms officers. *Law Enforcement Executive Forum, 8*(6), 107–138.

Lewinski, W. L., Dysterheft, J. L., Priem, M. M., & Pettitt, R. W. (2016). Police officers' actual vs. recalled path of travel in response to a threatening traffic stop scenario. *Police Practice and Research, 17*(1), 51–67.

Mack, A. & Rock, I. (1998). *Inattentional blindness.* Cambridge, MA: MIT Press.

Manson v. Brathwaite, 423 U.S. 98 (1977).

McGaugh, J. L. (2003). *Memory and emotion.* New York, NY: Columbia University Press.

Morgan III, C. A., Hazlett, G., Doran, T., Garrett, S., Hoyt, G., Thomas, P., Baranoski, M., & Southwick, S. (2004). Accuracy of eyewitness memory for persons encountered during exposure to highly intense stress. *International Journal of Psychiatry and the Law, 27*(3), 265–279.

Neria, Y., DiGrande, L., & Adams, B. G. (2011). Posttraumatic stress disorder following the September 11, 2001 terrorist attacks: A review of the literature among highly exposed populations. *American Psychologist [9/11: Ten Years Later]*, *66*(6), 429–446.

Pinizotto, A. J., Davis, E. F., & Miller, C. E. (2004). Intuitive policing: emotional/rational decision making in law enforcement. *FBI Law Enforcement Bulletin, 73*(2), 1–6.

Porter, S. & Peace, K. (2007). The scars of memory: A prospective, longitudinal investigation of the consistency of traumatic and positive emotional memories in adulthood. *Psychological Science, 18*(5), 435–441.

Purves, D., Wojtack, W. D., & Howe, C. (2008). Visual illusions: An empirical explanation. *Scholarpedia, 3*(6), 3706, doi:10.4249/scholarpedia.3706.

Ross, D. (2013). Assessing lethal force liability decisions and human factors research. *Law Enforcement Executive Forum, 13*(2), 85–107.

Ross, D. L., Murphy, R. L., & Hazlett, M. H. (2012). Analyzing perceptions and misperceptions of police officers in lethal force virtual simulator scenarios. *Law Enforcement Executive Forum, 12*(3), 53–73.

Ross, D. L. & Siddle, B. K. (2003). An analysis of the effects of survival stress in police use-of-force encounters. *Law Enforcement Executive Forum, 3*(2), 9–26.

Rossmo, K. (2009). *Criminal investigative failures*. Boca Raton, FL: CRC Press.

Sapolsky, R. M. (2004). Stressed out memories. *Scientific American Mind, 14*(5), 28–34.

Schacter, D. (2001). *The seven sins of memory*. New York, NY: Houghton Mifflin.

Sharps, M. J. (2010). *Processing under pressure: Stress, memory and decision making in law enforcement*. Flushing, NY: Looseleaf Law Publications.

Sharps, M. J., Barber, T., Stahl, H., & Villegas, A. B. (2003). Eyewitness memory for weapons. *The Forensic Examiner, 12*(3), 34–37.

Sharps, M. J. & Hess, A. B. (2008). To shoot or not to shoot: Response and interpretation of response to armed assailants. *The Forensic Examiner, 17*(4), 53–64.

Shomstein, S. & Yantis, S. (2004). Control of attention shifts between vision and audition in human cortex. *The Journal of Neuroscience, 24*(47), 10702–10706.

Simons, D. J. & Chabris, C. F. (1999). Gorillas in our midst: Sustained inattentional blindness for dynamic events. *Perception, 28*(9), 1059–1074.

Stone, M. P. & Berger, M. J. (2008). Appellate court confronts attack on sheriff's "Anti-Huddling Policy." *Legal Defense Trust Training Bulletin., 11*(7), 1–6.

Terry, R. A. (1997). Eyewitness identification. *The Forensic Examiner*, September–October, 21–24.

United States Department of Justice. (1999). *Eyewitness evidence: A guide for law enforcement*. Washington, DC: U.S. Department of Justice.

Vickers, J. N. (2007). *Perception, cognition, and decision training*. Champaign, IL: Human Kinetics.

Vickers, J. N. & Lewinski, W. L. (2012). Performing under pressure: Gaze control, decision making and shooting performance of elite and rookie police officers. *Human Movement Science, 31*(1), 101–117.

Wells, G. L. & Olson, E. A. (2003). Eyewitness testimony. *Annual Review of Psychology, 54*, 277–95.

Wells, G. L. & Quilivan, D. S. (2009). Suggestive eyewitness identification procedures and the Supreme Court's reliability test in light of eyewitness science: 30 years later. *Law and Human Behavior, 33*(1), 1–24.

6

OFFICER-INVOLVED INCIDENT INVESTIGATION GUIDELINES

Darrell L. Ross and Mark S. Dunston

Introduction

It has been established that officer-involved incidents resulting in a death of an arrestee or a detainee in custody are a rare occurrence. However, an incident resulting in a death or serious bodily injury requires an extensive investigation, while the integrity of the law enforcement or correctional agency is never more closely critiqued than during and following the incident. These incidents are considered high profile, meaning agency personnel, the county prosecutor, the public, the media, the plaintiff's attorney, and the judicial system will all closely scrutinize the investigation. It is incumbent upon all who respond to the scene and those assigned to conduct the investigation to work toward mitigating errors while performing the investigation.

Investigating an officer-involved arrest-related death incident or a custodial death involves many of the same components as other death investigations, but at the same time, they can be complex and encompass numerous variables to examine (Copeland, 1984; Frost & Hanzlick, 1988; Graham, 2014; Hiss & Kahana, 1996). Each incident contains potential social, civil, administrative, and criminal implications. Criminal and administrative investigations are common, which must follow appropriate procedures. The circumstances of these deaths require a detailed and methodological approach and frequently require a freeze-frame examination of the activities of all officers involved, as well as the decedent, which includes: the circumstances and nature of the incident, the behaviors and resistance of the decedent, pre-incident elements, the location of the incident, incident environmental components, reaction time, and the duration of the incident, to identify a few (Graham, 2014; Luke & Reay, 1992). Investigating a death of this nature includes numerous individuals who possess varying interests, skills, and abilities, while communication and a coordinated effort amongst them is needed in order to perform a complete and detailed investigation. Attending to the tasks and responsibilities of each of the varied parties involved in the investigation can appropriately address the complexities of the investigation, with the goal of minimizing potential errors.

Recognizing that supervisors and administrators from the involved agency and/or an outside agency may participate in the investigation, along with the medical examiner's office and the prosecutor's office, guidelines for conducting an investigation are needed. This chapter describes the guidelines and protocols needed to perform an investigation of an officer-involved incident that results in death or serious body injury. An officer-involved incident may include numerous types, and will be referred to in this chapter as a critical incident. For purposes of this chapter, a critical incident is defined as: a sudden event involving one or more police or correctional officers which requires responses of additional resources outside the normal call for service response, where a fatal injury or serious bodily injury of an arrestee or detainee occurs, resulting in an immediate investigation with no advance warning, and potentially resulting in suspension, termination, or arrest of the involved officer (Coviello et al., 2014). A critical incident may also be described as a life threatening survival stress situation which exposes the officer(s) or others to a traumatic experience, whereby activating a Sympathetic Nervous System discharge and creating a physiological and psychological stress response, which then disrupts the officer's values or assumptions about the environment, causing an unexpected and serious threat to the officer (Miller, 2006; Nielsen, 1981). Examples where these guidelines will be applicable include the following: intentional and accidental officer-involved shootings; arrest-related deaths after the use of non-deadly force measures; using a police vehicle as a technique to apprehend a suspect (pit maneuver, ramming, etc.); an in-custody death occurring in a detention facility or prison after the use of non-deadly force measures; and serious bodily injury after the major use of force sustained by an arrestee/detainee, innocent bystander, and/or the involved officer(s). Further, uninvolved officers on scene and the involved dispatcher may also experience a traumatic emotional reaction.

The guidelines presented in this chapter are designed to provide recommended steps and protocols, which provide discretion when considering their application to a given critical incident. They are obviously not mandatory nor are they definitive, and they are not intended to usurp an agency's decision or other procedures in a particular incident. Based on prior research and the experience and practices of criminal justice professionals and experts, these guidelines can assist in ensuring the integrity of the investigation is enhanced and that the appropriate outcome is accomplished. The guidelines may be used as a benchmark to assess procedures used by an agency in order to revise and develop the appropriate procedures proactively. They can assist the agency to be in the best position to respond to a critical incident, thereby reducing the chance of error during the investigation. The information in this chapter also provides considerations for appropriately approaching an involved officer who has just survived a traumatic and life threatening situation. Being mindful that all humans respond to and are affected differently by a stressful critical incident will assist in ensuring that all of the involved officers are treated humanely, respectfully, and professionally, while helping to obtain the most accurate information possible. Checklists are provided, which may be followed, to ensure thorough documentation is completed.

Pre-Incident Planning

Policy Implementation

Prior to the occurrence of a critical incident, it is recommended that the agency administrator have a current, comprehensive, and constitutional response to resistance policy developed and implemented. In *Monell v. Department of Social Services of the City of New York* (1978), the United States Supreme Court established that governmental liability maybe imposed under §1983 when the department's policy (or lack thereof), including customs and rules and regulations, was the "moving force" that created a constitutional injury. The decision has been affirmed in the Court's decision in *Los Angeles County v. Humphries* (2010). The application of these decisions as it relates to the use of force is for the agency administrator to develop and keep the department's response to resistance policy current within these decisions, state law, and within the purview of state standards.

The policy guides an officer in making justifiable field decisions, while procedures operationalize an officer's actions when encountering resistance. Well written policies aid in assisting officers to make the best decisions in the field, to make legally acceptable decisions, to generate the best report as feasible, and to assist in holding officers accountable (Brave, 2014a). At a minimum, a resistance to response policy should be framed by including components relating to objectives, definitions, and circumstances, as listed in Table 6.1 (Brave, 2014b; International Association of Chiefs of Police, 2015; Ross, 2013).

A separate policy should be developed and implemented which requires a force review by trained and authorized agency personnel, commonly referred to as a Force Investigation Team (FIT). Members of FIT should conduct a use of force review (above the level of the officer's supervisor) in the following situations: (1) the department receives a complaint of excessive use of force; (2) the supervisor recommends conducting a use of force review; (3) the encounter resulted in hospitalization of any person (including an officer); (4) the encounter resulted in death or serious bodily injury; or (5) the force recipient is a member of a special population.

Upon documented request, a force recipient shall be kept reasonably informed of the procedural status and final result of the review. Accidental weapon discharges shall be documented in a departmental memorandum explaining in detail how the discharge occurred (Brave, 2014b). Further, an agency administrator is encouraged to develop a separate policy which addresses and details the components of a post-critical incident investigation. The policy should outline all of the procedures to be employed and specifies all of the responsibilities of those assigned to conduct the investigation (discussed further in this chapter).

Training Officers, Supervisors, and Investigators

Agency administrators should develop and provide training to all officers, supervisors, and investigators in the response to resistance policy and their responsibility in using force measures in response to an arrestee/detainee's resistance. All personnel should be trained in the investigation protocols and guidelines so they have an understanding of the process. In accordance with the United States Supreme Court's decision in *City of Canton, Ohio v. Harris* (1989) and reaffirmed in *Connick v. Thompson* (2011), the Court established that the standard used to examine a claim of failing to train is deliberate indifference. This requires proof that the agency administrator purposely disregarded the "known or obvious consequence" that a particular omission in the department's training program would cause agency employees to violate a person's constitutional right. Further, the Court has stated that a "pattern" of similar constitutional violations is ordinarily necessary to demonstrate deliberate indifference. The Court opined that agency administrators must provide ongoing and realistic training commensurate to "obvious" recurring job functions.

The training should be provided on a regular basis, and should include: policies and procedures; all authorized use of force techniques, including aerosols, canines, weapons, and restraints; manufacturers' specifications for using force equipment; and the responsibilities of the supervisor, including writing

TABLE 6.1 Resistance to response policy

Objectives of the policy should be based on criteria established by the USSC	**Police Administrators**: *Graham v. Connor* (1989), *Tennessee v. Garner* (1985), *Brosseau v. Haugen* (2004), *Scott v. Harris* (2007), *Plumhoff v. Rickard* (2014), *City and County of San Francisco v. Sheehan* (2015), and *Mullenix v. Luna* (2015) [4th Amendment]. **Detention and Prison Administrators**: *Kingsley v. Hendrickson* (2015) [4th Amendment], *Hudson v. McMillian* (1992), *Wilkins v. Gaddy* (2010), and *Whitley v. Albers* (1986) [8th Amendment].
Definitions of these terms should be included in the policy	• Deadly force and non-deadly force • Justification(s) for using force and response to a person's behaviors • Defining objectively reasonable force • Distinguishing between imminent threat and immediate threat • Describing an officer's perception of the need of using force • Defining quantum of force • Response to subject resistance • Serious bodily injury • An arrest-related death • An in-custody death • All authorized force options, including verbal instructions, officer(s) presence, empty-hand control techniques, aerosols/intermediate weapons, canines, deadly force, authorized restraint equipment • Responding to an individual with an injury • Responding to special needs populations • Force used against animals • Unintentional discharge of a weapon • Reporting the use of force
Circumstance variables affecting the use of force should be described	• Describing the principles of escalation and de-escalation • Describing the prohibited use of force measures and warning shots • Describing the force used against a fleeing subject • Describing discharging a firearm from or at a moving vehicle • Describing pre- and post-incident medical care and monitoring the individual after the application of force • Describing arrestee or prisoner transport considerations • Describing the supervisor's response, actions and report

reports and submitting necessary forms and paperwork. All investigators should complete use of force training and be competent in all of the force measures authorized by the department in order to conduct a thorough investigation. On a regular basis, all personnel should be provided with dynamic realistic training which replicates field stressors, varying circumstances, and environmental conditions integrated with stress immersion principles geared toward activating the Sympathetic Nervous System. Training should be regularly provided which incorporates dynamic scenario-based training exercises and simulation training, as these methodologies have been shown to provide realistic stress-induced training (Armstrong, Clare, & Plecas, 2014; Atkins & Norris, 2007; Benell, Jones, & Corey, 2007; Lewinski, 2006; Lynch, 2005; Patton, Loukota, & Avery, 2013; Ross, Murphy, & Hazlett, 2012).

Administrators, supervisors, officers, and particularly investigators, should be trained on the science of human performance factors in order to gain an understanding of how the stress of participating in an officer-involved critical incident impacts the officer's perception and decision making in response to subject resistance, as well as the officer's post-incident thinking in response to stress, behaviors, and memory. In conjunction with this training, all agency personnel should be educated on what emotional and physical reactions are likely to be experienced by those involved officers or those officers who witnessed the incident, and also be educated on how to appropriately respond to an officer(s) who has been involved in a traumatic critical incident (Artwhol 2002; Artwhol & Christensen, 1997; Digiliani, 2012; International Association of Chiefs of Police, 2012, 2013; Ross et al., 2012, Ross, 2013; Sharps, 2010). Prior to the critical incident, agency administrators should designate and train personnel in the counseling options available to them after being involved in a critical incident. Agency personnel identified as a peer support team responder should be provided training and updated on a regular basis.

Moreover, all officers, dispatchers, supervisors, administrators, crime scene technicians, investigators, and support team personnel should receive training on their individual responsibilities and tasks immediately following a critical incident. Officers should be trained on the process and protocols involved with a critical incident investigation. All personnel should be provided with departmental procedures that outline the sequence of the tasks and responsibilities of those responding to the critical incident. Training in the policy should be provided with regular updates. A notification tree (as identified in an earlier chapter) should be developed and updated regularly by the agency administrator who will be summoned to the incident location. The tree should also contain contact information of family members and significant others that the involved officer desires to be contacted after a critical incident.

Critical incident investigators should complete training on the following subject matters as they relate to the topics addressed in this text: response to resistance policy and the critical incident investigation policy; crime scene management; crime scene sketching; evidence collection; human factors science; state and federal standards on use of force; cognitive interviewing; arrest-related and in-custody deaths; excited delirium syndrome and positional asphyxia; firearms, ballistics, and gunshot wounds; basic wounds and deaths from trauma; recognition of bloodstain patterns; photography and videotaping; autopsy procedures and toxicology testing; preparing reports; responding to the media; and testifying in court. Updated and advanced training should be provided to investigators on a regular basis.

Investigation Guidelines

The following discussion describes general investigatory guidelines, which are based on best practices and current research on responding to critical incidents. The recommendations are general in nature, are guidelines, and can be applied to officer-involved shootings, arrest-related deaths, sudden deaths in custody, as well as other critical incidents. It is acknowledged that every agency has its own practice and methods of conducting an investigation, and each critical incident will be unique with innumerable variables to be examined, and some recommendations may not be applicable. As these recommendations are reviewed, the reader should be mindful of his or her own agency's policies and state laws and standards, and where appropriate, modifications should be employed in order to enhance the efficiency of the investigation.

All personnel responding to the scene, whether providing support or conducting the investigation, including supervisors and command personnel, the agency head, all investigators, crime scene technicians, support team personnel, and the prosecutor, must recognize that an officer-involved shooting or a sudden arrest-related custodial death is not just another homicide. Civilian homicide investigations involve a murder, which is not justified, and the suspect should be arrested and afforded due process, and if convicted, should be incarcerated. Conversely, police and correction officers are hired and trained to use force, including deadly force. When the circumstances require it, these officers are legally authorized to use force and must follow constitutional standards. In an overwhelmingly high percentage of officer-involved shootings, arrest-related deaths, or sudden deaths in custody, the officer was performing his or her sworn duty, doing what he or she was hired to do, and responded as required.

Surviving a stressful and critical incident where an arrestee or detainee died can be traumatic for most officers, and a myriad of psychological and physiological responses may result immediately, within hours, or days later (Miller, 2006). Involved officers and officers on scene should be treated with respect, supported, and not treated like criminals. If the investigation turns into a criminal investigation, then the officer must be afforded the same constitutional rights as other suspects. The investigation must be performed professionally and conducted with integrity. Approaching the investigation with the mindset that a critical task of the officer is to use force assists in placing the investigation in proper perspective. All involved officers must obtain a fair and impartial investigation, allowing the evidence to form the basis of the final outcome.

Involved Officer

After a critical incident, the involved officer should contact dispatch, and the dispatcher will notify all persons on the notification tree. A supervisor and back-up personnel should be immediately requested to respond to the scene, and medical personnel should be summoned if not requested previously (Colorado 14th Judicial District, 2015; Davis, 2012; Hatch & Dickson, 2007; Ross, 2006; Seattle (WA) Police Department, 2015; Tracy, 2010). The arrestee or detainee should be assessed, secured, and medical attention provided as necessary. The officer should calm down, make sure all threats are ended, and check for any injuries that may have been sustained during the confrontation. Since an officer surviving a traumatic critical incident may not realize he or she has sustained an injury, all involved officers should be immediately checked for any personal injuries, first aid provided as needed, emotional first aid provided, and transported to a hospital as warranted (Artwhol & Christensen, 1997). If the officer is transported to the hospital, a support officer or supervisor should accompany the officer. An officer should be given the opportunity to voluntarily provide a toxicology sample. However, officers are generally advised by legal counsel not to submit to such tests. An officer should seek advice from his or her attorney prior to submitting to a toxicology sample. Intoxicant testing can only be compelled if there are indications of possible intoxication and legal standards have been met (Morrissey, 2015). All officers and supervisors on scene during the incident should be observed for emotional trauma and supervisors of dispatchers should also assess and monitor the involved dispatcher for a period of time (Bohrer & Chaney, 2010; Digiliani, 2012; Santa Clara County Police Chief's Association, 2012; Force Science News, 2006a; International Association of Chiefs of Police, 2012, 2013).

If the critical incident involved an officer shooting, the officer should secure the firearm in the holster, and it should not be unholstered so as to preserve critical evidence. In addition, the firearm should not be reloaded and shell casings should not be disturbed, nor should other firearms or evidence be disturbed. The officer should secure a shoulder weapon or other force devices (aerosol, CEW, baton, handcuffs, restraints, etc.) in the trunk or gunlock of the patrol car. If feasible, the involved officer(s) should secure the scene, preserve evidence, and identify witnesses. If practical, the officer should take photos of the scene (Colorado 14th Judicial District, 2015).

After the critical incident, the officer should step away from the scene and move to a quiet area on scene, away from other officers, the media, and community members. A support officer or friend of the officer's choice should accompany the officer. The officer should be monitored for emotional reactions and attended to as warranted (Force Science News, 2006a). An officer should not discuss the incident with other officers, support team officers, clergy, union representatives, or debriefing teams. The officer should, however, only make a brief public statement to a responding supervisor. As soon as practically possible, the involved officer(s) should contact family members or a significant other, contact the union representative where applicable, and contact his or her legal counsel. Officers on scene who were witnesses should contact their families and inform them they have been involved in a critical incident and advise them of their status. Moreover, the involved officer(s) should conduct a walkthrough of the incident scene with his or her legal counsel only, prior to the formal interview, and the walkthrough should preferably be performed as soon as possible after, and preferably at the same time of day/night as, the incident occurred (Coviello et al., 2014). Prior to the formal interview with investigators, the involved officer(s) should be allowed to review the video of the incident (Aitchison, 2014; Force Science News, 2009; International Association of Chiefs of Police, 2014; LePard & Collins, 2015; Miller, Toliver, & Police Executive Research Forum, 2014).

Supervisor on Scene

The responding supervisor serves an important role in attending to the involved officer(s) and managing the incident scene. Depending on the agency and the situation, the responding "supervisor" may include the rank of corporal, sergeant, lieutenant, captain, watch commander, or other first-line or second-line supervisor. The supervisor should adhere to agency procedures as he or she manages the incident scene, but also consider the innumerable variables contained within the incident circumstances as the process progresses. Once the supervisor is on scene, he or she should briefly explain to the officer(s) the process of the investigation. This will assist in keeping the officer(s) informed as the investigation moves forward. The supervisor should immediately attend to the involved officer(s), checking on his/her condition, assessing any injuries that may have been sustained, and providing first aid and emotional support as necessary. Supervisors are also reminded to be mindful of any psychological trauma exhibited by the officer and respond appropriately (International Association of Chiefs of Police, 2013).

The supervisor should establish control of the scene, protect the integrity of the scene, preserve perishable evidence, and double tape the scene (Colorado 14th Judicial District, 2015; Davis, 2012; Eliopulos, 2003; Force Science News, 2006b; Hanzlick, 2007; Hatch & Dickson, 2007; Laub, 2011; National Institute of Justice, 2011; Prahlow, 2010; Ross, 2006). An outer perimeter is helpful to provide a staging area where other arriving personnel may gather. When establishing the outer perimeter, consider the range of cameras of the media and community members and appropriately secure sensitive evidence like the body of the decedent, blood, weapons, and the involved officers. Consider securing a second scene if a pursuit or a foot chase was involved. A command post should be established and the supervisor should begin coordinating activities.

Additional personnel should be requested (from the notification tree) to respond to the scene, including: additional officers, emergency medical services personnel, a command officer, the agency administrator, agency investigator, crime scene technicians, the public information officer, support team officers, the prosecutor, the coroner/medical examiner, and the agency's risk manager. The supervisor should coordinate the activities of the responding personnel, assign an officer to each of the involved officers, and maintain a scene log documenting the date and time of the incident, as well as the names of all involved officers and others who respond and exit the scene, the purpose of their entrance on scene, and record all personnel who speak and interact with the involved officer(s).

The supervisor should move the involved officer(s) away from the primary scene, to a less stressful and less trafficked area, and away from the media. Witness officers should also be moved away from the scene area as well, and instructed not to discuss the incident with anyone. The supervisor should request that the officer(s) provide only a public safety statement and do not discuss the incident with anyone other than his or her attorney. The purpose of the public safety statement is to obtain basic and preliminary information from the officer(s), is limited in scope, and assists in managing the scene. Basic questions may include: are there injured people; what is the nature of the officer's condition and/or injuries; what weapons may be involved, including current location of the weapons; what is the level of threat existing for the community; what is the outstanding suspect information and vehicle information; who are the officer witnesses and other witnesses to the incident and their locations; and has the scene been secured, has evidence been secured, and what is the location of the evidence. The supervisor should also inquire if the officer's body camera was operating during the incident.

The officer should not be left unattended, therefore a peer support team officer should be assigned to remain with the officer, and instructed not to discuss the critical incident with the officer. The involved officer should be allowed to contact his or her legal counsel, clergy, his or her spouse or significant other, and the support team officer as soon as reasonably possible. The supervisor should check the uninvolved officer witnesses for injuries, check their firearms, and document the status of their firearms (Colorado 14th Judicial District, 2015; Santa Clara County Police Chief's Association, 2012; International Association of Chiefs of Police, 2016, 2012; Seattle (WA) Police Department, 2015; Spokane Investigative Regional Response Team, 2014).

The supervisor should assign an officer or crime scene personnel to take photos and/or videotape the scene as other personnel arrive and as paramedics attend to the arrestee/detainee/decedent, and/or all involved officers. Photographs of the involved officers should be taken in their uniform from 360-degrees, and all injuries sustained should be photographed. Photographs and the video will assist in documenting all of the activities as they are performed. In-car videos and body camera videos should be preserved as evidence.

The involved officer should not be transported to the police department in the back seat of a patrol vehicle, but rather the front seat. At the police department, a supervisor or crime scene personnel will obtain the involved officer's firearm with the gun belt, unless already secured on scene, and the officer will be provided with a replacement firearm immediately. This is a critical concern as removing an officer's firearm without providing a replacement firearm can create further emotional trauma for the officer. The firearm should not be removed from the holster on scene, which may cause the loss of trace evidence. Other use of force equipment and devices should be examined and collected as potential evidence. Crime scene personnel should collect evidence from the involved officer(s), including uniform clothing (replacement clothing should be provided) and completion of a gunshot residue (GSR) test. The involved officer should be allowed the opportunity to speak with his or her attorney before submitting to any intoxication test.

Prior to the ambulance departing the scene, the supervisor should obtain information from emergency medical and fire personnel about the status of the arrestee/detainee and document it. The supervisor should assign an officer to ride in the ambulance when an arrestee/detainee is being transported to the hospital, and assign a second officer to proceed to the hospital to speak with medical personnel and family members. The officer will provide custody escort for the arrestee/detainee and should be alert to: identify all statements made by the arrestee/detainee to medical personnel, including any utterances made; record any dying declarations made by the decedent; collect and preserve any evidence, including clothing of the decedent; and identify relevant witnesses, family members, and all medical personnel. If possible, an officer should take photographs of the arrestee/detainee's injuries and signs of trauma prior to surgery, and collect, preserve, and document all evidence recovered after surgery. The attending officers should be alert to the arrestee/detainee/decedent's family at the hospital and treat them with care and respect.

If medical personnel transport the officer to the hospital, the supervisor should assign one or more officers to proceed to the hospital. Even if it appears the involved officer is not injured, the officer should be transported to the hospital by an accompanying officer in order for the officer's vitals to be checked by medical personnel. The attending officer should work with the medical personnel to complete a GSR test, unless it was performed on scene (Colorado 14th Judicial District, 2015; Coviello et al., 2014; Force Science News, 2006a). After release from the hospital, a support team officer should transport the officer to the department. Once the officer is released from the department, a support team officer should transport him or her home.

The supervisor should locate, identify, and document contact information of all civilian witnesses, isolate them near the scene area, instruct them not to discuss the incident, and pass their contact information onto the critical incident investigator. Prior to the incident investigator arriving on scene, the supervisor should prepare a briefing. Once the incident investigator, command personnel, and crime scene technicians arrive on scene, the supervisor should provide a briefing of the incident. The supervisor should also provide a briefing with the prosecutor and the medical examiner as they respond to the scene. The supervisor should work with these individuals, informing them of the nature of the circumstances, the location of all scene evidence, the methods used to protect the scene, and identify any evidence that was moved or disturbed (Colorado 14th Judicial District, 2015; Digiliani, 2012; Santa Clara County Police Chief's Association, 2012; International Association of Chiefs of Police, 2016, 2013; Seattle (WA) Police Department, 2015; Spokane Investigative Regional Response Team, 2014; Tracy, 2010). Upon returning to the police department, the responding supervisor should submit a written report. A recommended supervisory report form and checklist is contained in Appendix A.

Agency Administrator

The agency administrator applies to the head administrator of the department as follows: Chief of Police, Sheriff, Jail Administrator, Warden, or Director of the agency. The agency administrator is responsible for ensuring that a fair, comprehensive, and thorough investigation is conducted and should ensure that all policies are followed. While each critical incident contains different and numerous variables, the agency administrator is responsible for balancing the need to perform a complete and thorough investigation with the need to ensure that the investigation is completed in a timely manner.

Surviving a stressful and traumatic critical incident can result in a myriad of psychological and physiological reactions. With this in mind, the agency administrator should respond to the incident location and maintain a supportive, caring, and professional demeanor (International Association of

Chiefs of Police, 2016, 2013; Miller, 2006). It is suggested that the agency administrator be mindful of any psychological trauma exhibited by the officer and respond appropriately. Primarily, the agency administrator should act as a resource for all responding personnel, and keep abreast of the activities occurring on scene without pressuring investigators, crime scene personnel, officers, or the medical examiner for information that is not confirmed.

On the incident location, the agency administrator should be briefed by the supervisor and informed of the activities accomplished at that time. It is recommended that the agency administrator speak briefly with the involved officer(s), offer him or her support, personal concern, and empathy. The agency administrator should avoid making physical contact with the officer so that physical evidence is not disturbed, and should not ask the officer to provide an explanation or description of what happened. The agency administrator should explain to the officer(s) how the investigation process will progress, and should not make any conclusory statements about the investigation or make any statements which may compromise any legal aspect of the investigation. The agency administrator should check to see if the officer(s) has contacted his or her family or significant other, if needs are being met, and/or if anything is needed. It is recommended that the agency administrator provide the involved officer(s) with a handout which describes the investigatory process and a handout which describes the possible psychological and physiological reactions which may occur, strategies for managing the stress, items to avoid, and information for contacting others for assistance (Colorado 14th Judicial District, 2015).

As part of the critical incident policy, the agency administrator should address the designated time period in which the officer(s) will be placed on administrative leave. The language in the policy should allow for flexibility of time, as recovery from a stressful critical incident is idiosyncratic. It is recommended that the involved officer should be placed on administrative leave for no less than three days (International Association of Chiefs of Police, 2013). The investigative interview should be conducted from 24 to 72 hours after the incident (Americans for Effective Law Enforcement, 2008; Colorado 14th Judicial District, 2015; Force Science News, 2006a; Geiselman, 2010; Tracy, 2010). Officers should be instructed to keep stimulants to a minimum, avoid the news on TV and the newspaper, and not to blog on social media. An officer should conduct a walk-through of the incident scene with his or her legal counsel only and preferably as soon as possible after the incident occurred (Coviello et al., 2014).

Prior to the involved officer(s) being transported home after the critical incident, the agency administrator should thoroughly explain the time period of the administrative leave, the process of the investigation, the process of returning to work, and remind the officer(s) that the leave is not disciplinary. In addition to the involved officer(s), the agency administrator should consider time off, or administrative leave, for those officers who were on scene but who did not shoot or personally participate in the critical incident.

The agency administrator or designee (i.e., public information officer (PIO)) should speak with the media within a reasonable time period, providing updates of the investigation and information that can be shared without jeopardizing or compromising the investigation. Responding to the media is addressed in more detail in Chapter 16.

After the involved officer's formal interview with an investigator (24–72 hours later), the agency administrator, or other command personnel designee, should speak with the involved officer, explain how the investigation process will proceed, and provide a written document that outlines the process. The officer(s) should be informed of the return to duty process and how that will be accomplished, should be encouraged to maintain contact with a support team officer and to voluntarily contact a mental health professional, and should provide a point of contact for command personnel should further questions arise. In some cases, command personnel require an involved officer to attend a counseling intervention session(s) with a trained and qualified mental health professional. In such cases, the mental health professional should be provided with a statement requesting that the officer's attendance at the session be verified without providing details of the intervention session (International Association of Chiefs of Police, 2013). At the appropriate time, command personnel should advise all officers of the agency as to the nature of the incident and ensure that the information provided is accurate.

Responsibilities of the Investigator

The assigned investigator plays a significant role in the investigation. Each critical incident requires that a thorough investigation be completed, in a manner which adheres to policies and procedures, follows appropriate protocols, and adheres to ethical principles, which ultimately will produce an accurate representation of the truth.

Depending on the situation, the investigator may be from the agency's Internal Affairs Unit, a detective from the Homicide unit, or an investigator from an external agency. It is important that the investigator protects the incident scene, while managing and controlling the investigation. The investigator will be working with numerous individuals on scene who will be performing various tasks and responsibilities, and a team approach is needed in order to minimize potential errors. In managing the investigation, the investigator is responsible for the dissemination of information, managing scene personnel, technology management, and logistics management (James, Nordby, & Bell, 2014). The successful outcome of securing the truth and minimizing error will improve by effectively coordinating these components through a collaborative team effort, and ensuring that ongoing communication occurs between all involved personnel throughout the entire investigation. The investigator must strive to thoroughly and accurately document all aspects of the investigation.

On the incident location, the investigator should make contact with the responding supervisor, agency administrator, medical examiner, and prosecutor to be briefed on the incident and the activities accomplished at that point. The investigator should elicit information from the initial responding supervisor, pertaining to: the location of the altercation; whether there was more than one location of contact between the officer(s) and the arrestee/detainee/decedent; the condition of the officer and the arrestee/detainee/decedent; the location of weapons; whether any evidence has been touched, disturbed or moved, and by whom; whether medical or fire personnel disturbed any evidence; whether any of the lighting conditions were altered; and whether any evidence needs immediate collection based on weather conditions or other factors. The investigator should err on the side of obtaining a search warrant to proceed further. If the investigator has any questions regarding securing a search warrant, the prosecutor should be contacted.

The investigator should start an incident scene log (Appendix B) of the inner perimeter, request additional resources as needed, and maintain timely communication with all personnel on scene and with personnel at the agency during the investigation. After being briefed, the investigator should conduct a preliminary walkthrough of the incident scene (Colorado 14th Judicial District, 2015; Eliopulos, 2003; Santa Clara County Police Chief's Association, 2012; Hanzlick, 2007; Laub, 2011; Spokane Investigative Regional Response Team, 2014; Tracy, 2010; Wagner, 2009). During the walkthrough, the investigator may take photographs to initially record the scene. The walkthrough serves as a mental beginning of the investigation and the investigator should be aware of: weather conditions; location and nature of the evidence; evidence that needs immediate preservation and collection; contamination of evidence by officers and emergency medical personnel, or by others; paths of travel during the altercation; and lighting conditions. A warrant is not required at this point as the walkthrough is not considered a search. The prosecutor, medical examiner, and other investigators should be allowed to perform a walkthrough of the incident scene, and the investigator should document the activity. After the walkthrough, the investigator should assess the scene, and based on the assessment, may: determine to expand the scene based on the circumstances of the incident; re-evaluate the media perimeter; determine that multiple scenes are needed to be secured and processed; determine the condition of the evidence; and determine what personnel and what resources are needed to process the scene. The involved officer(s) should not accompany the investigator during the walkthrough. The involved officer(s) should be allowed to walkthrough the scene with only his or her legal counsel prior to the formal interview, and as soon as possible after the incident occurred.

Once the crime scene technician(s) arrives, the investigator should brief him or her and assign the process of collecting evidence. Crime scene technicians should be allowed to perform a preliminary walkthrough to gain a perspective of the scene. If the decedent is still on location, the body should be processed as a "separate scene" (body as evidence) and the investigator and crime scene technicians should work closely with the medical examiner in processing the scene. Crime scene technicians should photograph the decedent's body prior to the medical examiner process (Colorado 14th Judicial District, 2015) (Appendix C).

Incident Scene

After the medical examiner has completed the assessment of the body, crime scene technicians may process the area. As the scene is processed, documentation is a must and serves as the most important component (Appendix D). Processing the incident scene encompasses key investigatory principles of recognition and identification, locating, photographing, collecting and seizing, preserving, transporting, storing, documenting, assessment and interpretation of the evidence, chain of custody, and reporting. Documentation of the scene involves four components: note taking, photography, videotaping, and scene sketching (James et al., 2014). All of the components are important and one is no more important than the others. Notes should reflect notification and arrival information; times of various tasks performed; briefing with personnel; personnel on scene and their tasks performed; assessment of the scene; description of all evidence; description of the environment and climatic conditions of the scene; arrestee/detainee/decedent description; description of all bodily fluids on scene; processing methods used; contacts with witnesses and their identification; description of all measurements taken; and reflect as a guide to who, what, where, when and how. Accurate note taking is important in documenting the investigation process, for preparing and writing the investigator's report, and for future investigations that may follow (Eliopulos, 2003) (Appendix D).

A crime scene technician should place numbered placards next to all pieces of evidence, as well as the body. If the scene is outside, partially spray painting near the evidence on the ground may be used to assist in documenting and outlining the positioning of certain items of evidence, including: vehicle tires, weapons, restraints, body position, position of the involved officers at the time of the altercation, location of shell casings, location of medical intervention by emergency medical personnel, and other pieces of evidence. In an officer-involved shooting incident, the crime scene technician or investigator should place adhesive labels with numbers next to bullet strike points on doors, walls, buildings, vehicles, windows, appliances, etc., then photograph and videotape. Any weapons handled or used by the decedent should be processed for fingerprints, photographed and videotaped, and bagged properly.

Investigators should ensure that photographs are taken of the overall incident location with a full 360-degree rotation. Other photographs should include: all pieces of evidence; the position of the decedent if still on the scene; body fluids on scene; injuries of the arrestee/detainee if still on scene; emergency medical vehicles, patrol vehicles, and fire vehicles; photographs from the perspective of the officers, witness officers, civilian witnesses, and arrestee/detainee/decedent; pathways of travel of the altercation; and aerial photos of the scene. Photographs should include views of the overall scene, as well as midrange, and close-up shots. Photographs of the trajectory of firearm rounds as reconstructed with measurements should be included. All photos taken must be recorded in a photo log (National Institute of Justice, 2011). If involved officers have not already been photographed, crime scene technicians should photograph them in their uniforms, from varying angles, and take pictures of all sustained injuries and abrasions, their gun belts, firearms, and all force equipment used.

The scene should also be videotaped and a sketch of the scene should be made. Videotaping the scene provides a better depth perception view not commonly provided by still photos. The sketch of the scene should include: measurements consistent with the evidence and location on scene, the position of the involved officer(s), the position of the decedent in proximity to the officer, and within the proximity to other pertinent items and evidence associated with the scene (Wagner, 2009).

Collecting and preserving the evidence comprises an important component of the investigation. The investigator should ensure that ample and varying types of containers are on location, with enough markers and sealing materials to package the evidence (Lothridge & Fitzpatrick, 2013). The nature or type of evidence will determine in what type of container the evidence is stored. For example, liquid or volatile types of evidence should be placed in airtight and unbreakable containers. Wet items can be temporarily packaged in airtight containers, allowed to air-dry, and then later repackaged within the original container. Dry clothing can generally be placed in paper bags and sealed. All pieces of evidence should be packaged separately to prevent cross-contamination between items of evidence. All containers must be sealed and marked at the time of the collection by the individual packaging the evidence, with identifying marks, normally with the investigator's initials (James et al., 2014). Investigators need to be mindful of the type of evidence and the type of container appropriate to package and preserve the evidence. A log of all collected evidence must be maintained which identifies the evidence, the time of packaging, and who packaged it. The investigator and crime scene technicians should follow safety procedures as they process the crime scene and collect evidence.

Identification of Witnesses

The investigator should identify and document all officer witnesses and supervisory witnesses who observed the critical incident for later interviews (Eliopulos, 2003). Responding emergency medical and fire personnel should be identified for later interviews. The investigator should contact all civilian witnesses, including any family members, and obtain preliminary information regarding the incident, and acquire their contact information for more detailed interviews at the agency. The investigator should obtain statements about the arrestee/detainee/decedent's behaviors or activities in the preceding hours, days, and weeks prior to police contact. This can assist in obtaining a full assessment of the person prior to police intervention or contact. Civilian witnesses should be asked if they made any video recording of the incident and the investigator should follow proper protocols in obtaining the video.

The investigator should conduct a detailed interview and obtain a written statement from both civilian and prisoner witnesses. The investigator should also consider videotaping transient witness interviews and those whom the investigator believes may change their statement later. If the critical incident occurred in a correctional facility, the investigator should obtain prisoner identification, housing unit location, and interview all prisoners who may have witnessed the incident or have information regarding the incident.

Radio Communications and Videos

An investigator should collect, review, assess, and preserve all radio communication recordings made between dispatch, officers, supervisors, fire and emergency medical services personnel, and individuals who called for police assistance. The computer-aided dispatch (CAD) logs should be collected and assessed. All video recordings made of the incident by the officer's body worn camera or in-car camera, surveillance recordings from nearby businesses or by civilian witnesses, or recordings from surveillance cameras in a correctional facility, should be collected, assessed, stored, and preserved.

At the Hospital

The hospital should be treated as a scene and the investigator should assign an additional investigator to the hospital to collect evidence and to interview appropriate medical personnel (Colorado 14th Judicial District, 2015). If the arrestee/detainee is still alive at the hospital, the investigator should work with hospital staff in photographing any wounds prior to surgery, noting any blunt trauma on the body and items that caused the injury, and photographing entrance and exit wounds and any powder tattooing, and noting any other bodily injuries. In accordance with legal requirements, the investigator should obtain samples of intoxicant testing, and should also collect, package, photograph, and document the arrestee/detainee's clothing. Statements and behaviors of the arrestee/detainee/decedent at the hospital should be documented as well as statements made by family and friends. The investigator should follow up with later interviews of family members and friends.

The investigator should interview the treating nurse and physician and obtain a copy of their medical reports, as well as determine if any evidence was removed from the arrestee/detainee/decedent and collect the evidence. The investigator should interview fire and emergency medical personnel and copies of run sheets and reports should be collected, reviewed, and preserved. The investigator should work with hospital personnel in obtaining access to interview the arrestee/detainee and if a dying declaration is made, it should be recorded when possible.

The Autopsy

In an officer-involved critical incident resulting in a death, an autopsy will be conducted by the medical examiner/pathologist and the investigator should attend (Colorado 14th Judicial District, 2015; Eliopulos, 2003; Hanzlick, 2007; Prahlow, 2010; Spokane Investigative Regional Response

Team, 2014; Wagner, 2009). The investigator should work closely with the medical examiner's office and form a professional working relationship. The fundamental function of the autopsy is to establish the cause and manner of death. The medical examiner may determine the manner of death from one of the following: accident, homicide, natural causes, accident, suicide, or undetermined (Graham, 2014; DiMaio, 2006; DiMaio & DiMaio, 2006).

It is important for the investigator to know the incident scene to know what will be important at the autopsy. The investigator should bring the clothes of the decedent and relevant scene photos to the autopsy so that evidence can be compared to the evidence found during the autopsy. The investigator should take photos of the decedent at the time of autopsy and focus on all injuries and trauma to the body, including: bruises, cuts, scrapings, contusions, marks, gunshot wounds (entrance and exit wounds), and any deformities. Small placards with numbers or letters should be placed near the wounds accompanied by a small scale to indicate the size of the wound, abrasions, or cuts. In officer-involved shooting incidents, the hands of the decedent should be tested for GSR. Regardless of the manner of death, the hands and all digits should be photographed and particularly the thumbs in arrest-related sudden custodial deaths.

If the incident involved an arrest-related custodial restraint death, the investigator should request that the pathologist conduct swabs of the nasal cavity, rectum, and vaginal areas, take a rectal temperature, and examine fingernail clippings. In addition, the following tests should be completed: histology, serology, toxicology, gastric contents, vitreous humor, bile and liver, and hair (DiMaio & DiMaio, 2006; Graham, 2014; James et al., 2014; Sathyavagiswaran, Rogers, & Noguchi, 2007). Graham (2014) also recommends that tissues be examined for sickle-cell trait condition. The structures of the neck should be carefully examined in cases where asphyxia is suspected (Vilke, 2006). The investigator should carefully review the reports and tests, including a review of the condition of the heart (e.g., the size of the heart and whether it was diseased) and other organs (e.g., the size and condition of the lungs, the condition of the brain, and artifacts that occurred post mortem), as well as signs of life saving efforts on the body (Ross, 2006). Since many arrest-related deaths are associated with excited delirium and mental illness, these tests and extensive analysis of the internal organs will assist in more specifically determining the cause of death. The investigator should not assume that all of these tests would be performed. The investigator should take photographs of the decedent's ankles and wrists to document the application of restraints, signature marks of the application of a CEW, and the use of an impact weapon (align with a scale) (Appendix E).

Although the investigator will obtain the autopsy report, the death certificate, and results of tests, he or she should take notes of personal observations of the decedent, describing signs of wounds and trauma, and documenting the photos taken. It is important to recognize that there will be post-mortem changes to the condition of the decedent's body, and that some marks on the body or fractures of bones will result as therapeutic artifacts (Hanzlick, 2007).

Personal History of the Decedent

In sudden arrest-related custody deaths, the investigator should conduct an extensive investigation into the background of the decedent (this can be useful in officer-involved shootings also) (Copeland, 1984; DiMaio & DiMaio, 1989; Eckert, 1983; Lawrence & Mohr, 2004; Ross 2006). The investigation should include the following historical aspects: family, residential, military employment, medical/mental health, arrest/conviction and incarceration, behavioral, and substance abuse. Acquiring a complete history of the decedent can provide additional information regarding his or her background. This is most useful in obtaining a complete understanding of the cause of death, which may be problematic when a negative autopsy is determined. The investigator should consider obtaining a search warrant to search the residence of the decedent for prescription, as well as illicit drugs, which may have been abused by the decedent.

Chain of Custody

The chain of custody must be followed by the investigator/team. The chain of custody helps to ensure the integrity of the investigation, documents how and by whom evidence was collected, shows that the evidence was not altered, and will show who had possession of the evidence at a particular time (Eliopulos, 2003; Hanzlick, 2007; Hundt & Wigger, 2013). At various points of time during the collection of evidence, investigators and crime scene technicians should document the evidence, the time, the person transporting the evidence, and the person receiving the evidence. Generally, the collected and packaged evidence is transported to the agency property room and itemized and documented upon receipt. Documenting the evidence provides a paper trail and shows where the evidence was during a certain time and who had possession of the evidence. Failing to document the evidence and maintain the proper chain of custody jeopardizes the integrity of the investigation, as well as heightens the suspicions of whether the investigation was performed in accordance with policy, professional guidelines, and ethics, and may prohibit the use of the evidence in legal proceedings.

Notification of the Family

As soon as reasonably possible, the investigator should make contact with the family or next of kin and notify them of the serious injury of the arrestee/detainee or death of the decedent (Hundt & Wigger, 2013). An investigator may consider making contact with the family with personnel from the medical examiner's office and/or the agency chaplain. It is important to provide factual information to the family and to treat them with respect. The investigator should also provide the family or next of kin with the status of the investigation and what remains to be accomplished. A date should be discussed with the family to determine when a formal interview with appropriate family members should be conducted, and the investigator should provide the family with his or her contact information.

Releasing the Scene

Prior to releasing the incident scene, the investigator should perform a final assessment to ensure that all elements of the scene investigation have been performed (Colorado 14th Judicial District, 2015). The investigator should not release the scene until after the autopsy has been performed, as questions may emerge about the evidence. The final assessment should include the following: conduct a final walkthrough of the scene; ensure all evidence has been collected, packaged, and has been fully documented; ensure all logs have been completed and collected; allow a walkthrough of the scene by the involved officer and his or her legal counsel; ensure to discuss the scene and evidence with all crime scene technicians, supervisors, command personnel, the prosecutor, and agency attorney; review all photographs that have been taken and determine if more are necessary, and re-check to ensure there is full documentation; recheck the listing of all witnesses and their contact information, including officer witnesses; ensure all scene logs are complete; review evidence and reports collected at the hospital of the arrestee/detainee/decedent and the involved officer(s); review agency policies to ensure compliance; and cross-check assessment against investigation checklists.

The investigator should review the critical incident with the department's firearm instructor and/or the department's subject control instructor. In some departments, this may include the members of the force investigation team (FIT). Once all evidence has been collected, the investigator should review the force policy, force techniques, and all force equipment used in the incident with the appropriate department instructor. If there is a video of the incident available, it should be reviewed by both the investigator and instructor. Conducting this review with the appropriate instructor will provide an additional perspective as it relates to the incident dynamics and the parameters of the policy and the training of the involved officer(s). The investigator should incorporate the instructor's review of the incident within the final investigation report identifying the date, time, location, and the specific instructor interviewed.

Investigator's Report

The objective of the investigator's report is to chronicle the process of the investigation and to provide a comprehensive and accurate summation of the critical incident. The prosecuting attorney will review the report to determine if criminal charges should be brought against the involved officer(s). The agency administrator will also review the report to determine whether the involved officer(s) violated any departmental policies, which could lead to either agency discipline or exoneration. The investigator should not interject his or her opinion into the report, nor make a recommendation regarding the involved officer(s), as any decision is the agency administrator's responsibility (Ross, 2006).

The report should contain, at a minimum, a written and thorough description of the following items:

- an executive summary discussing a brief synopsis of the incident, including the involved officers, their agency, and the arrestee/detainee/decedent;
- incident scene description and a description of all evidence located, collected, packaged, assessed, and stored (scene logs as attachment);
- a full description of any weapons handled or used by the decedent and the results of the tests performed on the weapon(s);
- a full description of the behaviors and statements made by the decedent (pre-, during, and post-incident);
- all scene photographs, videos, sketches, and measurements with documentation (with attachments);
- in-car camera videos, body worn camera videos, surveillance videos, and witness videos;
- computer-aided dispatch logs and all radio traffic/transmissions;
- typed transcripts of interviews of involved officer(s), supervisors, witness officers, scene witnesses, family members, responding emergency medical personnel, fire department personnel, attending hospital personnel, and written statements and reports generated;
- videos and/or audio recording of any interviews;
- statements made by the arrestee/detainee and family members at the hospital;

- injuries sustained by involved officers and the arrestee/detainee;
- firearms of involved officers (with photos) and tests performed;
- all use of force techniques, equipment, devices, aerosols, and restraints used (with photos);
- if a TASER was used, describe data port printout of dates and times used, and any tests conducted;
- ballistic tests performed with report (with photos);
- medical intervention by officers and by emergency medical personnel on scene and at the hospital;
- all reports generated by officers, supervisors, and medical and fire personnel;
- run sheets by emergency medical and fire personnel;
- decedent or arrestee/detainee history;
- scientific tests and reconstructions performed;
- shift logs;
- develop and include a time line of the events;
- death certificate, autopsy report, and all post-mortem tests performed with reports; and
- media accounts (TV and press).

Force Investigative Team

In major uses of force which result in a significant injury of the suspect the department's Force Investigation Team (FIT) may be assembled to review the officer's use of force. The purpose of the review is to serve as an administrative review to examine the officer's use of force as it relates to the department's use of force policy, training, and within the context of the dynamics of the confrontation. At a minimum, the team could comprise a supervisor at the rank of sergeant or higher, other appropriate command personnel, the department's subject control instructor, and the department's internal affairs investigator. A significant injury could mean that the suspect sustained treatable injuries by a medical professional on scene or at a hospital as a result of the officer's use of force. The review conducted by FIT should include the following items: involved officers' report, all videos and audio of the incident, officer witness reports, incident scene witnesses statements and/or interviews, arrestee statements/interview, citizen complaint, responding incident supervisor's report, all empty-hand control techniques used, all force equipment applied, emergency medical personnel reports and/or interviews, conducted energy device data printout, officer training records, department use of force policy, and interview of the officer. Once the FIT investigation is complete a report should be submitted to the agency executive for his or her review in order to determine the appropriate sanction as warranted. A checklist of these items is contained in Appendix E.

Summary

An officer-involved critical incident comprises innumerable variables that must be examined by the accomplished investigator. Pre-planning prior to an incident and following the guidelines presented in this chapter can assist in mitigating the potential errors that may arise from performing the investigation. Investigators are encouraged to integrate these protocols while conducting the investigation, and to cross-reference their work against the accompanying checklists.

Appendix A

Response to Resistance Supervisor's On-Scene After-Action Report

Incident Date: Incident Time: Case #:

Incident Location: Incident Type:

Rationale for Using Force:

☐ Effect an arrest ☐ Self-defense ☐ Defense of another ☐ Prevent a felony
☐ Prevent misdemeanor ☐ Field force operation ☐ For subject safety

Subject Resistance:

☐ Psychological intimidation ☐ Verbal non-compliance ☐ Passive resistance
☐ Pulling away/pushing/escape/fleeing ☐ Physical assault ☐ Deadly force assault
☐ Weapon(s) used: ______________________________
☐ Suspect injuries: ______________________________
☐ Medical/EMS intervention, describe: ______________________________

Officer Response:________ Number of involved officers: __________ Back-Up Requested

☐ Verbal instructions ☐ De-escalation techniques

Empty hand control used:
☐ Strikes ☐ Take down ☐ Control holds ☐ Neck restraint ☐ Pressure Points ☐ Escort

Force equipment used:
☐ Handcuffs ☐ Leg restraints ☐ Restraint Chair ☐ Aerosol ☐ Impact weapon ☐ Projectile

☐ Canine, Describe: ______________________________
☐ Lethal force
☐ FA Serial #:_____________
☐ TASER Serial #_______________________ Cartridge #___________
☐ Probe locations & # of applications _________________
☐ Drive stun locations & # of applications _____________
☐ Taser data printout

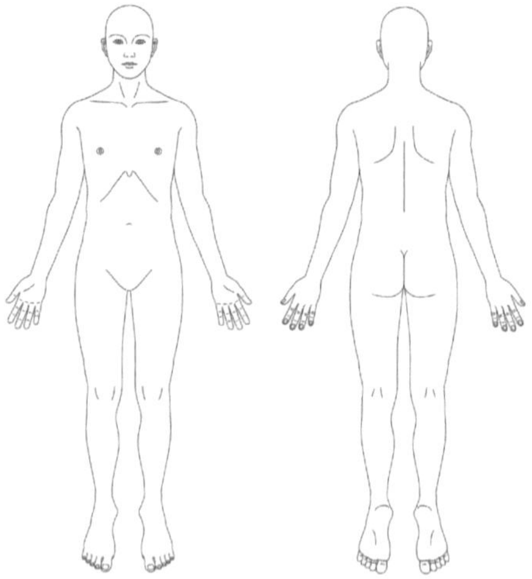

Response to Resistance Supervisor's On-Scene After-Action Report (cont.)

Describe the Circumstances and Temporal Aspects of the Incident:

Describe the Environment of the Scene:

Describe Officer Injuries:

Describe Officer Actions:

Witnesses and contact information:

Describe Supervisor Actions:

Method of transport and location of suspect:

Photos Taken:

Video of Incident:

On-scene investigation:

Officers Report:

Additional narrative:

Supervisor: Division: Executive:

Appendix B

Incident Scene Log

Case #:______________ Location:____________________________

Date:________________ Lead investigator:____________________

Name	*Rank*	*Unit*	*Time In*	*Time Out*
1.				
2.				
3.				
4.				
5.				
6.				

Appendix C

Evidence Collected and Photos

Date: __________ Investigator: ______________________________

Description	*Location*	*Photo Image*	*Placard #*
1.			
2.			
3.			
4.			
5.			
6.			
7.			
8.			
9.			
10.			
11.			
12.			
13.			
14.			
15.			

Appendix D

Officer-Involved Shooting Checklist

Notification List

☐ Supervisor ☐ Executive ☐ Investigator ☐ Crime scene technicians
☐ Medical examiner ☐ Prosecutor ☐ Legal counsel ☐ Risk manager
☐ Peer support team ☐ Chaplain

Preliminary Questions

Circumstances of the incident

☐ Location of incident ☐ Suspect behaviors ☐ Confrontation variables ☐ Climatic conditions
☐ Operating environment ☐ Weapon used by suspect ☐ Weapon accessible to suspect
☐ No weapon used by suspect ☐ Suspect used vehicle as weapon ☐ Officer dispatched or initiate contact
☐ Officer place him/herself in bad situation ☐ Verbal commands used ☐ Officer over-react/under-react
☐ Officer used verbal commands ☐ Tactics used by officer ☐ Cover available ☐ Policy issues
☐ Training issues ☐ Human factors ☐ Injuries sustained by officer ☐ Injuries sustained by suspect
☐ Public information statement of officer ☐ Search warrants needed ☐ Peer support team

Suspect Actions

☐ Weapon used by suspect ☐ Movements of suspect (contextual cues) ☐ Behaviors of suspect
☐ Type of resistance ☐ Threat of suspect ☐ Comments by suspect ☐ Injuries sustained

Suspect History

☐ Family ☐ Residential ☐ Military ☐ Criminal & confinement ☐ Employment
☐ Medical/Mental health ☐ Substance abuse ☐ Behavioral

Officer Actions

☐ Suspect's behavior precipitates officer response ☐ Actions of officer ☐ Tactics employed
☐ Back-up requested ☐ De-escalation techniques ☐ Supervisor requested ☐ EMS requested
☐ Distance from officer to suspect ☐ Verbal's attempted/used ☐ Officer perception
☐ Perceptual distortions ☐ Reactionary time (movement time, reaction time, & response time)
☐ Weapons used ☐ # of shots fired ☐ Work history of the officer (s) ☐ Training history
☐ Injuries sustained ☐ Transported to hospital

At the Scene

☐ Secure scene integrity (outer & inner perimeters) ☐ Medical treatment of officer
☐ Medical treatment of suspect ☐ Personnel at scene ☐ Scene log ☐ 360° walkthrough
☐ Video made ☐ Witness contacted & contact information ☐ Diagram/sketch made
☐ Measurements ☐ Preliminary statements made

Photos

☐ Photos of scene ☐ Photos of officer ☐ Photos of uniform/plain clothes ☐ Photos of decedent/subject
☐ Photos of police vehicles ☐ Photos of decedent vehicle

Officer-Involved Shooting Checklist (cont.)

Evidence Collection/Analysis

☐ All police equipment ☐ Officer uniform ☐ Officer vehicle ☐ Suspect vehicle
☐ Officer firearm (location/position) [serial #; model; caliber] ☐ Suspect weapon(s) [location/position]
☐ Objects used by suspect (bat, club, phone, stick, etc.) ☐ Shell casings (# & location) [officer & suspect]
☐ Rounds (location) ☐ Position of decedent when shot ☐ Position of officer when firearm fired
☐ Trajectory tests ☐ Ballistics tests ☐ Scene measurements ☐ Fingerprints ☐ Blood spatter
☐ Decedent clothing/personal affects ☐ Secure in-car video & body camera/video
☐ Dispatch tapes ☐ EMS run sheet ☐ ER personnel ☐ Evidence collected and bagged
☐ Evidence transported ☐ Chain of custody ☐ All tests performed

Autopsy

☐ Date and time ☐ Death certificate ☐ Toxicology performed ☐ Note all tests performed
☐ Note injuries, marks, tattoos, & trauma on the body ☐ Diseases of the body ☐ Photos of the body
☐ Entrance wounds ☐ Exit wounds

Reports

☐ Officer(s) ☐ EMS (run sheets/reports) ☐ Supervisors ☐ ER physicians ☐ Crime scene tech
☐ Corner/pathologist ☐ Autopsy ☐ Toxicology ☐ Tests performed

Interviews

☐ Witness & written statements ☐ EMS personnel ☐ Medical personnel ☐ Involved officer(s)
☐ Other officers ☐ Use of force/firearms instructor ☐ Follow-up interviews ☐ Retain all notes

Internal Affairs

☐ Garrity warnings ☐ Garrity statement ☐ Representation

Criminal Investigation

☐ Miranda rights ☐ Representation

Graham v. Conner standard of Objective Reasonableness

☐ Severity of crime at issue ☐ Suspect posed an immediate threat to the safety of the officer/others
☐ Suspect actively resisting arrest ☐ Circumstances tense, uncertain, &/or rapidly evolving
☐ Officer(s) perception ☐ Split-second decision making ☐ Totality of circumstances

Ongoing File

☐ All reports ☐ List of evidence & storage location ☐ List of witnesses/interviews & statements
☐ Retain interview tapes & statements ☐ Officer reports ☐ Relevant policies & procedures
☐ Rescue personnel reports ☐ All medical reports, statements, & interviews
☐ Dispatch tapes & transcripts ☐ Shift logs ☐ Autopsy reports & tests reports
☐ Firearms & tests performed ☐ All force equipment used ☐ Training records of officers
☐ Media accounts (TV & Press) ☐ Risk manager & legal counsel ☐ Prosecutor's report
☐ AG report ☐ Grand jury proceedings ☐ FBI investigation ☐ Develop timeline of events
☐ Maintain ongoing file as case develops

Appendix E

Sudden Arrest-Related Death Investigation Form

Investigation Data

Date:____________ Agency:____________________________________ Case:#__________________________

Investigated by:_________________________________County/State:___________________________________

Investigated by:_________________________________County/State:___________________________________

Decedent's Name: Last___________________ First______________________________ M_________________

Gender: ☐ Male ☐ Female DOB:_________________ Age:___________ SS#________________________

Phone #:______ Race: ☐ White ☐ African/Am. ☐ Hispanic/Latino ☐ Asian ☐ Am. Indian ☐ Other

Address:_______________________________________ City:_________________________ Zip_____________

Circumstances of Incident

Date of Death:_________ Time of Incident:_________________ Place of Death:_________________________

Incident Address:______________________________ City__________________________ Zip:_____________

Type/nature of call: ☐ Dispatch ☐ Patrol ☐ Serve order ☐ Assist medical/mental health:

____

____

Initial number of officers:___________ # of additional officers:_____________ # of supervisors_____________

Scene: ☐ Rural____

☐ Urban/suburban____

☐ Residential: ____

☐ Business:____

☐ Confinement facility:____

☐ Court House:____

☐ Mental health/medical facility:____

☐ Transport vehicle:____

Subject behaviors prior to police intervention:____

____

Sudden Arrest-Related Death Investigation Form (cont.)

Decedent Resistance

☐ Adopt threatening posture ☐ Verbal ☐ Passive ☐ Attempt to evade arrest/control
☐ Physical assault actions ☐ Lethal force assault ☐ Weapons ☐ Fight ☐ Duration of resistance

Describe resistance/struggle:____

____

Decedent Behaviors/Condition with Police

☐ Access to weapons ☐ Attempt to access officer weapons ☐ Stated nothing ☐ Stated can't breathe
☐ Stated needs help ☐ Stated needs medical ☐ Shouting ☐ Incoherent speech
☐ Threw objects ☐ Naked ☐ Partially naked ☐ Injured prior to police contact ☐ Bleeding
☐ Appeared mentally ill ☐ Appeared chemically impaired ☐ Sweating ☐ Severely agitated
☐ Increased strength ☐ High tolerance to pain ☐ Breathing difficulty ☐ Destroy property
☐ Violent behaviors toward self ☐ Violent behaviors toward others ☐ Struggle on ground
☐ Running ☐ Purposeless behaviors ☐ Hyperventilation ☐ Foaming at mouth ☐ Vomiting
☐ Spitting blood ☐ Spitting

Describe:____

____

Officer Response

Force justification:
☐ Control purposes ☐ Affect arrest ☐ Defend another ☐ Medical intervention ☐ Self-defense
☐ Back-up called ☐ Commitment Order ☐ Involuntary Commitment

Describe nature of contact:____

____

Levels of Force Used:
☐ Verbal ☐ Soft empty-hand ☐ Hard empty-hand ☐ Neck restraint ☐ OC ☐ Baton
☐ Flashlight ☐ ECD ☐ Handcuffs ☐ Other restraints used ☐ Restraint chair ☐ Canine
☐ Lethal force ☐ ECD discharge record ☐ Photos of equipment ☐ Other

Describe:____

____

Sudden Arrest-Related Death Investigation Form (cont.)

Actions After Control & Restraint

☐ Radio back-up ☐ Behaviors of decedent ☐ Subject verbal ☐ Decontamination procedures
☐ Decedent position ☐ Radio EMS ☐ Monitoring procedures ☐ Medical intervention by officers
☐ Medical intervention by EMS ☐ Subject calm ☐ Subject unresponsive ☐ Subject body temp.
☐ Subject's breathing patterns ☐ Skin color ☐ Trauma to subject ☐ Restraints removed
☐ Officer at medical facility ☐ Officer(s) Injuries ☐ Subject behaviors/statements during transport
☐ Vital signs ☐ AED printout ☐ Medications used ☐ Seizure ☐ Apnea ☐ Cyanosis
☐ Convulsions ☐ Barbs removed ☐ Length of time of struggle/in restraints
☐ Use of force after restraint

Describe:____

____

Arrival Times: Officers:________________ Back-up:________________ Supervisors:________________

EMS:________ Fire Dept.:________ Depart:________ Arrival at hospital:________ Arrival at jail:________

Incident Scene

☐ Briefing ☐ Walk through ☐ Log ☐ Photographs ☐ Measurements ☐ Diagrams ☐ Video of scene
☐ In-car video ☐ Body camera video ☐ Secure all force equipment ☐ Secure all firearms
☐ Secure officer uniforms ☐ Secure restraints used ☐ Property destroyed
☐ All evidence collected & tagged ☐ Log Personnel on scene ☐ Medical paraphernalia
☐ Blood ☐ Body fluids ☐ Environmental/climatic conditions noted

Describe:____

____

Scene Description:
☐ Indoor Temperature:________ Humidity:________ ☐ Outdoor Temperature:______ Humidity:________

Weather: ☐ Rainy ☐ Sunny ☐ Cloudy ☐ Windy Wind Chill:__________ Time:__________

Surface type/temp:____

____

Sudden Arrest-Related Death Investigation Form (cont.)

Witness Interviews

☐ Log ☐ Civilian ☐ Relatives ☐ Officers ☐ Supervisors ☐ EMS ☐ Fire personnel
☐ Physician ☐ Tapes ☐ Written statements

Name:______________________ Address:______________________
__________Phone #:__________ Date:__________ Time:__________
Name: ______________________ Address:______________________ Phone #:__________
Date:__________Time:__________

Witness:
Name:______________________ Address:______________________
__________Phone #:__________ Date:__________ Time:__________
Name: ______________________ Address:______________________ Phone #:__________
Date:__________ Time:__________

Name:______________________Address:______________________
__________Phone #:__________ Date:__________ Time:__________
Name: ______________________ Address:______________________ Phone #:__________
Date:__________Time:__________

Name:______________________ Address:______________________
Phone #:__________ Date:__________ Time: __________
Name: ______________________ Address:______________________

Transport

☐ Transport by police ☐ Transport by medical ☐ Transport to jail ☐ Transport to medical facility
☐ Position of subject during transport ☐ Position in vehicle ☐ Subject verbal
☐ Transported in restraints ☐ Medical care during transport ☐ Length of transport
☐ Monitoring during transport ☐ Behaviors during transport

Describe:____
____

At the Hospital

☐ Collect subject clothing (list) ☐ Emergency run sheets ☐ Subject behaviors at hospital
☐ Rescue efforts/procedures ☐ Medications ☐ Death pronouncement ☐ Statements of physicians

Statements by family/others Describe:____
____

Decedent Information

☐ Family history ☐ Social/residential history ☐ Employment history ☐ Educational history
☐ Military history ☐ Medical history ☐ Psychiatry history ☐ Hospitalization history
☐ Prior police contacts ☐ Prior criminal history ☐ Substance abuse history ☐ Medication history
☐ Behavioral & nutritional history

Sudden Arrest-Related Death Investigation Form (cont.)

Describe:____

____

Notification Procedures

☐ Identify & locate relatives ☐ Notify next of kin ☐ Notification of death
☐ Notify concerned agencies ☐ Media
Describe:____

____

Autopsy

Date:__________ Time:______________ Investigator:____________________________________

☐ Photos of body ☐ Post mortem changes ☐ Evidence of medical intervention
☐ External trauma to body ☐ Temperature of body ☐ Internal body organs exam
☐ Weight of organs ☐ Examination of brain ☐ Exam of eyes
☐ Respiratory exam ☐ Cardiovascular system ☐ Alimentary system ☐ Endocrine system
☐ Genitourinary system ☐ Orifice swabbing ☐ Fingernail clippings ☐ Body fluids
☐ Infectious diseases ☐ X-rays ☐ Microscopic exam ☐ Blood sample ☐ Organ abnormalities
☐ Pancreas ☐ Musculoskeletal system ☐ Head ☐ Neck ☐ Spine ☐ Scars
☐ Needle marks ☐ Artifacts ☐ Scalp ☐ Hair ☐ Urine ☐ Body deformities
☐ Digit exam ☐ Markings ☐ Autopsy report ☐ Toxicology report ☐ Serology report
☐ Histology report

Cause of death:____

____

Manner of death: ☐ Natural ☐ Homicide ☐ Suicide ☐ Accident ☐ Undetermined
Mechanism of death: ____________________________ Death certificate: ________________________
ME/Coroner ____
Pathologist:____

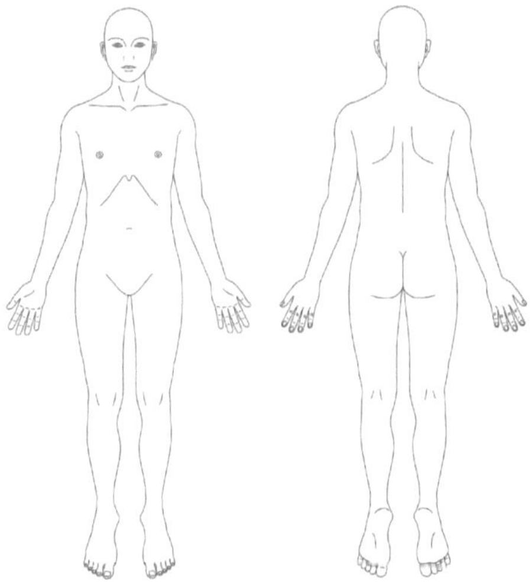

Sudden Arrest-Related Death Investigation Form (cont.)

Search Decedent's Property

Residence: ☐ All rooms ☐ Medicine cabinets ☐ Closets ☐ Refrigerator ☐ Kitchen
☐ Basement ☐ Garage ☐ Storage ☐ Vehicles ☐ Cell ☐ Clothing (list)
☐ Medications (list) ☐ Drugs (list) ☐ Photos ☐ Other

Officer(s) Items

☐ Collect officer uniform ☐ Photo officer ☐ Photo uniform ☐ Photo shoes
☐ Photo equipment ☐ Photo restraints

Investigator's Report/Ongoing File

ID all involved: ☐ officers ☐ supervisors ☐ witnesses ☐ rescue personnel ☐ physicians
Include investigation briefing process
Include reports/interviews of: ☐ officer ☐ supervisors ☐ witnesses ☐ rescue personnel
☐ physicians ☐ other
Include all circumstance scene evidence and how processed
Include all: ☐ Walk through ☐ photos ☐ videos ☐ diagrams ☐ scene measurements
☐ dispatch tapes/transcripts
Include all: ☐ tests ☐ examinations ☐ reconstructions performed

Complete written description of:

☐ All reports obtained ☐ Incident scene ☐ Uses of force ☐ Restraints ☐ Equipment
☐ Verbal instructions ☐ Intervention strategies ☐ Taser data printout
☐ Monitoring of subject after restraint by police and intervention efforts
☐ Medical intervention by officers
☐ Medical intervention by rescue personnel at scene and by whom (EMS/Fire rescue run sheets)
☐ Transport & by whom
☐ Medical intervention at hospital
☐ Autopsy, death certificate, & all scientific tests results performed
☐ Subject history and activities
☐ Develop timeline of events
☐ Final walk through, scene survey, & follow-up
☐ Media accounts (written & video)
☐ Shift logs
☐ Training records of officers
☐ Prosecutor review
☐ Grand jury hearing
☐ Agency counsel & risk manager

Appendix F

Force Investigation Team Investigation—Checklist

☐ Involved officer's report

☐ All videos and audio recordings

☐ Officer witness reports

☐ Arrestee injuries

☐ Medical personnel reports/treatment

☐ Responding supervisor's report

☐ Witness statements/interview

☐ Verbal commands provided

☐ Empty-hand control techniques used

☐ Force equipment used

☐ Arrestee statement/interview

☐ Citizen complaint

☐ TASER data port printout

☐ Officer training records

☐ Department use of force training

☐ Interview of officer

☐ Department use of force policy

☐ Report submitted

References

Aitchison, W. (2014, September). *Body worn cameras: A model policy*. Labor Relations Information Systems (LIRS). Retrieved from https://lris.com/2014/09/12/model-body-camera-policy.

Americans for Effective Law Enforcement. (2008). Administrative investigations of police shootings and other critical incidents: Officer statements and use of force reports, part one, the basics. *AELE Monthly Law Journal*, *8*(August), 201–215.

Armstrong, J., Clare, J., & Plecas, D. (2014). Monitoring the impact of scenario-based use-of- force simulations on police heart rate: Evaluating the Royal Canadian mounted police skills refresher program. *Western Criminology Review*, *15*(1), 51–59.

Artwhol, A. (2002). Perceptual and memory distortions in officer involved shootings. *The FBI Law Enforcement Bulletin*, *71*(10), 18–24.

Artwhol, A. A. & Christensen, L. W. (1997). *Deadly force encounters: What cops need to know to mentally and physically prepare for and survive a gunfight*. Boulder, CO: Paladin Press.

Atkins, V. & Norris, W. A. (2007). Simulation and technology for training. *The FLETC Journal*, *5*(1), 24–34.

Benell, B., Jones, N. J., & Corey, S. (2007). Does use of force simulation training in Canadian police agencies incorporate principles of effective training? *Psychology, Public Policy, and Law*, *13*(1), 35–58.

Bohrer, S. & Chaney, R. (2010). Police investigations of the use of deadly force can influence perceptions and outcome. *FBI Law Enforcement Bulletin*, January, 2–5.

Brave, M. (2014a). *Sample response to resistance procedural guidelines*. Phoenix, AZ: LAAW International, 1–9.

Brave, M. (2014b). *Developing a use of force policy*. PowerPoint presentation at the annual International Law Enforcement and Education Training Association conference, Wheeling, IL.

Brosseau v. Haugen, 543 U.S. 194 (2004).

City and County of San Francisco v. Sheehan, 135 S.Ct. 1765 (2015).

City of Canton, Ohio v. Harris, 489 U.S. 378 (1989).

Colorado 14th Judicial District. (2015). *Critical incident team policies and procedures & memorandum of understanding*. Retrieved from www.co.routt.co.us/DocumentCenter/View/4436.

Connick v. Thompson, 563 U.S. 131 S.Ct. 1350 (2011).

Copeland, A. R. (1984). Deaths in custody revisited. *American Journal Forensic Medicine and Pathology*, *5*(2), 121–124.

Coviello, M., Means, R., Presby, S., & Ross, D. L. (2014). Presentation for the Internal Affairs & Critical Incidents Seminar. *Labor Relations Information Systems Seminar*.

Davis, K. R. (2012). *Use of force investigation: A manual for law enforcement*. Bloomington, IN: Responder Media.

Digiliani, J. (2012). *Law enforcement incident handbook: Information for law enforcement involved in critical incidents*. Retrieved from http://post.nv.gov/uploadedFiles/postnvgov/content/Training/Critical%20Incident%20Handbook.pdf.

DiMaio, V. J. M. (2006). Deaths in custody investigations. In D. L. Ross & T. C. Chan (eds.), *Sudden deaths in custody* (167–172). Totowa, NJ: Humana Press.

DiMaio, D. J. & DiMaio, V. (1989). *Forensic pathology*. New York, NY: Elsevier.

DiMaio, T. G. & DiMaio, V. J. M. (2006). *Excited delirium syndrome: Cause of death and prevention*. Boca Raton, FL: CRC Press.

Eckert, G. (1983). Medicolegal investigation of problems involving criminals and criminal activity. *American Journal of Forensic Medicine and Pathology*, *4*(3), 279–286.

Eliopulos, L. N. (2003). *Death investigator's handbook* (expanded and updated edition). Boulder, CO: Paladin Press.

Force Science News. (2006a). How to assure fair, neutral & fact-finding officer-involved shooting investigations, part I (#41). Retrieved from www.forcescience.org/fsnews/41.html.

Force Science News. (2006b). More about how to assure fair, neutral & fact-finding OIS investigations: Suggestions for successfully mining memory, part II (#42). Retrieved from www.forcescience.org/fsnews/42.html.

Force Science News. (2009). Should officers see video of the encounters? Force science states its case (#114). Retrieved from www.forcescience.org/fsnews/114.html.

Frost, R. & Hanzlick, R. (1988). Deaths in custody. Atlanta and Fulton County Jail: 1974–1985. *American Journal Forensic Medicine and Pathology*, *9*(3), 207–211.

Geiselman, R. E. (2010). Rest and eyewitness memory recall. *American Journal of Forensic Psychology*, *28*(1), 65–69.

Graham v. Connor, 490 U.S. 386 (1989).

Graham, M. A. (2014). Investigation of deaths temporally associated with law enforcement apprehension. *Academic Forensic Pathology*, *4*(3), 366–389.

Hanzlick, R. (2007). *Death investigation: Systems and procedures*. Boca Raton, FL: CRC Press.

Hatch, D. E. & Dickson, R. (2007). *Officer-involved shootings and use of force: Practical investigation techniques* (2nd ed.). Boca Raton, FL: CRC Press.

Hiss, J. & Kahana, T. (1996). Medicolegal investigations of death in custody: A postmortem procedure for detection of blunt force injuries. *American Journal of Forensic Medicine and Pathology*, *17*(4), 312–314.

Hudson v. McMillian, 503 U.S. 1 (1992).

Hundt, P. & Wigger, A. (2013). *Guidelines for investigating deaths in custody*. Geneva, Switzerland: International Committee of the Red Cross.

International Association of Chiefs of Police. (2012). *Officer-involved shooting investigative protocols: A guide for law enforcement leaders*. Retrieved from www.theiacp.org/Portals/0/documents/pdfs/OIS_IP_Trifold_Web.pdf.

International Association of Chiefs of Police, Police Psychological Services Section. (2013). Officer-involved shooting guidelines. Retrieved from www.theiacp.org/portals/0/documents/pdfs/psych-officerinvolvedshooting.pdf.

International Association of Chiefs of Police. (2014, April). *Body worn cameras: Concepts and issues paper*. Alexandria, VA: IACP National Law Enforcement Policy Center.

International Association of Chiefs of Police. (2015). *Use of force: Concepts and issues paper*. Alexandria, VA: IACP National Law Enforcement Policy Center.

International Association of Chiefs of Police. (2016). *Office-involved shootings: A guide for law enforcement leaders*. Washington, DC: Office of Community Oriented Policing Services.

James, S. H., Nordby, J. J., & Bell, S. (2014). *Forensic science: An introduction to scientific and investigative techniques* (4th ed.). Boca Raton, FL: CRC Press.

Kingsley v. Hendrickson, 576 U.S. ______ (2015).

Laub, J. (2011). *Death investigation: A guide for the scene investigator, technical update*. Washington, DC: United States Department of Justice, National Institute of Justice.

Lawrence, C. & Mohr, W. (2004). Investigator protocol: Sudden in-custody death. *The Police Chief*, *71*(1), 25–31.

LePard, D. & Collins, J. M. (2015). Chief's counsel: Showing incident video to police officers under investigation—A best practice approach. *The Police Chief*, *82*(March), 20–24.

Lewinski, W. J. (2006, December). New findings about survival training and the stress of post-shooting interviews. *Force Science News*, *61*, 1–3.

Los Angeles County v. Humphries, 131 U.S. 447 (2010).

Lothridge, K. & Fitzpatrick, F. (2013). *Crime scene investigation: A guide for law enforcement*. Largo, FL: National Forensic Science Technology Center.

Luke, J. L. & Reay, D. T. (1992). The perils of investigating and certifying deaths in police custody. *American Journal of Forensic Medicine and Pathology*, *13*(2), 98–100.

Lynch, M. D. (2005). Developing a scenario-based training program: Giving officers a tactical advantage. *The FBI Law Enforcement Bulletin*, 74(10), 1–8.

Miller, L. (2006). Officer-involved shooting: Reaction patterns, response protocols, and psychological intervention strategies. *International Journal of Emergency Mental Health, 8*(4), 239–254.

Miller, L., Toliver, J., & Police Executive Research Forum. (2014). *Implementing a body-worn camera program: Recommendations and lessons learned.* Washington, DC: Office of Community Oriented Policing Services.

Monell v. Department of Social Services of the City of New York, 436 U.S. 658 (1978).

Morrissey, M. R. (2015). *Officer involved shooting protocol 2015.* Denver, CO: Denver District Attorney's Office. Retrieved from www.denverda.org/News_Release/Decision_Letters/OFFICER-INVOLVED%20 SHOOTING%20PROTOCOL%202015%20-revised%20May%202015%20.pdf.

Mullenix v. Luna, 577 U.S. _____ (2015).

National Institute of Justice. (2011). *A guide to death scene investigation.* Washington, DC: Office of Justice Programs. Retrieved from www.nij.gov/topics/law- enforcement/investigations/crime-scene/guides/death-investigation/pages/welcome.aspx.

Nielsen, E. (1981). *The law enforcement officer's use of deadly force and post-shooting reactions.* Salt Lake City, UT: Salt Lake City Police Department.

Patton, D., Loukota, P., & Avery, E. (2013). Using the immersive cognitive readiness simulator to validate the threat fire belt as an operational stressor: A pilot study. In B. Kennedy, D. Reitter, & R. St. Amant (eds.), *Proceedings of the 22nd Annual Conference on Behavior Representation in Modeling and Simulation* (1–8). Ottawa, Canada: BRIMS Society.

Plumhoff v. Rickard, 571 U.S. _____ (2014).

Prahlow, J. (2010). *Forensic pathology for police, death investigators, attorneys, and forensic scientists.* Totowa, NJ: Humana Press.

Ross, D. L. (2006). Administrative issues. In D. L. Ross & T. C. Chan (eds.) *Sudden deaths in custody* (203–228). Totowa, NJ: Humana Press.

Ross, D. L. (2013). *Civil liability in criminal justice* (6th ed.). Waltham, MA: Anderson Publishing.

Ross, D. L., Murphy, R. L., & Hazlett, M. H. (2012). Analyzing perceptions and misperceptions of police officers in lethal force virtual simulator scenarios. *Law Enforcement Executive Forum, 12*(3), 53–73.

Santa Clara County Police Chief's Association. (2012). *Officer involved incident guidelines.* Retrieved from www.sjpd.org/BOI/Homicide/images/Officer-Involved_Incident_Guidelines.pdf.

Sathyavagiswaran, L., Rogers, C., & Noguchi, T. T. (2007). Restraint asphyxia in in-custody deaths: Medical examiner's role in prevention of deaths. *Legal Medicine, 9*(2), 88–93.

Scott v. Harris, 550 U.S. 127 (2007).

Seattle (WA) Police Department. (2015). Use of force reporting and investigation (No. 8.400). *Seattle Police Department Manual*, 1–15.

Sharps, M. J. (2010). *Processing under pressure: Stress, memory and decision-making in law enforcement.* Flushing, NY: Looseleaf Publications.

Spokane Investigative Regional Response Team. (2014). *A protocol to investigate officer involved fatal incidents in the Spokane region.* Retrieved from www.spokanecounty.org/documentcenter/view/4288.

Tennessee v. Garner, 471 U.S. 1 (1985).

Tracy, D. J. (2010). Handling officer involved shootings. *The Police Chief*, 77(October), 38–48.

Vilke, G. M. (2006). Neck holds. In D. L. Ross & T. C. Chan (eds.), *Sudden deaths in custody* (15–38). Totowa, NJ: Humana Press.

Wagner, S. A. (2009). *Death scene investigation.* Boca Raton, FL: CRC Press.

Wilkins v. Gaddy, 130 S. Ct. 1175 (2010).

7

POSITIONAL AND RESTRAINT ASPHYXIA

Davut Savaser and Theodore C. Chan

Introduction

The use and implementation of physical restraint to control violent, uncooperative, or combative individuals is a common and expected intervention for law enforcement, as well as the pre-hospital and hospital setting. This has become an increasingly salient topic given current media discussion and coverage of events that highlight the use of force by law enforcement to restrain individuals. Often, the more violent, combative, or uncooperative an individual is, the greater the amount of force required to restrain. If significant injury or death occurs, there is concern whether or not the restraint process, including the position and method utilized, bear any causal relationship, or whether the death was predicated more upon the circumstances or predisposing factors that led to the person being restrained in the first place. Certainly, within law enforcement, there are specific restraint methods that have been proven to be harmful to individuals, and, as a result, are no longer used due to the risks they pose (see Chapter 8) (Reay & Eisele, 1982; Reay & Holloway, 1982).

In similar respects, the "hogtie," "hobble," or "prone maximal restraint" positions have also been scrutinized as potentially contributing to deaths of individuals brought into custody. The term "hobble" means to tie or strap together the legs to prevent movement. In the hogtie position, the individual is placed in a position with wrists handcuffed behind the back, ankles hobbled and secured, with varying degrees of freedom, to the handcuffs. The hogtie position can be prone (face down) or on the side. When the individual is in a hogtie restraint in a prone position, this is often referred to as the prone maximal restraint position (see Figure 7.1).

The literature does include reports of deaths of individuals placed into this position, with some attributing the cause of death to the restraint position (O'Halloran & Lewman, 1993; Reay et al., 1992; Stratton, Rogers, & Green 1995). The rationale for such conclusions is that the position impairs the ability of the individual to breathe and ventilate, such that hypoxemia (low oxygen levels in the blood) secondary to ventilatory insufficiency or failure, occur and that the degree and duration of the hypoxemia leads to an asphyxiation death. Some have also suggested that the position negatively impacts cardiac output by compression of the heart and great blood vessels, impacting blood flow and placing individuals at risk for cardiovascular collapse and death.

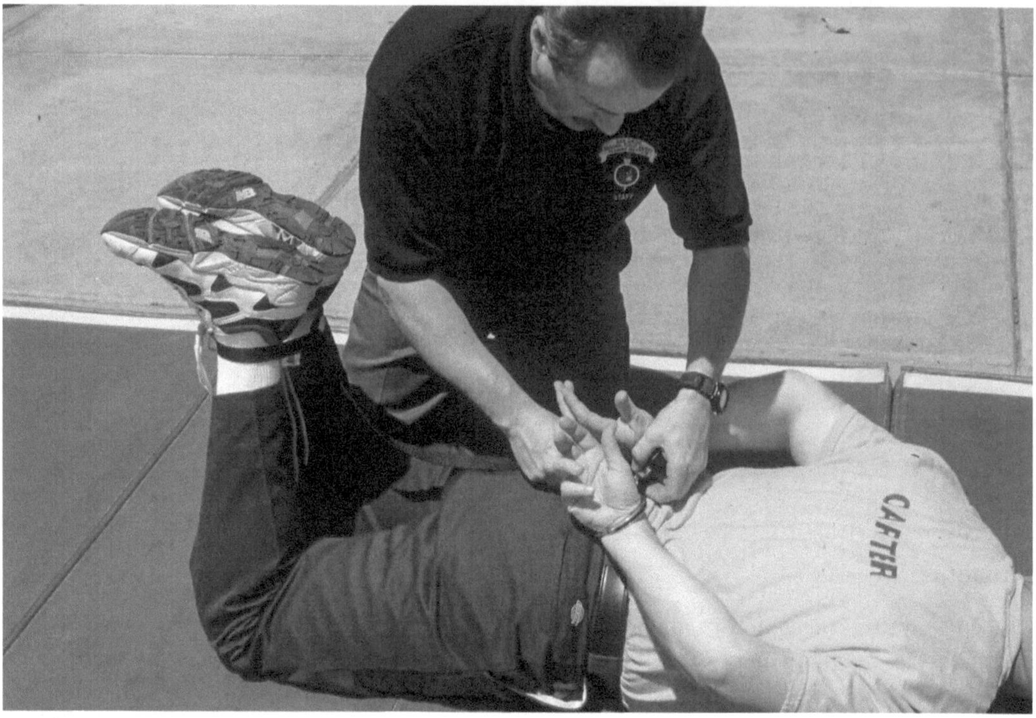

FIGURE 7.1 Hogtie or prone maximal restraint position.

Physiology of Ventilation and Gas Exchange

The process of asphyxiation itself is the ultimate death of the individual and the associated failure of organ systems secondary to a lack of oxygen supply and delivery to the organs. This oxygen delivery to the body relies upon many factors. For the purposes of this chapter, the most crucial factor is that oxygen can get into the blood to be transported to the tissues. Oxygenation of the blood can be divided into two parts: (1) ventilation and (2) gas exchange. The first and foremost process of ventilation is defined by adequate amounts of gas being delivered from the outside environment to the lung tissue for proper oxygenation of blood to occur, while carbon dioxide is removed. The second process, gas exchange, assuming adequate air movement via ventilation is present, allows for adequate exchanging of oxygen into the blood and removal of carbon dioxide from the blood in the small capillary beds and alveoli in the lungs. Both of these processes must occur for oxygenation of the blood.

Ventilation is a mechanical process whereby air from the outside environment is inhaled and exhaled through the airways to and from the lung tissues. Inhalation occurs with expansion of the chest thoracic cavity, primarily through contraction of the diaphragm and chest wall musculature, drawing air in through the mouth down through the airways into the bronchi and bronchioles of the lungs. Exhalation occurs with relaxation of these muscles and decrease in the volume of the thoracic cavity. Ventilatory parameters can be measured in a breathing individual by utilizing standard pulmonary function testing with spirometric functions serving as the most useful parameters when quantifying and evaluating gas movement.

Gas exchange occurs in the lung tissue alveoli, where gases in the air are exchanged with the blood through a process called diffusion. The oxygen concentration in the lungs is greater than in the blood and diffuses across the capillary beds into the blood to be circulated throughout the body. Similarly, the concentration of carbon dioxide in the blood is greater than that in the alveoli and thus diffuses out of the blood into the lung tissue where it will be exhaled out of the body. The actual measurement of gas exchange is difficult. The alveolar-arterial oxygen ($[A\text{-}a]O_2$) gradient is probably the most useful quantitative screening parameter to quantify the important process of gas exchange.

This quantity is calculated from the following equation:

$$(A\text{-}a)O_2 \text{ gradient} = (FIO_2 \times P_B - PaCO_2/RQ) - PaO_2$$

where FIO_2 is the fraction of inspired oxygen tension, P_B is the barometric pressure, $PaCO_2$ is the partial pressure of carbon dioxide in arterial blood, RQ is the respiratory quotient (respiratory exchange ratio) and PaO_2 is the partial pressure of oxygen in the arterial blood. A normal $(A\text{-}a)O_2$ gradient is less than 10–15 mmHg.

Gas exchange of carbon dioxide occurs rapidly in the lung tissue. As a result, carbon dioxide (CO_2) measurements (also known as end tidal CO_2, or the level of the gas in expired air as a reflection of carbon dioxide levels in the blood in the lungs) are a more sensitive measure of ventilation than oxygen levels. With impairment of ventilation, levels would rise early (as measured by end tidal CO_2). With continued impairment of ventilation at a significant amount, oxygen levels would drop over time. Over a significant period of time, low oxygen levels or hypoxemia can lead to organ dysfunction, cardiac dysrhythmias, and death.

CASE ONE

A 30-year-old male is found running naked in a park yelling that he is on fire because he is being attacked by fire-breathing dragons. Police and EMS are dispatched. The paramedics wait until the scene is safe and secured by police. The sweaty, agitated individual is taken down and restrained by three police officers. The entire process takes two to three minutes and the subject is screaming and squirming the entire time. The subject is placed into a hobble because he keeps kicking. Once restrained in the prone position there is only one officer holding modest pressure with a hand to the upper back to keep the subject from rolling. The subject continues to scream. As paramedics start their assessment, the subject stops yelling and moving. He is quickly found to be in cardiac arrest. Paramedics start CPR and artificial breathing. They place an end tidal CO_2 monitor on the airway and find and document a level of 16. They continue to treat the subject with advanced resuscitative measures and the individual regains a pulse. He is ultimately transferred to the hospital and maintained on life support. After five days, the efforts are deemed to be futile and he is removed from life support and expires. Blood drawn at the hospital at admission was saved for the medical examiner, who found high levels of cocaine in his system at the time of the cardiac arrest.

Comment

The initial end tidal CO_2, which is the measured amount of carbon dioxide being breathed out of the lungs, in cardiac arrest caused by an irregular heart beat (dysrhythmia) usually results in a low end tidal CO_2. If a person goes into cardiac arrest from ventilatory failure from a pulmonary condition or from asphyxiation, the CO_2 builds up in the blood stream prior to going into a cardiac arrest. When the paramedics start resuscitating the patient with ventilations, the initial end tidal CO_2 levels are indicative of the level in the blood of the lungs when the blood is circulated by chest compressions. Thus the high CO_2-laden blood is circulated to the lungs and is ventilated out resulting in a high end tidal CO_2 level initially (typically anywhere from 60–100 mmHg). The initial end tidal CO_2 levels in this case, along with the other features not supporting asphyxiation (such as the fact that the individual was yelling and screaming while restrained), indicate that this cardiac arrest was not from ventilatory failure (asphyxiation) but rather more consistent with a sudden cardiac arrest due to drug intoxication.

Historical Aspects

Historically, there have been a number of deaths that have occurred in individuals who have been placed in restraint positions. However, the definitive evidence of the actual physiologic role of the restraint position in these deaths remains uncertain. There is no argument against the existence of a phenomenon called positional asphyxia. Asphyxia, derived from the 18th-century Greek term for a (without) and sphuxis (pulse), is actually a misnomer when it comes to the true definition, which means "the state of not being able to breathe." As such, the state of not having a pulse will ensue if one is not able to breathe or adequately ventilate the lungs with air for a long enough period of a time. While the term was not coined until recently, the phenomenon of positional asphyxia has been reported to be in use as early as the 18th century in the form of a technique called "burking" (*Titlow v. Burt*, 2010), named after William Burke who, along with an accomplice in 1815, killed a number of people in the West Port murders and sold their bodies to medical schools in Edinburgh, Scotland. Burke's nefarious plan was to target intoxicated individuals who could be subdued easily without struggle, and who perhaps also had less social standing than would warrant attention after being murdered and suffocating them to death. Burke and his accomplice carried out the plan by one of them holding a hand over the victim's nose and mouth and pushing the victim's jaw up, while the other would compress the victim's torso until he or she died of asphyxia (*Tabish v. State*, 2003).

While positional asphyxia has been noted in the medical literature, the term was apparently first formally utilized by Bell et al. (1992), in a study of the deaths of 30 individuals in Dade and Broward County, Florida. No significant risk factors for death were identified in this original description of positional asphyxia. The unifying theme of the majority of these deaths was that individuals were discovered in positions that resulted in an upper airway obstruction. These positions included hyperflexion of the head and neck or lying face down on a suffocating object. Sedatives including alcohol and other depressant drugs were cited as a major risk factor in these cases and also explained why the individuals did not move from the position that caused the upper airway obstruction. In four of the cases, the torso was found to be hyperflexed, accounting for a mechanical inability to breathe or ventilate. In none of these original cases was the individual physically restrained in the prone or hobble position.

Another related form of asphyxia is termed mechanical asphyxiation. This term has been associated with the use of a vest, jacket, or even posy restraint, and has been primarily described in the geriatric nursing home population. In this instance, asphyxiation occurs when these restraints accidentally wrap around the neck of the individual which results in strangulation (Di Maio, Dana, & Bux, 1986; Dube & Mitchell, 1986; Katz, 1987; Miles, 1996). In other cases, individuals became suspended from either a bed or chair by their restraints, with resultant chest constriction causing mechanical ventilator impairment and death (Miles & Irvine, 1992; Emson, 1994).

There have been a number of case reports that document the deaths of individuals who are restrained by law enforcement; yet, such reports can only suggest the role of restraint in their respective deaths. In critical review of these cases, these reports only reveal a pattern of deaths that is, without question, very repetitive. Wetli and Fishbain (1985) reported seven cases of deaths in cocaine users, noting that five individuals were in police custody at the time, and that four were placed in hogtie like restraint positions. The authors suggest the amounts of cocaine found in the individuals did not support a sole diagnosis of "cocaine overdose" and believe the exact cause of death was indeterminate, offering speculation that the deaths may be the result of "autonomic reflexes, a toxic dysrhythmia, or 'restraint stress'" (Wetli & Fishbain, 1985).

Others have proposed that this restraint position impairs normal physiologic ventilatory function and directly places individuals at risk for death by asphyxiation. Based on this postulate, the term "positional asphyxia" has been used to describe these deaths, which also presents itself as an entirely different phenomenon than was initially associated with the term historically, as noted above. In 1992, Reay et al. reported three deaths which occurred in individuals who were restrained and placed in the back of police cars. All victims were violent, agitated, and uncooperative as a result of the use of various intoxicants or underlying psychiatric illness. The utilization of assistance of multiple officers was necessary in order to subdue these individuals and each one had become, at some point during transport, unresponsive. Upon autopsy, there was no clearly defined cause of death that could be determined and it was concluded that these deaths were the result of the combined ventilatory effects of the semi-prone position and the confined space of the patrol cars (Reay et al., 1992).

In 1993, O'Halloran and Lewman reported 11 cases of sudden death which occurred in subjects placed in the prone position. Nine of these individuals were placed in the hogtie restraint position. All of the subjects were combative, violent, and in an "excited delirious state" as a result of acute psychosis or drug ingestions (most commonly cocaine). Violent confrontation and struggle occurred in all cases. In fact, two of these cases were subjected to stun-gun or TASER shocks shortly before death. The authors asserted that the position, "clearly impairs breathing in situations of high oxygen demand by inhibiting chest wall and diaphragmatic movement" (O'Halloran & Lewman, 1993, 294). Additionally, in 1995, Stratton et al. were the first to report two individuals who died in the care of pre-hospital personnel and who had been placed in the prone restraint position for transport because of violent, agitated, and combative behaviors. Both were under the influence of drugs. The authors surmised that the prone restraint position leads to "restriction of motion of the diaphragm and chest," and that such positioning "can lead to asphyxia" (Stratton et al., 1995, 712).

In 1996, Ross reviewed 22 cases of sudden death in the prone hogtie position reported in the medical literature from 1988 to 1993. Of these deaths, 18 occurred in individuals placed in the hogtie restraint position, two were restrained prone on gurneys, and two were manually restrained in a prone position. All exhibited violent, combative behavior and fought or struggled with police. Drug use or alcohol intoxication was noted in 12 subjects. Positional asphyxia was listed as the sole cause of death in five cases and as a contributing cause of death along with drug intoxication in another six cases (Ross, 1996).

Hick, Smith, and Lynch (1999) describe five cases of individuals who were restrained and suffered cardiac arrest, resulting in four deaths. All cases demonstrated a profound acidosis and the authors suggest that the restraint process led to severe acidosis, which subsequently led to cardiovascular collapse (Hick et al., 1999). While these individuals demonstrated a profound acidosis, it is not clear that prone restraint (in fact, not all were restrained in the prone position) was the major factor resulting in the acidosis. Drug use (primarily cocaine) as well as physical exertion and a state of "excited delirium" no doubt were factors in developing acidosis (Wetli & Fishbain, 1985). Moreover, a good portion of the metabolic acidosis may have been due to the cardiac arrest itself, as sampling of blood took place after the initial arrest and resuscitation efforts (Chan et al., 1999).

These limited case reports are anecdotal and provide little in the way of definitive scientific evidence to support or refute any hypothesized cause of death. Unfortunately, the field of criminal justice offers an environment where theories that at first might appear to have some merit are put forth by experts and eventually become transitioned into apparent truths without adequate scientific evidence or support.

More recently, however, larger epidemiologic studies have been conducted that provide a strong scientific foundation upon which to base such conclusions. Hall et al. (2012) prospectively studied 1,269 subjects who were arrested, which included documentation of final resting position documented in 1,255 cases. Almost 43 percent (42.8%) were left in a prone position, of which none of them died, while one subject died in a non-prone position. Based on their data, the authors concluded that prone positioning was common and was not associated with death in their complete cohort of consecutive subjects following police use of force (Hall et al., 2012).

Additionally, Ross and Hazlett (2016) prospectively studied 1,085 violent arrestees who were restrained in the prone position by officers in 17 police agencies in the United States over one year. Officers used various types of use of force techniques and the use of the TASER as well as pepper spray to control the arrestees. All arrestees were controlled and restrained in the prone position from one to five minutes and were handcuffed. About 20 percent were further restrained through the use of hobbling the arrestee's ankles. None of the arrestees died, moderate injuries were sustained in about 16 percent, and treatable injuries were sustained in about 4 percent of the arrests. The researchers concluded that the officer's use of force was rare and restraining arrestees in the prone position is the preferred and a safe position to restrain violent arrestees.

Legal Aspects

Given the high-profile nature of these restraint-associated incidents, as well as the historical context and causal suppositions proffered in the past (even without supporting scientific evidence), it is not surprising that these events often end up in our legal system with accusations of wrongful death. The two legal cases summarized below highlight some of the issues involved in these cases, as well as the related scientific evidence and associated findings.

The theory of positional asphyxia was invoked by the plaintiffs in *Price v. County of San Diego* (1998). Daniel Price, a chronic abuser of methamphetamine, refused San Diego County deputies' demands to exit his vehicle and then proceeded to aggressively resist efforts to control and restrain him. Deputies utilized force, placing him in a facedown position on the road with his wrists handcuffed behind his back and ankles shackled. Despite these restraints, Price continued to kick at the deputies and, subsequently, a second pair of handcuffs was utilized to secure and connect the handcuffs, securing his wrists to the shackles on his ankles. Also known as the prone-maximal restraint (PMR) position, or hogtie position, deputies reportedly also applied pressure to Price's torso, restraining him with one deputy's knee placed on the back. Once in this position, paramedics were summoned to the scene and, upon arrival, found Price apneic and pulseless. Resuscitation efforts were initiated and Price was transported to the hospital, where he remained unconscious, culminating in his death.

Dr. John Eisele, a medical examiner for San Diego County, performed an autopsy and concluded that the cause of death was secondary to "restrictive asphyxia with cardiopulmonary arrest due to maximum restraint in a prone position" (*Price v. County of San Diego*, 1998). Dr. Eisele's findings relied on the research of Dr. Donald Reay, an expert for the plaintiff, who opined that prone restraint positions, such as the hogtie position, result in positional asphyxia because they prevent the body from achieving adequate oxygen levels due to the physical impairment of inhalation and exhalation. Reay's summation was a result of a previously conducted study of healthy volunteers, comparing placement in the hogtie position versus sitting after a period of short exercise. The researchers documented longer recovery times for oxygenation and heart rate in the hogtie position, suggesting physiologic impairment (Reay et al., 1988).

Dr. Thomas Neuman, defense expert, challenged Reay's findings. He noted that Reay's study utilized a cutaneous pulse oximeter to measure oxygen levels (which can be inaccurate at times, such as during exercise), with reported drops in oxygen levels with moderate exercise, which would not be expected in healthy subjects. Moreover, this drop was documented well before subjects were restrained, indicating that even if the decrease in oxygen was real, it was not caused by prone restraint (Chan, Vilke, & Neuman, 1998).

Prior to the *Price* case testimony, Dr. Neuman and a team of researchers performed a more comprehensive research study, investigating the physiology of prone restraint that was funded by the County of San Diego (Chan et al., 1997). In this study, the researchers measured ventilatory parameters, including forced vital capacity (FVC)—the amount of air an individual could exhale in a single breath—as well as forced expiratory volume in one second (FEV1)—the amount of air an individual could exhale rapidly in the first second of exhalation. These measures indicate the overall status of ventilatory function in an individual and are often used to assess patients with various lung conditions, including asthma. Interestingly, the researchers documented drops in these measures in the supine, prone, and prone maximal restraint positions when compared with sitting, suggesting some decrease in ventilation based on body position (including lying on the back). However, these measures have a range of normal that varies based on an individual's size and ethnicity, and in no cases were the parameters considered abnormal. On a physiologic level, this is consistent with prior work in respiratory physiology. The normal human body has excess ventilatory capacity such that lung function must be reduced significantly (i.e., less than 50 percent) to have an impact on oxygenation (Chan et al., 1997).

Accordingly, this research study was able to confirm that oxygenation of blood (as measured by actual blood sampling) did not decrease with mild or moderate exercise, refuting Reay and confirming well-documented exercise physiology findings in the medical literature. Similarly, the study demonstrated that carbon dioxide levels were no higher in those in the hogtie position versus sitting following exercise. Based on this work, Reay himself later wrote that the hogtie position was "physiologically neutral" (Reay, 1998). As a result of this work, the *Price* case concluded with a defense verdict, in support of the officers and the county of San Diego (the defendants), that the subject did not die from positional asphyxia.

In the case of *Lewis v. City of West Palm Beach, FL* (2009), restraint force was utilized to subdue a persistently combative individual, Donald George Lewis, who resisted arrest by law enforcement officers. The arrestee, Lewis, required multiple officers to restrain him, with one officer placing a knee on Lewis' upper back and neck, while handcuffs were secured. Lewis was then placed in a prone maximal restraint position, whereafter he lost consciousness, resulting in cardiopulmonary arrest. Despite resuscitative measures, Lewis subsequently died. The medical examiner determined that the cause of death was sudden respiratory arrest following physical struggle against restraints and cocaine-induced excited delirium.

Restraint asphyxia has been a term coined to suggest that while prone restraint may itself be "physiologically neutral," the addition of weight force, such as officers holding down an individual in this prone restraint position (e.g., with a knee on the back as in the *Lewis* case) may further limit ventilation to the point that the subject is at risk for asphyxiation. However, research studies looking at the impact of weight force have not provided any evidence to support this contention. In 2004, researchers conducted a study investigating weight force on the back and the ventilatory effects of that force (Chan et al., 2004). Ventilatory parameters (FVC and FEV1), as well as oxygen saturation (O_2 sat) and end tidal carbon dioxide ($ETCO_2$), were compared in the sitting position and in the prone maximal restraint position with 25 pounds and then 50 pounds of weight placed between the shoulder blades. There were no significant differences in either O_2 sat or $ETCO_2$ among the maximal restraint, prone position, sitting, or with the maximal restraint prone position with weight on the back (either 25 pounds or 50 pounds). There were decreases in FVC and FEV1 similar to those noted with weight force application, but these changes were similar to those seen in the earlier study conducted in 1997 by Chan et al. and, as such, did not produce any clinically relevant effects (Chan et al., 2004).

In another research study, Michalewicz et al. (2007) found that up to 225 pounds, applied and uniformly distributed, over the upper backs of subjects reduced maximal voluntary ventilation (MVV) up to 70 percent of seated values. Such small incremental changes with increasing amounts of weight on the back should be expected. The measure of maximal inspiratory pressure (MIP) is one of the best parameters to assess the ability of an individual to move gas or ventilate their lungs. Usually, the greatest inspiratory pressures are generated when the volume of a lung or lungs is at its lowest. To quote an extreme example, if one were to achieve maximal volume expansion of his lungs when full of air, the maximal inspiratory pressure would be zero; as lung volumes reduce secondary to an external load, it would be expected that the MIP that could be generated would increase, tending to preserve spirometric indices as external loads increase.

A short rebuttal to the argument that the ventilatory effects of additional body weight are worse in the prone position as compared to the supine position is inherent when one examines the experience in clinical medicine as well. It is common practice, in clinical medicine, that when gas exchange is severely impaired due to lung disease, critically ill patients have been repositioned to receive ventilation in the prone positions rather than in supine positions (Albert, 1997; Douglas et al., 1977; Langer et al., 1988; Mure, Martling, & Lindahl, 1997; Piehl & Brown, 1976). The evidence derived from the intensive care unit suggests that the prone position improves gas exchange compared with the supine position. And, in fact, there is increasingly clear evidence now that gas exchange is improved in the prone position and that abdominal distention with upward pressure on the diaphragm improves gas exchange as well (Mure et al., 1998). A study by Ward and Macklem (1990) also demonstrates that

CASE TWO

A 32-year-old male in a jail detoxification cell is reported to be pacing his cell, sweating, and banging his head against the cell door. Attempts at verbal de-escalation have failed to calm him down and the decision is made for a cell extraction using a tactical team and placement in a restraint chair. The tactical team enters the cell and the subject attacks. He is quickly taken to the ground. One officer has control of each of his extremities in a prone position while a fifth officer maintains the head and assesses the airway. The entire event is videotaped. During the cuffing process, the subject continues to struggle, yell, and spit. Just as the cuffs are placed, the subject is noted to stop fighting and is no longer making noise. He is pulled out of the cell and appears at that time to be flaccid and described by officers like carrying dead weight. He is immediately assessed by medical providers and is found to be in cardiac arrest. Resuscitation efforts are attempted but the subject ultimately expires. On autopsy, he is noted to have cocaine and cocaine metabolites in his system.

Comments

This is a classic case of sudden cardiac arrest occurring during restraint. The review of the video will allow for exact timing and quantification of how much weight was placed, where and for how long by each of the officers. It will also allow for assessment as to when the subject was talking or yelling—evidence that he was indeed moving air in and out of his lungs and was not having his ventilations completely restricted. For investigations in which there are no videos, belt tapes or 911 audio or bystander videos can be very helpful in establishing that the subject did not have a restriction in his breathing as evidenced by yelling and screaming on the audio. As asphyxiation takes time, a sudden death occurring in a subject who is fighting and screaming and suddenly goes flaccid is more consistent with sudden cardiac arrest, not asphyxiation.

while significant chest wall restriction may impede ventilation, restriction of abdominal motion should not influence ventilatory bellows function because diaphragmatic muscle contraction will occur at a more efficient length in the same fashion as higher MIPs can be generated with decreasing lung volumes.

Other studies have investigated the hobble restraint position, both with and without weight force, examining the potential hemodynamic effects of weight force and the hobble position on cardiac output as a measure of potential hemodynamic compromise, which has been suggested as another potential cause of death. A study by Ho et al. (2011) evaluated the placement of up to 147 pounds on the backs of subjects in a prone position to measure vena cava diameter. The researchers reported no difference in heart rate or blood pressure in any of the subjects with weight on them, implying that the heart was getting adequate blood return and functioning well enough to pump blood out and maintain blood pressure (Ho et al., 2011). This hemodynamic stability occurred even though there was a reported decrease in vena cava diameter in subjects with weight on them. In another randomized prospective crossover experimental study utilizing ultrasound to measure surrogate markers for cardiac output, decreases in the measurement of stroke volume for subjects restrained in the hogtie position (see Figure 7.2) as compared to the supine position were noted (Savaser et al., 2013).

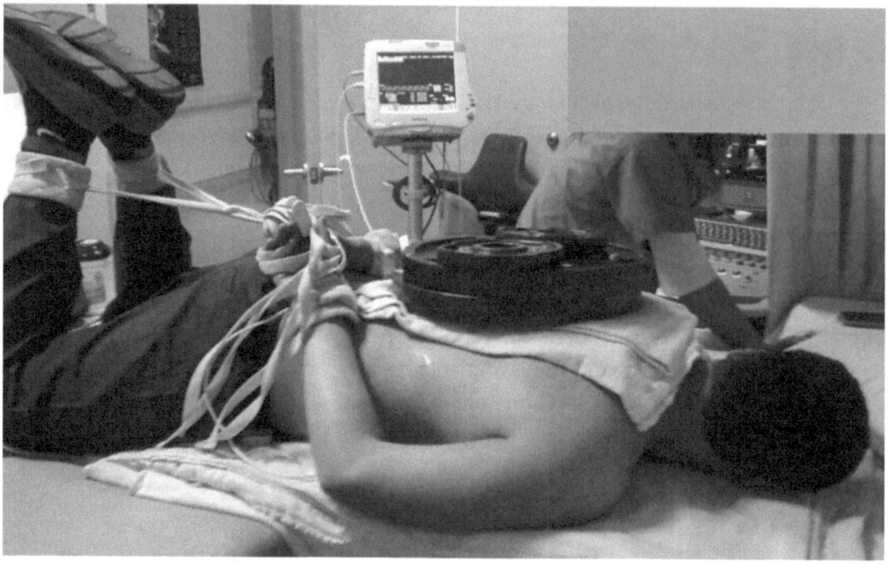

FIGURE 7.2 The prone maximal restraint position, aka "hogtie" position from the Savaser study.

However, when examining overall cardiac output, a measure of the amount of blood the heart pumps to the rest of the body, there were no significant differences when comparing all five positions studied, which included supine, prone, prone hogtie as well as hogtie position with respective weight forces of 50 and 100 pounds each, placed between the shoulder blades. The study ultimately revealed that there was no hemodynamic compromise in any of the restraint or hogtie positions when evaluating heart rate, blood pressure or O_2 saturation as well (Savaser et al., 2013).

Investigative Aspects

Individuals who are out of control and pose a risk to the general public or themselves will continue to attract the attention of law enforcement. As a result of their behaviors, such individuals may be predisposed not to want to readily comply with the instructions or direction of either police officers or pre-hospital personnel. Thus, intervention by the police will often be inevitable.

When a sudden, unexpected death occurs in such cases, it is important to consider whether the likely cause was respiratory or cardiac. Sudden cardiac death is defined as originating from cardiac etiology and is often brought on by a sudden and abrupt loss of consciousness within one hour of the onset of acute symptoms (Myerburg & Castellanos, 2005). The National Heart, Lung, and Blood Institute (NHLBI) describes the signs and symptoms of sudden cardiac arrest as including a loss of consciousness, a racing heartbeat, dizziness, and chest pain/shortness of breath, all within an hour of sudden cardiac arrest (National Heart, Lung, and Blood Institute, 2015). The most common cause is cardiac ischemia, causing an arrhythmia, termed ventricular fibrillation (V-fib) (Koplan & Stevenson, 2009). While underlying morbidity and co-morbid factors (e.g., diabetes, renal function, electrolyte levels) are contributing factors to the etiology of ventricular fibrillation, it is thought that left ventricular hypertrophy (LVH) is the leading contributing factor involved in sudden cardiac death in the adult population (Stevens, Reineir, & Chugh, 2013). The structural hypertrophy and non-compliance of the heart is associated as the underlying cause for increased cardiac irritability, arrhythmia, and, ultimately, by entering ventricular fibrillation, lost perfusion to the heart and brain, thereby leading to death.

Given the risk of the combinatory effects of underlying drugs, intoxicants, or ingestions and the exertion that is involved in these restraint scenarios, it is not surprising that sudden cardiac death may be a consequence of such an interaction. In many respects, such deaths are no more surprising than the death of an out-of-shape individual with cardiac disease playing aggressive weekend warrior basketball.

In comparison, respiratory arrest or respiratory failure is defined as inadequate ventilation or gas exchange by the respiratory system, whereby arterial oxygen and carbon dioxide levels are not adequately maintained in their normal ranges. Respiratory arrest results from the absence of adequate levels of oxygen in the blood due to respiratory failure. While the imbalance in arterial oxygen and carbon dioxide levels may be attributed to a variety of reasons, when one is either unable to provide sufficient oxygen to his or her tissues or eliminate a toxic level of tissue-generated carbon dioxide from the body via ventilation as well as adequate perfusion of the lungs, then respiratory arrest will result due to this imbalance.

Based on current data and studies that exist to date, the hogtie, maximal restraint position (hobble), or the prone position appear to be no more physiologically disruptive than any other position or even the supine position particularly in regards to respiratory and ventilatory function. The conjecture that the maximal restraint position (either hobble or hogtie) in some way places the restrained individual at increased risk for positional or restraint asphyxiation is not supported by the current literature and data that exist to date.

Investigation Checklist

As part of the investigation to assess for restraint asphyxia, the investigator will also need to assess for other possible etiologies for the death, including the findings of Excited Delirium Syndrome (please see Chapter 9 for the complete investigator checklist).

Historical Findings

- What type of restraint was used?
- How long did it take to place the restraint(s)?
- How many people were involved in the restraining process and what were their exact locations and body parts being held?
- How much did each person placing weight on the subject weigh?
- How long was each person placing his/her respective weight on the subject?
- Was the subject talking or yelling during the restraining process (indicating not a complete ventilation impedance)?
- What was the position of the subject? Was it constant or moving?
- Was there any arching or rolling during the restraining process?
- Was there loss of consciousness during the restraining process or afterwards?
- When did the loss of consciousness occur specifically in relation to the restraining process?
- What was each person's position at the time of the loss of consciousness?

- When was the subject first noted to not be breathing?
- When was the subject first noted to not be resisting or moving?
- Was there a color change of the subject's face? When did that occur?
- Other features of drug intoxication or ExDS (see checklist in Chapter 9).

Medical Findings

- Initial End-tidal CO_2 levels findings from the paramedics
- Urine toxicological screen results
- Initial electrocardiogram (ECG) rhythm and timing in relationship to loss of consciousness

Postmortem Findings

- Cardiac findings (hypertrophy)
- Pulmonary edema
- Airway or lung injuries
- Toxicological screen positive for stimulants
- Rib fractures, which ribs and location (if consistent with resuscitative efforts or not)

References

Albert, R. K. (1997). The prone position in acute respiratory distress syndrome: Where we are, and where do we go from here. *Critical Care Medicine, 25*(9), 1453–1454.

Bell, M. B., Rao, V. J., Wetli, C. V., & Rodriguez, R. N. (1992). Positional asphyxiation in adults: A series of 30 cases from the Dade and Broward County Florida medical examiner offices from 1982 to 1990. *American Journal of Forensic Medicine and Pathology, 13*(2), 101–107.

Chan, T. C., Neuman, T., Clausen, J., Eisele, J., & Vilke, G. M. (2004). Weight force during prone restraint and respiratory function. *American Journal of Forensic Medicine and Pathology, 25*(3), 185–189.

Chan, T. C., Neuman, T., Vilke, G. M., Clausen, J., & Clark, R. F. (1999). Metabolic acidosis in restraint-associated cardiac arrest [Letter to the editor]. *Academic Emergency Medicine, 6*(10), 1075–1076.

Chan, T. C., Vilke, G. M., & Neuman, T. (1998). Reexamination of custody restraint position and positional asphyxia. *American Journal of Forensic Medicine and Pathology, 19*(3), 201–205.

Chan, T. C., Vilke, G. M., Neuman, T., & Clausen, J. L. (1997). Restraint position and positional asphyxia. *Annals of Emergency Medicine, 30*(5), 578–586.

Di Maio, V. J. M., Dana, S. E., & Bux, R. C. (1986). Deaths caused by restraint vests. *Journal of the American Medical Association, 255*(7), 905.

Douglas, W. W., Rehder, K., Beynen, F. M., Sessler, A. D., & Marsh, H. M. (1977). Improved oxygenation in patients with acute respiratory failure: The prone position. *American Review of Respiratory Disease, 115*, 559–566.

Dube, A. H. & Mitchell, E. K. (1986). Accidental strangulation from vest restraints. *Journal of the American Medical Association, 256*(19), 2725–2726.

Emson, H. E. (1994). Death in a restraint jacket from mechanical asphyxia. *Canadian Medical Association Journal, 151*(7), 985–987.

Hall, C. A., McHale, A. M. D., Kader, A. S., Stewart, L. C., MacCarthy, C. S., & Fick, G. H. (2012). Incidence and outcome of prone positioning following police use of force in a prospective, consecutive cohort of subjects. *Journal of Forensic and Legal Medicine, 19*(2), 83–89.

Hick, J. L., Smith, S. W., & Lynch, M. T. (1999). Metabolic acidosis in restraint associated cardiac arrest: A case series. *Academic Emergency Medicine, 6*(3), 239–243.

Ho, J. D., Dawes, D. M., Moore, J. C., Caroon, L. V., & Miner, J. R. (2011). Effect of position and weight force on inferior vena cava diameter: Implications for arrest-related death. *Forensic Science International, 212*, 256–259.

Katz, L. (1987). Accidental strangulation from vest restraints. *Journal of the American Medical Association, 257*(15), 2032–2033.

Koplan, B. A. & Stevenson, W. G. (2009). Ventricular tachycardia and sudden cardiac death. *Mayo Clinic Proceedings, 84*(3), 289–297.

Langer, M., Mascheroni, D., Marcolin, R., & Gattinoni, L. (1988). The prone position in ARDS patients. A clinical study. *Chest, 94*(1), 103–107.

Lewis v. City of West Palm Beach, FL, 561 F.3d 1288 (11th Cir. 2009).

Michalewicz, B. A., Chan, T. C., Vilke, G. M., Levy, S. S., Neuman, T. S., & Kolkhorst, F. W. (2007). Ventilatory and metabolic demands during aggressive physical restraint in healthy adults. *Journal of Forensic Sciences, 52*(1), 171–175.

Miles, S. H. (1996). A case of death by physical restraint: New lessons from a photograph. *Journal of the American Geriatrics Society, 44*, 291–292.

Miles, S. H. & Irvine, P. (1992). Deaths caused by physical restraints. *The Gerontologist, 32*(6), 762–766.

Mure, M., Glenny, R. W., Domino, K. B., & Hlastala, M. P. (1998). Pulmonary gas exchange improves in the prone position with abdominal distention. *American Journal of Respiratory and Critical Care Medicine, 157*, 1785–1790.

Mure, M., Martling, C. R., & Lindahl, S. G. E. (1997). Dramatic effect on oxygenation in patients with severe acute lung insufficiency treated in the prone position. *Critical Care Medicine*, 25(9), 1539–1544.

Myerburg, R. J. & Castellanos, A. (2005). Cardiac arrest and sudden cardiac death. In Zipes, D. P., Libby, P., Bonow, R. O., & Braunwald, E. (eds.), *Braunwald's heart disease: A textbook of cardiovascular medicine* (865–908). Philadelphia, PA: WB Saunders Company.

National Heart, Lung, and Blood Institute. (2015). *What are the signs and symptoms of sudden cardiac arrest?* Retrieved from www.nhlbi.nih.gov/health/health-topics/topics/scda/signs.

O'Halloran, R. L. & Lewman, L. V. (1993). Restraint asphyxiation in excited delirium. *American Journal of Forensic Medicine and Pathology, 14*(4), 289–295.

Piehl, M. A. & Brown, R. S. (1976). Use of extreme position changes in acute respiratory failure. *Critical Care Medicine, 4*(1), 13–14.

Price v. County of San Diego, CA, 990 F.Supp. 1230 (S.D. Cal. 1998).

Reay, D. T. (1998). Death in custody. *Clinics in Laboratory Medicine*, 18(1), 1–22.

Reay, D. T. & Eisele, J. W. (1982). Deaths from law enforcement neck holds. *American Journal of Forensic Medicine and Pathology, 3*, 253.

Reay, D. T., Fligner, C. L., Stilwell, A. D., & Arnold, J. (1992). Positional asphyxia during law enforcement transport. *American Journal of Forensic Medicine and Pathology, 13*(2), 90–97.

Reay, D. T. & Holloway, G. A. (1982). Changes in carotid blood flow produced by neck compression. *American Journal of Forensic Medicine and Pathology, 3*, 199.

Reay, D. T., Howard, J. D., Fligner, C. L., & Ward, R. J. (1988). Effects of positional restraint on oxygen saturation and heart rate following exercise. *American Journal of Forensic Medicine and Pathology, 9*(1), 16–18.

Ross, D. L. & Hazlett, M. L. (2016). A prospective analysis of the outcomes of violent prone restraint incidents in policing. *Forensic Research & Criminology International Journal, 2*, January, 1–10.

Ross, D. L. (1996). An analysis of in-custody deaths and positional asphyxiation. *The Police Marksman*, March/April, 16–18.

Savaser, D. J., Campbell, C., Castillo, E. M., Vilke, G. M., Sloane, C., Neuman, T., & Chan, T. C. (2013). The effect of the prone maximal restrained position with and without weight force on cardiac output and other hemodynamic measures. *Journal of Forensic and Legal Medicine, 20*(8), 991–995.

Stevens, S. M., Reineir, K., & Chugh, S. S. (2013). Increased left ventricular mass as a predictor of sudden cardiac death: is it time to put it to the test? *Circulation Arrhythmia and Electrophysiology, 6*(1), 212–7.

Stratton, S. J., Rogers, C., & Green, K. (1995). Sudden death in individuals in hobble restraints during paramedic transport. *Annals of Emergency Medicine, 25*(5), 710–712.

Tabish v. State, 119 Nev. 293, 321 (Nev. 2003).

Titlow v. Burt, U.S. Dist. LEXIS 111459 (D. Mich. 2010).

Ward, M. & Macklem, P. T. (1990). The act of breathing and how it fails. *Chest, 97*(3), 36S–39S.

Wetli, C. V. & Fishbain, D. P. (1985). Cocaine-induced psychosis and sudden death in recreational cocaine users. *Journal of Forensic Sciences, 30*, 873–880.

8

NECK HOLDS

Michael Holman and Gary M. Vilke

Introduction

Neck holds are a technique used to subdue and control a violent subject with manipulation of the anterior neck. The carotid sleeper hold is a type of neck hold that has a record of being an extremely safe method of restraint. When used correctly, it utilizes the mechanism of temporarily disrupting the blood flow to the brain and rendering the subject unconscious. These holds have been used for centuries in the sport of Judo. Some of the Judo neck holds, called Shime-Waza, are essentially the same as those taught to law enforcement. We have learned much about neck holds used in law enforcement by studying Shime-Waza and how it has been used in a safe manner. There are other types of neck holds that may be less safe to use, such as the bar hold. Occasionally, deaths have occurred during or just after the application of a neck hold and the etiology of the death is often attributed to the actual maneuver itself. In these cases, careful examination must be given to the type of hold, the application, surrounding circumstances, and the associated physical findings.

This chapter will review the history of neck holds, types of holds, safety, associated deaths, and clinical research associated with neck holds. The anatomy of the neck will be defined so as to better understand the effects these holds can potentially have on an individual. The different types of neck holds will be discussed, including their applications, the potential risks, and complications. The physiological consequences of neck holds will also be reviewed. We will attempt to tease out myth from science as we explain what happens to the body with neck compression. There will be discussion about the management strategies for patients who are placed in neck holds and the potential need for medical assessment. Finally, we will review several cases in which the neck hold maneuver was utilized and provide a checklist for the investigator to help with evidence collection when there is a death with an associated neck hold.

Neck Anatomy

The neck is a complex pathway of nerves, blood vessels, and airway, that when thought of in a most simplistic form, is essentially a relay system connecting the head and brain with the rest of the body.

Neural transmissions go back and forth via the spinal cord as well as a complex integrated highway system of nerve fibers. The brain is nourished by blood flow originating from the heart, transported to and from the brain through the major blood vessels of the neck. There are specific regions of the neck that regulate this blood flow to the brain. This system includes specialized neuroendocrine and vascular tissue, such as the carotid bodies, which monitor blood pressure as well as blood oxygen and carbon dioxide levels, and adjusts blood flow parameters accordingly. The neck also serves as a conduit for food and liquid of the gastrointestinal tract via the esophagus, and as a pathway to get oxygen into the lungs and carbon dioxide out of the body for the respiratory system. Disruption of any of these pathways or processes has associated physiological effects. The normal cross-section anatomy of the neck is demonstrated in Figure 8.1.

Airway

The airway can be thought of as a breathing tube connecting the opening of the mouth and nose with the lungs. It includes the pharynx, larynx, and trachea. Its function is to facilitate the passage of air from outside of the body into the lungs.

Pharynx

The pharynx is the muscular posterior portion of the mouth that connects the oral cavity and nasal cavity to the larynx and esophagus. It is also a passageway for food to the esophagus and for air to the larynx. In Figure 8.1 the pharynx there is a division into the food conduit (esophagus) and air conduit (larynx and trachea).

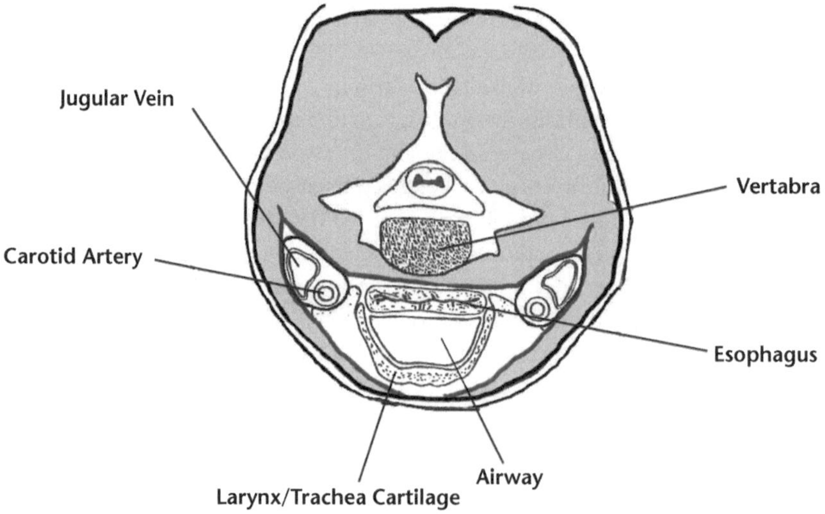

FIGURE 8.1 Cross section of neck: Demonstration of the normal cross section anatomy of the neck.
Source: Reprinted with permission from Springer.

Larynx

The larynx is a framework of cartilage that houses the vocal cords and is responsible for the production of vocal sounds. It serves as a passageway for air from the pharynx to the trachea. It is made of nine cartilages, which include the epiglottis, thyroid, cricoid, two cuneiforms, two corniculates, and two arytenoids that are bound together by ligaments and muscles. Above the cartilages there is a single bone, the hyoid bone, which helps the cartilages keep a firmly open airway. The prominence of thyroid cartilage of the larynx is often referred to as the Adam's apple.

Trachea

The trachea is the passageway for air from the larynx into the bronchial tree of the lungs. It is made of multiple cartilaginous rings and lies just below the skin, distal to the Adam's apple.

Vasculature

The neck vessels are the conduit of blood to and from the brain, an organ which requires a robust source of oxygen. The brain uses approximately 25 percent of the body's oxygen supply. The major vessels include the carotid and vertebral arteries and the jugular veins.

Carotid Arteries

The carotid arteries are the major sources of arterial blood flow to the brain. The common carotid artery on the left comes directly off of the aorta, whereas the right arises from the brachiocephalic artery, which originates from the aorta. Both ascend to about the level of the Adam's apple and then divide into internal and external carotid arteries. The internal carotid arteries supply the cerebrum, forehead, nose, eyes, and middle ear. The external carotid arteries supply the face, scalp, and neck.

Vertebral Arteries

The vertebral arteries transfer blood to the brain via a deeper route in the neck structures along the cervical spine vertebrae.

Jugular Veins

The jugular veins are the major vessels draining the blood flow from the head. Veins are much more pliable than arteries as they lack a thick muscular surrounding.

Musculoskeletal

The main bones of the neck include the cervical spine vertebrae and the hyoid bone.

Hyoid Bone

The hyoid bone is a free-floating U-shaped bone in the anterior portion of the neck that supports the tongue above and the larynx below. It is held in place by muscles and ligaments.

Cervical Spine

The cervical spine is a series of seven vertebrae that are stacked upon one another and house the spinal cord from the base of the skull to the thoracic spine. Between each bony vertebral body is an intervertebral disc.

Neck Muscles

The musculature of the neck is a complex combination of small muscles attaching adjoining vertebrae and longer strap muscles that offer support and strength over the cervical spine as a whole. The muscles are the semispinalis capitis, iliocostalis cervicis, longissimus cervicis, longissimus capitis, semispinalis capitis, obliquus capites superior and inferior, rectus capitis posterior minor and major, splenius capitis, splenius cervicis, levator scapulae, rhomboideus minor, trapezius, scalene anterior, middle, and posterior, thyrohyoid, omohyoid superior and inferior, and the sternohyoid, The sternocleidomastoid muscle runs from each clavicle to the lateral bases of the skull and is one of the most external muscles in the neck.

Spinal Cord

The spinal cord is the complex nervous tissue structure housed within the cervical spine that runs from the brainstem to the lower portion of the spine. Its function is to transmit neurological impulses between the brain and the rest of the body.

Other Related Structures

Several other important structures are housed within the neck region, including chemoreceptors, baroreceptors, and endocrine glands.

Carotid Bodies

The carotid bodies are small, highly vascular tissues located in the wall of the carotid artery at the site of its bifurcation. The bodies contain chemoreceptors that monitor the levels of carbon dioxide and oxygen in the blood. If the blood oxygen level is noted to fall, the chemoreceptors send impulses to the cardiac and respiratory centers in the brain to increase heart rate and respiratory rate.

Carotid Sinuses

The carotid sinuses are located near the carotid bodies and house baroreceptors that measure blood pressure coming to the brain. If blood pressure is low, the baroreceptors stop firing, as they are no longer being stretched. Neural impulses are then sent to the brain via the glossopharyngeal nerve (cranial nerve IX) triggering autonomic signals to stimulate the heart to beat faster and contract more forcefully, thus increasing cardiac output and improving blood flow to the brain. Compression of the carotid sinuses simulates elevated BP—thus the sinuses stimulate the vagus nerve to slow down heart rate and cardiac output as a way to drop blood pressure.

Thyroid Gland

The thyroid gland is a highly vascular endocrine gland located in the anterior neck just below the Adam's apple portion of the thyroid cartilage of the larynx. Its function is to produce and secrete thyroid hormone.

Parathyroid Glands

The parathyroid glands are four glands housed within the thyroid tissue of the neck that secrete parathyroid hormone, a regulator of blood calcium levels.

Tongue

The tongue is a muscular structure that attaches from the floor of the mouth and has several functions, including taste, speech, and manipulation of food down to the pharynx.

Esophagus

The esophagus is the muscular tube that transports food and liquid from the pharynx to the stomach. It is posteriorly located behind the airway but in front of the cervical spine.

History of Neck Holds

Use in Martial Arts

Shime-waza (neck hold) has been used in the sport of judo since 1882, when Professor Jigoro Kano founded the sport in Tokyo, Japan. *Shime*, meaning constriction, and *Waza*, meaning technique, can induce a state of unconsciousness (*Kodokan*) by temporarily stopping blood flow to the brain (Tezuka, 1978). The *shime-waza* hold results in victory when an opponent either indicates submission as a result of the technique, or having had the opportunity to submit, loses consciousness as a result of failing to do so. In both cases, it is accepted practice that the hold is maintained until the referee has announced the awarding of the point. The referees are typically trained to quickly detect loss of consciousness, and thus award the point and have the opponent release the hold (Owens & Ghadaili, 1991).

There are three forms of *shime-waza*: (1) *okurieri-jime*, the neck being squeezed as a whole; (2) *katajuji-jime*, the carotid arteries being compressed (similar to sleeper hold described later in the chapter); and (3) *hadaka-jime*, compression over the trachea (similar to a bar hold). *Kesa gatame* is an additional judo position that utilizes lateral neck compression by pinning the subject's arms upward to immobilize and render an opponent unconscious.

Individuals placed in the *katajuji-jime* hold are often not uncomfortable. In fact, in more novice judo participants who do not submit, loss of consciousness frequently occurs. The more experienced participants recognize the position and its likely outcome and will more frequently yield and submit before they lose consciousness. This is in contrast to *hadaka-jime*, which becomes painful early, given the direct pressure over the anterior structures of the neck, including the airway cartilage, and usually results in submission by the person being choked well before loss of unconsciousness. The discomfort of *okurieri-jime* tends to fall in between these two techniques. *Kesa-gatame* involves pinning the subject's arm up against the neck. The compression is over the lateral aspects of the neck and is typically not as painful as the *hadaka-jime* hold, and can render a subject unconscious in a short time.

Although there have been judo fatalities, a comprehensive search of the literature resulted in none due to *shime-waza* (Koiwai, 1981, 1987). Based on records from the International Judo Federation, World Class Championships, and Olympics and Junior World Judo Championships reported in 1979, there were no reported deaths from the 2,198 different techniques used to score, of which 97 (4.4 percent) involved the use of *shime-waza* (Barquin, 1979). Kamitani et al. (2013) looked at all catastrophic head and neck injuries in judo players in Japan from 2003 to 2010. Although they found 19 cervical spine neck injuries, none were from *shime-waza* (Kamitani et al., 2013).

Use in Law Enforcement

Neck holds have been used for decades by law enforcement agencies as a form of restraint in the continuum of the use-of-force progression. Typically, use of the neck hold is considered before moving on to more physically injurious force methods, such as impact weapons. Two basic types of neck holds that have been utilized are the bar hold and carotid sleeper hold, also known as the lateral vascular neck restraint (LVNR). A third hold, the shoulder pin restraint position, has been taught over the past two decades and is also utilized by law enforcement officers as a form of lateral neck restraint. Although there are several types of neck holds utilized by law enforcement, they are often erroneously collectively called "choke holds."

Similarly, confusion exists in terms of difference between strangulation and choking. Strangulation is defined as a form of asphyxia characterized by closure of the blood vessel or air passages of the neck as a result of external pressure on the neck (Iserson, 1984; Line, Stanley, & Choi, 1985). Choking is a more vague term and refers to either the violent act of strangulation, or aspiration of an object. "Choking out" or "choked out" are terms often used by law enforcement and medical care givers when a subject has had a neck hold placed. They are not specific to any particular holds and do not necessarily mean that the subject was actually restrained to the point of loss of consciousness. Thus, we discourage the use of these terms in medical or legal documentation.

Types of Neck Holds

The following section will review the types of neck holds and how they are placed.

Mechanical Hold

Occasionally, a mechanical restraint will be placed on the neck of a subject utilizing a large flashlight, a baton, or other bar-like device to compress the anterior portion of the neck. The hands of the restraining individual holding the bar device are placed around both sides of the subject's neck. The bar is pulled back, compressing the airway as well as the carotid arteries. The intent is to render the subject unconscious by compressing the carotid arteries and decreasing blood flow to the brain, or to gain control of the subject by submission due to the pain and uncomfortable nature associated with the hold. As there is direct pressure from a firm object across the airway, injury to underlying structures, including the larynx, trachea, and hyoid bone, is possible. Because of the risks associated with this neck hold, this technique has fallen out of favor and is not utilized as a primary neck hold by most law enforcement agencies.

Bar Hold

The bar hold, also known as the bar arm hold, is a restraint maneuver in which the forearm is placed straight across the front of the subject's neck while the restraining person is positioned behind the subject. This is similar to the mechanical hold but uses the forearm rather than an inanimate object. The free hand grasps the wrist of the "bar" arm, and pulls backward, putting pressure on the airway (see Figure 8.2).

The intended mechanism for rendering the subject unconscious is to occlude both carotid arteries, thus decreasing blood flow to the brain and inducing loss of consciousness. Like the mechanical hold, the risk of this hold is that too much pressure could cause injury to other vital structures of the neck. Given the anatomic location of the carotid arteries along the lateral aspect of the subject's neck, the hold typically will not induce loss of consciousness from arterial compression (see Figure 8.3).

This, in turn, may lead to greater force being applied and further potential serious injury, particularly to the airway structures. Because of the associated risks of injuries and death to subjects, this hold has fallen out of favor for the safer carotid sleeper hold.

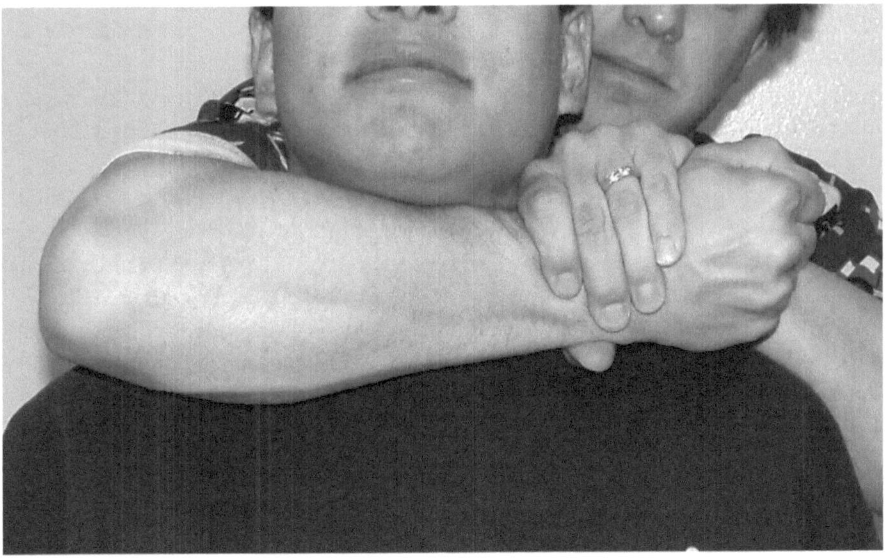

FIGURE 8.2 Bar hold: Demonstration of the proper technique for placement of the bar hold.

Source: Reprinted with permission from Springer.

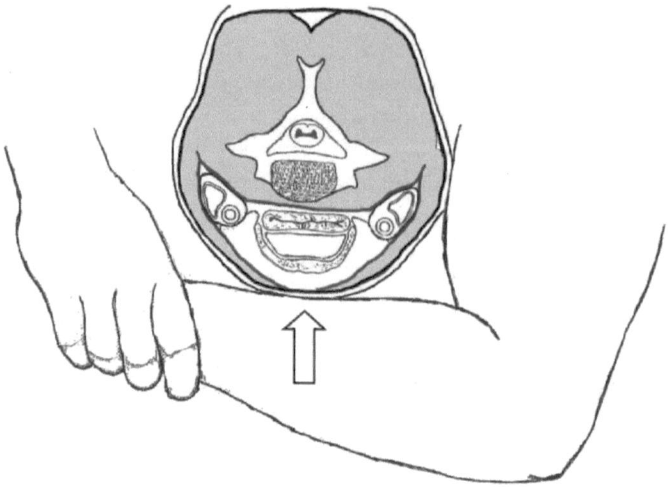

FIGURE 8.3 Bar hold: Demonstration of the neck in cross section with the pressure placed on the anterior airway structures by the forearm when the bar hold is implemented. The notable features are the compression of the airway structures with more deformation while the vascular structures are more spared in this hold.

Source: Reprinted with permission from Springer.

Lateral Vascular Neck Restraint (LVNR)

The Lateral Vascular Neck Restraint (LVNR), also known as the sleeper hold, carotid sleeper hold, or the carotid restraint, is a restraint maneuver in which the arm of the restraining person is held around the neck of the subject. The positioning is such that the crook, or anticubital fossa, of the elbow is over the anterior portion of the neck. The biceps region of the upper arm and the forearm are positioned to make a V-shape, with each region compressing the two sides of the neck. The free hand of the restraining person grasps the wrist of the restraining arm and pulls it back, thus creating a pinching effect (see Figure 8.4).

The tightening of the arm compresses the sides of the neck, compressing the carotid arteries, diminishing cerebral blood flow and causing unconsciousness (Mitchell et al., 2012). Since there is a fulcrum effect of the elbow at the anterior portion of the neck, there should be little pressure placed directly on the anterior airway, reducing the risk of collapse and injury (see Figure 8.5).

When appropriately placed, the carotid sleeper hold will typically cause loss of consciousness within ten to twenty seconds. At that point, the hold should be released and the unconscious period typically lasts up to thirty seconds after release. Theoretically, there should be no permanent sequelae after appropriate use of this hold. As with the *katajuji-jime* hold described previously, individuals being restrained in this manner are often not uncomfortable.

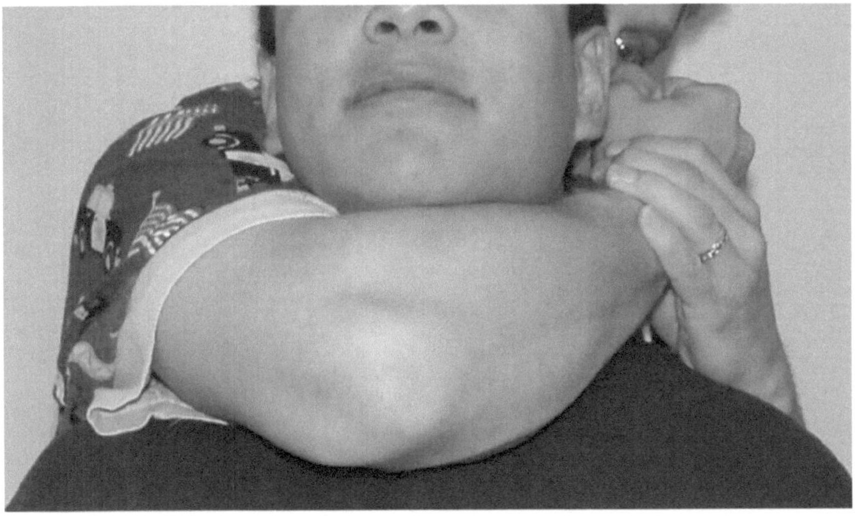

FIGURE 8.4 Carotid sleeper hold: Demonstration of the proper technique for placement of the carotid sleeper hold.

Source: Reprinted with permission from Springer.

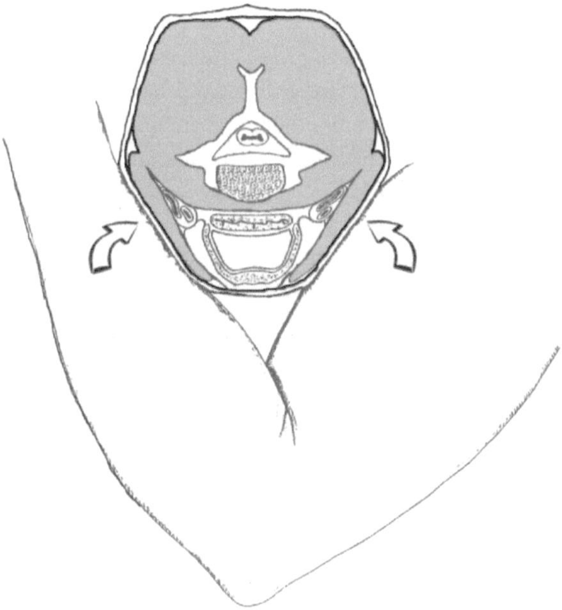

FIGURE 8.5 Carotid sleeper hold: Demonstration of the neck in cross section with force placed on it by a carotid sleeper hold. Note the compression on the carotid arteries by the forearm and upper arm, with sparing of pressure on the anterior airway structures by the crook of the arm when the carotid sleeper hold is properly implemented.

Source: Reprinted with permission from Springer.

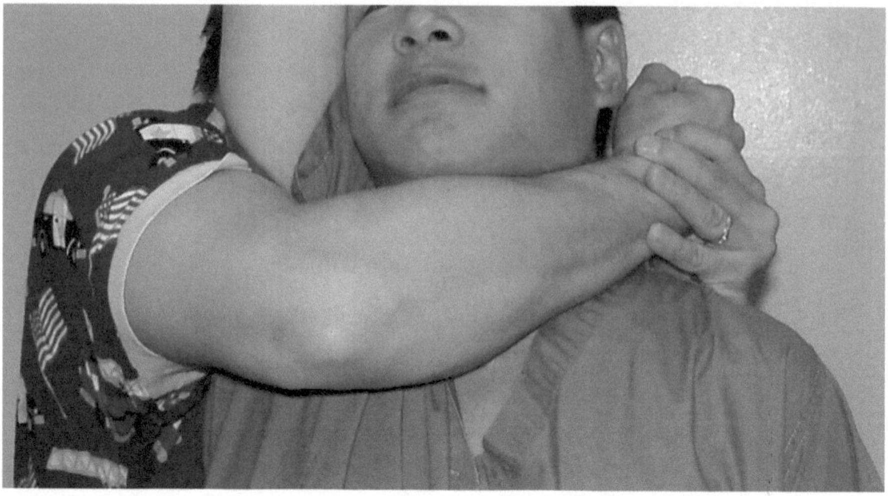

FIGURE 8.6 Shoulder pin restraint: Demonstration of the proper technique for placement of the shoulder pin restraint.

Source: Reprinted with permission from Springer.

Shoulder Pin Restraint

The shoulder pin restraint, derived from *kesa-gatame*, utilizes lateral neck compression to render the subject unconscious. Instead of wrapping the arm around both sides of the neck as in the carotid sleeper hold, one of the subject's arms is pinned upward along his own neck (see Figure 8.6).

The arm of the person placing the restraint is under the arm of the subject, below the subject's shoulder girdle so that the subject's arm is forced to rise above his head. The wrist of the restraining arm is then placed on the opposite side of the subject's neck, just below the mandible. The elbow of the restraining arm is centered on the sternum. The non-restraining hand grips the restraining hand and places pressure over the lateral neck of the subject. This hold, like the carotid sleeper hold, avoids pressure over the anterior airway structures. Like the other neck holds, if compression of the arteries is performed correctly, it will render the victim unconscious in ten to twenty seconds. Again, the hold should be released when the subject loses consciousness, with the unconscious period typically lasting up to thirty seconds.

Review of Neck Hold Related Deaths

Review of the Literature—Deaths

Reay and Eisele (1982) were the first to report deaths from law enforcement neck holds, describing a case of a 58-year-old man and a 35-year-old man who both had fractures of their thyroid cartilage on autopsy. The type of hold used was reported to be an attempted carotid sleeper hold that, because of the violent struggle, ended up becoming a bar hold (Reay & Eisele, 1982). It is questionable whether they died from the neck hold or their significant comorbidities exacerbated from the struggle. In these cases, there was no evidence linking the deaths directly to the use of the neck hold. Kornblum (1986a) reviewed the case records of 33 deaths associated with chokeholds. Many were associated with bar holds and several involved prolonged carotid restraint, from 1.5 to 3 minutes. He reported that 27 out of 33 individuals presented with abnormal behavior, 20 of which had confirmed toxicology screens that were positive for drugs or alcohol (Kornblum, 1986a)

Koiwai (1987) reported 14 fatalities in which the autopsy findings determined that the death was caused by the use of choke holds. The holds utilized in these cases included mechanical holds with a baton and a flashlight in two cases, bar holds in two cases, carotid sleeper holds in two cases, and unspecified neck holds in eight cases. All patients had evidence of injury to the neck, including bruises, ecchymosis, and hemorrhages on autopsy. Interestingly, there were five patients who suffered fractures of neck bones or cartilage (cricoid cartilage (1), hyoid bone (1), and thyroid cartilage (3)), and one of the intervertebral discs. These fractures occurred in subjects who died after either a mechanical hold or a bar hold. The other two cases occurred in one patient with a carotid sleeper hold and one in a patient with an undifferentiated neck hold. Other deaths in this series were attributed to asphyxia, with prolonged holds after loss of consciousness. It should be noted that one of the patients had taken lysergic acid diethylamide (LSD), one had taken heroin, one had taken ethanol and cocaine, and three had taken phencyclidine (PCP). Several patients had abnormalities noted of their hearts, including two with interstitial fibrosis, one with cardiomyopathy and one with atherosclerotic hypertensive heart disease, although it is unclear if these abnormalities played any role in the actual deaths. Similar cardiac findings were noted in a number of patients in Kornblum's (1986a) report as well.

Pollanen et al. (1998) reviewed 21 cases of deaths in police custody from excited delirium, and found that all were either laid in a prone position or had external pressure applied to the neck. Like previous studies, there was near 100 percent incidence of concomitant psychiatric disease or drug intoxication. In these cases, the cause of death was thought to be excited delirium and not from the neck pressure. The review also does not explain the type of neck pressure, nor was it indicated whether they were from a law enforcement neck hold.

Controversial Use in Law Enforcement

Because of multiple reported deaths occurring in custody associated with neck holds, police and neck hold techniques began to come under scrutiny (Reay & Mathers, 1983). Dr. Robert Kornblum, the acting medical examiner for Los Angeles County, wrote that a number of neck hold deaths occurring in his county led to a series of lawsuits and court actions that jeopardized the continued use of neck holds. One of these suits led to a ruling in 1981 by the United States Ninth District Court of Appeals that police officers could no longer use the choke hold unless "someone was threatened with serious bodily harm" (*Lyons v. City of Los Angeles*, 1981). A legislative proposal to eliminate the use of the bar hold and classify the carotid sleeper hold as a lethal weapon, thus restricting use to life threatening situations, was considered by the California State Legislature in 1983, but was not enacted (Kornblum, 1986b). Internal reviews by many agencies came to the determination that the bar hold placed individuals at risk for injury and death, and eventually this technique has been phased out of routine use by law enforcement. Many consider the use of the bar hold as inherently dangerous as the design is to obstruct the subject's airway, or to essentially force the person into submission.

Kornblum (1986b) also reported that when neck holds were restricted in use by the Los Angeles Police Department, there was a corresponding increase in the use of fists and night sticks to subdue violent suspects. This led to an increase in injuries to persons being arrested as well as injuries to police officers. He also reports that the police officers preferred the controlled neck holds at the time, rather than utilizing the more brutal baton.

In part because of these benefits, neck holds continue to be a common method of restraint by law enforcement agencies. Because of concerns regarding the potential risk of the mechanical bar hold, greater emphasis has now focused on the carotid sleeper hold. Use of this neck hold technique is currently taught in many law enforcement agencies and considered the hold of choice for safely gaining control of a subject. The technique is designed to render the subject unconscious in a brief period of time, while minimizing the risk of injury to the airway and other structures of the neck.

Anatomic Association

Death caused by neck holds is typically related to confounding anatomic or physiologic issues. These may be underlying medical conditions of the subject, or anatomic injury caused by the actual hold, especially if inappropriately placed. Clearly, if a hold were to be maintained in position well after the subject has lost consciousness, continued obstruction of cerebral blood flow would potentially lead to irreversible injury or death. In 1940, a team of doctors in Minnesota performed 341 carotid artery occlusion experiments on 126 men, ranging from 17 to 31 years of age. They placed a pneumatic cuff around their necks and occluded the carotid arteries, while the subjects were resting in a chair.

All 126 subjects lost consciousness within ten seconds. All regained consciousness in approximately the same amount of time. The researchers claimed, "All subjects could stand, walk out of the room, and go about their work within one or two minutes after the procedure, and no later effects were observed" (Rossen, Kabat, & Anderson, 1943, 513). This experiment was repeated up to four times in some of the subjects. In 11 subjects, the occlusion of blood flow to the brain was maintained after loss of consciousness for up to 100 seconds. All of these subjects regained consciousness within 40 seconds, walked out of the room within two minutes, and no late complications were observed (Rossen, Kabat, & Anderson, 1943). Kornblum (1986a) points out that how long one can safely occlude the carotids is likely decreased if there is a hyper-metabolic state. Exactly how much decrease is unknown and depends on the individual and the amount of exertion.

Airway Compromise

Bar holds directly place pressure on the anterior airway, which in turn may compress the airway, displace the tongue posteriorly, and potentially occlude the upper pharyngeal region. Too much pressure can collapse the airway. This pressure across the airway is often evidenced on autopsy as fractures of the larynx, its appendages, or the hyoid bone (Reay, 1998). A carotid sleeper hold is designed to better protect the airway, however, care must be given to maintain appropriate positioning, particularly in a struggling individual as the hold could shift into more of a bar hold, and thus put the airway at risk for compromise.

Vascular Injury

Patients with a significant medical history of atherosclerotic disease may be at risk for disruption of atherosclerotic material or plaque when a neck hold is used. This disruption of plaque could potentially result in a stroke from blockage of blood flow in the carotid arteries. Such cases have been reported in the medical field with the use of carotid sinus massage. Carotid sinus massage involves placing pressure directly over the carotid artery at the level of the carotid sinus and massaging the area, which has the effect of increasing neurologic discharge to slow down the heart rate. Munro and colleagues (1994) reported seven episodes of the neurological symptoms consistent with brain ischemia in older patients with the use of carotid sinus massage in 500 patients. The neurological findings of Munro et al. included weakness in five and visual field defects in two. Of these cases, five spontaneously resolved, one had persistent residual weakness on the same side as a pre-existing stroke, and another had permanent visual field loss (Munro et al., 1994). Richardson et al. (2000) had similar findings in 1,000 patients over 50 years of age, with nine patients reporting neurological complications possibly attributable to the carotid sinus massage, eight of which spontaneously resolved and one had persistent hand weakness. There were no sudden cardiac arrests or deaths reported in any of these case series.

Fortunately, atherosclerotic disease in the carotid arteries is most commonly found in the elderly population, a group less likely to require the use of a neck hold. However, the disease could be present in younger individuals. In most cases, it would be impossible for the restraining individual to know if this were the case at the time the subject requires restraint, as there are no physical attributes easily identifying a person at risk for stroke from compression of diseased carotid arteries.

Carotid Sinus Stimulation

Carotid sinus stimulation has been postulated as a possible etiology for sudden death in subjects undergoing neck holds. As noted above, pressure on the carotid sinus body causes a reflex vagal nerve discharge that can slow the heart rate. The belief is that marked compression of the carotid sinus can cause significant slowing of the heart (bradycardia) to the point of cardiac arrest and standstill (Line et al., 1985). This theory is based on the medical condition of carotid sinus syndrome (Line et al., 1985) and reports that some individuals can have marked bradycardia induced by neck massage (Arnold et al., 1991). Kornblum (1986a) also reports on this reflex action and states that, in rare cases, reflex cardiac arrest and sudden death can follow from pressure to this area. However, he provides no reference for this statement. Of the 1,000 patients who received carotid massage in the Richardson et al. (2000) study, none had any cardiac complications.

In a study performed by Solari et al. (2014), nearly 2,000 patients with a suspected hypersensitive carotid sinus had ten-second massages of both of their carotid arteries. Approximately 9 percent of these patients had a pause in their cardiac activity. On average, the pause lasted seven seconds, followed by a restart of the cardiac activity. The mean age was 77 and approximately 75 percent were male. About 70 percent of those with the sinus pause lost consciousness (Solari et al., 2014). There was not, nor has there ever been, a reported case of sustained asystole from carotid massage, even in those with carotid sinus syndrome. Our hearts are such that after a lack of activity from the normal contraction-stimulation cells, an integrated backup system will kick-in, providing electrical activity pump function.

The National Institute on Drug Abuse (NIDA) published *Phencyclidine Abuse: An Appraisal* in 1978. In a chapter on phencyclidine and use among youth, doctors Steven Lerner and Stanley Burns discuss how PCP can alter the carotid sinus reflex. They state that carotid sinus stimulation by external forces coupled with the effects of PCP on blood vessels may lead to an exaggerated bradycardia (Lerner & Burns, 1978). Again, this is a theory and there are no models in the medical literature proving this idea. A year later, in 1979, a civil law suit was brought against law enforcement personnel (*Burns v.*

City and County of Honolulu, 1982). Initially, the medical examiner had called the subject's cause of death asphyxiation. The cause of death was argued and it was postulated that the carotid restraint hold and PCP intoxication together may have caused an idiosyncratic bradycardic arrest. Whether the jury believed this to be true is unknown, but there was enough doubt about asphyxiation that the jury concluded there was no improper conduct by the police officers (Lerner & Burns, 1986).

The determination of death due to carotid sinus reflex is essentially impossible to determine at autopsy, particularly when alternative explanations for the cause of sudden death, such as excited delirium syndrome or acute drug intoxication exist. In one reported case in which the cause of death was listed as cardiac arrest from carotid sinus reflex, the patient had no neck injuries found on autopsy. The individual had been restrained because of psychotic behavior and delirium tremens from alcohol withdrawal. A neck hold was placed and the subject died suddenly while the force was being applied. The medical examiner reported that the diagnosis "almost certainly represents" death from carotid sinus stimulation, but this finding was made as a diagnosis of exclusion as such a cause would essentially be impossible to confirm (Koiwai, 1987).

While reflex bradycardia has been noted in a number of studies, there have been no reported deaths or bradycardic events to the point of requiring cardiac resuscitation in any of these studies (Arnold, 1999; Berk, Shea, & Crevey, 1991; Kornblum 1986a). Moreover, the medical literature is replete with studies looking at the use of carotid sinus massage as a diagnostic and therapeutic examination tool. In studies of thousands of uses on elderly patients, there were no complications of death or bradycardic events requiring treatment or resuscitation, even though this age group is traditionally more likely to have carotid sinus syndrome and more likely to be symptomatic from carotid sinus stimulation (Pollanen et al., 1998; Reay & Mathers, 1983). In fact, the diagnosis of carotid sinus syndrome, although well written about, is essentially unheard of in patients under the age of 50 years (Brignole & Menozzi, 1992; Coplan & Schweitzer, 1984; Kenny & Richardson, 2001; Mallet, 2003).

Given that sudden deaths associated with neck holds by law enforcement tend to be in younger subjects, the likelihood of carotid sinus stimulation syndrome is extremely unlikely. Additionally, in all of the clinical reports, reviews, and scientific studies of patients undergoing chokeholds or carotid sinus massage, there have been no reported deaths or bradycardic events requiring treatment or resuscitation. Although an interesting theory, the carotid sinus stimulation really should not be blamed for these sudden deaths.

Spinal Injury

Injury to the spinal column and spinal cord causing death from a neck hold is rare and typically associated with bar holds. In a case reported by Koiwai (1987), a 34-year-old patient who died following a bar hold was found to have intervertebral disc fractures between the third and fourth as well as fourth and fifth cervical vertebrae on autopsy. There was noted abnormal mobility of the cervical spine and a transverse tear of the ligamentum flavum, as well as an acute spinal epidural hematoma at the level of the third through eighth cervical disc. Death was determined to be from asphyxia from neck compression and not spinal cord injury. Kornblum (1986a) reports two subjects who suffered cervical spine injuries during neck holds. The first was a 53-year-old being detained by a citizen with an unknown type of choke hold, who on autopsy had third and fourth cervical vertebrae spinous process fractures and hemorrhage within the spinal canal that was pressing on the medulla oblongata. The second was a 34-year-old man who had a bar hold placed on him and was found to have hemorrhage in the anterior longitudinal ligament, an abnormal hypermobility of the vertebrae, and an epidural hematoma and a contusion of the spinal cord on autopsy.

In general, the extraordinary amount of force required to cause such injuries makes it extremely unlikely when a carotid sleeper hold is placed properly. The spinal cord injuries reported appear to be those in which bar holds were employed, with the exception of the one case of a non-trained person utilizing a neck hold. Higher risk patients would be those with underlying cervical spine pathology, such as ankylosing spondylitis or severe osteoporosis, who would be at higher risk for spinal injury with any neck manipulation. Again, these predisposing characteristics are found mostly in the elderly population, not younger subjects, who tend to be more subject to law enforcement holds.

Review of the Literature—Neck Hold Clinical Studies

Clinical studies on neck holds are predominantly performed on subjects with experience in judo or other related martial arts or on law enforcement officers. Neck holds in judo are remarkably similar to those used in law enforcement. The purpose of both is to subdue without inflicting injury. All of the studies discussed here have been in controlled scenarios with many not even going to the point of loss of consciousness from the hold. The focus of the studies tends to be non-invasive monitoring techniques in subjects who volunteer to be "choked out." Some of the techniques included evaluating brain waves utilizing electroencephalographs (EEG) or using transcutaneous technology to measure blood flow, vascular compliance, and cardiac pump function.

Electroencephalographic Studies

Very few clinical studies have been performed on the effects of performing neck holds on individuals. Rodriguez, Francione, and Gardella (1991) assessed EEG and regional cerebral blood flow (rCBF) utilizing the xenon 133 inhalation technique in ten judoka subjects undergoing *katajuji-jime* (carotid sleeper hold) to the point of unconsciousness. Baseline data of EEG and rCBF were obtained at rest, and EEG was done during choking and for ten minutes before and after the choking. rCBF was performed immediately after the recovery of physiological breathing. There were noted EEG changes (2–3 Hz delta waves in all cerebral regions but with an anterior predominance) that started about ten seconds after initiation of choking that lasted for five to six seconds. These findings were similar to the EEG findings of earlier studies, however, the clinical implications are unclear (Ikai, Ishiko, & Ueda, 1958; Suzuki, 1958). There was a slight decrease in rCBF in the measurement done after the chokehold was performed. These findings were not statistically significant, and it was concluded that rates of recovery are variable and depend on the individual (Rodriguez et al., 1991).

Rau and colleagues (1998) evaluated EEG findings in six healthy volunteers experienced in judo or ju-jitsu. EEG recordings were followed for 40 seconds, after which the volunteer was placed into a neck hold until he gave a sign to be released. None of the volunteers lost consciousness. EEG measurements continued for an additional 70 seconds. Average choking time was eight seconds (SD 1.8 seconds). They concluded that their testing did not find any appreciable changes in brain function during neck holds (Rau et al., 1998).

Vascular Flow Studies

Mitchell et al. (2012) evaluated the cause of unconsciousness during a carotid sleeper hold. Twenty-four healthy police officer volunteers had their carotid arteries compressed with this hold until the point of ocular fixation, a marker for unconsciousness. Vascular flow of the middle cerebral artery (MCA) was used to measure effectiveness of the cardiac artery compression. They found that the time to unconsciousness was approximately ten seconds after the hold. In successful maneuvers, neck pressures were at or exceeded 600mmHg and the MCA flows stopped to 0 cm/s. In unsuccessful maneuvers, the MCA flow never slowed below 30 cm/s. They also noted that neck pressure over the right carotid was greater than the left. This may have been related to the right-hand dominance of the investigator placing the neck hold. Although there was a decrease in the stroke volume and cardiac output at the time of hold application, the heart rate, mean arterial pressure, and ventricular contractility stayed constant and remained so for at least five minutes after the neck hold. This means that although there were some heart parameters that decreased, measurements of life-sustaining functions were never compromised. This again calls the theory of bradycardic arrest by carotid sinus stimulation into question. The authors concluded that the only mechanism for unconsciousness in a carotid sleeper hold is carotid artery compression, and thus a decrease in the brain's blood flow. They also concluded that this maneuver by law enforcement is a safe and effective intervention (Mitchell et al., 2012).

Hypophysio-Adrenocortical System Study

Ogawa and colleagues (1963) evaluated the effects of neck holds on five judo subjects, utilizing the *okurieri-jime* hold. Baseline and follow-up blood counts and urinalysis were checked on all subjects. Each subject was choked to the point of loss of consciousness, which took from 8–14 seconds and lasted from 10–20 seconds. All recovered without difficulty or complication. Transient decreases in pulse oximetry readings from an ear probe were noted with a baseline mean of 96 percent, decreasing to 86 percent with the hold, and returning back to baseline after removal of the neck hold. The authors also found increased total white blood cell counts as well as the level of 17-keto steroid in the urine, a hormone released by the adrenal cortex during stress. These are findings that would be expected as a result of the body's response to stress, thus the clinical applications are minimal, but did reflect that having a neck hold placed results in a physiologic stress response (Ogawa et al., 1963).

Evaluation of the "Choked Out" Patient

Very little has been studied on the medical evaluation of the patient who has been the recipient of a neck hold. Much of the work has come from those who work with judo participants, but formal protocols or guidelines do not exist. For victims of strangulation, reviews have suggested what imaging studies should be obtained to evaluate these patients, but given the retrospective nature of these studies, there was no opportunity to assess for sensitivity or specificity (McClane, Strack, & Hawley, 2001). An approach to evaluate the patient who has been "choked out" is described below.

History Taking

The clinical presentation, taken in context with the history, will drive what objective evaluation is indicated. Key elements that should be obtained regarding the neck restraint include: what hold was utilized; if it was properly placed; how long it was in place; whether the subject lost consciousness; and if it was promptly removed after loss of consciousness. Other important clinical elements include how long the subject was unconscious, whether the subject came back to an appropriate orientation upon awakening, and were there any other forms of force implemented (e.g., chemical agents, TASER, baton use). If the subject regains consciousness and then has a sudden cardiac arrest some time later, as long as there are no clinical findings of injury to the airway or vasculature enough to cause a cardiac arrest, the neck hold should be exonerated. Subjects will not regain consciousness then subsequently die or go into cardiac arrest in a delayed fashion. Mental status changes and neurological deficits, although difficult to ascertain in the agitated patient, can indicate injury. Other traditional historical questions about past medical history, medications, drug or alcohol use and allergies are also helpful if available from the subject. The review of any available video will help to evaluate the neck hold application, duration, and subject response prior to, during, and after the hold.

Physical Findings

In a subject who initially survives the neck hold, the airway will need to be assessed for compromise, including normal phonation, ability to speak in full sentences and lack of stridor (hoarseness). Examination should include assessment for tongue and facial swelling, oropharyngeal petechiae, swelling over the trachea, and speech and breathing patterns. Mild hoarseness or sore throat will require careful vigilance for any deterioration in airway status that would require additional intervention. Although initial presentation with non-focal findings is reassuring, close observation is

CASE ONE

Police responded to a person trying to break into a house. A 27-year-old shirtless combative male resisted arrest. He was taken to the ground with a single TASER activation but the struggle persisted. A neck hold was placed with an eventual loss of consciousness after about 30 seconds. He was handcuffed, then regained consciousness and started struggling violently against the handcuffs and kicking. Leg restraints were placed and paramedics were called. Officers held him in position on his side and then he went into cardiac arrest less than a minute before the ambulance arrived. He was unable to be resuscitated and was pronounced dead.

Comments

There is a significant time between the placement of the neck hold and the cardiac arrest. The key features in this case are to document the timeline. Much can be pieced together with dispatch data (when officers went hands on, when noted in custody, when the ambulance was called, when the ambulance arrived, etc.). The other key feature of this case is that the subject regained consciousness and returned to his baseline combative state well before his cardiac arrest.

important, particularly in patients with significant soft tissue trauma and bruising. Clearly, patients on anticoagulants are at increased risk for hematoma formation and airway compression, and should be watched closely and for longer periods of time. Important physical exam features for medical personnel to document after a neck hold placement include: (1) voice changes, (2) swallowing changes, (3) breathing changes, (4) mental status changes, (5) pain or deformity, (6) carotid artery bruits, (7) skin bruising or abrasions, (8) petechiae, (9) involuntary urination or defecation, (10) swelling of the neck, (11) chin or jaw injuries, (12) back and neck pain or deformity, (13) subconjunctival hemorrhage, (14) psychiatric changes, and (15) neurological deficits.

A careful neurological examination must be documented. Any abnormal findings would require additional objective evaluation. The examination should include cranial nerves, specific evaluation for Horner's syndrome (combination of lateralizing ptosis, myosis, and anhydrosis of the face indicating compromise of the cervical sympathetic nerves of the neck), motor examination, sensory examination, and cerebellar assessment. Finally, there should be a physical palpation of the neck. The cervical spine should have assessment for tenderness to palpation over the spinous processes. Additionally, the anterior components of the neck should be palpated with careful attention to the region over the carotid arteries and the anterior trachea. Range of motion should be assessed if there are no neurological findings and no tenderness to palpation over the spinous processes. The carotid arteries should be auscultated for bruits, and if none present, palpated for tenderness and thrills.

The findings to evaluate at autopsy in a subject who dies after the placement of a neck hold are noted below.

Diagnostic Imaging

Imaging in the patient who had a carotid restraint placed and initially survives is based on clinical findings. When determining which patients require imaging, the anatomic areas to consider include the airway, the spine, including the vertebrae and spinal cord, the esophagus, and the carotid arteries.

After appropriate steps have been taken to manage the patient's airway, imaging is directed at the patient's clinical presentation. All patients with stridor or change in speech require evaluation. Direct laryngoscopy or radiographic imaging, including computed tomography (CT) scanning, are two appropriate options, although direct laryngoscopy is preferred. If there is evidence of aspiration or involvement of the bronchi, then bronchoscopy would be necessary. Careful clinical monitoring is appropriate for mild cases.

If there is suspicion of cervical spine injury, particularly if there is point tenderness over the spinous processes of the cervical spine, radiographic imaging with computed tomography is the standard imaging modality used. We recommend using decision rules, such as the Canadian Cervical Spine Rules or NEXUS Criteria, if the practitioner needs additional guidance. If there is clinical evidence of a cervical spine injury, then the patient will likely require additional imaging, including CT or magnetic resonance imaging (MRI). Although extremely unlikely in an appropriately placed hold, special consideration should be given to patients with increased risk, including elderly patients, patients with significant osteoporosis, and patients with underlying spinal pathology, such as ankylosing spondylitis.

In neck holds, injury to the esophagus is very unlikely. The esophagus is a thick, muscular, pliable structure. If there is injury to the esophagus, it will likely be in conjunction with injury to the airway as well. In such a patient with significant injury, evaluation of the esophagus would be warranted, typically utilizing a swallow study or endoscopy. If there is any suspicion of injury, the patient should be kept NPO (nil per os).

The most challenging anatomic area to determine if evaluation is necessary lies with the carotid arteries. The injury that potentially can occur with blunt trauma is a carotid artery dissection. Dissection of the artery results from an intimal tear or primary hemorrhage of the vasa vasorum. Thrombus forms in the vessel and can lead to narrowing of the artery with reduced flow, or the thrombus may break free and become an embolic source for distal branch occlusion, causing stroke symptoms (Guyot, Kazmierczak, & Diaz, 2001). The patient with carotid artery dissection will suffer cerebral infarction in up to 82 percent of cases, and usually present within seven days (Biousse et al., 1995). Alimi et al. (1996) reported that only 56 percent of patients present with clinical findings in the first 24 hours and 66 percent within the first week. However, symptoms of stroke have been delayed up to several weeks. In patients presenting with spontaneous carotid dissection, the most common clinical findings include neck, jaw or head pain, Horner's syndrome, and tinnitus in up to 96 percent of the cases (Fisher, 1982).

There are several imaging modalities used to diagnose carotid artery dissection, including carotid ultrasound, computed tomography, magnetic resonance imaging/magnetic resonance angiography (MRI/MRA), and digital subtraction angiography (DSA). A literature review by Vilke and Chan (2011) revealed no case series or retrospective reviews on strangulation and carotid injury. They called for more studies to be done to better guide practitioners. The gold standard screening exam was traditionally digital subtraction angiography (DSA) of the cerebrovascular vessels. Recently, there has been a growing body of evidence showing that computed tomography angiography (CTA) had a sufficient negative predictive value to rule out carotid injury. This is likely due to the increasing sensitivity of new generation (64 channel) computed tomography (CT) scanners (Paulus et al., 2014). The non-inferiority of CTA was welcomed by many as DSA is relatively high in cost, invasiveness, resource demands, and complications.

Who to evaluate with a CTA is a common question. The infrequency of this diagnosis has made the creation of a practice and treatment guideline impossible. Previous work has reported screening criteria to include neurological examination not consistent with brain CT scan, development of lateralizing neurological deficits (hemiparesis, TIA, CVA, amaurosis fugax), Horner syndrome, signs of external cervical trauma, cervical bruits, basilar skull fracture and displaced mid-face or mandible fracture, massive epistaxis, severe flexion or extension cervical spine fracture, or neck hematoma (Biffl et al., 1998; Fabian et al., 1996; Kerwin, et al., 2001). We add that patients with persistent lateral neck pain, not consistent with paraspinous muscle strain solely after direct trauma, should have imaging strongly considered. Given the rarity of this diagnosis in blunt neck trauma patients, and that there has not yet been a published case report implicating a neck hold as a cause for carotid dissection, it would clearly be acceptable practice to advocate screening tests be reserved for patients with neurological deficits or findings of point tenderness over the carotid artery.

CASE TWO

Bystanders report a 27-year-old female walking in the street shouting obscenities. Police respond and find an agitated subject, resisting arrest. After a short pursuit, the subject is placed in a carotid neck hold. There was a slight struggle but the subject lost consciousness within 10 seconds. She was handcuffed. After regaining consciousness, she was cooperative with the officers. Complaining of anterior neck pain, she was brought to the nearest emergency department for medical clearance for jail.

In the Emergency Department, a careful examination of the patient's head, face, neck, and chest was performed. Slight erythema of the anterior neck was noted. The patient did not complain of pain on neck flexion or extension, difficulty swallowing, hoarse voice. Her vision was normal, there were no subconjunctival hemorrhages noted. There were no petechiae about her face. Her neurological exam was normal. She did not have any carotid bruits. Photographs of the patient's neck were taken by the police officers. Because of her unremarkable physical exam, x-rays, CT scans, and lab testing were deferred. The patient was discharged being medically clear for jail intake.

Several days later as an inmate in jail, the young female was seen at the jail medical clinic. The erythema about her neck had resolved and she was now asymptomatic.

Comment

Although this is not an in-custody death, it is a scenario that often results in litigation. Careful documentation of record and photo-documentation at the time will allow medical experts involved in the litigation to better opine that the neck hold did not have any short- or long-term clinical effects.

Autopsy Findings

It should be emphasized that there has never been a proven case of death due to a properly applied LVNR hold, however, some medical examiners have claimed a combination of carotid sinus stimulation and brain ischemia (Reay & Eisele, 1982). We argue that this is impossible to prove in a scientific manner. There are actually no physiological studies available to suggest that bradycardic arrest occurs from carotid stimulation during neck holds.

The carotid neck hold is extremely safe when used appropriately. It can be difficult to subdue a violent subject who may be under the influence of illicit substances, which can make him or her less responsive to pain. Multiple case reports have emphasized this violent behavior of those suffering from Excited Delirium Syndrome (ExDS) (Pollanen et al., 1998). ExDS, whether set off by psychiatric or illicit substance consumption, can give subjects a feeling of invincibility (Gerold et al., 2015). This can make for a dangerous struggle during which an extraordinary amount of force can accidentally be applied by the subduer. In cases in which there is a violent struggle, a core body temperature should be obtained if at all possible. This temperature could be documented by EMS providers or in the emergency department. If the patient ends up as a field cardiac arrest and the body is left at scene, a core liver temperature could be documented by the medical examiner's office. If significantly elevated, this may represent a case of acute drug intoxication or ExDS, both of which can cause sudden cardiac arrest.

An appropriately applied carotid neck hold should leave minimal abrasions and contusions, if any, around the neck. Signs and clinical findings should be specifically looked for and documented in cases in which a subject dies and a neck hold had been placed. These are listed in the checklist at the end of the chapter. Though each finding does not independently prove or even imply that a neck hold was placed incorrectly, each can be evaluated in the clinical context of the history. Findings, whether present or absent, that should be documented at autopsy include: (1) petechial hemorrhages, (2) subconjunctival hemorrhages, (3) jaw bone fractures or dislocations, (4) sternocleidomastoid muscle hemorrhages, (5) strap muscle hemorrhages, (6) posterior muscle or ligament injury, (7) vertebral injuries, (8) intervertebral disk injury, (9) esophageal injury, (10) thyroid cartilage fracture, (11) hyoid bone fractures, and (12) carotid artery dissection.

It is also important to obtain a comprehensive drug screen and note findings consistent with illicit substance abuse. A detailed medication screen is often of paramount importance, as many psychiatric medications have a narrow therapeutic index, some with known cardiotoxicity. And obviously careful attention to the rest of the autopsy, including heart size and cardiac vessel condition and distribution, is also important as part of the case evaluation.

Summary

The use of neck holds is a controversial issue. Although neck holds in judo have a long history of safety, their use by law enforcement has been questioned with cases of sudden death, which have received significant media and public attention. Their use has also come under fire by some who have reported theories of death which are not congruent with basic human physiology or available research. The data clearly indicate that the bar hold technique can result in an increased risk of significant injury to individuals and should not be routinely used for this reason. On the contrary, the carotid sleeper hold, when utilized in younger subjects appropriately, has a relatively solid safety profile and is an appropriate form of restraint and use of force method in law enforcement's force continuum.

Investigation Checklist

This checklist includes findings that are useful in evaluating the neck hold and better determine its role, if any, in the sudden death.

Historical Findings

- ☐ Type of hold placed
- ☐ How many times was the hold placed into position?
- ☐ How many times was pressure applied?
- ☐ What was the response to the pressure?
- ☐ Was there loss of consciousness?
- ☐ How long was the loss of consciousness?
- ☐ What was the activity level after the person "woke" back up?

- ☐ How long after "waking up" did the person go into cardiac arrest?
- ☐ Other uses of force used on or around the head and neck.
- ☐ Any injuries to the neck predating law enforcement involvement, like being choked by another individual or attempted hanging or strangulation.
- ☐ Other features of drug intoxication or ExDS (see checklist in Chapter 9).

Postmortem findings specific to neck holds

- ☐ External evidence of trauma
- ☐ Petechial hemorrhages
- ☐ Subconjunctival hemorrhages
- ☐ Jaw bone fractures or dislocations
- ☐ Sternocleidomastoid muscle hemorrhages
- ☐ Strap muscle hemorrhages
- ☐ Posterior muscle or ligament injury
- ☐ Vertebral injuries
- ☐ Intervertebral disk injury
- ☐ Esophageal injury
- ☐ Thyroid cartilage fracture
- ☐ Hyoid bone fractures
- ☐ Carotid artery dissection
- ☐ Toxicological screen positive for stimulants

References

Alimi, Y., Di Mauro, P., Fiacre, E., Magnan, J., & Juhan, C. (1996). Blunt injury to the internal carotid artery at the base of the skull: Six cases of venous graft restoration. *Journal of Vascular Surgery, 24*(2), 249–257.

Arnold, R. W. (1999). The human heart rate response profiles to five vagal maneuvers. *Yale Journal of Biology and Medicine, 72*(4), 237–44.

Arnold, R. W., Dyer, J. A., Gould, A. B., Hohberger, G. G., & Low, P. A. (1991). Sensitivity to vasovagal maneuvers in normal children and adults. *Mayo Clinic Proceedings, 66*(8), 797–804.

Barquin, R. C. (1979). *Handbook of the International Judo Federation.* Lausanne, Switzerland: International Judo Federation.

Berk, W. A., Shea, M. J., & Crevey, B. J. (1991). Bradycardic responses to vagally mediated bedside maneuvers in healthy volunteers. *The American Journal of Medicine, 90*(1), 725–729.

Biffl, W. L., Moore, E. E., Ryu, R. K., Offner, P. J, Novak, Z., Coldwell, D. M., Franciose, R. J., & Burch, J. M. (1998). The unrecognized epidemic of blunt carotid arterial injuries: Early diagnosis improves neurologic outcome. *Annals of Surgery, 228*(4), 462–470.

Biousse, V., D'Anglejan-Chatillon, J., Touboul, P. J., Amarenco, P., & Bousser, M. (1995). Time course of symptoms in extracranial carotid artery dissections: A series of 80 patients. *Stroke, 26*(2), 235–239.

Brignole, M. & Menozzi, C. (1992). Carotid sinus syndrome: Diagnosis, natural history and treatment. *European Journal of CPE, 2*, 247–254.

Burns v. City and County of Honolulu, 698 F.2d 1229 (1982).

Coplan, N. L. & Schweitzer, P. (1984). Carotid sinus hypersensitivity: Case report and review of the literature. *American Journal of Medicine*, 77(3), 561–565.

Fabian, T. C., Patton, J. H., Croce, M. A., Minard, G., Kudsk, K. A., & Pritchard, F. E. (1996). Blunt carotid injury: Importance of early diagnosis and anticoagulant therapy. *Annals of Surgery, 223*(5), 513–525.

Fisher, C. M. (1982). The headache and pain of spontaneous carotid artery dissection. *Headache: The Journal of Head and Face Pain, 22*(2), 60–65.

Gerold, K. B., Gibbons, M. E., Fisette, R. E., & Alves, D. (2015). Review, clinical update, and practice guidelines for excited delirium syndrome. *Journal of Special Operations Medicine, 15*(1), 62–69.

Guyot, L. L., Kazmierczak, C. D., & Diaz, F. G. (2001). Vascular injury in neurotrauma. *Neurological Research, 23*(2–3), 291–296.

Ikai, M., Ishiko, T., & Ueda, G. (1958). Physiological studies on "choking" in judo. *Bulletin of the Association for the Scientific Studies on Judo, Kokokan: Report 1*, 1–12.

Iserson, K. (1984). Strangulation: A review of ligature, manual and postural compression injuries. *Annals of Emergency Medicine, 13*(4), 179–185.

Kamitani, T., Nimura, Y., Nagahiro, S., Miyazaki, S., & Tomatsu, T. (2013). Catastrophic head and neck injuries in judo players in Japan from 2003 to 2010. *The American Journal of Sports Medicine, 41*(8), 1915–1921.

Kenny, R. A. & Richardson, D. A. (2001). Carotid sinus syndrome and falls in older adults. *American Journal of Geriatric Cardiology, 10*(2), 97–99.

Kerwin, A. J., Bynoe, R. P., Murray, J., Hudson, E. R., Close, T. P., Gifford, R. R. M., Carson, K. W., Smith, L. P., & Bell, R. M. (2001). Liberalized screening for blunt carotid and vertebral artery injuries is justified. *Journal of Trauma-Injury Infection and Critical Care, 51*(2), 308–314.

Koiwai, E. K. (1981). Fatalities associate with judo. *The Physician and Sportsmedicine, 9*(4), 61–66.

Koiwai, E. K. (1987). Deaths allegedly caused by the use of "choke holds" (shime-waza). *Journal of Forensic Sciences, 32*(2), 419–432.

Kornblum, R. N. (1986a). Medical analysis of police choke holds and general neck trauma (part 2). *Trauma, 28*, 13–64.

Kornblum, R. N. (1986b). Medical analysis of police choke holds and general neck trauma (part 1). *Trauma, 27*, 7–60.

Lerner, S. E. & Burns, R. S. (1978). Phencyclidine use among youth: History, epidemiology, and acute and chronic intoxication. In R. C. Peterson & R. C. Stillman (eds.), *Phencyclidine (PCP) abuse: An appraisal, NIDA research monograph 21* (1–17). Washington, DC: National Institute on Drug Abuse.

Lerner, S. E. & Burns, R. S. (1986). Legal issues associated with PCP abuse—The role of the forensic expert. In D. H. Clout (ed.), *Phencyclidine: An update, NIDA Research Monograph 64* (229–236). Washington, DC: National Institute on Drug Abuse.

Line, Jr., W. S., Stanley, Jr., R. B., & Choi, J. H. (1985). Strangulation: A full spectrum of blunt neck trauma. *Annals of Otology, Rhinology & Laryngology, 94*(6 Pt 1), 542–546.

Lyons v. City of Los Angeles, 656 F.2d 417 (1981).

Mallet, M. (2003). Carotid sinus syndrome. *Hospital Medicine, 64*(2), 92–95.

McClane, G. E., Strack, G. B., & Hawley, D. (2001). A review of 300 attempted strangulation case Part II: Clinical evaluation of the surviving victim. *Journal of Emergency Medicine, 21*(3), 311–315.

Mitchell, J. R., Roach, D. E., Tyberg, J. V., Belenkie, I., & Sheldon, R. S. (2012). Mechanism of loss of consciousness during vascular neck restraint. *Journal of Applied Physiology, 112*(3), 396–402.

Munro, N. C., McIntosh, S., Lawson, J., Morley, C. A., Sutton, R., & Kenny, R. A. (1994). Incidence and complications after carotid sinus massage in older patients with syncope. *Journal of the American Geriatrics Society, 42*(12), 1248–1251.

Ogawa, S., Akutsu, K., & Sugimoto, H. (1963). Physiologic studies on "choking" in judo with reference to hypophysio-adrenocortical system. *Bulletin of the Association for the Scientific Studies on Judo, Kokokan: Report 2*, 107–114.

Owens, R. G. & Ghadaili, E. J. (1991). Judo as a possible cause of anoxic brain damage. *Journal of Sports Medicine and Physical Fitness, 31*(4), 627–628.

Paulus, E. M., Fabian, T. C., Savage, S. A., Zarzaur, B. L., Botta, V., Dutton, W., & Croce, M. A. (2014). Blunt cerebrovascular injury screening with 64-channel multidetector computed tomography: More slices finally cut it. *Journal of Trauma and Acute Care Surgery, 76*(2), 279–285.

Pollanen, M. S., Chiasson, D. A., Cairns, T. J., & Young, J. G. (1998). Unexpected death related to restraint for excited delirium: A retrospective study of deaths in police custody and in the community. *Canadian Medical Association Journal, 158*(12), 1603–1607.

Rau, R., Raschka, C., Brunner, K., & Banzer, W. (1998). Spectral analysis of electroencephalography changes after choking in judo (juji-jime). *Medicine & Science in Sports & Exercise, 30*(9), 1356–1362.

Reay, D. T. (1998). Death in custody. *Clinics in Laboratory Medicine, 18*(1), 1–21.

Reay, D. T. & Eisele, J. W. (1982). Death from law enforcement neck holds. *American Journal of Forensic Medicine & Pathology, 3*(3), 253–258.

Reay, D. T. & Mathers, R. L. (1983). Physiological effects resulting from use of neck holds. *FBI Law Enforcement Bulletin, 52*, 12–15.

Richardson, D. A., Bexton, R., Shaw, F. E., Steen, N., Bond, J., & Kenny, R. A. (2000). Complications of carotid sinus massage—A prospective series of older patients. *Age and Ageing, 29*(5), 413–417.

Rodriguez, G., Francione, S., & Gardella, M. (1991). Judo and choking: EEG and regional cerebral blood flow findings. *Journal of Sports Medicine and Physical Fitness, 31*(4), 605–610.

Rossen, R., Kabat, H. & Anderson, J. (1943). Acute arrest of cerebral circulation in man. *Archives of Neurology and Psychiatry, 50*(5), 510–528.

Solari, D., Maggi, R., Oddone, D., Solano, A., Croci, F., Donateo, P., & Brignole, M. (2014). Clinical context and outcome of carotid sinus syndrome diagnosed by means of the "method of symptoms." *Europace, 16*(6), 928–934.

Suzuki, K. (1958). Medical studies on "choking" in judo, with special reference to electroencephalographic investigation. *Bulletin of the Association for the Scientific Studies on Judo, Kokokan: Report 1*, 23–48.

Tezuka, M. (1978). Physiological studies of the Ochi (unconsciousness) resulting from shime-waza (strangle-hold) in judo. *Bulletin of the Association for the Scientific Studies on Judo, Kodokan: Report*, 71–73.

Vilke, G. M. & Chan, T. C. (2011). Evaluation and management for carotid dissection in patients presenting after choking or strangulation. *The Journal of Emergency Medicine, 40*(3), 355–358.

9

EXCITED DELIRIUM SYNDROME (EXDS)

Christopher J. Coyne, Binh T. Ly, and Gary M. Vilke

Introduction

Excited delirium syndrome (ExDS) is generally defined as an alteration in mental status accompanied by severe agitation and frequent combativeness. This agitation may manifest as intense fear, paranoia, hyperactivity, shouting, panic, or violence. If left untreated, this syndrome has the potential to lead to a sudden cessation of struggling behavior in conjunction with cardiac or respiratory arrest (Wetli, Mash, & Karch, 1996). Although this clinical entity has been loosely described in the literature for 150 years, there remain no clearly defined diagnostic criteria for ExDS. Some of the clinical characteristics that one may see in these subjects include elevated temperature, enlarged pupils, high pain tolerance, superhuman strength, severe sweating, lack of fatigue, inappropriate clothing for the environment (little or no clothing despite a cold environment), combativeness, delirium, predilection toward glass or mirrors, and continued struggle despite restraint (Vilke et al., 2012a). One of the diagnostic dilemmas associated with ExDS is that many of these characteristics overlap with a variety of medical and psychiatric conditions, such as sepsis, stimulant drug intoxication, hyperthyroidism, seizure disorders, schizophrenia, and bipolar disease. It is only after these conditions are evaluated and controlled for that one can apply ExDS as the diagnosis.

Given that individuals with ExDS are confused or delirious, agitated, combative, and often destructive, law enforcement is often called on and their intervention is often necessary to mitigate the harm and damage that these persons may do to themselves or others. Many fatal cases of ExDS do occur while in police custody and generally involve some degree of struggle with medical staff or law enforcement followed by physical restraint (Grant et al., 2009). This has led to significant investigation and controversy surrounding the validity of ExDS, which has alternatively been described as "sudden in-custody death syndrome" (Robinson & Hunt, 2005). Although originally described post-mortem by medical examiners, the clinical entity of ExDS is now well recognized in emergency medicine, psychiatric, pre-hospital, and medico-legal literature (Debard, Adler, & Bozeman, 2009; Vilke et al., 2012b). Gill (2014) describes ExDS as a clinico-pathologic diagnosis that must be based on both the laboratory and toxicology results as well as the historical and clinical aspects of each case; however, most experts believe this is a clinical diagnosis that may have laboratory findings that are common and supportive, but not necessarily pathognomonic or diagnostic of ExDS. Given the complicated and controversial nature of ExDS and the context in which it generally occurs, it is imperative that investigators have a thorough understanding of the signs and symptoms of ExDS in order to assist with the confirmation of this diagnosis when appropriate (Gill, 2014; Lifschultz & Donoghue, 1991; Luke & Reay, 1992).

Historical Context

Luther Bell (1849) first described the clinical syndrome that is now known as ExDS in the 19th century. As primary psychiatrist for the McLean Asylum for the Insane in Massachusetts, Bell described the syndrome as an acute exhaustive mania that was fatal in over 75 percent of occurrences. He reported that out of the 1,700 patients he treated at his facility, 40 experienced the rapid onset of confusion, delusions, hallucinations, hyperactivity, sleeplessness, and fevers (Bell, 1849; Maldeniya & Vasudev, 2013). In the period following these initial reports, multiple names were applied to this condition, including Bell's mania, lethal catatonia, acute exhaustive mania, and agitated delirium (Sztajnkrycer & Baez, 2005; Takeuchi, Ahern, & Henderson, 2011). Most of these cases involved patients with psychiatric diseases, such as schizophrenia and bipolar disease, in an era before neuroleptics and other sedative medications. With the introduction of antipsychotic and mood-stabilizing medications in the 20th century, the number of deaths from ExDS began to fall steadily until the mid-1950s when the disease temporarily disappeared from the medical literature.

In the 1980s, many unexplained cases of in-custody deaths started to rise, with multiple case similarities to those previously described in the psychiatric literature. Although some were likely related to untreated psychiatric disorders, a majority of these cases were found to be related to the introduction and widespread abuse of cocaine in the United States (Fishbain & Wetli, 1981; Vilke et al., 2012; Wetli, 1987). In a study by Grant et al. (2007) that examined in-custody deaths using the Maryland Chief Medical Examiner database, of the 202 cases of ExDS between 1934 and 2004, there was a significant upswing in the 1980s that continued through the 2000s. In a follow-up study on patient demographics, approximately 80 percent of these predominantly middle-aged men were found to be positive for cocaine on post-mortem toxicology screens (Southall & Pestaner, 2003). The vast majority of subjects in these cases exhibited signs of ExDS, including severe agitation, altered mental status, superhuman strength, imperviousness to pain, and continuing to struggle despite restraint. As these cases became more frequent, medical scientists began exploring the pathophysiology behind these controversial deaths (Otahbachi, Cevik, & Bagdure, 2010).

Current Status of the Research

The vast majority of reported modern cases of ExDS appear to be related to stimulant drug abuse, as opposed to psychiatric or medical illness (Fink, 1999; Morrison & Sadler, 2001; Pollanen et al., 1998). Among cases of drug-related ExDS, cocaine appears to be the predominant precipitating substance, though cases involving phencyclidine (PCP), methamphetamine, lysergic acid diethylamide (LSD), and cathinones (bath salts) have been reported as well (O'Halloran & Lewman, 1993). Although one may expect levels of cocaine in post-mortem ExDS cases to be similar to those who died of cocaine intoxication, investigations by Pollanen et al. (1998) and Ruttenber, McAnally, and Wetli (1999) found that blood levels of cocaine in ExDS are generally much lower than in cocaine intoxication.

Chronic cocaine use with repeated binges have been associated with the development of fatal ExDS, as opposed to toxic levels (Stephens, Jentzen, Karch, Mash, & Wetli, 2004). Although drug exposure may be a precipitant of ExDS, this suggests that deaths may be due to a mechanism separate from acute drug poisoning.

Much of the research behind the pathophysiology underlying ExDS has been performed with the analysis of post-mortem brain tissue. In a typical ongoing cocaine user, there are actually physical changes in parts of the brain. In certain brain areas, there are changes in the nerve cell receptors and how the neurotransmitters bind and function at these sites. Specifically, there is a compensatory increase in the density of dopamine receptor binding, in addition to an increased amount of dopamine transporters in the regions of the brain that control reward (Mash & Staley, 1999; Staley et al., 1995). Serotonin transporters are similarly increased as a response to chronic stimulant use (Mash et al., 2000). These adaptive changes are thought to allow chronic users to respond to rapidly elevating levels of dopamine in the brain (Mash et al., 2003). In the brains of those individuals who die due to ExDS, there appear to be little or no adaptive changes to chronic cocaine use. Mash and Staley (1999) suggest that this lack of adaptive changes may be related to aberrant molecular processing in the brains of ExDS victims.

It has been postulated that this central dopamine stimulation, compounded with a relative lack of compensatory mechanisms, is what leads to the development of ExDS. One of the most compelling arguments that support this theory involves the profound elevated body temperatures (hyperthermia) experienced by many individuals who suffer from fatal ExDS. Dopamine is the central neurotransmitter that controls temperature regulation in the hypothalamus. Insufficient regulation of escalating dopamine levels by the neurotransporters in persons with ExDS may explain why many of these patients present with extremely high temperatures, beyond that which is expected relative to ambient temperature and degree of physical exertion (Allam & Noble, 2001). The involvement of hyperthermia in cases of ExDS has been demonstrated on the molecular level as well through post-mortem tissue analysis. In a case series by Mash et al. (2009), victims of ExDS were found to have elevated levels of heat shock proteins in brain tissue, up to four times higher than those levels found in matched controls. These heat shock proteins are specific proteins produced in brain tissue as a natural adaptation to protect cells from heat damage. In these same victims, there was an associated decrease in dopamine transporter levels, suggesting that the aberrant dopamine pathways and lack of compensatory changes are related to clinical manifestations of fatal ExDS.

Although this clinical condition was first described in psychiatric patients, modern cases of ExDS primarily related to mental illness have become uncommon. Although the exact causes of psychiatric illnesses such as schizophrenia and bipolar disorder are unknown, it is clear that abnormalities in dopamine and serotonin neurotransmission are involved in the pathogenesis. Cases of ExDS in patients with mental illness are likely uncommon due to the widespread use of medications that help treat these conditions by regulating these neurotransmitters, such as antipsychotics and antidepressants. Cases that involve mental illness appear to be more prevalent in individuals who abruptly discontinue their psychiatric medications (Morrison & Sadler, 2001). Rarely, cases of ExDS do occur in new-onset, untreated psychiatric illness with psychotic or manic features (Barnett et al., 2007).

Critical Issues and Factors

Due to the very visible context in which many of these cases present, such as destructive rampages or running around naked, deaths associated with ExDS have gained public attention. Whether this behavior and clinical presentation represent a true diagnosis or syndrome remains controversial in both the medical and legal literature. Fatal cases of ExDS frequently occur while in police custody after a period of struggle, which has led to speculation regarding the nature of these deaths (Karch & Stephens, 1999; O'Halloran & Lewman, 1993; Park, Korn, & Henderson, 2001; Pollanen et al., 1998; Sathyavagiswaran, Rogers, & Noguchi, 2007; Stratton et al., 2001). Although extensive post-mortem examinations often take place following deaths in custody, which lead to the description and establishment of ExDS initially as a pathological diagnosis, there are some who have argued that many of these cases may be causally related to other aspects of police use of force or restraining procedures. Some have even suggested that this is a fabricated diagnosis that was created to "cover up" police brutality (Vilke et al., 2012). Current data suggest that the incidence of death in persons that exhibit clinical signs and symptoms of ExDS is approximately 10 percent (DeBard et al., 2009; Stratton et al., 2001). Previous reports have suggested that approximately two-thirds of these fatal ExDS cases occur at the scene or while in police or medical custody (Stratton, Rogers, & Green, 1995). A study by Stratton et al., however, found that only 18 persons among 214 cases of ExDS died while being restrained by police (Ruttenber et al., 1999). Most cases of fatal ExDS have exhibited signs of pulmonary or cerebral edema on post-mortem exam, with non-lethal, self-inflicted wounds.

In response to claims of restraint-related asphyxia, multiple studies have been conducted to evaluate this potential cause of in-custody death. Given the severity of agitation and aggression encountered in cases of ExDS, it is no surprise that many of these individuals must be restrained prior to being arrested and transported. One of the most frequently utilized restraint methods involves placing the individual in a prone position, handcuffing behind the back and hobbling the feet together to minimize the risk of injury from kicking. Sometimes the subject will be placed into the prone maximal restraint position (PMRP) by attaching the hobble to the handcuffs for more limitation of movement. This is also called the hogtie position (Takeuchi et al., 2011). Additionally, personnel may additionally place a knee or elbow onto the subject's back with downward force in order to limit movement after restraint. Some researchers have postulated that persons in this position are more likely to asphyxiate due to an inability to maintain a patent airway, while also being unable to fully expand their chest wall and move their diaphragm (Pollanen et al., 1998; O'Halloran & Lewman, 1993). Clinical investigations have been conducted to evaluate this hypothesis, and have provided compelling evidence suggesting that the PMRP does not lead to asphyxia. Chan, Vilke, and Neuman (2000) conducted serial arterial blood gas measurements as well as pulmonary function tests on 12 healthy volunteers placed in the PRMP. The results of this study showed a decrease in normal chest expansion, though no associated drop in blood oxygen or rise in blood carbon dioxide, which would be expected with asphyxia (Chan et al., 2000). Multiple subsequent studies were performed to evaluate the addition of a downward force on a subject's back, typically a knee or elbow in the field, using up to 225 pounds of weights placed on the subject's back. These studies failed to demonstrate that the addition of weight to the back resulted in any clinically significant impacts on ventilation that would lead to asphyxiation (Chan, Neuman, & Clauson, 2004; Ho et al., 2011; Michalewicz et al., 2007; Savaser et al., 2013). These studies were notably conducted using healthy subjects under controlled conditions and therefore cannot completely exclude the possibility that restraint under "real world" conditions may contribute to death in extreme cases.

Some have postulated that in-custody death related to ExDS may be related to the use of conducted energy weapons (CEWs) such as the TASER electronic control device. In a case series of eight "clinically healthy" patients, Zipes (2012) suggests that these devices have the potential to externally "pace" the heart into a fatal arrhythmia, such as ventricular fibrillation or ventricular tachycardia. This was, however, a very small case series and the conclusions in it were strongly criticized. Multiple researchers responded to the publication with comments that questioned the lack of criteria for what was described as "clinically healthy." Seven of the eight patients had an enlarged heart or other evidence of heart disease, making them at particular risk for sudden cardiac death (Heegaard, Halperin, & Luceri, 2013; Ho & Dawes, 2013; Vilke, Chan, & Karch, 2013).

There remain no universally accepted diagnostic criteria that clearly define ExDS. The international classification of disease (ICD) database has multiple diagnoses that may be related to ExDS, such as "manic excitement" or "delirium of mixed origin," yet there is no code that uniquely defines ExDS at this time. Furthermore, the *Diagnostic Statistical Manual of Mental Disorders* (DSM), which establishes psychiatric diagnoses, also fails to clearly define this clinical entity, despite its presence in the literature. This lack of consensus is partially due to the fact that ExDS overlaps with many medical and psychiatric disorders. Additionally, it is possible that many psychiatrists and general medical practitioners are unfamiliar with this condition due to an absence of firsthand experience. As previously stated, some of these individuals do not arrive at the hospital for more advanced medical care prior to death. If these individuals do survive to receive care at the hospital, it is most likely that the care will be rendered by a physician specializing in emergency medicine. Furthermore, it is likely that emergency physicians are the most common medical providers to encounter individuals with ExDS and may be the only providers to witness the full spectrum of clinical findings prior to treatment. The American College of Emergency Physicians (ACEP) recently joined the National Board of Medical Examiners (NBME) as the first two organizations to recognize ExDS as a diagnostic entity. Subsequent studies have been performed to prospectively evaluate the signs and symptoms of ExDS to aid both law enforcement and medical personnel in the identification of these cases (DeBard et al., 2009; Hall et al., 2013; Stephens, Jentzen, Karch, Ross & Hazlett, 2016; Wetli, & Mash, 2004).

CASE ONE

On December 5th at approximately 9pm, a local business owner called 911 and stated that there was a "crazy" man acting strangely and breaking car windows along a busy urban street. The man was sweating profusely and was only wearing shorts, despite an ambient temperature of 40 degrees Fahrenheit. Bystanders noted that the man would stare into the windows of parked cars, apparently transfixed by his reflection, before suddenly using his fists to break the glass while screaming. The man had multiple abrasions and lacerations to his extremities, although he did not seem to be experiencing any pain.

Police responded to the scene at approximately 9:10pm and found the individual briskly walking down the middle of the street. They confronted the man, but he acted as though he did not hear or see the officers. Even after the officers ordered the man to stop walking and get down on the ground, he continued to walk along the street breaking car windows. Officers were eventually forced to act in the interest of public safety and stop the self-harming behavior;

however, four officers were required to take the man to the ground and a CEW was finally used to incapacitate him.

While in the back of the patrol vehicle, the man continued to struggle against his restraints. He thrashed violently from side to side and repeatedly kicked the backseat windows. Suddenly, the man stopped struggling and appeared to calm down. The officer then recognized that the man had actually lost consciousness. The officers diverted to the nearest emergency department where the man was found to be in cardiac arrest. Medical staff were unable to revive the man despite employing standard resuscitative efforts. His body was sent to the coroner for investigation.

On post-mortem analysis, the cause of death was unclear. There were no traumatic wounds to the head, neck, or torso that would have explained the individual's sudden cardiac arrest. Evaluation of the heart and lung tissue was unrevealing. Toxicological screening was positive for cocaine and THC, though not at toxic levels. Brain tissue exam revealed evidence of cerebral edema of unclear significance. On microscopic analysis there was evidence of elevated heat shock proteins, which indicated cerebral hyperthermia prior to death.

Comments

This case presents a classic presentation of ExDS. A key piece of information that would be good to obtain is a core body temperature on this individual as soon as possible. A skin or tympanic (ear drum) temperature given the ambient temperature of 40 degrees may read falsely low as the body typically shunts blood away from the periphery to the core organs of body. A rectal temperature in the Emergency Department is ideal and would likely have been significantly elevated in this case—lending strong objective support for the diagnosis of ExDS and better exonerating the other possible causes of death, like the TASER and restraint asphyxia, as neither of these cause an elevated temperature. The medical examiner in some cases, when picking up the body from the field, can obtain a core liver temperature. This is worth requesting. There have been cases in which the liver temperature was over 104 degrees Fahrenheit hours after the death.

Identification of Excited Delirium Syndrome

Although the medical literature had traditionally recognized the diagnosis of ExDS as having been established post-mortem, there are several perimortem signs and symptoms that can help investigators establish this diagnosis. The investigation should begin with a description of the subject's behavior prior to police interaction:

1. Were there witnesses who could describe the person's behavior? Was the individual displaying signs of agitation or confusion? Many persons with ExDS fail to interact normally with the others in their environment, including medical and law enforcement personnel. Even when they are directly addressed, they may act as though they do not hear or see others.
2. Was the individual acting delusionally? Many people suffering from ExDS have delusions of being on fire, seeing things that are not there, like dragons or demons, or other visions not based on reality.

3. Was the individual sweating profusely and breathing rapidly? Individuals with ExDS typically have profound hyperthermia related to extreme physical exertion as well as central nervous system hyperactivity. Sweating is a physiologic compensatory mechanism in humans to dissipate body heat.
4. What clothing was the patient wearing and was it appropriate for the environment? Given that these individuals may experience severe hyperthermia, there have been reports of people walking outside in extreme cold with very little clothing. In some cases they are completely naked, which often leads to the initial police involvement. Cases have been reported where victims of fatal ExDS were found lying next to icepacks and empty ice cube trays in failed attempts to cool themselves (Takeuchi et al., 2011).
5. Did the individual exhibit any abnormal attraction to glass or mirrors? It is unclear why, but in many cases, people with ExDS become abnormally focused on their reflection and sometimes become obsessed with the destruction of glass, mirrors, or reflective surfaces.
6. Did the individual exhibit constant or near constant activity with no signs of fatigue? Given the combination of central nervous system effects as well as the effects of stimulant drugs, many cases of ExDS involve persistent pacing, running, or constant movement of the extremities.

During the period of law enforcement involvement, there are many additional features that must be investigated to establish the diagnosis of ExDS:

1. Was the person hot to the touch? Again, hyperthermia is a harbinger of bad outcome in persons with ExDS. Often when going hands on, law enforcement officers will note that the subject was very hot when physical contact was made.
2. Does the individual display evidence of superhuman strength, extreme violence, and imperviousness to pain? These qualities may be experienced as law enforcement personnel are restraining the individual. It may be important to note how many officers or medical staff were required to restrain the individual. Also, in relation to the restraint process, it is important to investigate what techniques were used and how much force was applied. This may become important to establish whether the struggle or restraint process could have contributed to the patient's death. Though as previously discussed, if done correctly, the use of typical restraint techniques should not cause harm.
3. Was a CEW used to restrain the individual? Although the potential for a CEW, such as the TASER, to cause death is low and largely theoretical, it is important to document when the weapon was discharged in relation to when the person died, the mode used (probe or drive stun) and where the contact points were on the subject. If the cardiac arrest was minutes after the electric shock, it is highly unlikely that the CEW had any impact on the individual's mortality. Numerous studies have demonstrated the relative safety of CEWs (Kornblum & Reddy, 1991; Ho et al., 2006; Levine et al., 2007).

If the individual survives long enough to benefit from medical intervention, the investigation should include additional data such as vital signs and blood work. The most important data point at this phase is body temperature. If the patient is hyperthermic, in the setting of other historical features consistent with ExDS, then the diagnosis is likely. One should note the manner in which the temperature was taken (tympanic, temporal, oral, rectal, or bladder). Certain blood work may aid in supporting the

CASE TWO

On May 12th at approximately 2:30pm, emergency medical services were dispatched to an apartment complex where a man had recently been shot. According to witnesses, the injured individual had broken into an apartment while the resident was home. The man reportedly appeared to be "on something" and was not responding to the apartment resident, who threatened to shoot the subject if he did not leave his house. Witnesses report that the patient lunged at the resident, who proceeded to shoot the patient twice in the right leg. Despite his injuries, the man was able to escape the apartment complex, climb over a large wall, and run down the street, where he was eventually detained by police. EMS arrived to find the patient in a hobble position, very agitated and yelling at police.

With the assistance of law enforcement, paramedics were able to place the patient in bilateral ankle and wrist restraints as they transferred him onto a backboard and into the ambulance. Initial vital signs revealed a pulse of 140 beats per minute and a blood pressure of 180/105. His respiratory rate was 30 breaths per minute and his temperature was significantly elevated at 105°F. ECG electrodes were placed on the patient's chest that showed sinus tachycardia. The patient continued to resist restraint in the ambulance and required repeated doses of sedatives with little effect. Suddenly the patient stopped fighting and lost consciousness. At this time, the cardiac rhythm strip revealed an idioventricular (slow and widened) rhythm of 30 beats per minute, quickly followed by asystole (flatline). The paramedics initiated cardiopulmonary resuscitation (CPR) and an attempt at intubation was made. As the paramedic was attempting to place the endotracheal tube into the lungs, she noted a large amount of pink, frothy sputum in the airway suggestive of pulmonary edema. Eventually, the tube was placed, although the patient was very difficult to oxygenate.

Upon arrival to the hospital, CPR was ongoing and the patient was in critical condition. Laboratory tests were notable for an elevated creatinine phosphokinase (CPK) and an elevated creatinine. Full resuscitative measures were taken; however, attempts were unsuccessful and he was pronounced dead approximately 15 minutes after arrival at the emergency department. Cause of death was attributed to cardiac arrest of unclear etiology.

Comment

In this case the subject had a cardiac monitor in place at the time of his cardiac arrest, which is very fortuitous. This will better document the timing of the cardiac arrest. The paramedics were able to see the transition of a fast heart rate at 140 beats per minute (sinus tachycardia) to a rhythm incompatible with long-term survival, the slow idioventricular rhythm that quickly went to flatline. Most paramedic monitors have a memory chip that records the entire code and associated heart rhythms. This is an important piece of information to be used by the medical experts if litigation were to ensue. It can also be helpful for the medical examiner as well in making a cause of death determination. If the download from the cardiac monitor is not obtained in a timely manner, it will be overwritten by a subsequent patient's information and lost forever. So obtaining the download of the cardiac monitor as soon as is reasonable is very important.

diagnosis of ExDS, such as an elevated creatinine phosphokinase (CPK), which is indicative of muscle destruction resulting from extreme exertion. Urine toxicology screen may suggest recent stimulant use, however, drugs screens typically conducted by the hospitals may be misleading and positive results should be confirmed by a more sophisticated analytical method usually not available at the hospital. By the same token, negative results on the hospital drug screen do not exclude the presence of a substance that may have precipitated ExDS. Finally, serum creatinine may be elevated, which is indicative of kidney failure, although this is generally a finding observed hours to days later in the clinical course and may not be present during the initial evaluation or if the person dies early in the course of treatment (Maher et al., 2014).

Although there is no absolute confirmatory finding on autopsy that indicates ExDS as the cause of death, there are many features that may help the investigator to establish this diagnosis. First, however, the investigator must rule out trauma or specific medical causes of death. Although minor contusions, abrasions, and lacerations are often present on post-mortem analysis, signs of major trauma including damage to the brain, the spinal cord, or the airway would call into question the diagnosis of ExDS and require additional investigation. Toxicological evaluations should be conducted by one of a number of confirmatory analytical methods, such as gas or liquid chromatography/mass spectrometry, which can specifically identify both common and uncommon medications and street drugs with the potential to precipitate ExDS (Table 9.1).

TABLE 9.1 Examples of drugs with potential to precipitate ExDS

Amphetamines	Bromo-dimethoxyamphetamine (DOB)
	Bromo-methoxyphenylethylamine (2C-B)
	Dextro-amphetamine (Dexedrine, Dexy)
	Dimethoxyamphetamine (DOM/STP, serenity tranquility peace)
	Ephedrine (Ma-huang herbal products)
	Methamphetamine
	Methylenedioxyamphetamine (MDA, love drug)
	Methylenedioxyethamphetamine (MDEA, Eve)
	Methylenedioxymethamphetamine (MDMA, Adam, Molly, ecstacy, XTC)
	Methylphenidate (Ritalin, Concerta)
	Paramethoxyamphetamine (PMA, death)
Cathinones	"Bath Salts"
	Ethcathinone (ETH-CAT)
	Ethylone (MDEC, bk-MDEA)
	Mephedrone (drone, M-CAT, meow-meow)
	Methylenedioxypyrovalerone (MDPV)
	Methylone (MDMC, bk-MDMA)
	Pentedrone
	Khat (African plant containing cathinone)
Cocaine	
Dissociative Agents	Phencyclidine (PCP)
	Ketamine (Special K)
Hallucinogens	Dimethyltryptamine (DMT)
	Lysergic acid diethylamide (LSD)
	Mescaline (found in peyote cactus)
	Psilocin and psilocybin (found in hallucinogenic mushrooms)

On the other hand, ExDS has also been associated with abrupt cessation of medications taken for psychiatric illness, suggesting drug withdrawal or worsening of underlying psychiatric disease while untreated (Vilke, Payne-James, & Karch, 2012). Evaluation of brain tissue is likely the most helpful post-mortem examination in the evaluation of ExDS, though the research behind these analytical techniques is still ongoing (Johnson et al., 2012; Mash et al., 2009; Wetli et al., 1996). Characteristic abnormalities in dopaminergic and serotonergic processing pathways are suggestive of this condition. In the absence of other identifiable causes of death, these tissue findings in conjunction with the appropriate perimortem clinical characteristics are highly suggestive of ExDS.

CASE THREE

On August 5th at 2:45am law enforcement personnel were dispatched to a local park where a large man was found wandering naked. When asked what he was doing, the man did not respond appropriately, but instead started screaming that he was "on fire" and proceeded to run toward the police officers. Although he was difficult to restrain, officers were able to hold the man on the ground until paramedics arrived. On inspection, the man was covered in sweat and was noticeably hot to the touch.

In the ambulance, the patient required multiple doses of sedatives due to his extreme level of agitation. His heart rate, respiratory rate, and blood pressure were all elevated, though medics were unable to check the patient's oral temperature due to concern for biting. His pupils were notably dilated.

Upon arrival to the emergency department, the patient remained very aggressive and was threatening to hurt the staff. Emergency department personnel immediately transferred the patient to a gurney and restrained his wrists to the bed frame. Repeated doses of sedatives were given intramuscularly with moderate response. Blood work was performed that revealed evidence of kidney failure as well as profound muscle breakdown. The patient's core temperature was finally checked and was elevated at 107 degrees Fahrenheit.

After a period of observation, the patient was left alone in his hospital room for approximately ten minutes. There was a loud crash and the patient was found walking down the emergency department hallway toward the exit with the hospital gurney on his back, with his wrists still tied to the bedrails. A behavioral response code was called and multiple personnel were required to sedate the patient and place him back in his hospital bed. Shortly after the man was placed back in bed, he suddenly stopped breathing. His pulse was checked and was absent. After a prolonged period of attempted resuscitation, the patient was pronounced dead.

Post-mortem exam did not reveal a clear cause of the patient's cardiac arrest. Toxicological screening was positive for methamphetamines and PCP. There were no significant traumatic wounds that would explain the patient's death. The internal organs all appeared to be anatomically normal with the exception of an enlarged heart consistent with chronic drug use. The brain was sent for special histo-chemical staining and revealed evidence of heat shock proteins suggestive of cerebral hyperthermia prior to death.

Comment

This case demonstrates the usefulness of obtaining special evaluation of the brain for diagnosing ExDS. The University of Miami has been doing specific evaluations of brains of subjects who have died during what appears clinically to be an episode of ExDS for years. They use special techniques and stains to evaluate specific parts of the brain to help come to a diagnosis of ExDS, if appropriate. More information can be obtained at: http://exciteddelirium.org/. The decision of whether to send the brain or not has to be made by a medical examiner, but an investigator could certainly bring this opportunity to the attention of the ME.

Although all of the individuals in these example cases display findings that may be consistent with ExDS, none of these findings alone can lead to the diagnosis. After compiling information from bystanders, police, pre-hospital personnel and hospital staff, the investigator can build a case that is suggestive of ExDS. Using the following checklist, the investigator can collect the useful historical and clinical information that may help lead to an appropriate diagnosis of ExDS.

Investigation Checklist

Note that not all findings are necessary to diagnose ExDS. These findings together are suggestive of the disease in the correct context.

Historical Findings

- ☐ Extreme agitation or aggressiveness
- ☐ Delusional thoughts
- ☐ Profuse sweating
- ☐ Rapid breathing
- ☐ Hot to touch
- ☐ Attempted self-cooling
- ☐ Near constant physical activity
- ☐ Lack of fatigue
- ☐ High tolerance to pain
- ☐ Not responsive to police presence
- ☐ Inappropriate clothing for environment/naked
- ☐ Excessive/superhuman strength
- ☐ Glass attraction/destruction
- ☐ Keening (unintelligible animal-like sounds)

Medical Findings

- ☐ Rapid heart rate
- ☐ Elevated blood pressure

- ☐ Elevated respiratory rate
- ☐ Fever (over 100.4°F)
- ☐ Size of pupils
- ☐ Sweating or dry
- ☐ Elevated serum creatinine phosphokinase (CPK) or myoglobin
- ☐ Elevated serum creatinine (evidence of kidney failure)
- ☐ Low pH on blood gas testing
- ☐ Urine toxicological screen positive for stimulants (cocaine, methamphetamine, PCP, hallucinogens)
- ☐ History of antipsychotic or anticholinergic use
- ☐ Abnormal heart rhythm or electrocardiogram (ECG) prior to or after cardiac arrest

Post-mortem Findings

- ☐ Pulmonary edema
- ☐ Cerebral edema
- ☐ Toxicological screen positive for stimulants
- ☐ Neurochemical examination revealing abnormal dopamine synaptic markers or receptors in the striatum and hypothalamus
- ☐ Brain tissue analysis revealing elevated heat shock proteins
- ☐ Lack of other cause of death (trauma, asphyxiation, overdose, etc.)

References

Allam, S. & Noble, J. S. (2001). Cocaine-excited delirium and severe acidosis. *Anaesthesia, 56*(4), 385–386.

Barnett, J. H., Werners, U., Secher, S. M., Hill, K. E., Brazil, R., Masson, K., Pernet, D. E., Kirkbride, J. B., Murray, G. K., Bullmore, E. T., & Jones, P. B. (2007). Substance use in a population-based clinic sample of people with first-episode psychosis. *British Journal of Psychiatry, 190*(6), 515–520.

Bell, L. (1849). On a form of disease resembling some advanced stage of mania and fever. *American Journal of Insanity, 6*, 97–127.

Chan, T. C., Neuman, T., & Clausen, J. (2004). Weight force during prone restraint and respiratory function. *American Journal of Forensic Medicine and Pathology, 25*(3), 185–189.

Chan, T. C., Vilke, G. M., & Neuman, T. (2000). Restraint position and positional asphyxia. *American Journal of Forensic Medicine and Pathology, 21*(1), 93.

DeBard, M. L., Adler, J., & Bozeman, W. (2009). *White paper report on excited delirium syndrome. ACEP excited delirium task force.* American College of Emergency Physicians.

Fink, M. (1999). Delirious mania. *Bipolar Discord, 1*(1), 54–60.

Fishbain, D. A. & Wetli, C. V. (1981). Cocaine intoxication, delirium, and death in a body packer. *Annals of Emergency Medicine, 10*(10), 531–532.

Gill, J. R. (2014). The syndrome of excited delirium. *Forensic Science, Medicine and Pathology, 10*(2), 223–228.

Grant, J. R., Southall, P. E., Fowler, D. R., Mealy, J., Thomas, E. J., & Kinlock, T. W. (2007). Death in custody: A historical review. *Journal of Forensic Sciences, 52*(2), 1177–1181.

Grant, J. R., Southall, P. E., Mealey, J., Scott, S. R., & Fowler, D. R. (2009). Excited delirium deaths in custody: past and present. *American Journal of Forensic Medicine and Pathology, 30*(1), 1–5.

Hall, C. A., Kader, A. S., McHale, A. M. D., Stewart, L., Fick, G. H., & Vilke, G. M. (2013). Frequency of signs of excited delirium syndrome in subjects undergoing police use of force: Descriptive evaluation of a prospective, consecutive cohort. *Journal of Forensic and Legal Medicine, 20*(2), 102–107.

Heegaard, W. G., Halperin, H. R., & Luceri, R. (2013). Letter by Heegaard et al. regarding article, "Sudden Cardiac Arrest and Death Following Application of Shocks from a TASER Electronic Control Device." *Circulation, 127*(1), e260.

Ho, J. D. & Dawes, D. M. (2013). Letter by Ho and Dawes regarding article, "Sudden Cardiac Arrest and Death Following Application of Shocks from a TASER Electronic Control Device." *Circulation, 127*(1), e259.

Ho, J. D., Dawes, D. M., Moore, J. C., Caroon, L. V., & Miner, J. R. (2011). Effect of position and weight force on inferior vena cava diameter: Implications for arrest-related death. *Forensic Science International, 212*, 256–259.

Ho, J. D., Miner, J. R., Lakireddy, D. R., Bultman, L. L., & Heegaard, W. G. (2006). Cardiovascular and physiologic effects of conducted electrical weapon discharge in resting adults. *Academic Emergency Medicine, 13*(6), 589–595.

Johnson, M. M., David, J. A., Michelhaugh, S.K., Schmidt, C. J., & Bannon, M. J. (2012). Increased heat shock protein 70 gene expression in the brains of cocaine-related fatalities may be reflective of postdrug survival and intervention rather than excited delirium. *Journal of Forensic Sciences, 57*(6), 1519–1523.

Karch, S. B. & Stephens, B. G. (1999). Drug abusers who die during arrest or in custody. *Journal of the Royal Society of Medicine, 92*(3), 110–113.

Kornblum, R. N. & Reddy, S. K. (1991). Effects of the taser in fatalities involving police confrontation. *Journal of Forensic Sciences, 36*(2), 434–438.

Levine, S. D., Sloane, C. M., Chan, T. C., Dunford, J. V., & Vilke, C. V. (2007). Cardiac monitoring of human subjects exposed to the taser. *Journal of Emergency Medicine, 33*(2), 113–117.

Lifschultz, B. D. & Donoghue, E. R. (1991). Deaths in custody. *Legal Medicine, 1*, 45–71.

Luke, J. L. & Reay, D. T. (1992). The perils of investigating and certifying deaths in police custody. *American Journal of Forensic Medicine and Pathology, 13*(2), 98–100.

Maher, P. J., Walsh, M., Burns, T., & Strote, J. (2014). Prehospital resuscitation of a man with excited delirium and cardiopulmonary arrest. *Canadian Journal of Emergency Medicine, 16*(1), 80–83.

Maldeniya, P. M. & Vasudev, A. (2013). Is the concept of delirious mania valid in the elderly? A case report and a review of the literature. *Case Reports in Psychiatry, 5*, n.p.

Mash, D. C., Duque, L., Pablo, J., Qin, Y., Adi, N., Hearn, W. L., Hyma, B. A., Karch, S. B., Druid, H., & Wetli, C. V. (2009). Brain biomarkers for identifying excited delirium as a cause of sudden death. *Forensic Science International, 190*(1–3), e13–e19.

Mash, D. C., Ouyang, Q., Pablo, J., Basile, M., Izenwasser, S., Lieberman, A., & Perrin, R. J. (2003). Cocaine abusers have an overexpression of alpha-synuclein in dopamine neurons. *The Journal of Neuroscience, 23*(7), 2564–2571.

Mash, D. C. & Staley, J. K. (1999). D3 dopamine and kappa opioid receptor alterations in human brain of cocaine-overdose victims. *Annals of the New York Academy of Sciences, 877*, 507–522.

Mash, D. C., Staley, J. K., Izenwasser, S., Basile, M., & Ruttenber, A. J. (2000). Serotonin transporters upregulate with chronic cocaine use. *Journal of Chemical Neuroanatomy, 20*(3–4), 271–280.

Michalewicz, B. A., Chan, T. C., Vilke, G. M., Levy, S. S., Neuman, T. S., & Kolkhorst, F. W. (2007). Ventilatory and metabolic demands during aggressive physical restraint in healthy adults. *Journal of Forensic Sciences, 52*(1), 171–175.

Morrison, A. & Sadler, D. (2001). Death of a psychiatric patient during physical restraint. Excited delirium—A case report. *Medicine, Science and the Law, 41*(1), 46–50.

O'Halloran, R. L. & Lewman, L. V. (1993). Restraint asphyxiation in excited delirium. *American Journal of Forensic Medicine and Pathology, 14*(4), 289–295.

Otahbachi, M., Cevik, C., & Bagdure, S. (2010). Excited delirium, restraints, and unexpected death: A review of pathogenesis. *American Journal of Forensic Medicine and Pathology, 31*(2), 107–112.

Park, K. S., Korn, C. S., & Henderson, S.O. (2001). Agitated delirium and sudden death: Two case reports. *Prehospital Emergency Care, 5*(2), 214–216.

Pollanen, M. S., Chiasson, D. A., Cairns, J. T., & Young, J. G. (1998). Unexpected death related to restraint for excited delirium: A retrospective study of deaths in police custody and in the community. *Canadian Medical Association Journal, 158*(12), 1603–1607.

Robinson, D. & Hunt, S. (2005). Sudden in-custody death syndrome. *Topics in Emergency Medicine, 27*(1), 36–43.

Ross, D. L. & Hazlett, M. H. (2016). A prospective analysis of the outcomes of violent prone restraint incidents in policing. *Forensic Research & Criminology International Journal, 2*(1), 1–10.

Ruttenber, A. J., McAnally, H. B., & Wetli, C. V. (1999). Cocaine-associated rhabdomyolysis and excited delirium: different stages of the same syndrome. *American Journal of Forensic Medicine and Pathology, 20*(2), 120–127.

Sathyavagiswaran, L., Rogers, C.,, & Noguchi, T. T. (2007). Restraint asphyxia in in-custody deaths: Medical examiner's role in prevention of deaths. *Legal Medicine (Tokyo), 9*(2), 88–93.

Savaser, D. J., Campbell, C., Castillo, E. M., Vilke, G. M., Sloane, C., Neuman, T., Hansen, A. V., Shah, S., & Chan, T. C. (2013). The effect of the prone maximal restrained position with and without weight force on cardiac output and other hemodynamic measures. *Journal of Forensic and Legal Medicine, 20*(8), 991–995.

Southall, P. E. & Pestaner, J. P. (2003). Overwhelming number of AA deaths occur in police custody. *Journal of the National Medical Association, 95*(8), 754–755.

Staley, J. K., Welti, C. V., Ruttenber, A. J., Hearn, W. L., & Mash, D. C. (1995). Altered dopaminergic synaptic markers in cocaine psychosis and sudden death. *National Institute on Drug Abuse [NIDA] Research Monograph, 153*, 491.

Stephens, B. G., Jentzen, J. M., Karch, S., Mash, D. C., & Wetli, C. V. (2004). Criteria for the interpretation of cocaine levels in human biological samples and their relation to the cause of death. *American Journal of Forensic Medicine and Pathology, 25*(1), 1–10.

Stephens, B. G., Jentzen, J. M., Karch, S., Wetli, C. V., & Mash, D. C. (2004). National Association of Medical Examiners position paper on the certification of cocaine-related deaths. *American Journal of Forensic Medicine and Pathology, 25*(1), 11–13.

Stratton, S. J., Rogers, C., Brickett, K., & Gruzinski, G. (2001). Factors associated with sudden death of individuals requiring restraint for excited delirium. *American Journal of Emergency Medicine, 19*(3), 187–191.

Stratton, S. J., Rogers, C., & Green, K. (1995). Sudden death in individuals in hobble restraints during paramedic transport. *Annals of Emergency Medicine, 25*(5), 710–712.

Sztajnkrycer, M. D. & Baez, A. A. (2005). Cocaine, excited delirium and sudden unexpected death. *Journal of Emergency Medical Services, 34*(4), 77–81.

Takeuchi, A., Ahern, T., & Henderson, S. O. (2011). Excited delirium. *Western Journal of Emergency Medicine, 12*(1), 77–83.

Vilke, G. M., Chan, T. C., & Karch, S. (2013). Letter by Vilke et al. regarding article, "Sudden Cardiac Arrest and Death Following Application of Shocks from a TASER Electronic Control Device." *Circulation, 127*(1), e258.

Vilke, G. M., DeBard, M. L., Chan, T. C., Ho, J. D., Dawes, D. M., Hall, C., ... Bozeman, W. P. (2012a). Excited Delirium Syndrome (ExDS): Defining based on a review of the literature. *Journal of Emergency Medicine, 43*(5), 897–905.

Vilke, G. M., Payne-James, J., & Karch, S. B. (2012b). Excited delirium syndrome (ExDS): Redefining an old diagnosis. *Journal of Forensic and Legal Medicine, 19*(1), 7–11.

Wetli, C. V. (1987). Fatal cocaine intoxication. A review. *American Journal of Forensic Medicine and Pathology, 8*(1), 1–2.

Wetli, C. V., Mash, D., & Karch, S. B. (1996). Cocaine-associated agitated delirium and the neuroleptic malignant syndrome. *American Journal of Emergency Medicine, 14*(4), 425–428.

Zipes, D. P. (2012). Sudden cardiac arrest and death following application of shocks from a TASER electronic control device. *Circulation, 125*(20), 2417–2422.

10

AMPHETAMINES, CATHINONES (BATH SALTS), AND COCAINE

Stephen L. Thornton, Michael A. Darracq, and Binh T. Ly

Introduction

A stimulant is defined by the Merriam-Webster dictionary as "an agent (as a drug) that produces a temporary increase of the functional activity or efficiency of an organism or any of its parts" ("Stimulant," 2016). There are multiple substances, both legal and illicit, which can be considered stimulants. Caffeine, cocaine, amphetamines, and cathinones are among the more commonly encountered. This chapter will focus on the amphetamines, cathinones, and cocaine.

The history of amphetamines and cathinones usage in the United States is quite distinct. Amphetamine abuse first became an issue in the United States in the 1940s (Rasmussen, 2008). This was the result of the introduction and promotion of amphetamine, marketed under the trade name of Benzadrine in the 1930s, for various medical problems, ranging from congestion to depression to weight loss. Methamphetamine was introduced in the early 1940s for similar indications and also became widely abused (Vearrier et al., 2012). Gradually, the adverse health effects of amphetamines became recognized and restrictions were placed on them. This led to a rise in illicit manufacturing of amphetamines, primarily methamphetamine, in the 1960s. Both amphetamine and methamphetamine were scheduled by the Drug Enforcement Agency (DEA) in 1971 (Council on Scientific Affairs, 1978). While leading to a decrease in amphetamine abuse, it further drove illicit manufacturing. The 1980s saw a rise in methamphetamine abuse primarily from illicit manufacturing sources (Mooney, Rawson, & Gonzales, 2010). Currently, abuse of amphetamines, particularly methamphetamine, remains a significant problem with estimates of over 1.4 million individuals abusing methamphetamine or similar drugs in 2013 (Substance Abuse and Mental Health Services Administration, 2014).

Cathinone abuse and misuse only began to emerge in the United States around 2010 with the rise of "bath salts" (Centers for Disease Control and Prevention, 2011). Bath salts are synthetic chemicals derived from the naturally occurring cathinone found in khat (*Catha edulis*). Khat is a shrub or tree found in various regions of Africa and its leaves have been chewed for centuries for the stimulant effect (Wabe, 2011). This is similar to traditional use of coca leaves by South American natives (Blejer-Prieto, 1965). Though a DEA schedule I substance since 1987, complications from khat use in the United States has rarely been reported. In contrast, bath salts or synthetic cathinones have been associated with significant problems (Imam et al., 2013). Most synthetic cathinones are believed to be manufactured overseas, and then distributed via non-traditional routes, such as smoke shops and the Internet (Schneir et al., 2014). They are frequently packaged in brightly colored packets and labeled as "Not for Human Consumption" to avoid regulation by the Federal Analog Act (Schneir et al., 2014). Along with bath salts, they are also marketed as "plant food," "pond cleaner," and "skin treatment" (Murphy et al., 2013). The DEA has scheduled several of these synthetic cathinones, but newer, "legal," synthetic cathinones are constantly being introduced (Drug Enforcement Administration, 2014; Poklis et al., 2015). However, abuse of synthetic cathinones remains less prevalent than amphetamine (Drug Enforcement Administration, 2013).

It is important to appreciate that amphetamines and cathinones are two large classes of chemicals which share a common structural backbone—a benzene ring to which a two carbon chain is attached, which then ends with a nitrogen (Gerona & Wu, 2012). Figure 10.1 demonstrates this relationship. This shared structural backbone is also seen with epinephrine, norepinephrine, and dopamine, which are all neurotransmitters that activate the human sympathetic nervous system (Tank & Wong, 2015). As will be discussed, amphetamine and cathinones interact with these chemicals to cause clinical symptoms and toxicity (Kish, 2008; Rickli, Hoener, & Liechti, 2015). There are no naturally occurring amphetamines. Cathinones differ from amphetamines by having an additional oxygen atom bound to the carbon atom closest to the ring portion of the molecule (Gerona & Wu, 2012). Cathinone itself is a naturally occurring substance, but all of the bath salts or synthetic cathinones are man-made.

It is from these core structures that a wide variety of types or analogs of amphetamines and cathinones can be made. Through various chemistry techniques, different side chains or moieties can be added. The result is these analogs may have more potent or different effects from the parent compound. Perhaps the best example of this is methamphetamine, which differs from amphetamine by the addition of a carbon (methyl group) at the terminal nitrogen group. This is thought to make methamphetamine a more potent central nervous system stimulant than amphetamine, though human studies do not necessarily confirm this (Cox & Maickel, 1972; Kirkpatrick et al., 2012). Another example is methylenedioxymethamphetamine (MDMA, "ecstasy"), which is an analog of methamphetamine, but reported to have different psychoactive effects (Dumont and Verkes, 2006). There are similar examples with the cathinones as well. The presence of these analogs further complicates amphetamine and cathinone abuse in many cases, and law enforcement may not know exactly what substances are involved and thus toxicities of these substances may not be completely understood.

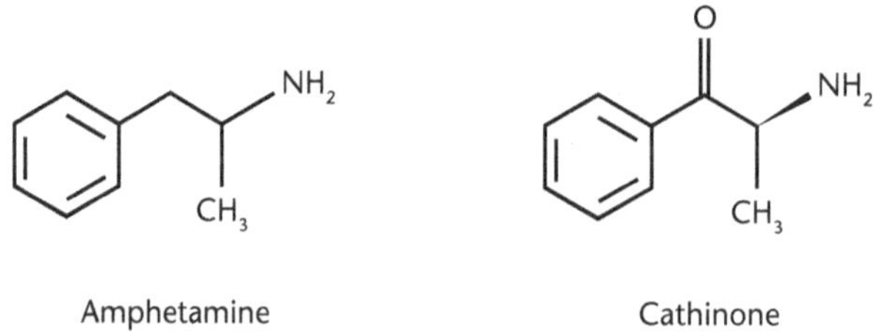

FIGURE 10.1 Chemical structures of amphetamine and cathinone.

The history of cocaine use is much longer than amphetamines and dates back to the 6th century, where there is evidence that humans chewed the leaves of the South American coca plant, *Erythroxylum coca* (Stolberg, 2011). Cocaine was isolated in 1859 and then became widely used, both medicinally and recreationally (Goldstein, DesLauriers, & Burda, 2009). In 1914, it was restricted to medicinal use by the Harrison Narcotic Act, but remained a substance of abuse. Cocaine use became popular in the 1970s and reached its peak in the 1980s with the introduction of the smokable form called crack, which is an anhydrous base of cocaine (Goldstein et al., 2009). It is estimated there are nearly 1.5 million current cocaine users in the United States (Substance Abuse and Mental Health Services Administration, 2013). Of note, cocaine use is reported to cause more emergency department visits than any other single substance (Substance Abuse and Mental Health Services Administration, 2013).

Clinical Manifestations

With few exceptions, the use and clinical effects of amphetamines and cathinones are similar. They can be taken orally, injected intravenously, insufflated into the nose, or inhaled via the lungs. They can also be absorbed through vaginal and rectal mucosal surfaces when placed in these orifices to conceal these substances. In all cases, absorption is rapid with time to peak levels being fastest for intravenous route followed by inhalation and intranasal (Harris et al., 2003; Lile et al., 2011). Once absorbed, amphetamines and cathinones cross the blood brain barrier and begin to affect the delicate balance of chemicals in the brain and nerve cells. They interfere with how brain and nerve cells package, release, and reabsorb chemicals, primarily norepinephrine, dopamine, and serotonin (Carvalho et al., 2012). All three of these chemicals are examples of neurotransmitters that play vital roles in normal function of the sympathetic nervous system, which is responsible for the "fight or flight" response. This system is particularly sensitive to the effects of amphetamines and cathinones (Schep, Slaughter, & Beasley, 2010). Dopamine is also thought to play an integral role in the addictive properties of stimulants (Verrico et al., 2013).

Ultimately, amphetamines and cathinones cause excessive amounts of norepinephrine and dopamine to be released and at the same time interfere with them being taken back up by nerve cells, which is necessary to stop their action (Elliott & Beveridge, 2005). The result is excessive norepinephrine and dopamine activity and increased activation of the sympathetic nervous system. To what degree the sympathetic nervous system is stimulated largely depends on the type and amount of amphetamine or cathinone used. Practically, a toxic dose of amphetamine or cathinone is one that causes undesirable effects. What constitutes an overdose or toxic dose of these agents will vary tremendously depending on the type of drug and the individual (Johanson & Schuster, 1981).

The acute signs and symptoms of amphetamine and cathinone toxicity are typically observed within one hour of exposure and present on a spectrum of toxicity, from mild to life threatening. Initially mild anxiety, elevated heart rate and blood pressure, enlarged pupils, dry mouth, and decreased appetite may be experienced and in smaller doses may be the extent of signs and symptoms. However, in larger exposures, users will start to develop agitation, violent behavior, and even psychosis (Thornton, Gerona, & Tomaszewski, 2012). Teeth grinding or bruxism is commonly seen and some individuals may use pacifiers to mitigate the discomfort. Heart rate and blood pressure can increase dramatically, sometimes to dangerous levels resulting in strokes and heart attacks (Christensen et al., 2013; Wijetunga et al., 2004). Extreme sweating and dilated pupils will be seen (Schep et al., 2010). Elevated body temperature can also occur and is a sign of severe toxicity (Chan et al., 1994; Schep et al., 2010). This constellation of psychomotor agitation, elevated heart rate, elevated blood pressure, sweating, and large pupils is called the sympathomimetic toxidrome (Schep et al., 2010). Muscle breakdown, called rhabdomyolysis, can also occur and result in kidney failure (O'Connor et al., 2015). Severe toxicity from amphetamines and cathinones can result in multi-organ failure and cardiovascular collapse potentially leading to death (Chan et al., 1994; Kamijo et al., 2002; Murray, Murphy, & Beuhler, 2012). It is important to note that these signs, symptoms, and complications are also seen in a condition called excited delirium (Vilke, Payne-James, & Karch, 2012), which is a true medical emergency and if not promptly treated, can be life threatening (Gill, 2014).

Acutely, the toxic effects of amphetamines and cathinones generally last anywhere from 6 to 24 hours (Schep et al., 2010). Again, this may vary depending on the exact drug, dose, and route of exposure. For example, ingestions of large amounts of amphetamines and cathinones may occur in "body stuffer" situations, where individuals swallow poorly wrapped drugs in an effort to avoid detection by law enforcement, and can result in both severe and prolonged symptoms or sudden death (West, McKeown, & Hendrickson, 2010).

Chronic, frequent use of amphetamines and cathinones leads to multiple adverse effects. This is best described with chronic methamphetamine use. Severe dental caries, so referred to as "meth mouth," result from the dry mouth and constant teeth grinding (Curtis, 2006). Chronic and potentially deadly heart and lung problems may also occur (Schaiberger et al., 1993; Won et al., 2013). Multiple permanent psychiatric problems, including psychosis, are attributed to chronic methamphetamine use (Rusyniak, 2013).

Cocaine is structurally distinct from amphetamines and cathinones. It is an example of an ester as shown in Figure 10.2.

Like the amphetamines and cathinones, cocaine has stimulant effects, but cocaine also has local anesthetic properties, which complicate its toxicity. Cocaine is rapidly absorbed and penetrates the central nervous system readily when insufflated, injected, or smoked (Jeffcoat et al., 1989). Once in the brain, cocaine's primary mechanism of action is to block the reuptake of all the aforementioned neurotransmitters at sympathetic nerve endings, in particular dopamine (Williams & Lacey, 1988). This results in excessive amounts of these chemicals being present and causes similar "fight or flight" reactions seen with the amphetamines and cathinones.

Acute symptoms seen with cocaine use include elevated heart rate, elevated blood pressure, dilated pupils, excessive sweating, agitation, and psychosis (Zimmerman, 2012). The effects of acute cocaine toxicity usually begin within minutes of use and last 1–2 hours (Zimmerman, 2012). As with any drug, the duration of action will depend on how much drug is used and by what route. In addition to its stimulant effect, cocaine also causes blood vessels to constrict, thereby causing the associated elevated blood pressure to be severe and may result in strokes, heart attacks, and aortic dissections (De Giorgi et al., 2012; Dean et al., 2014; Siniscalchi et al., 2015). More severe cases of cocaine toxicity

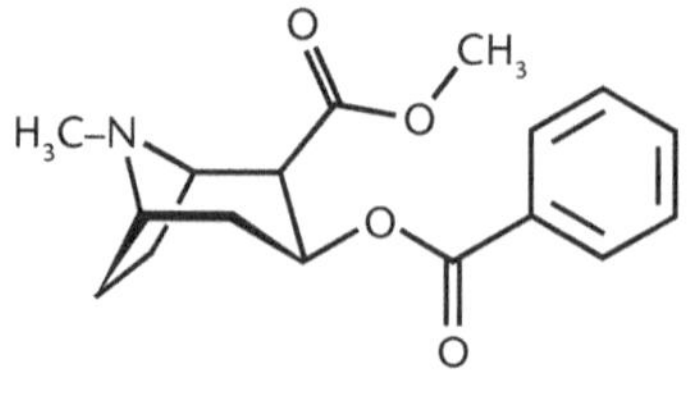

FIGURE 10.2 Chemical structure of cocaine.

can result in life threatening elevation in body temperature (hyperthermia), seizures, and life-threatening abnormal heart rhythms (Campbell, 1988; Lathers et al., 1988). Cocaine's ability to cause seizures and abnormal heart rhythms is due to its local anesthetic properties (sodium channel blockade) and are synergistic with its stimulant effects (Wood, Dargan, & Hoffman, 2009). The severity of symptoms depends on the amount of cocaine used. Use of cocaine is also described to cause formication ("cocaine bugs") and movement disorders ("crack dancing") due to its powerful dopamine effects (Brewer et al., 2008; Daras, Koppel, & Atos-Radzion, 1994). Chronic use of cocaine can lead to advanced atherosclerosis and heart disease (Kloner et al., 1992). Cocaine is also well described to cause cardiomyopathy, which are permanent structural changes in the heart (Cooper et al., 2013).

A large number of cocaine users will use it in conjunction with ethanol (McCance et al., 1995). This is important because cocaine and ethanol when used concurrently will be metabolized in the body to form a separate and toxic chemical called cocaethylene. This substance has similar effects to cocaine but is thought to be longer acting and probably more toxic to the heart and brain (Farooq, Bhatt, & Patel, 2009; McCance et al., 1995).

There is no conclusive information on what constitutes a toxic or lethal dose of cocaine. Studies have demonstrated that clinical toxicity does not seem to be related to blood concentrations of cocaine (Blaho et al., 2000).

Cocaine toxicity can be complicated by the fact that cocaine is often adulterated with other substances, which can contribute to unique clinical toxicity. The most commonly identified adulterant is levamisole, an anti-worming agent and former chemotherapeutic agent. It is estimated that nearly 70 percent of all cocaine in the United States contains levamisole (Centers for Disease Control and Prevention, 2009). Levamisole has been associated with inflammation of blood vessels, skin rashes, kidney problems, and bone marrow problems, leading to dangerously low blood cell counts (Buchanan et al., 2010; Nolan & Jen, 2015).

Legal Issues

Driving Under the Influence

Use of amphetamines and cathinones has been reported to impair driving ability (Knoy, Peterson, & Couper, 2014; Lemos, 2009; Logan, 1996; Musshoff & Madea, 2012; Stough et al., 2012). Interestingly, unexpected sedative-like effects have been described in cases of methamphetamine associated driving impairment (Logan, 1996; Musshoff & Madea, 2012). Other cases have shown widely divergent behavior, ranging from sedation to agitation with methamphetamine associated driving impairment (Lemos, 2009). Studies have been unable to find an association with drug levels and effect on impairment (Musshoff & Madea, 2012).

Driving under the influence of cocaine appears to be less common than with other drugs and little literature exists addressing the issue (Poklis, Maginn, & Barr, 1987a). A European study of drivers under the influence found positive cocaine results on screening and quantitative testing did not seem to be associated with clinical impairment (Arroyo et al., 2013). However, another study found that cocaine users were more likely per driver year to be in involved in "at fault" crashes than any other single substance, including ethanol (Chipman, Macdonald, & Mann, 2003).

Child Abuse or Neglect

Due to their prevalence as illicit substances in homes, stimulants such as methamphetamine and cocaine are often involved in suspected child abuse or neglect cases (Messina et al., 2014). Children will typically present with some form of agitation or abnormal behavior along with elevated heart rates and blood pressures (Matteucci et al., 2007; Pinto, Babu, & Jenny, 2013). Specifically with cocaine, positive qualitative immunoassay tests may be seen in cases where there was not initially suspicion of child abuse (Rosenberg et al., 1991). In these circumstances, quantitative laboratory testing of urine or blood should be obtained to confirm exposure, as this will have significant impact on the legal disposition of the child.

Death

Methamphetamine and its derivatives have been associated with fatal poisonings following oral and intravenous administration. As previously noted, there is a lack of correlation between drug levels and observed behaviors. Similarly, there is also a lack of correlation between drug levels and lethality with considerable overlap in drug levels of individuals who clearly died of violent traumatic means and those who died absent of a more obvious cause than drug intoxication alone. This is highlighted by a large series of fatalities, which found "lethal" methamphetamine levels to range from 0.05 mg/L to 9.3 mg/L (Logan, Fligner, & Haddix, 1998).

Fatalities due to cocaine are well described, though, as with amphetamines, studies have also demonstrated a wide range of "fatal" cocaine levels. One study found that in deaths attributed to cocaine, cocaine levels varied from 0.01 mg/L to 78 mg/L (Molina & Hargrove, 2011). This same study also found increased lethality when cocaine was used in combination with ethanol, heroin, opioids, antidepressant, and antipsychotic medications. Unique to cocaine, a New York study found that as ambient temperatures increased above 31.1°C (88°F), deaths attributed to cocaine also began to rise (Marzuk et al., 1998).

While many may view death as a termination of life and along with it a termination of all biological activity in the deceased organism, there are a number of processes that continue in the body following the termination of life. Both postmortem redistribution and metabolism can increase or decrease postmortem drug levels.

Case studies have demonstrated significant postmortem redistribution of methamphetamine, with postmortem methamphetamine levels 1.5 times higher than antemortem (pre-death) samples (McIntyre et al., 2013). There is also evidence that particular care should be taken in identifying the source of the blood from which the postmortem level is obtained. Studies have demonstrated that blood taken from the left heart had methamphetamine levels twice that of the right heart, and furthermore, pulmonary blood had higher levels than other sites (Miyazaki et al., 1993). Because of these factors, it is believed peripheral blood samples more accurately reflect circulating methamphetamine levels at the time of death and that a ratio of peripheral to central blood levels should be examined when possible (Barnhart, Fogacci, & Reed, 1999; McIntyre et al., 2013). There is little information available on the postmortem metabolism of amphetamines.

CASE ONE

On January 28 around 23:00, a man in his late 20s was frantically knocking on the door of multiple homes in a residential neighborhood, and stated to several of the residents that multiple individuals were chasing him. A 911 call was made and when police arrived, they witnessed the man ingest a bag containing an unknown substance. The individual subsequently barricaded himself in one of the homes and refused to follow the instructions of law enforcement officers. Over the next 30 minutes, the individual came out of the house and was described by multiple witnesses to be paranoid, acting bizarrely, freaking out, yelling loudly but unintelligibly, and removing his clothes. Suddenly, the individual fell to the ground and began to have generalized convulsions. Police officers immediately went to place the individual into custody but recognized that he was not conscious and having an acute medical emergency. Paramedics who were standing by on scene were immediately called to initiate medical aid. Physical examination on scene revealed that the individual was hot to the touch, sweating profusely, had "saucer sized pupils" and was having generalized convulsions, but he did have a strong rapid pulse. After about two minutes, the convulsions spontaneously ceased and the medics were able to administer oxygen and establish an IV, and loaded the patient into the ambulance for transport to the hospital. During the 15-minute transport period, the patient had multiple additional seizures without regaining consciousness, for which he was given multiple doses of IV midazolam in an effort to stop the seizure, all of which were unsuccessful. Upon arrival at the hospital, the individual was taken immediately to a resuscitation room where multiple advanced medical interventions were performed, including endotracheal intubation, mechanical ventilation, and administration of multiple additional anticonvulsant medications, which stabilized the patient. Core rectal temperature was 109°F. Urine drug of abuse screen was positive for "amphetamine/methamphetamine" and "marijuana." A head CT scan was performed in the emergency department and revealed a large intracranial hemorrhage that was deemed incompatible with survival. Following additional testing by the neurosurgeons and neurologists, the patient was pronounced brain dead and care was withdrawn. At autopsy, the medical examiner (ME) confirmed the intracranial hemorrhage as the cause of death. The ME also measured the following drug concentrations: Methamphetamine concentration was 15,875 ng/mL and amphetamine concentration was 1,203 ng/mL in a peripheral (femoral) blood sample. Delta-9-tetrahydrocannabinol and delta-9carboxy-tetrahydrocannabinol concentrations were 2.2 ng/mL and 11 ng/mL, respectively, in the same peripheral blood sample. Methamphetamine concentration was 2,850,000 ng/mL in a gastric fluid sample from the stomach.

Comments

This is a very typical case presentation of severe acute methamphetamine poisoning. The highlights of the clinical manifestations of this intoxication include enlarged pupils, sweating, paranoid delusions, elevated body temperature, and multiple seizures. Intracranial hemorrhage is an uncommon but well-known complication of acute methamphetamine toxicity. The very high concentration of methamphetamine detected in the sample from the stomach suggests that the individual orally consumed the drug in an effort to conceal the drug from law enforcement and also led to a very high concentration of methamphetamine in the blood. This practice is known as "body stuffing" and can result in lethal consequences as demonstrated in this case. Because many amphetamines and derivatives, including methamphetamine, may be legitimately prescribed by a physician, investigators should be aware of Prescription Drug Monitoring Programs (PDMP), which is a database of controlled substance prescriptions filled by pharmacies that is searchable by individuals receiving the medication. It is possible that the methamphetamine detected in this case resulted from ingestion of prescription tablets of Desoxyn® (methamphetamine). The amphetamine concentration detected in blood in this case is likely due to metabolism of methamphetamine, licit or illicit, in the body, but it is also possible that the individual was prescribed Adderal® (amphetamine and dextroamphetamine). However, taking Adderal® medicinally for attention deficit hyperactivity disorder (ADHD) does not explain the concomitant detection of methamphetamine. While methamphetamine metabolism results in the production of amphetamine, the converse is not true.

There is less literature regarding cathinones and postmortem redistribution. Reports examining deaths attributed to methylone and MDPV found that the cathinones did not appear to sequester or redistribute to any particular tissue (Cawrse et al., 2012; Wyman et al., 2013). Similar to amphetamines, there is little information available on the postmortem metabolism of cathinones.

Studies suggest that cocaine undergoes postmortem redistribution to urine, kidney, spleen, brain, lung and skeletal muscle, and post-mortem levels in these tissues are higher than blood samples (Poklis, Maginn, & Barr, 1987b). Postmortem metabolism of cocaine was demonstrated in one experiment, with only the brain and muscle retaining any significant amount of cocaine detectable after five days, while cocaethylene was noted to be stable over this time frame (Moriya & Hashimoto, 1996).

Biological Testing

Evaluation for amphetamine, cathinone, and cocaine toxicity focuses on the clinical presentation of the user. Laboratory tests and radiology tests may be helpful in some cases, but because of the limitations of the testing techniques, they may not provide definitive answers for legal purposes in many circumstances. Laboratory testing evaluating kidney function (serum creatinine) and breakdown of muscle cells (creatinine kinase) can help detect common complications from significant toxicity. Troponin, which is a measure of heart cell death, can help determine if acute injury to the heart has occurred. Urine drug immunoassay screens, commonly called urine drug screens, are often obtained to detect the use of amphetamine, methamphetamine, and cocaine, but unfortunately are of limited value for several reasons. These are only qualitative in nature and do not indicate how much drug the user may have been exposed to (Melanson, 2012). The amphetamine/methamphetamine screens are very non-specific and have multiple reported false positives (Saitman, Park, & Fitzgerald, 2014). False positives are when the test is positive for an amphetamine when amphetamine or methamphetamine were not taken. A common presumption in both the medical and legal setting is that the amphetamine detected is an illicit drug such as methamphetamine. However, common over-the-counter cold medications containing pseudoephedrine are notorious for causing false positives on these tests

(Moeller, Lee, & Kissack, 2008). In addition, several prescription medications such as methylphenidate (Ritalin®) and buproprion (Welbutrin®) may also cause false positives (Manzi, Law, & Shannon, 2002; Reidy, Walls, & Steele, 2011). Finally, these screens can remain positive for over 48 hours after exposure and therefore cannot determine exactly when a user might have been exposed or if the individual was acutely intoxicated at the time of the incident being investigated (Smith-Kielland, Skuterud, & Mørland, 1997). Because of all of these factors, it is important to remember a positive amphetamine or methamphetamine urine immunoassay drug screen does not necessarily indicate intoxication just proximate to the time of measurement. Cathinones are not commonly tested by urine drug immunoassay screens and similar limitations would apply.

Urine drug immunoassay screens for cocaine are actually detecting one of its main metabolites, benzoylecgonine. Unlike the amphetamine screen, the cocaine screen is both sensitive and specific, with no false positives reported (Johnson-Davis, Sadler, & Genzen, 2016). However, it is still a qualitative test, which does not indicate acute intoxication and can be positive for up to 48 hours (Melanson, 2012). As previously noted, crack cocaine is the anhydrous base of cocaine that is commonly smoked. When smoked, crack cocaine forms a unique chemical, anhydroecgonine methylester or methylecgonidine (Kintz et al., 1997). Detection of this chemical in biological fluids is indicative of crack cocaine exposure.

CASE TWO

A 52-year-old executive is pulled over by police for speeding. The officer noted the individual to have large pupils with minimal reaction when a penlight was shone into the eyes. During field sobriety testing, the individual was noted to be nervous, restless, and had hand tremors. He was taken into custody for suspicion of driving under the influence. At the jail, the nurse elicited a past medical history of diabetes and hypertension for which he was taking glyburide and benazepril, respectively. During evaluation by the nurse, which demonstrated a heart rate of 130 beats per minute (normal 60–100 beats per minute) and an elevated blood pressure of 180/110 mmHg, the individual reported acute onset of severe substernal crushing chest pain radiating to his jaw and was consequently referred to the nearby emergency department for medical evaluation. During transport to the hospital, the patient became pale and diaphoretic, with a low blood pressure of 80/50 and the heart rate had slowed to 45 beats per minute. On arrival at the hospital, an electrocardiogram was performed, demonstrating an acute heart attack. The patient then went into cardiac arrest, and despite aggressive resuscitative efforts in the emergency department, the patient died. Urine drug screen at the hospital was positive for cocaine and blood alcohol concentration was 0.240 g/dL (0.24%). Findings at autopsy included the following: chronic coronary atherosclerosis with acute thrombosis of the left main coronary artery and consistent with an acute myocardial infarction as the cause of death and hypertensive cardiovascular disease and cocaine intoxication were contributing factors. Cocaine, benzoylecgonine, and cocaethylene, and alcohol concentrations performed on postmortem peripheral blood were 0.26 mg/L, 0.85 mg/L, 0.32 mg/L, 0.21 g/dL (0.24%), respectively.

Comments

The concentrations of cocaine and metabolites in this case are below those typically detected in fatalities and suggest "recreational use" of cocaine. The detection of cocaethylene confirms concurrent use of cocaine and alcohol, but recall that cocaethylene is an active metabolite of cocaine and has toxic properties that are similar to its parent drug, cocaine. The investigation revealed that the decedent was at a party earlier in the evening and witnesses stated that he consumed numerous alcoholic beverages and snorted cocaine throughout the evening. The effects of both alcohol and cocaine likely led to him being pulled over by the police. The chest pain and subsequent heart attack were due to the vasoconstrictive effects of cocaine in a man under emotional stress of being in custody, who also had underlying atherosclerotic coronary artery disease.

Recently, many large commercial clinical laboratories have begun to offer drug screens, which are large panels aimed at detecting multiple amphetamines and cathinones. These tests are typically based on mass spectrometry technology. They are superior to the urine drug immunoassay screens in that they can be quantitative, whereby false positives should not occur. However, intoxication should not be determined based on a drug level in isolation and should be correlated with observed clinical as well as other investigative findings.

Quantitative urine and serum amphetamine, methamphetamine, and cocaine levels are sometimes obtained. These tests may be more clinically useful than the urine drug immunoassay screens, but must still be interpreted with caution and correlated to clinical findings. There is wide inter-individual variability in what constitutes a toxic or lethal methamphetamine level (Engblom et al., 2007; Verschraagen et al., 2007). It is again important to emphasize that one should not attempt to attribute specific behaviors or death to serum levels alone, even when quantitative serum levels are available, as clinical findings should be considered.

Hair testing is sometimes performed in an attempt to confirm exposure to one of these drugs, typically methamphetamine or cocaine. Improper sample collection and environmental contamination resulting in false positives is a potential limitation of hair testing (Romano, Barbera, & Lombardo, 2001; Romano et al., 2003). Furthermore, there are no agreed upon standards regarding reporting values or correlation to amount exposed (Pragst & Balikova, 2006).

Summary

Amphetamine, cathinones, and cocaine are all stimulants, which alter how the nervous system releases and uses norepinephrine, dopamine, and serotonin. Amphetamine abuse has been reported since the 1940s, while cathinone abuse is a relatively newer phenomenon. Cocaine abuse has been present for over a century. All three substances can be snorted, smoked, or injected and generally cause rapid onset of symptoms, which can last several hours. They cause diaphoresis, large pupils, agitation, psychosis, elevated heart rate, elevated blood pressure, seizures, and elevated body temperature. Cocaine can also cause life-threatening abnormal cardiac rhythms. Impaired driving can be seen with all three, and their detection is associated with child abuse and neglect. Cathinones are not routinely detected, but amphetamines and cocaine can be detected on common urine drug screens. However, these tests have limitations and should be cautiously interpreted. Correlating laboratory results with clinical and other investigative findings is essential in the evaluation of exposures to these stimulants.

Investigation Checklist

Note that not all findings are necessary to demonstrate stimulant exposure or toxicity but are corroborative in the proper context.

Historical Findings

- ☐ Chest pain
- ☐ Headache
- ☐ Nose bleeds
- ☐ Extreme agitation or aggressiveness
- ☐ Delusional thoughts
- ☐ Profuse sweating
- ☐ Rapid breathing
- ☐ Warm or hot to touch
- ☐ Attempted self-cooling
- ☐ Near constant physical activity
- ☐ Lack of fatigue
- ☐ High tolerance to pain
- ☐ Not responsive to police presence or instructions
- ☐ Inappropriate clothing for environment/naked
- ☐ Excessive/superhuman strength
- ☐ Establish a timeline for drug use and observed behaviors
- ☐ Quantify frequency of drug use and amount used on each occasion
- ☐ Obtain and retain samples of drugs for laboratory identification and analysis
- ☐ Prescription Drug Monitoring Program may demonstrate medically prescribed substances
- ☐ Medical records from other medical providers such as primary care physicians and consultants

Medical Findings

- ☐ Rapid heart rate
- ☐ Elevated blood pressure
- ☐ Elevated respiratory rate
- ☐ Elevated temperature (over 100.4°F)
- ☐ Enlarged pupils
- ☐ Sweating
- ☐ Elevated serum creatinine phosphokinase (CPK) or myoglobin
- ☐ Elevated serum creatinine (evidence of kidney failure)
- ☐ Low pH on blood gas testing
- ☐ Urine toxicological analysis positive for stimulants (amphetamines, cocaine metabolite)
- ☐ Abnormal heart rhythm or electrocardiogram (ECG) prior to or after cardiac arrest

Postmortem Findings

- ☐ Pulmonary edema
- ☐ Cerebral edema
- ☐ Brain hemorrhage
- ☐ Structural and microscopic cardiac abnormalities (necrosis, artherosclerosis)
- ☐ Toxicological analysis positive for amphetamines, cathinones, cocaine, or other stimulants
- ☐ Absence of other cause of death (trauma, asphyxiation, overdose, etc.)

References

Arroyo, A., Sánchez, M., Barberia, E., Barbal, M., Marrón, M. T., & Mora, A. (2013). Drivers under the influence of drugs of abuse: Quantification of cocaine and impaired driving. *Medico-Legal Journal, 81*(Pt 3), 135–143.

Barnhart, F. E., Fogacci, J. R., & Reed, D. W. (1999). Methamphetamine—A study of postmortem redistribution. *Journal of Analytical Toxicology, 23*(1), 69–70.

Blaho, K., Logan, B., Winbery, S., Park, L., & Schwilke, E. (2000). Blood cocaine and metabolite concentrations, clinical findings, and outcome of patients presenting to an ED. *American Journal of Emergency Medicine, 18*(5), 593–598.

Blejer-Prieto, H. (1965). Coca leaf and cocaine addiction—Some historical notes. *Canadian Medical Association Journal, 93*(13), 700–704.

Brewer, J. D., Meves, A., Bostwick, J. M., Hamacher, K. L., & Pittelkow, M. R. (2008). Cocaine abuse: Dermatologic manifestations and therapeutic approaches. *Journal of the American Academy of Dermatology, 59*(3), 483–487.

Buchanan, J. A., Oyer, R. J., Patel, N. R., Jacquet, G. A., Bornikova, L., Thienelt, C., … Lavonas, E. J. (2010). A confirmed case of agranulocytosis after use of cocaine contaminated with levamisole. *Journal of Medical Toxicology, 6*(2), 160–164.

Campbell, B. G. (1988). Cocaine abuse with hyperthermia, seizures and fatal complications. *Medical Journal of Australia, 149*(7), 387–389.

Carvalho, M., Carmo, H., Costa, V. M., Capela, J. P., Pontes, H., Remião, F., Carvalho, F., & Bastos, M. de L. (2012). Toxicity of amphetamines: An update. *Archives of Toxicology, 86*(8), 1167–1231.

Cawrse, B. M., Levine, B., Jufer, R. A., Fowler, D. R., Vorce, S. P., Dickson, A. J., & Holler, J. M. (2012). Distribution of methylone in four postmortem cases. *Journal of Analytical Toxicology, 36*(6), 434–439.

Centers for Disease Control and Prevention. (2009). Agranulocytosis associated with cocaine use—four States, March 2008—November 2009. *Morbidity and Mortality Weekly Report (MMWR), 58*, 1381–1385.

Centers for Disease Control and Prevention. (2011). Emergency department visits after use of a drug sold as "bath salts." Michigan, November 13, 2010–March 31, 2011. *Morbidity and Mortality Weekly Report (MMWR), 60*(19), 624–627.

Chan, P., Chen, J. H., Lee, M. H., & Deng, J. F. (1994). Fatal and nonfatal methamphetamine intoxication in the intensive care unit. *Journal of Toxicology. Clinical Toxicology, 32*(2), 147–155.

Chipman, M. L., Macdonald, S., & Mann, R. E. (2003). Being "at fault" in traffic crashes: Does alcohol, cannabis, cocaine, or polydrug abuse make a difference? *Injury Prevention, 9*(4), 343–348.

Christensen, M. R., Lesnikova, I., Madsen, L. B., Rosendal, I., & Banner, J. (2013). Drug-induced bilateral ischemic infarction in an amphetamine addict. *Forensic Science, Medicine, and Pathology, 9*(3), 458–461.

Cooper, C. J., Said, S., Alkhateeb, H., Rodriguez, E., Trien, R., Ajmal, S., Blandon, P. A., & Hernandez, G. T. (2013). Dilated cardiomyopathy secondary to chronic cocaine abuse: A case report. *BMC Research Notes, 6*, 536.

Council on Scientific Affairs. (1978). Clinical aspects of amphetamine abuse. *Journal of the American Medical Association, 240*(21), 2317–2319.

Cox, Jr., R. H. & Maickel, R. P. (1972). Comparison of anorexigenic and behavioral potency of phenylethylamines. *Journal of Pharmacology and Experimental Therapeutics, 181*(1), 1–9.

Curtis, E. K. (2006). Meth mouth: A review of methamphetamine abuse and its oral manifestations. *General Dentistry, 54*(2), 125–129.

Daras, M., Koppel, B. S., & Atos-Radzion, E. (1994). Cocaine-induced choreoathetoid movements ("crack dancing"). *Neurology, 44*(4), 751–752.

De Giorgi, A., Fabbian, F., Pala, M., Bonetti, F., Babini, I., Bagnaresi, I., ... Manfredini, R. (2012). Cocaine and acute vascular diseases. *Current Drug Abuse Reviews, 5*(2), 129–134.

Dean, J. H., Woznicki, E. M., O'Gara, P., Montgomery, D. G., Trimarchi, S., Myrmel, T., ... Bossone, E. (2014). Cocaine-related aortic dissection: Lessons from the International Registry of Acute Aortic Dissection. *American Journal of Medicine, 127*(9), 878–885.

Drug Enforcement Administration. (2013). *2013 National Drug Threat Assessment Summary, DEA-NWW-DIR-017-13.* United States Department of Justice.

Drug Enforcement Administration. (2014). Schedules of controlled substances: Temporary placement of 10 synthetic cathinones into Schedule I. *Federal Register, 79(*45), 12938–43.

Dumont, G. J. & Verkes, R. J. (2006). A review of acute effects of 3,4-methylenedioxymethamphetamine in healthy volunteers. *Journal of Psychopharmacology, 20*(2), 176–187.

Elliott, J. M. & Beveridge, T. J. (2005). Psychostimulants and monoamine transporters: Upsetting the balance. *Current Opinion in Pharmacology, 5*(1), 94–100.

Engblom, C., Gunnar, T., Rantanen, A., & Lillsunde, P. (2007). Driving under the influence of drugs—Amphetamine concentrations in oral fluid and whole blood samples. *Journal of Analytical Toxicology, 31*(5), 276–280.

Farooq, M.U., Bhatt, A., & Patel, M. (2009). Neurotoxic and cardiotoxic effects of cocaine and ethanol. *Journal of Medical Toxicology, 5*(3), 134–138.

Gerona, R. R. & Wu, A. H. (2012). Bath salts. *Clinics in Laboratory Medicine, 32*(3), 415–427.

Gill, J. R. (2014). The syndrome of excited delirium. *Forensic Science, Medicine, and Pathology, 10*(2), 223–228.

Goldstein, R. A., DesLauriers, C., & Burda, A. M. (2009). Cocaine: History, social implications, and toxicity—A review. *Disease-a-Month, 55*(1), 6–38.

Harris, D. S., Boxenbaum, H., Everhart, E. T., Sequeira, G., Mendelson, J. E., & Jones, R. T. (2003). The bioavailability of intranasal and smoked methamphetamine. *Clinical Pharmacology & Therapeutics, 74*(5), 475–86.

Imam, S. F., Patel, H., Mahmoud, M., Prakash, N. A., King, M. S., & Fremont, R. D. (2013). Bath salts intoxication: A case series. *Journal of Emergency Medicine, 45*(3), 361–365.

Jeffcoat, A. R., Perez-Reyes, M., Hill, J. M., Sadler, B. M., & Cook, C. E. (1989) Cocaine disposition in humans after intravenous injection, nasal insufflation (snorting), or smoking. *Drug Metabolism and Disposition, 17*(2), 153–159.

Johanson, C. E. & Schuster, C. R. (1981). A comparison of the behavioral effects of l- and dl-cathinone and d-amphetamine. *Journal of Pharmacology and Experimental Therapeutics, 219*(2), 355–362.

Johnson-Davis, K. L., Sadler, A. J., & Genzen, J. R. (2016). A retrospective analysis of urine drugs of abuse immunoassay true positive rates at a national reference laboratory. *Journal of Analytical Toxicology, 40*(2), 97–107.

Kamijo, Y., Soma, K., Nishida, M., Namera, A., & Ohwada, T. (2002). Acute liver failure following intravenous methamphetamine. *Veterinary and Human Toxicology, 44*(4), 216–217.

Kintz, P., Sengler, C., Cirimele, V., & Mangin, P. (1997). Evidence of crack use by anhydroecgonine methylester identification. *Human and Experimental Toxicology, 16*(2), 123–127.

Kirkpatrick, M. G., Gunderson, E. W., Johanson, C. E., Levin, F. R., Foltin, R. W., & Hart, C. L. (2012). Comparison of intranasal methamphetamine and d-amphetamine self-administration by humans. *Addiction, 107*(4), 783–791.

Kish, S. J. (2008). Pharmacologic mechanisms of crystal meth. *Canadian Medical Association Journal, 178*(13), 1679–1682.

Kloner, R. A., Hale, S., Alker, K., & Rezkalla, S. (1992). The effects of acute and chronic cocaine use on the heart. *Circulation, 85*(2), 407–419.

Knoy, J. L., Peterson, B. L., & Couper, F. J. (2014). Suspected impaired driving case involving α-pyrrolidinovalerophenone, methylone and ethylone. *Journal of Analytical Toxicology, 38*(8), 615–617.

Lathers, C. M., Tyau, L. S., Spino, M. M., & Agarwal, I. (1988). Cocaine-induced seizures, arrhythmias and sudden death. *Journal of Clinical Pharmacology, 28*(7), 584–593.

Lemos, N. P. (2009). Methamphetamine and driving. *Science & Justice, 49*(4), 247–249.

Lile, J. A., Babalonis, S., Emurian, C., Martin, C. A., Wermeling, D. P., & Kelly, T. H. (2011). Comparison of the behavioral and cardiovascular effects of intranasal and oral d-amphetamine in healthy human subjects. *Journal of Clinical Pharmacology, 51*(6), 888–889.

Logan, B. K. (1996). Methamphetamine and driving impairment. *Journal of Forensic Sciences, 41*(3), 457–464.

Logan, B. K., Fligner, C. L., & Haddix T. (1998). Cause and manner of death in fatalities involving methamphetamine. *Journal of Forensic Sciences, 43*(1), 28–34.

Manzi, S., Law, T., & Shannon, M. W. (2002). Methylphenidate produces a false-positive urine amphetamine screen. *Pediatric Emergency Care, 18*(5), 401.

Marzuk, P. M., Tardiff, K., Leon, A. C., Hirsch, C. S., Portera, L., Iqbal, M. I., … Hartwell, N. (1998). Ambient temperature and mortality from unintentional cocaine overdose. *Journal of the American Medical Association, 279*(22), 1795–1800.

Matteucci, M. J., Auten, J. D., Crowley, B., Combs, D., & Clark, R. F. (2007). Methamphetamine exposures in young children. *Pediatric Emergency Care, 23*(9), 638–640.

McCance, E. F., Price, L. H., Kosten, T. R., & Jatlow, P. I. (1995). Cocaethylene: Pharmacology, physiology and behavioral effects in humans. *Journal of Pharmacology and Experimental Therapeutics, 274*(1), 215–223.

McIntyre, I. M., Nelson, C. L., Schaber, B., & Hamm, C. E. (2013). Antemortem and postmortem methamphetamine blood concentrations: three case reports. *Journal of Analytical Toxicology, 37*(6), 386–389.

Melanson, S. E. (2012). The utility of immunoassays for urine drug testing. *Clinics in Laboratory Medicine, 32*(3), 429–447.

Messina, N., Jeter, K., Marinelli-Casey, P., West, K., & Rawson, R. (2014). Children exposed to methamphetamine use and manufacture. *Child Abuse & Neglect, 38*(11), 1872–1883.

Miyazaki, T., Kojima, T., Yashiki, M., Wakamoto, H., Iwasaki, Y., & Taniguchi, T. (1993). Site dependence of methamphetamine concentrations in blood samples collected from cadavers of people who had been methamphetamine abusers. *American Journal of Forensic Medicine and Pathology, 14*(2), 121–124.

Moeller, K. E., Lee, K. C., & Kissack, J. C. (2008). Urine drug screening: Practical guide for clinicians. *Mayo Clinic Proceedings, 83*(1), 66–76.

Molina, D. K. & Hargrove, V. M. (2011). Fatal cocaine interactions: A review of cocaine-related deaths in Bexar County, Texas. *American Journal of Forensic Medicine and Pathology, 32*(1), 71–77.

Mooney, L., Rawson, R. A., & Gonzales, R. (2010). The methamphetamine problem in the United States. *Annual Review of Public Health, 31*(1), 385–398.

Moriya, F. & Hashimoto, Y. (1996). Postmortem stability of cocaine and cocaethylene in blood and tissues of humans and rabbits. *Journal of Forensic Sciences, 141*(4), 612–616.

Murphy, C. M., Dulaney, A. R., Beuhler, M. C., & Kacinko, S. (2013). "Bath salts" and "plant food" products: The experience of one regional US poison center. *Journal of Medical Toxicology, 9*(1), 42–48.

Murray, B. L., Murphy, C. M., & Beuhler, M. C. (2012). Death following recreational use of designer drug "bath salts" containing 3,4-Methylenedioxypyrovalerone (MDPV). *Journal of Medical Toxicology, 8*(1), 69–75.

Musshoff, F. & Madea, B. (2012). Driving under the influence of amphetamine-like drugs. *Journal of Forensic Sciences*, *57*(2), 413–419.

Nolan, A. L. & Jen, K. Y. (2015). Pathologic manifestations of levamisole-adulterated cocaine exposure. *Diagnostic Pathology*, *10*, 48.

O'Connor, A. D., Padilla-Jones, A., Gerkin, R. D., & Levine, M. (2015). Prevalence of rhabdomyolysis in sympathomimetic toxicity: A comparison of stimulants. *Journal of Medical Toxicology*, *11*(2), 195–200.

Pinto, J. M., Babu, K., & Jenny, C. (2013). Cocaine-induced dystonic reaction: An unlikely presentation of child neglect. *Pediatric Emergency Care*, *29*(9), 1006–1008.

Poklis, A., Maginn, D., & Barr, J. L. (1987a). Drug findings in "Driving Under the Influence of Drugs" cases: A problem of illicit drug use. *Drug and Alcohol Dependence*, *20*(1), 57–62.

Poklis, A., Maginn, D., & Barr, J. L. (1987b). Tissue disposition of cocaine in man: A report of five fatal poisonings. *Forensic Science International*, *33*(2), 83–88.

Poklis, J. L., Wolf, C. E., ElJordi, O. I., Liu, K., Zhang, S., & Poklis, A. (2015). Analysis of the first- and second-generation Raving Dragon Novelty Bath Salts containing methylone and pentedrone. *Journal of Forensic Sciences*, *60*(S1), S234–240.

Pragst, F. & Balikova, M. A. (2006). State of the art in hair analysis for detection of drug and alcohol abuse. *Clinica Chimica Acta*, *370*(1–2), 17–49.

Rasmussen, N. (2008). America's first amphetamine epidemic 1929–1971: A quantitative and qualitative retrospective with implications for the present. *American Journal of Public Health*, *98*(6), 974–985.

Reidy, L., Walls, H. C., & Steele, B. W. (2011). Crossreactivity of bupropion metabolite with enzyme-linked immunosorbent assays designed to detect amphetamine in urine. *Therapeutic Drug Monitoring*, *33*(3), 366–368.

Rickli, A., Hoener, M. C., & Liechti, M. E. (2015). Monoamine transporter and receptor interaction profiles of novel psychoactive substances: Para-halogenated amphetamines and pyrovalerone cathinones. *European Neuropsychopharmacology*, *25*(3), 365–376.

Romano, G., Barbera, N., & Lombardo, I. (2001). Hair testing for drugs of abuse: Evaluation of external cocaine contamination and risk of false positives. *Forensic Science International*, *123*(2–3), 119–129.

Romano, G., Barbera, N., Spadaro, G., & Valenti, V. (2003). Determination of drugs of abuse in hair: Evaluation of external heroin contamination and risk of false positives. *Forensic Science International*, *131*(2–3), 98–102.

Rosenberg, N. M., Meert, K. L., Knazik, S. R., Yee, H., & Kauffman, R. E. (1991). Occult cocaine exposure in children. *American Journal of Diseases of Children*, *145*(12), 1430–1432.

Rusyniak, D. E. (2013). Neurologic manifestations of chronic methamphetamine abuse. *Psychiatric Clinics of North America*, *36*(2), 261–75.

Saitman, A., Park, H. D., & Fitzgerald, R. L. (2014). False-positive interferences of common urine drug screen immunoassays: A review. *Journal of Analytical Toxicology*, *38*(7), 387–396.

Schaiberger, P. H., Kennedy, T. C., Miller, F. C., Gal, J., & Petty, T. L. (1993). Pulmonary hypertension associated with long-term inhalation of "crank" methamphetamine. *Chest*, *104*(2), 614–616.

Schep, L. J., Slaughter, R. J., & Beasley, D. M. (2010). The clinical toxicology of metamfetamine. *Clinical Toxicology (Phila)*, *48*(7), 675–694.

Schneir, A., Ly, B. T., Casagrande, K., Darracq, M., Offerman, S. R., Thornton, S., ... Gerona, R. R. (2014). Comprehensive analysis of "bath salts" purchased from California stores and the Internet. *Clinical Toxicology*, *52*(7), 651–658.

Siniscalchi, A., Bonci, A., Mercuri, N. B., De Siena, A., De Sarro, G., Malferrari, G., ... Gallelli, L. (2015). Cocaine dependence and stroke: Pathogenesis and management. *Current Neurovascular Research*, *12*(2), 163–172.

Smith-Kielland, A., Skuterud, B., & Mørland, J. (1997). Urinary excretion of amphetamine after termination of drug abuse. *Journal of Analytical Toxicology*, *21*(5), 325–329.

"Stimulant." (2016). In *Merriam Webster Online*. Retrieved from www.merriam-webster.com/dictionary/stimulant.

Stolberg, V. B. (2011). The use of coca: Prehistory, history, and ethnography. *Journal of Ethnicity in Substance Abuse, 10*(2), 126–146.

Stough, C., Downey, L. A., King, R., Papafotiou, K., Swann, P., & Ogden, E. (2012). The acute effects of 3,4-methylenedioxymethamphetamine and methamphetamine on driving: A simulator study. *Accident Analysis & Prevention, 45*, 493–497.

Substance Abuse and Mental Health Services Administration. (2013). *Drug Abuse Warning Network, 2011: National Estimates of Drug-Related Emergency Department Visits*, HHS Publication No. (SMA) 13-4760. Rockville, MD: Substance Abuse and Mental Health Services Administration.

Substance Abuse and Mental Health Services Administration. (2014). *Results from the 2013 National Survey on Drug Use and Health: Summary of National Findings*, NSDUH Series H-48, HHS Publication No. (SMA) 14-4863. Rockville, MD: Substance Abuse and Mental Health Services Administration.

Tank, A. W. & Wong, D. L. (2015). Peripheral and central effects of circulating catecholamines. *Comprehensive Physiology, 5*(1), 1–15.

Thornton, S. L., Gerona, R. R., & Tomaszewski, C. A. (2012). Psychosis from a bath salt product containing flephedrone and MDPV with serum, urine, and product quantification. *Journal of Medical Toxicology, 8*(3), 310–313.

Vearrier, D., Greenberg, M. I., Miller, S. N., Okaneku, J. T., & Haggerty, D. A. (2012). Methamphetamine: History, pathophysiology, adverse health effects, current trends, and hazards associated with the clandestine manufacture of methamphetamine. *Disease-a-Month, 58*(2), 38–89.

Verrico, C. D., Haile, C. N., Newton, T. F., Kosten, T. R., & De La Garza, R. (2013). Pharmacotherapeutics for substance-use disorders: A focus on dopaminergic medications. *Expert Opinion on Investigational Drugs, 22*(12), 1549–1568.

Verschraagen, M., Maes, A., Ruiter, B., Bosman, I. J., Smink, B. E., & Lusthof, K. J. (2007). Post-mortem cases involving amphetamine-based drugs in The Netherlands. Comparison with driving under the influence cases. *Forensic Science International, 170*(2–3), 163–170.

Vilke, G. M., Payne-James, J., & Karch, S. B. (2012). Excited delirium syndrome (ExDS): Redefining an old diagnosis. *Journal of Forensic and Legal Medicine, 19*(1), 7–11.

Wabe, N. T. (2011). Chemistry, pharmacology, and toxicology of khat (catha edulis forsk): A review. *Addiction & Health, 3*(3–4), 137–149.

West, P. L., McKeown, N. J., & Hendrickson, R. G. (2010). Methamphetamine body stuffers: An observational case series. *Annals of Emergency Medicine, 55*(2), 190–197.

Wijetunga, M., Bhan, R., Lindsay, J., & Karch, S. (2004). Acute coronary syndrome and crystal methamphetamine use: A case series. *Hawai'i Medical Journal, 63*(1), 8–13, 25.

Williams, J. & Lacey, M. (1988). Actions of cocaine on central monoamine neurons: intracellular recordings in vitro. *National Institute on Drug Abuse (NIDA) Research Monograph, 90*, 234–242.

Won, S., Hong, R. A., Shohet, R. V., Seto, T. B., & Parikh, N. I. (2013). Methamphetamine-associated cardiomyopathy. *Clinical Cardiology, 36*(12): 737–742.

Wood, D. M., Dargan, P. I., & Hoffman, R. S. (2009). Management of cocaine-induced cardiac arrhythmias due to cardiac ion channel dysfunction. *Clinical Toxicology (Phila), 47*(1), 14–23.

Wyman, J. F., Lavins, E. S., Engelhart, D., Armstrong, E. J., Snell, K. D., Boggs, P. D., … Miller, F. P. (2013). Postmortem tissue distribution of MDPV following lethal intoxication by "bath salts." *Journal of Analytical Toxicology, 37*(3), 182–185.

Zimmerman, J. L. (2012). Cocaine intoxication. *Critical Care Clinics, 4*, 517–526.

11

CENTRAL NERVOUS SYSTEM DEPRESSANTS

Michael A. Darracq, Stephen L. Thornton, and Binh T. Ly

Introduction

Central nervous system depressants or sedatives are medications that are prescribed or abused with the intent to reduce excitability and trigger sedation, drowsiness, and sleep (hypnosis). All sedative-hypnotic medications induce central nervous system (CNS) depression. The majority of clinically important sedative-hypnotics exert this CNS depressant effect through modulation of the neurotransmitter gamma amino butyric acid (GABA), which is the principal inhibitory neurotransmitter in the brain. Ethanol (drinking alcohol), benzodiazepines, and barbiturates are classes of sedative medications that modulate GABA effects. Some other sedative-hypnotics may also act via other mechanisms.

Opiates are analgesics (pain-relieving compounds) that are found naturally in the opium poppy (*papaver somniferum*) that also induce central nervous system depression. Opiates include the compounds morphine, codeine, and thebaine. The broader term opioid refers to drugs that act similarly to opiates by binding to specific receptors in the brain and body. These agents include semi-synthetic opiates (structurally similar to morphine) such as heroin, hydrocodone, hydromorphone, oxycodone, and oxymorphone. Synthetic opioids are not derived from morphine and include fentanyl, methadone, and buprenorphine. Opioids and opiates are considered drugs of high abuse potential and are listed as such under the United States (US) Controlled Substance Act. In addition to pain-relieving effects, opiates and opioids are often associated with a sense of euphoria and may be abused for these mood-enhancing effects.

Use of sedatives, in particular benzodiazepines, is common in the US. Common uses for benzodiazepines include alcohol withdrawal, generalized anxiety disorder (GAD), panic disorder, insomnia, muscle relaxation, and seizures (Anderson, 2014). In 2015, it was estimated that 5.2 percent of US adults between the ages of 18 and 80 used a benzodiazepine. The use of benzodiazepines is also noted to increase with age: from 2.6 percent (18–35 years) to 5.4 percent (36–50 years) to 7.4 percent (51–64 years) to 8.7 percent (65–80 years) (Olfson, King, & Schoenbaum, 2015). Prescriptions for benzodiazepines are also described to be increasing. In 2012, a 17 percent increase in the number of prescriptions for benzodiazepines since 2006 was reported, with roughly 96 million prescriptions for benzodiazepines having been written in 2012. Alprazolam (Xanax), a benzodiazepine, prescriptions increased by 23 percent over the same period of time, making it the most prescribed psychiatric medication and eleventh most commonly prescribed medication overall (Miller, 2012).

In 2013, it was estimated that between 28 and 38 million people (0.6 to 0.8 percent of the global population between the ages of 15 and 65) had used opioids or opiates recreationally (United Nations Office on Drugs and Crime, 2015). In the US, it is estimated that 44 people die every day from prescription pain medication misuse (Centers for Disease Control and Prevention, 2016). The Substance Abuse and Mental Health Services Administration (SAMHSA) has described the considerable potential for morbidity and mortality related to benzodiazepine use. When combined with other agents such as alcohol and opioid pain medication, benzodiazepine-related emergency department visits resulted in 44 percent serious medical outcomes, including hospitalization or death. Benzodiazepine combination with ethanol similarly resulted in a 44 percent rate of serious medical outcomes (Substance Abuse and Mental Health Services Administration, 2014).

While many medications and drugs have sedating effects, it is beyond the scope of this chapter to present all classes of drugs that may have this undesirable adverse effect in their profile. However, a commonly prescribed and abused muscle relaxant, carisoprodol (Soma), deserves to be mentioned. Although its mechanism of action is not precisely known, carisoprodol has pronounced CNS sedating effects similar to benzodiazepines.

Clinical Manifestations

Following acute overdose of benzodiazepines or ethanol, initial signs and symptoms may manifest as incoordination, ataxia (unsteady gait), slurred speech, and excessive sleepiness. The majority of patients with pure benzodiazepine overdose will usually manifest with these CNS symptoms only. Gastrointestinal symptoms, such as nausea and vomiting, however, have been reported following acute overdose with benzodiazepines (Gaudreault et al., 1991). Paradoxical reactions such as increased anxiety, agitation, hallucinations, and delirium may also occur following benzodiazepine routine use or overdose (Garnier et al., 1984).

More serious and life-threatening toxicity is rare following pure benzodiazepine overdose, but may occur when combined with other CNS sedatives such as ethanol and opioids (Dart, 2003; Substance Abuse and Mental Health Services Administration, 2014). These symptoms and signs include deep and prolonged or cyclical coma, apnea (absent breathing), respiratory depression (both depressed rate and depth of respirations), hypoxia (inadequate oxygenation), hypothermia (depressed body temperature), bradycardia (abnormally slow heart rate), cardiac arrest, and pulmonary aspiration (Berger, Green, & Melnick, 1975; Busto, Kaplan, & Sellers, 1980; Greenblatt et al., 1977; Höjer, Baehrendtz, & Gustafsson, 1989; Welch, Rumack, & Hammond, 1977). The elderly and those with concomitant chronic medical problems are more at risk for lethal overdose from benzodiazepines even at relatively low doses (Brødsgaard, Hansen, & Vesterby, 1995; Gaudreault et al., 1991; Reidenberg et al., 1978; Sunter, Bal, & Cowan, 1988).

Following acute overdose of opioids, the most concerning adverse effects include excess sedation and respiratory depression (both depressed rate and depth of respiration). A typical sign of opioid intoxication is small pupils (miosis). In older adults, opioid use may be associated with increased risk of additional adverse effects, including sedation, nausea, vomiting, constipation, urinary retention, and falls (Baumann, 2009; Buckeridge et al., 2010).

Legal Issues

Driving-Related Impairments

Benzodiazepines and ethanol are well described to adversely affect driving-related performance. Serum benzodiazepine concentration and driving performance deficits for most of the benzodiazepines are essentially linear (Berghaus & Grass, 1997; O'Hanlon et al., 1995). Some studies suggest that even when tested the morning after use as a hypnotic agent, impairments are comparable to those seen in individuals with blood alcohol concentrations (BAC) of 0.05 to 0.10 percent, equal to or above the legal driving limit in a majority of US states (O'Hanlon & Volkerts, 1986).

Zolpidem (Ambien), zopiclone (Zimovane and Imovane), and zaleplon (Sonata, Starnoc, and Andante) are non-benzodiazepine sedative-hypnotics that have similarly demonstrated adverse driving effects. Drug manufacturers caution patients against use where complete mental alertness and coordination are necessary. Erratic driving (weaving, lane movement), slow and slurred speech, slowed or absent reflexes, disorientation, dazed or confused appearance, dilated pupils, somnolence, and poor performance on field sobriety testing have all been reported in cases in which zolpidem was the only drug detected in individuals cited for driving impairment (Logan & Couper, 2001; National Highway Traffic and Safety Administration, 2016).

Somnambulisms (Sleep-Related Activities)

Following commercial release, zolpidem (Ambien) was noted in post-marketing studies and case reports to also manifest complex behaviors, such as sleep driving, sleep cooking, sleep eating, sleep conversation, and sleep sex, accompanied by anterograde amnesia for the event. Other reported behaviors include manipulating objects (e.g., putting gasoline in a car) and cleaning the house (Dolder & Nelson, 2008). One case report describes a woman who wrote an email two hours following ingestion of zolpidem. She was able to logon and use her correct username and ID, however, the email was filled with odd grammar, punctuation, and format. The patient had no recollection of this event (Siddiqui, Osuna, & Chokroverty, 2009).

Post-marketing studies suggest a rate as high as 5 percent of patients taking zolpidem experiencing complex behaviors (Dolder & Nelson, 2008; Tsai et al., 2009). Because these behaviors often occur with amnesia, it is likely that they are underreported. These presumably non-voluntary behaviors have led to a number of legal claims and defenses. Both "sleep walking" and "the pill made me do it" defenses have been introduced as a means to reduce or eliminate criminal and civil liability in cases in which zolpidem was involved.

Daley, McNiel, and Binder (2011) describe 28 relevant legal cases in which zolpidem was involved. The defendants argued that use of zolpidem near the time of offense negated some of the criminal liability (Daley et al., 2011). In several of these cases, the defendant argued that the use of zolpidem resulted in an altered state of mind, leading to a lack of awareness of actions and that he or she was unaware at the time of ingestion of potential adverse effects (Myers, 1993). In cases where the defense is unable to demonstrate involuntary intoxication, the defense may argue for voluntary intoxication, which may reduce the severity of charges by negating specific intent of crime (i.e., premeditated murder).

In *Bingham v. State* (2009), Bingham shot his wife and stepson during a domestic argument. The wife died of injuries sustained while the stepson survived. Initially charged with first-degree murder and attempted murder, the defendant raised the defense of involuntary intoxication as a result of prescription drug use, including zolpidem. The defendant argued that he experienced a "distorted thought process." The jury found him guilty of the lesser charge of voluntary manslaughter and attempted murder. The court of appeals upheld the conviction, arguing that Bingham did not provide sufficient evidence of involuntary intoxication. Records were introduced that demonstrated that the defendant's physician had counseled him extensively about potential side effects of all of the medications prescribed (*Bingham v. State*, 2009).

Similar claims and defenses have been made for other sedative-hypnotics including benzodiazepines. In 1980, a woman was charged with murder after stabbing her husband to death with a kitchen knife during an argument. Previously, the defendant and her husband were in the midst of a divorce settlement. The defendant was understandably anxious and distressed as a result of this series of events and sought assistance from her primary medical provider. A prescription for diazepam (Valium) 5mg to be "taken as needed" and in an amount of 72 tablets was provided. In the hours preceding the stabbing incident, the defendant consumed six tablets over a six-hour period, with the last dose one hour prior to the argument. After arrest, the defendant took an additional tablet of diazepam. At trial, it was successfully argued that the 30mg of diazepam taken in the 12 hours prior to the stabbing incident was responsible for the paradoxical aggressive outburst by the defendant, and that she was not in full possession of her faculties at the time of the stabbing incident. The defendant was acquitted completely on the basis of an argument of involuntary intoxication. No records were introduced suggesting that the defendant had been warned or counseled about the potential adverse effects of diazepam (*Law Society Gazette*, 1987).

Triazolam (Halcion) has similarly been associated with aberrant behaviors and it was removed from the European market as a result (Dolder & Nelson, 2008; Myers, 1993). A successful product liability suit against the manufacturer of triazolam was awarded in the United States (*Freeman v. Upjohn Co.*, 1992).

In all successful defenses involving benzodiazepines or zolpidem, there has been a clear demonstration of intoxication, or impairment in perception and thought. In *People v. Hudon* (2009), testimony of witnesses was critical to the prosecution's case and successful defeat of the "zolpidem" defense. The prosecution produced witnesses who described the behavior and actions of the defendant immediately following a car chase and encounter with law enforcement.

Around 11:00pm, Hudon was observed driving in a reckless manner. A police chase ensued, which resulted in the defendant being cornered, where he resisted arrest and subsequently punched an officer in the face. A blood alcohol level was measured at 0.13 percent. The defendant described taking zolpidem at 9:30pm and denied any recollection of drinking alcohol, the police chase, or punching an officer. The defense relied on the testimony of a sleep medicine expert who described the known propensity of zolpidem to induce bizarre behaviors with amnesia. The nurse who treated Hudon shortly after his arrest described him as being of a normal mental status and answering all questions appropriately. One of the responding officers testified that the defendant's behavior was consistent with that of someone under the influence of alcohol rather than that of prescription medications. The presence of ethanol was viewed as evidence of voluntary intoxication and may have contributed to any reported amnesic effects experienced by the defendant. The jury convicted Hudon on all charges (*People v. Hudon*, 2009).

Because Hudon claimed an involuntary intoxication defense, the prosecution called into question the credibility of the defendant and was allowed to enter evidence that, under different circumstances, may have been excluded as prejudicial. The prosecution presented testimony of the arresting officer that Hudon claimed he was fleeing the police because of a prior DUI charge. This evidence directly contradicted the claim by the defense that the defendant was operating with a distortion of perception or thought and the innocent state of mind claimed by the defense (*People v Hudon*, 2009).

Potential motivation and pre-medicated state of mind is also critical to consideration of involuntary intoxication due to sedative-hypnotic. In the case of *Davidson v. State* (2006), Davidson was charged with murder after shooting the boyfriend of his ex-wife. The defendant claimed that he was involuntarily intoxicated as a result of zolpidem and therefore was in a dissociative state and not responsible for his actions. The prosecution entered evidence at trial that demonstrated that the defendant had maintained a sexual relationship with his ex-wife and witness testimony of previous statements by the defendant regarding his desire for the new boyfriend to be dead. The jury convicted the defendant of murder (*Davidson v. State*, 2006).

Biological Testing

Sedatives, including benzodiazepines, zolpidem, ethanol, and opioids, can be detected in various biological matrices including blood and urine. In the absence of biological testing, the court is dependent on statements made by the defendant as to whether the substance was taken prior to the contested act or behavior.

Blood samples may be used to approximate a time of ingestion or dose taken. Urine may confirm the presence of a sedative or opioid. There is, however, considerable individual variability in the absorption, distribution, metabolism, and excretion of these substances, limiting the accuracy of time of ingestion and dose estimation. Concomitant medication use, the timing of ingestion of food or beverage relative to ingestion of substance being tested may also influence absorption, distribution, metabolism, and excretion.

The blood alcohol concentration (BAC) represents the amount of ethanol that is present in the blood and can be measured in a number of ways. Law enforcement typically measures BAC in terms of a "whole" blood ethanol concentration, while serum or plasma ethanol concentrations (P-SAC) are most typically determined in a healthcare context. "Whole" blood represents the entirety of blood as it is removed from an individual, whereas serum or plasma blood represents what is left after red blood cells are removed. The actual amount of ethanol reported as present may be different depending on which testing is performed. For example, studies have reported serum/plasma ethanol concentration may be as high as 1.18 times the whole blood alcohol concentration (P-SAC/BAC = 1.18) (Barnhill, Herbert, & Wells, Jr., 2007). This has important implications for the legal determination of driving while intoxicated (DWI) or driving while under influence (DUI) and a knowledge of which testing method was used is important.

Sedatives such as benzodiazepines, ethanol, and opioids demonstrate tolerance, the progressive diminution of effect with repeated administration. In patients who take sedative-hypnotics chronically, progressively larger doses may be necessary to achieve an equivalent effect. Cross-tolerance between different classes of sedatives has been reported (Hu & Ticku, 1994). Tolerance and cross-tolerance severely limit the utility of biological testing in the determination of intoxication, and even when present, specific levels should be interpreted with caution, especially with regard to attribution of behavior or actions to substance use or intoxication. Specific blood or urine concentrations may or may not manifest clinically as intoxication, depending on the time these levels were obtained relative to ingestion, chronicity of use or abuse, concomitant sedative or other medication use or abuse, food or beverage ingestion, and individual variability in metabolism and excretion.

Investigator Key Components and Investigation Impact

The court is dependent on an accurate depiction of the mental state of the defendant at the time of commission of an alleged crime. The investigator is tasked with presenting an accurate picture of this mental state in determination of whether the defendant is in fact impaired or intoxicated. Critical information may be obtained through police reports and arrest records as well as eyewitness testimony. A field sobriety test may be especially helpful in determination of impairment. Information of when sedative medications were initiated and whether the individual was provided with information describing potential adverse side effects, including paradoxical aggressive behaviors and somnambulisms, such as sleep walking and sleep driving, are useful in determination of knowledge possessed by the accused prior to the use of these substances. This information may be contained in a patient medical or pharmacy record.

Complex behaviors are more likely to occur early in treatment, however, some reports describe these effects up to two years following initiation (Morgenthaler & Silber, 2002). The use of other psychotropic medications or ethanol may contribute to added risk for sleep-related, complex behaviors. Biological testing may be helpful in determining the presence of a particular substance of interest as well as additional substances that may be contributing to an alteration in mental status. Biological testing alone cannot and should not be used to confirm the presence of intoxication or degree of impairment. Intoxication is a clinical assessment based on behaviors and actions performed by the defendant following exposure to an intoxicant(s).

CASE ONE

On October 9th at approximately 5:00pm, a man was noted on video surveillance to possibly be shoplifting at a local retail store. Store security personnel contacted and detained the individual. The man was initially argumentative and they also noted that he may have been "under the influence of some type of intoxicant." While in the loss prevention office, the man was witnessed to ingest a handful of pills, stating he was very anxious and took some pills to relax. Subsequently, 911 was called and when local police arrived on scene, one of the police officers noted the man to be "drunk or on medication." The man reported that he was on a high dose of pain medicine. A search of the man's belongings revealed an unmarked pill bottle containing about 11 total pills of two different types. At about 5:30pm, police took custody of the man and transported him to the detention center.

At the detention center around 5:45pm, the booking process was attempted but the man was described to be very angry and uncooperative to a degree that prevented completion of the booking process. As a result, the man was placed in the "detox cell" for him to calm down and allow the booking process to continue. While in the detox cell, the man was being directly observed by a deputy sheriff. There were several other individuals in custody that were being held in adjacent cells. The man eventually calmed at around 6:30pm and sat in the cell quietly. Records at the jail demonstrate that the man remained in the seated position with his chin down but would respond verbally and with head bobs to the deputy when addressed approximately every 15 minutes. Following shift change, a different deputy was assigned to observe the sleeping man. He was noted to be breathing and bobbing his head but at 8:00pm, deputies noted minimal movement and checked to find him unresponsive. Paramedics were called to the jail for medical assistance. On scene in the cell, the man was noted by paramedics to have very weak pulses, shallow and slow respirations, and cyanosis. Resuscitative efforts were initiated and the man was transported to the regional medical center where he regained spontaneous respiratory effort and cardiac activity, but required supportive medical care on a mechanical ventilator. However, the man never regained consciousness and died six months later from pneumonia at a nursing facility.

Case Questions

1. ***How can the various types of pills be identified by law enforcement?***

Answer: Pharmaceuticals may be supplied in a number of different formulations. Examples include tablets, capsules, and liquids. The drug name(s) and dosages may be identified by noting the shape, size, color, and imprint codes on the pills. The regional poison control centers and various online search engines may be used for assistance with identification when some of the aforementioned characteristics of the pill are provided. *Pill 1 description*—round, blue, "R" imprinted on one side, "031" imprinted on the other side.

Pill 1 identification—alprazolam 1 mg. Alprazolam is a benzodiazepine marketed under the trademark name Xanax. While this particular pill contains 1 mg of alprazolam, other dosage formulations include 0.25, 0.5, and 2 mg.

Pill 2 description—oval, white, "M367" imprint on one side, scored in the middle on the other side.

Pill 2 identification—combination pharmaceutical containing both acetaminophen 325 mg (over-the-counter analgesic) and hydrocodone 10 mg (opioid). This is a very commonly prescribed and abused combination medication marketed under several other names (Vicodin, Lortab, Norco) and is also available in 5 mg dosages of the hydrocodone component.

Pill 3 description—round, white "2410 V" imprint.

Pill 3 identification—carisoprodol 350 mg, a muscle relaxant.

2. ***What specific behavioral and physical manifestations did security personnel at the retail store observe of the prisoner? Initially at the jail by deputies? At various intervals while the prisoner was being held in the detox cell?***

Answer: Certain behaviors are characteristic of intoxication from drugs. Phrases such as "under the influence" and "high on drugs" are vague and not as useful in determining the exact nature of intoxication. Some typical manifestations of alprazolam and carisoprodol intoxication include decreased level of alertness, somnolence, and unsteady gait. Typical manifestations of hydrocodone and other opioid intoxication include depressed level of alertness, slow and shallow respirations, and very small or even "pin point" pupils. Descriptions of the specific behaviors rather than impressions about the cause of the behavior should be elicited from witnesses and may be helpful in assessing the presence of suspected and unsuspected intoxicants.

3. ***What were the observations of the pre-hospital medical personnel? What vital signs and physical examination findings did paramedical personnel on scene note?***

Answer: Pre-hospital medical providers noted an unconscious man with a very weak pulse on palpation (hypotension), heart rate 30 beats per minute (normal adult heart rate is 60–100 beats per minute), and shallow respirations at a rate of four breaths per minute (normal adult respiratory rate is typically about 12–16 breaths per minute). These findings are indicative of intoxication from carisoprodol, alprazolam, and hydrocodone either independently or in combination.

4. ***What medical interventions were performed during their resuscitative efforts? What were the responses to each of the medical interventions?***

Answer: The medical interventions were establishment of intravenous (IV) access for administration of IV fluid and treatment of the low blood pressure. Also administered through the IV was naloxone, an antidote for opioid intoxication. The patient responded with an improvement in blood pressure from the IV fluid and improvement in respiratory status following naloxone administration. Typically, mental status depression would also improve following administration of naloxone. The absence of this improvement is suggestive of significant intoxication due to another agent such as alprazolam or brain injury due to prolonged hypoxia or anoxia.

5. ***At the hospital, what were the observations of the medical providers (doctors, nurses)?***

Answer: No major changes were identified at the hospital beyond those noted by the pre-hospital providers.

6. ***What diagnostic tests were performed? Were blood and body fluid specimens obtained for analysis by the laboratory? Were there any samples sent to the laboratory that were not used for analysis?***

Answer: A CT scan of the head was later performed and demonstrated cerebral edema suggestive of anoxic brain injury. Laboratory test performed at the hospital on blood specimens collected around 9:00pm demonstrated an acetaminophen concentration of 65 micrograms/milliliter (mcg/mL). The therapeutic range for acetaminophen is 10–25 mcg/mL, which suggests a significant overdose of acetaminophen. Because the concentration of hydrocodone is not typically assessed by hospital laboratories, its concentration can only be estimated to also be in overdose range due to the combination with acetaminophen. Blood alcohol concentration was 0.02%. This BAC, while detectable, is below the legal driving limit of 0.08% in most states and well below a level that would be considered to cause an individual to be in a comatose state. Most emergency departments will typically obtain more blood from critically ill patients than is typically needed for initial analysis. This is because medical providers will frequently ask for additional laboratory tests beyond those initial blood samples. Although highly variable, these samples are stored in the laboratory for a short period of time and if additional testing is not requested on these samples, they are discarded. These samples may also be requested for legal purposes should they not be used for the intended medical purpose.

7. ***After investigating the acute events, how can additional medical history be obtained?***

Answer: Additional medical history may be obtained from pre-existing hospital records, primary care or other consulting physicians. Evidence of previous medical care may also be obtained from employment, insurance, or other financial records.

Investigator Checklist

- ☐ Police report including any field sobriety testing
- ☐ Reports from prior encounters with law enforcement or the judicial system
- ☐ Obtain reports from pre-hospital emergency medical services
- ☐ Medication history including list of all medications prescribed, dates prescribed, and medication refill history. Records from primary care physicians, pharmacies, or insurance carriers may be helpful to establish the indication, duration, and frequency of use.
- ☐ Records from Prescription Drug Monitoring Program (PDMP)—state programs that keep records of all narcotic prescriptions filled by an individual.
- ☐ Timing and dosages of all medications and potential intoxicants including over-the-counter medications and use of herbal substances. Receipts from establishments providing intoxicants may be helpful in construction of a timeline.
- ☐ Documentation of discussion with the individual by prescribing provider or dispensing facility regarding potential adverse effects
- ☐ Documentation of discussion between the individual and provider or others regarding previously experienced adverse effects
- ☐ Quantification of how much and how often regarding the history of ethanol or other substance use or abuse. Nature of alcohol consumption as different beverages contain different amount of ethanol
- ☐ History of withdrawal from medication or ethanol following cessation or reduction of use
- ☐ Eyewitness descriptions of behavior, pupillary size (large, small, or normal), skin (absence or presence of sweating), unstable gait, nature of respirations, level of alertness at time of incident or shortly afterward
- ☐ If possible, obtain eyewitness descriptions of changes in behavior and degree of impairment at multiple time intervals
- ☐ Obtain reports from the health care facilities and medical examiner
- ☐ Biological testing results from the health care facilities, medical examiner, as well as current and prior employers

References

Anderson, L. (2014). *Benzodiazepines: Overview and use.* Retrieved from www.drugs.com/article/benzodiazepines.html.

Barnhill, Jr., M. T., Herbert, D., & Wells, Jr., D. J. (2007). Comparison of hospital laboratory serum alcohol levels obtained by an enzymatic method with whole blood levels forensically determined by gas chromatography. *Journal of Analytical Toxicology, 31*(1), 23–30

Baumann, S. (2009). A nursing approach to pain in older adults. *MEDSURG Nursing, 18*(2), 77–82.

Berger, R., Green, G., & Melnick, A. (1975). Cardiac arrest caused by oral diazepam intoxication. *Clinical Pediatrics, 14*(9), 842–844.

Berghaus, G. & Grass, H. (1997). Concentration-effect relationship with benzodiazepine therapy. *Proceedings of the 14th International Conference on Accidents, Drugs and Traffic Safety (ICADTS-T97)*, 705–709. Centre d'Etudes et de Recherches en Medicine du Trafic (CERMT) Annecy, FR.

Bingham v. State, No. 49A04-0808-CR-504 (Ind. App. 2009).

Brødsgaard, I., Hansen, A. C., & Vesterby, A. (1995). Two cases of lethal nitrazepam poisoning. *American Journal of Forensic Medicine and Pathology, 16*(2), 151–153.

Buckeridge, D., Huang, A., Hanley, J., Kelome, A., Reidel, K., Verma, A., ... Tamblyn, R. (2010). Risk of injury associated with opioid use in older adults. *Journal of the American Geriatrics Society, 58*(9), 1664–1670.

Busto, U., Kaplan, H. L., & Sellers, E. M. (1980). Benzodiazepine-associated emergencies in Toronto. *American Journal of Psychiatry, 137*(2), 224–227.

Centers for Disease Control and Prevention. (2016). *Understanding the epidemic.* Retrieved from www.cdc.gov/drugoverdose/epidemic/.

Daley, C., McNiel, D. E., & Binder, R. L. (2011). I did what? Zolpidem and the courts. *Journal of the American Academy of Psychiatry and the Law, 39*(4), 535–542.

Dart, R. C. (2003). *Medical toxicology* (3rd ed.). Philadelphia, PA: Lippincott Williams & Wilkins.

Davidson v. State, No. 849 N.E.2d 591 (Ind. 2006).

Dolder, C. R. & Nelson, M. H. (2008). Hypnosedative-induced complex behaviors; incidence, mechanisms and management. *CNS Drugs, 22*, 1021–1036.

Freeman v. Upjohn Co., No. 89-09648-A (Tex. Dist. Ct. 1992).

Garnier, R., Medernach, C., Harbach, S., & Fournier, E. (1984). Agitation and hallucinations during acute lorazepam poisoning in children: Apropos of 65 personal cases. *Annales de Pediatrie (Paris), 31*(4), 286–289.

Gaudreault, P., Guay, J., Thivierge, R. L., & Verdy, I. (1991). Benzodiazepine poisoning: Clinical and pharmacological considerations and treatment. *Drug Safety, 6*(4), 247–265.

Greenblatt, D. J., Allen, M. D., Noel, B. J., & Shader, R. I. (1977). Acute overdosage with benzodiazepine derivatives. *Clinical Pharmacology & Therapeutics, 21*(4), 497–514.

Höjer, J., Baehrendtz, S., & Gustafsson, L. (1989). Benzodiazepine poisoning: Experience of 702 admissions to an intensive care unit during a 14-year period. *Journal of Internal Medicine, 226*(2), 117–122.

Hu, X. J. & Ticku, M. K. (1994). Chronic benzodiazepine agonist treatment produces functional uncoupling of the gamma-aminobutyric acid-benzodiazepine receptor ionophore complex in cortical neurons. *Molecular Pharmacology, 45*, 618–625.

Law Society Gazette. (1987). Defendant acquitted of murder due to excessive prescriptive doses of valium. Retrieved from www.benzact.org/defendant%20aquit.htm.

Logan, B. K. & Couper, F. J. (2001). Zolpidem and driving impairment. *Journal of Forensic Sciences, 46*(1), 105–110.

Miller, L. (2012). Listening to xanax. *New York Magazine.* Retrieved from http://nymag.com/news/features/xanax-2012-3/index1.html.

Morgenthaler, T. I. & Silber, M. H. (2002). Amnestic sleep-related eating disorder associated with zolpidem. *Sleep Medicine, 3*(4), 323–327.

Myers, T. P. (1993). Halcion made me do it: New liability and a new defense—Fear and loathing in the Halcion paper chase. *University of Cincinnati Law Review, 62*, 603–653.

National Highway Traffic and Safety Administration. (2016). *Zolpidem (and Zaleplon, Zopiclone).* Retrieved from www.nhtsa.gov/people/injury/research/job185drugs/zolpidem.htm.

O'Hanlon, J. F., Vemeeren, A. K., Uiterwijk, M. M. C., van Vegel, L. M. A., & Swijgman, H. F. (1995). Anxiolytics: Effects on actual driving performance of patients and healthy volunteers in a standardized test: An integration of three studies. *Neuropsychobiology, 31*, 81–88.

O'Hanlon, J. F. & Volkerts, E. R. (1986). Hypnotics and actual driving performance. *Acta Psychiatrica Scandinavica, 74*(S332), 95–104.

Olfson, M., King, M., & Schoenbaum, M. (2015). Benzodiazepine use in the United States. *JAMA Psychiatry, 72*(2), 136–142.

People v. Hudon, No. D054442 (Cal. 4th App. 2009).

Reidenberg, M. M., Levy, M., Warner, H., Coutinho, C. B., Schwartz, M. A., Yu, G., & Cheripko, J. (1978). Relationship between diazepam dose, plasma level, age, and central nervous system depression. *Clinical Pharmacology & Therapeutics, 23*(4), 371–374.

Siddiqui, F., Osuna, E., & Chokroverty, S. (2009). Writing emails as part of sleepwalking after increase in zolpidem. *Sleep Medicine, 10*(2), 262–264.

Substance Abuse and Mental Health Services Administration, Center for Behavioral Health Statistics and Quality. (2014). *The DAWN report: Benzodiazepines in combination with opioid pain relievers or alcohol: Greater risk of more serious ED visit outcomes.* Retrieved from www.samhsa.gov/data/sites/default/files/DAWN-SR192-BenzoCombos-2014/DAWN-SR192-BenzoCombos-2014.htm.

Sunter, J. P., Bal, T. S., & Cowan, W. K. (1988). Three cases of fatal triazolam poisoning. *British Medical Journal, 297*(6650), 719.

Tsai, J. H., Yang, P., Chen, C. C., Chung, W., Tang, T. C., Wang, S. Y., & Liu, J. K. (2009). Zolpidem-induced amnesia and somnambulism: rare occurrences? *European Neuropsychopharmacology, 19*(1), 74–76.

United Nations Office on Drugs and Crime. (2015). *World Drug Report 2015.* Retrieved from www.unodc.org/documents/wdr2015World_Drug_Report_2015.pdf.

Welch, T. R., Rumack, B. H., & Hammond, K. (1977). Clonazepam overdose resulting in cyclic coma. *Clinical Toxicology, 10*(4), 433–436.

12

LESS LETHAL WEAPONS, NOT INCLUDING TASER

Christian Sloane and Gary M. Vilke

Introduction

Less lethal weapons have become a mainstay for law enforcement to use when confronting dangerous, combative individuals in the field. On the use of force continuum, these technologies occupy an intermediate level between verbal and physical control methods and lethal force, such as actual firearms. Less lethal weapons include riot control agents, electric stun devices such as TASERs, and other blunt projectile weapons. This chapter will cover the riot control agents and blunt projectile weapons, as TASERs are covered separately in Chapter 13. Use of these less lethal technologies increases both the safety of the intended target subject by supplanting the use of lethal force, as well as the user by controlling and subduing dangerous, combative individuals with a minimum of risk to the user. However, deaths have occurred in individuals following the use of these weapons, which were previously known as "less-than-lethal." A causal link between these various technologies and case fatalities remains controversial. Making matters more difficult, reporting practices vary, and consistent reporting and injury identification is problematic (Payne-James et al., 2014).

Riot control agents, such as tear gas, mace, and more recently oleoresin capsicum (OC), have been used by law enforcement to subdue violent individuals or crowds. Other less lethal weapons becoming increasingly popular include other electric stun devices and blunt projectile weapons used to control combative individuals, while maintaining some distance between the subject and the officer. This has the potential to lead to reductions in injuries to both officers and subjects (MacDonald, Kaminski, & Smith, 2009). Many of these products, like mace, OC spray, and stun guns, have been modified by manufacturers to be marketed to the public and often are used by people with little or no training. Although generally safe, there are certain specific concerns that should be addressed when evaluating a use of force incident that involves the devices. In this chapter, the different types of riot control agents and less lethal weapons will be discussed, including their history, mechanisms of action, intended and other physiologic effects, safety risks and complications, and key factors to evaluate in a death investigation. The associated research and case reports of injuries and deaths will be reviewed in detail.

Riot Control Agents

Riot control agents include a variety of substances that can be used to subdue individuals as well as large crowds. These agents include CN (Mace), CS, and Oleoresin Capsicum ("pepper spray"). These agents are commonly dispersed as gases, smoke, or aerosols against individuals or large gatherings and, as such, may affect the user as well as subject.

CN (1-chloroacetphenone)

History and Properties

CN, also known by the trade name Mace, was first synthesized in 1871 by Graebe and used in World War I. CN, 1-chloroacetophenone, was the primary tear gas used by law enforcement and the military up through the 1950s. This agent was also marketed for personal self-protection and was the product of choice until recently being replaced by oleoresin capsicum sprays. CN is a colorless crystalline substance that can be disseminated in a smoke form from an explosive device, such as a grenade, or propelled as a liquid or powder. Harassing concentrations for CN are typically 10 mg/m^3 with the human LCt50 (concentration at which fatalities in 50 percent of those exposed would be expected to occur) estimated at 7,000 mg min/m^3 for pure aerosol and 14,000 mg min/m^3 for a commercial grenade (McNamara, Vocci, & Owens, 1968).

Physiological Effects

CN acts as an irritant smoke when in contact with skin or mucous membrane tissues such as the eyes, nasal passages, oral cavity, and airway. Symptoms of exposure include coughing, sneezing, and increased airway secretions, as well as rhinorrhea and burning of the nasal passages and airways. Oral cavity and gastrointestinal exposure can result in the sensation of burning in the mouth, increased salivation, gagging, nausea, and vomiting. Ocular exposure to CN causes a burning sensation in the eye, injection of the conjunctiva, eye irritation, photophobia and tearing. Similarly, skin contact can result in burning, irritation, and erythema.

Case Reports

A prisoner was found dead under his bunk 46 hours after a "prolonged gassing" of inmates confined to individual cells with closed windows and doors and no ventilation. CN was used in the form of six thermal grenades, fourteen 100g projectiles and more than 500ml of 8 percent CS solution. The authors calculated the Ct to be 41,000 mg min/m^3. Details of other inmates' medical presentations were limited, but three were reported to require medical evaluation. The deceased inmate was found in rigor mortis and on autopsy was noted to have subpleural petechiae, hyperemia, mild edema, and patchy areas of consolidation in the lungs. His larynx, trachea, and bronchi were lined with an exudative pseudomembrane (Chapman & White, 1978). Another reported death occurred after exposure in a closed room with an estimated Ct of 142,500, ten times the LCt50. The individual survived to hospital admission, but ultimately died 12 hours later. On autopsy, there were similar findings as with the previous case, including pseudomembrane formation along the bronchial tree and associated edema and inflammation of the walls, as well as early patchy regions of pneumonia (McNamara et al., 1968).

One case series discusses the medical complications associated with prolonged exposure to CN in a prison incident. Surrounding circumstances include prolonged and recurrent exposures, and those that occurred in closed space with limited to no ventilation. Cutaneous complications included first and second degree burns over 25 percent of the total body surface area. Several patients required acute treatment with steroids and bronchodilators for laryngotracheo-bronchitis, but none reported any permanent medical issues. All ocular complaints were self-limited and there were no corneal injuries or permanent damage (Thorburn, 1982).

A few cases of allergic reactions have been reported, particularly in people who have a previous, even distant exposure in the past. A case of severe allergic reaction was reported in a military recruit who had been previously exposed to CN 17 years earlier, which had resulted in minimal itching at that time. He then went through the typical military CN training chamber in which he remained masked in the chamber for five minutes, then by protocol, removed the mask and exited the chamber. He developed generalized itching within minutes of exiting, which progressed over the next several hours to generalized erythema to all parts of his body, except the face portion covered by the mask and his feet. He developed a fever to 103 and by 48 hours, had diffuse vesication and edema, followed ultimately by desquamation of much of his skin. He improved over the next week (Queen & Standler, 1941). Other cutaneous reactions have been reported as well (Madden, 1951).

Ocular injuries have been reported with the use of CS, particularly when a tear gas cartridge is discharged at close range. In some cases, particles of agglomerated CS were driven into the eye tissue by the force of the dispersion device, most often a blast. In these cases, chemical reaction damage was noted over the course of months to years. These injuries were considered different than blast injuries in which particles other than CN would have been implicated (Levine & Stahl, 1968).

Research

There is limited research on the potential risks of CN and sudden arrest-related death. As noted above, most deaths reportedly associated with CN have evidence of significant airway and pulmonary injury on autopsy, suggesting that prolonged exposures to excessive concentrations of CN can cause significant respiratory damage and compromise.

In terms of other injuries, although permanent eye damage has been reported associated with the use of CN at close range, it is challenging to separate out whether the damage is from the CN or the actual weapon itself. However, at harassing or standard field concentrations, there is no evidence that CN causes permanent eye injury. Human studies placing 0.5 mg of CN on the skin for 60 minutes caused irritation and erythema for all participants, as compared with CS, which had no effects when used in amounts of less than 20 mg. When the skin was moist, 0.5 mg of CN caused vesication, while this was not seen in exposure to 30 mg or less of CS (Holland & White, 1972).

CS (o-chlorobenzylidene malononitrile)

History and Properties

CS, o-chlorobenzylidene malononitrile, is a riot control agent first synthesized in 1928 by Corson and Stoughton (the origin of its code name). CS replaced CN as the standard riot control irritant agent in the United States (U.S.) Army in 1959. By the late 1950s, it had replaced CN in most law enforcement agencies in the U.S. as well because of the perceived improved effectiveness of CS.

CS is a white, crystalline solid that is insoluble in water and only partially soluble in ethyl alcohol. Because of its low vapor pressure, CS is typically disseminated by dispersion of the powder or solution by explosion, spray, or smoke. Harassing concentrations are typically 4 mg/m^3. Because of its insoluble nature, decontamination of buildings or other items after exposure can be challenging. CS also has a high flammability rating and has been noted to cause some structure fires (Danto, 1987).

Physiological effects

The clinical effects that may be seen with the use of CS are similar to those of CN, resulting in irritation and inflammation of the skin, airways, and mucous membrane tissues on exposure. The effects typically start within minutes of exposure and will continue as long as the person is exposed to the material. The degree of symptoms tends to worsen based on concentration and duration of exposure, with mild exposures having tearing, watery eyes, nasal discharge, and coughing. As the exposure increases, this can worsen to gagging and vomiting, increased skin and mucus membrane burning, and subjective tightness in the chest. These effects improve after removal of the exposure and gradually resolve over 30 to 60 minutes, but some symptoms, such as skin erythema, may last up to several hours. Tolerance to CS has been demonstrated from prolonged or repeated exposures (Bestwick, Holland, & Kemp, 1972; Punte, Owens, & Gutentag, 1963).

CS has direct irritating properties to the skin. After minutes of exposure, a burning sensation may be noted, particularly over moistened or freshly shaven areas. This may lead to erythema, which will typically resolve in one to two hours after exposure. However, if the exposure is with a high concentration of CS, under high temperature or humid environmental conditions, severe erythema along with edema and vesication can follow. The time course of the development of vesicles can be delayed up to several hours, but typically occur within the first hour or so. During riots in Washington, DC, in 1968, firefighters were often exposed to CS when they entered buildings in which the agent had been used. The movement of the firemen and use of water hoses re-aerosolized the material. These unintended exposures resulted in erythema and edema on the skin of a number of firefighters (Rengstorff & Mershon, 1969a). In workers with repeated exposure and sensitization to CS, acquired contact dermatitis has occurred, confirmed by skin testing. Symptoms ranged from simple erythema to large vesicles and bullae. No pulmonary symptoms were reported (Shmunes & Taylor, 1973).

Case Reports

A four-month-old infant who was exposed for two to three hours to CS tear gas canisters fired into a house required hospital admission for frequent suctioning of upper airway secretions. He was treated with steroids and antibiotics as well as positive pressure ventilation for respiratory distress and wheezing within the first 48 hours, and slowly improved until he developed a pulmonary infiltrate on x-ray. He required ventilatory support and ultimately was discharged home fully recovered after 28 days (Park & Giammona, 1972).

Nine marines involved with strenuous exercise and exposure to CS in a field training exercise developed a transient pulmonary syndrome, presenting with cough, shortness of breath, and hemoptysis and hypoxia in several of those exposed. Some required close monitoring and treatment for hypoxia, but all nine demonstrated normal lung function on spirometry, pre- and post-exercise within a week after the exposure (Thomas et al., 2002). Hu and Christiani (1992) reported a case of exposure in an asthmatic who developed semi-chronic symptoms of cough and shortness of breath for up to two years after the exposure. Her FEV1 (Forced Expiratory Volume in 1 second) at four weeks post-exposure was 62 percent of predicted, and her FVC (Forced Vital Capacity) was 78 percent. At one and a half years after exposure, her FEV1 was 128 percent of predicted, with a 16 percent drop with brisk exercise in cool air (Hu & Christiani, 1992). Given the description, it is difficult to determine if her subjective symptoms of dyspnea were related to her underlying chronic asthma rather than the CS exposure.

Research

While these reports suggest that exposure to CS could be lethal by potentially causing pulmonary damage, injury, and pulmonary edema, there have been no case reports of human deaths associated with CS use to date in the medical literature. Moreover, these reports indicate that pulmonary injury would only potentially happen at concentrations several hundred times greater than typical irritating or incapacitating doses (Himsworth, 1971).

Moreover, there is little evidence that CS results in any permanent lung damage even after several exposures to field concentrations (Blain, 2003). Bestwick et al. (1972) found no change in tidal volume, peak flow, or vital capacity compared to pre-exposure values when measured immediately and at 24 hours after exposure to CS in 36 subjects. In another study on human subjects, Punte et al. (1963) reported that individuals subjected to daily exposures to CS (1–13 mg/m^3) showed no changes from pre-exposure levels of airway resistances measured two-four minutes after CS exposure, as well as on days four and ten after exposure.

In terms of other types of injuries, human studies have been performed to assess the effects of CS on skin using different concentrations and assessing the effects of various ambient temperatures and humidity levels. Subjects' developed first and second degree burns at different levels and the authors concluded that many variables affect the likelihood of blistering, making risk assessment difficult to predict (Hellreich et al., 1967; Hellreich et al., 1969). Spraying 0.1 percent or 0.25 percent CS carried in different solutions into the eyes of humans caused inability to open the eyes for 10 to 135 seconds. Post-exposure evaluation utilizing slit lamp evaluation noted a transient conjunctivitis, but no corneal damage (Rengstorff & Mershon, 1969a, 1969b).

Oleoresin Capsicum (OC) Spray

History and Properties

Oleoresin capsicum (OC) sprays, also known as pepper sprays, are derived from the natural oily extract of pepper plants in the genus Capsicum. In the 1980s and 1990s, the use of OC spray by law enforcement agencies increased as the use of CS was on the decline. By the 1990s, the majority of states in the U.S. had legalized the use of OC spray by the public (Smith & Greaves, 2002).

Oleoresin capsicum is made up of a mixture of fat-soluble phenols called capsinoids. Capsaicin typically makes up to 80–90 percent of these capsinoids and acts both as a direct irritant to nerve endings as well as a stimulant for the release of peripheral neuropeptides. Other capsinoid analogues include nordihydrocapsaicin, nonivamide, dihydrocapsaicin, homocapsaicin, and homodihydrocapsaicin. Capsaicin and dihydrocapsaicin are the two capsaicinoids with the highest sensory values, which are typically expressed in Scoville Heat units. The heat units were derived from an expert taste panel in conjunction with the Scoville Organoleptic Test, first employed in 1912 (Haas et al., 1997).

The contents of different OC sprays vary depending on manufacturer and capsicum concentrations may range from 1 percent to 15 percent. Commercially available OC typically is about 1 percent in concentration. OC is not considered flammable. Delivery modes include liquid stream spray, aerosol spray, and powder delivered as a projectile. The hand-held stream or aerosol OC spray is delivered by a propellant at a distance of approximately five to 15 feet. Other methods include delivery as an OC powder-filled projectile ball (Pepperball®) that is fired from a specialized launcher with a target range of 0–30 feet. When it hits the target, either the individual or a nearby object, the projectile ball breaks open and the powder is dispersed.

Physiological effects

Biochemically, capsacinoids stimulate chemo-nociceptors in primary afferent nerve endings, resulting in immediate pain and burning sensation over exposed areas of the skin, ocular, nasal, and oropharyngeal tissues. In addition, they cause the release of peripheral neuropeptides, including substance P. Substance P is a neurotransmitter that is involved in neurogenic inflammation and can cause vasodilatation, capillary leakage of plasma fluids, and pain sensation (Sanico et al., 1997).

OC spray can cause direct irritation to the eyes, skin, and mucous membranes. Onset of symptoms is almost instantaneous, causing burning and lacrimation of the eyes, as well as blepharospasm ranging from involuntary blinking to sustained closure of the eyelids. Cutaneous symptoms may include tingling, flushing, and intense burning sensation of the skin, particularly over recently shaved or abraded areas. Mucous membrane exposure, particularly of the nasal passages, will induce irritation, congestion, and rhinorrhea. Some subjects have complained of nausea as well. Exposure of the airway and respiratory tract to aerosolized OC may cause tingling, coughing, gagging, and shortness of breath. Some reports of a transient laryngeal paralysis with associated temporary inability to speak have also been reported (Steffee et al., 1995).

Case Reports

As OC spray is commonly used by many law enforcement agencies as a less lethal weapon, there are case reports and case series of deaths and injuries following OC use (Granfield, Onnen, & Petty, 1994; O'Halloran & Frank, 2000; Pollanen et al., 1998; Steffee et al., 1995). Amnesty International claims that over 90 persons have died after exposure to pepper spray in the U.S. since the early 1990s (Amnesty International, 2004).

Despite these reports, however, a causal connection between OC exposure and death remains controversial. In the early 1990s, Granfield et al. (1994) reported 30 cases of in-custody death following OC exposure, in a majority of which drugs and underlying natural diseases were a significant factor. Pollanan et al. (1998) reported 21 in-custody restraint deaths, of which four had been sprayed with OC. O'Halloran and Frank (2000) reported 21 cases of restraint in-custody death, of which ten of the restraint episodes were preceded by use of OC spray.

In nearly all of these cases, OC was determined not to have been the cause of death. In only one case was OC implicated on autopsy. In that case, Steffee et al. (1995) reported that a person who had a history of asthma and was sprayed with OC spray 10–15 times suffered a sudden cardiorespiratory arrest. Autopsy revealed severe epithelial lung damage, with the cause of death noted to be severe bronchospasm, probably precipitated by the use of pepper spray (Steffee et al., 1995).

Billmire et al. (1996) reported a case in which a four-week-old healthy male infant was sprayed in the face with a 5 percent OC spray when a key chain self-defense canister accidentally discharged. The child had sudden onset of gasping respirations, epistaxis, apnea, and cyanosis. The child required mechanical ventilation and ultimately extracorporeal membrane oxygen (ECMO). The child was discharged home after a 13-day hospitalization (Billmire et al., 1996). An 11-year-old boy required intubation and ventilation four hours after exposure for severe croup that resulted from intentional inhalation of OC spray. He was extubated two days later and recovered without sequelae (Winograd, 1977).

Other non-life threatening injuries have also been reported with OC exposure. As OC is commonly directed toward the face, symptoms often involve the eyes. Corneal abrasions have been reported in up to 8.6 percent of cases by Watson, Stremel, and Westdorp (1996) and 7 percent by Brown, Takeuchi, and Challoner (2000). These findings have been noted as transient and do not require any additional treatment beyond decontamination with water irrigation (Vesaluoma et al., 2000).

Research

Because of its ability to block pain sensation and pruritis, presumably by depletion of substance P and other neurotransmitters, capsaicin has been studied in many different human clinical models, such as the treatment of various medical conditions like post-herpetic neuralgia, osteoarthritis, psoriasis, lichen simplex chronicus, diabetic neuropathy, and osteoarthritis. These capsaicin-related pharmacotherapies have typically been associated with topical application of the agent. Given its ability to induce coughing, capsaicin has also been utilized in many studies investigating the cough reflex and the pulmonary system, as well as to induce cough activity in order to assess the efficacy of various cough suppressants (Foster, Yeo, & Ramsay, 1991).

Some animal and in-vitro human tissue studies have suggested that capsaicin increases airway resistance and bronchoconstriction (Hansson et al., 1992; Lundberg, Martling, & Saria, 1983). However, clinical studies in humans with nebulized capsaicin are less definitive. Fuller reported that inhaled nebulized capsaicin resulted in a transient dose-dependent increase in airway resistance that was maximal at 20 seconds and lasted less than 60 seconds (Fuller, Dixon, & Barnes, 1985). Blanc et al. (1991) and Collier and Fuller (1984) reported no significant decrease in FEV1 in subjects who inhaled nebulized capsaicin at concentrations sufficient to induce cough. However, direct bronchoconstriction caused by capsaicin may be masked by cough and deep inhalation as both have bronchodilatory effects. In fact, sub-tussive doses of inhaled capsaicin have been shown to cause changes in airway resistance and pulmonary function (Fuller, 1987; Hathaway et al., 1993; Maxwell, Fuller, & Dixon, 1987).

Unlike capsaicin, there is only limited research on the human effects of OC spray (Ross & Siddle, 1996). A number of observational reports have been published assessing safety of OC spray use. A two-year joint study by the FBI and U.S. Army reported that OC spray was not associated with any long-term health risks (Onnen, 1993).

Chan et al. (2002) conducted a randomized, cross-over controlled trial in 35 volunteer human subjects who were exposed to either OC spray or placebo propellant without OC, followed by a ten-minute period of being placed in either the sitting or prone maximal restraint position. Pulmonary function testing was performed and arterial blood gases monitored during this time. OC exposure did not result in abnormal pulmonary dysfunction, hypoxemia, or hypoventilation when compared to placebo in either the sitting or restraint positions. However, there was an increase in mean heart rate and blood pressure in subjects exposed to OC that did not occur in the placebo group. The investigators concluded that OC spray did not result in any evidence of respiratory compromise with and without restraint that would make OC inherently lethal. The changes in cardiovascular parameters, however, indicated the need for additional study (Chan et al., 2002).

Beyond research in the clinical laboratory setting, OC use has been widespread and a number of epidemiologic studies have been reported on its use and safety. The California State Attorney General reported that no fatal consequences occurred in over 23,000 exposures to OC spray (Lundgren, 1996). Watson et al. (1996) reviewed 908 exposures to OC spray in their region and found less than 10 percent of subjects exposed required any medical attention. Additionally, less than 1 percent complained of respiratory symptoms which required medical attention, and none of these were determined to have any significant injuries. There were no deaths reported in either of these studies. Yeung and Tang (2015) found in a review paper that dermatological injury was reported and ranged from acute burning pain, tingling, erythema, edema, and itching, that may persist for several hours to blister formation if prolonged contact.

Overall, OC spray has been used hundreds of thousands of times with no long-term health effects reported. Although there are case reports of death following the use of OC spray, other causes, such as drug intoxication, excited delirium, or underlying medical conditions, have been implicated as the primary cause of death, rather than the OC exposure, in the large majority of these cases. Moreover, clinical and epidemiologic studies on OC have yet to report any compelling evidence that OC is inherently dangerous or lethal when used as directed.

CASE ONE

A 44-year-old male was stopped by police after driving erratically on the highway. During the ensuing encounter, he began to resist arrest, and, in the process, he was sprayed with OC spray to the face. As the struggle ensued, he began to cough, wheeze, and officers noted he broke out in a rash. On arrival of EMS, he was noted to be tachycardic (elevated heart rate), wheezing, and had hives on his body. He had conjunctival injection (red eyes). He complained of shortness of breath. On further review, he had a history of asthma. Treatment with bronchodilators was initiated, and he was transported to the hospital. En route, his breathing became more labored and he went in to respiratory arrest. Resuscitative efforts were unsuccessful.

Comments

It is important in this case to know that he had a history of asthma. While OC and other inhaled agents can cause mild bronchospasm, rarely is it fatal. In this case, the key here was noting that not only did he have some signs of an allergic reaction like hives, but he also had a history of asthma that was likely set off by the inhalation of the OC spray. Other facts that would be critical to an investigation would be the reported lung compliance by the medics (how hard it was to squeeze air into his lungs). If the lungs were easily bagged, and there was minimal wheezing, then the OC spray is unlikely to be the cause of death. If, on the other hand, poor compliance and wheezing were noted, it is possible that the OC caused an acute allergic asthma reaction and thus may have been a contributing factor in the death.

Blunt Projectiles

History and Mechanics

Blunt projectiles were first used during the Hong Kong Riots of the 1950s and 1960s. Initial projectiles were made of wood. Similar devices were also used during the Northern Ireland conflict and Israeli-Palestinian conflicts of the 1970s and 1980s. Early devices included hard rubber missile-shaped projectiles that were so inaccurate that hits to the head, face, and chest could not be avoided. Later versions evolved into PVC-type bullets, modern-day blunt rubber bullets, and beanbag type rounds, which are currently in use by various law enforcement agencies in the United States. While the specifics of each type of projectile are beyond the scope of this chapter, they in general all involve a blunt type projectile that can impart energies on the order of 100–200 Joules depending on the type of round and the distance from firing at impact.

Physiologic Effects

Blunt projectiles are used as an alternative to regular firearms when trying to disperse a crowd from a distance or when trying to subdue a combative, dangerous individual without the use of lethal force. The action of the blunt projectile is to induce pain, irritation, and often minimal injury to the subject without causing any life-threatening injuries that occur with the use of actual lethal force, such as firearms. The physiologic effects of blunt projectiles are directly related to anatomic location where the blunt projectile strikes the subject and induces blunt force trauma to the individual.

Case Reports and Research

The association of blunt projectiles and severe injuries mainly stems from risk of a direct blow to the chest, inducing a cardiac dysrhythmia such as VF. This problem has a clinical name—commotio cordis—which is a rare, but reported syndrome in which apparently young healthy individuals suddenly suffer cardiac arrest after blunt chest trauma, usually related to a sports activity such as baseball, hockey, lacrosse, and softball. Commotio cordis is characterized by a sudden disturbance of cardiac rhythm in the absence of demonstrable signs of significant mechanical injury to the heart that is induced by a direct blow to the chest. This is separate from direct injury to the heart leading to myocardial contusion, valvular disruption, or pericardial effusion. Through animal studies, researchers found that impacts that were reliably timed to that part of the cardiac cycle that occurred between 15 and 30 milliseconds preceding the peak of the electrocardiographic T wave were able to induce an irregular heartbeat known as ventricular fibrillation (VF) consistently. There is still debate, however, as to the precise pathophysiologic mechanisms at work (Zangwill & Strasburger, 2004).

CASE TWO

A 40-year-old woman was waving a knife and threatening neighbors. Police were summoned to the scene, and attempts at verbal de-escalation were unsuccessful. The subject was shot in the left chest with a beanbag round. She immediately fell to the ground and was unresponsive. Police attempted to stimulate the patient but were unable to arouse her. EMS was already staged at the scene, and found her to have a strong odor of alcohol, and to be in cardiac arrest. They began cardiac resuscitation and found her heart to be in ventricular fibrillation and ultimately resuscitation attempts were unsuccessful. On post mortem, she was found to have left sided parasternal rib fractures, as well as underlying lung and pericardial contusions. The remainder of the exam was normal. The cause of death was surmised to be from commotio cordis due to blunt chest trauma.

Comments

While this subject did sustain several injuries that were of significance, i.e., rib fractures, lung contusions, pericardial contusion, none of these were sufficient to cause an immediate collapse and loss of responsiveness. In this case of sudden cardiac arrest, some other etiology must be sought. It is certainly possible that she had a cardiac event such as heart attack, but in the absence of findings on autopsy to support this, along with the timing of the presentation, one is left with the likely cause of commotio cordis—trauma-induced ventricular fibrillation.

The energies involved in the use of less lethal projectiles are on the order of the same energies that are involved in some of the aforementioned sporting events. Therefore, one could speculate that these devices would have the same risk of causing VF. As of the date of this publication, there have been no direct cases described of commotio cordis from flexible baton or beanbag rounds.

One specific case report of a death following use of the devices was published in 1998. A 61-year-old woman was facing police in a threatening manner, brandishing a butcher knife. After two unsuccessful deployments of a stun gun, she was subsequently shot in the chest using a plastic bullet (AR-1 baton round). She stumbled back and collapsed. She had labored breathing and subsequently suffered cardiac arrest. Autopsy showed she had sustained multiple rib fractures to the left chest, an underlying lung laceration, and heart lacerations that led to significant bleeding into the chest cavity. A toxicology screen was negative. The cause of death was certified as "blunt force injuries of chest due to plastic bullet wound" (Chute & Smialek, 1998).

A severe injury from a Flash Ball® projectile was reported in 2015 (Hiquet & Gromb-Monnoyeur, 2015). A healthy 34-year-old male victim of a Flash-Ball® was shot during a riot following a sports event. The man sustained serious craniocerebral injuries with a left temporal fracture, moderate cerebral edema, fronto-temporal hemorrhagic brain contusion along with an extra-dural hematoma, and subarachnoid hemorrhage. His injuries required significant neurological and rehabilitation care for two months, leaving him with significant neurological deficits.

Several studies have examined the injury patterns from the use of plastic and rubber bullets. Their conclusions all tend to show that while generally regarded as less lethal weapons, significant injuries including death can occur when the weapons strike the chest, abdomen, or head. Millar et al. (1975) reviewed 90 patients who had sustained injuries to various parts of their bodies, concluding that the eyes, face, skull, bones, and brain are at greatest risk of injury from rubber bullets. The distance at which the rubber bullets resulted in serious injury ranged from 17 to 25 meters (Millar et al., 1975). Additionally, the French, who have experience using the stinger grenade®, a device in widespread use, reported several significant injuries from the device, including facial lacerations, eye injury, and large bruises (Scolan et al., 2012).

Another study noted that of 80 subjects injured by rubber bullets, four died, three from ventricular dysrhythmias secondary to cardiac contusion and one from a hemopneumothorax (blood and air collapsing the lung in the chest cavity). Ritchie and Gibbons (1990) evaluated 19 patients who required hospitalization and had serious chest wounds. They postulated a mechanism of injury involving shock waves producing shearing stresses and compression to soft tissue and bony structures, resulting in contusions and fractures. Based on their finding, they state that any injury to the chest from one of these devices should be regarded as serious, requiring close observation (Ritchie & Gibbons, 1990).

Suyama et al. (2003) evaluated a series of cases that arose from a period of civil unrest in Cincinnati in 2001. The officers involved used two types of beanbag rounds, and one type of foam projectile. They reported that significant morbidity was found in seven (28 percent) cases with no fatalities; three (12 percent) individuals, with the diagnoses of pulmonary contusion, liver laceration, and Achilles tendon rupture, required admission; while two (8 percent) individuals had delayed complications of pneumonia and post-concussive syndrome (Suyama et al., 2003).

De Freminville et al. (2011) performed a study on human cadavers to try to establish the type of wounds causes by hybrid less lethal projectiles, using a cadaveric forensic flap-by-flap procedure. They examined what force was required to fracture bones in various parts of the body as a function of velocity of the projectile, using a Heckler & Koch (H&K) 69 rifled-bore Handgun Launcher. They found no significant correlation between degree of skin injury and likelihood of fracture, but were able to establish velocities needed to fracture bones. This correlated with the distance between the subject and the projectile at the point of fire, but had many variables including temperature and angle. However, they concluded that it is difficult to establish distance range from the shooter when evaluating lesions in the cadaver (de Freminville et al., 2011; 2010).

Kobayashi and Mellen (2009) described the difficulty that forensic pathologists face when evaluating subjects on whom these less lethal devices are used. A recognized possible challenge is that interpretation of the rubber bullet injuries is unfamiliar to the majority of forensic pathologists. Some injuries during riot, such as a fatal injury caused by either a rubber bullet shot by a law enforcement personnel or a stone thrown by riot crowds, can be difficult to differentiate and interpret and also socially problematic with an increased chance for public scrutiny. It is crucial for forensic pathologists to be aware of the variation of rubber bullet injuries and understand the relation between the types of rubber bullets and injuries they produce.

De Brito et al. (2001) examined 39 men and one woman between the ages of 16 and 77 who were shot by officers of either the Los Angeles Police Department or the Los Angeles Sheriff's Department. There was one fatality cause by massive hemothorax (bleeding into the lung cavity) after thoracic penetration of the beanbag. The locations of serious penetrating injuries included the thoracic cavity, eye, abdomen, arm, and leg. Blunt injuries included splenic rupture, pneumothorax, compartment syndrome, testicular fracture, subcapsular liver hematoma, and cardiac contusion. Complications included hemothorax, pneumopericardium (air around the heart), wound infection, compartment syndrome, and osteomyelitis. The majority of the subjects involved had psychiatric diagnoses. All but one had toxicology screenings performed, of which 29 (74.4 percent) were positive. Of those 29 positive results, 15 (51.7 percent) were positive for alcohol and eight (27.6 percent) were positive for cocaine.

Patel, Toohey, and Boysen-Osborn (2014) reported a case of a splenic laceration in a schizophrenic who was shot by police using a beanbag round (type unspecified and no range data provided). Additionally, Thakur et al. (2013) reported a penetrating chest injury from a beanbag round.

CASE THREE

A 26-year-old male with schizophrenia presented to the emergency department after being shot by law enforcement with two beanbag rounds. He was shot once in the upper abdomen. He reportedly turned and was shot again in the left flank; both shots were at an estimated distance of 15 feet. On arrival, the patient's blood pressure was 90/60 and heart rate was 130 beats per minute. The patient was agitated and given 5 mg intramuscular (IM) haloperidol, and 2 mg intravenous lorazepam. The patient's chest and back exam revealed a 2.0 cm abrasion and contusion to the left flank. His lung examination was normal. His abdomen was thin, soft, and non-tender. He had another 2.0 cm circular abrasion to the upper abdomen just below the sternum. Initial hemoglobin was 13.4 g/dL. A Focused Assessment with Sonography for Trauma (FAST ultrasound) examination demonstrated free fluid in the abdominal cavity. Computed tomography of the abdomen and pelvis with intravenous contrast revealed the following:

moderately displaced fractures of the left 11th and 12th ribs, a grade 3 splenic laceration with moderate perisplenic hematoma, and anterior abdominal wall/ rectus sheath hematoma. The patient was treated conservatively and after several days of observation in the hospital, was transferred to the local county jail.

Comments

In this case, it is important to note where exactly the beanbags hit and what brand they were. Also, what was the distance from the muzzle to the subject, as kinetic energy drops off rapidly with distance. Also important to note are other signs of trauma that may have caused the injuries instead of the beanbag rounds. Significant life-threatening injuries can occur from these projectiles causing intra-abdominal bleeding.

Investigator Key Components and Investigation Impact

Riot Control Agents and OC Sprays

For the riot control agents and OC sprays, the circumstances surrounding the exposure are critical. Was the exposure in a closed space such as a room or in the open? A closed space exposure potentially allows for a higher concentration to cause adverse events. Was there reported shortness of breath or wheezing on the part of the subject? Was the subject gasping? This would support some degree of respiratory compromise.

As for ocular complaints, was the exposure directly to the eyes and did the subject complain of burning and tearing, and blurring of vision? Did investigators note eye redness? Given that these agents can cause corneal anesthesia, was the subject placed face down in the dirt, and did dirt get in the eyes, which perhaps was not felt by the subject because of the anesthesia?

Nature of the exposure is important to ascertain—intentional or accidental; concurrent disease and health of the victim; varying distances from spray; environmental conditions; and crowd size. Were glasses or goggles used to protect the eyes?

Blunt Projectiles

The type of firing device and projectile size needs to be determined. Additionally, the distance from muzzle to subject allows one to assess the degree of kinetic energy that possibly struck the subject. All locations of impact on the body need to be noted. Photographs should be taken of all impact sites. If there is a reported loss of consciousness, duration, and circumstances should be noted. Any strike to the chest followed by an immediate loss of consciousness should raise concern for a commotio cordis type event. Results of any imaging tests are important, as internal injury caused by the device, though rare, must be documented. Interestingly, as noted in the de Freminville et al. (2011) report, there was no correlation between soft and bone tissue observed lesions and impact velocity (correlated to distance range). So while photos and injury need to be noted, conclusions can be difficult to draw and every area struck by the projectile should be fully evaluated.

Summary

Riot control agents and less lethal weapons are criticized by some as inhumane and may be associated with significant injury or death. However, these agents hold an important role in the escalation of force continuum to maintain safety for law enforcement officers, while offering the ability to incapacitate and mitigate at-risk individuals. These agents and weapons have saved countless lives by enabling law enforcement to avoid the need to use deadly force, and although not truly "non-lethal," these less lethal agents have an overall excellent safety profile. Investigations into deaths involving the use of these tools should be straightforward and guided by the physical nature of the injuries.

Investigator Checklist

Sprays

Scene

- ☐ Type of spray, brand, dispersement method
- ☐ Concentration of material
- ☐ Distance from source
- ☐ Subject medical conditions
- ☐ Illicit substance use
- ☐ Areas of contact by the agent
- ☐ Nature of contact (crowd, closed space, sprayed from bottle)
- ☐ Patient physiologic response
- ☐ Patient verbal complaints
- ☐ Type of decontamination

EMS or hospital information

- ☐ Initial cardiac rhythm
- ☐ Lung sounds
- ☐ Oxygenation saturation levels
- ☐ Vital signs
- ☐ Lung compliance (how hard is it to ventilate?)
- ☐ Was there a rash

On Autopsy

- ☐ Injuries and evidence of hemorrhage or other causes of death
- ☐ Condition of the lungs, evidence of bronchospasm, hemorrhage, pulmonary edema
- ☐ Skin condition—burns, blisters
- ☐ Eyes—corneal abrasions, edema

Projectiles

Scene

- ☐ Exact projectile used
- ☐ Distance from muzzle or grenade to subject if possible to ascertain
- ☐ Location of injuries on the body
- ☐ Comorbid medical conditions and medications such as stimulants or blood thinners
- ☐ Use of illicit substances
- ☐ Other potential projectiles that might cause impact
- ☐ Was there a fall secondary to the impact?

EMS or hospital information

- ☐ Initial cardiac rhythm
- ☐ Oxygenation saturation levels
- ☐ Vital signs
- ☐ Lung compliance (how hard is it to ventilate?)
- ☐ All radiographic studies performed
- ☐ Location of injuries

References

Amnesty International. (2004). Retrieved from www.amnestyusa.org/node/55449?page=72.

Bestwick, F. W., Holland. P., & Kemp, K. H. (1972). Acute effects of exposure to ortho-chlorobenzylidene malononitrile (CS) and the development of tolerance. *British Journal of Industrial Medicine, 29*(3), 298–306.

Billmire, D. F., Vinocur, C., Ginda, M., Robinson, N. B., Panitch, H., Friss, H., … Wiley, J. F. (1996). Pepper-spray-induced respiratory failure treated with extracorporeal membrane oxygenation. *Pediatrics, 98*(5), 961–963.

Blain, P. G. (2003). Tear gases and irritant incapacitants: 1-chloroacetophenone, 2-chlorobenzylidene malononitrile and dibenz[b,f]-1,4-oxazepine. *Toxicological Reviews, 22*(2), 103–110.

Blanc, P., Liu, D., Juarez, C., & Boushey, H. A. (1991). Cough in hot pepper workers. *Chest, 99*(1), 27–32.

Brown, L., Takeuchi, D., & Challoner, K. (2000). Corneal abrasions associated with pepper spray exposure. *American Journal of Emergency Medicine, 18*(3), 271–272.

Chan, T. C., Vilke, G. M., Clausen, J., Clark, R. F., Schmidt, P., Snowden, T., & Neuman, T. (2002). The effect of oleoresin capsicum "pepper spray" inhalation on respiratory function. *Journal of Forensic Sciences, 47*(2), 299–304.

Chapman, A. J. & White, C. (1978). Death resulting from lacrimatory agents. *Journal of Forensic Sciences, 23*(3), 527–530.

Chute, D. J. & Smialek, J. E. (1998). Injury patterns in a plastic (AR-1) baton fatality. *American Journal of Forensic Medicine and Pathology, 19*(3), 226–229.

Collier, J. G. & Fuller, R. W. (1984). Capsaicin inhalation in man and the effects of sodium cromoglycate. *British Journal of Pharmacology, 81*(1), 113–117.

Danto, B. L. (1987). Medical problems and criteria regarding the use of tear gas by police. *American Journal of Forensic Medicine and Pathology, 8*(4), 317–322.

de Brito, D., Challoner, K. R., Sehgal, A., & Mallon, W. (2001). The injury pattern of a new law enforcement weapon: The police bean bag. *Annals of Emergency Medicine, 38*(4), 383–390.

de Freminville, H., Prat, N., Rongieras, F., & Voiglio, E. J. (2010). Less-lethal hybrid ammunition wounds: A forensic assessment introducing bullet-skin-bone entity. *Journal of Forensic Sciences, 55*(5), 1367–1370.

de Freminville, H., Rongieras, F., Prat, N., & Voiglio, E. J. (2011). The flap by flap dissection in terminal ballistic applied to less lethal weapons. *American Journal of Forensic Medicine and Pathology, 32*(2), 149–152.

Foster, G., Yeo, W. W., & Ramsay, L. E. (1991). Effect of sulindac on the cough reflex of healthy subjects. *British Journal of Clinical Pharmacology, 31*(2), 207–208.

Fuller, R. W. (1987). Pharmacology of inhaled capsaicin in humans. *Respiratory Medicine, 85*(supp. A), 31–34.

Fuller, R. W., Dixon, C. M. S., & Barnes, P. J. (1985). Bronchoconstrictor response to inhaled capsaicin in humans. *Journal of Applied Physiology, 58*(4), 1080–1084.

Granfield, J., Onnen, J., & Petty, C. S. (1994). Pepper spray and in-custody deaths. *International Association of Chiefs of Police Executive Brief.*

Haas, J. E., Whipple, R. E., Grant, P. M., Andresen, B. D., Volpe, A. M., & Pelkey, G. E. (1997). Chemical and elemental comparison of two formulations of oleoresin capsicum. *Science and Justice, 37*(1), 15–24.

Hansson, L., Wollmer, P., Dahlback, M., & Karlsson, J. A. (1992). Regional sensitivity of human airways to capsaicin-induced cough. *American Review of Respiratory Disease, 145*(5), 1191–1195.

Hathaway, T. J., Higenbottam, T. W., Morrison, J. F. J., Clelland, C. A., & Wallwork, J. (1993). Effects of inhaled capsaicin in heart-lung transplant patients and asthmatic subjects. *American Review of Respiratory Disease, 148*(5), 1233–1237.

Hellreich, A., Goldman, R. H., Bottiglieri, N. G., & Weimer, J. T. (1967). *The effects of thermally-generated CS aerosols on human skin (Technical report 4075).* Edgewood Arsenal, MD: Medical Research Laboratories.

Hellreich, A., Mershon, M. M., Weimer, J. T., Kysor, K. P., & Bottiglieri, N. G. (1969). *An evaluation of the irritant potential of CS aerosols on human skin under tropical climatic conditions (Technical report 4252).* Edgewood Arsenal, MD: Medical Research Laboratories.

Himsworth, H. (1971). *Report of the enquiry into the medical and toxicological aspect of CS (ortho-chlorobenzylidene malononitrile) II: Enquiry into toxicological aspects of CS and its use for civil purposes.* London: HM Stationery Office.

Hiquet, J. & Gromb-Monnoyeur, S. (2015). Severe craniocerebral trauma with sequelae caused by Flash-Ball® shot, a less-lethal weapon: Report of one case and review of the literature. *Medicine, Science and the Law, 55*(3), ii.

Holland, P. & White, R. G. (1972). The cutaneous reactions produced by o-chlorobenzylidene malononitrile and 1-chloroacetophenone when applied directly to the skin of human subjects. *British Journal of Dermatology, 86*(2), 150–154.

Hu, H. & Christiani, D. (1992). Reactive airways dysfunction after exposure to teargas. *The Lancet, 339*(8808), 1535.

Kobayashi, M. & Mellen, P. F. (2009). Rubber bullet injury: Case report with autopsy observation and literature review. *American Journal of Forensic Medicine and Pathology, 30*(3), 262–267.

Levine, R. A. & Stahl, C. J. (1968). Eye injury caused by tear gas weapons. *American Journal of Ophthalmology, 65*(4), 497–508.

Lundberg, J. M., Martling, C. R., & Saria, A. (1983). Substance P and capsaicin-induced contraction of human bronchi. *Acta Physiologica Scandinavica, 119*(1), 49–53.

Lundgren, D. E. (1996). Oleoresin capsicum (OC) usage reports: Summary information. *Report of the California State Attorney General.*

MacDonald, J. M., Kaminski, R. J., & Smith, M. R. (2009). The effect of less-lethal weapons on injuries in police use-of-force events. *American Journal of Public Health, 99*(12), 2268–2274.

Madden, J. F. (1951). Cutaneous hypersensitivity to tear gas (chloroacetophenone). *AMA Archives of Dermatology and Syphilology, 63*(1), 133–134.

Maxwell, D. L., Fuller, R. W., & Dixon, C. M. S. (1987). Ventilatory effects of inhaled capsaicin in man. *European Journal of Clinical Pharmacology, 31*(6), 715–717.

McNamara, B. P., Vocci, F. J., & Owens, E. J. (1968). *The toxicology of CN. (Technical report 4207).* Edgewood Arsenal, MD: Medical Research Laboratories.

Millar, R., Rutherford, W. H., Jonston, S., & Malhotra, V. J. (1975). Injuries caused by rubber bullets: A report on 90 patients. *British Journal of Surgery, 62*(6), 480–486.

O'Halloran, R. L. & Frank, J. G. (2000). Asphyxial death during prone restraint revisited: A report of 21 cases. *American Journal of Forensic Medicine and Pathology, 21*(1), 39–52.

Onnen, J. (1993). Oleoresin capsicum. *International Association of Chiefs of Police Executive Brief.*

Park, S. & Giammona, S. T. (1972). Toxic effects of tear gas on an infant following prolonged exposure. *American Journal of Diseases of Children, 123*(3), 245–246.

Patel, A., Toohey, S., & Boysen-Osborn, M. (2014). Splenic laceration and pulmonary contusion injury from bean bag weapon. *Western Journal of Emergency Medicine, 15*(2), 118–119.

Payne-James, J. J., Rivers, E., Green, P., & Johnston, A. (2014). Trends in less-lethal use of force techniques by police services within England and Wales: 2007–2011. *Forensic Science and Medical Pathology, 10*(1), 50–55.

Pollanen, M. S., Chaisson, D. A., Cairns, J. T., & Young, J. G. (1998). Unexpected death related to restraint for excited delirium: A retrospective study of deaths in police custody and in the community. *Canadian Medical Association Journal, 158*(12), 1603–1607.

Punte, C. L., Owens, E. J., & Gutentag, P. J. (1963). Exposures to ortho-chlorobenzylidene malononitrile. *Archives of Environmental Health: An International Journal, 6*(1), 72–80.

Queen, F. B. & Standler, T. (1941). Allergic dermatitis following exposure to tear gas (chloroacetophenone). *Journal of the American Medical Association, 117*(22), 1879.

Rengstorff, R. H. & Mershon, M. M. (1969a). *CS in trioctyl phosphate: Effects on human eyes (Technical report 4376).* Edgewood Arsenal, MD: Medical Research Laboratories.

Rengstorff, R. H. & Mershon, M. M. (1969b). *CS in water: Effects on human eyes (Technical report 4377).* Edgewood Arsenal, MD: Medical Research Laboratories.

Ritchie, A. J. & Gibbons, J. R. P. (1990). Life threatening injuries to the chest caused by plastic bullets. *British Medical Journal, 301,* 1027.

Ross, D. & Siddle, B. (1996). Use of force policies and training recommendations: Based on the medical implications of oleoresin capsicum. *PPCT Research Review, 4,* 1–9.

Sanico, A. M., Atsuta, S., Proud, D., & Togiaas, A. (1997). Dose-dependent effects of capsaicin nasal challenge: In vivo evidence of human airway neurogenic inflammation. *Journal of Allergy and Clinical Immunology, 100*(5), 632–641.

Scolan, V., Herry, C., Carreta, M., Stahl, C., Barret, L., Romanet, J. P., & Paysant, F. (2012). Risks of non-lethal weapon use: Case studies of three French victims of stingergrenades. *Forensic Science International, 223*(1–3), e18–21.

Shmunes, E. & Taylor, J. S. (1973). Industrial contact dermatitis: Effects of the riot control agent ortho-chlorobenzylidene malononitrile. *Archives of Dermatology, 107*(2), 212–216.

Smith, J. & Greaves, I. (2002). The use of chemical incapacitant sprays: A review. *Journal of Trauma, 52*(3), 595–600.

Steffee, C. H., Lantz, P. E., Flannagan, L. M., Thompson, R. L., & Jason, D. R. (1995). Oleoresin capsicum (pepper) spray and "in-custody deaths." *American Journal of Forensic Medicine and Pathology, 16*(3), 185–192.

Suyama, J., Panagos, P. D., Sztajnkrycer, M. D., FitzGerald, D. J., & Barnes, D. (2003). Injury patterns related to use of less-lethal weapons during a period of civil unrest. *Journal of Emergency Medicine, 25*(2), 219–227.

Thakur, S., Teloken, P. E., Gilfillan, I., & Sharma, S. (2013). Non-lethal? Penetrating chest injury due to beanbag bullet. *BMJ Case Reports,* doi: 10.1136/bcr-2012-008482.

Thomas, R. J., Smith, P. A., Rascona, D. A., Louthan, J. D., & Gumpert, B. (2002). Acute pulmonary effects from o-chlorobenzylidenemalonitrile "tear gas": A unique exposure outcome unmasked by strenuous exercise after a military training event. *Military Medicine*, *167*, 136–139.

Thorburn, K. M. (1982). Injuries after use of the lacrimatory agent chloroacetophenone in a confined space. *Archives of Environmental Health: An International Journal*, 37(3), 182–186.

Vesaluoma, M., Muller, L., Gallar, J., Lambiase, A., Moilanen, J., Hack, T., ... Tervo, T. (2000). Effects of oleoresin capsicum pepper spray on human corneal morphology and sensitivity. *Investigative Ophthalmology & Visual Science*, *41*(8), 2138–2147.

Watson, W. A., Stremel, K. R., & Westdorp, E. J. (1996). Oleoresin capsicum (Cap-Stun) toxicity from aerosol exposure. *Annals of Pharmacotherapy*, *30*(7–8), 733–735.

Winograd, H. L. (1977). Acute croup in an older child: An unusual toxin origin. *Clinical Pediatrics*, *16*(10), 884–887.

Yeung, M. F. & Tang, W. Y. M. (2015). Clinicopathological effects of pepper (oleoresin capsicum) spray. *Hong Kong Medical Journal*, *21*, 542–552.

Zangwill, S. D. & Strasburger, J. F. (2004). Commotio cordis. *Pediatric Clinics*, *51*(5), 1347–1354.

13

TASER—CONDUCTED ELECTRICAL WEAPONS

Mark W. Kroll and Michael A. Brave

Introduction

The mass media and legal system possess and promulgate deep misunderstandings of the basic concepts, operation, and effects of the modern Conducted Electrical Weapon (CEW). Many of these misunderstandings emanate from electrophobia (an unreasonable fear of electricity) and a lack of appreciation of the small amount of current a CEW actually delivers to a subject. Just as recreational and industrial balls vary in mass (e.g. ping-pong ball, baseball, bowling ball, and wrecking ball), so do electrical shocks. Even physicians will often equate a lightning strike or a high-voltage powerline exposure to a CEW application, which is analogous to comparing an iron-wrecking ball to a ping-pong ball.

CEW benefits are well established in the peer-reviewed literature and explain why these weapons are so widely adopted throughout the industrialized world (107 countries). With the use of CEWs, injury rates are reduced by approximately two-thirds. In other words, the use of alternative force options, including hands-on or physical force, tends to triple (3x) the injury rate compared to the CEW (Bovbjerg et al., 2007; Bozeman et al., 2009; Haileyesus, Annest, & Mercy, 2011; Ho, Clinton et al., 2010; Jenkinson, Neeson, & Bleetman, 2006; MacDonald, Kaminski, & Smith, 2009; Mesloh, Henych, & Wolf, 2008; Vilke, Bozeman, & Chan, 2011; Strote, Verzemnieks et al., 2010; Taylor et al., 2009). The number of law enforcement uses of lethal force prevented has been estimated at over 165,000 based on the 3.05 plus million field uses at more than 18,000 agencies (Brewer & Kroll, 2009; Eastman et al., 2008). In agencies using the CEW with minimal restrictions, the *fatal* officer-involved shooting rate falls by approximately two-thirds (Ferdik et al., 2014).

The primary demonstrated and theoretical lethal risks supported by the existing literature are outlined in Table 13.1.

TABLE 13.1 Primary literature-supported lethal risks from electronic control

	Probe mode	*Drive-stun*	*Notes*
Fatal injury from uncontrolled fall	Fatalities demonstrated (Fox & Payne-James, 2012: Kroll et al., 2016). Non-fatal injuries demonstrated (Haileyesus et al., 2011; Mangus et al., 2008).	Unlikely. Has not been reported in the literature.	These fatalities almost always represent a head injury; a theoretical exception is a cardiac blunt trauma injury.
Fume ignition	Fatalities demonstrated (Clarke & Andrews, 2014; Kroll, 2011).	Unlikely. Has not been reported (Kroll, 2011).	
Electrocution	Theoretical possibility with probe directly over heart in subjects under 46 lbs. (Kroll et al., 2014a). In general, the electrocution risk in adults is an urban legend (Council of Canadian Academies & Canadian Academy of Health Sciences, 2013; Kroll et al., 2014a). Theoretical VF risk estimated at less than 1 in 2.5–2.9 million cases, consistent with epidemiological CEW experience (Kroll et al., 2011; Panescu, Kroll, & Brave, 2015).	Essentially impossible. Even swine are not electrocuted with a drive-stun (Lakkireddy et al., 2008; Valentino, Walter, Dennis, Nagy et al., 2008; Valentino, Walter, Dennis, et al., 2007; Valentino, Walter, Nagy et al., 2007).	Present CEWs satisfy all world electrical safety standards including those for the electric fence (Nimunkar & Webster, 2009; Panescu, Nerheim, & Kroll, 2013).

The most common contribution to a CEW-temporal fatality is a secondary injury from a fall from height or a head impact from an uncontrolled fall, often with momentum. If the subject is running or is above a hard surface and receives a probe deployment to the back, the unbroken fall can cause a serious head injury—there have been 16 such deaths (Fox & Payne-James, 2012; Kroll et al., 2016). The most severe head injuries are usually to the back of the head, rather than the forehead. This has not been reported as an issue with the drive-stun application mode as there is no CEW-induced muscle lock-up. (Note that head injuries are probably more common with other control options (Cox, Buchholz, & Wolf, 1987).)

There have been a handful of secondary injury fatalities in which flammable fumes were ignited, possibly by an electrical spark from the CEW (Clarke & Andrews, 2014). In some reported cases, the often-suicidal subject appears to have ignited the fuel with a cigarette lighter before the CEW probes were deployed. However, there are at least three cases where it is clear that the CEW ignited the flammable fumes. This has not been reported with drive-stuns, although that remains a very unlikely theoretical possibility.

The most misunderstood and exaggerated theoretical risk is that of electrocution or the electrical induction of VF (ventricular fibrillation). This is extremely unlikely as the output of existing CEWs satisfies all relevant world electrical safety standards, including those for the ubiquitous electric fence (Nimunkar & Webster, 2009; Panescu et al., 2013).

Fatal Fall Injury

By the end of 2015, there were almost 20 cases of fatal fall injuries with CEW involvement with 17 causal (Kroll et al., 2014b), while there were 16 probable cases of fatal brain injuries (Kroll et al., 2016). Out of three million field uses, this gives a risk of 5.3 ± 2.6 PPM, which is higher than the theoretical risk of electrocution. The mean age was 46 ± 14 years, which is significantly greater than the age of the typical arrest-related death (ARD) (36 ± 10). There is also a single case of a fatal neck injury due to a fall caused by electronic control.

An illustrative example of a fatal brain injury is the case of Mr. James Sizer (Austin, TX, 2015). Police received a call from the elderly man who reported a family disturbance. He told dispatchers that he had a gun and had already fired three rounds. When officers arrived, they confronted the man, who refused to comply with their orders to get on the ground. An officer deployed a CEW into the man's back, causing him to hit the back of his head when he fell to the concrete driveway. He was treated and released from a hospital for the laceration to his head. However, he died eight days later from complications of injuries sustained in the fall. According to litigation filings, the autopsy found the cause of death to be "blunt force head trauma."

The single case of a fatal neck injury was Mr. Estyl Hall (age 68) who was involved in a disturbance with his landlord. When police arrived, the man had locked himself in a trailer and refused to come out. Believing he was armed, officers cut into the trailer. One officer deployed a CEW at the man, hitting him in the face and causing the man to fall and injure his neck. An ambulance transported him to a hospital where he died from complications of his injuries seven days later. Media reported that the autopsy found the cause of death to be "spinal cord injury due to cervical spine fractures due to blunt face and neck injury."

Not all of the CEW-involved fatal arrest-related falls have been due to a head injury. Nor have all of the falls been caused by the CEW. For example, Mr. Curtis Sloan (Bloomington, IL, 2006), fell on his left chest and broke several ribs. One of the broken ribs cut into the left ventricle of his heart. However, the CEW was only relevant in that it was blocked by clothing and failed to stop Mr. Sloan from running from arrest. The officer then ran after and tackled Mr. Sloan, with both falling over a low chain-link fence, with the officer landing on top of him.

There are many cases where the CEW fall did not contribute to the fatal head injury. Mr. Carlos Claros-Castro (Chapel Hill, NC, 2006) was a 28-year-old who, while in custody, was involved in an altercation with jailers. Multiple CEW drive-stuns were used in the control attempts. Significant findings at autopsy included multiple blunt trauma injuries of the head, torso, and extremities, including patterned contusions, extensive multifocal subgaleal hematomas and multifocal right parietal subarachnoid hemorrhage, as well as evidence of asphyxiation characterized by periorbital, scleral and conjunctival petechiae, and multifocal hemorrhage in the right sternocleidomastoid muscle. Contusions on the back suggested an element of mechanical asphyxiation. The medical examiner's opinion was that the cause of death for Mr. Claros-Castro was due to multiple injuries, including blunt trauma to the head and asphyxiation. There was no mention of a fall.

Mr. Jorge Trujillo-Hernandez (San Jose, CA, 2006) was a 34-year-old victim of an assault (hit repeatedly with a baseball bat) by unknown suspects. He was able to flee the scene on foot and bystanders called police, who were able to make contact with Mr. Trujillo. He reportedly was combative with police, who struck him with a baton and used a CEW to control him. He was brought under control and taken to a hospital where he expired. Table 13.2 lists the diagnostic issues for a death from a suspected CEW-induced fall.

TABLE 13.2 Diagnosis of fatal fall injury induced by CEW

Item	*Notes*
Death was due to head injury from fall.	Note the Claros-Castro case where head-trauma and asphyxiation were given equal weights. Also, the Hall case of a fatal cervical fracture but only minor head injury.
There was no competing cause of the fall such as a tackle or intentional grounding.	See Sloan case where fall was from a tackle.
No competing cause of the head injury.	Note the Claros-Castro case where it was not clear what caused the head trauma. And, Trujillo-Hernandez where it is believed that a baseball bat did the damage. Eliminate vehicle crash or other such source of traumatic injury.
Fall was caused by the CEW probe-mode application inducing motor-nerve mediated muscle lock-up.	Expect probe application with probe spread > 9 inches on back or 12 inches on front chest for rapid takedown (Ho et al., 2012).

Fatal Burn Injury from Fume Ignition

We are aware of six fatal and six non-fatal cases of fire or explosion proximate to and possibly related to a CEW discharge. Of the fatal cases, we believe that at least three were ignited by the CEW.

In October 2005, Mr. Richard McKinnon was eluding a Cumberland County, NC, sheriff's deputy when he crashed his van. This caused him to be doused with gasoline from a can that had been sitting in the front seat. After exiting the vehicle, he threatened the deputy and she deployed her CEW, which ignited the gasoline fumes coming from Mr. McKinnon's clothing, causing a fire and his eventual death.

There are other cases with a CEW and gasoline burns, but they had confounding causation with another source of flame in the subject's hand. A fatality case occurred in 2013 in Plymouth, United Kingdom (UK) when the suspect, Andrew Pimlott, doused himself with gasoline and threatened suicide while holding a cigarette lighter (Clarke & Andrews, 2014). It is not clear what caused the ignition.

A very tragic case involved a suicidal man, Mr. David Riley, who turned on the natural gas in his home (Joplin, MO, 2004). Shortly after officers arrived for a welfare check, Mr. Riley was engaged and a CEW was subsequently deployed, after which the house exploded, killing Mr. Riley and Officer Timothy Nielson. The Missouri Division of Fire Safety report found there was not enough conclusive evidence to determine the cause of the explosion. It may or may not have been the CEW.

Other cases involve a cigarette lighter with the subject threatening suicide by lighting gasoline-soaked clothes with a lighter. For example, Mr. Shawn Mohney (Clarion Cty, PA, 2009) had an open lighter in his right hand near his upper body when officers deployed CEW probes to his left side. Flames were first seen on his right side, suggesting that the lighter in his right hand caused the fire. Another case with a cigarette lighter (as a possible source of ignition) is Mr. Flores-Lopez (San Angelo, TX, 2007).

These rare cases are best diagnosed with the criteria listed in Table 13.3.

TABLE 13.3 Diagnosis of fatal fire injury induced by CEW

Item	*Notes*
Death was due to smoke inhalation or burns.	
There was no competing cause of the fire ignition such as cigarette lighter.	This was an issue in three cases: Pimlott, Mohney, and Florez-Lopez.
Fire occurred coincident with the CEW application.	There can be delays of up to one or two seconds (Clarke & Andrews, 2014).

Electrocution: Chasing Bigfoot

There is no debate that it is theoretically possible for a CEW to electrocute a human (Harrison, 2007; Kroll et al., 2011; Panescu et al., 2015). If a probe tip were to nearly touch the right ventricle of the heart, because of an extremely emaciated build and a freak landing of the CEW dart in the small "sweet spot" directly over the heart, with full dart depth penetration, this could indeed happen. While there are contrary published opinions, we have investigated every case in which electrocution was alleged and with the information available to us, we can say with confidence that it has not yet occurred. Nevertheless, we are all well aware of the urban myth that people have been electrocuted by a CEW (Council of Canadian Academies & Canadian Academy of Health Sciences, 2013; Kroll et al., 2014a; Zipes, 2014). These are listed in Table 13.4.

Scientifically, it is almost trivial to eliminate CEW-induced electrocution. To begin with, all present CEWs deliver less than the 2.5 watts of power as allowed by the international electric fence safety standard (International Electrotechnical Commission, 2006; Kroll, Perkins, & Panescu, 2015; Nimunkar & Webster, 2009). If modern CEWs could be proven to actually electrocute, then millions of miles of electric fences would have to be removed from gardens, farms, and ranches around the world. However, a major driver of the electrocution myth is the non-specialist's intellectual inability to differentiate between a mild 2 mA (milliampere) pulsatile shock of a CEW and a lethal 500 mA alternating current shock. An important but subtle point is that the modern CEWs do not even have pulse charges sufficient to stimulate muscle. Instead, the pulses are tuned for motor-nerve mediated stimulation, which requires significantly less delivered charge than a charge that directly stimulates the muscle. Even without knowing the exact weights, everyone has an intuitive idea that being hit by a bowling ball could be lethal while being hit by tennis ball is at most irritating.

However, because of the general ignorance of invisible electricity, and the popularity of the CEW-electrocution myth, the CEW is judged guilty until proven innocent, and the investigator is given the

TABLE 13.4 Electrocution myth drivers

Item	*Notes*
1. Ignorance of levels of electrical current	A tennis ball is not a bowling ball
2. Diagnosis of exclusion	Guilty until proven innocent
3. Amnesty International fundraising	Implies that residual ARDs were electrocutions
4. Electrocution of small swine	Implies a risk to humans ≤ 46 lbs
5. Sensationalistic headlines	Typically imply that any ARD involving electronic control was an electrocution

difficult challenge of proving that Bigfoot does not exist. After all, it is theoretically possible that a gorilla-sized animal has been hiding in the United States but has not been shot or captured.

Another driver of the CEW-temporal electrocution myth is what physicians call a "diagnosis of exclusion" and lawyers call "guilty until proven innocent." In other words, if another obvious cause-of-death the physician actually knows about is not found, then the CEW must be blamed. First, the "diagnosis of exclusion" never includes all potential causes or contributors to death; it only includes a partial sampling. Such a diagnosis by exclusion is, of course, illogical when it fails to consider other potential mechanisms. It also ignores the fact that modern CEWs satisfy all relevant electrical safety standards and thus the CEW should be excluded, not favored, as the cause of an ARD.

The records of the Salem witchcraft trials provide an infamous example. In early 1692, 11-year-old Abigail Williams and 9-year-old Elizabeth Parris begin behaving very strangely, and then other Salem girls begin acting similarly. Local physician, Dr. William Griggs, suggested that witchcraft could be the cause of their strange behavior, as he could find no natural cause. Dr. Griggs' diagnosis, by exclusion, led directly to the death by hanging of 19 men and women, as well as seven others who expired in prison.

Many medical examiners fail to appreciate how a physically and emotionally stressful event can cause sudden cardiac death (SCD) (Krexi et al., 2016). Stressful events, such as an altercation (45 percent), physical restraint (31 percent), just being in police custody (10 percent), examinations or school or job stress (7 percent), receiving bad news (4 percent), or a car accident without injuries (3 percent), have been known to induce SCD. And, 53 percent of these SCD cases died with a negative autopsy and a morphologically normal heart (Krexi et al., 2016). Consider the deaths of the law enforcement officers who did *not* receive any electrical current. Their SCD risk is 34–69 times higher during restraints or altercations, 32–51 times higher during pursuits, 20–23 times higher during physical training, and 6–9 times higher during medical or rescue operations (Varvarigou et al., 2014). Authorities and the public expect that modern medicine and advanced diagnostic testing will always find a clear cause, and this pressures medical examiners to sometimes blame the thing that they understand the least—invisible electricity—much like Dr. Griggs blamed witchcraft over three centuries ago.

Another major driver of this electrocution myth appears to be the fundraising material of Amnesty International that lists ARDs with CEW temporal involvement along with the innuendo that the CEW somehow caused the death. Imagine that someone invented a pill that reduced the mortality rate of malaria by two-thirds. The inventor would receive acclaim and likely a Nobel Prize. No one would turn this upside-down and accuse the pill of killing the residual one-third of malaria patients. Nevertheless, that is exactly what Amnesty does with its favorite fundraising material. Notably, it has never attempted to explain how a CEW that satisfies all relevant world electrical safety standards could electrocute an adult human. At least Amnesty is careful enough to point out that the CEW is not mentioned, in the autopsy report, almost 90 percent of the time. However, Amnesty also seems to be contradictory in reporting its examination of hundreds of deaths following the use of a TASER, in that although "medical examiners have listed Tasers as a cause or contributing factor in more than 60 deaths," most deaths "have been attributed to other causes ... and in a number of other cases the exact cause of death is unknown" (Amnesty International, 2012).

Just like most medical examiners, Amnesty does not: (1) distill or explain the mechanism of alleged causation or contribution to death, (2) state to what degree of certainty, or (3) provide scientific justification or citations to its bald assertions. Surprisingly, in some rare instances, medical examiners have inappropriately embellished (or simply misunderstood) Amnesty's temporal fatality numbers as implying causality: "The use of Taser conducted energy devices by police has been criticized in the media, and Amnesty International reports 540 deaths in the United States as the result of their use since 2001" (Mathis, 2014; Shuman, 2013). Note the distortion as these residual ARDs are now described as *the result of* electronic control and not just *coincident* with it. Most medical examiners are board-certified forensic pathologists, and we hope that they would not confuse fundraising material with peer-reviewed scientific literature, but as shown, this is not always the case.

Another myth driver is that small swine can occasionally be electrocuted by a CEW. The largest swine electrocuted by an X26 CEW weighed 36 kg (79 lbs) (Valentino, Walter, Dennis, Margeta et al., 2008). Nanthakumar et al. (2006) also electrocuted a *single* 50 kg (110 lbs) swine, but a drug trick was used, which made the swine's weight equivalent to about 30 kg (66 lbs). Hence, the largest swine ever directly electrocuted by a normal CEW output weighed only 36 kg.

The levels of dangerous electrical current scale with body mass. Walcott, Kroll, and Ideker (2015) showed that swine are three times as sensitive to electrical current as humans. Thus, we can translate the 36 kg pig to a human (Walcott, Kroll, & Ideker, 2015). The amount of current required for electrocution conservatively scales with the square root of body mass (Geddes et al., 1973). For example, if the weight is quadrupled, then the amount of electrical current required for electrocution is doubled. Utilizing such a relationship, the 36 kg pig is equivalent to a 21 kg (46 lb) human. Hence, the best evidence suggests that the risk of CEW electrocution is limited to humans with a body mass under 46 lbs and with a very small DTH (dart-to-heart) distance.

The more recent driver of this urban myth is the litigation partnership of an anti-police attorney (John Burton) and a controversial retired cardiologist expert witness (Douglas P. Zipes). In May 2012, they published an anecdotal case series paper with summaries of eight of their litigated cases, and unsurprisingly argued electrocution by the CEW (Zipes, 2012a). The paper originally failed to make any mention of the lawyer co-author and only listed the cardiologist. The case series was rife with errors, including the comment that the subjects were "clinically normal." As a result, this error was corrected in an addendum after being brought to light in a deposition (Zipes, 2012b). Numerous other errors have been noted, including the listing of a case where the CEW probes missed the subject and thus could hardly be blamed for contributing to his death (Heegaard, Halperin, & Luceri, 2013; Ho & Dawes, 2013; Vilke, Chan, & Karch, 2013). Subsequently, the journal required the cardiologist to acknowledge the plaintiffs' attorney as a contributor to the case series (Zipes, 2013).

The Council of Canadian Academies and the Canadian Academy of Health Sciences convened an expert panel and reviewed the scientific literature on CEWs and specifically commented on the Zipes/Burton case series, stating, "The study by Zipes (2012) is particularly questionable since the author had a potential conflict of interest and used eight isolated and controversial cases as part of the analysis" (Council of Canadian Academies & Canadian Academy of Health Sciences, 2013, 36). Incidentally, occurring at the same time, *Circulation*, the publisher of the Zipes' case series, solicited a refutation paper published in January 2014 (Kroll et al., 2014a). It methodically considered the available evidence and showed that none of Zipes' expert witnessing anecdotes represented electrocution by the CEW.

The final promoter of the electrocution myth is the sensationalistic headline. As shown in Figure 13.1, of the typical 5,000 CEW uses, there is a single overlap with the 20 ARDs.

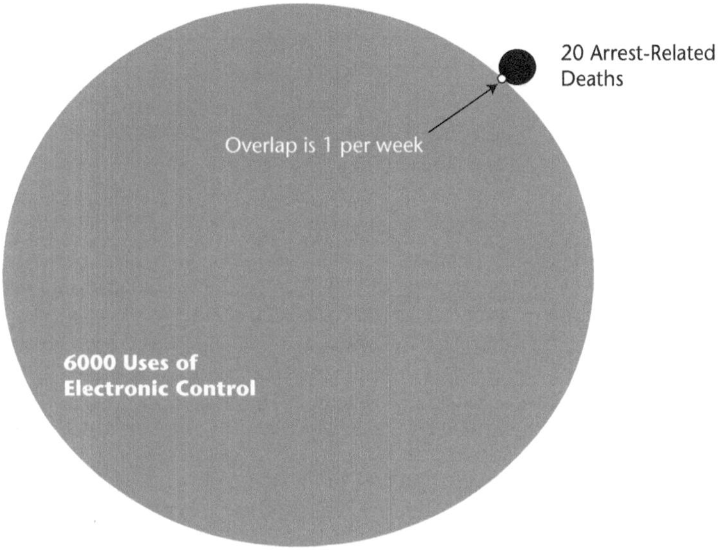

FIGURE 13.1 CEW uses and ARDs.

In an ideal world, there might be some newspaper headlines pointing to the fact that the main cause of ARDs is the failure to use electronic control. However, the day after an ARD, where electronic control was used or attempted, the local headline will be, "Man dies after police use TASER." Of course there is no autopsy report to confirm or deny the statement, but the headline inappropriately reinforces the idea that electronic control kills people. Usually, from 60–180 days after the headline first appears, the autopsy report is released and will show the cause of death being something like: complications of methamphetamine intoxication. However, rather than retract the initial headline, often the subsequent headline will still imply an electrocution by stating, "Autopsy report released in Taser death."

How to Diagnose a CEW Electrocution

Fortunately, objective criteria can be given for an electrocution diagnosis for an electronic control incident. As shown in Table 13.5, there are six criteria on which to identify an electrocution by a CEW, and each criterion must be satisfied in order to make a decision on the CEW electrocution.

Asystole (flat-line) and PEA (pulseless electrical activity) are not inducible with electrical stimulation (Zima et al., 2006). Asystole is rarely confused by EMS personnel, and almost never if multiple leads were used (Cummins & Austin, 1988). Electrically-induced VF does not deteriorate to asystole in swine in < 20 minutes and the median time is 34 minutes (Kroll, Walcott et al., 2012). The delay is longer with chest compressions (White, Goodman, & Svoboda, 2011).

The best current evidence suggests that electrocution in a human would require that the tip of the probe be within approximately 4 mm of the epicardium (outer surface of the heart). Even Zipes (the most common electrocution-asserting expert) has testified that he cannot say to a reasonable degree of certainty that in a case with a DTH > 16.7 mm, as seen in most all CEW-temporal deaths, the CEW induced cardiac capture, let alone ventricular fibrillation (Zipes, 2012b). The electrocution

TABLE 13.5 Diagnosis of electrocution by CEW. Each criterion must be satisfied

Item	*Notes*
1. Presenting rhythm is VF (Zima et al., 2006).	Asystole and Pulseless Electrical Activity (PEA) are not inducible with electrical stimulation (Zima et al., 2006).
2. Dart-to-epicardial distance is ≤ 4 mm (Wu et al., 2008).	The critical DTH distance is 5.8 ± 2.1 mm in swine (Wu et al., 2008). A probe in the sternum is considered too far away as the sternum is an insulator in adults (Panescu et al., 2014).
3. No documented pulse after CEW application.	If a responder is pushed to find a pulse in 10 seconds or less, about 30% of the responders will fail to find one. Given a full minute, they will almost always find the pulse with 97% accuracy (Bahr et al., 1997). Here the question is about false positives, i.e. what are the chances that the officer would detect a pulse that is not there? Studies show that when a pulse is detected, this has a 95% accuracy (Dick et al., 2000).
4. Cessation of normal breathing within 60 seconds of CEW application (Haouzi et al., 2010; Zuercher et al., 2010).	
5. Cessation of agonal breathing within 6 minutes of CEW application (Clark et al., 1992; Zuercher et al., 2010).	Commonly referred to as "dying gasps" and not confused with normal breathing.
6. If defibrillation (up to 3 shocks) is attempted within 10 minutes (or 14 minutes with CPR) it is successful (Kroll et al., 2012a).	Electrically-induced VF is defibrillated with a 95% success rate at 10 minutes with any chest compressions (Kroll et al., 2012a).

concern is not an issue with the drive stun, as no probes penetrate the skin to get sufficiently close to the heart. With any chest compressions, defibrillation has a 90 percent success rate after 10 minutes of electrically induced VF, with three or fewer shocks (Kroll, Fish, Calkins et al., 2012). Hence, the failure of prompt defibrillation exculpates an electrical cause for VF.

After a cardiac arrest, normal breathing ceases in 12–60 seconds (Haouzi et al., 2010; Zuercher et al., 2010). However, some subjects will also have "agonal" breathing (dying gasps) for a maximum total of six minutes (Clark et al., 1992).

Note that Table 13.5 does not include the application duration, number of CEW trigger pulls, or the timing to a collapse to the ground. There is a widespread mythical misunderstanding that electrical current builds up like poison and that the number of CEW trigger pulls, or total duration of delivered current, are relevant for electrocution. As discussed in the following section, this is simply not true. The timing to postural collapse is often stressed by non-specialists with a statement like "the victim collapsed to the ground immediately with the start of the CEW discharge." The innuendo is, of course, that the CEW caused his cardiac arrest, but in fact an immediate collapse to the ground is a *primary goal* of the use of the weapon in probe-deployment mode.

Here is a classic case of a CEW-involved ARD.

Since items 2, 3, and 4 in Table 13.5 quickly eliminate so many alleged electrocution cases, anti-law-enforcement litigators and their experts sometimes rely on a creative theory that the CEW *infected* the heart with a VT (ventricular tachycardia) and that allowed the subject to have a pulse, continue

ALLEGED ELECTROCUTION CASE

In the early morning hours of 28 August 2008, an officer of the Moberly (MO) Police Department made a traffic stop on 23-year-old Mr. Stanley Harlan on suspicion of drunk driving. When Mr. Harlan fled, and resisted, an officer used a TASER X26 CEW to attempt to control him. Mr. Harlan was then walked over to the curb and placed in a seated position. The uncontroverted witness and video evidence shows Mr. Harlan had a pulse and was breathing for about 13 minutes after the seating placement. After this time, Mr. Harlan suffered cardiac arrest and died. The presenting cardiac arrest rhythm was asystole (flat-line), which is not inducible with electrical stimulation. The medical examiner found that the sternum was between the CEW probe and the heart, thus precluding a sufficiently short current path for VF induction. Cardiac pathology showed lymphocytic myocarditis. Myocarditis is a common cause of stress-related sudden death in younger men (Amital et al., 2004; Phillips et al., 1986).

Note that in this case, the first four items in Table 13.5 veto the electrocution.

resisting, and keep breathing for many minutes until the onset of cardiac arrest. A complete discussion of this (frankly desperate) theory goes beyond the scope of this chapter, but a five-point refutation can be found in Kroll et al., 2014a.

Baseball, Poison, and Other Common Myths

Table 13.6 provides another list of common myths associated with the use of a CEW. Each of the myths identified will be discussed in detail below.

Myth 1 may derive from a confusion of the CEW with a firearm. After all, every time the trigger on a pistol is pulled, it will launch a bullet until the weapon is empty. The CEW looks somewhat like a pistol and is occasionally mislabeled as a "stun gun." This further allows the non-specialist to perhaps make a subconscious connection that forms the misplaced intuition that every time the trigger is pulled, something powerful is launched toward the subject. The high (up to 85 percent) effectiveness rate tends to also give the impression that the device must be extremely powerful (Brandl & Stroshine, 2015). It is not; it is just very optimized to do its job with minimal power.

Myth 1 is also closely tied to the false intuition that the number of trigger pulls is somehow related to the severity of the CEW application. This is incorrect for no less than three reasons: (1) the popular X26 CEW delivers 18.3 pulses per second. Thus, with a five-second trigger pull and a good connection, it will deliver 91 pulses. If the trigger is held down continuously for a single long pull of three minutes (and this has happened), then the weapon will deliver about 3,294 pulses. Now, consider a case with five pulls each of two seconds, which will deliver about 183 pulses. Hence, it is easily seen that the number of trigger pulls has no direct relationship to the number of electrical pulses delivered. (2) With the important probe-mode applications, an increased number of trigger pulls usually means that *less* current is being delivered, as the additional trigger pulls are often due to the failure of the connection either from a broken wire, dislodged probe, or clothing disconnect. (3) Even if the number of trigger pulls was somehow correlated with the seconds of current delivery, it would

TABLE 13.6 More myths and misunderstandings

Myth	*Facts*
1. The number of CEW trigger pulls, or duration of delivered current, is relevant to electrocution.	The number of trigger pulls is among the least relevant facts surrounding a CEW usage.
2. Electricity builds up like poison. I.e. the number of seconds of CEW exposure increases the risk of serious injury or death.	If an electrical current is strong enough to electrocute it will do so in 1–5 seconds (Kroll & Panescu, 2012; Kroll, Fish, Lakkireddy et al., 2012). Prolonged delivery of weaker currents has essentially no effect (Kroll et al., 2010; Scott et al., 1973).
3. The CEW delivers enormous currents.	Commercial CEWs deliver a mild current causing moderate motor-nerve mediated muscle contractions with sufficient probe spread (Gregory et al., 2007; Ho et al., 2012; Sweeney, 2009). The strength of the muscle contractions is less than half (≈46%) of what someone would voluntarily develop during recreational weight lifting (Gregory et al., 2007; Sweeney, 2009).
4. Humans have a delayed recovery to a CEW application.	Recovery is essentially (≈1 second) instantaneous (Criscione & Kroll, 2014). See also Jauchem "Misconceptions" paper (Jauchem, 2015).
5. TASER CEW delivers a 50,000 volt (V) pulse to the body.	The actual pulse voltage is 600 V (Dawes, Ho, Kroll et al., 2010).
6. The CEW is safe on healthy people but could kill someone on drugs.	Electrocution is a stand-alone cause of death and not like a soup recipe where salt and pepper both add to the overall flavor (Kroll, Fish, Lakkireddy et al., 2012; Lakkireddy et al., 2006).
7. The CEW pain could kill.	Unsupported and unscientific speculation. None of the 2.0+ million law enforcement training exposures led to a death.

still be irrelevant since the effects of electrical current do not build up beyond about five seconds (Scott, Lee, & Zoledziowski, 1973).

Myth 1 has been further reinforced by some American baseball and incarceration rules, which have limits of three strikes. Some self-styled CEW experts have taken this "three-strike" philosophy and turned it into an unscientific excessive force rule. The scientific arm of the United States Department of Justice (DOJ) is the National Institute of Justice (NIJ). A lengthy NIJ review has criticized the originator of this unscientific three-strike dogma with strong language: "After a review of anecdotes that seemed to indicate that multiple exposures were more hazardous, one researcher recommended in 2005—without supporting documentation—that law enforcement agents should ... limit the number of TASER® exposures when possible (3 is probably a reasonable number)" (Laub, 2011, 26 [referring to the Czarnecki (2005) recommendations]).

The utter logical failure of the three-strike rule can be seen from the fact that no department we are aware of has a similar rule, such as: three verbal warnings, three chemical agent exposures, three hand strikes, three baton strikes, or limiting firearm magazines to three cartridges even though baton strikes and bullet wounds actually may have a foreseeable cumulative effect. Ironically, the DOJ funded an outside think tank to provide recommendations for the Philadelphia (PA) Police Department (Fachner & Carter, 2015). These recommendations apparently ignored some of the scientific work of the DOJ and surprisingly repeated the baseball rule by referencing White and Ready (2009) and stating, "The PPD should limit the use of ECW in any circumstances to three cycles, equaling 15 seconds" (Fachner & Carter, 2015, 50).

In fact, White and Ready (2009) state the exact opposite. They point out in Table 2 and Table 3 of their article that fatal incidents involve more CEW trigger pulls. However, they then point out that the number of trigger pulls is *absolutely not* a statistically significant predictor of fatality. They point out that the most statistically significant predictors were: (1) the subject was armed with a weapon, or (2) under the influence of drugs. *The number of trigger pulls did not increase mortality*. Thus, not only did these promoters of the unfounded baseball rule misquote the peer-reviewed literature, they also ignored DOJ's five years of scientific work.

A closely related misunderstanding is Myth 2 that electricity builds up like poison, such that the number of seconds of CEW exposure increases the risk of serious injury or death. In fact, if an electrical current is strong enough to electrocute, it will do so in one to five seconds (Kroll, Fish, Lakkireddy et al., 2012; Kroll & Panescu, 2012). Prolonged delivery of weaker currents has essentially no effect (Kroll et al., 2010; Scott et al., 1973).

Another popular misunderstanding is Myth 3, which promotes that the CEW delivers enormous currents. The commercial CEWs deliver a mild current causing only moderate motor-nerve mediated muscle contractions (assuming sufficient probe spread) (Gregory, Dixon, & Bickel, 2007; Ho et al., 2012; Sweeney, 2009). The strength of the muscle contractions is less than half (approximately 46 percent) of what someone would voluntarily develop during recreational weight lifting (Gregory et al., 2007; Sweeney, 2009).

Myth 4 is that humans have a delayed recovery to a CEW application. This myth is so widespread that it earned a special section in Jauchem's "Misconceptions" paper (Jauchem, 2015). With zero evidence, various authors have speculated arbitrary effects, such as subjects are "incapacitated, left dazed and weak for at least five, perhaps, fifteen minutes" (OMEGA Foundation, 2000). Or, that an individual would be "rendered … physically incapacitated … for up to 10 min" (Layman, 2000, 97). Fortuitously, such creative thoughts are usually confined to the political and psychological literature, as well as theatrical productions, so far.

The media favorite is the voltage myth, Myth 5. The actual pulse voltage is 600 V (Dawes, Ho, Kroll et al., 2010). Media reporters prefer to mention the 50 kilovolts (kV) (which serves only to arc thru clothing and initiate the connection), as it is more sensationalistic than the actual 600 V pulse delivered to the body. Finally, voltage is not directly relevant to electrocution.

Myth 6 reflects a popular false intuition among lay people: "since drugs are bad, then they must really be 'badder' in the presence of electricity." In fact, the opposite is true. Electrocution is not like a soup recipe where salt and pepper both synergistically add to the overall flavor. For example, if someone with late-stage cancer were to receive a large current, they would be dead within seconds, but the cancer had nothing to do with the death. However, if the same person received a lower level of current and died 30 days, or even five minutes later, that person was not electrocuted. With rare partial exceptions, generally not salient to ARDs, the presence of other disease states does not make someone significantly harder or easier to electrocute. Conversely, low-power electrical currents (such as those from TASER CEWs) do not hasten deaths from other diseases.

The soup-recipe analogy actually works in reverse for some drugs. Cocaine has many deleterious effects on the body, and the heart in particular. However, a surprising effect, to many, is that cocaine makes it more difficult to electrocute someone (electrically induce VF), not easier (Lakkireddy et al., 2006; Tisdale et al., 1996). The technical reason is that cocaine is a sodium-channel blocker and thus it tends to make it harder for the electrical stimulus to affect the heart (Fenelon et al., 2003).

Finally, we have the "lethal pain" myth, Myth 7, which purports that the CEW caused great pain and this led to increased catecholamines, which caused the death. Catecholamines are the "hyper" hormones of epinephrine, norepinephrine, and dopamine. It is easy to refute the speculation that the presence of agitation along with the pain of a CEW application would lead to a surge of catecholamines, which could contribute to a sudden death. There have been over 2.0 million CEW training applications, all painful, and there have been no deaths. Cardiac arrest is not induced from the pain associated with severe back problems, headaches, broken bones, childbirth, or kidney stones. While emotionally appealing, this specious speculation is unsupported by any science and runs contrary to extensive experience. People can faint from pain, but they do not die. Most arrest-resisting subjects (73–82 percent) are also well anesthetized from alcohol, illegal drugs, schizophrenic psychosis, or the endorphins from their resistance (Hall et al., 2015; Strote, Verzemnieks et al., 2010; Strote, Walsh et al., 2010). The over 2.0 million CEW officer-training exposures did not involve anesthesia and no officers died.

It is also important to remember that all force options involve the infliction of and experience of pain. That is why some are often referred to as "pain control" or "pain compliance" techniques, weapons, or force options.

A study compared a 10-second TASER X26 CEW *probe-mode* exposure to pepper (oleoresin capsicum) spray, 45 seconds of striking a heavy bag (simulated physical resistance), sprinting 150 meters and hurdle (simulated flight from arrest), and a fleeing and resistance exercise involving a law enforcement canine (Ho, Dawes et al., 2010). The greatest increases in catecholamines were obtained from punching and sprinting. The next highest increase was seen with the canine threat. The lowest increase (immediately after the exposure) was with pepper spray, while the TASER CEW was the second lowest. However, after three minutes, the pepper (OC) spray stress began to increase and after four minutes post-exposure, the X26 CEW had the lowest level of catecholamines.

For completeness, we should discuss an earlier concern over acidemia. Swine, undergoing full-trunk CEW applications, have been reported to develop acidemia or acidic blood (Dennis et al., 2007; Jauchem, 2010; Jauchem et al., 2006; Walter et al., 2008). There had been speculation that a similar effect could be seen in humans, and that the acidemia could be severe enough to cause injury or death. This concern can be eliminated for several reasons:

1. The anesthetized animals that developed acidemia (with up to three minutes of CEW current) had their ventilator turned *off* during the CEW exposures (Dennis et al., 2007; Jauchem, 2010; Jauchem et al., 2006; Walter et al., 2008). Thus, they were not able to compensate for the acidemia by breathing.
2. With a ventilator running with the extreme 30-minute (not 30 seconds!), Hughes et al. (2007) reported that no swine died from acidemia.
3. Humans do not develop acidemia from CEW exposures (Dawes, Ho, Reardon et al., 2010; Ho, Dawes et al., 2010; Ho et al., 2006; Ho, Dawes, Bultman et al., 2009; Ho, Dawes, Cole et al., 2009; Ho et al., 2013). There is a very slight initial pH shift similar to that seen with mild exercise (running 20 yards), which then stabilizes (Ho et al., 2013). Breathing actually increases slightly.
4. Since a broad probe-spread CEW application induces muscle contractions of less than half (< 50 percent) of voluntary weight lifting, it cannot be that stressful on the body (Sweeney, 2009). More importantly, five seconds of CEW-induced muscle contractions causes less muscle effects and acidemia than running 20 yards (Ho et al., 2013).

Summary

Conducted electrical weapons are, after all, weapons, and are used in violent and dangerous situations. They have indeed contributed to deaths from head injuries and ignition of flammable fumes. While electrocution remains a theoretical possibility, the notion that an electrical weapon has ever electrocuted anyone is an urban myth.

Investigator Checklist

Highly Perishable Evidence

- ☐ **AED/Cardiac Monitor Downloads:** Get the AED (Automated External Defibrillator) or cardiac monitor downloads, including rhythm strips, electronic data downloads, and technical operational downloads. This is often erased or deleted when the next paramedic shift starts. This information can eliminate "electrocution" by the TASER CEW (Conducted Electrical Weapon) 95% of the time (Swerdlow, Fishbein, Chaman, Lakkireddy, & Tchou, 2009). However, it is erased 80% of the time. Note that there can be four or more defibrillators/heart monitors: (1) squad car, (2) paramedics, (3) ambulance, and (4) hospital.
- ☐ **Person's Clothing:** Acquire and handle as perishable evidence the person's clothing, especially any clothing where a CEW probe may have struck, punctured, or attached.
- ☐ **CEW Wires/Probes/Cartridges:** ***Maintain as evidence the CEW wires, probes and cartridges!*** Microscopic analysis of the probes and wires can often show that no electrical current was delivered (as a probe missed) and eliminate the TASER CEW as a factor (Wyant & Hinz, 2009). DNA analysis of the probes may show who, if anyone, had a probe insertion. Do NOT let anyone put the probes/wires into a "sharps" container. These are valuable evidence.
- ☐ **Probe Impact, Attach or Penetrate:** Carefully acquire all data regarding probes and where and if they impacted, attached or penetrated clothing or skin. Millimeters matter, thus, very carefully acquire this information and fully document (with complete annotations).
- ☐ **CEW Spark Tests/Cartridge Removal Discharges:** Carefully determine and document any CEW spark tests or cartridge removals, including "3-point" deployments or drive stun after cartridge removal, and drive stun with deployed cartridge remaining in place on the CEW.
- ☐ **Core (rectal or liver) Body Temperatures:** Taken as close as possible to time of collapse. Not always thought important by Emergency Medical Services (EMS) or Emergency Department (ED) staff for therapy, but may be important for Excited Delirium diagnosis, ***so politely ask for it!*** (Karch, 2012; Vilke, Payne-James, & Karch, 2012).
- ☐ **Pulse Oximeter:** Paramedic pulse oximeter recording, if available.
- ☐ **Antemortem (pre-death) Blood Sample(s):** From ED grey-top vacutainer tubes for "quantitative" analysis—not just "qualitative" analysis. The "grey-tops" contain sodium fluoride, which will prevent the breakdown of cocaine. Note that the subject is a "patient" up until death is pronounced and only then becomes a body for the coroner/ME investigation. The ED is doing you a big favor if he/she will share a 10ml antemortem blood sample.
- ☐ **Postmortem Blood Sample(s):** Get several blood samples (especially peripheral samples) and place in "grey-top" tubes for quantitative analysis. Be sure to fully document where blood was taken from and time of sample acquisition. Be extra nice here. Law enforcement has a right to

evidence to help the coroner/ME investigation but the ED staff does *not have* to take these blood samples for you.

☐ **Urine Samples**.

Important Requests for ME (Medical Examiner)

☐ Hair sample and chronic drug use analysis ($75). At least save a sufficient head hair sample (pencil thick when twisted) and a pubic hair sample (Berankova et al., 2005; Paterson, Cordero, & Stearns, 2009; Politi, Zucchella, Morini, Stramesi, & Polettini, 2007).

☐ Dr. Deborah Mash Miami brain test ($400), (1-800-UM-BRAIN and www.exciteddelirium.org) (Mash et al., 2009; Mash et al., 2003; Stephens, Jentzen, Karch, Wetli, & Mash, 2004). Must be properly collected, prepped and frozen, usually within 24 hours of death. Ideally frozen in dry ice. Otherwise, collect coronal slices flat in bags and freeze in normal freezer (–4°F or –20°C).

☐ If cocaine is suspected, request analysis of brain for cocaine and its metabolite.

☐ Due to the importance of the hair and brain test, the LEA (Law Enforcement Agency) should offer to pay for them. The $475 is nothing compared to the typical $1 million settlement, or thousands in attorney's fees, for an ARD (arrest-related death).

☐ Save the heart (histologic heart blocks may be very important). Heart tissue slides can be critical in establishing myocarditis, which is a very common cause of exertional sudden death in young men (Amital et al., 2004; Kroll et al., 2014a; Phillips et al., 1986).

☐ If any TASER CEW probes were within 5 cm (2 inches) of the heart, ME should measure the exact distance (in millimeters) from the tip of the probe to the outer surface of the heart (Kroll et al., 2011; Rahko, 2008). Document all probe locations. Fully document what tissues a probe penetrated (entered) and perforated (went through), starting at the outside of the skin and moving closer to the heart, including, but not limited to: epidermis, dermis, dermal fat layer, skeletal muscle, intercostal muscle, pericardial sac. Document if probe was in bone. Document if bone, including sternum, was between the CEW probe and the heart. *Have a histological section taken of all probe marks.*

☐ Save blood sample for genetic testing for "long QT" syndrome.

☐ The entire gastric content should be submitted for drug analysis and the total amount of drug remaining in the stomach should be quantified.

☐ Test for the classical drugs (heroin, methamphetamine, MDMA, LSD, and cocaine). Also, test for THC as this is being increasingly linked to unexpected death (Bachs & Morland, 2001; Sattout & Nicol, 2009). Also, request testing for newer dangerous synthetics, such as K2/Spice, bath salts and JWH-018 (found in fake marijuana) (Angoa-Perez et al., 2011; Murray, Murphy, & Beuhler, 2012; Prosser & Nelson, 2011; Rosenbaum, Carreiro, & Babu, 2012; Ross, Watson, & Goldberger, 2011; Spiller, Ryan, Weston, & Jansen, 2011). (See Chronic Medical Information section.)

☐ Test premortem, postmortem, vitreous, and urine samples.

☐ There is no need to interfere with organ and tissue donation prior to autopsy, unless the ME cannot examine the body before procurement. Protocols have been established to allow the ME to examine the body prior to procurement of organs. The ME has the authority to restrict the taking of certain organs or tissues, depending on the circumstances of death, but a blanket denial is not justified. The issue has been thoroughly addressed by the National Association of Medical Examiners and published as a position paper several years ago. It is about to be revised but blanket denials will still be unjustified in the update. Note, however, that in areas where there is no ME or Forensic Pathologist, then a blanket denial may be justified. Hopefully, that would be a rare occurrence in the U.S. The main thing is to be sure the ME is apprised of the circumstances of death and has the ability to examine the body prior to organ procurement (virtually all tissues can be obtained after autopsy).

- ☐ If the victim is African-American or of African descent, request a hemoglobin electrophoresis. This is the best method to determine sickle cell trait.

Acute Medical Information

- ☐ Body Core (rectal or liver) temperature at time of death and as close to collapse as possible (Karch, 2012; Kroll et al., 2009; Vilke et al., 2011; Vilke et al., 2012).
- ☐ (Premortem) Collect 10 ml (milliliters) of blood as soon as possible after ED arrival for later quantitative drug testing.
- ☐ Document (ideally photograph) all TASER CEW probe and wound locations and marks. Be sure to photograph for context—including inch or cm rulers and body landmarks. Record if they removed the probes or subject arrived without. Millimeters matter, thus, it is very important to carefully document exact locations of probes, marks, etc.
- ☐ Within 24 (preferably less than 12) hours of collapse, brain samples must be properly collected and frozen. Call 1-800-UM-BRAIN (also www.exciteddelirium.org) for shipping instructions.
- ☐ In suspected cocaine, methamphetamine, PCP, LSD, THC, etc., smoking cases, swabs of mouth and bronchial tree are helpful for chemical analysis.
- ☐ Politely remind treating physicians to keep documentation objective and do not speculate or write or document about things they do not understand. Occasionally hospital records will include statements about a "TASER" wound even though there was no TASER CEW used near that specific location.
- ☐ Preemptively stop anyone from attempting to harvest or harvesting any organs or body materials for transplant or other purposes prior to autopsy.

Chronic Medical Information

- ☐ Obtaining hair and toenail samples (Berankova, Habrdova, Balikova, & Strejc, 2005; Paterson, Cordero, & Stearns, 2009; Politi, Zucchella, Morini, Stramesi, & Polettini, 2007). Twist strands of longest head hair available like a lock, about as thick as a pencil lead, hold together to keep strands aligned. Try to include the hair root so the time of drug ingestion can be estimated. Transfer lock to tin foil or paper, fold (to hold together), and secure. Collect similar samples from longest pubic or groin hair.
- ☐ Collect three "gray top" tubes of peripheral blood (or cardiac if necessary) for possible later testing of synthetic drugs such as "bath salts" etc. Note that the normal toxicology laboratory used by your medical examiner is probably not equipped to do these tests (Banks, Worst, Rusyniak, & Sprague, 2014; Smith, Metters, Khreit, Sutcliffe, & Banks, 2014).
- ☐ Obtain all available past medical records.
- ☐ Obtain all psychological/psychiatric records (Karch, 2012; Vilke et al., 2012).
- ☐ Obtain printouts from pharmacies used by suspect for past two years.
- ☐ Obtain all rehabilitation and treatment records.

Circumstances Regarding Arrest

- ☐ Create highly detailed fully annotated timeline of event, clearly noting those times which are beyond dispute (e.g., dispatch records with dispatch time stamping tied to Internet time).
- ☐ Distance CEW deployed (fired), probe spread, *probe locations*, number of cycles, timing of cycles, and duration of cycles.
- ☐ Download CEW as soon as reasonably possible after event. Carefully set internal clock (as necessary) to determine clock drift.
- ☐ TASER CEW effects (such as change in behavior).
- ☐ Subject's influence (drugs, alcohol, emotionally disturbed).
- ☐ Any other use of force employed?
- ☐ Was an AED, defibrillator, or cardiac monitor used? (Note ownership, manufacturer, model, serial number, and all recent maintenance records.)
- ☐ Did the AED report a shockable rhythm? (Very important to determine which type of shockable rhythm.) Did the AED or defibrillator operator manually trigger a defibrillation shock?
- ☐ Expeditiously acquire clean printout (download), electronic data download and maintenance download from the AED or cardiac monitor.
- ☐ How long between the CEW exposure and the subject's collapse? Specifically detailed chronicle of all witnessed behaviors, actions, inactions, physiological status, etc. Plaintiff's lawyers will try to confuse postural collapse (falling down) with cardiovascular collapse (cardiac arrest). Do not add to this confusion.
- ☐ Was the subject walking, fighting, talking, moaning, groaning, or breathing after the CEW exposure? And, for how long—*do not guess*—be as precise as possible. Normal breathing ceases within 12–60 seconds of cardiac arrest (Haouzi et al., 2010; Zuercher et al., 2010).
- ☐ Carefully document all signs of life including pulse (where on body taken, for how long, and by whom), breathing, moving, moaning, and groaning, and carefully include in fully annotated event timeline.
- ☐ Collect all clothing and treat as evidence: especially any clothing where a CEW probe may have landed, penetrated, punctured, or attached.
- ☐ ME contact info or supporting info from medical attendants and ED.
- ☐ Hospital exam information (if conducted).

Interviews

- ☐ First, expeditiously create *known* timeline—dispatch times, CEW downloads (with clock drift corrections), video/audio recordings, AED/cardiac monitor downloads, hospital emergency records, ambulance/fire dispatch, and action times. Then, use the interviews to carefully fill in and document the time line—with full annotations.
- ☐ *Treat the EMTs (Emergency Medical Technicians) and Paramedics at the scene like any other witnesses.* Get complete readable, detailed, time chronological statements from them about what they observed and what interventions they made. EMTs do not always perfectly document the event. However, they can make medical observations that the LEOs (Law Enforcement Officers) might not realize are important but they will have forgotten by the time their depositions are taken two or three years later. Where did the probes land? *Don't assume that their standard report has enough information—it does not.*

- ☐ Try to get eyewitness statements that address the rapidity with which the subject went from screaming, struggling, and yelling to unconscious, not breathing and pulseless. (Remember a respiratory death takes minutes, whereas a cardiac death takes only a few seconds.) Try to specifically determine the time sequence as clearly and carefully as possible in the early phase of the investigation. Advise LEOs to collect as much information about the passage from activity to unconsciousness as possible. The sequence of events for a sudden cardiac-arrest death as opposed to a respiratory death are markedly different and chronicling exactly what happened, how fast, when, and whether there was resistance, exertion, struggling, or fighting until "all of a sudden" or like a "light switch" things changed, can be the most important information.
- ☐ Get statements that include whether or not the subject could be heard to be breathing, screaming, yelling, or moaning throughout their confrontation against LEOs' efforts to capture, control, and restrain. Screaming and yelling require that air is moving over the vocal cords and demonstrate that at least some degree of ventilation had to take place. How much yelling and screaming?
- ☐ Debrief LEOs and witnesses regarding words and actions manifested by subject. Get details of patterns of walking, talking, gestures, facial expressions, breathing, pulse, etc. Ask interviewees to replay their memory with attention to DUI (Driving Under the Influence)/DRE (Drug Recognition Expert) type details. Sounds, even grunts, growls, and snarls, can be important. Get collaborative reports.
  - Was suspect growling? How?
  - Keening or wailing?
  - What words could you make out?
  - Huffing and puffing?
  - Sweating?
  - Drooling?
  - Eye movements?
  - Balance?
- ☐ If subject is only injured and survives, debrief as soon as possible about subjective feelings, thoughts, and drug effects. They were the only ones inside their bodies and looking out so ask how they saw and heard the world. Don't translate anything into your own words but describe mannerisms and expressions accompanying their descriptions.
- ☐ Sounds: Ask all witnesses to describe any unusual sounds they heard. If they describe sounds like "arcing" or "electrical short" there was probably a connection break and the suspect was not getting current delivered at that time. Even "clicking" heard in a noisy situation or from less than 10 feet in a quiet situation, is indicative of a broken connection. Like a car or refrigerator, when the TASER CEW is making noise, there is usually something wrong. Adverse witnesses love to go on about hearing the electrical noise, thinking they are hurting the police when the opposite is true.
- ☐ Blue lights or lighting: determine whether anyone saw "blue lights" or "lightning" in the LEO's hand. This indicates that the CEW is arcing at the CEW and not delivering an electrical charge to the person.

Evidence Collection

- ☐ Photos, including contextual, of wounds, marks, etc., and CEW probe or drive-stun impacts with ruler.

- ☐ Photos showing distance of probe or drive-stun spread (i.e., with ruler).
- ☐ Keep the original CEW battery in the CEW (*do not remove*). This will maintain the integrity of the internal clock.
- ☐ Do not discard probes or wires (treat them as evidence). Do not let EMS place probes in "sharps" container as information can be gathered from the probes and wires as to whether or not they actually delivered current.
- ☐ Download CEW data as expeditiously as reasonable (at least within 48 hours) of the event and maintain evidentiary copy of download (including time drift and time drift correction).
- ☐ Collect two to three AFID (Anti-Felon Identification) tags and note their location; this will be helpful if multiple CEWs or cartridges were deployed.
- ☐ Collect all audio recordings. Computer analysis can differentiate between the "crackling" sound of a missed (or broken) connection and the "clicking" sound of a good connection. These recording sources may include:
  - Dash cameras
  - TASER CAM
  - TASER Axon
  - Tactical radio
  - 911 recordings
  - Witness mobile phones

Medical/Autopsy Data and Tissues

- ☐ All treatment records
  - EMS
  - Emergency department
- ☐ Autopsy report
- ☐ Autopsy microscopic slides (if any were prepared)
- ☐ Autopsy gross tissues (if any were retained)
  - Heart is especially useful
- ☐ Autopsy photos (it is just as important to determine that there is no mark or sign of injury on the body as it is to show what injuries did occur).

If the CEW Did Not Perform as Expected

- ☐ What was the failure or challenge?
- ☐ What was the subject wearing (especially multiple or thick layers or loose clothing)?
- ☐ Was the CEW dropped or subject to a high-moisture environment?
- ☐ What were the operating conditions?
- ☐ Did the CEW fire?
- ☐ Did LEOs hear loud arcing—especially across the front of the CEW?
- ☐ Drive-stun or probe deployment?
- ☐ When was a last successful download or spark test done?

References

Amital, H., Glikson, M., Burstein, M., Afek, A., Sinnreich, R., Weiss, Y., & Israeli, V. (2004). Clinical characteristics of unexpected death among young enlisted military personnel: Results of a three-decade retrospective surveillance. *Chest*, *126*(2), 528–533.

Amnesty International. (2012). *USA: Stricter limits urged as deaths following police taser use reach 500.* Retrieved from www.amnesty.org/en/latest/news/2012/02/usa-stricter-limits-urged-deaths-following-police-taser-use-reach/.

Angoa-Perez, M., Kane, M. J., Francescutti, D. M., Sykes, K. E., Shah, M. M., Mohammed, A. M. et al. (2011). Mephedrone, an abused psychoactive component of 'bath salts' and methamphetamine congener, does not cause neurotoxicity to dopamine nerve endings of the striatum. *Journal of Neurochemistry*, doi:10.1111/j.1471-4159.2011.07632.x.

Bachs, L., & Morland, H. (2001). Acute cardiovascular fatalities following cannabis use. *Forensic Science International*, *124*(2–3): 200–3.

Bahr, J., Klingler, H., Panzer, W., Rode, H., & Kettler, D. (1997). Skills of lay people in checking the carotid pulse. *Resuscitation*, *35*(1), 23–26.

Banks, M. L., Worst, T. J., Rusyniak, D. E., & Sprague, J. E. (2014). Synthetic cathinones ("bath salts"). *The Journal of Emergency Medicine*, *46*(5): 632–42.

Berankova, K., Habrdova, V., Balikova, M., & Strejc P. (2005). Methamphetamine in hair and interpretation of forensic findings in a fatal case. *Forensic Science International*, *153*(1): 93–7.

Bovbjerg, V. E., Kenny, J. M., Heal, C. S., & Murray, W. B. (2007). Field-based evaluation of non-lethal weapons: Conducted energy weapons. *Office of Naval Research Monograph (NTIC Subcontract N. 03-740).*

Bozeman, W. P., Hauda II, W. E., Heck, J. J., Graham, Jr., D. D., Martin, B. P., & Winslow, J. E. (2009). Safety and injury profile of conducted electrical weapons used by law enforcement officers against criminal suspects. *Annals of Emergency Medicine*, *53*(4), 480–489.

Brandl, S. G. & Stroshine, M. S. (2015). Oleoresin capsicum spray and TASERs: A comparison of factors predicting use and effectiveness. *Criminal Justice Policy Review*, doi: 0887403415578732.

Brewer, J. & Kroll, M. (2009). Field statistics overview. In M. Kroll & J. Ho (eds.), *TASER Conducted Electrical Weapons: Physiology, Pathology, and Law*. New York, NY: Springer-Kluwer.

Clark, J. J., Larsen, M. P., Culley, L. L., Graves, J. R., & Eisenberg, M. S. (1992). Incidence of agonal respirations in sudden cardiac arrest. *Annals of Emergency Medicine*, *21*(12), 1464–1467.

Clarke, C. & Andrews, S. (2014). The ignitability of petrol vapours and potential for vapour phase explosion by use of TASER® law enforcement electronic control device. *Science & Justice*, *54*(6), 412–420.

Council of Canadian Academies and Canadian Academy of Health Sciences. (2013). *The health effects of conducted energy weapons*. Ottawa, ON: The Expert Panel on the Medical and Physiological Impacts of Conducted Energy Weapons. Council of Canadian Academies and Canadian Academy of Health Sciences.

Cox, T. C., Buchholz, D. J., & Wolf, D. J. (1987). Blunt force head trauma from police impact weapons: Some skeletal and neuropsychological considerations. *Journal of Police Science and Administration*, *15*(1), 56–92.

Criscione, J.C., & Kroll, M.W. (2014) Incapacitation recovery times from a conductive electrical weapon exposure. *Forensic Science, Medicine, and Pathology*, *10*(2), 203–7. doi:10.1007/s12024-014-9551-x.

Cummins, R. O. & Austin, Jr., D. (1988). The frequency of "occult" ventricular fibrillation masquerading as a flat line in prehospital cardiac arrest. *Annals of Emergency Medicine*, *17*(8), 813–817.

Czarnecki, F. (2005). Recommendations for the use of the TASER by law enforcement officers. *International Association of Chiefs of Police Conference, Legal Officers Section.*

Dawes, D. M., Ho, J. D., Kroll, M. W., & Miner, J. R. (2010). Electrical characteristics of an electronic control device under a physiologic load: A brief report. *Pacing and Clinical Electrophysiology*, *33*(3), 330–336.

Dawes, D. M., Ho, J. D., Reardon, R. F., & Miner, J. R. (2010). The cardiovascular, respiratory, and metabolic effects of a long duration electronic control device exposure in human volunteers. *Forensic Science, Medicine, and Pathology, 6*(4), 268–274.

Dennis, A. J., Valentino, D. J., Walter, R. J., Nagy, K. K., Winners, J., Bokhari, F., … Roberts, R. R. (2007). Acute effects of TASER X26 discharges in a swine model. *Journal of Trauma-Injury Infection & Critical Care, 63*(3), 581–590.

Dick, W. F., Eberle, B., Wisser, G., & Schneider, T. (2000). The carotid pulse check revisited: What if there is no pulse? *Critical Care Medicine, 28*(11), N183–185.

Eastman, A. L., Metzger, J. C., Pepe, P. E., Benitez, F. L., Decker, J., Rinnert, K. J., … Friese, R. S. (2008). Conductive electrical devices: A prospective, population-based study of the medical safety of law enforcement use. *Journal of Trauma-Injury Infection & Critical Care, 64*(4), 1567–1572.

Fachner, G. & Carter, S. (2015). *Collaborative Reform Initiative: An assessment of deadly force in the Philadelphia Police Department.* Washington, DC: U.S. Department of Justice, Office of Community Oriented Policing Services.

Fenelon, G., Uchoa, J., Otobone, J. R., Reis, M., do Amaral, J. L. G., & de Paola, A. A. V. (2003). Characterization of the in vivo cardiac electrophysiologic effects of high-dose cocaine in closed-chest, anesthetized dogs with normal hearts. *Arquivos Brasileiros de Cardiologia, 81*(1), 29–34.

Ferdik, F. V., Kaminski, R. J., Cooney, M. D., & Sevigny, E. L. (2014). The influence of agency policies on conducted energy device use and police use of lethal force. *Police Quarterly, 17*(4), 328–358.

Fox, A. W. & Payne-James, J. J. (2012). Conducted energy devices: Pilot analysis of (non)attributability of death using a modified Naranjo algorithm. *Forensic Science International, 223*(1–3), 261–265.

Geddes, L. A., Cabler, P., Moore, A. G., Rosborough, J., & Tacker, W. A. (1973). Threshold 60-Hz current required for ventricular fibrillation in subjects of various body weights. *IEEE Transactions on Biomedical Engineering, 20*(6), 465–468.

Gregory, C. M., Dixon, W., & Bickel, C. S. (2007). Impact of varying pulse frequency and duration on muscle torque production and fatigue. *Muscle & Nerve, 35*(4), 504–509.

Haileyesus, T., Annest, J. L., & Mercy, J. A. (2011). Non-fatal conductive energy device-related injuries treated in US emergency departments, 2005–2008. *Injury Prevention, 17*(2), 127–130.

Hall, C., Votova, K., Heyd, C., Walker, M., MacDonald, S., Eramian, D., & Vilke, G. M. (2015). Restraint in police use of force events: Examining sudden in custody death for prone and not-prone positions. *Journal of Forensic and Legal Medicine, 31*, 29–35.

Haouzi, P., Ahmadpour, N., Bell, H. J., Artman, S., Banchs, J., Samii, S., … Gleeson, K. (2010). Breathing patterns during cardiac arrest. *Journal of Applied Physiology, 109*(2), 405–411.

Harrison, D. (2007). Science undecided on safety of stun guns. *CanWest News Service*. Retrieved from www.nationalpost.com/news/story.html?id=77a7c7b7-daf6-4c93-a198-efb34afb8a06.

Heegaard, W. G., Halperin, H. R., & Luceri, R. (2013). Letter by Heegaard et al regarding article, "Sudden cardiac arrest and death following application of shocks from a TASER electronic control device." *Circulation, 127*(1), e260.

Ho, J. D. & Dawes, D. M. (2013). Letter by Ho and Dawes regarding article, "Sudden cardiac arrest and death following application of shocks from a TASER electronic control device." *Circulation, 127*(1), e259.

Ho, J. D., Clinton, J. E., Lappe, M. A., Heegaard, W. G., Williams, M. F., & Miner, J. R. (2010). Introduction of the conducted electrical weapon into a hospital setting. *Journal of Emergency Medicine, 41*(3), 317–323.

Ho, J. D., Dawes, D. M., Bultman, L. L., Moscati, R. M., Janchar, T. A., & Miner, J. R. (2009). Prolonged TASER use on exhausted humans does not worsen markers of acidosis. *American Journal of Emergency Medicine, 27*(4), 413–418.

Ho, J. D., Dawes, D. M., Cole, J. B., Hottinger, J. C., Overton, K. G., & Miner, J. R. (2009). Lactate and pH evaluation in exhausted humans with prolonged TASER X26 exposure or continued exertion. *Forensic Science International, 190*(1–3), 80–86.

Ho, J., Dawes, D., Miner, J., Kunz, S., Nelson, R., & Sweeney, J. (2012). Conducted electrical weapon incapacitation during a goal-directed task as a function of probe spread. *Forensic Science, Medicine, and Pathology, 8*(4), 358–366.

Ho, J. D., Dawes, D. M., Nelson, R. S., Lundin, E. J., Ryan, F. J., Overton, K. G., ... Miner, J. R. (2010). Acidosis and catecholamine evaluation following simulated law enforcement "use of force" encounters. *Academic Emergency Medicine, 17*(7), e60–e68.

Ho, J. D., Dawes, D. M., Nystrom, P. C., Collins, D. P., Nelson, R. S., Moore, J. C., & Miner, J. R. (2013). Markers of acidosis and stress in a sprint versus a conducted electrical weapon. *Forensic Science International, 233*(1–3), 84–89.

Ho, J. D., Miner, J. R., Lakkireddy, D. R., Bultman, L. L., & Heegaard, W. G. (2006). Cardiovascular and physiologic effects of conducted electrical weapon discharge in resting adults. *Academic Emergency Medicine, 13*(6), 589–595.

Hughes, E., Kennett, M., Murray, W., Werner, J., & Jenkins, D. (2007). *Electro-muscular disruption (EMD) bioeffects: A study on the effects of a continuous application of the TASER X26 waveform on swine.* Philadelphia, PA: Penn State University Press.

International Electrotechnical Commission. (2006). Household and similar electrical appliances—Safety—Part 2-76: Particular requirements for electric fence energizers. *International Electrotechnical Commission (IEC 60335-2-76).*

Jauchem, J. R. (2010). Repeated or long-duration TASER electronic control device exposures: Acidemia and lack of respiration. *Forensic Science, Medicine, and Pathology, 6*(1), 46–53.

Jauchem, J. R. (2015). TASER conducted electrical weapons: Misconceptions in the scientific/medical and other literature. *Forensic Science, Medicine, and Pathology, 11*(1), 53–64.

Jauchem, J. R., Sherry, C. J., Fines, D. A., & Cook, M. C. (2006). Acidosis, lactate, electrolytes, muscle enzymes, and other factors in the blood of *Sus scrofa* following repeated TASER exposures. *Forensic Science International, 161*(1), 20–30.

Jenkinson, E., Neeson, C., & Bleetman, A. (2006). The relative risk of police use-of-force options: Evaluating the potential for deployment of electronic weaponry. *Journal of Clinical Forensic Medicine, 13*(5), 229–241.

Karch, S. (2012). Possible strategies for the diagnosis of fatal excited delirium syndrome. *Academy of Forensic Pathology, 2*(3): 273–83.

Krexi, L., Georgiou, R., Krexi, D., & Sheppard, M. N. (2016). Sudden cardiac death with stress and restraint: The association with sudden adult death syndrome, cardiomyopathy and coronary artery disease. *Medicine, Science and the Law, 56*(2), 85–90.

Kroll, M. (2011). TASER® conducted electrical weapons. In M. Stark (ed.), *Clinical forensic medicine: A physician's guide.* New York, NY: Springer.

Kroll, M., Adamec, J., Wetli, C., & Williams, H. (2016). Fatal traumatic brain injury with electrical weapon falls *Journal of Forensic and Legal Medicine, 43*: 12–9.

Kroll, M. W., Fish, R. M., Calkins, H., Halperin, H., Lakkireddy, D., & Panescu, D. (2012). Defibrillation success rates for electrically-induced fibrillation: Hair of the dog. *Annual International Conference of the IEEE Engineering in Medicine and Biology Society, 34*, 689–693.

Kroll, M. W., Fish, R. M., Lakkireddy, D., Luceri, R. M., & Panescu, D. (2012). Essentials of low-power electrocution: Established and speculated mechanisms. *Annual International Conference of the IEEE Engineering in Medicine and Biology Society, 34*, 5734–5740.

Kroll, M. W., Lakkireddy, D., Rahko, P. S., & Panescu, D. (2011). Ventricular fibrillation risk estimation for conducted electrical weapons: Critical convolutions. *Annual International Conference of the IEEE Engineering in Medicine and Biology Society, 33*, 271–277.

Kroll, M. W., Lakkireddy, D. R., Stone, J. R., & Luceri, R. M. (2014a). TASER electronic control devices and cardiac arrests: Coincidental or causal? *Circulation, 129*(1), 93–100.

Kroll, M. W., Lakkireddy, D. R., Stone, J. R., & Luceri, R. M. (2014b). Response to letter regarding article, "TASER electronic control devices and cardiac arrests: Coincidental or causal?" *Circulation, 130,* e168.

Kroll, M. W., & Panescu, D. (2012). Physics of electrical injury. In: Ho, J. D., Dawes, D. M. & Kroll, M. W. (eds.) *Atlas of conducted electrical weapon wounds and forensic analysis*. New York, NY: Springer; pp. 25–45.

Kroll, M. W., Panescu, D., Hinz, A. F., & Lakkireddy, D. (2010). A novel mechanism for electrical currents inducing ventricular fibrillation: The three-fold way to fibrillation. *Annual International Conference of the IEEE Engineering in Medicine and Biology Society, 32,* 1990–1996.

Kroll, M., Perkins, P., & Panescu, D. (2015). Electric fence standards comport with human data and AC limits. *Annual International Conference of the IEEE Engineering in Medicine and Biology Society, 37,* 1343–1348.

Kroll, M. W., Walcott, G. P., Ideker, R. E., Graham, M. A., Calkins, H., Lakkireddy, D., ... Panescu, D. (2012). The stability of electrically induced ventricular fibrillation. *Annual International Conference of the IEEE Engineering in Medicine and Biology Society, 34,* 6377–6381.

Kroll, M., Wetli, C., Mash, D., Karch, S. Graham, M., & Ho, J. (2009). Excited delirium syndrome checklist. In M. Kroll & J. Ho (eds.), *TASER conducted electrical weapons: Physiology, pathology, and law*. New York, NY: Springer-Kluwer.

Lakkireddy, D., Wallick, D., Ryschon, K., Chung, M. K., Butany, J., Martin, D., ... Tchou, P. J. (2006). Effects of cocaine intoxication on the threshold for stun gun induction of ventricular fibrillation. *Journal of the American College of Cardiology, 48*(4), 805–811.

Lakkireddy, D., Wallick, D., Verma, A., Ryschon, K., Kowalewski, W., Wazni, O., ... Tchou, P. J. (2008). Cardiac effects of electrical stun guns: Does position of barbs contact make a difference? *Pacing and Clinical Electrophysiology, 31*(4), 398–408.

Laub, J. (2011). *Study of deaths following electro muscular disruption*. Washington, DC: U.S. Department of Justice, National Institute of Justice.

Layman, E. L. (2000). How therapeutic are Tasers? *Journal of the American Psychiatric Nurses Association,* 6(3), 97–99.

MacDonald, J. M., Kaminski, R. J., & Smith, M. R. (2009). The effect of less-lethal weapons on injuries in police use-of-force events. *American Journal of Public Health, 99*(12), 2268–2274.

Mangus, B. E., Shen, L. Y., Helmer, S. D., Maher, J., & Smith, R. S. (2008). Taser and Taser associated injuries: A case series. *American Surgeon, 74*(9), 862–865.

Mash, D. C., Duque, L., Pablo, J., Qin, Y., Adi, N., Hearn, W. L. et al. (2009). Brain biomarkers for identifying excited delirium as a cause of sudden death. *Forensic Science International. 190*(1–3): e13–9.

Mash, D. C., Ouyang, Q., Pablo, J., Basile, M., Izenwasser, S., Lieberman, A. et al. (2003). Cocaine abusers have an overexpression of alpha-synuclein in dopamine neurons. *Journal of Neuroscience, 23*(7): 2564–71.

Mathis, M. (2014). Autopsy findings for Willie James Sams. *Miami-Dade Medical Examiner Report, 19055.*

Mesloh, C., Henych, M., & Wolf, R. (2008). Less lethal weapon effectiveness, use of force, and suspect & officer injuries: A five-year analysis. *Report to the National Institute of Justice (2005-IJ-CX-K050).*

Murray, B. L., Murphy, C. M., & Beuhler, M. C. (2012). Death following recreational use of designer drug "bath salts" containing 3,4-Methylenedioxypyrovalerone (MDPV). *Journal of Medical Toxicology, 8*(1): 69–75.

Nanthakumar, K., Billingsley, I. M., Masse, S., Dorian, P., Cameron, D., Chauhan, V. S., ... Sevaptsidis, E. (2006). Cardiac electrophysiological consequences of neuromuscular incapacitating device discharges. *Journal of the American College of Cardiology, 48*(4), 798–804.

Nimunkar, A. J. & Webster, J. G. (2009). Safety of pulsed electric devices. *Physiological Measurement, 30*(1), 101–114.

OMEGA Foundation. (2000). *Crowd control technologies: An appraisal of technologies for political control*. Luxembourg, Germany: European Parliament, Directorate General for Research.

Panescu, D., Kroll, M., & Brave, M. (2015). Cardiac fibrillation risks with TASER conducted electrical weapons. *Annual International Conference of the IEEE Engineering in Medicine and Biology Society, 37,* 323–329.

Panescu, D., Kroll, M., Iverson, C., & Brave, M. (2014). The sternum as an electrical shield. *Annual International Conference of the IEEE Engineering in Medicine and Biology Society, 36*, 4464–4470.

Panescu, D., Nerheim, M., & Kroll, M. (2013). Electrical safety of conducted electrical weapons relative to requirements of relevant electrical standards. *Annual International Conference of the IEEE Engineering in Medicine and Biology Society, 35*, 5342–5347.

Paterson, S., Cordero, R., & Stearns, E. (2009). Chronic drug use confirmed by hair analysis: its role in understanding both the medical cause of death and the circumstances surrounding the death. *Journal of Forensic and Legal Medicine, 16*(3): 143–7.

Phillips, M., Robinowitz, M., Higgins, J. R., Boran, K. J., Reed, T., & Virmani, R. (1986). Sudden cardiac death in Air Force recruits. A 20-year review. *Journal of the American Medical Association, 256*(19), 2696–2699.

Politi, L., Zucchella, A., Morini, L., Stramesi, C., & Polettini, A. (2007). Markers of chronic alcohol use in hair: Comparison of ethyl glucuronide and cocaethylene in cocaine users. *Forensic Science International, 172*(1): 23–7.

Rahko, P. S. (2008). Evaluation of the skin-to-heart distance in the standing adult by two-dimensional echocardiography. *Journal of the American Society of Echocardiography, 21*(6): 761–4.

Prosser, J. M., & Nelson, L.S. (2011). The toxicology of bath salts: A review of synthetic cathinones. *Journal of Medical Toxicology*, doi:10.1007/s13181-011-0193-z.

Rosenbaum, S., Carreiro, S. P., & Babu, K. M. (2012). Here today, gone tomorrow … and back again? A review of herbal marijuana alternatives (K2, spice), synthetic cathinones (bath salts), kratom, salvia divinorum, methoxetamine, and piperazines. *Journal of Medical Toxicology, 8*(1), 15–32.

Ross, E. A., Watson, M., & Goldberger, B. (2011). "Bath salts" intoxication. *New England Journal of Medicine, 365*(10): 967–8.

Sattout, A. H., & Nicol, M. F. (2009). Cardiac arrest following cannabis use: a case report. *Cases Journal, 2*: 208.

Scott, J. R., Lee, W. R., & Zoledziowski, S. (1973). Ventricular fibrillation threshold for AC shocks of long duration, in dogs with normal acid-base state. *British Journal of Industrial Medicine, 30*(2), 155–161.

Shuman, M. (2013). Autopsy findings for Israel Hernandez. *Miami-Dade Medical Examiner Report, 2043.*

Smith, J. P., Metters, J. P., Khreit, O. I., Sutcliffe, O. B., & Banks, C. E. (2014). Forensic electrochemistry applied to the sensing of new psychoactive substances: Electroanalytical sensing of synthetic cathinones and analytical validation in the quantification of seized street samples. *Analytical Chemistry, 86*(19): 9985–92.

Spiller, H.A., Ryan, M.L., Weston, R. G., & Jansen, J. (2011). Clinical experience with and analytical confirmation of "bath salts" and "legal highs" (synthetic cathinones) in the United States. *Clinical Toxicology (Phila), 49*(6): 499–505.

Stephens, B. G., Jentzen, J. M., Karch, S., Wetli, C. V., & Mash, D. C. (2004). National Association of Medical Examiners position paper on the certification of cocaine-related deaths. *The American journal of Forensic Medicine and Pathology, 25*(1): 11–3.

Strote, J., Verzemnieks, E., Walsh, M., & Hutson, H. R. (2010). Use of force by law enforcement: An evaluation of safety and injury. *Joural of Trauma-Injury Infection & Critical Care, 69*(5), 1288–1293.

Strote, J., Walsh, M., Angelidis, M., Basta, A., & Hutson, H. R. (2010). Conducted electrical weapon use by law enforcement: An evaluation of safety and injury. *Journal of Trauma-Injury Infection & Critical Care, 68*(5), 1239–1246.

Sweeney, J. (2009). Transcutaneous muscle stimulation. In M. Kroll & J. Ho (eds.), *TASER conducted electrical weapons: Physiology, pathology, and law.* New York, NY: Springer-Kluwer.

Swerdlow, C. D., Fishbein, M. C., Chaman, L., Lakkireddy, D. R., & Tchou, P. (2009). Presenting rhythm in sudden deaths temporally proximate to discharge of TASER conducted electrical weapons. *Academic Emergency Medicine, 16*(8): 726–39.

Taylor, B., Woods, D., Kubu, B., Koper, C., Tegeler, B., Cheney, J., … Kappelman, K. (2009). Comparing safety outcomes in police use-of-force cases for law enforcement agencies that have deployed conducted energy devices and a matched comparison group that have not: A quasi-experimental evaluation. *Police*

Executive Research Forum. Retrieved from www.policeforum.org/assets/docs/Free_Online_Documents/Use_of_Force/conducted%20energy%20devices%20matched%20agency%20study%202009.pdf.

Tisdale, J. E., Shimoyama, H., Sabbah, H. N., & Webb, C. R. (1996). The effect of cocaine on ventricular fibrillation threshold in the normal canine heart. *Pharmacotherapy, 16*(3), 429–437, May–June.

Valentino, D. J., Walter, R. J., Dennis, A. J., Margeta, B., Starr, F., Nagy, K. K., … Roberts, R. R. (2008). Taser X26 discharges in swine: Ventricular rhythm capture is dependent on discharge vector. *Journal of Trauma-Injury Infection & Critical Care, 65*(6), 1478–1487.

Valentino, D. J., Walter, R. J., Dennis, A. J., Nagy, K., Loor, M. M., Winners, J., … Roberts, R. (2007). Neuromuscular effects of stun device discharges. *Journal of Surgical Research, 143*(1), 78–87.

Valentino, D. J., Walter, R. J., Dennis, A. J., Nagy, K., Loor, M. M., Winners, J., … Roberts, R. (2008). Acute effects of MK63 stun device discharges in miniature swine. *Military Medicine, 173*(2), 167–173.

Valentino, D. J., Walter, R. J., Nagy, K., Dennis, A. J., Winners, J., Bokhari, F., … Roberts, R. (2007). Repeated thoracic discharges from a stun device. *Journal of Trauma-Injury Infection & Critical Care, 62*(5), 1134–1142.

Varvarigou, V., Farioli, A., Korre, M., Sato, S., Dahabreh, I. J., & Kales, S. N. (2014). Law enforcement duties and sudden cardiac death among police officers in United States: Case distribution study. *British Medical Journal, 349*, g6534.

Vilke, G. M., Bozeman, W. P., & Chan, T. C. (2011). Emergency department evaluation after conducted energy weapon use: Review of the literature for the clinician. *The Journal of Emergency Medicine, 40*(5): 598–604.

Vilke, G. M., Chan, T. C., & Karch, S. (2013). Letter by Vilke et al regarding article, "Sudden cardiac arrest and death following application of shocks from a TASER electronic control device." *Circulation, 127*(1), e258.

Vilke, G. M., Debard, M. L., Chan, T. C., Ho, J. D., Dawes, D. M., Hall, C., … Bozeman, W. P. (2011). Excited delirium syndrome (ExDS): Defining based on a review of the literature. *Journal of Emergency Medicine, 43*(5), 897–905.

Vilke, G. M., Payne-James, J., & Karch, S. B. (2012). Excited delirium syndrome (ExDS): Redefining an old diagnosis. *Journal of Forensic and Legal Medicine, 19*(1), 7–11.

Walcott, G. P., Kroll, M. W., & Ideker, R. E. (2015). Ventricular fibrillation: Are swine a sensitive species? *Journal of Interventional Cardiac Electrophysiology, 42*(2), 83–89.

Walter, R. J., Dennis, A. J., Valentino, D. J., Margeta, B., Nagy, K. K., Bokhari, F., … Roberts, R. R. (2008). TASER X26 discharges in swine produce potentially fatal ventricular arrhythmias. *Academic Emergency Medicine, 15*(1), 66–73.

White, M. D. & Ready, J. (2009). Examining fatal and nonfatal incidents involving the TASER: Identifying predictors of suspect death reported in the media. *Criminology & Public Policy, 8*(4), 865–891.

White, R. D., Goodman, B. W., & Svoboda, M. A. (2011). Neurologic recovery following prolonged out-of-hospital cardiac arrest with resuscitation guided by continuous capnography. *Mayo Clinic Proceedings, 86*(6), 544–548.

Wu, J. Y., Sun, H., O'Rourke, A. P., Huebner, S. M., Rahko, P. S., Will, J. A., & Webster, J. G. (2008). Taser blunt probe dart-to-heart distance causing ventricular fibrillation in pigs. *IEEE Transactions on Biomedical Engineering, 55*(12), 2768–2771.

Wyant, R., & Hinz, A. (2009). Examination of Electronic Control Device Probes to Determine Duration of Application. *Proceedings of the American Academy of Forensic Science.*

Zima, E., Gergely, M., Soos, P., Geller, L. A., Nemes, A., Acsady, G., & Merkely, B. (2006). The effect of induction method on defibrillation threshold and ventricular fibrillation cycle length. *Journal of Cardiovascular Electrophysiology, 17*(4), 377–381.

Zipes, D. P. (2012a). Sudden cardiac arrest and death following application of shocks from a TASER electronic control device. *Circulation, 125*(20), 2417–2422.

Zipes, D. P. (2012b). Deposition in Jacobs v TASER. *Texas District Court, District of Travis County*, vol. D-1-GN-10-003622, 1–44.

Zipes, D. P. (2013). Acknowledgement of Atty. John Burton for sudden cardiac arrest and death following application of shocks from a TASER electronic control device. *Circulation, 127*, e839.

Zipes, D. P. (2014). TASER electronic control devices can cause cardiac arrest in humans. *Circulation, 129*(1), 101–111.

Zuercher, M., Ewy, G. A., Otto, C. W., Hilwig, R. W., Bobrow, B. J., Clark, L., ... Kern, K. B. (2010). Gasping in response to basic resuscitation efforts: observation in a Swine model of cardiac arrest. *Critical Care Research and Practice, 10*(1), 1–7.

14

CUSTODIAL DEATHS IN DETENTION

Darrell L. Ross

Introduction

While rare in occurrence, a custodial death of a detainee confined in a detention facility should not be unexpected (Copeland, 1984; Hundt & Wigger, 2013; Noonan, Rohloff, & Ginder, 2015). Detainees enter a period of confinement with diverse criminal backgrounds and diverse medical and mental health conditions. Maruschak, Berzofsky, and Unangst (2015) report that 45 percent of the jail population enters a period of confinement with varying chronic medical conditions, including: cancer, heart problems, high blood pressure, diabetes, kidney disease, AIDS, and asthma. Further, about 15 percent of the jail detainee population possesses an infectious disease, and about 62 percent are overweight, obese, or morbidly obese. It is estimated that about 54 percent of the jail population enters confinement under the influence of alcohol, prescription medication, or illicit drugs. Moreover, James and Glaze (2006) reported that 64 percent of the jail prisoners were clinically diagnosed with a mental disorder, and 76 percent of these detainees were dependent on or abused drugs.

Given these conditions, it should not be unexpected that a custodial death may occur. As reported in an earlier chapter, the most common causes of death from 2000 to 2013 included: illness (54 percent); suicide (31 percent); drugs/alcohol (5 percent); accident (3 percent); homicide (2 percent); and other or unknown (5 percent). Deaths caused by an illness or suicide account for about 75 percent of all deaths in a detention facility. Deaths from an illness include heart disease and stroke related problems, AIDS-related, cancer, liver disease, asthma, and respiratory disease. Characteristics of the typical detainee decedent include 87 percent white male, average age 35 (70 percent), and in confinement less than seven days (40 percent).

Further, given the millions of jail detainees admitted annually, their medical and mental health condition and unhealthy lifestyles, it is not surprising that a death in confinement may occur. Still, the likelihood of such a death occurring in a detention facility is statistically rare. As discussed earlier, the reported custodial deaths in jails showed that from 1978 to 2013, 17,544 detainees died in jail custody, which averages to about 800 deaths annually. The average daily population (ADP) during that time was 685,000 detainees, with an increase of 79 percent during the time period. However, during this time period, the estimated likelihood of a custodial death in jail was 0.0012 percent.

In a review of the time period from 2000 to 2013, detainee deaths increased to an average of 978 annually, which mirrored a five percent increase in the ADP to 721,143 detainees. However, as with the expanded time period, even with these increases during the 14-year period, the statistical likelihood of a death during jail confinement only rose to 0.0014 percent, still a negligible percentage at less than one percent.

Even allowing for under-reporting and by doubling the average number of jail deaths to 1,956, the estimated likelihood of a death occurring in a jail remains negligible at 0.0027 percent. Of the six reported manners of death, about 80 percent of these deaths included natural illness, suicides, and AIDS. Deaths due to alcohol/drug intoxication accounted for about five percent of all deaths. A detainee death by homicide accounted for less than one percent of the total deaths in jail.

The occurrence of a death of a state prisoner followed slightly different trends than their jail counterparts. From 2001 to 2013, deaths from natural causes and natural illnesses accounted for 90 percent of the deaths, which included: cancer, heart disease, AIDS-related, respiratory disease, liver disease, and other causes. Prisoner deaths by suicide accounted for about 6 percent, homicides accounted for about 1.4 percent, deaths from drug/alcohol intoxication accounted for 1.2 percent, and accidents accounted for 0.8 percent (Carson, 2014). From 2001 to 2013, there were 42,157 prisoner deaths reported and the average prisoner population was 1,172,175. Based on the reported prisoner deaths, it is estimated that the likelihood of a death in prison is about 0.04 percent. The argument that a custodial death during jail or prison confinement is highly likely is not supported by the statistics, and remains at less than one percent of the jail annual daily population or average annual prison population.

Several case studies of a custodial death in a detention facility are illustrative. First, suicides account for about one-third of all detention deaths and that number has remained stable for about 35 years. A detainee was admitted into the jail on an outstanding warrant for first degree sexual conduct from another state. The booking officer noted that he could smell a strong odor of alcohol on the breath of the detainee and heard him say that he should be given a gun to shoot himself. The booking officer followed the standard intake procedures and took the detainee's shoes, belt, jacket, and wallet, but allowed him to retain his jeans and t-shirt. The detainee was given a blanket, and placed in a holding cell, near the booking station, but was not placed on suicide watch.

The detainee was monitored and checked twice during the first hour of his confinement. Detention personnel and the booking officer's attention was diverted from monitoring the detainee for about 30 minutes as they had to assist in controlling a violent and disruptive detainee brought in by a state trooper. At some point later, a detention officer went to check on the detainee and found him slumped over in the cell, unconscious, with the blanket tied around his neck, secured to a narrow pipe in the cell. Officers immediately removed the blanket from the detainee's neck, began CPR, and summoned emergency medical service (EMS) personnel, who responded in about five minutes. Resuscitation efforts were unsuccessful and the detainee died. A $10 million §1983 lawsuit was filed against the officers, the sheriff, and the county on claims of failure to protect the detainee.

The sheriff assigned a detective to investigate the death and the detective submitted a three-page report. However, the detective failed to take any photos of the cell or the blanket, did not inspect the cell, failed to collect and preserve the blanket, did not interview other detainees close to the detainee's cell, failed to review the booking forms and the records of the detainee, and only interviewed two of the four detention officers on shift that night. The court granted summary judgment on behalf of the officers, the sheriff, and the county, concluding that the detainee's own actions caused his death.

Similarly, an alcoholic detainee was admitted into the jail on a probation violation at about 1:00pm. The detainee had been confined in the jail on four prior occasions over several years, and was well known to the detention officers. The detainee was booked into the jail in accordance with standard admission procedures and because he blew a 0.21 blood alcohol content, was placed in an observation cell with a glass front. The detainee refused the evening meal and refused his medication at 8:00pm. The officers documented the detainee's refusal to take his medication but they did not contact his physician. The detainee began trembling, shaking, and stumbling in the cell. When he tried to walk in the cell he lost his balance and hit the glass window several times.

One of the three officers on shift decided to video tape the detainee in the cell so that he could use the video later in a DARE class with local middle school students. The video captured about five minutes of the detainee staggering and stumbling in the cell, striking his head on the glass of the cell several times, and collapsing on the cell floor. The video also showed the detainee picking imaginary bugs off of the glass window. About an hour later, the detainee died from alcohol poisoning. Because of the video, the investigator performed a minimal investigation into the incident. The estate of the detainee filed a civil action and the county settled the case out of court for $2 million.

In another case, a detainee diagnosed as a paranoid schizophrenic was being admitted into the jail for attempting to enter a pre-school with a weapon and partially naked. While standing at the booking counter, with his hands handcuffed behind his back, he refused to cooperate and answer the booking questions. Ten minutes into the booking process, he suddenly turned and kicked the sergeant in the head, splitting his ear. Three officers took him to the floor and secured him in leg restraints, but were unsuccessful in placing him in a restraint chair as he violently struggled with the officers. Officers then carried the detainee to an observation cell, where they removed his leg restraints and attempted to restrain him with a restrain strap, so that medical care could be provided. The strap broke as the detainee continued to violently kick. The officers secured him in leg irons and additional handcuffs and placed him in on his stomach in the cell. The prisoner was placed on a 15-minute watch. When officers returned to the cell within 12 minutes, they discovered him unresponsive, and initiated lifesaving procedures. The detainee died in the ambulance during transport to the hospital.

The detainee had a history of mental illness, with a history of cocaine and alcohol abuse, and had been off of his medication for nine days. An autopsy showed bruising on his wrists and ankles (from struggling against the restraints) and a few cuts to his legs and arms. The decedent's heart weighed 510 grams (grossly enlarged), however, no other internal organ abnormalities were noted. The cause of death was classified as an accident with contributing factors of excited delirium psychosis, associated with physical activity, catecholamine surge, heart abnormality, and physical restraint. An investigation revealed that the decedent had an extensive cocaine use history, had been admitted to Veterans Administration hospitals on over 20 occasions for mental health and drug reasons, and had been four-pointed restrained during a significant number of these admissions. The case settled for about $10 million.

A custodial death in confinement will always raise a myriad of questions and requires a full and complete investigation (Hanzlick, 2007; Wangmo et al., 2014). As observed in the incidents described above, the estate will generally file a civil lawsuit alleging that the decedent's constitutional rights under the Eighth and Fourteenth Amendments were violated (Ross, 2010). A wrongful death lawsuit commonly asserts that the detention officers failed to protect the detainee, failed to provide access to medical or mental health care, and in some incidents allege that the officers used excessive force which contributed to the death (Ross, 2013). The case examples also demonstrate that a full and complete investigation was lacking, which impeded a complete review of the evidence. Allegations of the lawsuit will also routinely assert that an inadequate investigation was conducted, which ratified the actions of the officers.

Every state requires an investigation of a suspicious death and when a death in custody occurs, an investigation is also required. As in any death investigation and consistent with the theme of this text, the circumstances of custodial deaths must be clearly established, which requires a careful examination of the circumstances, the incident scene, the actions of detention officers and supervisors, the collection and analysis of the evidence, the interviews of witnesses and involved officers, and a careful review of the detainee's records and past history. Failure to conduct a thorough and complete investigation means that critical evidence that can reveal the truth of the incident is not collected, which is needed to assist the medical examiner in having "all" pertinent information to determine the cause or mechanism of death (Southall et al., 2008).

As the above case examples illustrate, there is always a question of criminal and civil liability and every effort must be made to conduct a death investigation so that the true cause and manner of death can be determined (Eckert, 1983). The involved officers seek exoneration for their actions and the family seeks retribution for the death (Reay, 1998). The purpose of the investigation will assist the medical examiner in determining the manner of death, will identify the circumstances surrounding the death, will assist in eliminating unfounded rumors and speculation which may emerge, will exonerate or find culpability of the involved officers, and is in the best interests of the department, the decedent's family, the involved officers, and the criminal justice system. Luke and Reay (1992) note that in deaths in custody, the pathology is often less important than are the investigative circumstances.

The purpose of this chapter is to identify investigation guidelines when conducting an investigation of a custodial death in confinement. There are differences between investigating an arrest-related death, an officer-involved shooting, and a custodial death of a detainee or prisoner found dead in a cell. Many of the investigation guidelines addressed in other chapters are applicable to a custodial confinement death investigation. Additional components, however, specific to the confinement setting not addressed in those other chapters will be addressed here so that the investigator will ensure to perform the most complete and thorough custodial death investigation possible. In addition, the guidelines presented in other chapters will not be repeated here, but the investigator tasked with investigating a custodial death in confinement should consider the following guidelines in conjunction with guidelines presented for arrest-related death or officer-involved shooting investigations. A thorough, well-documented investigation is an important step toward managing the difficult problems deaths in custody may present (Lifschultz & Donoghue, 1991). This chapter presents eleven components that should be considered in conjunction with other investigation recommendations previously discussed when performing a detainee death in custody investigation.

Death Scene Circumstances

In a high percentage of custodial deaths in a confinement facility, a detention officer, medical personnel, or other detainee will likely discover the detainee unresponsive in a cell, which becomes the death scene. A detainee, while in an observation cell, segregation cell, or general population cell, found hanging from an apparent suicide, is one example of discovering a custodial death. Hanging is the most common method of detainee suicide in detention facilities and detainees have used blankets and sheets, clothing, ropes, shoestrings, belts, and towels to commit the act (Hayes, 2010). In one incident, where county administrators settled the case out of court, the detainee tightly rolled his

T-shirt and stuffed it down his throat with about two inches dangling from his mouth, asphyxiating himself. Other less common methods of suicide include cutting a wrist or the neck with a razor or sharp object, overdosing on drugs, jumping off of a walkway of the cellblock, and asphyxiation from placing a plastic bag over the head.

In other circumstances, a detainee may be found unresponsive in a cell and die later in the hospital due to cardiorespiratory complications or other medical conditions. A few detainees have died in the jail while going through a period of supervised alcohol withdrawal. As a further example, a once violent or combative detainee who vigorously fought with detention officers may be secured in a restraint chair or restrained in a cell may be discovered unresponsive during a security check. These examples portray some circumstances in which a decedent detainee is discovered.

Once a detainee is discovered unresponsive in the cell, the practice is for the detention officer to summon additional assistance from other officers, a supervisor, jail medical personnel, and to request outside EMS personnel. It is not uncommon for fire and rescue personnel to respond as well. If the detainee is found hanging, the officers will remove any ligature around the neck and/or remove any other object used to commit the act. Once this is accomplished, the officers may initiate resuscitation procedures and relinquish these efforts when jail medical and/or EMS personnel arrive and attend to the detainee. Depending on the circumstances, officers will commonly relocate other detainees to other cells and lock down the area.

In responding to the emergency situation, officers will most likely move the position of the detainee to render medical care, which will contaminate the scene. If the detainee is secured in a restraint chair, the responding officers will remove the detainee from the chair and remove additional restraints if they were applied. Frequently, because of the small size of the cell and the number of personnel who typically respond to render lifesaving procedures, the detainee may be moved outside of the cell to a hallway or in a corridor in order to provide more room for the procedures. Handling the unresponsive body may add injury or trauma to the body. For example, a detainee may sustain injury to the head, neck, or spine when he or she is cut down from hanging and accidently dropped on the cell floor. Trauma may be sustained when removing the detainee from a restraint chair and removing additional restraints. Rendering resuscitative procedures may also produce injuries. It is not uncommon for a detainee to sustain trauma to the sternum and rib fractures from chest compressions. The detainee may also sustain injury to the larynx through intubation by attending EMS personnel.

In a majority of incidents, the detainee will be transported from the detention facility to the hospital before the assigned investigator arrives on scene. Managing the scene area is critically important. A supervisor or appropriate agency individual should begin contacting the sheriff or warden, the undersheriff, jail administrator, medical examiner, department investigator, crime scene technicians, prosecutor, risk manager, department chaplain, and agency attorney to respond to the facility. The responding supervisor or assigned officer should secure the scene, protect it, limit individuals from entering the area, and begin a log which records everyone who entered and exited the area. Visitation and treatment programs should be postponed and all detainees placed on lockdown until the investigation is completed. A supervisor should ensure other detainees do not enter the scene area and do not allow any trustee to enter the area to clean the scene. Unbelievably, this has happened in a few incidents. Items associated with the death found in the cell or moved outside of the cell, including medical equipment, should not be disturbed and left in their position.

Once the decedent is removed from the confinement facility, involved personnel should be separated, instructed not to discuss the incident with one another, and provide a preliminary statement.

All involved officers, supervisors, and jail medical personnel should be identified and their level of involvement documented. Administrators should not conduct an interview with the involved officers or with responding jail medical personnel. If an officer sustained an injury during a use of force incident, a supervisor or investigator should take photos of the injuries and the officer in full uniform. The officer(s) should be escorted to the hospital by a fellow officer and treated. Documentation of hospital treatment should be maintained and the uniform collected and preserved.

Responding to and attending to the death of a detainee can be traumatic for the involved officers and they should be allowed to contact their family and their attorney. Involved officers should be escorted home by a peer support officer, placed on administrative leave for a minimum of three days, and return to work for a formal interview within 24 to 72 hours. Prior to the interview, involved personnel should be able to view the video of the incident if one exists. Involved officers should be referred to mental health counseling as appropriate. A supervisor or administrator should fully explain the investigation process to the involved officers and provide them with updates as the investigation progresses.

Investigator on Scene

The assigned investigator(s) should respond to the sheriff, undersheriff, or jail administrator's office and receive a briefing on the incident. One investigator should conduct the investigation at the facility while another should be assigned to the hospital. The investigator should refrain from forming a biased opinion about the circumstances just because it appears the detainee committed suicide or died from natural causes in the confinement facility. The investigation should be performed in an objective manner, consistent with procedures that guide all death investigations. During the briefing, the investigator should obtain the following information: circumstances of the death; how, where, and when the detainee was discovered; a description of the position of the detainee as discovered in the cell; a description of who discovered the detainee; the activities of all involved officers and supervisors once the detainee was discovered; the actions of responding jail medical personnel; and the actions of all responding EMS personnel (Eliopulos, 2003). The investigator assigned to the facility should perform a walkthrough of the area where the detainee was discovered, take photos of the scene, and begin recording notes of his or her observations.

Incident Scene

Once crime scene technicians arrive at the jail, the investigator should perform a briefing with them and conduct a walkthrough of the scene area. An incident scene log should be started and maintained through the end of the investigation. Like other death scenes, assigned technicians should place numbered placards next to items of evidence and photograph them, documenting these items of evidence on a photo log. Technicians should videotape the incident scene as well. All items found on the scene should be collected, documented, and bagged appropriately, with the person bagging the items placing his or her initials on the bag. Bodily fluids of the detainee should be collected, preserved, and stored appropriately. A log of all items collected should be documented and the name of the person collecting and bagging the evidence should be recorded. The chain of custody must be maintained of all collected and bagged evidence and documented. The investigator and technicians should adhere to safety procedures when processing the scene and collecting evidence. The investigator should not release the crime scene until the autopsy has been finalized and a final walkthrough has been accomplished, ensuring that all of the evidence has been collected and all photos have been taken. The investigator should cross reference all evidence and photos taken against the custodial deaths investigator checklist (see Appendix A).

Components of the Custodial Death Investigation

Facility Documents

There are numerous facility documents and items associated with custodial deaths which need to be collected and analyzed by the investigator. Due to the differences in detention facilities, not all of the documents or forms identified may be used or available at all detention facilities. All documents associated with the booking and intake process should be collected, which may include: arrest report of the arresting agency; the booking and intake observation form/questionnaire; medical and mental health screening form; housing and security classification forms; medical assessment at time of booking; booking photograph; fingerprint card; detainee property inventory form; the video of the booking process; and the video of cell and/or pod surveillance. The investigator should collect any documents or directives initiated by detention supervisors directing officers in the frequency of conducting security checks of the detainee. Officer reports of responding to the death scene and their involvement should be retrieved and assessed

Detainee Medical Records

The detainee's medical file should be collected and analyzed. Documents pertinent to the investigation should include: medical assessment and screening of the detainee after admission by medical personnel; sick call records; any referrals to mental health and any treatment and treatment plans developed mental health during confinement; any transport to a medical or mental health facility during confinement; medical treatment provided by jail medical personnel and/or hospital personnel; jail nurse/physician medical notes and file; escorts by detention personnel for medical purposes; a listing of all medications prescribed for the detainee; the log of all medications dispensed; and referrals or reports prepared by detention officers or supervisors regarding the participation in providing the detainee access to medical care. The health care contractor agreement should be collected.

Detainee Supervision Logs and Video

The investigator should collect all logs or forms that are associated with supervising the detainee, which may include: medical observation chart; suicide watch monitoring chart; drug withdrawal monitoring chart; chart for monitoring the detainee restrained in a restraint chair or after a use of force requiring restraints or after using a conducted energy weapon (CEW); detainee daily activity log; detainee phone log with audio recordings of the calls; detainee visitation log; cell check monitoring log; officer daily activity log; and a log documenting escorting the detainee outside the facility. The investigator should collect and analyze all surveillance videos and logs that are associated with the death of the detainee.

Use of Force

If the death of the detainee is associated with a use of force incident, the investigator should collect and assess the appropriate incident documents and equipment. Such documents and items may include officer reports and a description of all restraints that were used, including the restraint chair, aerosol, CEW, impact weapon, and spit guard. Photographs of all equipment used in controlling the detainee should be taken. The CEW data printout should be collected and assessed. Manufacture specifications should be assessed to determine whether the equipment was used appropriately. If there is surveillance video available, which recorded the force incident, monitoring of the detainee in the restraint chair or in the cell, and shows officers providing medical attention to the detainee, the investigator should collect, preserve, and analyze it. The investigator should meet with the department's use of force instructor to review the video and to review the empty-hand control techniques and equipment used by the involved officers.

Other Documents

The investigator should obtain additional documents pertinent to the death. These documents may include: jail floor plan and cell design; appropriate policies and procedures of the department relevant to the incident; EMS and fire rescue run sheets; hospital emergency room medical reports and records; and suicide note if one exists (which should be preserved). The investigator should collect, preserve, and analyze radio communications within the jail if they exist, as well as recordings of dispatch communications.

At the Hospital

The investigator assigned to the hospital should work with hospital personnel in taking photos of the detainee, if death has not yet occurred, documenting all signs of injuries and trauma. The investigator should collect and preserve the detainee's clothes and photograph and bag them appropriately. Any statements and behaviors of the detainee at the hospital should be documented, as well as statements made by family members and friends. If the detainee made a dying declaration, it should be recorded if feasible and documented if not recorded. The investigator should conduct interviews of EMS and/or responding firefighters, attending emergency room medical personnel, and surgeon at the hospital, if surgery was performed. Copies of medical treatment records rendered at the hospital and tests performed should be obtained.

Autopsy

Consistent with other death investigations, the investigator should attend the autopsy. Even though the cause of death may appear to be obvious, from natural causes, accident or by suicide, the medical examiner or pathologist performing the autopsy will make the final classification of death, and the investigator should be in attendance. In cases where the cause of death may be classified as undetermined, as a result of a negative autopsy or in cases where the cause of death is classified as a homicide, the investigator needs to be in attendance at the autopsy. During the autopsy, the investigator should take notes, take photographs of the procedure, obtain a copy of the death certificate, obtain the autopsy report, and obtain a report of all tests performed on the decedent. In deaths classified as undetermined or as a homicide, the investigator should request toxicology tests be performed, including: the urine, the blood, gastric contents, vitreous humor, bile and liver, and hair (DiMaio & DiMaio, 2006; Graham, 2014; James & Nordby, 2012; Sathyavagiswaran, Rogers, & Noguchi, 2007).

The tissues of the heart, brain, lungs, and other organs should also be tested in incidents where the detainee vigorously fought against physical control measures, CEW, aerosol, and restraint equipment used by the officers. All signs of trauma identified on the body should be examined and noted (Hiss & Kahana, 1996). Documentation of needle marks or tracks on the body should be noted (Eckert, 1983). Graham (2014) also recommends that tissues be examined for sickle-cell trait condition. The structures of the neck should be carefully examined in cases where asphyxia is suspected (Vilke, 2006). In cases of a sudden death after a violent restraint use of force confrontation, the investigator should carefully review the histology, serology, and toxicology reports, as well as other tests, including a review of the condition of the heart (e.g., the size of the heart and whether it was diseased) and other organs (e.g., the size and condition of the lungs, the condition of the brain, and artifacts that occurred post mortem), as well as signs of life saving efforts on the body (Ross, 2006). The investigator should take photographs of the decedent's ankles and wrists to document the application of restraints, signature marks of the application of a CEW, and the use of an impact weapon (align with a scale).

Detainee Personal History

The investigator should collect and analyze the personal history of the detainee. As discussed in another chapter, the investigator should conduct an investigation into the background of the detainee, which will provide additional information about the detainee's medical and mental health condition (DiMaio & DiMaio, 1989; Laub, 2011; Lawrence & Mohr, 2004; Ross, 2006). The investigation should include the following historical components: family, residential, military, employment, medical and mental health, arrest/conviction and confinement, parole and probation records, behavioral, and substance abuse records.

Interviews

Consistent with other death investigations, the investigator should conduct interviews with all personnel involved in the incident, including the involved officers, involved detention medical personnel, and involved supervisors. The investigator should identify, document, and also interview: the arresting officers; other officers who may have witnessed the officer's response; other detention facility personnel who may have witnessed the officer's response, such as teachers, social workers, chaplain, etc.; other detainees in proximity to the detainee's cell; and the jail administrator and command personnel overseeing the shift. Contact information of the witnesses should be documented and written statements obtained from the witnesses.

Notifying the Family

The investigator should make contact with the detainee's family or next of kin as soon as possible and inform them of the death. As feasible, the investigator, along with the medical examiner and the department chaplain, should make contact at the family member's residence and treat all family members with respect and dignity. The family should be alerted to the time and date of the autopsy. The investigator should explain the investigation process to the family and keep them informed as to the progress of the investigation. The investigator should schedule a formal interview with appropriate family members and provide them with his or her contact information. Personal belongings of the detainee should be returned to the family as soon as reasonably possible.

Investigation Report

Once all of the investigatory tasks are accomplished, the investigation report must be developed and submitted. Writing the report is as important as ensuring that all the evidence is properly collected, preserved, and documented. The detainee's death produces potential implications of criminal and/or civil liability and potential policy violations regarding the actions of detention officers, supervisors, and detention medical personnel. Hence, the report should document the culmination of a complete, thorough, and unbiased investigation upon which important decisions will be made.

The components of the investigation report were previously described in another chapter. In conjunction with those report components, the investigator should also include the following items as they relate to a custodial death in confinement: a review of the detention booking and intake documents; a review of the observation and medical assessment of the detainee at time of booking; a review of the access to and medical and mental health treatment of the detainee; a review of all photos taken; a review of the condition of the cell in which the detainee was discovered; a review of all the detention medical and mental health records; a review of detainee supervisory logs and activity reports; interviews of all detainee witnesses and detention personnel witnesses; a review of the detainee's criminal history and incarceration history; housing and classification forms; charting and monitoring documents of the detainee on medical watch, suicide watch, substance withdrawal watch, in restraint chair, or after the use of force; a review of the cell check and activity logs; a description of the use of force measures used by the officers to control a resisting and combative detainee; a review of the medical attention provided to the detainee once discovered unresponsive; a review of when EMS was called, responded, and when EMS left the facility en route to the hospital with the detainee; and a review of the intervention provided by the hospital emergency room personnel. The investigator should assemble the incident information into a "freeze frame" assessment by developing a time line which chronicles the dates and times of the events and officer actions and response regarding the detainee custodial death (Luke & Reay, 1992).

Summary

This chapter has described the guidelines for investigating a custodial death of a confined detainee. The discussion has primarily focused on deaths in detention facilities, although the guidelines have applicability to deaths of prisoners confined in state and federal prison. The guidelines are based on published works and best practices in the field. The guidelines discussed in this chapter should also be combined with the guidelines presented in other chapters. Carefully following the guidelines, combined with using investigation checklists, will ensure the investigation is thoroughly performed, thereby minimizing potential errors that may emerge.

Appendix A

Custodial Deaths Investigator Checklist

Incident Scene Log

☐ Officers on scene ☐ Administrator ☐ Jail medical personnel ☐ Paramedics
☐ Detainees ☐ Crime scene technicians ☐ Other personnel
☐ Walk through ☐ Photos ☐ Photo log ☐ Evidence collected/preserved

Location of Death (Fully Describe)

☐ Cell ☐ Shower ☐ Day room ☐ Common area of pod
☐ Medical unit ☐ Restraint chair ☐ Hospital ☐ Other

Instrumentality of Death

☐ Bedding ☐ Plastic bag ☐ Weapon ☐ Glass ☐ Razor/sharp instrument
☐ Clothing ☐ Towel ☐ Cord/rope ☐ Other

Facility Documents

☐ Booking/admission ☐ Booking photo ☐ Arrest report ☐ Medical/mental health screening
☐ Property inventory ☐ Classification ☐ Housing assignment ☐ Criminal history
☐ Finger print card ☐ Disciplinary actions ☐ Court contacts ☐ Activity logs
☐ Security checks ☐ Visits ☐ Phone calls ☐ Video surveillance
☐ Officer reports ☐ All relevant policies ☐ Prior confinements ☐ Other

Medical/Mental Health Records

☐ Health appraisal ☐ Medication distribution log ☐ Nurse notes ☐ Mental health appraisal
☐ Jail physician exam ☐ Sick call records ☐ Treatment plans ☐ Mental health referral
☐ Escorts to hospital ☐ Medical treatment ☐ Medical response of personnel ☐ Other

Observation Cell Watch

☐ Video ☐ Initiation of watch ☐ Security checks ☐ Suicide observation chart
☐ Withdrawal observation chart ☐ Medical personnel checks ☐ Restraint chair observation chart
☐ Other

Use of Force

☐ Officer reports ☐ Intermediate weapons used ☐ Aerosol ☐ All restraints used ☐ Spit guard
☐ Restraint chair ☐ Photos of all equipment ☐ TASER printout
☐ Collect and preserve all evidence ☐ Video of incident ☐ Medical assistance ☐ Other

Other Documents

☐ Jail floor plan ☐ Cell design ☐ Pod design ☐ Radio communications ☐ Dispatch tapes
☐ Suicide note ☐ Other

Interviews

☐ Officers ☐ Supervisors ☐ Detainee witnesses ☐ Visitors ☐ Medical personnel
☐ Arresting officer ☐ Teachers ☐ Social workers ☐ Chaplin ☐ Administrators
☐ Other

At the Hospital

☐ EMS/fire rescue run sheet ☐ Paramedics ☐ Fire rescue ☐ ER nurse ☐ ER physician
☐ Family members ☐ Dying declaration ☐ Photo decedent ☐ Photo clothes
☐ Photos of officers ☐ Other

Detainee Personal History

☐ Family ☐ Employment ☐ Military ☐ Education ☐ Criminal ☐ Medical
☐ Mental health ☐ Probation ☐ Parole ☐ Behavioral ☐ Substance abuse ☐ Residential

References

Carson, E. A. (2014). *Prisoners in 2013.* Washington, DC: United States Department of Justice, Bureau of Justice Statistics.

Copeland, A. R. (1984). Deaths in custody revisited. *American Journal Forensic Medicine and Pathology, 5*(2), 121–124.

DiMaio, D. J. & DiMaio, V. (1989). *Forensic Pathology.* New York, NY: Elsevier.

DiMaio, T. G. & DiMaio, V. J. M. (2006). *Excited delirium syndrome: Cause of death and prevention.* Boca Raton, FL: CRC Press.

Eckert, G. (1983). Medicolegal investigation of problems involving criminals and criminal activity. *American Journal of Forensic Medicine and Pathology, 4*(3), 279–286.

Eliopulos, L. N. (2003). *Death investigator's handbook: Expanded an updated edition.* Boulder, CO: Paladin Press.

Graham, M. A. (2014). Investigation of deaths temporally associated with law enforcement apprehension. *Academic Forensic Pathology, 4*(3), 366–389.

Hanzlick, R. (2007). *Death investigation: Systems and procedures.* Boca Raton, FL: CRC Press.

Hayes, L. M. (2010). *National study of jail suicide: 20 years later.* Washington, DC: United States Department of Justice, National Institute of Corrections.

Hiss, J. & Kahana, T. (1996). Medicolegal investigations of death in custody: A postmortem procedure for detection of blunt force injuries. *American Journal of Forensic Medicine and Pathology, 17*(4), 312–314.

Hundt, P. & Wigger, A. (2013). *Guidelines for investigating deaths in custody.* Geneva, Switzerland: International Committee of the Red Cross.

James, D. J. & Glaze, L. E. (2006). *Mental health problems of jail inmates.* Washington, DC: United States Department of Justice, Bureau of Justice Statistics.

James, S. H. & Nordby, J. J. (2012). *Forensic science: An introduction to scientific and investigative techniques* (Third edition). Boca Raton, FL: CRC Press, Taylor and Francis Group.

Laub, J. (2011). *Death investigation: A guide for the scene investigator, technical update.* Washington, DC: United States Department of Justice, National Institute of Justice.

Lawrence, C. & Mohr, W. (2004). Investigator protocol: Sudden in-custody death. *The Police Chief, 71*(1), 46–49.

Lifschultz, B. D. & Donoghue, E. R. (1991). Deaths in custody. *Legal Medicine, 1*, 45–71.

Luke, J. L. & Reay, D. T. (1992). The perils of investigating and certifying deaths in police custody. *American Journal of Forensic Medicine and Pathology, 13*(2), 98–100.

Maruschak, L. M., Berzofsky, M., & Unangst, J. (2015). *Medical problems of state and federal prisoners and jail inmates: 2011 to 2012.* Washington, DC: United States Department of Justice, Bureau of Justice Statistics.

Noonan, M., Rohloff, H., & Ginder, S. (2015). *Mortality in local jails and state prisons, 2000 to 2013—Statistical tables.* Washington, DC: United States Department of Justice, Bureau of Justice Statistics.

Reay, D. T. (1998). Death in custody. *Clinics in Laboratory Medicine, 1*, 1–22.

Ross, D. L. (2006). Administrative issues. In D. L. Ross & T. C. Chan (eds.) *Sudden deaths in custody* (203–228). Totowa, NJ: Humana Press.

Ross, D. L. (2010). The liability trends of custodial suicides. *American Jails Magazine, 24*(1), 37–47.

Ross, D. L. (2013). *Civil liability in criminal justice* (6th ed.). Waltham, MA: Anderson Publishing.

Sathyavagiswaran, L., Rogers, C., & Noguchi, T. T. (2007). Restraint asphyxia in in-custody deaths: Medical examiner's role in prevention of deaths. *Legal Medicine, 9*(2), 88–93.

Southall, P., Grant, J., Fowler, D., & Scott, S. (2008). Police custody deaths in Maryland, USA: An examination of 45 cases. *Journal of Forensic and Legal Medicine, 15*(4), 227–230.

Vilke, G. M. (2006). Neck holds. In D. L. Ross & T. C. Chan (eds.), *Sudden deaths in custody* (15–38). Totowa, NJ: Humana Press.

Wangmo, T., Ruiz, G., Sinclair, J., Mangin, P., & Elger, B. S. (2014). The investigation of deaths in custody: A quantitative analysis of problems and prospects. *Journal of Forensic and Legal Medicine, 25*(July), 30–37.

15

CONDUCTING THE INVESTIGATIVE INTERVIEW

R. Edward Geiselman, James F. Wilson, and Alexis Artwohl

Introduction

Officer-involved shooting (OIS) investigations are directed at the determination of whether the shooter officer's decision to use deadly force was "objectively reasonable under the totality of the circumstances confronting the officer," and thus was both lawful and within department policy. An adversarial relationship between the investigator and the involved officer can be created if the investigator conducts the interview of the "subject" officer more from the perspective of a suspect interrogation rather than that of a witness interview. It therefore is important that use of force investigators recognize that officers who have been involved in an OIS incident are *not* suspects in any wrongdoing (unless and until evidence of wrongdoing has been developed). Rather, they are law enforcement professionals who have been trained, equipped, and sent out to deal with critical incidents on society's behalf, and who have just witnessed and experienced such an incident in the line of duty.

In the context of determining the "objective reasonableness" of an officer's use of force, the only facts and circumstances which have any legal relevance are those that were known to that officer at the moment that the decision to use force was made. In each OIS investigation, therefore, the accurate determination of the question at hand turns on the collection of all available data concerning exactly what constituted the "totality of the circumstances" confronting the officer at the time of the decision to use deadly force. As a result, the goal of the OIS investigator should be to obtain as complete and accurate an understanding of the involved officer's perception of those circumstances as is possible. In order to do so, the investigator must conduct the interview of the involved officer in such a manner as to maximize the "take" from the interview. The interview protocol currently used in some jurisdictions for conducting the OIS investigation can create circumstances that are less than ideal to achieve that goal.

Sometimes, the investigative questioning carries unintended overtones of suspicion and accusations against the involved officer. These interviews tend to be conducted in a choppy question and answer (Q&A) type format that tends to disrupt the officer's train of thought and deters in-depth memory recall. This can create a non-optimal outcome scenario as follows. Considerable research shows that most deceptive persons tend to offer minimal, bare-bones reports (McCormack et al., 2009), but with an adversarial approach to OIS investigations, truthful officers can be just as hesitant to give complete reports. This limits the development of adequate justification for the action and almost guarantees later additions to the report (reminiscent memories). The preferred option, then, should be to reset the mission procedurally, where there are no "bad guys"; where the OIS investigators and involved officers constitute a team with the common goal of gathering and reporting the "totality of the circumstances" to which the officer was responding with the use of deadly force; and where the standing presumption is honesty. Certainly, the interviewer must challenge the involved officer if a challenge appears warranted, but research shows that this challenge should come late in the information-gathering interview, not from the outset (Geiselman, 2012; Hartwig et al., 2006). While this reset of the mission may seem like special treatment, such treatment is justified under the special circumstances presented in a duty-related OIS.

The Cognitive Interview Approach

The interviewing technique known as the cognitive interview (CI) offers OIS investigators the opportunity to achieve the goal of maximizing the "take" from the interview of an officer who has been involved in a critical incident (Fisher & Geiselman, 1992; Geiselman & Fisher, 1997, 2014). The CI is a systematic approach to interviewing victims and witnesses toward increasing the amount of relevant information obtained without compromising the rate of accuracy.

The CI is based on scientifically derived principles of memory and communication theory as well as extensive analyses of law-enforcement interviews. The CI has been found in both scientific laboratory and field studies to produce significantly more information than standard police Q&A interviews, and the protocol is legally acceptable to the courts. The CI provides a template for conducting any investigative interview (Appendix A), but it also supplies the interviewer with a toolbox of specific techniques designed to elicit specific kinds of information. Several elements of the CI are directly relevant to a good-practice approach to OIS investigative interviews. First, the CI relies on the witness to provide the needed information via open-ended questions. This approach is witness-centered rather than interviewer-centered, in that it is driven by the witness's recollection of events, and not by the interviewer's preconceived notions of what information is important to the outcome of the investigation. After all, the involved officer has the needed information (i.e., the facts and circumstances known by him/her at the moment of decision), not the interviewer. Second, the CI encourages the witness to be complete in his/her report and utilizes reliable memory-enhancement techniques to achieve this goal. Third, the communications elements of the CI establish a solid social foundation that is conducive to reporting information. Fourth, research has shown that the CI effectively addresses psychological stressors like those frequently encountered following an OIS incident.

The CI approach has been implemented for several years as standard practice in the conduct of victim/witness interviews in criminal investigations at many federal, state, and local policing agencies nationwide, as well as in other countries (e.g., the UK). The principal elements of the CI were included in the DOJ Federal Guidelines on handling and preserving eyewitness evidence in 1999 (National Institute of Justice, 1999). Just as the CI has been helpful for interviewing lay victims and witnesses of crime, it has proven valuable for interviewing officers involved in shootings and other critical incidents. A manual for conducting the full CI was published in 1992 (Fisher & Geiselman, 1992).

The CI has been tested as an information-gathering technique in over 100 laboratory studies, most of which were conducted in the United States, England, Germany, or Australia. In these studies, volunteer witnesses observed either a live event or a videotape of a simulated crime. Shortly thereafter (ranging from a few hours to several days), the witnesses were interviewed by a trained researcher—or in some cases by experienced police officers—who conducted either a CI or a control interview. The control interview was either modeled after a typical police Q&A interview or after another generally accepted interview protocol (e.g., stepwise interview). Across these studies, the CI typically elicited between 25 and 50 percent more correct statements than did the control interview. The effect is also extremely reliable. For example, Koehnken et al. (1999) examined 55 experiments in one meta-analysis, and found that in 53 of the experiments, the CI elicited more information than did the comparison interview (median increase of 34 percent). Equally important, accuracy was as high or slightly higher in the CI interviews (accuracy rate of .85) than in the comparison interviews (accuracy rate of .82) (Koehnken et al., 1999). The reliability of the CI for improving memory recall was replicated in a more recent, second meta-analysis that included more studies (Memon, Meissner, & Fraser, 2010). The CI also was successfully field tested as an interview procedure in actual criminal cases with real witnesses and victims of crime (Fisher, Geiselman, & Amador, 1989; Geiselman & Fisher, 1997; George & Clifford, 1992), and has been credited with aiding in the solution of many celebrated criminal cases.

How the CI Works

The CI approach builds upon the standard police interview in several important ways. First, the CI expands the rapport development phase of an interview by engaging the witness with interview preparation instructions to clarify the nature and purpose for the interview up front, as well as to clarify the role to be played by the witness. These instructions include building teamwork for the interview, securing concentration, and encouraging completeness. Suggested wording for this phase of the interview specifically crafted for use in OIS interviews is presented later in this chapter.

The CI also utilizes reliable memory jogging techniques taken from the field of cognitive psychology that have been demonstrated in experiments to reliably enhance accurate memory recall. For example, the narrative account from the witness is preceded by a mental reinstatement of the physical and emotional context that existed just before and during the incident, and the narrative ultimately is requested a second time but in reverse chronological order to elicit additional details. The CI technique also includes guidelines for developing a plan during the initial narrative for asking follow-up questions. The follow-up questioning relies heavily on asking open-ended questions such as, "Tell me in detail more about 'xyz' if you can." The interviewer should slow down the pace of the questioning and allow a brief pause following each answer. These communication measures will increase the likelihood that the witness will search memory thoroughly. To carry out the follow-up questioning plan, the CI utilizes a toolbox of specific memory jogging techniques for eliciting specific kinds of information, such as person descriptions, names, and numbers. The CI protocol is in stark contrast with a standard Q&A approach, where only specific short-answer questions are asked of the witness, with frequent interruptions, and without any memory-jogging initiatives.

Near the end of the CI protocol, the witness is asked to give the narrative a second time, but this time to begin with the last thing that happened in the incident and then to describe in detail the events moving backward in time systematically until the witness reaches the beginning of the incident.

Questions such as, "What happened right before that?" and "What were you thinking and looking at right before that?" are useful as prompts during the reverse-order recall and can elicit additional details. Reverse-order recall tends to slow down the action in the witness's mind and allows for a more exhaustive search of the memory record, frame by frame.

Also near the end of the CI interview, the witness is asked to consider the different perspectives that he/she may have had on the events during the incident and/or to think about the incident again from the perspective of someone else present at the scene. Asking the witness to draw a diagram of the events, indicating where he/she was located during the incident, and to think about what he/she was able to see from each location are useful aids in enhancing the "take" from this phase of the interview. The change-perspectives technique is a memory-jogging tool that also has been shown to increase the amount of details recalled. Throughout the interview, the witness should be cautioned against speculating or guessing, but rather to report only what he/she believes to have happened.

It is important that the interviewer not interrupt the witness during the interview. Instead, the interviewer should take limited notes during the narrative phase of the interview, jotting down key words or phrases from the witness so that the "scenes" from the narrative can be probed later with follow-up questions. The interviewer must devote full attention to the narrative without interrupting the witness's concentration. More detailed notes can be taken during the follow-up questioning, but consider using a secondary interviewer who can take detailed notes throughout the interview while the primary interviewer manages the flow of the interview. The interviewer(s) will review the notes with the witness before concluding the interview to insure accuracy and to allow for changes and/or additions to the record.

The CI Compared to Conventional Q&A Interviews

With conventional Q&A interviews, victims and witnesses often report that they feel like suspects when they are asked a string of very specific, closed questions at the outset of the interview. In comparison, when witnesses are permitted to give an open-ended narration at the beginning of a CI, they report that they feel as if the interviewer trusts them, and is listening to them. Not surprisingly, feeling like a trusted person rather than a suspect should contribute to the witness's perception of dignity and respect and enhance the witness's commitment to participate fully in the effort to mine his/her memory.

Victims and witnesses often will be anxious about the interview process because they are uncertain about what is expected of them and how the process will transpire (Sydeman et al., 1997). CI interviewers attempt to reduce that uncertainty by previewing the structure of the interview, and especially by explaining the "ground rules" of the interview. Furthermore, victims are encouraged to ask questions about the process. Foreshadowing the interview should reduce victims' anxiety about the process as it reduces uncertainty. These measures will likely contribute to a more successful search of the involved officer's memory for details of the incident as well as the officer's ongoing state of mind.

Conventional Q&A interviews rely heavily on asking many closed questions, relegating the interviewee to the role of question answerer. In comparison, the CI relies more heavily on eliciting information via open-ended questions, inducing witnesses to narrate about the topics of investigative interest. It is common for people to comment that the CI does not seem like an interview at all, because the interviewer asks so few questions, and the witness seems merely to be telling a story. By allowing interviewees to talk more, and especially in the form of a narration, the CI has an enabling effect by affording more control to the interviewees to give voice to their stories. The free narrative format also allows interviewees to relate their stories in a non-coercive fashion. Fisher, Mello, and McCauley (1999) found that CI interviews were rated as being less manipulative and less coercive than interviews conducted in a Q&A fashion.

In a typical Q&A interview, the investigator controls the social dynamics, and structures the interview around the interviewer's own cognitive needs and preconceptions as to what sort of information is important to the success of the interview. For instance, interviewers frequently interrupt witnesses' narrations to ask follow-up questions, because interviewers are concerned that they will forget to ask the follow-up questions, and consider only secondarily, or not at all, that their interruptions disrupt the witnesses' thought processes. By comparison, in a CI, the witness plays the central role—the witness's thoughts and emotions drive the interview process, and the interviewer alters his/her questions in response to the witness's recollections. It is likely that the witness's greater control over the interview process in the CI leads to a greater sense of self-efficacy than in the typical police interview, where the witness plays a more subordinate role.

The CI witness likely concentrates more intensely during the interview, than does a conventional interview witness. That comes about for a variety of reasons: (a) CI interviewers ask fewer questions and are less likely to disrupt the witness's concentration; (b) the CI is conducted at a slower pace; (c) the CI witness is encouraged to close his/her eyes (if desired); and (d) the CI encourages witnesses to provide long narrative responses, in which they become increasingly focused as the narrative develops. It is likely that the resulting heightened concentration allows witnesses to be more relaxed during the interview, and that this confers a greater sense of control and mastery when thinking about the critical event.

The aforementioned are the major differences between the CI and conventional Q&A interviews. It is interesting to note that some schools of journalism offer teaching modules on good practice interviewing techniques for use with victims and witnesses to traumatic events, and the suggestions in these modules are very similar to the elements of the CI protocol (Cote & Simpson, 2000). Explaining the ground rules up front and fostering a sense of teamwork are considered central. Building rapport, effective listening, and sharing control with the interviewee are also key. Thus, cognitive interviewing and journalistic interviewing are largely consistent with respect to recommended questioning of victims and witnesses of stressful events.

Other Considerations

Electronic recording of an OIS investigative interview is controversial in part because in some states, as soon as the investigation is complete, the recording becomes a public record. On the one hand, reliving the events of the OIS incident during this post-incident interview often is a highly emotional experience, especially when the interview is not delayed, and the officer's emotions (e.g., sorrow, anger) should be protected from unfettered public scrutiny. In fact, one powerful memory-jogging tool from the CI protocol is the mental reinstatement of the emotional context that the officer experienced during the incident. The officer should not be deterred from reliving these emotions because in doing so, memory retrieval is expected to be more complete. On the other hand, recording the interview would reduce some of the cognitive load placed on the interviewer by the need to take detailed notes during the interview, such that the interviewer could concentrate more on managing the flow of the interview. Furthermore, a show of emotion by the officer or candid comments such as, "I'm angry that the suspect made me use deadly force," could be turned to the advantage of the defense should that be necessary in litigation, which might subsequently arise against the involved officer and/or his/her employing entity. Such statements can be used to illustrate to the jury that the officer was upset by having been required to use deadly force and is not the sort of person who goes to work expecting to, or looking forward to, using deadly force on the citizenry. A middle-ground option that addresses concerns on both sides might be to employ a stenographer to memorialize the verbalizations during the interview.

Prior to the investigative interview, any "walk-through" of the scene should be conducted by the involved officer and his or her legal representative, and should be unaccompanied by those investigating the incident, and/or any audio or video recording device. It should take place under similar lighting conditions to those that existed at the time of the incident, if possible, to preserve the environmental context, and any conversation with an accompanying person should be avoided to prevent possible contamination of the involved officer's memory record.

The viewing of video recordings of the incident by the involved officer(s) has been discussed in Force Science News (2009, 2010) and should be considered carefully based on department policy. Video recordings have the potential to provide for additional clarity and/or memory enhancement, but video recordings also have the potential to be misleading, depending on the camera's perspective and quality. Therefore, a compromise middle-ground position is to interview the involved officer(s) prior to viewing the video recordings and then to allow for additional elaborations and/or revisions after viewing the video recordings.

As discussed below, some inconsistencies and delayed recollections are to be expected following stressful encounters, and these natural phenomena of memory are not to be automatically taken as signs of dishonesty (Fisher, Brewer, & Mitchell, 2009; Fisher & Cutler, 1995). If the compromise middle-ground option is adopted, then we suggest using an advisory similar to that suggested by the Force Science Institute (Force Science News, 2010). The suggested advisory for use with involved officers in an OIS investigation is as follows:

> You are about to view a camera recording of a use-of-force event in which you were involved. Understand that while this recording depicts visual information from the scene, the human eye and brain are highly likely to perceive some things in stressful situations differently than a camera records them, so this photographic record may not reflect how you actually perceived the event. The recording may depict things that you did not see or hear. You may have seen or heard things that were not recorded by the camera. Depending on the speed of the camera, some action elements may not have been recorded or may have happened faster than you could perceive and absorb them. The camera has captured a 2-dimensional image, which may be different from your 3-dimensional observations. Lighting and angles may also have contributed to different perceptions. And, of course, the camera did not view the scene with your unique experience and training. Hopefully, this recording will enhance your understanding of the incident. Keep in mind, though, that these video images are only one piece of evidence to be considered in reconstructing and evaluating the totality of the circumstances. Some elements may require further exploration and explanation before the investigation is concluded.

Likewise, any pre-interview conference between or among the involved officers should be approached with caution and each officer must remain objective. Research from cognitive psychology using laypersons raises caution that a dominant person in the group could convince the others that his/her recollections constitute the historical truth (Paterson, Kemp, & Ng, 2011). If a pre-interview conference is permitted, the involved officers must strive to consolidate everyone's recollections into a more complete version of the historical truth without one person dominating everyone else. Fortunately, police officers are used to conferring about more "routine" calls during debriefings and integrating information from multiple sources.

A pre-interview conference among the officers who were involved in an OIS is not without legal implications, however, because each officer may then be responsible for more than his/her own narrative version of the truth (Stone, 2008). Justification for each involved officer's conduct during the OIS incident turns on the reasonableness of the force, if any, that was used by that officer when viewed in light of the totality of the facts and circumstances that confronted him/her at the moment of decision. The only facts and circumstances that are relevant to that evaluation are those that were known to the involved officer at that moment. Therefore, it is critical to capture the recollections of each involved officer for only those facts and circumstances of the incident that each perceived, and to which each reacted. Because no two witnesses or participants in any dynamic encounter will have identical perceptions of the event, any interaction and discussion between the officers could cause the tainting of each officer's recollections with things observed by other officers that this subject officer did not see or hear. For that reason, pre-interview conferences among multiple officers who were involved in an OIS incident are to be discouraged.

Reset the Mission

OIS investigators should approach their task with the involved-officer interview as objective fact gatherers, whose goal is to collect and report a complete factual account of the incident (Wilson & Geiselman, 2011). The investigator should convey this commitment to the officer during the "rapport building" phase of the interview. This approach can make good progress toward dispelling any preconceived negative perceptions held by the officer about the OIS investigation process, and can obtain the officer's buy-in to the cognitive effort that will be required to produce the most complete statement possible. Only after this foundation has been laid and the officer has bought into the concept should the actual interview be commenced, using the CI techniques described above. The following is suggested language for the rapport-development phase during OIS investigative interviews:

> The goal of my investigation is to collect evidence that will help determine whether the facts of the incident in which you were involved show that the use of force was within the law and/or department policy, and/or whether there is a need for the department to modify its policies or procedures, or to provide its officers with more, better or different training. This will be an objective investigation of the incident, and my role is to gather information. It is not my job to form any opinions about the incident, or to make any recommendations about it. I am tasked only with gathering all of the information and evidence that may be available about the incident so that it can be transmitted in my report to those whose job it is to arrive at conclusions and make decisions about the results of the investigation.
>
> The purpose of my interviewing you is for me to obtain as much information as possible about the totality of the circumstances that confronted you in this incident, and how those circumstances affected the decisions that you made and the actions which you took. With that

> in mind, it is obvious that as we proceed, you should be doing most of the talking during the interview. This is because you have the information that is needed, not me. I was not there.
>
> I will be asking questions that tend to call for narrative answers. Please give each question careful thought and try to answer as fully and completely as you can. More is better. Please do not try to filter your answers by excluding information that you may think is unimportant or irrelevant. Such details may well prove to be very important and highly relevant to the investigation, and omissions could adversely affect the accuracy of the investigation.
>
> As we proceed, you may recall a detail related to a previous question that you did not remember when you gave your answer. It is not unusual for that to happen. Please provide that additional information immediately so as to avoid forgetting the information. The same is true with regard to subsequent recollections that may seem to contradict something that you may have stated in answer to a previous question. Keep in mind that we are here to collect accurate information, and it is not unusual for people to have such contradictory recollections as they search their memories. Some later recollection may trigger a different, more accurate or more detailed memory. It is far better to correct an earlier oversight or mistaken recollection immediately than to attempt to do so at some later time.
>
> I probably will have some follow-up questions at various points during the interview, and I may revisit aspects of the incident about which you have already given information. My reason for doing so will be to give me a better understanding of what you have already told me, or to explore your memory for more details than you have already provided. If you do not know the answer to a question or if you cannot remember something, then simply tell me that you do not know or cannot remember. Do not guess at answers.
>
> The process of exploring your memory of this incident for detailed information may take some time, and will require concentration on your part. It is critically important to the success of this investigation that you are willing to work with me in collecting as much detail as possible from your memory. If you need to take a break at any point during the interview, please let me know.

An important factor that is unique to OIS investigative interviews is that the interviewer and the subject of the interview are both peace officers. As a result, an officer-to-officer dynamic may take shape, whereby many unspoken assumptions are made that are neither articulated during the interview nor written into the text of the interview report. The unspoken assumptions sometimes include the involved officer's background, training, and mindset going into the incident. Such omissions can rob the investigative report of crucial background context that would add materially to the creation of a complete accounting of the "totality of the circumstances" that confronted the officer during the incident. The officer-to-officer interview dynamic may also result in the use of jargon not familiar to those reading the report later, and/or the omission of details regarding police training and procedure. It would therefore be advisable for investigators to avoid the use of police jargon in their reports, and to assume ignorance by the reader of police procedures and protocols. Special effort should be made to draw out all details of the event and the factors that went into the making of the officer's use of force decisions, including, where appropriate, details of the officer's prior training and/or experience regarding incidents of a similar type to the one in question. This will assist lay readers in fully understanding why the involved officers acted as they did.

The involved officers and their employing entities are forced to live with the content of the statements that are provided to the OIS investigators within hours or days of the incident. It can be problematic later to "fill in the blanks" with facts that have been left out of the initial investigative report. Subsequent additions and clarifications to the investigative report can be viewed with suspicion. This could become a major issue in any civil litigation that arises from the incident. It is, therefore, best to maximize the completeness of the information that is obtained in the initial, and perhaps only, interview that the involved officers may provide, and to accurately and completely memorialize the obtained information in the investigative report.

With that in mind, there is a need to understand the full scope of the factual information that falls within the definition of the "totality of the circumstances" that faced the officer at the moment of the use of force decision. Investigators must ensure that a full sweep of this information is executed and that this information is captured and included in the investigative report.

The state of mind of the involved officer is directly relevant to the analysis of the threat assessment made by the officer as the critical incident unfolded. State of mind speaks to the reasonableness of the use of force decisions made in dealing with the threat. A full and accurate depiction of the officer's evolving state of mind in response to the dynamic circumstances of the incident will include more than "just the facts" of the incident. State of mind will be influenced by the training and experience of the officer as it relates to the type of incident that was being handled when the need to use force arose, as well as by the information received from dispatch and/or eyewitnesses before and during the incident, and the officer's own observations during the incident. The investigator also should probe the involved officer's memory for information regarding the options, if any, that were open to the officer at key junctures in the evolution of the threat, including the choices made by the officer at each juncture, and the reasons for one option being selected and others rejected. There are checklists that can be used to ensure that these areas are covered adequately, and one such use-of-force checklist is presented in Appendix B.

Components of the basic CI template are ideally suited for eliciting information about state of mind and threat assessment. The reinstatement of the context should start with the beginning of the shift and progress to the time just before the initial contact in the incident under investigation. The interviewer should address what information was given to the officer at the outset of the incident, establish the nature of the response that was initially planned, and elicit the officer's perceptions upon arrival on scene. The instruction to be complete should include a request that the officer provide an ongoing account of his/her threat assessment as the incident developed, as well as any perceived early threat warning signs and any unusual circumstances noted during the contact. The ongoing account should also include the officer's decision-making process while responding to the various stimuli encountered in gaining and maintaining control of the subject(s)/incident, and the officer's follow through after stabilization of the incident. Witness-centered questioning should be used to elicit emotions and thoughts, training elements triggered, and reactions to the situation. The interviewer must be careful to avoid any attempt to convince the officer of what happened or to change his/her mind. Specific questions to elicit the officer's thoughts and emotions during the incident might include: "What were you thinking right then?" "Just before then, what were you looking at?" "What were you thinking right before that?"

In summary, OIS investigators should be well versed in the kinds of information that must be sought out and preserved in the investigation (Appendix B) and be proficient in the techniques for eliciting that information using the CI protocol (Appendix A).

When to Conduct the Full Investigative Interview

Immediately following an OIS incident, the involved officer is likely on an adrenalin rush that eventually may give way to exhaustion. It is reasonable to expect that a well-rested eyewitness would produce more complete and more accurate recall than would a less-rested eyewitness, especially in the wake of high-stress situations (Artwohl, Chapter 5, this volume; Geiselman, 2010). It is well documented within the field of eyewitness psychology that police officers show the same deleterious effects of heightened stress on memory performance as civilians (Zimmerman, 2003). Unfortunately, the decision to possibly delay the full investigative interview to allow for rest typically must be made based on surface indicators of officer stress. Some officers might appear quite calm shortly after participating in a shooting and may prefer to give or even demand a full interview at that time. Nevertheless, it often is best for officers to sleep first and give their statement later (Artwohl, 2002). The recommended CI protocol requires time and requires the officer's full cooperation and exhaustive participation. This does not preclude a limited request to provide enough information to get the investigation started.

How might rest contribute to more complete and accurate eyewitness recall? One hypothesis is that REM (rapid eye movement) sleep plays an important role in the consolidation of memories (see Stickgold, 2005 for a review) and therefore recall should be more complete following sleep. It is well known that stress can typically cause an increase in cortisol (hormone) and while it is thought that cortisol may sometimes *enhance the formation of memories*, it has been found that the remaining presence of increased cortisol can *impair memory retrieval* (Ackerman et al., 2013). Recent research also suggests that sleep deprivation may contribute to the generation of false memories (Fenn et al., 2009). Interestingly, the generation of false memories caused by sleep deprivation has been found to be largely reversed with the administration of caffeine, "indicating that adenosinergic mechanisms can contribute to the generation of false memories associated with sleep loss" (Diekelmann et al., 2008).

In a rare study of high intensity stress at the time of experiencing the event that was actually induced by the event (as opposed to "artificially"), Morgan et al. (2004) found that witness memory performance 24 hours later was poorer for those who had undergone the high stress versus the low stress (prior) experience. They concluded that high stress may have contributed to a disruption of memory encoding. They also noted that other studies:

> have shown that the consolidation of memory may occur over a number of days after stress exposure. It is possible that memory for the low-stress condition consolidated more rapidly than for the high stress condition and that an assessment at a later time point may have reduced the observed differences in memory between the two conditions.
>
> *(Morgan et al., 2004, p. 276)*

Indeed, when discussing their 2004 stress event, Morgan, Colwell, and Hazlett (2011) commented that in their prior studies they noted that after exposure to high stress, their participants had increased hormone levels "for at least 24 hours" (p. 1232).

While perhaps the definitive experimental test has yet to be conducted, in light of these research data showing positive effects of rest and negative effects of sleep deprivation, the expression "let me sleep on it" appears to have some validity as it applies to eyewitness memory recall performance. Obtaining the needed rest prior to a full investigative interview could be difficult to achieve after stress-inducing OIS incidents. Klinger (2001) reported that 46 percent of officers involved in shootings experience difficulty sleeping within the first 24 hours and approximately one-third of the officers still experienced difficulty sleeping after one week. If the full investigative interview is delayed to allow for rest and for the dissipation of stress, investigators should use the CI protocol to conduct the interview. As described above, the CI protocol contains techniques for reconstructing the sensory and emotional context that existed at the time of the event as well as techniques for enhancing memory retrieval following some forgetting. These techniques also have been found to circumvent certain post-event sources of contamination (Geiselman et al., 1986; Memon, Zaragoza, Clifford, & Kidd, 2010; Milne & Bull, 2003). Therefore, a CI goes a long way toward counteracting any negative effects on memory recall caused by a delay of the full investigative interview to allow for rest and stress reduction. Furthermore, research has shown that the various elements of the CI do not themselves produce false memories (Sharman & Powell, 2013). Given all factors considered, a delay of 48-hours seems to be a reasonable and prudent practice. A delay also would afford the investigator more time to prepare for the interview and to study the factual information that is available from other sources in the case in advance.

Summary: Lessons Learned from Past Interviews

The following are some of the more important lessons for investigators and for the involved officers garnered from a review of several OIS investigative interviews.

For Investigators

Lesson 1

Understand that police officers have the same perceptual and memory systems as civilian witnesses—we're all human, and subject to the same human limitations. Research shows that, with some exceptions, police officers are affected by situational factors such as stress and weapon focus and they react to leading questions much like civilian witnesses. In the midst of a high stress encounter, such as a deadly force confrontation, perceptual distortions and exclusions caused by stress may well cause an involved officer to fail to perceive (and thus fail to recall) events that occurred in his/her immediate presence during the incident.

Police officers also exhibit certain memory failures such as inconsistencies and delayed recollections much like civilian witnesses, especially under conditions of lingering stress and sleep deprivation. Admonish the involved officer from the beginning of the interview to tell you if he/she does not recall something, and to avoid speculating or guessing. The involved officer should not be encouraged to stretch his/her memory recall beyond its limitations.

It is important for the interviewer to thank the involved officer periodically during the interview for his/her ongoing concentration and effort, but not for speculation or guessing. Never tell the involved officer that if you (the interviewer) had been there, you would have remembered "that."

Lesson 2

Given the nature of human memory, it is important to conduct the investigative interviews using a cognitive-interview, information-gathering approach rather than a confrontation-interrogation type approach (at least throughout most of the interview). Address the "totality of the circumstances" that faced the officer at the moment of the use of force decision, so as to maximize the likelihood that the necessary information can be included in the investigative report. A confrontational approach in this context often is counterproductive and it could also cause the involved officer to second-guess and otherwise question his/her own memory. Under persistent and leading questioning, the officer may begin to speculate as to how the incident happened for which he/she has no clear memory. The creation of new memories from confused memories using persistent leading and suggestive questioning is one of the more reliable phenomena and easiest to demonstrate in the research field of eyewitness psychology. It is also one that should be scrupulously avoided by the OIS investigator.

Lesson 3

Do not overly apply any training that you may have had on detecting deception such that the interview becomes contaminated with confirmatory bias. Keep in mind that some classic "signs" of deception also are signs of intense concentration, such as long pauses, deep breaths, and gaze aversions. A witness who is working hard to mine his/her memory in a CI interview must engage in intense concentration, and thus is likely to exhibit some of these "signs" of deception.

Remember that all signs of deception are hot spots or red flags only. Throughout the investigative interview, the default assumption about delayed recollections and inconsistencies should be that they reflect natural memory phenomena until it is determined otherwise. Ask the involved officer to address any confusing elements of the story during the later phases of the interview.

Lesson 4

Consider delaying the full investigative interview for 24 to 48 hours. Keep in mind that the involved officer is in a unique situation where he/she is both a victim and a potential suspect. State of mind in approaching the interview is relevant. The involved officer may face consequences for employment, civil litigation or even a criminal indictment as a result of his/her involvement in the incident under investigation. If the involved officer is sleep deprived with lingering signs of stress, understand that his/her recollections may be incomplete, disorganized, and more open to suggestion. If the goal is to minimize inconsistencies within an interview, as it should be, then delaying the interview until after the incident has been well thought out by the involved officer could be a wise choice. If the interview is not delayed under these conditions, expect inconsistencies and delayed recollections, and do not automatically label these possible memory failures as indications of deception and dishonesty. Keep an open mind throughout the interview.

Lesson 5

It is important to conduct the investigative interviews of any civilian eyewitnesses to the officer-involved critical incident using the same cognitive-interview, non-leading approach as used with the involved officer. It is important to consider the basic principles of eyewitness psychology when evaluating the perceptions and recollections of the eyewitnesses. In particular, do not "join the prosecution team" in the presence of these eyewitnesses so as to contaminate their recollections going forward. Do not comment on the evidence or the possible actions of the involved officer. Understand that the manner in which you frame the incident during the interview can artificially conform the thinking of an eyewitness to fit your hunch. Never make comments such as, "I think there is some truth in what everyone is telling me. If someone is abusing their authority, then this has to be dealt with, maybe even from a criminal standpoint. What he/she has done is wrong." Instead, remain in the information-gathering mode.

For the Involved Officers

Lesson 1

Understand the strengths and weaknesses of your own perceptual and memory systems. During the interview, do not hesitate to state "I don't know" and then maintain that you do not know if that is the truth. However, it is important to spontaneously correct inconsistencies and offer additional recollections as they come to mind without delay. These are natural phenomena of memory, especially under these conditions, and to avoid them could create the suspicion of deception and dishonesty.

Lesson 2

Interrogate your own memory both prior to and during the full investigative interview. Become familiar with the memory-enhancement elements of the cognitive interview and use them to help you recollect what happened. These include reconstruction of the circumstances surrounding the incident, thinking in detail, going through the scenario in reverse as well as in forward order, and considering the different perspectives that you had on the incident. It is important to be as complete as possible early on as you are being interviewed in the investigation.

Lesson 3

Inform the interviewer when you are taking the time to concentrate during the interview. This will enable you to perform optimally in an unfettered manner without feeling the need to maintain an artificial appearance of truthfulness in your body language. Remember that the bodily signs of intense concentration somewhat resemble some of the recognized signs of deception.

Lesson 4

Make a request for a delay of the full investigative interview if you believe that you are not in a frame of mind at the time to perform adequately due to lingering stress and/or sleep deprivation. Do not minimize your mental and physiological state in an attempt to appear strong in the face of these potentially negative factors. At least make the request.

Lesson 5

Address critical issues in your recitation if the interviewer fails to do so. In particular, comment spontaneously on your state of mind throughout the incident. This would include your understanding of the advance information that you were given from dispatch and others at the time. Also, comment on your threat assessment throughout the incident. This would include elements of your training and experience that were triggered in your mind by the circumstances as they unfolded.

Acknowledgment

The inspiration for and the framework upon which the above checklist was constructed were taken directly from a Street Survival Seminars Dispute Resolution Model UOF Reporting Checklist for Investigators that was published on PoliceOne.com in November, 2007, and is still available in the *PoliceOne* archives.

References

Ackerman, S., Hartman, F., Papassotiropoulos, A., de Quervain, D., & Rasch, B. (2013). Association between basal cortisol levels and memory retrieval in healthy young individuals. *Journal of Cognitive Neuroscience, 25*(11), 1896–1907.

Artwohl, A. (2002). Perceptual and memory distortion during officer-involved shootings. *FBI Law Enforcement Bulletin, 18*, 18–24.

Cote, W. & Simpson, R. (2000). *Covering violence: A guide to ethical reporting about victims and trauma.* New York, NY: Columbia University Press.

Diekelmann, S., Landolt, H. P., Lahl, O., Born, J., & Wagner, U. (2008). Sleep loss produces false memories. *PLoS One, 3*(10), e3512.

Fenn, K. M., Gallo, D. A., Margoliash, D., Roediger, H. L., & Nusbaum, H. C. (2009). Reduced false memory after sleep. *Learning and Memory, 16*, 509–513.

Fisher, R. P., Brewer, N., & Mitchell, G. (2009). The relation between consistency and accuracy of eyewitness testimony: Legal versus cognitive explanations. In T. Williamson, R. Bull, & T. Valentine (eds.), *Handbook of psychology of investigative interviewing: Current developments and future directions.* Hoboken, NJ: John Wiley & Sons.

Fisher, R. P., & Cutler, B. L. (1995). Relation between consistency and accuracy of eyewitness testimony. In G. M. Davies, S. Lloyd-Bostock, M. McMurran, & C. Wilson (eds.), *Psychology and law: Advances in research* (pp. 21–28). Berlin: DeGruyter.

Fisher, R. P. & Geiselman, R. E. (1992). *Memory-enhancing techniques in investigative interviewing: The cognitive interview.* Springfield, IL: C.C. Thomas.

Fisher, R. P., Geiselman, R. E., & Amador, M. (1989). Field test of the cognitive interview: Enhancing the recollection of actual victims and witnesses of crime. *Journal of Applied Psychology, 74*(5), 722–727.

Fisher, R. P., Mello, E. W., & McCauley, M. R. (1999). Are jurors' perceptions of eyewitness credibility affected by the cognitive interview? *Psychology, Crime and Law, 5*(1–2), 167–176.

Force Science News. (2009). Should officers see video of their encounters? Force science states its case (#114). Retrieved from www.forcescience.org/fsnews/114.html.

Force Science News. (2010). Do head cameras always see what you see in a force encounter? (#145). Retrieved from www.forcescience.org/fsnews/145.html.

Geiselman, R. E. (2010). Rest and eyewitness memory recall. *American Journal of Forensic Psychology, 28*(1), 65–69.

Geiselman, R. E. (2012). The cognitive interview for suspects (CIS). *American Journal of Forensic Psychology, 30*(1), 1–12.

Geiselman, R. E. & Fisher, R. P. (1997). Ten years of cognitive interviewing. In D. Payne & F. Conrad (eds.) *Intersections in basic and applied memory research* (pp. 291–310). New York, NY: Lawrence Erlbaum.

Geiselman, R. E. & Fisher, R. P. (2014). Interviewing victims and witnesses. In Michel St. Yves (ed.), *Investigative interviewing: Handbook of best practices.* Toronto: Thomson Reuters Publishers.

Geiselman, R. E., Fisher, R. P., Cohen, G., Holland, H. L., & Surtes, L. (1986). Eyewitness responses to leading and misleading questions under the cognitive interview. *Journal of Police Science and Administration, 14*(1), 31–39.

George, R. C. & Clifford, B. (1992). Making the most of witnesses. *Policing, 8,* 185–198.

Hartwig, M., Granhag, P. A., Strömwall, L. A., & Kronkvist, O. (2006). Strategic use of evidence during police interviews: When training to detect deception works. *Law and Human Behavior, 30*(5), 603–619.

Klinger, D. (2001). *Police responses to officer-involved shootings.* U.S. Department of Justice, National Institute of Justice, NCJ 192285, Washington, DC.

Koehnken, G., Milne, R., Memon, A., & Bull, R. (1999). The cognitive interview: A meta-analysis. *Psychology, Crime & Law, 5*(1–2), 3–27.

McCormack, T., Ashkar, A., Hunt, A., Chang, E., Silberkleit, G., & Geiselman, R. E. (2009). Indicators of deception in an oral narrative: Which are more reliable? *American Journal of Forensic Psychiatry, 30,* 49–56.

Memon, A., Meissner, C. A., & Fraser, J. (2010). The cognitive interview: A meta-analytic and study space analysis of the last 25 years. *Psychology, Public Policy, and Law, 16*(4), 340–372.

Memon, A., Zaragoza, M., Clifford, B., & Kidd, L. (2010). Inoculation or antidote? The effects of cognitive interview timing on false memory for forcibly fabricated events. *Law and Human Behavior, 34*(2), 105–117.

Milne, R. & Bull, R. (2003). Does the cognitive interview help children to resist the effects of suggestive questioning? *Legal and Criminological Psychology, 8*(1), 21–38.

Morgan III, C. A., Colwell, K., & Hazlett, G. (2011). Efficacy of forensic statement analysis in distinguishing truthful from deceptive eyewitness accounts of highly stressful events. *Journal of Forensic Sciences, 56*(5), 1227–1234.

Morgan III, C. A., Hazlett, G., Doran, T., Garrett, S., Hoyt, G., Thomas, P., ... Southwick, S. (2004). Accuracy of eyewitness memory for persons encountered during exposure to highly intense stress. *International Journal of Psychiatry and the Law, 27*(3), 265–279.

National Institute of Justice (1999). *Eyewitness evidence: A guide for law enforcement.* NCJ 178240, Washington, DC.

Paterson, H. M., Kemp, R. I., & Ng, J. R. (2011). Combating co-witness contamination: Attempting to decrease the negative effects of discussion on eyewitness memory. *Applied Cognitive Psychology, 25*(5), 43–52.

Sharman, S. J. and Powell, M. B. (2013). Do cognitive interview instructions contribute to false beliefs and memories? *Journal of Investigative Psychology and Offender Profiling, 10*(1), 114–124.

Stickgold, R. (2005). Sleep-dependent memory consolidation. *Nature, 437,* 1272–1278.

Stone, S. (2008). Appellate court confronts attack on Sheriff's "anti-huddling policy." *Training Bulletin, 11*(7), 1–6.

Sydeman, S. J., Cascardi, M., Poythress, N. G., & Ritterbrand, L. M. (1997). Procedural justice in the context of civil commitment: A critique of Tyler's analysis. *Psychology, Public Policy, and Law, 3*(1), 207–221.

Wilson, J. F. & Geiselman, R. E. (2011). Training for the aftermath of an officer-involved shooting. *International Law Enforcement Educators and Trainers Association (ILEETA) Use of Force Journal, 11,* 24–28.

Zimmerman, L. A. (2003). Recent research: Effects of stress on police and citizen eyewitness recall. *Canadian Journal of Police and Security Services, 1*(4), 377–380.

Appendix A

General Cognitive Interview Template

Rapport and Interview Instructions

- Ask who they are and what do they do.
- Explain who you are and your function in this case.
- Explain transfer of control (they have the information, you were not there).
- Explain this will require considerable concentration on their part.

Narrative

- Re-create context leading up to the incident.
- Ask to be complete, report everything.
- Ask them to take their time, go slowly, close eyes if they want, and to concentrate.
- Do not interrupt.
- Take limited notes about scenes to probe later; rank scenes on which might have most information (to be probed first).

Specific Questions Phase

- Use their words to focus on richest scene.
- Use open-ended question first ("tell me more about...").
- Do not interrupt, use pauses effectively.
- Stick with one scene before moving on to another.
- Go through each scene on your list.
- Now use reverse-order recall.
- Now use change perspectives recall.

Review

- Ask them to interrupt you if they want to add or change anything.
- Use their words to re-tell event from beginning to end.
- Stop periodically to see if they want to add anything.

Closure

- Thank them for their efforts.
- Offer contact information

Appendix B

OIS Incident Investigative Interview Checklist

Approach Considerations

A. Decision making—why did you initiate contact, i.e., justification and desirability?
  1. General Info: duty assignment; uniformed/plain clothes; marked unit?
    a. Equipment carried on your person.
    b. Additional equipment in your unit (not carried on the person).
  2. How contact initiated: dispatched to scene; observation; flagged by citizen (give details).
  3. Initial information regarding the incident.
    a. information provided in call by dispatch/initial personal observations regarding an "on sight" incident/initial information provided by citizen informant.
    b. prior information known to officer about location/subject(s)
      – prior history of criminal activity and/or violence.
      – subject(s) trained in martial arts and/or having propensity for violence.
      – known presence of weapons.
    c. additional information obtained while en route/upon arrival on scene.
    d. relevant training and experience of the responding officer regarding the type of incident being handled that provided the officer with context for an initial threat assessment and plan of action.
  4. Initial plan for handling incident.
    a. personal thoughts on how to handle the situation.
    b. discussion, if any, had with other officers responding to the scene by way of initial tactical plan.
  5. How contact evolved/developed.
    a. Reasonable Suspicion.
    b. Probable Cause.
    c. Other justification.

B. Tactical deployment—how did you approach?
  1. Control of distance.
  2. Positioning.
  3. Team tactics.

On Scene Development of Situational Information

A. Observations made upon arrival at the scene.
  1. Nature of the activity observed.
  2. Reaction of the people present to the arrival of officer(s).
  3. Number and location of people present.
  4. Information gathered from people initially contacted at scene.
  5. Initial observations made of subject(s) of the call.
  6. Seriousness of the crime(s) in progress/which have occurred.

B. Threat assessment.
   1. Levels of resistance—Describing what the subject is doing.
      a. Unresponsive (Subject apparently unconscious).
      b. Non-responsive (Subject conspicuously ignoring).
      c. Dead-weight tactics (Subject passively resists being moved).
      d. Resistive tension (Subject tightening up muscles).
      e. Defensive resistance (Subject attempting to get away).
      f. Aggressive/active resistance (See caveat below).
      g. Physical assault (Subject striking at officers w/ or w/o weapon).
      h. Great bodily harm assault (Subject's actions/ability to cause harm).
      i. Life-threatening assault (Subject's ability to cause death).
      j. Life-threatening weapon assault (Subject's ability to cause death).
   2. Early warning signs? Explain.
      a. Conspicuously ignoring.
      b. Excessive emotional attention.
      c. Exaggerated movement.
      d. Ceasing all movement.
      e. Known violent background.
      f. Verbalization of threats.
      g. Scanning the area.
   3. Pre-attack postures? Explain.
      a. Stance—describe in detail (e.g., "the subject dropped his right leg back, bladed his body to me, slightly bent his knees so as to lower his center of gravity, and brought his hands to chest level in a fighting stance").
      b. Hand set (open handed or clinched fist).
      c. Shoulder shift.
      d. Target glance.
      e. Thousand-yard stare.
      f. Hands in pockets.
   4. Subject apparently "emotionally disturbed" (i.e., mentally ill, under influence of drugs and/or alcohol, or is obviously in crisis and out of control)? Explain how subject's apparent emotional condition affected the threat assessment.
   5. Weapon threat assessment.
      a. What weapons have you brought to the scene?
      b. What weapons has the subject brought to the scene?
      c. What other weapons are available? Explain.

Dynamics of the Contact

A. What were the officer/subject factors?
   1. Number of participants (officers and subjects)?
   2. Individual factors officer(s)/subject(s).
      a. Relative ages.
      b. Relative strengths.

        c. Relative sizes.
        d. Relative skill levels.

B. Were there any special circumstances, such as:
    1. Your reasonable perception of threat.
    2. Sudden assault.
    3. Your physical positioning.
    4. Subject's ability to escalate force rapidly.
    5. Your special knowledge about the subject.
    6. Your injury or exhaustion.
    7. Other special circumstances.

C. Tactical considerations relevant to the scene, such as:
    1. Lighting conditions.
        a. If lighting conditions were poor, what, if any, light source did you/other officers use?
    2. Describe the tactical effect, if any, of the surface conditions at the scene (slippery, wet, loose gravel, broken pavement, debris scattered about).
    3. Describe cover/concealment, if any, that was available to you/other officers and/or the subject(s).
        a. Was it used, and, if so, by whom and how?

D. Gaining/maintaining control of the subject: Demonstrate adherence to the Principle of Escalation and De-escalation of Force if force is applied in order to overcome resistance to lawful detention or arrest, prevent escape, or act in defense of self or others.
    1. Within the context of the factors set forth above, describe the circumstances of suspect's actions that gave rise to the application of force.
        a. Include a description of the reactions of other officers on scene to suspect's actions that you observed, and how they affected your tactical decisions, if at all.
        b. Describe what commands and/or warnings, if any, were given to the suspect, and by whom.
            - if any language in addition to English was used, identify it.
            - did the suspect appear to understand the commands/warnings.
            - how did the suspect react to the commands/warnings, if at all?
            - if the giving of a warning was not feasible prior to the application of force, or if the giving of such a warning would have merely been a futile gesture, and therefore none was given, articulate the reason(s) why.
    2. Describe the options that were available to you in order to respond to the suspect's actions at each stage as the contact evolved.
    3. Articulate the force option chosen and the reason(s) for rejecting any other option at each stage as the contact evolved.
    4. Describe the level/stage/degree of stabilization, if any, achieved at each point of the contact:
        a. Presence stabilization—describe type and degree to which the officer's or officers' physical presence stabilized the scene.
        b. Verbal stabilization—describe type and degree to which the officer's verbal commands stabilized the scene.
        c. Standing stabilization—describe type, degree of stabilization, and if restraints were on yet.

d. Wall stabilization—describe type, degree of stabilization, and if restraints were on yet.
e. Ground stabilization—describe type, degree of stabilization, and if restraints were on yet.
f. Special restraints—describe type, degree, and degree of immobilization.

E. Follow-through considerations.
1. Stabilization/application of restraints.
2. Monitoring/debriefing.
3. Searching.
4. Escorting.
5. Transportation.
6. Transfer of custody.

Caveat

The foregoing checklist is an attempt to provide officers with a methodical and comprehensive guide for use in preparing to report on the use of force. It by no means purports to be an all-inclusive or exhaustive list of the factors that should be considered and included in any such report, either written or oral. Indeed, every use of force incident is unique. Some of the factors listed above may not come into play in any particular incident, whereas other factors that are not listed above, and which cannot be foreseen in creating a theoretical reporting framework, may prove to be crucial to the complete and accurate analysis of that incident. Care should be taken by the officer when preparing to give his or her account of a use of force to insure that such factors, which have not been foreseen here, are retrieved from memory and included in any report on the incident.

16

EFFECTIVE AGENCY RESPONSE TO THE MEDIA IN USE OF FORCE INCIDENTS

Todd A. Lough

Introduction

Though it may be an inconvenient truth, the news media provide the primary conduit through which police departments communicate with the communities they serve, especially when that communication relates to a critical incident. This is problematic, given the media have historically played the roles of both partner and critic of the police. Which role the media assume in any particular incident can be heavily influenced by the policies, choices, and behavior of the police themselves. In this chapter, we examine the fundamental nature of the relationship between law enforcement and the media, discuss ways of improving and sustaining that relationship, and offer suggestions for police administrators as to how to engage the media following use of force incidents in a way that best accomplishes the goals of their agencies. Though it can be an uneasy alliance, when approached and managed properly, the media can act as an important partner of law enforcement in conveying vital information to the citizens of a community.

The Evolution of Police Media Relations

The news as presented by the electronic and print media is, at best, only an approximation of reality. Because of their unique position, the news media have a central role in what Lawrence (2000) calls the social construction of reality. Social groups, institutions, and ideologies are in an ongoing struggle to influence the construction of that reality (Gurevitch & Levy, 1985), with Gans (1979) describing journalists as the primary mediators of this struggle. The results of this constant struggle to define reality explain why events that police departments define as isolated incidents, and unrepresentative of the daily performance of a department, can come to be catalysts for negative public perception of the police, and the exaggeration of perceived community problems. Because most citizens have little or no actual interaction with the police, media stories and images can play an influential role in shaping public opinion regarding the police and their performance. Lawrence (2000) describes this as a "social constructionist" approach that stresses the paramount importance of public perception of societal problems, with the news media playing a key role in the social construction of those problems.

According to this approach, problems are what the public perceives them to be, regardless of whether those perceptions are contradicted by the facts on the street. Through the content and editorial choices they make, the news media play a significant role in shaping public perception or, at the very least, in influencing about what issues citizens are thinking. As journalists act as information managers, they are also operating as opinion gatekeepers, determining what competing groups and viewpoints will receive a public audience. In the simplest terms, a community's problems are whatever citizens believe them to be, and the news media play an influential role in not only shaping those beliefs, but in determining whose opinions get expressed in a public forum.

The relationship between the police and the media, in many jurisdictions, tends to be somewhat erratic. This stems, in part, from a traditional lack of trust and respect between the two groups (Garner, 1984), and from the fact that cops and reporters often hold differing political viewpoints and opinions regarding the role of the press in a democracy. To individuals working in law enforcement, it is no surprise that those in the media tend to be more ideologically liberal than the average police officer, and more likely to oppose police efforts to control the flow of information (Altschull, 1975). This tendency of the average police officer and journalist to view the world around them differently seems to start at a very early stage in their respective careers. After surveying both police cadets and journalism students, Selke and Bartoszek (1984) found both groups generally distrustful of one another, and likely to develop negative views of the other's profession during the course of their academy or university training. In addition, those in law enforcement often believe the media have a limited capacity to fully grasp the role of the police in society, or to understand the bureaucratic and economic constraints departments and officers face (Skolnick & McCoy, 1984; Ziembo-Vogl, 1998).

Though philosophical and educational factors certainly play a role in fostering an atmosphere of distrust between the police and the media, they are still not the primary cause of suspicion between the two groups. Negativity on the part of law enforcement agencies toward the press stems in largest part from the way the media report police errors of omission and commission, as well as acts of intentional misconduct. Fairly or unfairly, the police can come to view the media as "creators of scandal" (Caeti, Liederbach, & Bellew, 2004; Sherman, 1974). Throughout American history, whether through the printed word, the still photograph, or the video clip, the news media have acted as a beacon, shedding light on the conduct, both good and bad, of the police.

Negative media coverage of police action first became nationally relevant during the political turmoil of the 1960s. As television images of police dogs and fire hoses being used on civil rights protestors in Selma, and images of police batons striking political protestors in Chicago were broadcast throughout the country, citizens began to see law enforcement in a different light. In addition, as the number of media outlets has grown over time, competition to "get the scoop" has led to greater motivation on the part of the media to find important stories, such as cases of police corruption (Surrette, 1998).

Despite the often-contentious role the media play in publicizing police deviance, in the majority of police/media interaction, the relationship is pragmatic and mutually beneficial. Just as with other agents of the government, police officials, through their provision of information regarding crime and police activity, are normally "primary definers" of the news (Hall et al., 1978). Police officials act as primary content providers for journalists and media organizations seeking to fill space and airtime, with stories likely to best capture the interest of their readers or viewers (Bennett, 1990; Lawrence, 2000). This arrangement provides police spokespersons the opportunity to describe or frame issues and incidents involving crime and police activity in a manner most likely to elicit public support or minimize public criticism for their department. Thus, both police officials and the news media have an interest in, and benefit from, routinizing the exchange of information regarding day-to-day police activity in a community (Gans, 1979; Lawrence, 2000).

This cooperative relationship, however, becomes less mutually beneficial when a newsworthy event involving police error or misconduct occurs. Here the relationship becomes strained, as both sides try to interpret and give meaning to the facts. As Lawrence states,

> the news is an arena of struggle over the meaning of events, the existence of problems, and the search for solutions. Events can play a dynamic role in these struggles because the news assigns definitions and significance to events whether or not officials successfully control that process. Officials must work to frame and contain the definitions journalists construct around evocative news events ... such as police shootings.
>
> *(Lawrence, 2000, p. 36).*

Because use of force cases often qualify as "evocative news events," they pose a special challenge to law enforcement agencies. The way police agencies respond to media scrutiny, then, plays a large role in determining the ultimate "definition" of individual use of force cases.

The incident that has perhaps most affected the modern relationship between the media and police is that of the videotaped beating of Rodney King by officers of the Los Angeles Police Department (LAPD) in 1991. The 81-second video of officers repeatedly striking King with their batons ushered in the media practice of the video presentation of police misconduct. This practice has only grown over time, and demonstrated the power of images to significantly affect policing. In the aftermath of the King beating, and the riots that followed the officers' acquittal, citizens groups and local, state, and federal officials launched investigations, applied political pressure, and made recommendations that eventually led to LAPD Chief Daryl Gates' resignation. Significant changes in department policy and the federal indictment of several officers for civil rights violations eventually ensued as well. This pattern of the media broadcasting video of police officers in acts of apparent misconduct, followed by public outrage, leading to changes in department leadership and the suspension or indictment of the offending officers, has only reinforced the air of distrust between the media and law enforcement.

These types of incidents can also significantly erode overall public support for the police; both Lasley (1994) and Tuch and Weitzer (1997) found evidence that surveyed citizens expressed reduced levels of support for the police following highly-publicized accounts of excessive use of force by law enforcement. This drop in public support following an excessive force incident has been found to be greatest among minority citizens (Jefferis et al., 1997). This disparity is especially important given the traditionally tenuous levels of trust between many police agencies and the minority groups they serve. When imagery is broadcast of excessive force being used against a minority suspect, there always exists the potential for the media to frame the incident in racial terms, and reinforce stereotypes that undermine law enforcement's relationship with the community. As will be discussed later, this is one of several reasons it is imperative that police agencies build relationships with the media that afford them some influence over how unexpected incidents are interpreted and presented by the media.

A failure to quickly grasp the significance of changes in communications technology has exacerbated the difficulties police departments face in dealing with the media. Within several minutes of the shootings at Virginia Tech in 2007, a student was able to upload audio of the event captured on a cell phone camera to a Cable News Network (CNN) website, where it was later broadcast worldwide. In an age where everyone with a cell phone camera is potentially a journalist, police agencies have been surprisingly slow to change their training and practices to confront this new reality. This "cultural lag" has undermined the legitimacy of police departments in various jurisdictions, as unexpected video clips surface following incidents which show either apparent acts of misconduct or excessive force, or "prove the lie" later when officers' paperwork doesn't match the events depicted in the video (Lovell, 2003). More media savvy departments now train their officers to use the concept of an "imaginary video camera" as a reminder that they should constantly operate under the assumption that their actions are being video recorded, and act appropriately. Likewise, officers and agencies have been traditionally reluctant to fully accept cameras in their cars and interrogation rooms. Fortunately, this attitude is changing within policing, as officers come to understand that the same camera that can indict, can also exonerate.

Both the confrontational aspects and public nature of police work invite media analysis and criticism in a way not experienced by most other governmental actors. In their efforts to publicize police corruption and misconduct, the media have become a primary catalyst for change in policing. A recent study using traffic stop data in Rhode Island found that between 2001 and 2005, racial disparities in vehicle searches were significantly reduced when news media coverage was creating pronounced pressure on police organizations to make changes in leadership (Warren & Farrell, 2009). The issues the media choose to focus upon do create pressure that can accelerate policy change. As Lovell (2003, p. 5) states,

> it must be acknowledged up front that media do not "cause" police reform, as the social conditions necessary for reform always predate the catalyst; but media are effective in directing enough attention to the potential causes both before and more significantly after the pivotal event, thus allowing the police reform to occur.

Besides significant changes in use of force policy, the investigations following the Rodney King case eventually led to an increased commitment nationwide for the accelerated implementation of community policing principles and practices (Lawrence, 2000). Throughout the country, as new video recordings of police officers using force, both necessary and excessive, have been broadcast, police departments have responded with policy changes, increased training, and renewed efforts to strengthen the bonds between agencies and the communities they serve. Although changes in policing methods can always be potentially beneficial, most police supervisors would prefer to proactively introduce that change, rather than have it occur as a response to an embarrassing or scandalous incident. When such incidents do occur, however, those agencies with the best ability to work with and influence the media will have the best chance of mitigating any potential damage to their department's relationship with the community.

The Foundations of Good Police/Media Relations

As previously discussed, the normal working relationship between the media and most police departments is one of cooperation and mutual reliance. This type of relationship is developed and fostered on the part of police departments through the establishment and maintenance of coherent policy and proper staff training. In the following sections of this chapter, we will examine some of the best policies that have been developed by police agencies for promoting and sustaining effective relationships with the media, examine the role of public information officers or department spokespersons, and make specific policy and practice recommendations for properly engaging the media in response to publicized use of force incidents.

It is imperative that every law enforcement agency has a formal media policy that both establishes guidelines for its employees and promotes a positive and pragmatic attitude toward the media. The police and the media need one another to effectively do their jobs, and respect for this symbiotic relationship should be evident in a department's media policy. Accentuating the positive aspects of productive media relations will help to bolster its acceptance within the department. Because a law enforcement agency's media policy is a matter of public record and will be read by the media, it should provide guidelines for both the police and reporters as to the ground rules that will guide their interactions. The policy should stress to police officers that each of them, and their actions, represent the entire department, and provide clear instruction as to how reporters should be treated. Reporters should be able to discern from the policy that the department recognizes its occupational responsibilities and will do what is possible to assist them with their jobs (Donlon-Cotton, 2005).

An effective law enforcement agency media policy must also distinguish what subjects or areas of police work are off limits to the media. Topic areas that are not to be discussed, such as legal issues, details of ongoing investigations, or personnel issues, must be clearly delineated in the policy, as well as an admonition to officers that they offer only facts and not speculate when providing information to the press (Donlon-Cotton, 2005). Most journalists are aware of their responsibilities and legal constraints in regard to reporting on police matters, and understand their access to future information from the police is predicated in part on their avoiding interference with, or the undermining of, police investigations.

Those working in a department or agency must also have a clear understanding of the existing chain of command, where they function in that chain, and what individuals are authorized to communicate with the media on behalf of the organization. The media relations chain of command may or may not correspond with the normal rank-driven order of authority. The size and budget of a department, the community being served, the level of criminal activity, and other considerations may all affect the structure an agency employs for media relations. An agency can employ one or more of the following approaches in deciding who will speak with the media on behalf of the department: only the agency head speaks, anyone can speak, only designated people can speak, the senior officer on the scene can speak, or the public information officer can speak (Donlon-Cotton, 2005). Smaller police departments, with limited resources, will normally have the agency head or their first deputy act as spokesperson, with larger, busier departments normally creating a media relations office or division with one or more Public Information Officers to handle most media inquiries.

For those departments with the necessary resources, a Public Information Officer (PIO) is an invaluable asset. Just as the media act as information gatekeepers between law enforcement and the public, so the PIO assumes the responsibility of acting as a buffer between the media and police personnel. Though it is usually best for the agency head or a member of the command staff to be the department spokesperson in the case of a high-profile use of force incident, for the more routine communications between the police and the media, a PIO may be preferable. Among many benefits, the utilization of a PIO frees-up command staff to focus on the numerous other administrative and supervisory tasks they face.

The potential duties of the PIO are numerous and include both working to mitigate bad press and identifying opportunities to publicize positive stories about the police. By focusing full-time on the media's coverage of the department and public opinion of police service in the community, a PIO can anticipate potential problems. PIOs are often better able to keep abreast of changes in public opinion, demonstrated through both traditional media sources and through the monitoring of sources of information utilized by younger citizens, such as social networking sites and blogs.

A good media relations officer will also cultivate good relationships with members of the press, will have a working knowledge of their methods and deadlines, and will work with the media in a way that builds trust and respect between the two organizations. Although reporters will always be wary of manipulation, they will be potentially grateful when a PIO offers a public interest story of a police action or program that has a significant impact on their readers or viewers. Media outlets need interesting and relevant content, and if a PIO presents a story in a compelling way, it is often hard for the media to resist. More importantly, through working cooperatively and respectfully with the press, and by providing them interesting content and access, the PIO is building a legacy of trust that will serve a police department well when controversial incidents surface, such as those involving use of force. A police department's reputation for honesty, respect, and cooperation is built over time, and a good PIO can greatly help in the development of that reputation.

The reality, though, is that many smaller departments simply cannot afford a full-time media relations expert. In such cases, it is essential that the agency head and his or her command staff be prepared to handle media inquiries, both routine and unexpected, and that if possible, first-line officers be trained to act as at least temporary intermediaries. As mentioned earlier, this requires both sufficient media relations training for officers and a clear understanding of the department's media policy.

Managing the Media: Use of Force Incidents

Engaging the press effectively is an essential task for any police agency, but it is an especially important responsibility following an incident where force is used in a manner or context that attracts significant media attention. Years of departmental efforts at cultivating trust with the community and local media organizations can be undermined rapidly through the misguided or incompetent handling of a use of force investigation. In the final section of this chapter, we examine some of the practices and policies that can be employed by law enforcement agencies following use of force incidents to best manage media coverage of the event. As with any task in policing, prior training and preparation make for better performance when an incident occurs. Department command staff and media relations officers should have extensive training in, and familiarity with, the agency's protocol for officer-involved shootings and other serious use of force incidents. Regular training is especially important in those police departments where officers are rarely involved in shootings and thus the command staff gets little practice in handling such incidents.

How a police department engages the media following a significant use of force incident involving an officer can greatly influence how the story is framed or defined once it is broadcast. Pat Camden, former Deputy Director of News Affairs for the Chicago Police Department, advises agencies to get out in front of the story as much as possible and remember that the media can act as a public communications tool in such cases. He suggests that a department spokesperson rather than the chief of the involved department call the local media outlets first and provide them whatever preliminary information can be given. The head of the law enforcement agency will likely eventually engage in dialogue with the media, depending on the nature of the incident and the size of the department. But, in those departments with a PIO or other media relations officer, and where shootings are not uncommon, it is better not to risk attracting undue media attention with significant early involvement by the head of the agency (Camden, 2010).

Often, the more information that can be safely released following an incident, the better the department can define the incident. Remember, in those cases where a police department fails to frame or define an incident for the media, the media will take that task on for themselves, often with less desirable public relations results for the police. Department spokespersons are advised to permanently eliminate the phrase "no comment" from their vocabularies. Responses in that vein lead the press to be automatically suspicious and distrustful and will lead to journalists looking to "uncover" a story or scandalous angle to an incident that does not actually exist. Following a high-profile incident, updates should be given to the media by agency spokespersons, either through briefings or eventually a press conference involving command staff. General rules for such press conferences include preparing before the event for likely press questions, following department policy regarding the naming of involved officers or victims, and having a predetermined exit point in mind. Generally, when good news is being presented, department spokespersons should be in uniform, when bad news is being presented, formal business attire may project a better departmental image (Camden, 2010).

Following highly publicized use of force incidents, especially officer-involved shootings, it is also a department's responsibility to protect and advise the affected officers. Patrol officers involved in such cases should be discouraged from reading or watching news accounts of the incident, and likewise should avoid viewing blogs that might contain posts discussing the event. For most officers, such an incident might be the most traumatic experience of their careers, and regardless of the legal outcomes of the case, could significantly affect their confidence and performance in the future.

Despite an agency's best efforts at media and public relations, there are still times when particular use of force incidents occur that will elicit an immediate and negative response from the press and the public. A policy of swift and aggressive damage control needs to be employed in particularly ugly situations, such as when an unarmed suspect is shot by the police, when a disproportionate number of rounds are fired by officers in a deadly force encounter, or when video surfaces which appears to show excessive force being used by the police (Rosenthal, 2005). In cases such as these, where there is great potential for a police department to be perceived by the public as either incompetent, reckless, or criminally brutal, it is imperative that the agency head take the lead in communicating the organization's response to the incident.

Though most of the rules for handling the press that were discussed earlier still apply, when an incident has the potential to be portrayed by the media and perceived by the public as a serious scandal, the Chief must present himself or herself as fully in charge and engaged in a swift investigation of the incident. It is especially important during such cases to communicate regularly with the media and keep them, to the extent possible, apprised of what actions are being taken by the department. Any significant delay in conveying information, or appearance that the department is stalling or deflecting media inquiries, increases the likelihood the press will frame the story as one of potential police misconduct or corruption. The agency head can help define the narrative surrounding the episode by showing himself or herself in the neighborhood where the incident occurred, and speaking to members of the community that were affected. Images of the Sheriff/Chief speaking with citizens near the scene of the controversy, listening to their concerns and showing empathy, are very powerful and are unlikely to be ignored by the media.

Once the investigation of a use of force incident concludes that the police acted improperly, it is time for the agency to admit the mistakes, take responsibility, and outline what changes it plans to implement to prevent the error from occurring again. Actions taken against responsible agency personnel should also be outlined in whatever detail is permissible. This "mea culpa" should be given at a time and in a manner that demonstrates the department's understanding of the significance of the event. A formal press conference led by the agency head at a time that is respectful of the media's production schedules sends the best message. Though formally admitting error is unlikely to aid in deflecting lawsuits related to the incident, apologizing and promising to do better in the future will almost certainly improve the image of the agency head and department in the eyes of the majority of citizens they serve.

Summary

It is essential for law enforcement leaders and their agencies to be able to effectively communicate with the public through the media. Although this will never be a simple or completely predictable task, there are policies and practices that police and sheriff's departments can employ to cultivate good relationships with the media. The ability of a law enforcement agency to work cooperatively and respectfully with the press is especially important following high-profile events, such as controversial use of force incidents, when both the credibility of an agency head and the entire organization is potentially at stake. Some of the best recommendations for fostering effective police/media relations, especially following use of force incidents, are summarized below:

- Law enforcement agencies must constantly work to cultivate a relationship of respect and trust with the news media. The time for cultivating this respect and trust is before a use of force incident arises.
- Work to understand the press, their goals, methods of operation, and production schedules. View them dispassionately as merely individuals doing a job.
- Use the media when possible to publicize positive stories about your agency, its accomplishments, and community reductions in crime. Such stories help promote higher levels of public support and trust which will be important to counteract potential negative stories.
- When possible, employ a Public Information Officer, or designate an officer, to act as primary agency liaison with the media. Provide as much training in media relations as possible to all personnel in the agency.
- Never mislead the media or use the term "no comment" in response to inquiries. Once trust is lost with the press it is very difficult to rebuild.
- Get out in front of problem situations. Contact the media before they contact the agency in response to controversial use of force incidents. Ensure that command staff and department spokespersons are trained and practiced in handling media inquiries into such incidents.
- Don't wait for the entire inquiry into a use of force incident to conclude before providing the media with information. As long as it doesn't hinder the investigation, provide the press with information as it becomes available, and at regular intervals. If an agency creates an information void in regard to an incident, the media may fill it with inaccurate and negative conjecture.
- The agency head and command staff need to appear engaged and in charge of investigations into controversial use of force incidents. The chief/sheriff should travel to the scene of the controversy at some point to listen and empathize with the citizens' concerns.

- As the saying goes, "Dress Up and Fess Up." When mistakes are made, the agency head needs to publicly recognize the errors, apologize when appropriate, and provide a detailed description of what policies or practices are being put in place to correct the errors in judgment or action. Specify whether and how responsible personnel are being disciplined.
- Try to use a potentially negative situation in the most positive terms possible by demonstrating responsiveness and accountability to community concerns. Some positives can be created from negative situations.

The duties of police administrators and officers are diverse and complicated. Adding to the complexity of the law enforcement role is the speed of current communications technology and the media saturated nature of contemporary society. Though this complexity cannot be completely overcome, it can be managed. This chapter has outlined some of the practices and policies that can help agencies effectively accomplish that task, and come to recognize the potential benefits of working effectively with the media.

Acknowledgment

Translated and reprinted by permission of ILETSBEI. This article was originally published under the English title "Use of Force and Responding to the Media" by Todd Lough and Vladimir Sergevnin in 2011. Copyright © 2011 by ILETSBEI. This translation, Copyright © 2011. Reprinted with Permission by Law Enforcement Executive Forum, IL Executive Institute (12/11; pp. 87–98).

References

Altschull, J. (1975). The press and the police: News flow and ideology. *Journal of Police Science and Administration, 3*(4), 425–433.

Bennett, W. L. (1990). Toward a theory of press-state relations in the United States. *Journal of Communication, 40*(2), 103–125.

Caeti, T. J., Liederbach, J., & Bellew, S. (2004). Police-media relations at critical incidents: Interviews from Oklahoma City. *International Journal of Police Science & Management*, 7(2), 86–97.

Camden, P. (2010). *Use of force and responding to the media.* Breakout Session from Use of Force Executive Summit, Chicago, IL.

Donlon-Cotton, C. (2005). Model media policy. *Law & Order, 53*(10), 18–20.

Gans, H. J. (1979). *Deciding what's news.* New York, NY: Vintage Books.

Garner, G. (1984). *The police meet the press.* Springfield, IL: Charles C. Thomas Publisher.

Gurevitch, M. & Levy, M. R. (1985). Preface. In M. Gurevitch & M. R. Levy (eds.), *Mass communication review yearbook* (5th ed.). Beverly Hills, CA: Sage Publications.

Hall, S., Critcher, C., Jefferson, T., Clarke, J., & Roberts, B. (1978) *Policing the crisis.* New York, NY: Holmes and Meier Publishers, Inc.

Jefferis, E. S., Kaminski, R. J., Holmes, S., & Hanley, D. E. (1997). The effect of a videotaped arrest on public perceptions of police use of force. *Journal of Criminal Justice 25*(5), 381–395.

Lasley, J. R. (1994). The impact of the Rodney King incident on citizen attitudes toward police. *Policing and Society, 3*(4), 245–255.

Lawrence, R. G. (2000). *The politics of force: media and the construction of police brutality.* Berkeley: University of California Press.

Lovell, J. S. (2003). *Good cop/bad cop: Mass media and the cycle of police reform.* Monsey, NY: Criminal Justice Press.

Rosenthal, R. (2005). Managing the media in ugly situations. *Sheriff*, 57(Sep/Oct), 53–56.

Selke, W. L. & Bartoszek, G. M. (1984). Police and media relations: The seeds of conflict. *Criminal Justice Review*, *9*(2), 25–30.

Sherman, L. W. (1974). *Police corruption: A sociological perspective*. Garden City, NY: Anchor Press.

Skolnick, J. H. & McCoy, C. (1984). Police accountability and the media. *American Bar Foundation Research Journal*, *9*(3), 521–557.

Surrette, R. (1998). *Media, crime, and criminal justice: Images and realities* (2nd ed.). Belmont, CA: Wadsworth Publishing.

Tuch, S. A. & Weitzer, R. (1997). Racial differences in attitudes toward the police. *Public Opinion Quarterly*, *61*(4), 642–663.

Warren, P. Y. & Farrell, A. (2009). The environmental context of racial profiling. *The Annals of the American Academy of Political and Social Sciences*, *623*, 52–63.

Ziembo-Vogl, J. (1998). Exploring the functions of the media in community policing. *Police Forum*, *8*(1), 1–12.

INDEX

Locators in *italics* refer to figures and those in **bold** to tables. Alphabetization is word-by-word.